YEAR
AROUND
COOKBOOK

SARAH LEAH CHASE'S

YEAR
AROUND
COOKBOOK

Illustrations by Judith Shahn & Gretchen Shields

Two volumes in one:

Nantucket Open House Cookbook
&
Cold Weather Cooking

Tess
Press

This edition published by arrangement with
Workman Publishing Company

Published by
      Tess Press an imprint of Black Dog & Leventhal Publishers, Inc.
      151 West 19th Street
      New York, NY 10011

ISBN: 1-57912-131-4

Manufactured in the United States of America

Library of Congress Cataloging-in-Publication Data

Chase, Sarah Leah.
Sarah Leah Chase's year around cookbook.
p.cm.
"Two volumes in one, Sarah Leah Chase's Nantucket open house
cookbook & Sarah Leah Chase's Cold weather cookbook."
ISBN: 1-57912-131-4
1. Entertaining. 2. Cookery. I. Chase, Sarah Leah. Nantucket open-house
cookbook. II. Chase, Sarah Leah. Cold weather cooking. III. Title.

TX731. C543 2000
641.5--dc21   00-027319

For K.
Who encouraged me to write before he encouraged me to cook, and who has always provided islands of inspiration in both. Thank you for teaching me that clouds may indeed be embraced . . .

Dedication
A thanksgiving of appreciation to the generations of consummate women in my family who have fired my culinary imagination and nurtured my hungry soul with good food. Stockpots of love and never ending soupçons of admiration for my talented and perfect Mother, voraciously generous Grandmother Florian, elegantly Polish Graminski, and outrageously gastronomic Auntie Diane!

CONTENTS

Thinking Thanksgiving Part 2:

NANTUCKET OPEN-HOUSE COOKBOOK

Que Sera Sarah

We owe much to the fruitful meditation of our sages, but a sane view of life is, after all, elaborated mainly in the kitchen.
—JOSEPH CONRAD

A long time ago, I used to study language philosophy late into the night. I would lie awake pondering whether language determined reality, or reality language. I dreamed of becoming a semiologist, not a chef.

Today, I still possess a restlessness that keeps me awake and curious at odd hours of the night. Now, however, more often than not I am lost in a mouthwatering mound of the latest cooking publications. I worry less about which came first—the chicken or the egg—and more about the best ways to roast a chicken, hard boil an egg, roll a grape leaf, or intensify the flavor of a sorbet. This transformation from the world of ideas to the art of creating gastronomic delights occurred through nothing more extraordinary, than falling in love.

But the circumstances were not quite so predictable: an irresistibly arrogant and nimble French chef didn't whisk me away to a three-star auberge to live plumply ever after; a dark, alluring Italian count didn't twirl my tender heart helplessly like just so many strands of fettuccine; an elegant sushi roller didn't set my romantic sensibilities blindly ablaze with a fiery blast of wasabi paste; and a gorgeous, young California Adonis posing as a culinary star didn't bring about a confusion between passion fruit and true fulfillment. No, I fell irrevocably in love—not with a person or an ideal or even a cuisine, but with of all things, an island—Nantucket Island.

There was absolutely nothing subtle about this seduction, as Nantucket has it all and almost too much: lucent baby blue skies; blustery cumulus days; impenetrable fogs and gentle lavender mists; waters that sparkle, lap, wave, and enchant everywhere in dramatic cliffside seascapes, cozy harbors, sensuously duned beaches, and even secluded inland ponds. There is sun that shines often, hugging people, hydrangeas, and curious old attics alike and rains that intimidate with fervent but cleansing tantrums. Graceful old elms and oaks shade, pine forests remain hidden secrets, and twisted lanes and cobblestoned streets captivate with quaintness. Stately old sea captains' homes cluster throughout the town as if to lend historical anchor to the island's etherealness; but, then, they too are imbued with spirituality as legends of household ghosts are common and whisper of long lost others who could never bear to leave Nantucket, either.

In retrospect, I should have grasped that cooking would become my creative and emotional outlet. I was thirteen years old when I first came to Nantucket to summer as a mother's helper for a favorite aunt and uncle who ran a fascinating antiques business on the island. I was warmly welcomed into their immaculately restored sea captain's house. My sunny golden bedroom served as a microcosm of Nantucket history as it was filled with island treasures—old lightship baskets, whirligigs, seafaring chests, whaling journals, island-loomed blankets, and just-polished brass candlesticks. I loved to gaze down at the wisteria bordered patio below or dream for long hours in front of the sparkling harbor view. But, my very favorite part of the house was the kitchen—a singular blending of early American antiques, state-of-the-art appliances, and irresistible new aromas. My aunt was (and always will be) a fabulous cook. While every little aspect of Nantucket seemed to strike my fancy with magical power, it was in truth the creations and flavors of my aunt's kitchen that were to linger the most indelibly.

My favorite chores as a mother's helper became those of assisting in the family meals and learning hors d'oeuvre assembly for the busy entertaining schedule. As a neophyte, I was initially astounded by the amounts of food my aunt would prepare. My most repeated refrain became, "Auntie Diane, why are you preparing so much food?" It didn't take long to grasp the answer and it was at this point that I learned several essential lessons that were to have a grand influence on the development of my own approach to cooking. First, I noted that imaginative and skilled cooks attract an entertaining array of charismatic and appreciative friends, well versed in the art of spontaneously "dropping by" and loving to be unexpectedly fed. In short, plentiful food and exciting people go together.

Next, I was quick to glean that if one is to expend the effort and emotion required of the best culinary triumphs, it makes sense to prepare generous quantities to cover the next day's inevitable cravings. The third and most important insight for me, however, was realizing that there was something in my aunt's style of cooking that intuitively captured the very essence of Nantucket. Indeed, a meal in my aunt and uncle's Union Street home—the setting, the conversation, and of course the food—was capable of communicating almost all that needed to be known about the highly specialized art of loving Nantucket. In subtle but unforgettable ways, all the generosity and outrageous-ness of Nantucket abounded at their dinner table. (Leftovers, if any, never lasted more than 24 hours.)

It took some maturing to sort out the real significance of all my impressions. I continued to summer on Nantucket and to visit whenever possible. In the meantime, I also took the usual collegiate plunge into exploring the philosophical purpose of life. A strange but satisfying balance ensued in spending part of my year searing swordfish steaks and simmering batches of rata-touille and the rest dancing upon Nietzschean tightropes, dipping into existential abysses, and waiting for Godot. An undeniable clue to my future occurred when I realized that my stack of *Gourmet* magazines had superceded in thickness my senior hon-ors thesis on language. At that point I concluded I might fare better by shedding the encumbering words of my abstract essays and instead confront my love for Nantucket with the seemingly more supple medium of cooking. Bertrand Russell beckoned no longer and instead Brillat-Savarin blazed the path to new ways of communication and fulfillment—"Tell me what you eat, and I will tell you what you are!"

As I was understandably nervous about my leap from scholar to shopkeeper, I decided to name my food business "Que Sera Sarah," reasoning that if one questionable course of life failed, the name was versatile enough to sustain a few more trial ventures. Perserverance prevailed and eventually gained me an adorable and affordable pink (Heaven!) shuttered shop in a former rooming house in the heart of town.

Once I got the life's investment of kitchen equipment—which was too wide to pass through the narrow Nantucket doorways—off the street and into the shop, I hired the artist/tenant on the floor above me, to help with the chopping, dicing, and dishing of both salads and people. I also snagged a beautiful wandering student, who read *Women in Love* during the store's initial slow moments, to sell the first culinary creations. I had no real scheme in mind except to cook the foods I liked most, which were predominantly cold preparations, utilizing Nantucket's ocean bounty in combination with inspirations from European travels. I hoped that if I approached this task with enough integrity and passion, other lovers of Nantucket would share in an appetite for my personal culinary whims. The transition to the professional field of cooking was not terribly difficult, as I soon discovered that my Sabatier chopping knives were almost as dangerous as collegiate nihilism, and that the very hands that once beheld being and nothingness so well adjusted amiably to onions and potatoes.

From the beginning, the Que Sera Sarah shop exuded a cross-section of Nantucket's iconoclastic artistic energy. It was never my policy to hire highly trained professional cooks, as I preferred surrounding myself with an eclectic range of painters, carpenters, writers, designers, philosophers, and entrepreneurs. I found that their interpretation of food as well as their knowledge of passing topics, staved off any forms of culinary drudgery.

For example, Sterling captured on canvas the odd pieces of cake or stray caviar eggs that did not sell and gave the most accurate astrological forecasts daily, predicted according to the ease with which the croissant dough rolled out. Elena would titillate, amuse, and shock with random excerpts from a current writing assignment—about her life with an emotional vampire—while tossing a batch of Kielbasa Vinaigrette. Olga knew every scandalous event that had occurred on the island in the last fifteen years (let alone past fifteen minutes) and possessed a unique talent for making up instant song lyrics. A kitchen favorite began: "I know it's late, I know you're weary. Why don't we bake?" Through all this chatter, Jane could be found quietly kneading peasant bread in a far corner to the rhythmic meter of her next poetry endeavor. And in the midst of these wonderfully inspiring scenes, I would take on the role of kitchen choreographer. I drained Moroccan Carrots, snatched the oatmeal cookies from the oven at the perfect moment, whisked in an egg yolk here and there to bind a mayonnaise back together, and always placed the hearts tenderly on each sausage in brioche. A sane view of life was, after all, elaborated mainly in the kitchen.

The past six years spent cooking have successfully provided the chance to take the beautiful raw ingredients of my beloved island and evoke through taste and personal stylization, many other sensory appeals of my life on Nantucket. I have learned how to cook fish so that it summarizes the sea, to arrange tomatoes in alternating splashes of red and orange in tribute to Madaket sunsets, and to seal memories of September in jars of beach plum jam. The endless hours I devote to the perfection of foods in the Que Sera Sarah shop are seldom questioned because only an environment as generous as that of Nantucket can inspire such devotion and loyalty. The kitchen days that still begin at 6 A.M. and end near midnight bring to mind the saying: "Cooking is like love—it should be entered into with abandon or not at all." Such a sentiment seems to go hand in hand with the abandon it takes to live, laugh, and thrive on an island thirty miles out to sea.

Sarah Leah Chase
Nantucket Island, May 1987

Appetizers and Favorite Nibbling Foods

"When shall we live if not now?"
—SENECA

It seems clear to me that those who lead the most enviable lives in a summer retreat are endowed with natural spontaneity and guiltless abandon. When there are warming rays of the sun to absorb, endlessly cresting waves to ride, billowing spinnakers to sail, wild pink roses to inhale, ripening blueberries and raspberries to gather, monumental novels to escape into, cool silver shooting stars to gaze at, and indeed all of summer's sizzling passion to savor, there is little time left to think of meals in a traditional and boringly balanced fashion. Nonetheless the food consumed should have an intensity equal to the life sustained. Nibbling at whim on selective, seductive, and savory morsels has always seemed to me the perfect way to breeze through summer holidays.

The recipes that make up this versatile collection were born out of enjoying many, many summers of plenty on Nantucket Island. Share them with lots of friends or simply secrete them away for private indulgence when the mood strikes.

Scallop Puffs Que Sera

A very favorite Nantucket hors d'oeuvre among friends and customers. The recipe makes twelve dozen puffs, but they need not be made all at once. The scallop mixture keeps for a week in the refrigerator, so that you can make them as needed for spur-of-the-moment entertaining.

3 tablespoons unsalted butter

1 pound bay scallops, quartered

2 teaspoons finely minced lemon zest

3 cloves garlic, minced

3 tablespoons chopped fresh dill

2 cups grated Swiss or Gruyère cheese

2¼ cups Hellmann's mayonnaise

Freshly ground pepper to taste

12 dozen 1-inch bread rounds cut from good-quality commercial white sandwich bread, lightly toasted

Sweet Hungarian paprika

Lemon slices and dill sprigs for garnish

1. Melt the butter in a medium skillet or sauté pan over medium-high heat. Add the scallops, lemon zest, and garlic. Cook, stirring constantly, until the scallops are just barely cooked through, 2 to 3 minutes. Add the dill and cook 30 seconds longer. Let cool to room temperature.

2. Add the cheese, mayonnaise, and pepper to the scallop mixture and stir to combine well. Refrigerate in a covered bowl until ready to use, but no longer than a week.

3. Preheat the broiler.

4. Place the toast rounds ½ inch apart on baking sheets. Top each toast round with a heaping teaspoon of the scallop mixture and sprinkle lightly with paprika.

5. Broil the puffs 5 inches from the heat until puffed and golden, 2 to 3 minutes. Transfer the puffs to platters and garnish with lemon slices and dill sprigs. Serve hot.

Makes 12 dozen.

CAVIAR TARTINES
OR
THE BEST WAY TO EAT CAVIAR

To begin with, the best way to eat caviar is to eat only the best—Russian Beluga. Next, the pomp and circumstance of elaborate caviar paraphernalia must be removed in favor of somewhat more peasanty infusions—fresh crusty bread and slabs of sweet butter. A 125-gram tin of Beluga is the preferred size, for anything smaller is too dainty. The company should be kept to a minimum, perhaps, to just your favorite person in the entire world. There must definitely be drink; either your most coveted bottle of French Champagne or crystal shooters of iced 100-proof vodka would do. Moonlight and the sound of the surf breaking in the background are lovely too but not entirely necessary.

The scene set, the bread must be sliced—about ½ inch thick—and then spread generously with sweet butter. Sterling silver is always appropriate for this action. Then, literally slather the buttered bread with a fortune of the precious eggs—more than you would ever dare be caught consuming in public. This is your basic caviar tartine—a fabulous balance of extravagance and simple peasantry.

Repeat over and over again breaking only for sighs of ecstacy and sips of Champagne or shots of vodka. For the duration of the caviar supply and the period of ensuing afterglow, you will know what it is like to leave the shadowy world of earthly foods and ascend to the purest level of Platonic inception.

Caviar Ceviche

S erve this loosely interpreted ceviche on dainty glass plates as a sophisticated starter at a formal party. Small flutes of iced vodka would make a perfect accompaniment.

1 pound bay scallops
½ cup fresh lemon juice
3 tablespoons vodka
2 teaspoons very finely
   grated lemon zest
¾ to 1 cup crème fraîche
   or sour cream

1 jar (30 grams) Sevruga
   caviar
Thin lemon slices and
   fresh parsley or other
   leafy herb for garnish

1. Toss the scallops, lemon juice, vodka, and lemon zest together in a mixing bowl. Cover and let marinate in the refrigerator for 4 hours.

2. Just before serving, drain the scallops thoroughly and toss with enough crème fraîche to bind. Quickly and gently fold in the caviar, being careful not to break the delicate eggs. Spoon the ceviche on 8 plates and garnish with lemon slices and a sprig or two of parsley.

Makes 8 appetizer servings.

Cornmeal Blinis with Favorite Caviars

T hese fluffy little golden pancakes make an elegant first course when served on individual plates or quite the decadent nibble when passed hors-d'oeuvre style at parties. I like to top these blinis with three caviars. If you are feeling extravagant, try Beluga, Ossetra, and Sevruga, although a selection of good American caviars such as golden, salmon, and sturgeon will sparkle as well.

1 package (¼ ounce)
  active dry yeast
½ cup warm water (105°
  to 115° F)
1 cup light cream
1 cup unbleached
  all-purpose flour
½ cup yellow cornmeal

3 large eggs, separated
1 teaspoon sugar
½ teaspoon salt
½ cup (1 stick) unsalted
  butter, melted and cooled
1 cup crème fraîche
3 jars (2 ounces each) of
  3 different caviars

1. Sprinkle the yeast over the warm water in a small bowl and let stand for 5 minutes. Pour the yeast mixture into a blender and add the cream, flour, cornmeal, egg yolks, sugar, salt, and melted butter. Blend until smooth. Pour into a large bowl, cover with plastic wrap, and let rise in a warm, draft-free place until doubled in bulk, 1 to 1½ hours.

2. Beat the egg whites in a mixing bowl until soft peaks form. Gently fold the whites into the batter just until incorporated.

3. Heat a griddle over medium-high heat and brush lightly with butter. Drop the batter 2 tablespoons at a time onto the griddle to make little pancakes 1½ inches in diameter. Cook, turning once, until lightly browned on both sides. Transfer the blinis to a baking sheet. Place in a single layer. Repeat with the remaining batter until all are cooked.

4. When you are ready to serve, warm the blinis briefly in a skillet or in a preheated 350°F oven just until warm to the touch. Top each blini with a dollop of crème fraîche and then a small spoonful of one of the caviars. Serve at once.

Makes about 3½ dozen.

LIGHT CREAM

If you have any problem finding light cream, half and half can be substituted although the results will be slightly less rich. You can also approximate commercially packaged light cream by blending equal amounts of whole milk and heavy or whipping cream. For example, to make 1 cup light cream, mix together ½ cup milk and ½ cup heavy cream.

Steamed Clams Que Sera

Charting the tides, squinting in search of myopic clam holes, and breaking a fingernail or two while furrowing for bivalves are among the simpler summer pleasures of shore living, but cooking up a great feast of one's labor makes the day one of the most rewarding of the lazy sunny season.

5 dozen littleneck or
  steamer clams
⅓ cup olive oil
3 cloves garlic, minced
4 ounces hard Italian
  sausage, cut into
  ¼-inch dice
3 ripe medium tomatoes,
  seeded and cut into
  ½-inch dice
1 tablespoon dried
  oregano

1 teaspoon dried red
  pepper flakes
1 teaspoon fennel seeds
Salt and freshly ground
  pepper to taste
1½ cups dry white wine
3 tablespoons fresh lemon
  juice
3 tablespoons chopped
  fresh basil

1. Scrub and rinse the clams under cold running water to make sure they are free of sand and grit.

2. Heat the oil in a pot large enough for cooking the clams over high heat. Add the garlic, sausage, and tomatoes and cook, stirring constantly, for 5 minutes. Add the oregano, red pepper flakes, fennel seeds, salt, and pepper; cook 1 minute longer.

3. Pour the wine and lemon juice into the pot and then add the clams. Sprinkle the basil over the top and cover the pot tightly. Cook the clams just until they all open.

4. Ladle the clams and cooking liquid into shallow bowls and serve with crusty bread.

Makes 12 to 15 appetizer servings, or 4 to 6 light entrée servings.

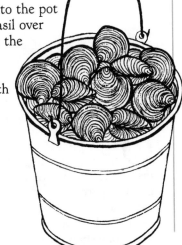

Roasted Garlic

This is a perfect example of very simple food that is purely fabulous. While squeezing the garlic out of the roasted husks can be a bit messy, it is part and parcel of the whole sensual enjoyment of this preparation.

8 whole heads fresh garlic
⅓ cup extra-virgin olive
   oil
1½ teaspoons coarsely
   ground pepper

1½ teaspoons dried
   thyme
1 teaspoon salt

1. Preheat the oven to 350°F.
2. Trim the point off each garlic head to expose the tops of the cloves. Place the heads next to each other in a shallow baking dish, such as a 9-inch pie plate. Drizzle the heads with the oil and sprinkle evenly with the pepper, thyme, and salt.
3. Roast the garlic for 30 minutes. Reduce the temperature to 250°F and cook 1 hour longer.
4. Serve the garlic with slices of crusty French bread, butter, and goat cheese if you like. Pop the cloves out of the skins and spread on the bread.
   Makes 8 servings.

French Onion Tart

One bite of this delectably rich and savory tart creates instant transport to the sybaritic south of France. It makes a popular party hors d'oeuvre when cut into small squares and garnished with olives and springs of fresh herbs. Cut into large squares, the tart is an indulgent form of luncheon sustenance to fuel a day spent lazing on a sandy beach.

½ recipe Pizza Dough (see page 80)

ANCHOVY PESTO SPREAD:

3 cans (2 ounces each) anchovy fillets (about 20)

3 cloves garlic, minced

2 tablespoons balsamic vinegar

½ cup fresh parsley leaves

1 teaspoon dried thyme

2 large egg yolks

1 cup fresh white bread crumbs

¾ cup olive oil

Freshly ground pepper to taste

1 to 2 tablespoons fresh lemon juice

FILLING:

¼ cup olive oil

4 very large Spanish onions, cut into thin rings

1 tablespoon sugar

2 cloves garlic, finely minced

Niçoise olives and parsley sprigs for garnish

1. Make the pizza dough up to the point it is ready to roll out.

2. Prepare the anchovy pesto spread: Place the anchovies, garlic, vinegar, parsley, and thyme in a food processor fitted with the steel blade. Process to a smooth paste. Add the egg yolks and bread crumbs and process again until smooth. With the machine running, pour the oil through the feed tube in a thin, steady stream and process until the mixture is thick and creamy. Season to taste with pepper and lemon juice.

3. Prepare the filling: Heat the oil in a 4-quart pot over medium-high heat. Add the onions and cook, stirring frequently, for 10 minutes. Reduce the heat to medium-low and continue to cook, stirring frequently, for another 10 minutes. Stir in the sugar and cook 5 minutes longer. Finally, stir in the garlic and cook another 5 minutes. Remove from the heat.

4. Preheat the oven to 375°F. Brush a 15 x 10-inch baking sheet lightly with olive oil.

5. To assemble the tart, roll out the pizza dough to fit the baking sheet. Place the dough in the pan and crimp the edges decoratively. Using a rubber spatula, spread about 1 cup of the anchovy pesto spread in a thin even layer over the dough. (The remaining spread can be stored in the refrigerator up to 2 weeks and used for another tart or as a sandwich spread or vegetable

dip.) Spread the onion filling evenly over the anchovy spread.

6. Bake the tart until the edges are crusty and golden brown, 30 to 40 minutes. Let cool to room temperature. Cut into small or large squares and garnish with Niçoise olives and parsley sprigs.

Makes 15 x 10-inch tart.

Marinated Goat Cheeses

I always have a large platter of these dumplinglike cheeses marinating on one of the store counters. They are so beautiful spattered with brilliant green summer basil and pretty pink peppercorns shimmering under a bath of rich olive oil. The crusty heel of a loaf of French bread and, perhaps, a smear of two of roasted garlic are natural accompaniments.

8 Crottin goat cheeses
  (2 to 3 ounces each) or
  other small, round,
  hard goat cheeses
1½ cups extra-virgin
  olive oil
4 bay leaves
1 tablespoon mixed
  white, black, and green
  peppercorns

1½ tablespoons dried
  thyme
3 large cloves garlic, cut
  into slivers
3 tablespoons slivered
  fresh basil
1 tablespoon dried pink
  peppercorns

1. Place the goat cheeses on an ovenproof platter or flat dish large enough to hold the cheeses without touching. An earthenware pie plate works well.

2. Heat the oil, bay leaves, mixed peppercorns, and dried thyme in a small saucepan over medium-high heat until you hear the mixture begin to sizzle and pop. Immediately remove from the heat and pour over the cheeses.

3. Scatter the slivered garlic in the marinade and sprinkle with the basil and pink peppercorns. Let marinate in the refrigerator overnight to firm up the cheeses. Bring to room temperature before serving.

Makes 8 appetizer servings or 24 hors d'oeuvre servings.

Sausage in Brioche

Decorative and delicious, sausages in brioche are equally popular for an impulse breakfast, lunch, or snack or, sliced into bite-size rounds, as a cocktail nibble. The plump little dough heart adorning each sausage adds great flair.

BRIOCHE DOUGH:
1 package (¼ ounce) active dry yeast
1 tablespoon sugar
⅔ cup milk, heated just until warm to the touch (110 to 115° F)
4 large eggs

4 to 4½ cups unbleached all-purpose flour
1 cup (2 sticks) unsalted butter, melted and cooled
2 teaspoons salt

FILLING:
8 tablespoons Dijon mustard
16 thin slices Provolone cheese

16 cheddarwurst sausages or other plump smoked sausages 5 to 6 inches long

EGG WASH:
1 large egg

1 tablespoon water

1. The day before you plan to serve the sausages, prepare the brioche dough: Place the yeast and sugar in a mixing bowl and pour in the warm milk. Let stand until puffed and foamy, about 5 minutes. Whisk in 2 of the eggs and about ¾ cup flour to make a mixture of the consistency of pancake batter. Cover the bowl with plastic wrap or a damp towel. Let rise in a warm, draft-free place until tripled or more in size, 1½ hours.

2. Transfer the mixture to a heavy-duty mixer fitted with a dough hook or a large mixing bowl if making the dough by hand. Add the remaining 2 eggs, the butter, and salt and mix until well combined. Gradually work in the remaining flour to make a soft (not stiff) elastic dough.

3. Transfer the dough to a clean large bowl. Cover with plastic wrap or a damp towel and let rise overnight in a cool spot or in the refrigerator.

4. The following day, preheat the oven to 375°F. Line 2 large baking sheets with parchment paper.

5. Roll out half the dough ¼ inch thick on a lightly floured surface. Cut the dough into eight 5-inch squares. Reserve the scraps for making the decorations later.

6. Spread ½ tablespoon Dijon mustard down the center of each square. Top with 1 slice of the Provolone. Place a sausage on the cheese. Roll up the sausage in the dough and seal the seam (not the ends) with your fingertips. Place the rolls seam side down and 2 inches apart on the prepared baking sheet. Repeat with the remaining dough, mustard, cheese, and sausages.

7. Mix the egg and water in a small bowl. Using a pastry brush, brush each roll with the egg wash. Gather all the scraps of dough together and roll out ¼ inch thick. Cut out hearts (or another shape) with a 1- to 1½-inch cookie cutter and place 1 heart on the top of each roll. Brush the rolls again with the egg wash.

8. Bake the rolls until light golden brown all over, 25 to 30 minutes. Serve the sausages hot or at room temperature. They can also be reheated in a 350°F oven for 5 to 7 minutes.

Makes 16 servings.

BRIE IN BRIOCHE

*B*rioche dough can also be used to enclose 8 to 10 baby ½-pound wheels or two 1 kilo wheels of Brie. Roll the dough into a circle large enough to completely cover each wheel. Wrap the wheel in dough, trim any excess, and place seam side down on a parchment-lined baking sheet. Brush the top and side of the dough with egg wash and decorate with shapes cut from the scraps of dough. Strips of dough braided or woven into a lattice make pretty designs. Brush the dough again with the egg wash and bake in a preheated 375°F oven until light golden brown about 25 to 30 minutes. Be careful not to overbake; if the Brie melts too much it will ooze out of the dough.

Serve the Brie at room temperature, for if it is hot it will be too runny and messy to eat. The baby wheels make great picnic fare, and the larger wheels always make a dressy and delicious presentation for cocktail parties.

Country Pâté with Beer and Fennel

This recipe has been a longtime favorite. It is a rather coarse-textured pâté packed with strong, distinctive flavors. While delightful served in the traditional manner with a crock of tart cornichons, it is even more irresistible when tucked into a crusty loaf of French bread with lots of mustard. The best part of making this pâté is that a good swig or two of the cooking beer always seems to make the assembly of the recipe seem almost effortless.

5 tablespoons unsalted butter
2 large onions, chopped
5 cloves garlic, minced
1 bunch scallions (white bulbs and green stalks), sliced
1½ cups fresh parsley leaves, minced
½ cup shelled pistachios
2 tablespoons fennel seeds
3 pounds sweet Italian sausage, removed from casings

2 cups beer, preferably imported
1 pound lean ground veal
1 pound sliced bacon
1 package (8 ounces) Pepperidge Farm's herb-seasoned crumb stuffing
4 or 5 large eggs
Salt and freshly ground pepper to taste
6 whole bay leaves

1. Melt the butter in a large skillet over medium-high heat. Add the onions, garlic, and scallions and cook until soft and translucent, about 7 minutes, stirring occasionally. Transfer the onion mixture to a large mixing bowl. Stir in the parsley, pistachios, and fennel seeds.

2. Sauté the sausage in 2 batches in the same skillet over medium-high heat. Cook each batch for 2 or 3 minutes, crumbling the sausage into smaller pieces with the back of a wooden spoon. Add ½ cup of beer to each batch and cook just until the sausage is no longer pink. Add each batch to the mixing bowl and stir to combine with the onions.

3. Add the ground veal to the same skillet and cook with another ½ cup beer just until the veal is no longer pink. Add to the mixing bowl.

4. Cut 6 slices of bacon into ½-inch dice. Cook in the same skillet until the bacon renders some of its fat; do not let it begin to become crisp. Add the crumb stuffing and the remaining ½ cup beer. Cook, stirring constantly, for 30 seconds and then add to the mixing bowl.

5. Add 4 eggs to the pâté mixture and beat to make a moist, but not wet, meat-loaf-like mixture. Add the last egg if necessary to bind the mixture. Season with salt and freshly ground pepper.

6. Preheat the oven to 350°F.

7. Place 3 bay leaves in a row down the center of each of two 9 x 3-inch loaf pans. Line each pan with the remaining bacon slices by arranging the strips crosswise in the pan to line both the sides and bottom. Let the ends of the slices hang over the edges of the pan.

8. Pack the pâté mixture very tightly into the pans, pressing down firmly with the back of a spoon or your hands. Fold the overhanging bacon over the top of each pâté. Completely wrap each pan tightly with aluminum foil. Place the pans in a larger baking pan and fill the pan with enough hot water to come halfway up the sides of the pâté pans.

9. Bake the pâtés for 1½ hours. Remove the pâtés from the oven and weight for several hours with a heavy object (such as a 5-pound bag of flour or a large can of tomatoes) placed on each pâté. Refrigerate for several hours.

10. To unmold the pâtés, run a knife around the sides of each pan and invert the pâté onto a clean surface.

11. The pâté will keep up to 2 weeks, tightly wrapped in the refrigerator. The pâté can also be frozen, tightly wrapped in plastic wrap and then in aluminum foil, up to 2 months.

Makes two 9 x 3-inch pâtés.

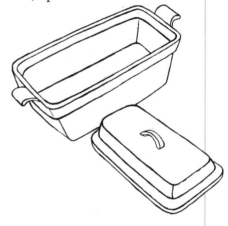

Sicilian Loaf

I used to make this recipe years ago as a hot meat leaf when it was my turn to cook a family meal. Over the years my fanaticism for cold foods has given reincarnation to Sicilian Loaf as one of my shop's most popular chilled pâtés. When sliced thinly, the roulade effect of the baked prosciutto and provolone makes a very pretty presentation. Leftovers make robust sandwiches layered with strong mustard, lettuce, and sliced garden tomatoes.

1½ pounds ground beef
   sirloin
1 pound ground veal
1 medium onion, chopped
4 cloves garlic, minced
2 tablespoons dried
   Italian herb blend
½ cup chopped fresh
   parsley
2½ cups fresh bread
   crumbs

2 large eggs
1 cup tomato juice
1 tablespoon salt
2 teaspoons freshly
   ground pepper
8 ounces thinly sliced
   ham or prosciutto
12 ounces sliced
   Provolone cheese

1. Place the sirloin, veal, onion, garlic, Italian herbs, parsley, and bread crumbs in a large mixing bowl and mix it together with your hands. Add the eggs and tomato juice and blend it in with your hands to bind the mixture. Season to taste with salt and freshly ground pepper.

2. Preheat the oven to 350°F.

3. Place a large sheet of parchment or waxed paper on a work surface. Shape the meat mixture into a 15 x 10-inch rectangle on the paper. Arrange the ham in an even layer over the meat mixture. Cover the ham with 8 ounces of the sliced cheese. Starting from one long side of the rectangle, roll up the meat loaf like a jelly roll and pat the ends gently to make a good loaf shape.

4. Pulling on the paper, carefully slide the meat loaf onto a large baking sheet. Bake for 50 minutes. Arrange the remaining cheese over the top of the meat loaf and bake until the cheese is lightly browned and bubbling, about 10 minutes longer.

5. Let the loaf cool to room temperature, then wrap it in aluminum foil and refrigerate for several hours or overnight. Using a serrated knife, slice it into ¼-inch slices.

Makes 8 entrée servings or 20 to 25 hors d'oeuvre servings.

Smoked Bluefish Pâté

A popular and very Nantucket appetizer.

1 pound smoked bluefish,
  skinned and flaked
12 ounces cream cheese,
  at room temperature
  and cut into small
  chunks
6 tablespoons unsalted
  butter, at room
  temperature and cut
  into bits
1 medium red onion,
  minced

¼ cup chopped fresh dill
2 tablespoons capers,
  drained
3 tablespoons fresh lemon
  juice
2 tablespoons Cognac
Freshly ground pepper to
  taste
Lemon wedges and capers
  for garnish
French Toast Rounds
  (recipe follows)

1. Beat the bluefish, cream cheese, and butter in a mixing bowl with a hand mixer just until combined. Add the onion, dill, capers, lemon juice, and Cognac; beat until blended but do not overbeat so that the pâté will have some texture. Season to taste with pepper.

2. Pack the pâté into small crocks or 1 large one. Cover and refrigerate for a few hours to mellow the flavors. Garnish with lemon wedges and capers and serve at room temperature with toast rounds.

Makes about 3 cups.

French Toast Rounds

While these toasts were invented simply as a way to use up stale bread, they have developed such a devoted following that we now have to bake extra bread just to meet the demand. One customer from Connecticut is so addicted to these that we have named him "Mr. Toast." The toast rounds do add a nice homemade look when serving cheeses and pâtés, and I must admit these are indeed quite delicious.

2 loaves day-old French
    bread, cut into ¼-inch-
    thick slices
½ cup olive oil

1½ tablespoons fines
    herbes or Italian herb
    blend

1. Preheat the oven to 350°F.

2. Arrange the bread slices in a single layer on baking sheets. Lightly brush 1 side of each slice all over with oil, then sprinkle lightly with the herbs.

3. Bake just until crisp and light golden brown, 12 to 15 minutes. Let cool to room temperature and store in an airtight container.

Makes 4 to 5 dozen.

Pastel Chicken Pâté

This pâté is full of the complex flavors of other pâtés but is lighter in texture and summery in color.

8 whole boneless, skinless
    chicken breasts, cut
    into ½-inch chunks
1 cup plus 3 tablespoons
    snipped fresh chives
5 tablespoons chopped
    fresh tarragon
1¼ cups diced thinly
    sliced baked ham
½ cup shelled pistachios
5 tablespoons pink
    peppercorns

⅔ cup Cognac
2 teaspoons salt, or more
    to taste
1 teaspoon freshly ground
    black pepper, plus
    additional
2 large eggs
2 large egg whites
½ teaspoon grated
    nutmeg
2½ cups heavy or
    whipping cream

1. Place one-quarter of the chicken breasts in a large mixing bowl. Add 1 cup chives, 3 tablespoons tarragon, the ham, pistachios, pink peppercorns, ⅓ cup Cognac, 2 teaspoons salt, and 1 teaspoon black pepper; toss together. Let the mixture marinate at room temperature for 30 minutes.

2. Meanwhile, place the remaining chicken breasts in a food processor fitted with the steel blade and process until the meat is ground. Add the eggs and egg whites and process until smooth.

Add the remaining ⅓ cup Cognac, 3 tablespoons chives, 2 tablespoons tarragon, and the nutmeg and process until blended. With the machine running, pour the heavy cream through the feed tube and process until thoroughly blended.

3. Preheat the oven to 350°F. Brush a 16 x 5-inch loaf pan with vegetable oil.

4. Add the processed mixture to the marinated mixture in the mixing bowl and stir until well combined. Spoon the pâté mixture into the prepared pan. Cover with aluminum foil. Place the pan in a larger baking pan and fill the larger pan with enough hot water to come halfway up the sides of the pâté pan. Bake until the top of the pâté is just firm to the touch, about 1 hour. Let cool to room temperature. Invert onto a clean surface, wrap in plastic wrap, and refrigerate until ready to serve.

Makes 16 x 5-inch pâté.

June Taylor Chicken Legs

I was at first dismayed when I realized that of all the esoteric fare available at the store these simple chicken drumsticks were one of the most popular items. Then I thought of the little legs in a chorus line, and that infused enough humor into the daily preparation of trays and trays to make it enjoyable.

20 to 24 chicken drumsticks	Salt and coarsely ground black pepper to taste
⅓ cup vegetable oil	1½ cups fresh bread crumbs
½ cup Dijon mustard	
⅓ cup dry white wine	

1. Preheat the oven to 350°F.

2. Arrange the drumsticks in rows on a large baking sheet. Using a pastry brush, brush each drumstick lightly with oil. Whisk the mustard and wine together in a small bowl and brush this mixture generously over each drumstick. Sprinkle the drumsticks with salt and pepper, then sprinkle the bread crumbs evenly over all the drumsticks.

3. Bake the drumsticks for 50 to 60 minutes. Cover the drumsticks with aluminum foil if they seem to be getting too brown. Serve the drumsticks warm or at room temperature arranged on a large platter in a chorus line.

Makes 10 to 12 hors d'oeuvre servings.

Summer
Steak Tartare

This wonderful rendition of classic steak tartare captures the flavors and fragrances of summer and takes a delicious bit of license with the standard presentation.

1½ pounds finely ground
  very lean beef
  tenderloin
3 shallots, minced
1 clove garlic, minced
1½ tablespoons capers,
  drained
½ cup chopped fresh basil
½ cup chopped fresh
  parsley
10 sun-dried tomatoes,
  packed in oil, drained
  and minced

2½ tablespoons Dijon
  mustard
2 tablespoons Cognac
  (optional)
2 large egg yolks
Salt and freshly ground
  pepper to taste
1 bunch arugula
2 ounce wedge Parmesan
  cheese
2 hard-cooked egg yolks,
  pressed through fine
  sieve

1. Using your hands, thoroughly combine the beef, shallots, garlic, capers, basil, parsley, sun-dried tomatoes, mustard, and Cognac in a mixing bowl. Blend in the raw egg yolks and season the mixture with salt and pepper.

2. Line a serving plate with arugula leaves. Mound the steak tartare on the center of the plate. Shave the wedge of Parmesan cheese with a vegetable peeler to make thin shards and scatter them over the steak tartare and arugula leaves. Sprinkle the sieved egg yolks over all to create a fine spattered effect. Serve at once with toast points.

Makes 8 servings.

Orange Rosemary Muffins with Sliced Duck Breast

The pronounced flavors in these savory bite-size sandwich hors d'oeuvres capture the essence of summer lushness.

ORANGE ROSEMARY MUFFINS:

½ cup (1 stick) unsalted butter, at room temperature
1 cup sugar
2 large eggs
2 cups unbleached all-purpose flour
1 teaspoon baking soda

½ teaspoon salt
1 cup sour cream or well-shaken buttermilk
1 cup golden raisins
1 large orange, zest grated, orange juiced
1 tablespoon dried rosemary

DUCK BREASTS:

3 whole boneless duck breasts
¼ cup fresh orange juice
2 tablespoons orange-flavored liqueur

¼ cup fruity olive oil
Salt and freshly ground pepper to taste
Honey mustard

1. Prepare the muffins: Preheat the oven to 375°F. Lightly grease miniature muffin cups, 1½ inches in diameter.

2. Using an electric mixer, beat the butter and sugar in a mixing bowl until smooth and creamy. Beat in the eggs, one at a time, then continue beating until light and fluffy.

3. Sift the flour, baking soda, and salt together. Add the flour mixture to the butter mixture alternately with the sour cream, blending thoroughly after each addition.

4. Place the raisins, orange zest, and rosemary in a food processor fitted with the steel blade and process until finely minced. Stir the raisin mixture into the batter.

5. Spoon the batter into the muffin cups, filling each cup almost to the top. Bake until light golden brown, 10 to 12 minutes. Remove the muffins from oven and brush the tops lightly with the orange juice. Turn out onto a wire rack and let cool completely. You will have enough batter for about 5 dozen muffins.

6. Prepare the duck breasts: Grill the duck on an outdoor grill, preferably over mesquite or another flavorful wood chip.

Grill the breasts, skin side down, until the skin is well browned, 4 to 5 minutes. Turn the duck and grill 2 minutes longer for rare meat. Let the duck cool, then cut diagonally into thin slices.

7. Place the meat in a shallow bowl. Add the orange juice, liqueur, oil, salt, and pepper and toss to combine. Let marinate for at least 1 hour.

8. To serve, split each muffin in half and spread the bottoms with a generous dab of honey mustard. Fold a slice of marinated duck breast in half and place over the mustard. Replace the top on each muffin and when all are assembled, arrange in a flat basket or on a serving platter. These will hold unrefrigerated for to 2 to 3 hours if covered with a lightly dampened cloth.

Makes 5 dozen.

Sweet-Potato and Peanut Chips

A simple and irresistible nosh that finds its inspiration way down in the land of Dixie. When not serving them as a fast-to-disappear party hors d'oeuvre, try them as an accompaniment to barbecued ribs or Southern fried chicken.

¾ cup honey roasted
  peanuts
2 large sweet potatoes,
  peeled and sliced ⅛
  inch thick

½ cup (1 stick) unsalted
  butter, melted
Salt to taste

1. Preheat the oven to 475°F. Line 2 large baking sheets with aluminum foil. Lightly butter the foil.

2. Process the peanuts in a food processor fitted with the steel blade until finely chopped but not powdered; transfer to a bowl. Dip the potato slices in the melted butter to coat both sides. Arrange the slices on the prepared pans in rows that are close together but not overlapping. Sprinkle the top of each potato slice generously with peanuts.

3. Bake the chips until the tops are lightly browned and the potatoes are just tender, 15 to 20 minutes. Watch carefully that they do not burn. Transfer the chips to paper towels to drain off any excess butter. Let cool 5 minutes. Taste and sprinkle with additional salt if desired. Arrange the chips on trays and serve.

Makes about 4 dozen.

Baby Chiles Rellenos

Although quite a bit of work to make, the delectable results make it all worthwhile. I love these.

2 cans (4 ounces each)
  whole green chiles
1 can (8 ounces) whole
  pimientos
8 ounces Monterey Jack
  cheese

8 ounces Monterey Jack
  cheese with jalapeño
  peppers

BATTER:

2 cups unbleached
  all-purpose flour
1 tablespoon ground
  cumin

2 teaspoons salt
2 cups beer, preferably
  imported

CORIANDER DIPPING SAUCE:

3 cloves garlic, minced
8 canned whole tomatillos
1 cup fresh coriander
  leaves
½ cup whole or slivered
  blanched almonds

⅓ cup fresh lime juice
½ cup olive oil
Salt and freshly ground
  pepper to taste

Vegetable oil for deep frying

1. Drain the cans of green chiles and pimientos. Cut the chiles and pimientos into ½-inch-wide strips. Cut both cheeses into ½-inch cubes. Wrap the green chile strips around the plain Monterey Jack cheese and the pimiento strips around the jalapeño Jack cheese, securing each with a wooden toothpick. Place them all on a tray and refrigerate for a few hours.

2. Meanwhile, prepare the batter: Stir the flour, cumin, and salt together in a mixing bowl. Add the beer and whisk until smooth. Let stand at room temperature for at least 1 hour.

3. Prepare the dipping sauce: Place the garlic, tomatillos, coriander, and almonds in a food processor fitted with the steel blade; process until smooth. Add the lime juice and olive oil and process until blended. Season with salt and pepper. Transfer to a small bowl.

4. Pour 1 inch vegetable oil into a large skillet and heat to 400°F. Dip the chilled cheese morsels, one at a time, in the beer batter and immediately drop in the hot oil. Do not crowd the pan. Fry, turning once, until light golden brown. Drain on paper towels. Serve immediately with the dipping sauce. (The chiles rellenos can be fried up to 3 hours in advance and reheated in a 375°F hot oven for 5 minutes, just before serving.)

Makes 4 to 4½ dozen.

Stuffed Grape Leaves (Dolmas)

I like my grape leaves cold or at room temperature and therefore prefer a filling without ground meat. These are done in the Persian tradition with the sweet addition of currants, cinnamon, and nutmeg balancing the saltiness of the brine-packed grape leaves in mysterious ways. The only problem with grape leaves is the time-consuming labor of rolling each individual one. During the late summer cocktail party frenzy, I often think I would trade all my food processors, attachments included, for an automatic grape-leaf roller. Short of that, friends' Greek mothers are always welcomed with open arms in late August.

FILLING:

½ cup plus 3 tablespoons olive oil
1 medium onion, minced
1½ cups converted rice
4 cups chicken stock, preferably homemade
½ cup dry white wine
⅔ cup currants
2 tablespoons ground cinnamon

1 teaspoon grated nutmeg
½ cup pine nuts, lightly toasted
1 cup minced fresh parsley
Salt and freshly ground pepper to taste

1 jar (16 ounces) grape leaves packed in brine (preferably from California, for they tend to be better than the imported Greek brands)

½ cup fresh lemon juice
½ cup water
Lemon slices and fresh mint sprigs for garnish

1. Heat 3 tablespoons oil in a large skillet over medium-high heat. Add the onion and cook for 4 minutes. Stir in the rice and cook 2 minutes longer, stirring to coat the rice well with the oil.

2. Reduce the heat to medium and pour in 2 cups of the chicken stock and the wine. Add the currants and simmer uncovered, stirring occasionally, for 10 minutes. Add 1½ cups more chicken stock and simmer 5 minutes longer. Add the remaining ½ cup chicken stock and cook another 5 minutes, watching the rice carefully throughout and stirring occasionally to prevent burning.

3. Reduce the heat to low, stir in the cinnamon and nutmeg, and cook 1 minute. Let cool, stirring occasionally to fluff the rice. Add the pine nuts and parsley and toss to combine. Season to taste with salt and pepper. (Be careful not to salt heavily as the grape leaves are quite salty.)

4. Rinse the grape leaves under cold running water and pat dry. Place 1 leaf, vein side up, on a dry working surface. Place about 1 tablespoon filling at the center stem end of the leaf. Shape the filling into a compact log, about 1 inch long, and roll up the leaf as tightly as possible, folding in the sides as you roll to make a compact bundle. Repeat with the remaining grape leaves and filling.

5. Line the bottom of a 4-quart pot with any torn grape leaves to prevent the stuffed leaves from burning and sticking to the pot. Pack the stuffed leaves in concentric circles in the pot, making as many layers as necessary.

6. Pour the lemon juice, ½ cup olive oil, and the water over the grape leaves. Place a heatproof plate on top of the grape leaves with a heavy can (such as tomatoes) on top. Simmer the grape leaves over medium heat for 40 minutes. Let cool completely with the plate and can still on top.

7. Arrange the grape leaves on a platter and garnish with lemon slices and sprigs of mint. Serve at room temperature or slightly chilled. Store any extra or leftover grape leaves in the refrigerator.

Makes about 60.

Sunny
Sauces, Sips,
and Skinny
Dips

Those languorous spells of hot, hot, and hazy summer days call for effortless sustenance in a soothing variety of cooling liquid forms. The splendid selection of sauces in this chaper can all be made ahead and either dolloped on an entanglement of pasta or splashed atop sizzling fare from the grill at the last minute. The dips require just a flick or two of the food processor blade or, at most, a rhythmic flexing of the chopping knife. The sips—the most cooling enticement of all—demand only a good supply of ice, a liberal pouring hand, and a few choice libations spiked with a dash or two of island mixing secrets.

Great Guacamole

While it is not difficult to make authentic tasting Mexican guacamole, I find that few people north of Texas seem to develop the instincts for such. To be truly transported to the land of tequila, tacos, and mañana, a scoop of guacamole should be chunky in texture, balanced perfectly between the fire of jalapeño peppers and the soothing cool of lime juice, and spiced liberally with aromatic fresh coriander leaves. This much admired version is made daily in my shop.

8 Hass avocados (dark green small) or 4 large, smooth-skinned Florida avocados, at the peak of ripeness
4 ripe medium tomatoes, seeded and cut into ¼-inch dice
1 small red onion, coarsely chopped
2 fresh jalapeño peppers, seeded and finely chopped
½ cup fresh lime juice
3 tablespoons chopped fresh coriander leaves
Salt to taste
3 tablespoons Hellmann's mayonnaise
⅓ cup sour cream

1. Peel and pit the avocados and mash the pulp in a medium mixing bowl to a chunky consistency. A large wooden spoon or potato masher works well, but do not use a food processor or blender or the mixture will become too smooth.

2. Add the tomatoes, onion, and jalapeño peppers to the avocados and stir to combine. Stir in the lime juice, coriander, and salt. Fold in the mayonnaise to keep the guacamole from discoloring. Transfer the guacamole to an earthenware or ceramic serving dish; make an indentation in the center and spoon in the sour cream. Serve with plenty of your favorite corn tortilla chips.

Makes 4 to 4½ cups.

Tomatillo Salsa

A slippery green version of the more traditional red salsa. Use as a dip for tortilla chips or as a sauce with cold poached chicken or shellfish.

3 cups whole tomatillos,
   fresh or canned, peeled
2 ripe medium tomatoes,
   seeded and finely
   chopped
1 small red onion,
   minced
1 clove garlic, minced
2 fresh jalapeño peppers,
   seeded and finely chopped

½ yellow bell pepper,
   seeded and finely
   chopped
½ cup fresh lime juice
¼ cup fruity olive oil
¼ cup freshly chopped
   coriander
Salt and freshly ground
   pepper to taste

Purée the tomatillos in a blender or food processor fitted with the steel blade until smooth. Transfer to a mixing bowl. Stir in the remaining ingredients. Refrigerate a few hours to allow the flavors to blend, then serve.

Makes about 1 quart.

Mexican Salsa

This salsa bears little resemblance to the red sauce served in typical American Mexican restaurants. I believe this to be the perfect summer dip.

1 bunch scallions,
   chopped
3 ripe large tomatoes,
   seeded and chopped
2 fresh jalapeño peppers,
   seeded and minced
1 green bell pepper,
   seeded and diced
½ red bell pepper, seeded
   and diced

½ yellow bell pepper,
   seeded and diced
1 can (35 ounces) whole
   tomatoes, puréed with liquid
½ cup water
½ cup fresh lime juice
2 tablespoons fruity olive oil
2 tablespoons chopped coriander
Salt and freshly ground
   pepper to taste

Combine the scallions, fresh tomatoes, and peppers in a large mixing bowl. Stir in the puréed tomatoes, water, and lime juice. Stir in the oil and coriander and season with salt and pepper. Refrigerate covered until ready to serve. Serve with your favorite corn tortilla chips.

Makes 8 cups.

WIDOW'S WALK COCKTAILS

Stuffed Grape Leaves
Roasted Garlic
Marinated Goat Cheeses • French Toast Rounds
Sicilian Loaf
Hummus bi Tahini

Lillet Martinis
Hammie Heard's Bloody Marys

Hummus bi Tahini

The Que Sera version of hummus acquires more devoted followers every summer season. It is no wonder, for this recipe for hummus is by no means the bland chick-pea paste you may have tasted elsewhere, but a voluptuous spread with lots of garlic, lemon, and cumin. It is perfect and versatile fare to pack for the beach, to dip into in the late afternoon, or to serve with pre-dinner cocktails. Accompaniments are simple—fresh pita triangles for scooping and, perhaps, some deep purple Mediterranean olives.

3 large cloves garlic,
   minced
½ cup fresh lemon juice
1 cup sesame tahini paste
1 cup water
6 cups canned chick-peas,
   rinsed and drained
1½ tablespoons ground
   cumin

Salt to taste
3 tablespoons fruity olive
   oil
Sweet Hungarian paprika
Lemon slices, Greek
   olives, and fresh mint
   or parsley sprigs for
   garnish

1. Place the garlic, lemon juice, and tahini in a food processor fitted with the steel blade; process to a smooth paste.

2. Add the water and chick-peas and process until the mixture is very smooth, almost fluffy. Season with the cumin and salt to taste.

3. Transfer the hummus to an earthenware bowl. Pour the oil over the top and swirl lightly with the tip of a knife. Sprinkle with the paprika, and garnish with lemon slices, olives, and mint or parsley sprigs.

Makes about 6 cups.

Baba Ghanouj

A close cousin to hummus, this Middle Eastern dip is often referred to as eggplant caviar.

2 medium eggplants
¾ cup sesame tahini
  paste
½ cup fresh lemon juice
2 cloves garlic, minced
Salt and freshly ground
  pepper to taste
1 small red onion,
  minced

2 ripe medium tomatoes,
  seeded and finely diced
¾ cup chopped fresh
  parsley
2 tablespoons fruity olive
  oil

1. Preheat the oven to 375°F.

2. Place the whole eggplants on a lightly oiled baking sheet. Roast the eggplants, turning once halfway through cooking, until the flesh is quite soft, about 45 minutes. Let stand until cool enough to handle.

3. Cut off the stems and peel the skin from the eggplants. Place the pulp in a food processor fitted with the steel blade and process until smooth. Add the tahini, lemon juice, and garlic and process again until smooth. Season to taste with salt and pepper.

4. Transfer the eggplant mixture to a mixing bowl. Add the onion, tomatoes, ½ cup of the parsley, and the oil and stir until blended. Refrigerate a few hours to mellow the flavors. Garnish with the remaining ¼ cup chopped parlsey and serve with fresh pita triangles for dipping.

Makes about 3 cups.

Roasted Red Pepper Dip

Save this sunset-colored dip for the ripest of summer's vegetables plucked warm from the vine.

2 red bell peppers, roasted, peeled, and seeds removed	3 tablespoons fruity olive oil
1 whole head roasted garlic (see page 20), pulp squeezed and skins discarded	5 tablespoons minced fresh basil
	1 tablespoon chopped fresh rosemary
	Pinch cayenne pepper
8 ounces Montrachet or other mild, soft goat cheese, without ash	Salt and freshly ground pepper to taste

Place the red peppers, garlic, and cheese in a blender or food processor fitted with the steel blade; purée until smooth. Transfer the mixture to a mixing bowl and stir in the oil, basil, rosemary, and cayenne. Season to taste with salt and pepper. Refrigerate covered to firm the dip. Serve with your favorite dipping vegetables.

Makes about 1½ cups.

Tomato Béarnaise Mayonnaise

A fabulous accompaniment to both cold sliced tenderloin and whole poached salmon, this mayonnaise also adds extra zest to spur-of-the-moment sandwiches.

4 shallots, minced	2 tablespoons fresh lemon juice
3 heaping tablespoons dried tarragon	1¼ cups vegetable oil
⅓ cup tarragon vinegar	1 cup olive oil
⅓ cup dry white wine	¼ cup tomato paste
3 large egg yolks	Salt and freshly ground pepper to taste
2½ tablespoons Dijon mustard	

1. Place the shallots, tarragon, vinegar, and wine in a small saucepan. Heat to boiling over high heat and reduce until just 1 tablespoon liquid remains. Set aside.

2. Process the egg yolks, mustard, and lemon juice in a food processor fitted with the steel blade for 10 seconds. With the machine running, add the oils in a thin, steady stream through the feed tube to make a thick emulsion. Add the tomato paste and the shallot mixture; process until blended. Season to taste with salt and pepper. Refrigerate covered until ready to serve.

Makes about 4 cups.

Basil Parmesan Mayonnaise

This pesto-inspired mayonnaise was developed as a salad binder when working with The Silver Palate on the *Good Times Cookbook*. As it was soon discovered to be sensational just on its own, I decided to adapt the recipe into a crudite dip. The fresh green color and clear basil flavor provide instant transport to the middle of a garden patch and the mayonnaise contrasts beautifully with Roasted Red Pepper Dip on large vegetable platters.

1 large egg	3 tablespoons fresh lemon
2 large egg yolks	juice
2 tablespoons Dijon	2 cups olive oil
mustard	1½ cups vegetable oil
½ cup finely grated	Salt and freshly ground
Parmesan cheese	pepper to taste
½ cup minced fresh basil	

Place the egg, egg yolks, mustard, Parmesan, basil, and lemon juice in a food processor fitted with the steel blade; process for 10 seconds. With the machine running, add the oils in a thin, steady stream through the feed tube to make a thick emulsion. Season the mayonnaise to taste with salt and freshly ground pepper. Refrigerate covered until ready to serve.

Makes about 4 cups.

Aioli

I think almost everything tastes better with a little dab of aioli on it. Two of my most favorite dippers are blanched green beans and chunks of steaming lobster meat.

1 thick slice day-old
    French bread
3 tablespoons light cream
    (see Index) or half and
    half
5 or 6 cloves garlic,
    minced
2 large egg yolks

1 tablespoon Dijon
    mustard
1 cup vegetable oil
¾ cup olive oil
2 to 3 tablespoons fresh
    lemon juice
Salt and freshly ground
    pepper to taste

1. Trim the crust from the bread and tear the bread into irregular pieces. Combine the bread and cream in a small bowl and let stand for 5 minutes. Gather the bread into a ball and squeeze out as much liquid as possible.

2. Place the bread, garlic, egg yolks, and mustard in a food processor fitted with the steel blade; process until smooth. With the machine running, pour the oils in a thin, steady stream through the feed tube to make a thick emulsion.

3. Season to taste with lemon juice, salt, and pepper. Refrigerate covered until ready to serve.

Makes about 2 cups.

Remoulade Sauce

One of the most flavorful homemade mayonnaises: Besides being the perfect accompaniment to codfish cakes, remoulade sauce is great dolloped on top of grilled hamburgers, spread on your favorite club sandwich, or tossed with a julienne of fresh celeriac to make the classic version of the French bistro salad, celeriac remoulade.

1 large egg
2 large egg yolks
6 anchovy fillets, drained
2 tablespoons capers,
    drained
4 cornichons, minced
2 cloves garlic, minced
2 tablespoons Dijon
    mustard
⅓ cup minced fresh
    parsley

2 tablespoons minced
    fresh tarragon or 1
    tablespoon dried
    tarragon
2 tablespoons balsamic
    vinegar
2 tablespoons fresh lemon
    juice
1¾ cups olive oil
Salt and freshly ground
    pepper to taste

Place the egg, egg yolks, anchovies, capers, cornichons, garlic, mustard, parsley, tarragon, vinegar, and lemon juice in a food processor fitted with the steel blade; process to combine, 15 seconds. With the machine running, pour the oil through the feed tube in a thin, steady stream to make a thick emulsion. Season the sauce with salt and pepper to taste. Store covered in the refrigerator for up to 1 week.

Makes about 2½ cups sauce.

Cold Pine Nut Sauce for Seafood

This sunny yellow sauce adds a new dimension to the accompaniments usually served with cold poached seafood. The inspiration for this recipe is of obscure Mexican origins.

⅓ cup pine nuts, toasted
3 hard-cooked large egg
    yolks
1 cup sour cream
¼ cup Hellmann's
    mayonnaise

2 tablespoons fresh lime
    juice
2 tablespoons minced
    fresh coriander
Salt to taste

Place the pine nuts and egg yolks in a food processor fitted with the steel blade; process until finely minced. Add the sour cream, mayonnaise, and lime juice and process until smooth. Stir in the coriander and season with salt. Refrigerate covered until cold. Serve with your favorite cold poached seafood.

Makes 1½ cups.

Tomato Cognac Sauce for Chilled Mussels

An elegant hors d'oeuvre sauce to be spooned over cold steamed mussels that have been nestled back into the half shell.

¼ cup tomato paste	½ cup water
2 tablespoons fresh lemon juice	1½ cups Hellmann's mayonnaise
1 tablespoon dry sherry	½ cup sour cream
3 tablespoons Cognac	2 heaping tablespoons (or to taste) prepared horseradish with beets
2 cloves garlic, minced	
1 small Bermuda onion, minced	

1. Place the tomato paste, lemon juice, sherry, Cognac, garlic, onion, and water in a small saucepan and cook, stirring occasionally, over medium heat until the mixture is reduced by half. Be careful not to let the mixture burn on the bottom of the pan. Transfer to a mixing bowl and let cool to room temperature.

2. Fold the mayonnaise, sour cream, and horseradish into the tomato mixture. Refrigerate the sauce for a few hours to allow the flavors to blend and mellow.

Makes about 2¼ cups.

Liptauer

This delicious Hungarian spread is an excellent accompaniment to sliced smoked salmon with dark bread.

8 ounces cream cheese, cut into small pieces	1½ tablespoons sweet Hungarian paprika
4 tablespoons (½ stick) unsalted butter, cut into small pieces	1 teaspoon Dijon mustard
	1 teaspoon anchovy paste
1 small onion, minced	2 teaspoons caraway seeds
1 tablespoon capers, drained	

Place the cream cheese, butter, onion, capers, paprika, mustard, and anchovy paste in a food processor fitted with the steel blade; process until combined but not smooth or puréed. Add the caraway seeds and process quickly just to combine. Transfer the mixture to a small serving bowl and refrigerate for several hours to allow the flavors to mellow.

Makes about 1½ cups.

Red Clam Sauce

A traditional Italian sauce for pasta, but try it also as a base for a seafood pizza.

¼ cup olive oil
1 large onion, chopped
6 cloves garlic, minced
2 cans (28 ounces each) Italian plum tomatoes, undrained
¼ cup (or as needed) tomato paste
½ cup (or as needed) dry red wine
¾ cup bottled clam juice

1 teaspoon dried red pepper flakes
3 tablespoons dried oregano
Salt and freshly ground pepper to taste
3½ cups minced cooked clams, fresh or canned
¼ cup chopped fresh basil
¼ cup chopped fresh parsley

1. Heat the oil in a large pot over medium-high heat. Add the onion and garlic and cook, stirring frequently, for 10 minutes. Add the tomatoes, paste, wine, clam juice, red pepper, and oregano. Simmer 30 minutes, adding more wine if the sauce seems too thick or more tomato paste if too thin. Season to taste with salt and pepper.

2. Stir the clams, basil, and parsley into the sauce and simmer 10 minutes longer.

Makes about 3 quarts.

White Clam Sauce

An easy sauce that always wins raves from friends and guests.

¾ cup dry white wine
4 dozen littleneck clams, scrubbed
½ cup fruity olive oil
6 cloves garlic, minced
1 tablespoon dried oregano

3 tablespoons minced fresh parsley
½ cup chopped fresh basil
Salt and freshly ground pepper to taste
1 pound linguine, cooked al dente

1. Pour the wine into a large pot. Add the clams and cook covered over high heat until the clams open. Remove the clams from the pot with a slotted spoon. Remove the meat from the shells and set aside. Discard the shells. Strain the cooking liquid through a fine mesh sieve and reserve.

2. Heat the oil in a large skillet over medium heat. Add the garlic, reduce the heat to low, and cook, stirring frequently, just until the garlic is light golden. Add the oregano and the reserved cooking liquid. Heat to boiling, then simmer for 10 minutes.

3. Stir the clams, parsley, and basil into the sauce. Season to taste with salt and pepper. Simmer 5 minutes longer. Serve the sauce tossed with the linguine.

Makes 4 to 6 servings.

Onion Marmalade

This is fantastic on top of grilled hamburgers or as an accompaniment to other summer barbecue fare.

2 extra large yellow onions (2½ to 3 pounds), each cut into 10 wedges
1½ cups chicken stock
½ cup medium-dry sherry

2 tablespoons sherry vinegar
2 teaspoons sugar
Salt and freshly ground pepper to taste
½ cup crème fraîche

Place the onions in a medium saucepan. Add the chicken stock, sherry, sherry vinegar, and sugar. Heat to boiling. Reduce the heat and simmer covered, stirring occasionally, until most of the liquid evaporates, about 45 minutes. Season to taste with salt and pepper. Stir in the crème fraîche and cook over low heat 10 minutes longer. Serve warm or at room temperature. Store any extra covered in the refrigerator. It will keep for up to 1 week.
Makes about 2½ cups.

Elena's Grandfather's Peasant Sauce

My close friend Elena escaped the trials and tribulations of writing magazine articles and reading screenplays in New York one summer and blessed my kitchen with her unique sense of humor and some treasured old family recipes. Both my staff and customers fell madly in love with a very simple and straightforward recipe for her grandfather's meatless tomato sauce. The secret to its unique appeal lies in the large ratio of onions to tomatoes and the resulting smoky sweet taste that the slow sautéing of the onions in fruity olive oil imparts to the overall taste of the sauce. While always comforting in its traditional use on pasta, I'm also partial to a spoonful or two of Peasant Sauce over charcoal grilled hamburgers.

½ cup fruity olive oil
3 large yellow onions, chopped medium fine
1 tablespoon salt
2½ tablespoons tomato paste
1 can (35 ounces) Italian plum tomatoes, undrained

1 pound vermicelli or capellini, cooked al dente
Freshly grated Parmesan or Romano cheese

1. Heat oil in a large saucepan over high heat until sizzling hot. Add the onions and sauté, stirring frequently, for 5 minutes. Reduce the heat to medium and cook the onions, stirring frequently, just until beginning to turn golden brown, about 25 minutes.

2. Stir in the salt and tomato paste. Stir in the canned tomatoes and simmer the sauce uncovered for 30 minutes.

3. Toss the hot pasta with just enough of the sauce to keep it from sticking together. Serve the remaining sauce on the side and pass the cheese.

Makes 4 to 6 servings.

ELENA'S STORY

"My grandfather grew up in San Polo di Cavalieri, a tiny hill town outside of Rome where Italian messengers were sent for an ancient version of rest and relaxation. When he came to this country, he brought with him many treasures, none of which were packed in his small valise. Among my favorites is his recipe for a sauce that made meatless Catholic Fridays a joy.

When visiting his family in Rome last summer, I offered to make this sauce which I had always thought of as his creation. But the very next day his niece prepared—il pranzo—the midday meal—and lo and behold, it was my grandfather's sauce! More than any history or stories that we shared, this sauce said we were family."

Hammie Heard's Bloody Mary

Years ago I was invited to a Sunday afternoon picnic on the sunny deck of Hammie Heard's Hulbert Avenue home. He served absolutely the best Bloody Mary I have ever tasted. Hammie graciously offered to share his blending secrets provided that we could test the recipe together and perfect it several times over!

6 ounces Beefamato
Dash Jane's Crazy
  Mixed-Up Salt
Few grinds of the
  peppermill
Few shakes Tabasco sauce

Few drops Worcestershire
  sauce
1 generous shot vodka
Ice cubes
Juice of ½ lime

Stir the Beefamato, salt, pepper, Tabasco, and Worcestershire together in a large glass. Stir in the vodka and then add enough ice to fill the glass. Stir like crazy. Squeeze some of the lime juice around the rim of the glass and squeeze the rest over the drink. Savor!

Makes 1 drink.

CHAMPAGNE

Champagne is a luxury for the unluxurious moment, the moment of monetary, or, worse, emotional poverty. When despair has tightened your throat so, you can't swallow anything, and you have to speak by hand signals. When no human comfort can reach you, and you must rely, helpless, on the beneficience of the generous sound of pouring wine. When the kindest hand would be too heavy. The voice of sympathy, abrasive as a badly stroked cello. When the heartache you've always read about in the distance turns out to be your own. When love has been mistaken, gone, died. Champagne is for laughing-in-spite-of-your-tears, a shout of defiance, an act of faith, a promise of renewal. Champagne is best when your world is falling apart.

—JEANINE LARMOTH
The Passionate Palate

Pink Bellinis

Those who have traveled to Venice are no doubt familiar with the magical Venetian cocktail, the Bellini—a quenching froth of fresh peach juice and Italian Prosecco. While it is hard to find good Prosecco in this country and our peaches differ in intensity from those grown in Italy, I feel I have devised a rather irresistible facsimile using dry pink Champagne and orchard ripe peaches.

Every summer I spend an annual Bellini afternoon on the

beach with my special friend and children's author, Joan Walsh Anglund. We swim in the surf, nibble on grapes and olives, get lost in deep spiritual conversation, and usually end up sipping this sunset-colored cocktail right into the moonlight.

2 ripe large peaches	1 cup small ice cubes
2 tablespoons fresh lemon juice	1 bottle (750 ml) dry pink Champagne, cold
3 tablespoons fresh orange juice	

Drop the peaches into a small saucepan of boiling water, blanch for 2 minutes, and drain. Remove the skins and pits from the peaches. Purée the peaches, lemon and orange juices in a blender. Add the ice and Champagne and blend until smooth and frothy. Pour into 8 chilled champagne flutes and serve.

Makes 8 Bellinis.

Lillet Martini

The French aperitif Lillet is the light drink I prefer to sip through the summer. However, for those days when something far more potent than the traditional Lillet and soda is needed I have devised this outrageous martini.

1¼ cups vodka	2 thin strips orange zest for garnish
¼ cup Lillet Blanc	
2 large strips (2 inches wide) orange zest	

1. The day before you think you might need a strong martini, mix the vodka and Lillet and pour into a freezer container. Add the 2 large strips of orange zest. Freeze covered for at least 12 hours.

2. When ready to serve, remove the orange zest from the martini and pour into 2 chilled martini glasses. Garnish with the thin strips of orange zest. For added drama, twist the thin zest strips to release the oils and ignite them with a match before dropping into the martini glass.

Makes 2 very strong martinis.

Las Palmas

In the early days of Que Sera when the shop was tucked into a pink shuttered cubbyhole at 21 Federal Street, and town zoning regulations were still lax enough to allow a creative soul to open a business spontaneously, my neighbor in the apartment above my shop opened a free-spirited clothing store named Zecchino. To infuse a touch of established class into this ephemeral operation, she decided that she needed two locations printed on her sign. She chose Nantucket and Las Palmas—the latter being the warmest possible spot she might long for deep in the raw chill of a Nantucket winter. That summer she and her roommate, my artist friend Sterling, collaborated on tropical rum concoctions and sent them floating down to my shop in the late afternoon. In memory of Zecchino and in honor of her wonderful spirit, here is the drink recollected.

½ cup Mount Gay or
   other good-quality dark
   rum
1½ tablespoons brown
   sugar
1 can (6 ounces)
   pineapple juice
Juice of 3 limes

½ cup diced ripe
   cantaloupe, peach, or
   nectarine
½ ripe banana
⅓ cup fresh raspberries
1 cup ice cubes
Lime slices for garnish

Place all the ingredients, except the garnish, in a blender and blend until smooth and frothy. Pour into 3 glasses, garnish with lime slices, serve, and savor.

Makes 3 drinks.

Soup
Sorcery

When she knew that he [Denys] was coming she would have his favorite dish for him. This was "clear soup," Kamante's exquisite consommé. Perhaps the making of this soup taught Karen Blixen something about writing stories. The recipe calls for you to keep the spirit but to discard the substance of your rough ingredients: eggshells and raw bones, root vegetables and red meat. You then submit them, like a storyteller, to the "fire and patience." And the clarity comes at the end, a magic trick."

Isak Dinesen: The Life of a Storyteller
—JUDITH THURMAN

I believe that soup making is one of the most gratifying experiences of all in the vast spectrum of culinary activities. Tender stirring and simmering cannot help but bring forth the loving and nurturing instinct of every soup maker, but it is the finished product that contains the power to assuage the parched palate or soul in truly magical ways.

On New England islands such as Nantucket, where old tourist brochures would boast that "Summer is five Septembers long," soup sorcery takes on many different forms. Chilled soups are in demand on the hot, high noon days when even chewing seems too difficult, while creamy rich soups are needed when pure self-indulgence is in order. The heartier soups, bursting with hominess and nourishment, acknowledge the first signs of summer's fading and the invigorating chill in the air. This coveted collection of soup recipes, ranging from a silky avocado to peasanty potato and kale, is guaranteed to provide many sips of contentment, whatever the climate or occasion.

Smoky Clam Chowder

Every cook harbors secret inexplicable idiosyncracies. One of mine is that making clam chowder sends me into a state of pure rapture. I always rely on my instincts to add extra generous amounts of my favorite chowder ingredients and believe this particular version is made extraordinary by the addition of smoky finnan haddie to the usual clam base.

8 slices bacon, cut into
   ½-inch dice
2 tablespoons unsalted
   butter
1 large onion, chopped
2 quarts water
2 cups dry white wine
3 large boiling pototoes,
   peeled and cut into
   ½-inch dice (about 4½
   cups)

1 pound finnan haddie
2 cups milk
4 cups canned or fresh
   clams with juice
2 cups half and half
1 cup heavy or whipping
   cream
2 teaspoons dried thyme
1 teaspoon paprika
Salt and freshly ground
   pepper to taste

1. Fry the bacon in a large stockpot over medium-high heat, stirring frequently, until crisp. Using a slotted spoon, transfer the bacon to paper towels to drain. Set aside.

2. Add the butter to the bacon fat in the pot and heat over medium heat. Add the onion and cook, stirring occasionally, for 10 minutes.

3. Pour the water and wine into the pot, then add the potatoes. Simmer uncovered until the potatoes are tender, about 25 minutes. Measure 3 cups of the soup with potatoes into a blender and process until smooth. Return the purée to the soup and stir.

4. While the soup is simmering, cut the finnan haddie in half and place it in a saucepan. Cover with the milk. Heat to boiling. Reduce the heat and simmer for 20 minutes. Pour the poaching liquid into the soup. Flake the finnan haddie into small pieces. Add the fish and clams with juice to the soup.

5. Stir the half and half and cream into the soup. Add the thyme and paprika and season with salt and pepper to taste. Simmer 10 to 15 minutes. Stir in the bacon just before serving.

Makes about 3½ quarts.

My Aunt's Cold
Clam Chowder

As with most of the fabulous and abundant creations of my aunt's Nantucket kitchen, we would discover the next day that we loved the leftovers cold from the refrigerator. I became so fond of this clam chowder that whole batches were frequently made just for chilling.

5 ounces salt pork, cut
   into ¼-inch dice
1 large onion, diced
4 cups clam juice
   (combination bottled
   and fresh from the
   shucked clams)
1 cup dry white wine
4 cups peeled potato
   cubes (bite size)
2 pounds shelled fresh
   clams, chopped,
   drained, juice reserved

½ teaspoon dried thyme
½ teaspoon dried dill
Few shakes Tabasco sauce
2½ cups heavy or
   whipping cream
Salt to taste
⅓ cup Dry Sack sherry or
   other good-quality dry
   sherry
Chopped pimiento and
   fresh parsley for
   garnish

1. Fry the salt pork in a large stockpot over medium-high heat until browned and crisp. Remove with a slotted spoon and save for another use or discard.

2. Add the onion to the fat in the pot and cook, stirring occasionally, over medium-high heat until tender, 10 to 15 minutes. Add the clam juice, wine, and potatoes. Simmer just until the potatoes are tender, about 25 minutes.

3. Add the clams, thyme, dill, and Tabasco to taste to the soup. Simmer 5 minutes longer. Stir in the cream and season with salt to taste. Heat the soup almost to a boil, then stir in the sherry. Remove from the heat and let cool.

4. Purée the soup in a food processor fitted with the steel blade. Refrigerate until cold, about 3 hours. Ladle the cold chowder into soup bowls and garnish with a sprinkling of chopped pimiento and fresh parsley.

Makes about 3 quarts.

Meursault and Escargot Bisque

Two of Burgundy's famed products star in this truly graceful bisque. I like to make this soup when I am longing for my days spent bicycling through the vineyards of the Côte d'Or.

3 dozen canned escargot
(snails), rinsed under
cold water
1 bottle (750 ml)
Meursault wine
12 tablespoons (1½
sticks) unsalted butter
4 shallots, minced
½ cup unbleached
all-purpose flour
2 quarts fish stock (recipe
follows)
2 teaspoons dried thyme
2 carrots, peeled and cut
into fine julienne
strips, 2 inches long
2 leeks, rinsed, dried,
and cut into fine
julienne strips, 2
inches long

2 ribs celery, cut into fine
julienne strips, 2
inches long
1 yellow bell pepper,
seeded and cut into
fine julienne strips, 2
inches long
2½ cups heavy or
whipping cream
2 large egg yolks
1 tablespoon fresh
lemon juice
Salt and freshly
ground white
pepper to taste
Finely chopped
fresh parsley
for garnish

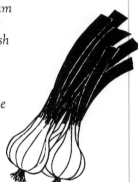

1. Place the escargot in a saucepan and cover with the Meursault. Heat just to boiling. Reduce the heat and simmer for 5 minutes. Remove from the heat. Drain the snails, reserving the cooking wine.

2. Melt 10 tablespoons of the butter in a large stockpot over medium-high heat. Add the shallots and cook for 5 minutes. Whisk in the flour and cook, stirring constantly, for 2 minutes. Gradually whisk in the fish stock, the reserved cooking wine, and the thyme. Reduce the heat to low and simmer the soup uncovered for 30 minutes.

3. Meanwhile, melt the remaining 2 tablespoons butter in a large skillet over medium-low heat. Add all the julienned vegetables and toss to coat with the butter. Cook, stirring occasionally,

just until the vegetables are tender, about 5 minutes. Remove the vegetables from the heat and set aside.

4. Stir 2 cups of the cream into the soup. Whisk the remaining ½ cup cream with the egg yolks and lemon juice in a small mixing bowl. Whisk ½ cup of the hot soup into the egg yolk mixture, then whisk it back into the soup. Add the escargot and julienned vegetables to the soup. Season the soup to taste with salt and white pepper. Serve the soup hot in wide soup bowls. Garnish with a sprinkling of finely chopped parsley.

Makes 10 to 12 servings.

Fish Stock

Bottled clam juice may provide a convenient substitute for recipes calling for fish stock, but it cannot replace the rich ocean flavors achieved from making fish stock from scratch. I suggest making a big batch and storing pint containers in the freezer to defrost and use as needed.

1 large Spanish onion, thinly sliced	2 teaspoons dried thyme
1½ cups minced fennel bulb or celery ribs	3 bay leaves
2 carrots, peeled and sliced into rounds	1 tablespoon black peppercorns
2 cloves garlic, peeled	4 cups dry white wine
1 lemon, sliced	1 tablespoon salt
6 sprigs fresh parsley	4 pounds fish heads, bones, and trimmings
	2½ quarts cold tap water

Place all of the ingredients in a large heavy stockpot. Bring to a boil over medium-high heat and then lower the heat and simmer, uncovered, for 45 minutes. Strain the stock through a fine sieve, discarding all of the solids. Store in covered plastic containers in the refrigerator for 2 to 3 days or in the freezer for up to 3 months.

Makes about 3 quarts.

Mexican Corn Soup with Shrimp and Cilantro Purée

I always felt that corn chowder was about the most unpleasant looking dish ever invented. Then all of a sudden hot restaurants across the country began making smooth corn soups swirled with a variety of contrasting purées. While the soups were certainly more pleasing to the eye, I was still disappointed by the bland flavor. I became determined to invent a corn soup that even I could adore. This recipe is the result. The contrast between the pastel yellow of the soup, the coral of the shrimp, and the vibrant green of the cilantro is spectacular.

1 bottle (12 ounces) beer preferably imported
3½ cups water
1 bay leaf
½ teaspoon dried red pepper flakes
1 pound medium (24 to 35 per pound) shrimp, shelled and deveined
5 tablespoons unsalted butter
1 large onion, minced
3 ribs celery, minced
2 carrots, peeled and minced
½ yellow bell pepper, seeded and diced

1 tablespoon dried oregano
1 tablespoon ground cumin
1 teaspoon dried thyme
3 tablespoons unbleached all-purpose flour
1½ cups bottled clam juice or fish stock (see facing page)
4½ cups fresh corn kernels (6 to 8 ears)
1½ cups heavy or whipping cream
1 cup milk
¼ cup fresh lime juice
Salt and freshly ground pepper to taste

CILANTRO PURÉE:
1 can (4 ounces) green chiles, drained
1 cup fresh cilantro (coriander) leaves

¼ cup olive oil

1. Heat the beer, 2 cups of the water, the bay leaf, and red pepper flakes in a 2-quart saucepan to boiling. Add the shrimp and cook just until done, 2 to 3 minutes. Drain the shrimp and

return the cooking liquid to the saucepan. Boil the cooking liquid over high heat until reduced by one-half.

2. Meanwhile, melt the butter in a large stockpot over medium heat. Add the onion, celery, carrots, and bell pepper. Cook, stirring frequently, for 15 minutes. Stir in the oregano, cumin, thyme, and flour. Cook and stir for 2 minutes.

3. Add the reduced cooking liquid, the clam juice, remaining 1½ cups water, and the corn to the pot. Simmer uncovered for 20 minutes.

4. Cut each shrimp into 4 pieces and add half the shrimp to the soup. Remove from the heat and stir in the cream, milk, and lime juice. Purée the soup in batches in a blender. Press through a sieve or food mill back into the pot. Season to taste with salt and pepper. Stir in the remaining shrimp and keep warm over low heat.

5. Prepare the cilantro purée: Place the chiles, cilantro, and oil in a food processor fitted with the steel blade and process until smooth.

6. Ladle the soup into serving bowls and swirl a couple tablespoons of the cilantro purée on top of each serving.

Makes 8 to 10 servings.

Cream of Sweet Onion and Sauternes Soup

My very favorite way to enjoy Georgia's famous Vidalia onion.

½ cup (1 stick) unsalted butter

4 Vidalia onions, sliced lengthwise into thin slivers

2 medium red onions, sliced lengthwise into thin slivers

3 tablespoons sugar

¼ cup unbleached all-purpose flour

4 cups Sauternes wine

2 quarts chicken stock, preferably homemade

2½ cups heavy or whipping cream

Salt and freshly ground white pepper to taste

Snipped fresh chives and whole chive blossoms for garnish

1. Melt the butter in a stockpot over medium-high heat. Stir in the onions and cook, stirring constantly, for 5 minutes. Reduce the heat to low. Place a sheet of waxed paper on top of the onions and sweat the onions until very tender and translucent, about 20 minutes.

2. Remove and discard the waxed paper. Stir in the sugar and cook the onions for 3 minutes to caramelize them. Stir in the flour and cook for another 2 minutes. Gradually whisk in the wine and chicken stock. Simmer the soup uncovered for 10 minutes.

3. Stir the cream into the soup and season to taste with salt and pepper. Keep the soup warm over low heat until ready to serve. Garnish with a few snipped chives and a purple chive blossom in the center of each serving.

Makes 8 to 10 servings.

Cream of Cauliflower Soup

My friend Elena, known for her grandfather's peasant sauce (see Index) among other things, believes that some food is meant for blonds only. Being a blond myself, I happen to agree. To my mind cream of cauliflower soup is quintessential blond food.

5 tablespoons unsalted butter	6 cups chicken stock, preferably homemade
1 leek, rinsed, dried, and minced	Salt and freshly white ground pepper to taste
1 medium onion, chopped	1 head cauliflower,
1 carrot, peeled and minced	steamed just until barely tender, then
1 teaspoon dried tarragon	broken into small
½ teaspoon dried thyme	flowerets
¼ cup unbleached all-purpose flour	1 cup milk
1 cup dry white wine	1 cup heavy or whipping cream

1. Melt the butter in a stockpot over medium-high heat. Add the leek, onion, and carrot and cook, stirring occasionally, for 10 minutes. Stir in the tarragon and thyme and cook 1 minute longer.

2. Add the flour and cook, stirring constantly, for 1 minute. Reduce the heat to medium and gradually stir in the wine and chicken stock. Season the soup with salt and white pepper and add the cauliflower flowerets. Simmer the soup uncovered, stirring occasionally, for 30 minutes.

3. Purée the soup in batches in a blender and return to the pot. Stir in the milk and cream. Gently heat just until heated through. Taste and adjust the seasonings. Serve the soup hot.

Makes about 2½ quarts.

VARIATION

CAULIFLOWER CHEESE SOUP Stir 2½ cups grated Swiss cheese into the soup after the milk and cream have been added and heat until the cheese is melted.

Roasted Yellow Pepper Soup with Parmesan Gremolata

This sunshine-colored soup is laden with the smoky sweet flavor of roasted peppers. The gremolata—a traditional Italian mixture of lemon zest, garlic, and parsley—adds harmonious contrast.

6 tablespoons extra-virgin olive oil

1 large yellow onion, chopped

2 carrots, peeled and minced

2 ribs celery, minced

2 cloves garlic, minced

4 sun-dried tomatoes, packed in oil, drained and minced

8 yellow bell peppers, roasted, peeled, seeded, and chopped

2 quarts chicken stock, preferably homemade

1 cup dry white wine

5 tablespoons chopped fresh basil

½ cup light cream (see Index)

Salt and freshly ground pepper to taste

PARMESAN GREMOLATA:

Finely chopped zest of
  2 lemons
4 cloves garlic, minced
5 tablespoons chopped
  fresh basil

1 bunch parsley, stems
  trimmed and leaves
  minced
5 ounces Parmesan
  cheese, freshly grated

1. Heat the oil in a stockpot over medium-high heat. Stir in the onions, carrots, celery, garlic, and tomatoes; cook, stirring frequently, for 5 minutes. Reduce the heat to medium and cook, stirring occasionally, 15 minutes longer.

2. Stir in the yellow peppers, chicken stock, and white wine and simmer for 15 minutes.

3. Stir in the basil and simmer for 2 minutes. Remove from the heat and stir in the cream. Purée the soup in batches in a blender and return to the pot. Season to taste with salt and pepper. Bring the soup just to a simmer.

ROASTING PEPPERS

*T*here are several methods for roasting peppers, but my favorite is oven broiling. A gas stove works best, but an electric broiler will suffice, although it may require a bit more time to char the peppers adequately.

Preheat the broiler. Lay whole peppers on a baking sheet and place them 4 inches from the heat. Broil until the peppers are charred black, then turn each one-quarter turn to char again. Repeat the process until the peppers are blackened all over. Immediately transfer the peppers to a large plastic bag and seal the top of the bag to create a steam vacuum of sorts. Let the peppers stand in the bag until cool enough to handle, 10 to 15 minutes. Remove them from the bag and slip off and discard the blackened outer skins.

Stem and seed the peppers. Use at once or store covered in the refrigerator for up to 3 days.

4. Prepare the gremolata: Toss together in a small mixing bowl all the ingredients until mixed.

5. Ladle the hot soup into bowls and top each serving with a heaping spoonful of the gremolata.

Makes 10 to 12 servings.

Tomato Soup Provençal

A n uninhibitedly flavorful interpretation of tomato soup— great for September lunches served with lots of crusty bread.

⅓ cup fruity olive oil
4 leeks, rinsed, dried, and minced
3 carrots, peeled and minced
1 medium red onion, chopped
3 cloves garlic, minced
Grated zest of 1 orange
1 tablespoon dried thyme
1 teaspoon fennel seeds
1 teaspoon saffron threads

12 ripe large tomatoes, seeded and diced
3 cans (35 ounces each) Italian plum tomatoes, undrained
2 quarts chicken stock, preferably homemade
1 cup orange juice
Salt and freshly ground pepper to taste
1 cup chopped fresh basil
Crumbled goat cheese for garnish

1. Heat the oil in a large stockpot over high heat. Add the leeks, carrots, onion, and garlic and cook, stirring frequently, for 15 minutes.

2. Add the orange zest, thyme, fennel seeds, and saffron; cook, stirring frequently, for 3 minutes.

3. Add the fresh and canned tomatoes, chicken stock, and orange juice and stir to combine. Simmer the soup uncovered over medium heat for 30 minutes. Remove from the heat and purée in batches in a blender or food processor fitted with the steel blade. Season to taste with salt and pepper.

4. Return the soup to the pot and bring just to a simmer. Just before serving, stir in the basil. Garnish each serving with a little goat cheese.

Makes 4 quarts.

Potato Soup with Quattro Formaggi

The Italians have a wonderful way of making starchy excess ever so satisfying. Here I have borrowed their *quattro formaggi* (four cheese) concept for pasta and melted it into a smooth and comforting potato soup.

6 tablespoons (¾ stick)
  unsalted butter
1 large yellow onion,
  chopped
2 quarts chicken stock,
  preferably homemade
2 cups dry white wine
2 large boiling potatoes,
  peeled and diced
1½ cups milk
2 cups heavy or whipping
  cream
4 ounces shredded
  mozzarella

4 ounces shredded Italian
  Fontina cheese
4 ounces crumbled
  Gorgonzola
4 ounces freshly grated
  Parmesan cheese
2 large egg yolks
½ teaspoon grated
  nutmeg
Salt and freshly ground
  white pepper to taste
Croutons for garnish (see
  page 117)

1. Melt the butter in a stockpot over medium-high heat. Stir in the onion and cook until softened, about 10 minutes. Add the chicken stock, wine, and potatoes; simmer uncovered until the potatoes are tender, about 25 minutes.

2. Stir in the milk and 1½ cups of the cream. Purée the soup in batches in a blender, then return it to the pot.

3. Heat the soup over medium-low heat. Add all the cheese and heat, stirring frequently, until the cheese is completely melted.

4. Whisk the egg yolks and remaining ½ cup cream in a small bowl until blended. Whisk ½ cup of the hot soup into the cream mixture, then whisk this mixture into the hot soup. Stir in the nutmeg and season to taste with salt and pepper. Be careful not to let the soup boil, or it will separate. Ladle the hot soup in earthenware crocks and garnish with croutons.

Makes 10 to 12 servings.

Portuguese Kale Soup

Everyone in New England coastal towns has a favorite recipe for the hearty Portuguese specialty, kale soup. Knowing how to make this soup well can increase one's chances of acceptance in the local community from summer tourist to nearly native. The soup keeps well and even improves with age, so I think it best to make a large pot full.

6 tablespoons fruity olive oil
3½ to 4 pounds beef neck bones or other meaty soup bones
2 large onions, coarsely chopped
6 cloves garlic, minced
3 carrots, peeled and cut into ¼-inch dice
1 cup minced fresh fennel or celery
4 quarts water
1 cup dry red wine
1 can (35 ounces) whole tomatoes, coarsely chopped, with juice

2 bay leaves
Salt and freshly ground pepper to taste
4 large potatoes, peeled and cut into ¾-inch dice
1½ pounds linguica sausage
1½ pounds Polish kielbasa
1½ pounds fresh kale, rinsed and cut into long thin strips
Freshly grated Parmesan cheese and olive oil for garnish

1. Heat 4 tablespoons of the oil in a large stockpot over medium-high heat. Add the beef bones and brown on all sides, about 15 minutes. Remove the bones from the pot.

2. Add the onions to the pot and cook, stirring occasionally, for 10 minutes. Add the remaining 2 tablespoons oil and then the garlic, carrots, and fennel. Cook, stirring occasionally, for 10 minutes.

3. Return the beef bones to the pot. Add the water, wine, tomatoes, bay leaves, salt, and pepper. Simmer the soup uncovered over low heat for 2 hours. Remove the bones from the pot again and let stand until cool enough to handle.

4. Meanwhile, add the potatoes to the pot and simmer the soup 30

minutes longer, stirring occasionally.

5. Place the *linguica* and kielbasa in a separate pot, add water to cover, and heat to boiling. Reduce the heat and simmer 5 minutes. Drain.

6. Tear the beef from the bones into fine shreds. Cut the sausages into ¼-inch-thick slices. Add the beef and sausage to the soup.

7. Stir in kale and simmer the soup for 1 hour. If the soup seems to be too thick, thin it with water.

8. Serve the soup steaming hot in large deep bowls. Sprinkle the top with a healthy amount of Parmesan and drizzle a little fruity olive oil over the top too.

Makes about 6 quarts.

Mushroom and Hazelnut Soup

T his is an outrageous soup that is velvety rich and soothing. Serve it in precious portions to your most elegant and appreciative friends.

6 cups chicken stock, preferably homemade
5 tablespoons sweet Marsala wine
7 tablespoons unsalted butter
½ cup unbleached all-purpose flour
12 ounces fresh white mushrooms, cleaned
2 tablespoons fresh lemon juice

1 cup milk
½ cup hazelnuts, lightly toasted and finely ground
2 large egg yolks, at room temperature
1 cup light cream (see Index)
Pinch grated nutmeg
Salt and freshly ground pepper to taste

1. Heat the chicken stock and 3 tablespoons of the Marsala in a medium saucepan until quite hot to the touch.

2. Meanwhile, melt 4 tablespoons of the butter in a heavy stockpot over medium heat. Whisk in the flour and cook, stirring constantly, until the roux is light golden, 3 to 4 minutes. Gradually add the hot stock mixture, whisking until smooth. Heat to boiling. Reduce the heat to low and simmer uncovered, stirring occasionally, for 40 minutes.

3. Finely chop the mushrooms by hand or in a food processor fitted with the steel blade. Toss with the lemon juice to prevent discoloration. Melt the remaining 3 tablespoons butter in a skillet over medium-high heat. Add the mushrooms and cook, stirring constantly, until all the moisture evaporates. Remove from the heat.

4. Stir the mushrooms into the stock. Stir in the milk and then the hazelnuts over low heat.

5. Whisk the egg yolks and light cream together in a small bowl. Whisk in 1 cup of the hot soup, then gently whisk it back into the soup. Be careful at this point not to let the soup boil or it will curdle. Stir in the remaining 2 tablespoons Marsala and season with the nutmeg, salt, and pepper. Serve hot.

Makes 6 to 8 small servings.

Olga's Avgolemono Soup

It is far easier to describe's Olga's *avgolemono* than it is to describe Olga. No person has ever made me laugh as long and as much; at the same time, no person has ever made me see, feel, and appreciate life as much as Olga. Our lives intertwined very closely during the initial years of Que Sera Sarah. Without Olga's presence, neither my shop nor my life on Nantucket would have been the same. While I would really like her recipe for life, I have settled momentarily for her recipe for this refreshing Greek soup.

2 small chickens, cut into
   serving pieces
1 tablespoon salt
1 tablespoon freshly
   ground pepper
1 tablespoon dried
   oregano

½ cup (1 stick) butter,
   melted
½ cup white rice
6 large eggs, separated
1 cup water
Juice of 3 lemons

1. Place the chickens in a stockpot and add water to cover. Sprinkle with salt and pepper to taste. Heat to boiling. Reduce the heat and simmer covered for 1 hour.

2. Preheat the oven to 350 F.

3. Remove the chickens from the pot and place in a roasting pan. Sprinkle with the oregano and more salt and pepper and drizzle with the melted butter. Roast for 30 minutes.

4. Meanwhile, strain the chicken broth and spoon off the fat. Taste and adjust the seasoning. Heat the broth in the stockpot to boiling. Stir in the rice and simmer covered just until the rice is tender, about 15 minutes. Remove from the heat.

5. Beat the egg whites in a large mixing bowl until fluffy but not stiff. Gradually beat in the egg yolks and then the water. While still beating, slowly drizzle in the lemon juice. Beat in the hot broth, 1 ladle at a time, until all is added (The rice will sink to the bottom of the pot and should not be ladled in with the broth.) Return the soup to the pot, stir up the rice, and serve immediately with the chicken alongside.

Makes 4 to 6 servings.

OLGA WRITES:

Sitting around on a rainy day brings out the best and worst in people. Some find good books and other sit and lament the state of their lives. As a friend, you can either give advice or be smart and get up and make this soup. It soothes, it nourishes, and it keeps you out of trouble!

If you or your friend are feeling particularly infantile or fragile it's okay to add shredded pieces of chicken to the soup.

Some of my best memories are of standing at my mother's stove whisking an Avgolemono. Wonderful conversations would spring up—secrets exchanged or announcements made.

Minestrone Freddo

Several years ago I slipped into a little Florentine restaurant tucked away on a side street near the busy Ponte Vecchio and discovered this fabulous cold version of classic Italian minestrone. I make at least one big batch of this healthy vegetable soup every summer. It seems to improve with age and is perfect sustenance on hot days.

3 tablespoons olive oil
4 ounces pancetta, cut
    into small dice
4 ounces prosciutto, cut
    into small dice
1 large onion, minced
4 cloves garlic, minced
2 carrots, peeled and cut
    into ¼-inch dice
1 large zucchini, rinsed
    and cut into ½-inch
    dice
1 large yellow summer
    squash, rinsed and cut
    into ½-inch dice
2 baking potatoes, peeled
    and cut into ¼-inch
    dice
5 tomatoes, seeded and
    cut into ½-inch chunks
3 quarts plus 3 cups (15
    cups) chicken stock,
    preferably homemade

1 cup dry white wine
1 pound green beans,
    trimmed and cut into
    2-inch lengths
1 small green cabbage,
    cored and shredded
1 pound fresh spinach,
    stems trimmed, and
    leaves cut into thin
    strips
1 large can (1 pound 3
    ounces) cannellini
    beans, rinsed and
    drained
2 cups cooked Italian
    short-grain rice
    (Arborio) or converted
    rice
½ cup chopped fresh basil
Salt and freshly ground
    pepper to taste
Freshly grated Parmesan
    cheese

1. Heat the oil in a large stock pot over medium-high heat. Add the pancetta and prosciutto and cook just until crisp and light brown, 7 to 10 minutes.

2. Stir in the onion, garlic, carrots, zucchini, summer squash, and potatoes; cook, stirring frequently, for 10 minutes. Stir in the tomatoes and cook 5 minutes longer. Pour in the chicken stock and wine, then add the green beans, cabbage, and spinach. Simmer the soup uncovered, stirring occasionally, for 45 minutes.

3. Stir the cannellini beans, rice, and basil into the soup. Season to taste with salt and pepper. Simmer for 10 minutes.

4. Let the soup cool completely, then store covered in the refrigerator. Remove about 30 minutes before serving. The soup should be slightly chilled and served in large bowls with plenty of Parmesan cheese.

Makes 14 to 16 servings.

Peruvian Avocado Soup

This soup was inspired by the brilliant Peruvian chef at The Ballroom Restaurant in New York City. It is the best and most unusual avocado soup I have ever tasted.

4 Hass avocados (dark green small) at the peak of ripeness
1 tablespoon fresh lemon juice
6 tablespoons (¾ stick) unsalted butter
1 large onion, chopped
3 cloves garlic, minced
2 small fresh jalapeño peppers, seeded and minced
1 cup minced celery
1 tablespoon chopped fresh tarragon
1 tablespoon ground cumin
½ teaspoon grated nutmeg

3 tablespoons unbleached all-purpose flour
2 quarts chicken stock, preferably homemade
Salt and freshly ground pepper to taste
½ yellow bell pepper, seeded and diced
1 red bell pepper, seeded and diced
3 tablespoons chopped fresh coriander
3 tablespoons chopped fresh basil
2 tablespoons chopped fresh mint

HYDRANGEAS AND HIGH NOON

Peruvian Avocado Soup

Classic Chicken and Grape Salad
Moroccan Carrots
Green Beans in Dill Walnut Sauce

Lace Cookies

Iced Tea

1. Peel and pit the avocados and put them in a bowl of cold water mixed with the lemon juice to keep them from discoloring.

2. Melt the butter in a stockpot over medium-high heat. Add the onion, garlic, jalapeño peppers, and celery; cook, stirring frequently, for 5 minutes. Reduce the heat to low and cook, stirring occasionally, until the vegetables are soft, 15 minutes.

3. Stir in the tarragon, cumin, and nutmeg and cook a few minutes longer. Stir in the flour and cook 1 minute. Gradually stir in the chicken stock. Increase the heat and heat to boiling. Reduce the heat and simmer uncovered for 15 minutes. Remove from the heat and let cool for 15 minutes.

4. Drain the avocados, cut into pieces, and add to the soup. Process the soup in batches in a blender until smooth. Season to taste with salt and freshly ground pepper. Refrigerate until cold.

5. Ladle the soup into bowls and sprinkle with the yellow and red peppers and the fresh herbs.

Makes 8 to 10 servings.

Que Sera Gazpacho

While gazpacho lost its sense of foreign intrigue years ago, it is still one of the most irresistible summer soups. The secret of making the best gazpacho is to start with a bread-crumb base and only make the soup when intensely flavored farm vegetables are available.

3 slices fresh white bread, preferably homemade, crusts removed

5 cloves garlic, peeled

3 tablespoons fresh lemon juice

10 ripe large tomatoes, seeded and cut into ¼-inch dice

2 bunches scallions, minced

3 cucumbers, peeled, seeded, and cut into ¼-inch dice

2 green bell peppers, seeded and diced

1 red bell pepper, seeded and diced

1 yellow bell pepper, seeded and diced

1 large can (46 ounces) V-8 juice

3 tablespoons balsamic vinegar

5 tablespoons fruity olive oil

Salt and freshly ground pepper to taste

Croutons for garnish (see page 117)

1. Place the bread, garlic, and lemon juice in a blender or food processor fitted with the steel blade and process to a smooth paste. Transfer to a large mixing bowl.

2. Add all the vegetables to the bread paste and toss to combine. Stir in the V-8, then the vinegar, oil, salt, and pepper.

3. Purée half the soup in the food processor or blender and combine with the remaining soup. Refrigerate until very cold. Serve the soup garnished with a couple of croutons.

Makes 12 to 15 servings.

Chilled Potato, Pear, and Arugula Soup

The rather strange-sounding combination of ingredients work together in this exceptional cold soup.

4 tablespoons (½ stick) unsalted butter
1 medium red onion, minced
3 ribs celery, minced
2 quarts chicken stock, preferably homemade
1 cup dry white wine
2 large potatoes, peeled and cut into small dice
5 ripe pears, peeled, cored, and sliced

4 cups arugula, rinsed and stems removed, plus additional for garnish
1 cup light cream (see Index)
1 cup heavy or whipping cream
2 teaspoons ground coriander seeds
Salt and freshly ground white pepper to taste

1. Melt the butter in a stockpot over medium-high heat. Add the onion and celery and sauté, stirring frequently, for 7 minutes.

2. Add the chicken stock, wine, and potatoes. Simmer the soup just until the potatoes are tender, about 25 minutes.

3. Add the pears and arugula to the soup and simmer 5 minutes longer. Remove from the heat and stir in the light and heavy creams. Stir in the coriander. Process the soup in batches in a blender until smooth. Season to taste with salt and white pepper.

4. Refrigerate the soup until cold. To serve, ladle the cold soup into bowls and garnish each serving with a whole arugula leaf.

Makes 10 to 12 servings.

Beet and Beaujolais Soup

This soup has an intense deep ruby color but a light texture. The beets, pear, and raspberry vinegar all blend wonderfully with the fruitiness of Beaujolais wine. The soup is most refreshing during the hot summer months, but the color makes it an elegant choice to serve throughout the holidays. Try making it with Beaujolais Nouveau after mid-November.

8 medium beets, peeled and cut into ½-inch dice
1 small red onion, chopped
1 ripe medium pear, peeled, cored, and cut into ½-inch dice
3 tablespoons raw white rice
4½ cups water
1 tablespoon sugar
3 tablespoons raspberry vinegar
2 cups Beaujolais wine
Salt and freshly ground pepper to taste
2 teaspoons finely grated lemon zest
Crème fraîche for garnish

1. Place the beets, onion, pear, and rice together in a large saucepan. Add the water and heat to boiling over high heat. Reduce the heat and simmer uncovered until the beets are very tender, about 30 minutes.

2. Stir the sugar, vinegar, and wine into the soup. Purée the soup in batches in a blender. Season to taste with salt and pepper.

3. Strain the soup through a fine-mesh sieve to make it very smooth. Stir in the lemon zest. Serve the soup hot or very chilled. Garnish each serving with a small dollop of crème fraîche.

Makes 8 to 10 servings.

Summer
Savories

This chapter contains the recipes for the most irresistible food baked at Que Sera Sarah: pizzas, frittatas, calzones, turnovers and empanadas. California health crazes and Perrier preachings aside, East Coast saltwater seasons inspire hearty appetites and unrelenting cravings for carbohydrates. Every morning one entire counter of my shop is aromatically overladen with this collection of savories still sizzling from the oven. The hand-formed crusts are filled with nooks and crannies that support an almost unbearable amount of temptation: luscious local vegetables, shiny and smoky black Mediterranean olives, splashes of fiesta-colored peppers, fragrant green herbs, spicy cured meats and sausages, and spatters of pungent melted cheeses.

Whether these guilt-inducing specialties go on board boats, to the beach, nearest park bench, or are stashed furtively for bedtime snacks, I do not know. But I do know that by midafternoon of any given summer day, there is scarcely a stray pepperoni from a pizza or lone olive from a empanada left resting on the counter.

Deep-Dish Broccoli Pizza

Once upon a sunny summer morning in the early days of Que Sera Sarah, I found that I had a surplus of broccoli. I consulted local chef Marian Morash's superb *Victory Garden Cookbook* for inspiration; this recipe was the delicious best-selling result. I now make at least one of these outrageous pizzas every single day in the store, and, more often than not, I find I never have enough broccoli to keep up with the deep-dish devotees.

Olive oil and yellow
   cornmeal for the pan
1 recipe Pizza Dough
   (recipe follows)
1½ cups Pizza Sauce
   (recipe follows)
8 sweet Italian sausage
   (about 1 pound),
   casings removed
1 tablespoon fennel seeds
2 cups sliced fresh
   mushrooms

⅓ cup dry white wine
½ teaspoon coarsely
   ground pepper
2 quarts water
2 large bunches broccoli
4½ cups shredded
   mozzarella cheese
3 to 4 tablespoons olive
   oil

1. Brush a 14-inch deep-dish pizza pan lightly with olive oil and dust with cornmeal. Roll out two-thirds of the pizza dough into an 18-inch circle on a lightly floured surface. Fit the dough into the prepared pan, letting the excess dough hang over the edges.

2. Spread the pizza sauce evenly over the dough in the bottom of the pan.

3. Brown the sausage, crumbling it with a wooden spoon, and the fennel seeds in a large skillet over medium-high heat. Remove the sausage but keep the fat in the skillet. Add the mushrooms, wine, and pepper to the fat and cook, scraping up any browned bits on the bottom of the pan, just until the mushrooms are cooked through and most of the liquid has evaporated.

4. Preheat the oven to 400°F.

5. While the sausage and mushrooms are cooking, heat the water to boiling in a large pan. Trim off and discard the tough lower stalks on the broccoli. Slice the remaining stalks ½ inch thick. Separate the flowerets. When the water boils, add the

broccoli stalk pieces and cook for 4 minutes. Then add the flowerets and cook until barely tender, 2 to 3 minutes. Drain well in a colander.

6. Spread the cooked mushrooms over the pizza sauce in the pan. Top with 2 cups of the mozzarella.

7. Roll the remaining one-third of the dough into a 14-inch circle and place on top of the cheese layer. Press the edges into the dough-lined sides of the pan to secure. Slash the dough a few times with a sharp knife to create steam vents.

8. Spoon the sausage over the dough and top with all the broccoli. Sprinkle with the remaining 2½ cups mozzarella. Drizzle the top with the olive oil. Fold the edge of the dough over and crimp to form a thick rim.

9. Bake the pizza until the crust is browned and the cheese is bubbling, 40 to 45 minutes. Let stand for 5 to 10 minutes before cutting into wedges. The pizza is also delicious served at room temperature.

Makes 10 to 12 hearty slices.

Pizza Dough

I make pizza dough at least once a day in the shop and it is much more sturdy than most people would imagine. While it is often hard to make just the right amount of dough needed for a given recipe, I have found that trimmings and leftovers are amazingly resilient when tucked away in the refrigerator or freezer in anticipation of the next craving.

1 package active dry yeast	4½ teaspoons fruity olive oil
3 cups warm water (105° to 115°F)	¼ cup rye flour
2 teaspoons salt	8 to 9 cups unbleached all-purpose flour

1. Sprinkle the yeast over the warm water in a large bowl or heavy-duty mixer bowl and let stand for 5 minutes. Stir in the salt and oil, then the rye flour. By hand or machine, gradually mix in enough of the unbleached flour to make a moderately stiff dough. Knead the dough until smooth and satiny, 10 to 15 minutes.

2. Place the dough in a large bowl. Cover with plastic wrap or a damp towel and let rise in a warm place for 2 hours or in a cool spot overnight. Punch the dough down and use as called for

in the recipes. Any remaining dough can be double-wrapped in plastic wrap and stored in the refrigerator for 2 to 3 days or in the freezer up to 1 month. Let the dough come to room temperature before using.

Makes enough dough for two 15x10-inch pizzas or twelve 6-inch pizzas.

Pizza Sauce

A versatile, all-purpose, aromatic tomato sauce. In a pinch it can be used over spaghetti or in making lasagne.

¼ cup olive oil
1 large Spanish onion, chopped
6 cloves garlic, minced
2 cans (28 ounces each) Italian plum tomatoes, with juice
1 can (14½ ounces) whole tomatoes, with juice

5 tablespoons tomato paste
¾ cup dry red wine
¼ cup dried Italian herb blend
Salt and freshly ground pepper to taste

1. Heat the oil in a large saucepan over medium-high heat. Add the onion and garlic and cook, stirring frequently, for 10 minutes.

2. Stir in the canned tomatoes, tomato paste, and red wine. Season the sauce with the Italian herbs, salt, and pepper. Simmer, uncovered, over medium heat, stirring occasionally with a large spoon to break up the tomatoes, for about 45 minutes.

Makes 2 quarts.

Pizza Bianca

The crispness and saltiness of this pale pizza balances beautifully with Champagne bubbles. I often pass it on silver trays at the beginning of a wedding reception or other festive Champagne occasion.

*Yellow cornmeal for the
  baking sheet*
*½ recipe Pizza Dough
  (see page 80)*
*½ cup extra-virgin
  olive oil*
*2 teaspoons coarse or
  kosher salt*

*3 tablespoons chopped
  fresh rosemary*
*1 dozen whole fresh sage
  leaves*
3 cloves garlic, minced
*½ cup finely chopped (not
  grated) Parmesan
  cheese*

1. Preheat the oven to 400°F. Lightly sprinkle one 18 x 12-inch baking sheet with cornmeal.

2. Roll out the pizza dough as thinly as possible into a rough rectangle, 18 x 12 inches, on a lightly floured surface. Place the dough on the prepared baking sheet, stretching a bit if necessary.

3. Spread the olive oil evenly over the dough with a pastry brush. Sprinkle evenly all over with the salt and rosemary. Arrange the sage leaves artistically over the dough, then sprinkle with the garlic and Parmesan.

4. Bake pizza until crisp and light golden brown, 20 to 25 minutes. Let the pizza cool to room temperature, then cut into small irregular squares to serve.

Makes one 18 x 12-inch pizza.

DINNER UNDER THE SPELL OF SUMMER

Que Sera Gazpacho
Pizza Bianca

Grilled Lobster with Champagne
Perfect Potato Salad
Caesar Salad Embellished with Sun-Dried Tomatoes
Honey-Herb Rolls

Double Raspberry Tart

Champagne

Pizza with a Few of My Favorite Things

Yellow cornmeal for the
  baking sheet
½ recipe Pizza Dough
  (see page 80)
1 cup Pizza Sauce
  (see page 81)
4 ounces prosciutto,
  thinly sliced
4 ounces crumbled
  Gorgonzola or blue
  cheese

8 sun-dried tomatoes
  packed in oil, drained
  and cut into slivers
½ cup pitted Niçoise olives
½ cup chopped fresh basil
½ cup freshly grated
  Parmesan cheese
2 tablespoons pine nuts,
  lightly toasted
3 tablespoons extra-virgin
  olive oil

1. Preheat the oven to 375°F. Lightly sprinkle cornmeal on a 15 x 10-inch baking sheet.

2. Roll out the dough into a 16 x 11-inch rectangle on a lightly floured surface. Place on the baking sheet and crimp the edges.

3. Spread the pizza sauce over the dough. Top with the prosciutto, then scatter the Gorgonzola, tomatoes, and olives over the prosciutto. Sprinkle with the basil, Parmesan, and pine nuts. Drizzle the oil evenly over the top.

4. Bake the pizza until the crust is golden brown and the topping is bubbling, 40 to 45 minutes. Let the pizza cool slightly, then cut into 8 squares and serve.

Makes 8 servings.

Pizza Rustica

This peasanty layered pizza makes perfect picnic fare. The colored stratified layers are an impressive sight, and the pizza will tote easily for an afternoon sail or a day's beach excursion.

*Olive oil and yellow
   cornmeal for the pan*
*1 recipe Pizza Dough
   (see page 80)*
4 tablespoons olive oil
*1 medium red onion,
   minced*
2 cloves garlic, minced
*2 packages (10 ounces
   each) frozen spinach,
   thawed, steamed,
   squeezed dry, and
   chopped*
*2 tablespoons dry white
   wine*
*2 tablespoons heavy or
   whipping cream*

*¼ cup freshly grated
   Parmesan cheese*
*Salt and freshly ground
   pepper to taste*
*4 ounces mozzarella
   cheese, thinly sliced*
*¾ pound prosciutto,
   thinly sliced*
*1 can (16 ounces) whole
   pimientos, drained*
*12 ounces Provolone
   cheese, thinly sliced*
*10 sun-dried tomatoes,
   packed in oil, drained*

1. Preheat the oven to 375°F. Lightly oil a 9½-inch springform pan and dust with cornmeal. Line 2 baking sheets with parchment paper.

2. Roll out half of the dough into 2 thin 9½-inch circles on a lightly floured surface. Transfer the circles to the lined baking sheets. Bake until lightly browned, 10 to 15 minutes. Let cool.

3. Meanwhile, heat 2 tablespoons of the oil in a medium skillet over medium-high heat. Add the onion and garlic and sauté, stirring occasionally, for 10 minutes. Stir in the spinach, wine, and cream and simmer until most of the liquid evaporates. Stir in the Parmesan and heat just until melted. Season to taste with salt and pepper and remove from heat.

4. Roll out two-thirds of the remaining dough into a 15-inch circle. Line the prepared springform pan with the dough and trim any overhanging dough.

5. Arrange all the mozzarella over the bottom of the dough and cover with one-third of the spinach mixture. Top with a layer of the prosciutto and then half the pimientos spread out flat. Top with a layer of the Provolone and follow with 1 of the baked dough circles. Press the layers lightly as you work.

6. Top the baked dough with another third of the spinach mixture and follow with a layer of prosciutto, all the sun-dried tomatoes, and then Provolone. Top with the second baked dough circle.

7. Make final layers with the remaining spinach mixture, prosciutto, pimientos, and Provolone.

8. Roll out the remaining dough into a 11-inch circle. Place over the top of the torte and join and decoratively crimp the edges to seal. Cut a few steam vents in the dough and brush with the remaining 2 tablespoons oil.

9. Place the torte on a baking sheet to catch any drips and bake until the top is light golden brown, 50 minutes to 1 hour. Let the pizza cool for at least 20 minutes. Remove the pizza from the pan. Serve, cut into wedges, warm or at room temperature.

Makes 8 to 10 servings.

Baby Pizzas

No pizza parlor can ever match the flavor or personality of these hand-formed miniature pizzas.

Olive oil and yellow
cornmeal for the
baking sheets
½ recipe Pizza Dough
(see page 80)
2½ cups Pizza Sauce
(see page 81)
1 small summer squash,
sliced into thin rounds
6 thin slices prosciutto

1 green bell pepper, sliced
into thin rings
1 can (14½ ounces)
artichoke hearts,
drained and thinly
sliced
6 whole basil leaves
3 tablespoons olive oil
2½ cups shredded
mozzarella

1. Preheat the oven to 375°F. Lightly oil two 15 x 10-inch baking sheets and sprinkle lightly with cornmeal.

2. Divide the pizza dough into 6 equal pieces. Roll out each piece into a 6- to 7-inch circle on a lightly floured surface. Place 3 dough circles on each baking sheet.

3. Spread a thin coating of the pizza sauce over each dough circle. Arrange the summer squash over one-quarter of each circle, the prosciutto over another quarter, the bell pepper over another quarter, and the artichoke hearts over the remaining quarter. Place 1 basil leaf in the center of each pizza and drizzle lightly with the oil.

4. Bake the pizzas until the crusts have just begun to color, 12 to 15 minutes. Scatter the cheese evenly over the pizzas and bake until the cheese is melted and bubbling, another 5 to 7 minutes. Serve hot or at room temperature.

Makes 6 baby pizzas.

Goat Cheese Calzones

A great filling for this hearty Italian turnover.

2 pounds ricotta cheese
8 ounces Montrachet
  goat cheese, without
  ash
4 ounces prosciutto,
  minced
2 ripe medium tomatoes,
  seeded and chopped
1 cup finely chopped
  mushrooms, squeezed
  dry in kitchen towel
¼ cup pine nuts, lightly
  toasted

1 cup grated mozzarella
  cheese
½ cup freshly grated
  Parmesan cheese
1 tablespoon dried Italian
  herb blend
3 tablespoons chopped
  fresh basil
Salt and freshly ground
  pepper to taste
½ recipe Pizza Dough
  (see page 80)
3 tablespoons fruity olive oil

1. To make the calzone filling, place the ricotta and goat cheese in a mixing bowl and beat until light and fluffy. Stir in the prosciutto, tomatoes, mushrooms, and pine nuts. Fold in the grated cheeses. Season the mixture with the Italian herb blend, basil, salt, and pepper.

2. Preheat the oven to 400°F. Line 2 baking sheets with parchment paper.

3. Divide the dough into 9 equal pieces and roll out each piece into a thin circle, about 5 inches in diameter, on a lightly floured surface. Place a heaping spoonful of the filling on half of each circle. Fold the dough over and moisten the edges with a little water to seal. Crimp the edges together as you would a pie shell.

4. Place the calzones on the lined baking sheets and brush with oil. Bake until puffed and lightly golden, 25 to 30 minutes. Serve hot or at room temperature.

Makes 9 calzones.

Tex-Mex Turnovers

T hese are one of my personal favorites. I love the way the creaminess of the cheese soothes the fire of the jalapeños. Some summer mornings when caffeine alone doesn't get me going, a nibble or two on a spicy turnover seems to do the trick. For more conventional noshing, make these for lunch or in miniature for a cocktail party.

CREAM CHEESE DOUGH:
12 ounces cream cheese,
   cold
1½ cups (3 sticks)
   unsalted butter, cold
¼ teaspoon salt
3 cups unbleached
   all-purpose flour

TEX-MEX FILLING:
12 ounces cream cheese,
   at room temperature
1 boneless skinless whole
   chicken breast, poached
   and diced
2 fresh jalapeño peppers,
   seeded and minced, or
   1 can (4 ounces)
   chopped green chiles,
   drained
½ red bell pepper, seeded
   and diced
5 scallions, chopped
4 ounces Cheddar or
   Monterey Jack cheese,
   shredded
1 tablespoon ground
   cumin
Salt and freshly ground
   pepper to taste

EGG WASH:
1 large egg
1 tablespoon water

1. Prepare the dough: Cut both the cream cheese and butter into small pieces and place in a food processor fitted with the steel blade. Add the salt and the flour. Process the mixture just until it sticks together and begins to gather into a ball. Remove the dough from the machine, wrap in plastic wrap, and refrigerate at least 1 hour.

2. Prepare the filling: Place all the filling ingredients in a mixing bowl and beat with an electric mixer until well blended.

3. Preheat the oven to 350°F. Line 2 baking sheets with aluminum foil or parchment paper.

4. Divide the dough in half and roll out 1 piece ⅛ inch thick on a lightly floured surface. Using a pastry cutter or knife, cut out as many 5-inch squares as possible. Reserve the dough scraps.

5. Place 2 heaping tablespoons of the filling on half of each square. Fold each square neatly in half to form a triangle. Seal by

pressing around the edges with the tines of a fork. Place the turnovers on the lined baking sheets.

6. Repeat with the remaining dough and filling. You should have about 16 turnovers.

7. Make the egg wash by beating the egg and water together. Brush the egg wash over the turnovers. Roll out the dough scraps and cut out using a small star cookie cutter. Place a star on top of each turnover and brush again with the egg wash.

8. Bake the turnovers until lightly browned all over, 25 to 30 minutes. Serve hot or at room temperature.

Makes about 16 turnovers.

Empanadas

Oil for the baking sheets
2 packages (17¼ ounces
    each) frozen puff
    pastry
Flour for the pastry sheets

2 large eggs
2 tablespoons water
Lamb and Pine Nut
    Filling or Picadillo
    Filling (recipes follow)

1. Thaw the puff pastry according to package directions. Line two 15 x 10-inch baking sheets with parchment paper. Place each sheet of pastry on a lightly floured surface and roll lightly in all directions to smooth the dough and expand the size slightly.

2. Cut 3 of the puff pastry sheets into 6 equal squares each; reserve the fourth sheet for decorations. Beat the egg and water together and brush lightly around the edges of each square. Place a heaping spoonful of either filling on half of each square. Fold dough squares over to make triangles and seal the edges by pressing together with the tines of a fork. Place the empanadas a couple inches apart on the baking sheets.

3. Lightly flour the remaining sheet of puff pastry and cut out using a 2-inch star cookie cutter or other cutter of your choice. Place a star on each turnover. Brush the turnovers all over with the egg wash and refrigerate for 20 minutes.

4. Preheat the oven to 400°F.

5. Bake the empanadas until toasty brown all over, 25 to 30 minutes. Serve hot or at room temperature.

Makes 18 empanadas.

Note: Baked empanadas can be frozen in plastic bags. Heat frozen empanadas on baking sheets in a 400°F oven. Additionally, baby empanadas make great hors d'oeuvres and can be made in the same manner using 2-inch squares of puff pastry.

Lamb and Pine Nut Filling

2 tablespoons olive oil	¼ cup pine nuts, lightly
1 medium red onion,	toasted
minced	1 cup crumbled feta
3 cloves garlic, minced	cheese
1½ pounds ground lean	3 tablespoons chopped
lamb	fresh mint
½ cup currants	Salt and freshly ground
½ cup dry red wine	pepper to taste

1. Heat the oil in a large skillet over medium-high heat. Stir in the onion and garlic and sauté for 5 minutes. Add the lamb to the skillet and cook, crumbling the meat with a fork or the back of a wooden spoon, just until the meat is no longer pink.

2. Stir in the currants and wine. Simmer uncovered for 20 minutes.

3. Stir in the pine nuts and feta and cook 2 minutes longer. Remove from the heat. Stir in the mint and season with salt and pepper.

Makes 6 cups.

Picadillo Filling for Empanadas

3 tablespoons olive oil	1 cup tomato sauce
2 green bell peppers,	1 cup dry red wine
seeded and diced	1 cup dark raisins
1 red bell pepper, seeded	1 cup Spanish olives,
and diced	sliced
1 large onion, chopped	½ cup capers, drained
1½ pounds ground lean	Salt and freshly ground
beef	pepper to taste
3 cloves garlic, minced	

1. Heat the oil in a large skillet over medium-high heat. Add the peppers and onion and sauté for 10 minutes.

2. At the same time, cook the ground beef in another skillet,

just until it is no longer pink. Add to the pepper mixture, then stir in the garlic, tomato sauce, wine, raisins, olives, and capers. Season with salt and pepper. Simmer uncovered, stirring occasionally, for 40 minutes.

Makes 6 cups.

FROZEN PUFF PASTRY

In the process of writing this cookbook, I have realized that there are certain ingredient revelations that might shock devoted customers and serious cooks. One example is the fact that I make my empanadas with frozen rather than homemade puff pastry. Although I am fanatically opinionated about all sorts of food preparations, tastes, and techniques, I am not so holy that I will not nab a good convenience product when it comes along. My three favorites are Hellmann's mayonnaise, Pepperidge Farm Herb Stuffing crumbs, and frozen puff pastry.

In the case of puff pastry, I find that my empanada fillings are so flavorful that they would overpower the delicacy of the best and most time-consuming homemade puff pastry. While I would never dream of using frozen puff pastry for making feathery light Napoleons or Feuilletés, it makes little qualitative difference in a hearty empanada recipe. And I must confess that as intimately engrossed as I am with food preparation, I don't mind saving a little time here and there to allow for a perusal of a current best-seller or a sunny siesta at the beach.

September Stuffed Cabbage

I always herald September in the shop by placing one of these fabulous peasanty stuffed cabbages on a pedestal next to all the pizzas. Making this brings out all my Polish instincts.

1 head Savoy or other
   leafy green cabbage
   (about 2½ pounds)
3 tablespoons unsalted
   butter
1 medium onion, chopped
2 leeks, rinsed, dried,
   and chopped
3 cloves garlic, minced
12 ounces sweet Italian
   sausage, casings removed
1 pound Polish kielbasa,
   cut into ¼-inch dice

1 tablespoon caraway seeds
1½ cups Riesling wine
2 packages (10 ounces each)
   frozen chopped spinach,
   cooked and drained
1½ cups cooked rice
1½ cups grated Gruyère
2 large eggs
2 teaspoons dried thyme
Pinch grated nutmeg
Salt and freshly ground
   pepper to taste
4 slices bacon

1. Heat a large pot of water to boiling. Remove the outer leaves from the cabbage that come off easily and remain whole. Blanch the leaves in the boiling water for 3 minutes and remove to cool and drain. Add the remaining cabbage in 1 piece to the boiling water and cook until tender, 7 to 10 minutes. Drain, cool, and slice the cabbage into thin strips.

2. Melt the butter in a large skillet over medium-high heat. Add the onion, leeks, and garlic and sauté for 5 minutes. Add the Italian sausage and cook, crumbling with the back of a wooden spoon, until the meat is no longer pink. Stir in the kielbasa and the caraway seeds. Add ½ cup of the wine and cook until most of the liquid evaporates, about 10 minutes.

3. Transfer the meat mixture to a large mixing bowl and combine with the shredded cabbage, spinach, rice, and cheese. Beat in the eggs to bind the mixture. Season with the thyme, nutmeg, salt, and pepper.

4. Preheat the oven to 375°F. Lightly butter a 9-inch round ovenproof bowl.

5. Cross 2 slices of the bacon over the bottom of the bowl. Line the bowl with the whole cabbage leaves, letting the edges hang over the edge of the bowl and reserving 1 leaf for the top. Gently pack the meat mixture into the bowl. Top with the reserved cabbage leaf and fold the hanging leaves toward the center. Crisscross the remaining bacon over the top.

6. Pour the remaining wine over the top and let it seep between the sides of the bowl and the cabbage leaves. Cover the top of the cabbage with a piece of buttered aluminum foil and bake for 1 hour. Remove from the oven and let stand for 15 minutes. Carefully invert onto a platter and serve.

Makes 8 servings.

Mexican Torta

This impressive savory torte is a Mexican-food lover's dream come true.

3 tablespoons olive oil	1 tablespoon chili powder
2 cloves garlic, minced	½ cup fresh lime juice
1 medium onion, chopped	½ cup dry red wine
3 small fresh jalapeño peppers, seeded and minced	½ cup raisins
	½ cup slivered almonds, toasted
	1 can (16 ounces) refried beans
1 green bell pepper, seeded and minced	2 tablespoons chopped fresh coriander
1 red bell pepper, seeded and minced	Salt and freshly ground pepper to taste
1½ pounds lean ground beef	1½ pounds Monterey Jack cheese, thinly sliced
2 tablespoons ground cumin	Butter for the aluminum foil

1. Heat the oil in a large skillet over medium-high heat. Stir in the onion and garlic and cook 2 minutes. Add the jalapeños, and green and red peppers and cook, stirring occasionally, 5 minutes.

2. Add the ground beef and cook, crumbling with a wooden spoon, just until the meat is no longer pink. Stir in the cumin and chili powder and cook 1 minute. Stir in the lime juice, wine, and raisins; simmer uncovered for 20 minutes.

A great many people, to be sure, visit the Island every summer for quite other purposes. They go to have a good time at a summer resort. But like the case of the man who went to church to scoff and remained to pray, the Island lays its spell over every one of them; they come to love best of all its ancient flavor; they choose by preference its oldest houses to live in; they resent every suggestion that the cobblestones be removed from Main Street in favor of asphalt; they walk at sunset down the ancient, crooked streets and call Nantucket "home."

—Guide to Nantucket 1932

3. Stir in the almonds, beans, and coriander. Season to taste with salt and pepper and remove from the heat.

4. Preheat the oven to 350°F.

5. Line the bottom and sides of a 3-quart soufflé dish with the sliced Monterey Jack. Pack one-third of the meat mixture into the dish and top with a layer of the cheese. Repeat the layers 2 more times, ending with cheese.

6. Cover the dish with a buttered sheet of aluminum foil. Place the dish in a larger baking pan and pour enough hot water into the pan to come halfway up the side of the dish. Bake until firm, 50 minutes. Remove the dish from the water bath and let stand for 15 minutes. Unmold the torta onto a serving platter. Cut into wedges and serve at once.

Makes 8 servings.

Italian Ricotta Pie

Every once in a while I crave the robust quality of Italian pastries. They're the thing to eat when I want to feel like I've really eaten something. I particularly like the combination of sweet, savory, and smoky in this recipe, which traces its origins to cooking traditions of the Renaissance.

CRUST:

2¼ cups unbleached
  all-purpose flour
⅓ cup sugar
½ teaspoon salt

1 cup lard, cold, cut into
  small pieces
3 large egg yolks, lightly beaten
3 tablespoons cold water

FILLING:

2 pounds ricotta cheese
5 large eggs
12 ounces fresh
  mozzarella cheese, cut
  into ¼-inch dice
5 ounces prosciutto,
  minced

½ cup freshly grated
  Pecorino Romano cheese
1 tablespoon dried oregano
Salt and freshly ground
  pepper to taste

EGG WASH:

1 large egg

1½ tablespoons water

1. Prepare the crust: Place the flour, sugar, salt, and lard in a food processor fitted with the steel blade. Process until the mixture resembles coarse meal. Add the egg yolks and cold water and process just until the dough begins to gather into a ball. Wrap the dough in plastic wrap and refrigerate at least 1 hour.

2. Prepare the filling: Beat the ricotta and eggs together in a large mixing bowl until smooth. Stir in the mozzarella, prosciutto, and Pecorino Romano. Season with the oregano, salt, and pepper.

3. Preheat the oven to 350°F.

4. Roll out two-thirds of the dough into a 12-inch circle on a well-floured surface. Carefully fit the dough into a 9½-inch springform pan. Pour the filling into the pan. Roll out the remaining dough into a 10½-inch circle and place on top of the pie. Crimp the edges together and trim in a decorative fashion.

5. Make the egg wash by beating the egg and water together. Brush the egg wash over the top of the pie with a pastry brush. You can decorate the top of the pie with cutouts from the dough scraps. Brush the decorations with egg wash.

6. Bake the pie until golden brown, 1¼ hours. Let cool at least 30 minutes before cutting into wedges. Serve warm or at room temperature.

Makes 12 servings.

Lobster Frittata

A more sumptuous rendition of the Vegetable Frittata!

3 tablespoons olive oil
1 medium red onion,
    thinly sliced
2 cloves garlic, minced
3 summer squash, sliced
    ¼ inch thick
1 yellow bell pepper,
    seeded and cut into
    ¼-inch-thick strips
2 red bell peppers, seeded
    and cut into ¼-inch-
    wide strips
6 large eggs
¼ cup heavy or whipping
    cream

1 teaspoon saffron
    threads
3 tablespoons chopped
    fresh basil
Salt and freshly ground
    pepper to taste
2 packages (5 ounces
    each) Boursin cheese
1 pound cooked fresh
    lobster meat, cut into
    bite-size chunks
2 cups grated Gruyère
    cheese

1. Preheat the oven to 350°F. Butter the bottom and sides of a 10-inch springform pan.

2. Heat the oil in a large pot over medium-high heat. Add the onion, garlic, squash, and peppers; sauté, stirring frequently, until crisp-tender, 10 to 15 minutes.

3. While the vegetables are cooking, whisk the eggs and cream together in a large mixing bowl. Whisk in the saffron, basil, salt, and pepper. Crumble the Boursin into small pieces and stir into the egg mixture. Stir in the lobster meat and sautéed vegetables. Then add the Gruyère and stir well to combine. Pour the mixture into the prepared pan.

4. Place the pan on a baking sheet to catch any leaks. Bake just until firm throughout, 45 to 60 minutes. Let cool for 10 minutes and then cut into wedges.

Makes 6 to 8 servings.

Vegetable Frittata

This spectacular vegetable frittata is more dramatic than most because it is baked in a springform pan for added height and richness. Depending on the weather or the occasion, it is equally delicious hot, at room temperature, or cold—for a lazy summer brunch, a boat picnic, or late night alfresco nibble.

3 tablespoons olive oil
1 large Spanish onion,
    thinly sliced
3 cloves garlic, minced
3 medium summer
    squash, sliced ¼ inch
    thick
3 medium zucchini,
    sliced ¼ inch thick
1 red bell pepper, seeded
    and cut into ¼-inch-
    wide strips
1 yellow bell pepper,
    seeded and cut into
    ¼-inch-thick strips
1 green bell pepper,
    seeded and cut into
    ¼-inch-thick strips

8 ounces fresh
    mushrooms, sliced
6 large eggs
¼ cup heavy or whipping
    cream
2 teaspoons salt
2 teaspoons freshly
    ground pepper
2 cups stale French bread
    cubes (½-inch pieces)
8 ounces cream cheese,
    crumbled into small
    bits
2 cups grated Swiss
    cheese

1. Preheat the oven to 350°F. Grease the bottom and sides of a 10-inch springform pan.

2. Heat the oil in a large pot over medium-high heat. Add the onion, garlic, summer squash, zucchini, peppers, and mushrooms; sauté, stirring and tossing the vegetables occasionally, until crisp-tender, 15 to 20 minutes.

3. While the vegetables are cooking, whisk the eggs and cream together in a large mixing bowl. Season with salt and pepper. Stir in the bread, cream cheese, and Swiss cheese.

4. Add the sautéed vegetables to the egg mixture and stir until well combined. Pour into the prepared pan and pack the mixture tightly.

5. Place the pan on a baking sheet to catch any leaks. Bake the frittata until firm to the touch, puffed, and golden brown, about 1 hour. If the top of the frittata is getting too brown, cover it with a sheet of aluminum foil.

6. Serve the frittata hot, at room temperature, or cold. It can also be reheated in a 350°F oven until warmed through, about 15 minutes.

Makes 8 servings.

Nantucket Farm Vegetables

*If thou art wise, lay thee down now and steep thyself
in a bowl of summer-time.*
—Virgil

One of the very first things that lured me to living on Nantucket was the spectacular array of locally grown vegetables abundantly displayed on rickety old carts throughout the morning on Main Street. To this day I remain convinced that I will never taste more intensely flavored and perfect vegetables anywhere in the world.

Farm vegetables have come to symbolize for me the essence of what it means to live on and love Nantucket. The cascading heads of light and leafy lettuces refresh like the froth of the ocean waves, the deep purple eggplants brood like the early morning fog of the moors, the dusty beets and potatoes concentrate the earthy taste of the salt-misted shores, the plump red and yellow tomatoes overwhelm as the most brillant of Madaket sunsets, and the baskets of fresh herbs intoxicate in the way of all the best of Nantucket.

Tian of Just Picked Vegetables

A tian is a large round earthenware dish used in Provence for baking gratins. Vegetable tians make great accompaniments to grilled foods.

3 medium zucchini,
 sliced ¼ inch thick
Salt
3 medium summer
 squash, sliced ¼ inch
 thick
1 large eggplant, sliced ¼
 inch thick
5 ripe medium tomatoes,
 sliced ¼ inch thick
¾ cup olive oil
2 large yellow onions,
 chopped

4 cloves garlic, minced
1½ cups fresh bread
 crumbs
Freshly ground pepper to
 taste
1 bunch fresh parsley,
 minced
Very finely chopped zest
 of 1 lemon
1 cup freshly grated
 Parmesan cheese

1. Place the zucchini and summer squash in a bowl, sprinkle lightly with salt, and toss to combine. Let stand 1 hour. Repeat the process with the eggplant and tomatoes in separate bowls.

2. Meanwhile, heat ¼ cup of the oil in a large skillet over medium-high heat. Add the onions and sauté, stirring frequently, for 5 minutes. Stir in the garlic, reduce the heat to medium, and cook, stirring occasionally, 10 minutes longer.

3. Remove the onion mixture from the heat. Stir in the bread crumbs. Season to taste with salt and pepper. Sprinkle half the mixture over the bottom of a 12-inch round or oval gratin dish.

4. Drain the zucchini and summer squash and pat dry with paper towels. Repeat with the eggplant and tomatoes.

5. Preheat the oven to 350°F.

6. Alternately layer the vegetables over the bread mixture in the dish. Sprinkle each layer with salt and pepper and drizzle with the remaining oil. Top with the remaining bread mixture.

7. Cover the dish tightly with aluminum foil and bake for 30 minutes. Combine the parsley, lemon zest, and Parmesan cheese.

Remove the foil from the dish and sprinkle the parsley mixture evenly over the top. Bake uncovered until the top is nicely browned and the vegetables are tender, 20 to 25 minutes. Let stand several minutes and then serve.

Makes 8 to 10 servings.

Oil-Roasted Farm Vegetables

This is one of the simplest, most colorful, and absolutely ravishing ways I know of preparing summer vegetables warm from the vine.

3 large or 12 small red
   potatoes, scrubbed
¾ to 1 cup olive oil
Coarse (kosher) salt and
   freshly ground pepper
   to taste
1 medium eggplant
2 medium zucchini
2 medium summer
   squash

2 yellow bell peppers
2 red bell peppers
2 medium red onions,
   peeled
3 ripe medium tomatoes,
   seeded and cut into
   ½-inch wedges
¼ cup chopped fresh basil

1. Cut the potatoes into ⅛-inch-thick slices. Arrange the slices in a single layer in a 12 x 9-inch baking dish and drizzle lightly with some of the oil. Sprinkle lightly with salt and pepper.

2. Cut the unpeeled eggplant into ½-inch-thick slices, then cut the slices crosswise in half. Slice the zucchini and summer squash in the same manner. Core and seed the peppers, cut into ½-inch-thick rings, and then in half to make half rings. Finally, cut the red onion into ¼-inch-thick half circles.

3. Preheat the oven to 375°F.

4. To form a rainbow of colors, arrange all the vegetables over the potatoes in compact, alternating rows, each vegetable slice standing balanced on its straight edge. Drizzle the vegetables with about ½ cup oil and sprinkle with salt and pepper.

5. Cover the dish very tightly with aluminum foil. Bake for 1¼ hours. Remove the foil and insert the tomato wedges ran-

domly between the rows of vegetables. Sprinkle the basil over the top and drizzle with a bit more olive oil if the vegetables seem to be drying out. Bake the vegetables uncovered 30 to 40 minutes longer. Serve the vegetables warm or at room temperature.

Makes 8 to 10 servings.

Summer Squash Casserole

T his was one of my favorite things to make and eat during the summers I spent with my aunt and uncle on Nantucket. It is still, in my opinion, the most delicious way to savor summer squash.

2 tablespoons olive oil
10 medium summer squash, sliced ¼ inch thick
2 medium red onions, thinly sliced
Salt and freshly ground pepper to taste
Fines herbes or your favorite blend of salad herbs to taste

10 ounces sharp Cheddar cheese, sliced ¼ inch thick
8 ounces Havarti, Monterey Jack, or Swiss cheese, sliced ¼ inch thick

1. Preheat the oven to 375°F.

2. Brush a 10-inch round casserole or soufflé dish with the oil. Arrange a layer of summer squash slices evenly in the bottom of the casserole. Top with a layer of onion and sprinkle with salt, pepper, and herbs. Dot with slices of Cheddar cheese. Repeat the layers, alternating the Havarti and Cheddar. Finish with a layer of cheese. Cover the casserole with aluminum foil.

3. Bake for 35 minutes. Remove the foil and continue to bake until the squash is tender and the cheese is bubbly and browned, about 30 minutes. Let stand 5 minutes before serving.

Makes 8 to 10 servings.

Stuffed Summer Tomatoes

I first discovered baked stuffed tomatoes in Rome and couldn't wait to try the recipe using Nantucket tomatoes. I am happy to report that the dish loses none of its delectable appeal in translation. Serve on a patio as a summer luncheon entrée or as a peasanty first course at dinner time.

6 firm ripe large tomatoes
Coarse (kosher) salt and
    freshly ground pepper
    to taste
3 tablespoons olive oil
1 medium yellow onion,
    chopped
3 cloves garlic, minced
6 sweet Italian sausages
    (about ½ pound),
    casings removed
2 tablespoons balsamic
    vinegar
1 cup cold cooked
    long-grain or
    Arborio rice

3 tablespoons chopped
    fresh basil
3 tablespoons chopped
    fresh parsley
1 large egg
¼ cup pine nuts, lightly
    toasted
½ cup shredded
    mozzarella cheese
½ cup freshly grated
    Parmesan cheese

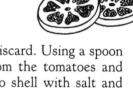

1. Slice the tops off the tomatoes and discard. Using a spoon or small paring knife, remove the pulp from the tomatoes and reserve. Sprinkle the inside of each tomato shell with salt and pepper. Invert the shells onto paper towels and let drain for 20 minutes.

2. Meanwhile, heat the oil in a medium skillet over medium-high heat. Add the onion and garlic and sauté for 5 minutes. Add the sausage and cook, crumbling the meat with a fork or wooden spoon into small pieces, just until the meat begins to lose its pink color. Stir in the reserved tomato pulp and the vinegar; simmer uncovered for 15 minutes.

3. Reduce the heat to low and stir in the rice, basil, and parsley. Season to taste with salt and pepper. Cook 2 minutes and remove from the heat. Lightly beat the egg and stir it into the filling mixture. Stir in the pine nuts, half the mozzarella, and half the Parmesan.

4. Preheat the oven to 375°F.

5. Place the tomato shells in a baking dish just large enough

to hold them. Spoon the filling into the shells, mounding it slightly on top. Sprinkle with the remaining mozzarella and Parmesan. Bake the tomatoes for 25 to 30 minutes. Serve slightly warm or at room temperature.

Makes 6 servings.

Bruschetta

Bruschetta is a simple but superb Italian appetizer of thick slices of toasted bread spread with a garden-fresh topping of marinated deep red tomatoes, basil, and olive oil. This is my friend Elena's version, learned from her relatives in Italy but made with the local Nantucket tomatoes and Portuguese bread.

3 cups diced, seeded,
   peeled ripe tomatoes
5 tablespoons chopped
   fresh basil
1 tablespoon minced
   garlic
¼ cup extra-virgin
   olive oil

Salt and freshly ground
   pepper to taste
6 thick (½ to ¾ inch)
   slices Italian or
   Portuguese bread,
   toasted

1. Combine the tomatoes, basil, garlic, and oil in a mixing bowl. Season to taste with salt and pepper. Let the mixture marinate at room temperature for 45 minutes.

2. Spoon the mixture generously over the toasted bread. Serve with a knife and fork as an appetizer or antipasto.

Makes 6 servings.

Just Tomatoes

I have never been quite certain whether there is something in the salt-misted air or mysterious elements in the soil, but I think that the Nantucket tomatoes of August and September are the best-tasting tomatoes in the entire world. I eat them every single day of their short season and find that they need very little embellishment. This is how I like to prepare them.

4 vine-ripened very large tomatoes	Coarse (kosher) salt and freshly ground black
3 to 4 tablespoons extra-virgin olive oil	pepper to taste
1½ tablespoons balsamic vinegar	3 tablespoons thinly slivered fresh basil

About 30 minutes before serving, cut the tomatoes into thick ½-inch slices and arrange them on a flat platter. Drizzle with the oil and vinegar and sprinkle with salt and pepper. Scatter the basil over the top. Let stand at room temperature for 30 minutes. Then savor and understand why tomatoes were created.

Makes 4 servings.

Tomato Relish

My aunt makes this relish every September with the ripest summer tomatoes. We love it as a condiment with red meat, game, grilled sandwiches, or even spooned directly from the jar onto the tip of the tongue.

21 pounds ripe red tomatoes	4 pounds sugar
2 pints white distilled vinegar	4 bottles (6 ounces each) liquid pectin
½ cup fresh lemon juice	4 cinnamon sticks
	1 cup bourbon

1. Core the tomatoes and chop them into coarse chunks. Place the tomatoes, vinegar, and lemon juice in a large non-aluminum stockpot. Heat to boiling. Reduce the heat and simmer uncovered for 30 minutes. Remove from the heat and drain the liquid from the tomatoes in a colander.

2. Return the tomatoes to the pot and stir in the sugar, pectin, and cinnamon. Simmer 20 minutes. Stir in the bourbon and simmer 10 minutes longer. Let the tomato relish cool for several hours or overnight.

3. Ladle the relish into sterilized jars and seal according to manufacturer's instructions.

Makes about 12 pints.

Ratatouille

Ratatouille is the perfect dish to make when all of summer's vegetables are at their peak. It is a wonderful warm accompaniment to grilled fare and a refreshing cold salad the next day. However, my very favorite way to enjoy ratatouille is to stir in cubes of mozzarella just after the mixture has finished cooking and pack it into a pocket of fresh Syrian bread. It makes a luscious, though slightly messy, stuffed sandwich.

½ cup olive oil
4 large Spanish onions, thinly sliced
6 cloves garlic, minced
2 medium eggplants, unpeeled, cut into 1- to 1½-inch cubes
2 green bell peppers, seeded and cut into ½-inch-wide strips
2 red bell peppers, seeded and cut into ½-inch-wide strips
3 medium zucchini, sliced ¼ inch thick
3 medium summer squash, sliced ¼ inch thick

3 tablespoons dried oregano
1 tablespoon dried marjoram
Salt and freshly ground pepper to taste
4 ripe medium tomatoes, seeded and cut into ¾-inch dice
1 pound fresh small mushrooms
½ cup chopped fresh basil
½ cup chopped fresh parsley
12 ounces mozzarella cheese, cut into ½-inch dice

1. Heat the oil in a very large pot over medium-high heat. Add the onions and sauté, stirring occasionally, until soft and translucent.

2. Add the garlic and eggplant to the pot and cook until the eggplant begins to soften, about 10 minutes. Add the bell peppers, zucchini, summer squash, oregano, marjoram, and salt and pepper to taste. Stir and cover the pot. Reduce the heat and simmer for 30 minutes.

3. Stir in the tomatoes and mushrooms and cook uncovered, stirring occasionally, 10 minutes longer. Stir in the basil and parsley and cook 5 more minutes. Remove from the heat and let cool a bit. Stir in the diced mozzarella and serve.

Makes 12 servings.

Green Beans with Warm Mustard Vinaigrette

A perfect last-minute accompaniment for many summer dishes. Use only the most tender green beans.

---

2 pounds fresh green beans, ends trimmed	½ cup olive oil
2 shallots, minced	Salt and freshly ground pepper to taste
2 tablespoons Dijon mustard	¼ cup chopped fresh dill
2 tablespoons balsamic vinegar	

1. Heat a large pot of water to boiling. Add the green beans and cook until crisp-tender, 2 to 4 minutes. Drain well.

2. While the beans are cooking, place the shallots, mustard, vinegar, oil, salt, and pepper in a small saucepan. Heat, whisking constantly, just until the mixture is hot to the touch.

3. Toss the hot green beans with the dressing to coat. Quickly add the dill and toss to combine. Serve at once.

Makes 6 to 8 servings.

Baby Carrots with Dill and Capers

The bunches of baby Nantucket carrots with their feathery green tops always look so adorable that I have a hard time deciding between using them decoratively on the table or delectably on the dinner plate.

Salt
1 pound baby carrots,
  trimmed and lightly
  peeled

4 tablespoons (½ stick)
  unsalted butter, melted
¼ cup chopped fresh dill
1½ tablespoons minced capers

1. Heat a pot of salted water to boiling. Add the carrots and cook just until barely tender. Drain well and return to the pot.

2. Toss the hot carrots with the butter, dill, and capers. Keep warm on the stove until ready to serve.

Makes 6 servings.

Fresh Peas with Prosciutto

When fresh peas are available on Nantucket, I can rarely restrain myself from popping them raw from the shell directly into my mouth. When I can muster up enough discipline, this is the way I like to cook farm peas.

4 tablespoons (½ stick)
  unsalted butter
1 small red onion,
  minced
4 cups (4 pounds in the
  pod) shelled fresh peas
1 tablespoon sugar
1 cup chicken stock,
  preferably homemade

4 ounces thinly sliced
  prosciutto, cut into
  thin strips
Salt and freshly ground
  pepper to taste
2 tablespoons chopped
  fresh parsley

1. Melt the butter in a medium saucepan over medium-high heat. Add the onion and cook, stirring occasionally, just until softened, about 5 minutes.

2. Stir in the peas, sugar, and chicken stock and simmer covered until the peas are barely tender, about 5 minutes. Stir in the prosciutto and cook 1 minute longer.

3. Using a slotted spoon, transfer the peas and prosciutto to a warmed serving bowl. Reduce the liquid remaining in the saucepan over high heat to a thin syrupy glaze. Pour the glaze over the peas and season with salt and pepper. Sprinkle with parsley and serve at once.

Makes 6 to 8 servings.

Corn Pudding

A while ago I was researching old Nantucket recipes and came across many for corn pudding. This is my updated version. It is a creamy and comforting way to enjoy corn off the cob.

5 to 6 ears fresh corn	*Pinch grated nutmeg*
1 large egg	*Salt and freshly ground*
¾ cup light cream	*pepper to taste*
(see Index)	*½ cup plus 3 tablespoons*
½ cup heavy cream or	*crumbled Ritz crackers*
whipping cream	*4 tablespoons (½ stick)*
1 tablespoon brown sugar	*unsalted butter, melted*
2 tablespoons snipped fresh	
chives	

1. Preheat the oven to 350°F. Butter a 6- to 8-cup casserole.
2. With a sharp knife, split each row of corn kernels on each ear of corn down the center. Scrape enough kernels off the cobs to measure 3½ cups.
3. Beat the egg, light cream, heavy cream, and brown sugar in a mixing bowl just until blended. Stir in the chives and nutmeg. Season to taste with salt and pepper. Stir in the corn.
4. Toss ½ cup cracker crumbs with 3 tablespoons of the melted butter in a large mixing bowl, then stir in the corn mixture. Pour the corn mixture into the prepared casserole. Toss the remaining 3 tablespoons cracker crumbs with remaining 1 tablespoon butter. Sprinkle the crumbs over the top of the pudding.
5. Bake the pudding uncovered until light golden brown and slightly firm to the touch, 45 to 50 minutes.
   Makes 6 servings.

Brussels Sprouts with Poppy Seeds and Sherry

A quick and delicious way to prepare this plump little autumn vegetable.

1½ pounds Brussels
   sprouts, trimmed and
   cut with X on bottom
3 tablespoons unsalted
   butter
2 tablespoons sherry

1½ tablespoons poppy
   seeds
Pinch grated nutmeg
Salt and freshly ground
   pepper to taste

1. Steam the Brussels sprouts in a vegetable steamer over boiling water just until crisp-tender. Drain.

2. Meanwhile, melt the butter in a small saucepan. Stir in the sherry and the poppy seeds and simmer for 3 minutes. Stir in the nutmeg, salt, and pepper to taste. Pour the butter over the hot Brussels sprouts in a serving bowl; toss to coat well. Serve at once.

Makes 6 servings.

Broccoli with Balsamic Butter

The rich tang of Balsamic vinegar splashed over vibrant green summer broccoli makes for an irresistible vegetable.

1 large head broccoli,
   trimmed and broken
   into large flowerets
2 tablespoons balsamic
   vinegar
2 tablespoons dry
   red wine

6 tablespoons unsalted
   butter, cold and cut
   into small pieces
Salt and freshly ground
   pepper to taste

1. Steam the broccoli in a vegetable steamer over boiling water just until crisp-tender.

2. Meanwhile, combine the vinegar and wine in a small saucepan and cook over medium-high heat until reduced by half. Remove from the heat and whisk in the butter, bit by bit until all is incorporated and the sauce is creamy. Season to taste with salt and pepper.

3. Pour the balsamic butter over the broccoli and toss to coat well. Serve at once.

Makes 4 to 6 servings.

Braised Cauliflower

One evening I was discussing favorite foods with a group of friends. One person mentioned that his favorite vegetable was cauliflower cooked in chicken stock. As I am a great lover of the vegetable, I decided to experiment and discovered the method to be a nice enrichment to the subtle flavor of cauliflower.

1 large head or 2 small
   heads cauliflower
4 tablespoons unsalted
   butter
1 carrot, peeled and
   minced

2 shallots, minced
1 cup chicken stock,
   preferably homemade
3 tablespoons dry vermouth
Salt and freshly ground
   pepper to taste

1. Prepare the cauliflower by discarding the outer green leaves and cutting out the thick center core. Break the head into flowerets, then cut each floweret into ½-inch-thick slices. Set aside.

2. Melt the butter in a large skillet over medium-high heat. Add the carrots and shallots and sauté for 3 minutes. Stir in the cauliflower pieces and toss to coat with the vegetables and butter. Pour in the chicken stock and vermouth. Reduce the heat to medium, cover the pan, and braise the cauliflower just until crisp-tender, about 7 minutes. Season with salt and pepper to taste. Serve at once.

Makes 6 servings.

Beets with Raspberry Vinegar

The taste of these raspberry-infused beets makes them a passion, but I also love the intense burst of color they bring to the dinner table.

12 medium beets,
   trimmed, washed, and
   peeled
3 tablespoons unsalted
   butter

2 tablespoons raspberry
   vinegar
Salt and freshly ground
   pepper to taste

Place the beets in a large saucepan and cover with water. Bring to a boil over medium-high heat, then reduce the heat and simmer uncovered until the beets are just tender. Drain and return the beets to the saucepan. Add the butter and raspberry vinegar. Cook over low heat until the butter is melted and the beets are lightly glazed, about 5 minutes. Season with salt and pepper to taste and serve at once.

Makes 6 servings.

Purée of
Fresh Beets with
Horseradish

While color alone makes me adore this recipe, the taste is quite sensational as well.

8 medium beets, trimmed, washed, peeled, and diced	2 teaspoon fresh lemon juice
5 tablespoons unsalted butter, cut into tablespoons	3 tablespoons prepared horseradish
½ cup heavy or whipping cream	Salt and freshly ground pepper to taste
1 teaspoon sugar	Fresh dill sprigs and pink peppercorns for garnish

1. Place the beets in a medium saucepan and add cold water to cover. Heat to boiling, then reduce the heat and simmer uncovered until quite tender. Drain.

2. Purée the beets in a blender or food processor fitted with the steel blade. Add the butter, cream, sugar, lemon juice, horseradish, salt, and pepper and process until blended. Strain the purée through a sieve into the saucepan.

3. Gently reheat over very low heat, stirring frequently to prevent it from sticking to the bottom of the pan. Spoon the purée onto serving plates and garnish each serving with a sprig of dill and a few pink peppercorns.

Makes 6 servings.

Kale au Gratin

I made this one evening in a little seaside cottage that was provisioned with an interesting range of odd seasonings, though lacking in the most common herbs and spices. The results were serendipitous and instantly made confirmed kale eaters of the guests. It is an excellent accompaniment to pork or any red meat.

2 pounds fresh kale,
   stems removed and
   leaves rinsed
4 tablespoons (½ stick)
   unsalted butter
1 small red onion,
   coarsely chopped
1 cup heavy cream
½ teaspoon ground
   cumin

½ teaspoon Chinese
   five-spice powder
½ cup grated Gruyère
   cheese
Salt and freshly ground
   pepper to taste
1½ cups coarse fresh
   bread crumbs
¼ cup freshly grated
   Parmesan cheese

1. Heat a large pot of water to boiling. Add the kale and cook for 10 minutes. Drain well, then squeeze out any remaining water with your hands. Remove the tough center rib from each kale leaf and tear the leaves into irregular pieces.

2. Preheat the oven to 350°F. Butter a 7-inch soufflé or gratin dish.

3. Melt 2 tablespoons butter in a small skillet over medium-high heat. Add the onion and sauté 5 minutes. Stir in the cream and heat to boiling. Reduce the heat and simmer for 5 minutes to reduce the cream slightly. Stir in the cumin and five-spice powder. Stir in the Gruyère cheese and heat, stirring constantly, just until it melts. Season with salt and pepper.

4. Stir the kale and cream sauce together and place it into the prepared dish. Sprinkle with the bread crumbs, dot with the remaining 2 tablespoons butter, and sprinkle with the Parmesan.

5. Bake until bubbling and the top turns a light golden brown, 30 to 35 minutes. Serve immediately.

Makes 4 to 6 servings.

Potato Gratin with Minced Black Truffle

This recipe takes the extravagant liberty of infusing earthy Nantucket potatoes with a hint of precious black truffle. It is a wonderful accompaniment to steak and lamb entrées.

4 tablespoons (½ stick)
    butter, melted
6 medium red-skinned
    potatoes
1 canned black truffle,
    ¾ to 1 inch in
    diameter, finely minced

3 tablespoons minced
    fresh chives
Salt and freshly ground
    pepper to taste
⅔ cup heavy cream

1. Preheat the oven to 350°F. Brush a little of the butter in a 4- to 6-cup soufflé dish.

2. Scrub the potatoes well and cut into ⅛-inch-thick slices. Make a double layer of the potato slices in the prepared dish. Drizzle with a little butter and scatter some of the truffle and chives over the top. Sprinkle lightly with salt and pepper. Repeat the layers. Pour the heavy cream over the top.

3. Bake the potato gratin until the potatoes are tender and the top is lightly browned, about 1 hour.

Makes 6 servings.

Potatoes Persillade

The French parsley sauce—Persillade—infuses little new potatoes with a rich flavor and provides a striking contrast to their rosy-hued skins. They team up beautifully with grilled fish.

24 small red-skinned
    potatoes, scrubbed
4 tablespoons unsalted
    butter
1 shallot, minced
3 cloves garlic, minced

1 bunch fresh parsley,
    stems trimmed, minced
¾ cup fresh bread crumbs
Salt and freshly ground
    pepper to taste

1. To make the potatoes look decorative, peel a stripe of skin around the center of each potato with a paring knife or vegetable peeler, leaving the rest of the skin intact. Place the potatoes in a large saucepan, cover with water, and bring to a boil over high heat. Lower the heat and simmer the potatoes just until tender, 25 minutes.

2. Meanwhile, prepare the persillade: Melt the butter in an 8-inch skillet over medium heat. Add the shallot and garlic and sauté for 3 minutes. Stir in the parsley and bread crumbs and continue to cook, stirring frequently, until the bread crumbs turn light golden brown, about 10 minutes. Season the mixture with salt and pepper to taste.

3. Drain the potatoes very well. Transfer them to a mixing bowl or clean saucepan and toss with the persillade mixture to coat thoroughly. Serve at once.

Makes 6 to 8 servings.

Basic Herb Vinaigrette

This is a good and flavorful dressing to have on hand during the salad season.

4 cloves garlic, finely minced	½ cup vegetable oil
3 tablespoons Dijon mustard	3 tablespoons dried Italian herb blend
¾ cup red wine vinegar	Salt and freshly ground pepper to taste
2 cups olive oil	

1. Whisk the garlic and mustard together in a mixing bowl. Whisk in the vinegar.

2. While continuing to whisk, pour in the olive and vegetable oils in a thin, steady stream. Season with the herbs and salt and pepper to taste. Let stand at room temperature for several hours to allow the flavors to mellow. Store covered in the refrigerator. Let warm to room temperature before using.

Makes about 4 cups.

Lemon Leek Salad Dressing

This is a favorite salad dressing that is both rich and tart. It combines well with most green salads. Because I love eating salads every day in the summertime, I make lots of dressing at one time and keep it in the refrigerator, where it actually improves with age as the flavors mellow. Remember to bring the dressing to room temperature before serving.

1 large egg yolk
2 tablespoons Dijon
  mustard
½ cup fresh lemon juice
3 tablespoons tarragon
  vinegar
1 leek, rinsed well, white
  bulb and green stalk
  finely minced

3 tablespoons dried
  tarragon
1½ cups vegetable oil
1 cup extra-virgin olive
  oil
Salt and lots of freshly
  ground pepper to taste

1. Whisk the egg yolk and mustard together in a mixing bowl, then whisk in the lemon juice and vinegar. Add the leek and tarragon and whisk to combine.

2. While continuing to whisk, pour in the vegetable and olive oils in a thin, steady stream. Season to taste with salt and pepper. Store covered in the refrigerator.

Makes 5 cups.

Lemon Dill Vinaigrette

I often poach a variety of farm vegetables until barely tender, arrange them on a large platter, and drizzle with this vinaigrette. Just looking at this vegetable garden on the table makes me feel healthy.

½ cup fresh lemon juice
2½ tablespoons Dijon
  mustard
1¾ cups olive oil

½ cup chopped fresh dill
Salt and freshly ground
  pepper to taste

Whisk the lemon juice and Dijon mustard together in a mixing bowl. Gradually whisk in the oil, then whisk in the dill and season to taste with salt and pepper. Let stand at room temperature several hours to allow the flavors to mellow.

Makes about 2¼ cups.

Warm Port Vinaigrette

This is a great autumn salad dressing for greens mixed with crumbled blue or Stilton cheese and perhaps a crunchy apple or pear.

3 shallots, minced	2½ tablespoons honey
2½ cups extra-virgin olive oil	2 tablespoons fresh lemon juice
½ cup port	Salt and freshly ground
¼ cup balsamic vinegar	pepper to taste

1. Place the shallots in a skillet and pour the oil over them. Heat over medium-high heat just until it starts to sizzle. Reduce the heat and simmer for 2 minutes and remove from the heat.

2. Meanwhile, whisk the port, vinegar, honey, and lemon juice together in a mixing bowl. Whisk in the hot oil and shallots. Season with salt and pepper to taste.

3. When ready to use the dressing, heat the amount you need in a small skillet until it starts to sizzle. Pour the dressing over the salad, toss, and serve at once. Store the dressing covered in the refrigerator. It will keep for several weeks.

Makes about 3 cups.

Cream Dressing

With all the fancy salad ingredients available in today's market, there is often a tendency to make overly elaborate salads. I believe the art of restraint could stand a bit of reviving in order to rediscover the joys of a simple green salad. This is the dressing I like to drizzle over silky leaves of Boston or butter lettuce. Feel free to substitute minced shallot for the garlic if you prefer a milder dressing.

1 clove garlic, minced
2 teaspoons Dijon
  mustard
2 tablespoons white wine
  vinegar
1 tablespoon fresh lemon
  juice
½ cup extra-virgin
  olive oil

½ cup heavy or whipping
  cream
Salt and freshly ground
  pepper to taste
2 tablespoons snipped
  fresh chives

Purée all the ingredients except the chives in a blender until smooth and thick. Stir in the chives. Toss your favorite greens with just enough dressing to coat the leaves lightly. Store the dressing covered in the refrigerator.

Makes about 1 cup.

Salad Croutons

Learning the subtle art of sautéing a batch of crunchy, garlicky croutons should be a prerequisite for every aspiring salad maker.

3 tablespoons olive oil
3 tablespoons unsalted
  butter
4 cups day-old ½-inch
  bread cubes
1 clove garlic, minced
2 teaspoons mixed dried
  herbs (your favorite
  blend)

Salt and freshly ground
  pepper to taste
½ cup freshly grated
  Parmesan cheese

1. Heat the oil and butter in a large skillet over medium heat. Add the bread cubes and toss to coat with the oil and butter. Reduce the heat to low and sauté the bread, stirring frequently, until toasted light golden brown, 15 to 20 minutes.

2. Stir in the garlic, herbs, and salt and pepper to taste; sauté 5 minutes longer. Remove from the heat and transfer to a mixing bowl. Add the Parmesan and stir until the croutons have cooled. Refrigerate in an airtight container or bag. The croutons can be recrisped on a baking sheet in a 275°F oven for 10 minutes or so.

Makes 4 cups.

Beach Plum Jam

While beach plums are certainly not a vegetable, I couldn't resist including this recipe here because they are a special Nantucket treat. Indeed, gathering dusty blue, purple, and ruby beach plums while surrounded by windswept ocean vistas is one of the great pleasures of September seashore living. Hunting for a plentiful picking spot can be great sport, although pitting all the berries is quite tedious. But there is nothing that can come close to the sweet-tart flavor of beach plum jam which compensates for the intensive work of making an annual batch of this Cape and Island specialty.

Don't limit this jam to the usual morning toast or croissant routine as it is a delicious condiment with grilled lamb chops or finishing glaze for roasted chicken.

12 cups beach plums, stems and leaves removed	*1½ cups Grand Marnier*
	Finely chopped zest of 2 oranges
1 cup water	*4 to 4½ cups sugar*

1. Rinse the beach plums under cold running water. Place in a large saucepan and add the water along with 1 cup of the Grand Marnier. Heat to boiling over medium-high heat. Reduce the heat and simmer uncovered for 15 minutes. Remove from the heat and let cool to room temperature.

2. Remove the pits from the beach plums by squeezing them out individually with your fingers. (It will help to be engrossed in some riveting television mini-series or movie while doing this.) Discard the pits and place the pulp and any remaining liquid in a clean saucepan.

3. Stir in the orange zest. Simmer uncovered, stirring occasionally, over medium-low heat until the mixture is quite thick, about 45 minutes. Stir in 4 cups sugar, taste, and add more sugar if needed. Stir in the remaining ½ cup Grand Marnier and simmer 15 minutes longer.

4. Ladle the jam into sterilized jam jars and seal according to manufacturer's instructions.

Makes 6 cups.

Open-House
Salads

Paprika-perfumed Moroccan carrots, rich red cabbage and Roquefort, slender green beans feathered with dill pesto, plump garden vegetables splashed with citronnade, perfect potato salad, a Caesar enriched with sun-dried tomatoes, or a spicy blend of crunchy Oriental pods and sprouts—these are among the lighter salads that celebrate lazy summer days at Que Sera Sarah.

More often than not, vacation-style entertaining is casual—a sunset barbecue, a shady picnic, boating expedition, or deckside potluck supper—where guests are asked to contribute a favorite side dish to the feasting. This chapter, with its vast array of portable salads, adds just the right pizzazz to such open-air, open-house occasions. At first glance, these recipes may seem to yield rather large quantities, but experience has proven that the spontaneous gatherings of unpredictable numbers of family, friends and their houseguests so characteristic of "easy" summertime living, call for plentiful cooking. Making a salad to feed twelve to fifteen people requires almost the same amount of time and preparation as making the same recipe for four to six people. Since the majority of salads in this chapter keep for quite a few days, they can be prepared in advance, and dividends include a relaxed host or hostess by the time company arrives and an inspiring refrigerator of terrific leftovers for refreshing lunches or snacks.

Salad making is my passion, and I firmly believe that salads meant as accompaniments must be as memorable as every other serving on the dinner plate. As my quest for preventing a lethargic August palate is never ending, the inspiration for these cooling salads comes from all parts of the globe as well as the backyard where the best flavors of home-grown abound.

Mushrooms à la Grecque

Serve these aromatic mushrooms as an accompaniment to grilled meats, or spoon them into an earthenware crock and serve them with toothpicks for a light summer hors d'oeuvre.

¾ cup olive oil
¼ cup red wine vinegar
2 tablespoons fresh lemon
   juice
2 tablespoons ground
   coriander seeds

1 tablespoon dried
   oregano
Salt and freshly ground
   pepper to taste

BOUQUET GARNI:
1 teaspoon dried
   marjoram
1 teaspoon dried thyme
½ teaspoon crumbled
   dried sage

2 teaspoons fennel seeds
2 bay leaves, broken in
   half
3 garlic cloves, unpeeled,
   slightly crushed

4 pounds small white
   mushrooms, rinsed and
   patted dry

Chopped fresh parsley
   and/or fresh sage
   sprigs for garnish

1. Mix the oil, vinegar, lemon juice, coriander, oregano, salt, and pepper in a large stockpot.

2. Make the bouquet garni by placing all the herbs and the garlic in the center of a double 3-inch square of cheesecloth. Tie it with kitchen string and add to the oil mixture in the pot.

3. Heat the oil mixture to boiling over medium-high heat. Reduce the heat and simmer several minutes. Gradually add the mushrooms to the pot, stirring with a wooden spoon to coat with the hot sauce. Simmer the mushrooms, stirring occasionally, over medium heat for about 20 minutes.

4. Let the mushrooms cool in the pot to room temperature, about 2 hours. Remove and discard the bouquet garni. Transfer the mushrooms and liquid to a serving bowl. Garnish with chopped parsley and/or sage sprigs if desired. Serve at room temperature. They will keep in the refrigerator for at least 1 month.

Makes about 3 quarts.

Vegetables Citronnade

A colorful and crunchy blend of vegetables bathed in a refreshing, light, citrus-spiked mayonnaise.

1 large head cauliflower, broken into 1½-inch flowerets
1 large head broccoli, broken into 1½-inch flowerets, tender stalks cut into ¾-inch pieces
1½ pounds carrots, peeled and sliced diagonally ½ inch thick

2 medium summer squash, sliced ¼ inch thick
2 medium zucchini, sliced ½ inch thick
1½ pounds sugar snap or snow peas, strings removed
1 red bell pepper, cut into thin julienne strips

CITRONNADE MAYONNAISE:
1 large egg yolk
1 large egg
2 tablespoons Dijon mustard
2 cloves garlic, minced
¼ cup fresh lemon juice
1½ cups vegetable oil
Salt and freshly ground pepper to taste

1 tablespoon finely grated lemon zest
½ cup chopped fresh parsley for garnish
1 tablespoon grated orange zest for garnish

1. Steam each vegetable except for the red pepper separately just until crisp-tender. Refresh under cold running water and drain. Combine all the vegetables, including the red pepper, in a large mixing bowl.

2. Prepare the citronnade mayonnaise: Place the egg yolk, egg, mustard, garlic, and lemon juice in a food processor fitted with the steel blade; process just until blended. With the machine running, add the oil in a thin, steady stream through the feed tube to make a thick emulsion. Season with salt and pepper to taste. Add the grated lemon zest and process just to blend.

3. Toss the steamed vegetables with the mayonnaise to coat. Transfer to a large serving bowl and sprinkle the top of the salad with the chopped parsley and orange zest. Refrigerate several hours but no longer than 12 hours before serving.

Makes 15 to 20 servings.

Moroccan Carrots

A wonderful and very popular summer vegetable salad that is quick and easy to make and glistens with exotic flavor. This salad has been a favorite at Que Sera Sarah ever since the store opened.

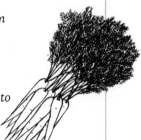

> 3 pounds carrots, peeled, trimmed, and cut on sharp diagonal into ⅓-inch slices
> 1 cup fruity olive oil
> ¼ cup balsamic vinegar
> ¾ cup red wine vinegar
> ¼ cup sweet Hungarian paprika
>
> ¼ cup ground cumin
> 5 large cloves garlic, coarsely chopped
> 1 cup finely minced fresh parsley
> 1 tablespoon salt or to taste

1. Place the carrots in a large pot and add cold water to cover. Cook over high heat just until the carrots are crisp-tender. Drain immediately. Do not rinse with cool water.

2. While the carrots are cooking, make the dressing: Whisk the oil, balsamic vinegar, and red wine vinegar together in a large mixing bowl. Whisk in the paprika, cumin, and salt.

3. Add the hot carrots to the dressing and stir to coat. Add the garlic and the parsley and toss to combine. Let the salad cool to room temperature, then serve. The salad can be stored in the refrigerator for several days. For the best flavor, let it warm to room temperature before serving.

Makes 10 to 12 servings.

Summer Vegetable Couscous

This Moroccan-style salad looks like intense summer sunshine and lures with hints of exotic flavors. A wonderful luncheon salad by itself or an unusual accompaniment to grilled chicken.

1 quart chicken stock,
  preferably homemade
¼ cup olive oil
1 tablespoon turmeric
1 tablespoon ground
  cinnamon
1 tablespoon ground
  ginger
1 package (17 ounces)
  couscous
½ cup golden raisins
½ cup diced pitted dates
1 large summer squash,
  cut into ¼-inch dice

1 large zucchini, cut into
  ¼-inch dice
4 carrots, peeled and cut
  into ¼-inch dice
1 large red onion,
  chopped
3 ripe medium tomatoes,
  seeded and cut into
  ¼-inch dice
1 cup cooked chick-peas
1 cup slivered almonds,
  lightly toasted

DRESSING:
½ cup olive oil
½ cup fresh lemon juice

Salt to taste

1. Place the chicken stock, oil, turmeric, cinnamon, and ginger in a large saucepan. Heat to a full boil and gradually stir in the couscous. Cook until most of the liquid has been absorbed, about 2 minutes. Remove from the heat and stir in the raisins and dates. Cover the pot tightly and let stand undisturbed for 15 minutes.

2. Meanwhile, combine all the chopped vegetables in a large mixing bowl. Add the chick-peas and almonds and toss to combine. Add the couscous mixture and stir until well combined.

3. Prepare the dressing: Whisk the oil and lemon juice together. Pour the dressing over the salad and toss to coat. Season to taste with salt. Serve the couscous slightly chilled or at room temperature. This salad will keep up to a week stored in the refrigerator.

Makes 15 to 20 servings.

Tabouleh
with Feta

In the early seventies when I was summering with my aunt and uncle on Nantucket, we made at least one batch of tabouleh a week, each more outrageous than the last. The final version I remember was gilded with clusters of green grapes and jumbo shrimp. Fortunately, time has brought with it some well-advised restraint. This recipe is what I believe to be the perfect rendition of this refreshing salad.

2 pounds bulgur wheat
1½ cups fresh lemon
   juice, plus additional
   to taste
6 cups hot water
3 medium cucumbers,
   seeded and chopped
   very small
8 ripe medium tomatoes,
   seeded and chopped
   very small
1 medium red onion,
   minced

2 cloves garlic, minced
3 bunches parsley, finely
   chopped
5 tablespoons minced
   fresh mint
2 cups (8 ounces)
   crumbled feta cheese
1½ cups (or as needed)
   olive oil
Salt and freshly ground
   pepper to taste

1. Place the bulgur in a large mixing bowl and pour over 1½ cups fresh lemon juice and the hot water. Let stand until the bulgur is tender, 30 to 40 minutes. Drain off any excess liquid.

2. Add the cucumbers, tomatoes, onion, garlic, parsley, mint, and feta to the bulgur and toss to combine. Dress with enough of the olive oil and additional lemon juice to make the salad moist but not runny. Season with salt and pepper.

3. Refrigerate the salad for several hours to allow the flavors to blend. Serve cold or at room temperature accompanied with pita bread.

Makes 14 to 16 servings.

Mixed Vegetables
à la Russe

1 medium-large turnip, peeled and cut into ¼-inch dice	2 large egg yolks
	4 cornichons, minced
2 medium boiling potatoes, peeled and cut into ¼-inch dice	2 teaspoons Dijon mustard
	1 tablespoon capers, drained
½ cup small cauliflower flowerets	3 tablespoons fresh lemon juice
5 carrots, peeled and cut into ¼-inch dice	½ cup olive oil
2 cups shelled fresh peas	1 to 1½ cups vegetable oil
1 medium red onion, minced	Salt and freshly ground pepper to taste
1 small red bell pepper, seeded and diced	1 cup chopped fresh parsley

1. Cook the turnip, potatoes, cauliflower, and carrots separately in boiling salted water until crisp-tender. Drain and refresh under cold running water. Combine the cooked vegetables, and the peas, onion, and red pepper in a mixing bowl.

2. Place the egg yolks, cornichons, mustard, capers, and lemon juice in a food processor fitted with the steel blade; process 30 seconds to blend. With the machine running, pour the oils in a thin, steady stream through the feed tube to make a thick emulsion. Season with salt and pepper.

3. Toss the salad with the mayonnaise to bind. Stir in the parsley and refrigerate until ready to serve.

Makes 10 to 12 servings.

Potato Boursin Salad

This is a luscious and rich potato salad that can keep fine company with lobster feasts or the choicest cuts of meat seared over the summer grill.

3½ pounds small Red
   Bliss potatoes,
   scrubbed but not
   peeled
5 large eggs, hard-cooked,
   shelled, and coarsely
   chopped

4 large ribs celery,
   chopped
1 can (6 ounces) pitted
   large black olives,
   sliced

DRESSING:
2½ packages (5 ounces
   each) Boursin cheese
1 cup olive oil

⅓ cup fresh lemon juice
Salt and freshly ground
   pepper to taste

1½ cups chopped fresh
   parsley

1. Place the potatoes in a large pot and add water to cover. Heat to boiling, then lower the heat and simmer uncovered just until fork-tender, 25 minutes. Drain in a colander and let cool slightly.

2. Cut the warm potatoes into large bite-size chunks. Toss the potatoes, eggs, celery, and olives together in a large bowl.

3. Prepare the dressing: Crumble the cheese into small pieces and place it in a food processor fitted with the steel blade. Purée until smooth. Add the oil and lemon juice and process until smooth. Season to taste with salt and pepper.

4. Add the dressing to the warm potato mixture and toss until thoroughly coated. Add the parsley and toss to combine. Transfer to a serving platter or refrigerate until ready to serve.

Makes 10 to 12 servings.

Perfect Potato Salad

There is a great deal of satisfaction that comes from making popular foods well. Modesty aside, we make terrific potato salad at Que Sera, and I believe the secret to our potato salad, or any good potato salad, lies in tossing the hot potatoes in an aromatic vinaigrette before proceeding with the rest of the recipe.

6 pounds small Red Bliss
 potatoes, scrubbed but
 not peeled
4 carrots, peeled and cut
 into ¼-inch dice
6 ribs celery, coarsely
 chopped
1 large red onion, minced
1 cup chopped fresh dill
1 cup Basic Herb
 Vinaigrette (see Index)

½ cup dry white wine
1½ cups Hellmann's
 mayonnaise
¾ cup sour cream
Salt and freshly ground
 pepper to taste
Chopped fresh dill for
 garnish

1. Place the potatoes in a large pot and add water to cover. Heat to boiling, then lower the heat and simmer uncovered until fork-tender, 25 minutes. Drain in a colander.

2. Place the carrots, celery, red onion, and dill in a large mixing bowl. Cut the hot potatoes into uneven chunks and combine with the vegetables in the bowl. Toss with the vinaigrette and the white wine.

3. Add the mayonnaise and sour cream and toss well. Season with salt and pepper to taste and refrigerate the salad for a few hours to mellow the flavors. Serve with an additional sprinkling of chopped fresh dill.

Serves 15 to 20.

A sojourn upon the island has been likened to an ocean voyage with the disagreeable features eliminated. There is always a breeze and the pure invigorating salt air and bright sunshine, with the peace and quiet which pervades, are most soothing alike to the tired brain-worker and to those of nervous temperment. Relief from hay fever is assured and malaria is unknown. That the climate is most beneficial for recuperative purposes is the unanimous indorsement of many prominent members of the medical profession.

—Guide to Nantucket 1928

Mr. Power's Potatoes

There is an absolute bevy of blond and red-headed Powers girls that come to my rescue every summer. Their mother is in the catering business in Weston, Connecticut, and all five daughters—from age 14 to 26—possess unbelievable food savvy. I could scarcely imagine a family of so many good cooks when to my amazement I learned that the gregarious father of this clan cooked as well! Here is his recipe for a family favorite.

4 pounds small Red Bliss
    potatoes, scrubbed but
    not peeled
2 cups heavy or whipping
    cream

2 cups well-flavored
    chicken stock,
    preferably homemade
1 cup dry white wine

SHERRY VINAIGRETTE:
1 cup sherry vinegar
2 teaspoons dry mustard
1 teaspoon dried thyme

1 cup olive oil
Salt and freshly ground
    pepper to taste

1 bunch scallions, white
    bulbs and green stalks,
    chopped
1 medium red onion,
    minced

1 cup minced fresh
    parsley
Salt and freshly ground
    pepper to taste

1. Place the potatoes in a large pot and add water to cover. Heat to boiling, then lower the heat and simmer uncovered until fork-tender, 25 minutes. Drain in a colander. Using a serrated knife, slice the potatoes about ⅓ inch thick.

2. Cover the warm potato slices with the cream, chicken stock, and wine in a large bowl. Marinate for 15 minutes, then pour off any excess liquid.

3. Prepare the sherry vinaigrette: Whisk the vinegar, mustard, and thyme together in a medium mixing bowl. Whisk in the oil and season to taste with salt and pepper. Pour the vinaigrette over the potatoes and toss to combine.

4. Add the scallions, onion, and parsley to the salad and toss to combine. Taste and adjust the seasonings. Serve the salad warm or at room temperature.

Makes 14 to 16 servings.

Mexican Fiesta

A unanimous choice for the most refreshing of summer salads. It is great as an accompaniment to heartier salads and grilled fare, or by itself as a cooling low-calorie crunch.

2 large zucchini, scrubbed	1 red bell pepper, seeded and diced
2 large summer squash, scrubbed	1 yellow bell pepper, seeded and diced
3 medium cucumbers	1 green bell pepper, seeded and diced
1¼ cups tarragon vinegar, plus additional to taste	½ cup chopped fresh coriander
2 medium red onions, chopped	1½ cups olive oil
8 ripe medium tomatoes, seeded and cut into ¼-inch dice	Salt and freshly ground pepper to taste

1. Trim the zucchini and summer squash, cut lengthwise into long strips, then cut into ¼-inch dice. Peel and seed the cucumbers, then cut into ¼-inch dice. Place the squash and cucumbers in a large mixing bowl. Add 1¼ cups of tarragon vinegar and toss to combine. Let marinate for 45 minutes at room temperature.

2. Meanwhile, combine the onions, tomatoes, bell peppers, and coriander in another large mixing bowl.

3. Drain the squash mixture in a colander. Add to the onion mixture and toss to combine. Dress the salad with the olive oil, salt, and pepper. Taste and add more vinegar if needed. Refrigerate at least 2 hours before serving.

Makes 12 to 16 servings.

Red Cabbage and Roquefort

A simple and quick salad to prepare, yet absolutely spectacular in presentation.

2 medium heads red
cabbage
1½ cups crumbled
Roquefort cheese
2 cups chopped fresh
parsley

½ cup grainy Dijon
mustard
3½ cups Hellmann's
mayonnaise

1. Remove the outer leaves from each head of cabbage and reserve. Using a sharp knife, core the cabbages and finely shred them. Place the shredded cabbage in a large mixing bowl. Add 1 cup of the Roquefort and 1 cup of the parsley; toss to combine.

2. Whisk the mustard and mayonnaise together in another mixing bowl. Add to the cabbage mixture and toss to coat thoroughly.

3. Line a large serving bowl with the reserved cabbage leaves. (I like to use a deep blue bowl, which contrasts strikingly with the deep red of the cabbage.) Spoon the cabbage mixture into the leaves and garnish with the remaining Roquefort and parsley. Refrigerate at least 2 hours before serving.

Makes 16 servings.

Carolina Coleslaw

This is the type of great coleslaw that they serve way down in the land of Dixie and induces cravings for a piece or two of crispy fried chicken and a few hush puppies.

1 head red cabbage,
finely shredded
1 head green cabbage,
finely shredded
4 carrots, peeled and
grated
1 large yellow onion,
chopped
2 green bell peppers,
seeded and cut into
julienne strips
1 yellow bell pepper,
seeded and cut into
julienne strips

1 red bell pepper, seeded
and cut into julienne
strips
2 cups tarragon vinegar
1½ cups vegetable oil
1 cup sugar
1½ tablespoons dry
mustard
1½ tablespoons celery
seeds
Salt and freshly ground
pepper to taste

1. Combine the red and green cabbages, carrots, onion, and bell peppers in a large mixing bowl.

2. Mix the vinegar, oil, sugar, mustard, and celery seeds in a medium saucepan. Heat just to boiling. Reduce the heat and simmer 1 minute. Pour the dressing over the coleslaw and toss well. Season to taste with salt and pepper.

3. Transfer the coleslaw to a serving dish and refrigerate for several hours to allow the flavors to mellow.

Makes 16 to 20 servings.

Lone Star Slaw

A tribute to the spicy palates of the dedicated Texas contingent who summer on Nantucket.

1 large head red cabbage, shredded	1 cup sour cream
5 carrots, peeled and grated	3 tablespoons heavy or whipping cream
1 large green bell pepper, seeded and diced	2 heaping tablespoons Dijon mustard
1 large yellow onion, chopped	1 tablespoon chili powder
12 slices bacon	1½ tablespoons cumin
2 cups Hellmann's mayonnaise	Salt and freshly ground pepper to taste
	¼ cup chopped fresh parsley

1. Toss the cabbage, carrots, green pepper, and onion together in a large mixing bowl.

2. Fry the bacon in a skillet until crisp. Drain on paper towels and crumble into small bits.

3. Add the mayonnaise and sour cream to the bacon fat in the skillet and whisk until smooth. Whisk in the cream, mustard, chili powder, and cumin. Season to taste with salt and pepper.

4. Add half the bacon to the cabbage mixture. Add the dressing and toss well to coat. Transfer to a serving bowl and garnish the salad with the remaining bacon and the parsley. Serve slightly chilled or at room temperature.

Makes 10 to 12 servings.

Green Beans in Dill
Walnut Sauce

A vibrant salad when green beans are tender and fresh from a local farm.

3 pounds green beans, trimmed	½ cup walnut halves
1 bunch scallions, white bulbs and green stalks, minced	¼ cup fresh lemon juice
	1½ cups olive oil
	Salt and freshly ground pepper to taste
1 bunch fresh dill, chopped	Cherry tomatoes, quartered (optional)
½ cup minced fresh parsley	

1. Heat a large pot of water to boiling. Add the green beans and boil until crisp-tender. Drain immediately, then immerse in a large bowl of ice water to prevent further cooking and retain the bright green color.

2. Meanwhile, make the sauce: Place the scallions, dill, parsley, walnuts, and lemon juice in a blender or food processor fitted with the steel blade; process until smooth. With the machine running, pour the olive oil in a thin, steady stream through the feed tube to make a thick green sauce. Add salt and pepper to taste.

3. Drain the beans and dry with a towel. Toss the beans with the dressing in a mixing bowl. Add the cherry tomatoes for color contrast, if desired. Transfer the beans to a flat serving bowl. Serve slightly chilled or at room temperature.

Makes 10 to 12 servings.

White Bean and
Goat Cheese Salad

This is the best bean salad I have ever tasted. I'm particularly fond of the way the toasted pine nuts are camouflaged in the beans and then surprise one with an intense little crunch.

1 pound dried small white beans, picked over, soaked overnight in cold water, and drained
6 cups chicken stock, preferably homemade
3 carrots, peeled and cut into ¼-inch dice
2 bay leaves
2 cloves garlic, minced
1½ tablespoons grainy Dijon mustard

⅓ cup fresh lemon juice
1¼ cups olive oil
Salt and freshly ground pepper to taste
1 medium red onion, chopped
12 ounces Montrachet goat cheese, crumbled
½ cup pine nuts, toasted
1 bunch parsley, chopped

1. Place the beans, chicken stock, carrots, and bay leaves in a large saucepan. Heat to boiling, skimming off any foam that rises to the surface. Reduce the heat and simmer uncovered just until the beans are tender, 25 to 30 minutes. Remove from the heat and drain.

2. Meanwhile, mix the garlic, mustard, and lemon juice in a small mixing bowl. Whisk in the oil and season to taste with salt and pepper. Toss the warm beans with the dressing.

3. Add the onion, goat cheese, pine nuts, and parsley to the salad and toss to combine well. Serve at room temperature.

Makes 8 to 10 servings.

Indian Cauliflower with Toasted Mustard Seeds

In Indian cuisine this is served to cool the fire of a hot curry. I am so fond of it, however, that I often enjoy it as a salad on its own.

3 heads cauliflower, broken into bite-size flowerets, steamed just until crisp-tender, and drained
6 tablespoons unsalted butter

⅓ cup golden mustard seeds
4 cups plain yogurt
Salt to taste

1. Place the cauliflower in a large mixing bowl and let cool to room temperature.

2. Melt the butter in a small skillet over medium heat. Add the mustard seeds to the butter and immediately cover the skillet. Cook just until you hear the first mustard seeds popping against the cover (similar to popcorn). Remove from the heat but do not uncover until the popping ceases, about 5 minutes.

3. Add the toasted mustard seeds with the butter to the cooled cauliflower and toss to coat. Stir in the yogurt and season to taste with salt. Refrigerate several hours before serving.

Makes 8 to 10 servings.

Asparagus with Sesame Mayonnaise

Thisis crisp Oriental-style salad partners perfectly with cold sliced steak.

3 pounds asparagus
2 cloves garlic, minced
1½ tablespoons chopped fresh ginger
⅓ cup soy sauce
2 tablespoons rice wine vinegar
2 tablespoons brown sugar
1 large egg yolk

1 large egg
1 tablespoon fresh lemon juice
1½ tablespoons Dijon mustard
1¼ cups vegetable oil
¼ cup Oriental sesame oil
⅓ cup sesame seeds, lightly toasted

1. Cut off the tough lower stalks of the asparagus and discard. Cut each stalk diagonally into 2 or 3 pieces; keep the tip pieces separate from the rest, as they need less time to cook. Steam the asparagus tips and stalks separately in steamers placed over boiling water. Steam just until crisp-tender and remove from the heat immediately.

2. Make the sesame mayonnaise: Place the garlic, ginger, soy sauce, vinegar, and brown sugar in a small saucepan. Heat to boiling. Reduce the heat and simmer until reduced by about half.

3. Place the egg yolk, egg, lemon juice, and mustard in a food

processor fitted with the steel blade; process for 10 seconds. With the machine running, pour the vegetable and sesame oils in a thin, steady stream through the feed tube to form a thick emulsion. Add the reduced soy mixture and process until well blended.

4. Toss the asparagus with the sesame mayonnaise and transfer to a serving bowl. Sprinkle the salad with the sesame seeds. Refrigerate at least 2 hours before serving.

Makes 8 servings.

Stuffed Artichokes Vinaigrette

An intriguing way to dress up a steamed artichoke.

4 artichokes, trimmed
8 tablespoons olive oil
3 shallots, minced
1½ cups finely chopped
   mushrooms
3 tablespoons dry white
   wine
2 tablespoons
   Champagne vinegar
1½ tablespoons fresh
   lemon juice

1 large clove garlic,
   minced
½ cup finely shredded
   prosciutto
3 tablespoons freshly
   grated Parmesan cheese
Salt and freshly ground
   pepper to taste

1. Sit the artichokes upright on a vegetable steamer placed in a large saucepan. Pour in enough water to come just level with the top of the steamer. Cover the pan and gently simmer the artichokes until tender, 45 minutes to 1 hour. Remove the artichokes and set aside to cool.

2. Heat 2 tablespoons of the oil in a small skillet over medium heat. Add the shallots and sauté just until tender, about 5 minutes. Stir in the mushrooms and sauté 3 minutes longer. Transfer the mixture to a mixing bowl.

3. Add the wine, vinegar, lemon juice, garlic, prosciutto, Parmesan, and remaining 6 tablespoons oil to the mushroom mixture and toss to combine. Season to taste with salt and pepper. Let marinate at room temperature for 30 minutes.

4. Pull out enough center leaves of each artichoke to reach the choke. Scrape out the prickly hairs with a spoon and discard. Spoon the dressing into the artichokes. Serve the stuffed artichokes at room temperature.

Makes 4 servings.

Eggplant and Peppers in Hoisin Marinade

This unusual salad looks like the autumn leaves in New England at their peak of color.

8 tablespoons vegetable oil
4 tablespoons Oriental sesame oil
3 medium eggplants, unpeeled, cut into 3 x ½-inch strips
2 red bell peppers, seeded and cut into ½-inch-wide strips
2 yellow bell peppers, seeded and cut into ½-inch-wide strips

1 green bell pepper, seeded and cut into ½-inch-wide strips
1 can (6 ounces) pitted black olives, drained
1 jar (5 ounces) hoisin sauce
½ cup soy sauce
3 tablespoons honey
Several drops hot chili oil
3 tablespoons chopped fresh coriander

1. Heat 2 tablespoons vegetable oil and 1 tablespoon sesame oil in a large skillet over high heat. Add as many of the eggplant strips as will fit in a single layer and stir-fry just until crisp-tender, about 5 minutes. Repeat with the remaining eggplant and the peppers, adding vegetable oil and sesame oil as needed. Transfer all the vegetables to a large mixing bowl.

2. Add the olives to the salad and toss to combine. Add the hoisin sauce and toss well. Stir in the soy sauce, honey, and chili oil to taste. Transfer to a serving bowl and sprinkle the top of the salad with the coriander. Serve at room temperature or slightly chilled.

Makes 10 to 12 servings.

Mixed Greens with Fennel, Pears, and Parmesan Shards

A harmonious combination of ingredients that makes either a nice first-course salad or an after-dinner salad with pasta or other Italian fare.

2 bunches watercress, tough stems removed

3 cups coarsely torn salad lettuce

1 small head radicchio, leaves separated

1½ cups sliced fresh fennel stalks

3 tablespoons pine nuts, toasted

2 ripe Bosc pears, peeled, cored, and thinly sliced

1 cup shaved Parmesan cheese (use vegetable peeler)

⅔ cup Lemon Leek Dressing (see Index)

Toss the watercress, lettuce, radicchio, and fennel together in a large salad bowl. Scatter the pine nuts, pears, and Parmesan over the greens. Toss the salad with enough dressing to coat. Serve immediately.

Makes 6 servings.

ASPIRING TO BE ITALIAN

Bruschetta

Linguine with White Clam Sauce

Mixed Greens with Fennel, Pears, and Parmesan Shards

Espresso-Walnut Cake

Chilled Orvieto

Vegetables Chinois

A light salad that is always welcome during the really scorching spells of summer heat.

¾ cup dried Chinese
  mushrooms
1 pound snow peas,
  strings removed
3 cups fresh bean sprouts
1 red bell pepper, seeded
  and cut into thin
  julienne strips
1 yellow bell pepper,
  seeded and cut into
  thin julienne strips

2 cans (8 ounces each)
  water chestnuts,
  drained and thinly
  sliced
1 can (8 ounces) sliced
  bamboo shoots,
  drained
1 bunch scallions, white
  bulbs and green stalks,
  sliced diagonally

DRESSING:
2 cloves garlic, minced
3 tablespoons rice wine
  vinegar
¼ cup sweet sherry
1½ tablespoons sugar

2 tablespoons Oriental
  sesame oil
¼ cup vegetable oil
¼ cup soy sauce
Hot chili oil to taste

1. Soak the Chinese mushrooms in boiling water for 20 minutes, drain, pat dry, and slice.

2. Blanch the snow peas in boiling water for 30 seconds. Run under cold water to stop the cooking, drain, and pat dry.

3. Toss all the vegetables together in a large mixing bowl.

4. Prepare the dressing: Whisk the garlic, vinegar, sherry, and sugar together in a small mixing bowl. Whisk in the oils, soy sauce, and chili oil to taste. Pour the dressing over the vegetables and toss to coat. Refrigerate until cold.

Makes 8 to 10 servings.

Caesar Salad Embellished with Sun-Dried Tomatoes

With sun-dried tomtoes the current rage, they seem to pop up almost everywhere. This is one place that I feel they really belong.

1 large head romaine lettuce	2 cups fresh spinach leaves

SUN-DRIED TOMATO DRESSING:

1 large egg yolk	½ cup vegetable oil
1 tablespoon grainy Dijon mustard	1 cup olive oil
1 tablespoon anchovy paste	2 teaspoons dried thyme
3 tablespoons balsamic vinegar	Salt and freshly ground pepper to taste
2½ tablespoons fresh lemon juice	1 cup Croutons (see Index)
2 cloves garlic, minced	1 cup freshly grated Parmesan cheese
8 sun-dried tomatoes packed in oil, finely chopped	

1. Tear the lettuce and spinach into large irregular pieces and toss together in a large salad bowl. Refrigerate until ready to serve.

2. Prepare the dressing: Whisk the egg yolk, mustard, and anchovy paste together in a small mixing bowl until smooth. Gradually whisk in the vinegar and lemon juice, then stir in the garlic and sun-dried tomatoes.

3. Combine the vegetable and olive oils and pour into the dressing in a thin, steady stream, whisking constantly. Whisk in thyme and season to taste with salt and pepper. Let stand at room temperature several hours to allow the flavors to mellow.

4. Toss the salad greens with enough dressing to coat generously. Add the croutons and Parmesan and toss to combine. Serve at once.

Makes 8 servings.

Salad Stars

From time to time, in the daily course of salad making at Que Sera Sarah, a real salad star is born. While I always try to infuse every salad with its own unique intensity, I find there is no predicting what serendipitous kitchen methodology leads to the creation of a star. The discerning public taste responds equally to the simplicity of a chunky chicken salad, the exoticism of shrimp bathed in raspberries and mint, or the extravagant complicity of plump Italian tortellini dressed with an entire jar of puréed sun-dried tomatoes.

While there are plenty of salads in this chapter with universal appeal, Nantucketers are always particularly fond of salads from the sea. Indeed, a summer spent by the ocean invites culinary exploration as much as it does sportive enjoyment. The pastel colors of crustaceans in varying shades of coral, salmon, apricot, and opalescent pearl seem to appeal to the eye as much as the palate. No summer on Nantucket is ever complete without at least a few fishing expeditions—either casting offshore, braving the high seas, wrestling with the rocks for mussels, or simply vying for a parking space in front of the local fish market.

Whether from land or sea, these are cherishable salads meant to take center stage whenever an impressive meal of cool and elegant fare is in order.

Lobster Salad with Mayonnaise du Midi

Fresh lobster salad in its extravagant simplicity is perfect for those peak summer days when excess seems to be just enough.

3 pounds fresh cooked
lobster meat (about six
1¼ pound whole
lobsters, steamed), cut
into large chunks

4 inner white ribs celery,
cut into ½-inch dice
3 shallots, minced

MAYONNAISE:
1 large egg yolk
1 large egg
2½ tablespoons fresh
lemon juice
1 tablespoon Dijon
mustard

Finely grated zest of 1 lemon
½ teaspoon saffron threads
½ teaspoon dried thyme
1½ cups best-quality olive oil
Salt and freshly ground
pepper to taste

1. Combine the lobster, celery, and shallots in a mixing bowl.
2. Prepare the mayonnaise: Place the egg yolk, egg, lemon juice, mustard, lemon zest, saffron, and thyme in a food processor fitted with the steel blade; process for 10 seconds. With the machine running, add the oil in a thin, steady stream through the feed tube to form an emulsion. Season the mayonnaise to taste with salt and pepper.
3. Combine the lobster mixture with enough mayonnaise to bind. Cover and refrigerate at least 1 hour. Serve in generous portions with little else to accompany.
Makes 8 servings.

Insalata di Frutti di Mare

In Venice, restaurant windows frequently display alluring platters of mixed seafood marinating in a glistening bath of olive oil. This is my own local version of this sumptuous Italian classic.

2 pounds jumbo shrimp
(12 to 15 per pound)
peeled, deveined, and
cooked just until
opaque (see box, page
148)
1½ pounds fresh cooked
lobster meat
5 ribs celery, sliced
diagonally ½ inch
thick
1 medium red onion,
sliced into thin rings
1½ cups dry white wine
1½ cups water
1½ pounds sea scallops
2 pounds squid, cleaned
and cut into rings

1¾ cups fruity olive oil
3 cloves garlic, minced
2 teaspoons dried oregano
½ teaspoon dried red
pepper flakes
¼ cup fresh lemon juice
1 cup chopped fresh
parsley
½ cup chopped fresh basil
2 tablespoons Pernod
2 ripe medium tomatoes,
seeded and cut into
¼-inch dice
Salt and freshly ground
pepper to taste

1. Mix the shrimp, lobster, celery, and red onion together in a large bowl.

2. Heat the wine and water in a deep skillet just to simmering. Add the scallops and simmer just until opaque, 1½ to 2 minutes. Remove from the liquid with a slotted spoon, cool, and add to the seafood in the bowl. Add the squid to the poaching liquid and simmer just until tender, about 3 minutes. Remove with a slotted spoon, cool, and add to the seafood. Boil the poaching liquid until it is reduced by half and then remove from the heat.

3. Pour the olive oil into another skillet and heat over medium heat. Stir in the garlic, oregano, and red pepper flakes and simmer for 10 minutes. Stir in the lemon juice, ¾ cup of the reduced poaching liquid, the parsley, basil, and Pernod. Simmer 5 minutes longer. Stir in the tomatoes, season to taste with salt and pepper, and simmer another 5 minutes.

4. Pour the hot dressing over the seafood and toss thoroughly to coat. Transfer the salad to a serving dish and refrigerate for several hours before serving.

Makes 10 to 12 servings.

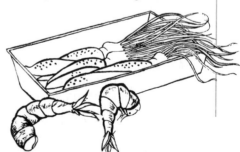

: N/A

Scallop Ceviche

Ceviche is one of the most cooling of all summer salads and is inspired by the fiery cuisines of Latin America.

3 pounds fresh sea or bay
   scallops
1 cup fresh lime juice
⅓ cup fresh lemon juice
3 ripe medium tomatoes,
   seeded and cut into
   ¼-inch dice
1 yellow bell pepper,
   seeded and cut into
   ¼-inch dice
1 red bell pepper, seeded
   and cut into ¼-inch
   dice
1 green bell pepper,
   seeded and cut into
   ¼-inch dice

2 fresh jalapeño peppers,
   seeded and minced
1 bunch scallions, white
   bulbs and green stalks,
   minced
½ cup minced fresh
   coriander
¼ cup fruity olive oil
Salt and freshly ground
   pepper to taste
Lime wedges for garnish

1. Place the scallops in a large mixing bowl and pour over the lime and lemon juices. Add the tomatoes, peppers, and scallions and toss together. Add the coriander, oil, salt, and pepper and toss thoroughly to coat.

2. Transfer the ceviche to a serving bowl and refrigerate covered several hours to allow the lime juice to "cook" the scallops and the flavors to blend. Serve cold on small salad plates, garnished with lime wedges.

Makes 10 to 12 servings.

Smoked Mussels Vinaigrette

A quick and tasty way to dress up smoked mussels for an unusual summer salad or great seaside cocktail fare. As a salad, spoon it into avocado halves or on leafy garden greens. As an hors d'oeuvre, simply supply lots of toothpicks and perhaps a salt-rimmed margarita or two.

1½ pounds smoked
  mussels, preferably
  freshly smoked from a
  reputable smokehouse
5 scallions, white bulbs
  and green stalks, sliced
½ red bell pepper, seeded
  and diced

½ yellow bell pepper,
  seeded and diced
3 tablespoons chopped
  fresh coriander
½ cup fresh lime juice
½ cup fruity olive oil
Freshly ground pepper to
  taste

1. Toss the mussels, scallions, peppers, and coriander together in a mixing bowl.

2. Whisk the lime juice and olive oil together in a small mixing bowl and pour over the mussels. Toss thoroughly to coat. Sprinkle with pepper to taste. Serve at room temperature.

Makes 8 servings.

Mussels Gribiche

A simple yet richly delicious way to serve chilled mussels.

3 pounds shucked cooked
  mussels (about 8 to 10
  pounds in the shell)
2 large egg yolks
2 tablespoons balsamic
  vinegar
1 tablespoon fresh lemon
  juice
2 tablespoons minced
  fresh tarragon
3 tablespoons minced
  fresh parsley

¾ cup olive oil
¾ cup vegetable oil
8 cornichon pickles,
  minced
2 tablespoons capers,
  drained
2 hard-cooked eggs,
  minced
Salt and freshly ground
  pepper to taste
Capers and lemon
  wedges for garnish

1. Drain the mussels and place in a large mixing bowl.

2. To make the gribiche sauce, place the egg yolks, vinegar, lemon juice, tarragon, and parsley in a food processor fitted with the steel blade and process for 10 seconds. With the machine running, add the oils in a thin, steady stream through the feed

tube to make an emulsion. Transfer the mayonnaise to a mixing bowl and stir in the cornichons, capers, and eggs. Season to taste with salt and pepper.

3. Add the gribiche sauce to the mussels and toss to coat. Refrigerate several hours before serving. Spoon onto salad plates and garnish with capers and lemon wedges.

Makes 6 to 8 servings.

Scallops with Orange and Chervil Vinaigrette

A refreshing change of pace for those who are squeamish about eating scallops raw in ceviche.

2½ pounds sea scallops	Finely chopped zest of 1
2 cups orange juice	orange
2 cups dry white wine	3 tablespoons chopped
1 bunch scallions, white	fresh chervil
bulbs and green stalks,	1 tablespoon capers,
sliced	drained
⅓ cup Niçoise olives,	1 cup fruity olive oil
pitted and coarsely	Salt and freshly ground
chopped	pepper to taste
3 ripe medium tomatoes,	
seeded and cut into	
¼-inch dice	

1. Place the scallops in a large skillet and pour over the orange juice and wine. Heat to boiling, then reduce heat to low and simmer the scallops just until barely cooked through, 2 to 3 minutes. Using a slotted spoon, transfer the scallops to a mixing bowl. Reduce the remaining liquid in the pan over high heat to ½ cup. Remove from the heat and set aside.

2. Add the scallions, olives, tomatoes, orange zest, chervil, and capers to the scallops; toss to combine.

3. Whisk the reduced poaching liquid and the olive oil together. Season the dressing to taste with salt and freshly ground pepper. Pour over the scallop salad and toss to coat. Serve at once or refrigerate until ready to serve.

Makes 6 servings.

Shrimp in a Bath of Raspberry Vinegar and Mint

The perfect way to infuse irresistible jumbo shrimp with the sparkle of summer.

5 pounds jumbo (12 to
   15 per pound) shrimp,
   peeled, deveined, and
   cooked until opaque
   (see box, below)
1 cup Champagne
   vinegar
1 cup raspberry vinegar

6 tablespoons sugar
3 tablespoons fresh lemon
   juice
1½ cups chopped fresh
   mint
1½ cups fruity olive oil
Salt and freshly ground
   pepper to taste

1. Place the shrimp in a large mixing bowl. Whisk the vinegars and sugar together in a small mixing bowl until the sugar dissolves. Whisk in the lemon juice and mint, then the olive oil. Season with salt and pepper. Pour the dressing over the shrimp and toss well to coat. Marinate in the refrigerator at least 3 hours before serving.

2. Serve the shrimp either as a salad on plates garnished with

COOKING SHRIMP

I like to cook shrimp in a combination of dry white wine and water infused with lemon, herbs, and spices. A ratio of 2 cups wine to 8 cups water works well. I then add 2 or 3 bay leaves, 1 lemon, quartered, 2 teaspoons mustard seeds, and a dash or two of dried red pepper flakes and bring the liquid to a full boil before dropping in the shrimp. I cook the shrimp over high heat just until opaque in the center. Large shrimp generally take 3 to 4 minutes, while small shrimp need only cook 1½ to 2 minutes. The shrimp should be drained immediately, then covered with ice cubes to arrest the cooking and cool them quickly. Drain again and use as called for in the recipes.

sprigs of fresh mint or serve as an hors d'oeuvre on a shallow platter with toothpicks.

Makes 10 to 12 salad servings or 20 to 25 appetizer servings.

Seashells with Shrimp and Sugar Snap Peas

An alliterative and scrumptious combination of ingredients make this coral-hued salad a favorite in the cold pasta category.

3 pounds large (16 to 24 per pound) shrimp, peeled, deveined, and cooked just until opaque (see box, facing page)

2 pounds small pasta shells, cooked al dente, rinsed under cold water, and drained

1 bunch scallions, white bulbs and green stalks, sliced

1 red bell pepper, seeded and cut into fine julienne strips

1½ pounds sugar snap peas, blanched in boiling water for 30 seconds, cooled under cold running water, and drained

DRESSING:

3 tablespoons tomato paste

3 tablespoons fresh lemon juice

½ cup dry vermouth

4 hard-cooked eggs

3 tablespoons chopped fresh tarragon

3 cups Hellmann's mayonnaise

Salt and freshly ground pepper to taste

2 tablespoons Pernod

1. Place 2½ pounds of the shrimp in a large mixing bowl. (Reserve the remaining ½ pound for the dressing.) Add the pasta and peas to the shrimp and toss to combine. Stir in the scallions and red pepper.

2. Prepare the dressing: Place the reserved shrimp, tomato paste, lemon juice, eggs, and tarragon in a food processor fitted with the steel blade; process until smooth. Add the mayonnaise and process again until smooth. Season to taste with salt and pepper and add the Pernod. Process once more just to blend. Pour the dressing over the pasta salad and toss thoroughly to coat. Transfer the salad to a serving bowl. Serve at once or refrigerate covered several hours and serve cold.

Makes 10 to 12 servings.

Paella Salad

This dramatic cold interpretation of classic Spanish paella is a fabulous dish to prepare for guests on hot summer evenings.

2 quarts chicken stock,
  preferably homemade
1 tablespoon curry powder
1 teaspoon saffron threads
1 teaspoon fennel seeds
1 teaspoon dried red
  pepper flakes
6 tablespoons olive oil
1 large red onion, minced
5 cloves garlic, minced
3 cups long-grain rice
3 boneless, skinless whole
  chicken breasts, cut
  into ¾-inch chunks
5 ribs celery, chopped
1 bunch scallions, white
  bulbs and green stalks,
  sliced
2 red bell peppers, seeded
  and cut into ¼-inch dice
1 yellow bell pepper, seeded
  and cut into ¼-inch dice

1 cup pitted black olives, sliced
2 cans (14 ounces each)
  artichoke hearts, drained
  and sliced
1 pound fresh cooked crabmeat
3 pounds large (16 to 24
  per pound) shrimp,
  peeled, deveined, and
  cooked just until
  opaque (see box, page 148)
3 dozen cooked fresh
  mussels, shucked
8 ounces hard sausage,
  thinly sliced
½ cup fresh lemon juice
2 to 2½ cups Hellmann's
  mayonnaise
Salt and freshly ground
  pepper to taste
Lemon slices, red bell
  pepper strips, and
  black olives for garnish

1. Combine the chicken stock, curry powder, saffron, fennel seeds, and red pepper flakes in a medium saucepan and heat just to boiling.

2. Heat the oil in a very large skillet over medium-high heat. Stir in the red onion and garlic and cook, stirring frequently, for 5 minutes. Add the rice and stir to coat with the oil. Cook 2 minutes longer. Gradually stir in the chicken stock mixture. Reduce the heat and simmer covered, stirring occasionally, until half the liquid has been absorbed, 15 to 20 minutes.

3. Stir the chicken into the rice mixture and continue to simmer until all the liquid has been absorbed and the rice is tender, 20 to 25 minutes longer. Remove from the heat and let cool to room temperature, stirring occasionally.

4. When the rice is cooled, transfer it to a large mixing bowl. Add the celery, scallions, peppers, olives, artichoke hearts, crabmeat, shrimp, mussels, and sausage. Toss to combine all the ingredients thoroughly. Stir in the lemon juice and enough mayonnaise to lightly bind. Season to taste with salt and pepper. Transfer the salad to a large shallow serving dish. Garnish with lemon slices, red pepper strips, and whole olives. Refrigerate covered at least 2 hours before serving.

Makes 18 to 20 servings.

Egg and Smoked Salmon Salad

Serve this salad in tomato shells for a light luncheon or on rye or pumpernickel bread for great sandwiches.

12 large eggs, hard-cooked, shelled, and coarsely chopped	5 ounces smoked salmon, cut into ¼-inch dice
2 ribs celery, chopped	1 cup (or as needed) Hellmann's mayonnaise
1 small red onion, minced	Salt and freshly ground pepper to taste
3 tablespoons chopped fresh dill	

1. Place the eggs, celery, onion, dill, and salmon in a mixing bowl and toss to combine.

2. Stir in enough mayonnaise to bind the salad, being careful not to make it too wet. Season to taste with salt and pepper. Refrigerate for several hours to allow the flavors to blend.

Makes 6 servings.

Tuna Tonnato

In culinary experimentation, redundancy can sometimes achieve a triumph of flavor intensity, as is the case with this salad in which seared chunks of fresh tuna are tossed with a classic Italian tonnato sauce with a canned tuna base. A most elegant interpretation of the forever popular tuna fish salad!

3 pounds fresh tuna, cut
  into ¾-inch chunks
¾ cup fresh lemon juice
½ cup olive oil
2 shallots, minced
Salt and freshly ground
  pepper to taste
1 cucumber, peeled,
  halved lengthwise,
  seeded, and sliced
  diagonally ¼ inch
  thick

2 yellow bell peppers,
  seeded and cut into
  ½-inch squares
5 ripe medium tomatoes,
  seeded and sliced ½
  inch thick
1 medium red onion, cut
  into thin slivers
½ cup chopped fresh dill

TONNATO SAUCE:
2 large egg yolks
1 large egg
5 anchovy fillets, drained
  and chopped
1½ tablespoons capers,
  drained
3 tablespoons fresh lemon
  juice

1½ tablespoons Dijon
  mustard
1 can (12 ounces) white
  meat tuna packed in
  oil (don't drain)
1½ cups olive oil
Salt and freshly ground
  pepper to taste

1. Place the chunks of tuna in a wide shallow bowl. Whisk the lemon juice, oil, shallots, salt, and pepper together in a small mixing bowl and pour over the tuna. Marinate, turning the fish occasionally, for 3 hours in the refrigerator.

2. Combine the cucumber, yellow peppers, tomatoes, onion, and dill in a large mixing bowl. Heat a large skillet over high heat until quite hot. Add the tuna with the marinade and stir-fry just until the tuna is cooked through, 5 to 7 minutes. Add the tuna to the vegetables and toss to combine.

3. Prepare the tonnato sauce: Place the egg yolks, egg, anchovies, capers, lemon juice, mustard, and canned tuna with

its oil in a food processor fitted with the steel blade; process until smooth. With the machine running, slowly pour the oil in a thin, steady stream through the feed tube to make a sauce the consistency of mayonnaise. Season the sauce with salt and pepper to taste. Pour the sauce over the salad ingredients and toss thoroughly to coat. Refrigerate the salad at least 2 hours before serving.

Makes 6 to 8 servings.

Blackened Snapper Vinaigrette

By substituting olive oil for butter in the traditional recipe for blackened snapper, the fish can be served slightly chilled or at room temperature. It's a great way to enjoy this New Orleans specialty when it is just too hot to heat up the cast-iron skillet right before eating.

2 cups olive oil	2 teaspoons dried red
½ cup fresh lemon juice	pepper flakes
2 tablespoons dried thyme	2 teaspoons salt
3 tablespoons dried basil	8 red snapper fillets,
1 tablespoon dried	about 8 ounces each
oregano	3 tablespoons shredded
1½ tablespoons coarsely	fresh basil
ground pepper	1 lemon, cut into wedges

1. Heat the oil in a medium skillet and add the lemon juice, thyme, basil, oregano, pepper, red pepper flakes, and salt. Simmer over low heat for 10 minutes, then remove from the heat.

2. Dip the fish fillets, one at a time, in the oil mixture, coating both sides heavily with herbs. Place the fillets on a flat tray and freeze until very cold, 15 to 20 minutes.

3. Heat a large cast-iron skillet over very high heat. Arrange as many fillets as will fit in a single layer in the skillet and quickly sear and blacken both sides, about 4 minutes. Transfer the fillets to a serving platter and refrigerate for several hours. Repeat with any remaining fillets. Serve cold or at room temperature, sprinkled with the basil and garnished with the lemon wedges.

Makes 8 servings.

Steak, Mushroom, and Hearts of Palm with Béarnaise Mayonnaise

Many of the components of a great steak dinner translated into an extravagant and refreshing summer salad.

1 boneless top round steak, 3 pounds, 2 to 2½ inches thick	12 ounces fresh mushrooms (as white as you can find), thinly sliced
1 tablespoon dried mustard	2 cans (14 ounces each) hearts of palm, drained and cut into ½-inch slices
Salt and freshly ground pepper to taste	
1 bunch scallions, white bulb and green stalks, sliced	½ cup chopped fresh parsley

BÉARNAISE MAYONNAISE:

3 shallots, peeled and minced	1 tablespoon Dijon mustard
2½ tablespoons dried tarragon	½ cup olive oil
½ cup dry white wine	1 cup vegetable oil
¼ cup tarragon vinegar	Salt and freshly ground pepper to taste
2 large egg yolks	
2 tablespoons fresh lemon juice	Sliced tomato and fresh tarragon or parsley sprigs for garnish

1. Preheat the broiler.

2. Rub the steak all over with the dried mustard and sprinkle generously on both sides with salt and pepper. Broil the steak about 6 inches from the heat, turning once, until cooked medium-rare. Let cool several minutes, then cut the steak into thin strips, 2½ to 3 inches long. Combine the steak, scallions, mushrooms, hearts of palm, and parsley in a mixing bowl.

3. Prepare the mayonnaise: Place the shallots, tarragon, wine, and vinegar in a small saucepan and cook over high heat until just 1 tablespoon liquid remains.

4. Place the egg yolks, lemon juice, and mustard in a food

processor fitted with the steel blade; process for 10 seconds. With the machine running, pour the olive and vegetable oils in a thin, steady stream through the feed tube to make a thick emulsion. Add the reduced shallot mixture to the mayonnaise and process to blend. Season the mayonnaise to taste with salt and pepper.

5. Bind the steak salad with the mayonnaise. Refrigerate covered at least several hours but no longer than 12 hours. Garnish with tomato slices and a sprig or two of fresh tarragon or parsley.

Makes 8 servings.

Ham, Cheese, Mushroom, and Walnut Salad

A personal favorite that reminds me of the robust salads I savored in Germany during adolescent bicycle meanderings.

1½ pounds baked ham,
   thinly sliced
1½ pounds Swiss cheese,
   thinly sliced
1 pound fresh
   mushrooms, thinly
   sliced

3 cups chopped fresh
   parsley
¼ cup fresh lemon juice
¼ cup olive oil

DRESSING:
1¾ cups chopped walnuts
5 cloves garlic, minced
¼ cup fresh lemon juice
2½ cups olive oil

½ teaspoon cayenne
   pepper
Salt and freshly ground
   pepper to taste

1. Cut the ham and cheese into ¼-inch squares and toss together in a large mixing bowl. Add the mushrooms and parsley and toss to combine. Drizzle with the lemon juice and oil and toss once more.

2. Prepare the dressing: Place the walnuts, garlic, and lemon juice in a food processor fitted with the steel blade; pulse just to combine but not purée. Add the oil ½ cup at a time and pulse a

few times after each addition until blended, being careful not to lose the texture of the walnuts. Season the dressing with the cayenne and salt and pepper to taste. Bind the salad with the dressing. Serve at once or refrigerate until ready to serve.

Makes 10 to 12 servings.

Kielbasa Vinaigrette

If I were stranded on a desert isle and allowed only one food, it would probably be kielbasa. A kielbasa supper was always my favorite home-cooked meal when I was growing up. I later devised this salad so I could indulge my passion for cold foods and Polish sausage at the same time.

This salad is very popular with my customers both as a main course and an hors d'oeuvre.

3½ pounds smoked
   kielbasa sausage
1 jar (4 ounces) chopped
   pimientos, drained
1 can (6 ounces) large
   pitted, black olives,
   sliced

1 bunch scallions, white
   bulbs and green stalks,
   sliced
1 cup chopped fresh
   parsley
1½ cups Basic Herb
   Vinaigrette (see Index)

1. Put the kielbasa in a large pot and add enough water to just cover the sausage. Heat to boiling over high heat. Reduce the heat and simmer uncovered for 10 minutes. Drain in a colander and let cool just until you can easily slice the sausage without burning your fingers.

2. Using a serrated knife, cut the sausage on a sharp diagonal angle into ½-inch-thick slices. Place the sausage in a large mixing bowl. Add the pimientos, olives, scallions, and parsley and toss to combine. Add the vinaigrette and toss to coat. Serve at room temperature. The salad keeps well in the refrigerator, but it must be warmed to room temperature before serving.

Makes 8 main-course servings or 15 to 20 hors d'oeuvre servings.

Lamb, Eggplant, and Orzo Salad

A Mediterranean-flavored salad that makes great use of leftover lamb in an unusual variation on cold pasta salads.

2 large eggplants, cut into
  ¾-inch chunks
¾ cup olive oil
3 cloves garlic, minced
2 pounds orzo, cooked in
  large pot of boiling
  water until al dente,
  drained, and cooled
  under cold running
  water
2½ pounds rare lamb,
  cut into ¾-inch chunks
1½ cups pitted Greek
  olives, cut in half

1 medium red onion,
  minced
2 yellow bell peppers,
  seeded and cut into
  ½-inch dice
1 cup yellow or red cherry
  tomatoes, quartered
½ cup pine nuts, lightly
  toasted
1 bunch fresh parsley,
  minced
3 tablespoons chopped
  fresh rosemary

LEMON GARLIC DRESSING:
2 large egg yolks
1 large egg
⅓ cup fresh lemon juice
1 tablespoon dried
  oregano
6 cloves garlic, minced

2 teaspoons grated lemon
  zest
2½ cups olive oil
Salt and freshly ground
  pepper to taste

1. Preheat the oven to 375°F.

2. Place the eggplant in a baking pan. Drizzle with the olive oil, add the garlic, and toss to combine. Bake, stirring occasionally, until the eggplant is tender, 30 to 40 minutes. Let cool.

3. Combine the orzo, lamb, olives, onion, yellow peppers, tomatoes, pine nuts, parsley, and rosemary in a large mixing bowl. Add the roasted eggplant and toss all the ingredients together well.

4. Prepare the dressing: Place the egg yolks, egg, lemon juice, oregano, garlic, and lemon zest in a food processor fitted with the steel blade; process for 10 seconds. With the machine running, pour the oil in a thin, steady stream through the feed tube to

make a thick mayonnaise. Season to taste with salt and pepper.

5. Bind the salad with the dressing and transfer to a serving bowl. Garnish with fresh sprigs of rosemary. Serve slightly chilled or at room temperature.

Makes 12 to 15 servings.

Cold Chinese Noodles

Since day one, customers have coveted these noodles. One man from Washington has consumed so many of them over the summers that he is now known by all on Nantucket as the "Big Noodle." This salad is indeed the sort for which midnight cravings are made.

1 boneless, skinless whole
    chicken breast, poached,
    cooled, and cut into
    thin julienne strips
    (see box, page 163)
5 ounces boiled or baked
    ham, sliced and cut
    into thin julienne strips
1 bunch scallions
    (including green tops),
    cut into 2-inch lengths,
    then into julienne
    strips
½ cup coarsely chopped
    walnuts
1 pound thin vermicelli,
    angel hair, or Chinese
    rice stick noodles,
    cooked until al dente,
    drained, and cooled
    under cold running
    water

1 cup vegetable oil
2½ tablespoons Oriental
    sesame oil
2 tablespoons sesame
    seeds
3 tablespoons ground
    coriander seeds
¾ cup soy sauce
1 scant teaspoon (or to
    taste) hot chili oil

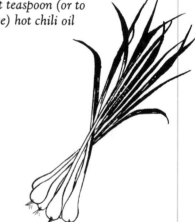

1. Combine the chicken, ham, scallions, and walnuts in a large mixing bowl. Add the pasta.

2. Heat the vegetable and sesame oils and sesame seeds in a small saucepan over medium heat just until the sesame seeds

turn light brown. Remove from the heat. Stir in the coriander and soy sauce; stand back as you do this for the mixture will crackle and sizzle. Stir in the chili oil.

3. Pour the hot dressing over the noodles and toss to coat evenly. The very best way to do this is with your hands. Inevitably at the moment you are up to your elbows in Chinese noodles the phone will ring—it is part of the fun.

4. Transfer the noodles to a serving bowl—again with your hands—and refrigerate until cold, about 3 hours.

Makes 6 to 8 servings or 4 true Chinese-noodle–aficionado servings.

Indonesian Noodles

A more complex, though equally favored, version of the cold Chinese noodles.

2 pounds angel hair or Oriental rice stick noodles, cooked until al dente, drained, and cooled under cold running water

1 bunch scallions white bulbs and green stalks, cut into 2-inch lengths, then into julienne strips

1 pound snow peas, strings removed, blanched in boiling water for 30 seconds, rinsed under cold running water, and then cut lengthwise in half

1 red bell pepper, seeded and cut into thin julienne strips

1 yellow bell pepper, seeded and cut into thin julienne strips

1 can (8 ounces) water chestnuts, drained and thinly sliced

2 cans (8 ounces each) sliced bamboo shoots, drained

1 jar (7¼ ounces) pickled baby corn, drained and cut lengthwise into quarters

½ cup chopped fresh coriander

2½ pounds small (35 to 40 per pound) shrimp, peeled, deveined, and cooked just until opaque (see box, page 148)

¾ cup salted peanuts

¼ cup Oriental sesame oil

¾ cup soy sauce

3½ cups Hellmann's mayonnaise

Hot chili oil to taste

1. Place the drained pasta in a large mixing bowl. Add the julienned vegetables, the water chestnuts, bamboo shoots, baby corn, coriander, shrimp, and peanuts; toss to combine.

2. Whisk the sesame oil, soy sauce, and mayonnaise together in a small mixing bowl. Pour the dressing over the noodles and mix thoroughly with your hands to ensure that the salad is evenly coated. Season with drops of hot chili oil to taste. Refrigerate covered the salad for several hours and serve as a main course.

Makes 10 to 12 servings.

Tortellini with Sun-Dried Tomato Pesto

This is an irresistible way of serving tortellini. My customers have told me that the dish is so good they often can't wait to serve it as the main course and instead spear the tortellini on toothpicks as an hors d'oeuvre.

SUN-DRIED TOMATO PESTO:

½ stick pepperoni (about ¼ pound), cut into small dice
3 tablespoons Dijon mustard
4 cloves garlic, minced
1 tablespoon fennel seeds
1 jar (7 ounces) sun-dried tomatoes packed in oil

1½ cups olive oil
2 tablespoons fresh lemon juice
Salt and freshly ground pepper to taste

SALAD:

2 pounds cheese- or meat-filled tortellini, cooked and drained
2 ripe medium tomatoes, seeded and chopped
1 yellow bell pepper, seeded and diced

1 stick pepperoni, thinly sliced
½ cup chopped fresh parsley
3 tablespoons chopped fresh basil

1. Prepare the pesto: Place the pepperoni, mustard, garlic, fennel seeds, and sun-dried tomatoes with oil in a food processor fitted with the steel blade; process until smooth. With the machine running, pour the olive oil in a thin, steady stream through the feed tube and continue processing until the mixture is smooth. Season with the lemon juice and salt and pepper to taste.

2. Combine the tortellini, tomatoes, yellow pepper, and pepperoni in a large mixing bowl. Add the pesto and toss to coat. Sprinkle with the parsley and basil. Serve warm or at room temperature.

Makes 8 to 10 servings.

Duck and Wild Rice à l'Orange

An expensive combination of the best ingredients, this woodsy salad tastes as fabulous as one would expect.

2 cups wild rice
4 tablespoons (½ stick) unsalted butter
4 carrots, peeled and cut into ¼-inch dice
1 large red onion, minced
3 cups chicken stock, preferably homemade
4 boneless whole duck breasts

1 bunch scallions, white bulbs and green stalks, sliced on slight diagonal
1 cup golden raisins
1½ cups pecan halves
Grated zest of 2 oranges
¾ cup fresh orange juice
¾ cup best-quality olive oil
Salt and freshly ground pepper to taste

1. Place the wild rice in a small bowl, add cold water to cover, and let soak for 1 hour. Drain. Heat a 2-quart pot of water to boiling. Add the rice and boil for 5 minutes. Drain again and set aside.

2. Preheat the oven to 375°F.

3. Melt the butter in a large skillet over medium-high heat. Add the carrots and onion and sauté, stirring frequently, for 10 minutes. Add the rice, stir to coat it with the butter, and cook several minutes longer.

4. Transfer the rice mixture to a lasagne-type baking pan, 13 x 11-inches, and pour in the chicken stock. Cover the pan

tightly with aluminum foil and bake until the liquid is absorbed and the rice is tender, 40 to 45 minutes.

5. Meanwhile, place the duck breasts flat on a baking sheet, skin side up, and bake 15 to 20 minutes for rare meat. Remove the duck from the oven and let stand until cool enough to handle. Remove the skin from the meat and return it to the baking sheet. Bake the skins until very crispy, 30 to 40 minutes.

6. Transfer the rice to a large mixing bowl. Cut the duck meat into long, narrow strips and combine it with the rice. Add the scallions, raisins, pecans, and orange zest; toss to combine. Dress the salad with the orange juice and olive oil. Season to taste with salt and pepper.

7. Transfer the salad to a serving bowl. Cut the crisp duck skin into bits and scatter them over the salad. Serve slightly warm or at room temperature.

Makes 8 to 10 servings.

Curried Chicken Salad

Customers at Que Sera are generally divided into two camps of those who favor the chicken and grape salad and those who favor the curried chicken. Then there is a small diplomatic core that often orders a pint of each. The curried chicken recipe is quite simple for a curry. I am convinced that the secret is the addition of the wine in which the raisins are simmered, as it thins the mayonnaise into more of a light curry sauce.

3 pounds boneless, skinless chicken breasts, poached just until tender and cooled to room temperature (see box, facing page)

3 ribs celery, coarsely chopped

2 Granny Smith apples, cored and cut into chunks

¾ cup golden raisins

1 cup dry white wine

2 tablespoons fresh lime juice

2 tablespoons ground ginger

2½ to 3 tablespoons good-quality curry powder

1½ cups Hellmann's mayonnaise

Salt to taste

Sliced Granny Smith apples and curry-colored summer flowers (marigolds, zinnias) for garnish

1. Cut the chicken breasts into ¾- to 1-inch chunks, removing and discarding any tough tendons as you go along. Toss the
chicken, celery, and apples together in a large bowl.

2. Place the raisins and wine in a small saucepan. Heat to
boiling over medium-high heat. Reduce the heat and simmer for 3
to 4 minutes. Add the raisins and liquid to the chicken and toss
to combine.

3. Add the lime juice, ginger, and curry powder and toss
again. Bind the salad with the mayonnaise and season to taste
with salt.

4. Transfer the salad to a serving bowl and garnish with the
apple slices and summer flowers. Refrigerate at least 1 hour
before serving.

Makes 6 to 8 servings.

POACHING CHICKEN BREASTS

As reigning queen of chicken salad sales on Nantucket
Island in the summertime, I poach zillions and zillions of
chicken breasts. The process is much less of a technique
and more of a habit that has become second nature to me.

I start by filling a large saucepan with water and spike
it with a few splashes of white wine or dry vermouth. I
scatter in several onion slices and/or carrot slices, celery
leaves, and parsley sprigs over the top, season with a dash
of salt and grinding of pepper, then add the chicken
breasts. Next I bring the pan to a full boil, and then turn
it off, letting the heat of the liquid finish the cooking
process. This method seems to keep the breasts especially
moist and tender.

When all has cooled, I remove the chicken breasts with
a slotted spoon and proceed with the salad making. The
poaching liquid can be strained and used for stock in soup
recipes.

When I have to poach several batches of chicken
breasts over a short period of time, I use the same strained
stock over and over again to produce a super rich and
wonderfully flavored stock that is great for hearty soup
bases and for braising.

Classic Chicken and Grape Salad

Every year about mid-July, I begin to suspect that my entire life revolves around poaching countless ten-pound bags of chicken breasts. Little did I know years ago, when I tried to surprise my uncle on his birthday with a batch of chicken salad as wonderful as that which he raved about at Boston's Ritz Carlton, that so much of my catering reputation and fortune would come to center on that recipe.

While ingredients such as dried thyme, garlic powder, and store-bought mayonnaise reflect the culinary naïveté of my adolescence, the insuing years of food sophistication spent cultivating window boxes of fragrant fresh herbs and whisking together countless varieties of homemade mayonnaise have yet to yield a more perfectly comforting and soothing chicken salad than this original "Ritz" rendition.

3½ pounds boneless, skinless chicken breasts, poached just until tender and cooled to room temperature (see box, page 163)
5 ribs celery, coarsely chopped
1½ cups seedless green grapes, cut in half

1½ teaspoons dried thyme
1½ teaspoons garlic powder (fresh garlic is overpowering)
Salt and freshly ground pepper to taste
3 cups (or as needed) Hellmann's mayonnaise

1. Cut the chicken breasts into ¾- to 1-inch chunks, removing and discarding any tough tendons as you go along.

2. Toss the chicken, celery, and grapes together in a large bowl. Season with the thyme, garlic powder, salt, and pepper. Bind the salad with the mayonnaise. You want to use a lot of mayonnaise to make the salad very moist and creamy.

3. Transfer the salad to a serving bowl and refrigerate covered at least 1 hour before serving.

Makes 6 to 8 servings.

Chicken and Apricot Salad with Double-Mustard Mayonnaise

Chicken salad seems capable of sustaining an amazing number of incarnations. This autumnal version was created in response to a favorite customer's suggestion.

3 pounds boneless,
 skinless chicken breasts,
 poached just until
 tender and cooled to
 room temperature (see
 box, page 163)
1 cup dried apricots, cut
 into ¼-inch strips
⅓ cup cream sherry
3 ribs celery, coarsely
 chopped

4 scallions, white bulbs
 and green stalks,
 trimmed and sliced on
 diagonal
½ cup slivered almonds,
 lightly toasted
3 tablespoons chopped
 fresh rosemary

DOUBLE-MUSTARD MAYONNAISE:
2 large egg yolks
2 tablespoons fresh lemon
 juice
2 tablespoons grainy
 Dijon mustard

¾ cup vegetable oil
⅔ cup olive oil
¼ cup honey mustard
Salt and freshly ground
 pepper to taste

Fresh rosemary sprigs for
 garnish

1. Cut the poached chicken breasts into 2 x ¾-inch strips and place them in a large mixing bowl.

2. Place the apricots and sherry in a small saucepan. Heat to boiling. Reduce the heat and simmer for 3 minutes. Add the apricots with the liquid to the chicken.

3. Add the celery, scallions, almonds, and rosemary to the salad and toss to combine.

4. Prepare the mayonnaise: Place the egg yolks, lemon juice, and grainy mustard in a food processor fitted with the steel blade; process for 10 seconds. With the machine running, pour the vegetable and olive oils in a thin, steady stream through the feed tube to make an emulsion. Add the honey mustard and process until smooth. Season to taste with salt and freshly ground pepper. Bind the salad with the mayonnaise.

5. Transfer the salad to a serving bowl and garnish with the rosemary sprigs. Refrigerate covered at least 2 hours before serving.

Makes 6 to 8 servings.

Indian Chicken Salad

This is the most adventuresome chicken salad made at Que Sera Sarah. Lovers of Indian tandoor cooking will appreciate this chilled salad version.

4 pounds boneless,
    skinless chicken breasts,
    cut into 1-inch chunks
5 cloves garlic, minced
3 tablespoons chopped
    fresh ginger
2 tablespoons ground
    coriander seeds
2 tablespoons fennel seeds
1 tablespoon cumin seeds
1 tablespoon turmeric
1 tablespoon ground
    cinnamon

1½ teaspoons ground
    ginger
3 tablespoons tomato
    paste
3 tablespoons fresh lemon
    juice
1 can (28 ounces)
    tomatoes packed in
    purée
Salt to taste
2 tablespoons fresh
    coriander leaves for
    garnish

1. Arrange the chicken in a single layer in a shallow glass or enamel baking dish.

2. Place the garlic, fresh ginger, coriander seeds, fennel, cumin, turmeric, cinnamon, ground ginger, tomato paste, and lemon juice in a food processor fitted with the steel blade; process to a thick paste. Add the tomatoes and process until well

blended. Season to taste with salt. Pour the spice mixture over the chicken. Let marinate covered overnight in the refrigerator, stirring occasionally.

3. Preheat the oven to 450°F.

4. Bake the chicken, stirring frequently, just until it is cooked through, 20 to 25 minutes. Let cool to room temperature.

5. Transfer the salad to a serving bowl and garnish with the fresh coriander. Serve the salad at room temperature or refrigerate for an hour or so.

Makes 8 servings.

Smoked Turkey with Artichoke Hearts

A pretty pastel salad that you can assemble quickly on a hot, hot day when any movement seems overwhelming.

3 pound piece smoked
    turkey, cut into ¾-inch
    chunks
1 large red onion, cut
    into thin slivers
2 cans (14 ounces each)
    artichoke hearts,
    packed in water,
    drained and thinly
    sliced

4 ribs celery, minced
5 tablespoons fresh lemon
    juice
7 tablespoons olive oil
1 teaspoon salt
1 teaspoon freshly ground
    pepper

GREEN-PEPPERCORN
TARRAGON MAYONNAISE:
2 large egg yolks
1 large egg
1½ tablespoons Dijon
    mustard
1½ tablespoons green
    peppercorns packed in
    brine, drained

2½ tablespoons minced
    fresh tarragon
3 tablespoons fresh lemon
    juice
1¼ cups olive oil
1½ cups vegetable oil
Salt to taste

1. Combine the turkey, onion, artichoke hearts, and celery in a large mixing bowl. Drizzle with the lemon juice and oil and sprinkle with the salt and pepper. Toss to combine. Let marinate at room temperature for 30 minutes.

2. Prepare the mayonnaise: Place the egg yolks, egg, mustard, green peppercorns, tarragon, and lemon juice in a food processor fitted with the steel blade; process for 20 seconds. With the machine running, pour the olive and vegetable oils in a thin, steady stream through the feed tube to make a thick mayonnaise. Season the mayonnaise with salt to taste.

3. Bind the salad with mayonnaise. Refrigerate several hours before serving.

Makes 8 to 10 servings.

Eclectic
Dinner
Fare

One might suspect a certain lack of worldliness to prevail on a tiny New England island isolated by thirty miles of ocean, but throughout its history the spirit of Nantucketers has never been in the least bit provincial. From the island's prosperous whaling beginnings in the 1700s to the stylish present, the person lured to living or vacationing on Nantucket has always seemed capable of balancing a restless curiosity for the nooks and crannies of the globe with a strong attachment to Nantucket as home.

The joy of creating dinners for such clients is that they immediately understand and appreciate both foreign and native inspirations of a meal. While the rest of America appears to be intently focused on the revival of regional cooking, a wonderful culinary eclecticism thrives on this island. Local Nantucket provisions are always enthusiastically welcomed for preparations that may find their origins in the lagoons of Venice, the olive groves of Greece, the vineyards of Burgundy, the *pousadas* of Portugal, the extremities of Baja, the glitz of New York, or the traditions of New England. The supreme enjoyment of sharing dinner with friends on Nantucket is that the boundaries of one island oasis can expand to include so many imaginative culinary voyages around the world.

Cuban Pork Roast

This is a great feast for a balmy summer evening. The flavorings take their inspiration from a friend's recollections of growing up in Havana and my own personal fascination with Caribbean cuisine. In addition to the recipes for Black Beans and Baked Bananas included here, you may want to serve a side of white rice to make this unusually spiced meal complete.

6 cloves garlic
4 scallions, white bulbs and green stalks, minced
½ cup pine nuts
1 fresh jalapeño pepper, seeded and minced
2 cups minced fresh coriander leaves
⅔ cup fruity olive oil
½ cup plus 3 tablespoons fresh lime juice
⅓ cup Niçoise or Greek olives, pitted and minced

Salt and freshly ground pepper to taste
1 boneless pork loin roast (4 pounds)
½ cup fresh grapefruit juice
½ cup fresh orange juice
½ cup hot pepper jelly (available at specialty food stores)

BLACK BEANS AND BAKED BANANAS: (recipes follow), as accompaniments

1. On the day before you plan to serve the pork, prepare the filling and marinade: Place the garlic, scallions, pine nuts, jalapeño pepper, and coriander in a food processor fitted with the steel blade. Process to form a thick paste. With the machine running, pour the olive oil in a thin, steady stream through the feed tube until all is incorporated. Remove to a small bowl and stir in the lime juice, olives, and salt and pepper to taste.

2. If the pork roast is tied, untie it and roll it out flat. Spread two-thirds of the garlic-coriander paste over the meat. Reroll the roast and tie it.

3. Stir the grapefruit, orange, and lime juices into the remaining garlic-coriander paste. Make shallow incisions over the surface of the roast with the tip of a sharp knife. Place the roast in a shallow dish or pan and pour over the marinade. Let marinate in

the refrigerator, turning occasionally, for 24 hours.

4. Preheat the oven to 375°F.

5. Remove the roast from the marinade and place it in a roasting pan. Roast uncovered, basting occasionally with any leftover marinade, for 1¾ hours. Brush the roast all over with the hot pepper jelly and bake 15 minutes more or until cooked to desired doneness.

6. Let the roast rest out of the oven for 10 minutes, then carve into ½-inch-thick slices and serve.

Makes 8 servings.

Black Beans

The seasoning or "sofrito" for these beans has been derived from recipes of many different Caribbean islands. The annatto seeds add authentic flavoring subtleties and impart a bright orange-red color, but are not essential to the success of this dish if they are difficult to locate in your area.

1 pound black beans,
     soaked overnight in
     cold water
1½ tablespoons annatto
     seeds (available in
     specialty food stores)
⅓ cup olive oil
1 medium onion, diced
2 scallions, white bulbs
     and green stalks,
     minced
4 cloves garlic, minced
½ green bell pepper,
     seeded and diced
½ red bell pepper, seeded
     and diced
1 fresh jalapeño pepper,
     seeded and minced

2 tablespoons tomato
     paste
3 tablespoons red wine
     vinegar
1 tablespoon dried
     oregano leaves
1 tablespoon ground
     cumin
3 tablespoons minced
     fresh coriander leaves
1 tablespoon salt
2 teaspoons freshly
     ground pepper

1. Drain the beans and place in a large saucepan or stockpot with water to cover. Heat to boiling over medium-high heat, then

lower the heat and simmer for 1¼ hours. Add more water if necessary to keep the beans moist. Do not drain the cooked beans.

2. Meanwhile, make the sofrito: If you are using the annatto seeds, place them in a small saucepan with the olive oil. Heat over medium heat just until the annatto seeds release their color, 5 to 7 minutes. Strain out the seeds and discard.

3. Heat the flavored oil (or plain olive oil) in a medium skillet over medium-high heat. Add the onion, scallions, garlic, bell peppers, and jalapeño and sauté, stirring frequently, for 7 minutes. Stir in the tomato paste and vinegar, then add the oregano, cumin, coriander, salt, and pepper. Reduce the heat to medium and cook for 5 minutes more. Remove from the heat.

4. Add the sofrito to the cooked beans (there should still be a fair amount of liquid with the beans) and simmer uncovered until the mixture becomes quite thick, 30 minutes. You can serve the beans at once or set aside. (Many cooks like to make black beans in advance as they feel the flavor improves with a little age and reheating.) Reheat the beans covered over low heat.

Makes 8 servings.

Baked Bananas

These provide an interesting sweet balance to the spiciness of the pork and black beans.

4 ripe bananas, peeled, cut crosswise in half, then halved lengthwise	1 tablespoon fresh lime juice
4 tablespoons (½ stick) unsalted butter	⅓ cup loosely packed brown sugar
2 tablespoons dry sherry	1 teaspoon ground cinnamon

1. Preheat the oven to 375°F. Arrange the bananas in a single layer in an 11 x 9-inch glass baking dish.

2. Melt the butter in a small saucepan over medium heat, then stir in the sherry and lime juice. Heat thoroughly, then pour over the bananas. Dot with the brown sugar and cinnamon. Bake in the oven until lightly browned and bubbly, 12 to 15 minutes.

Makes 8 servings.

Filet Mignon with Herbes de Provence and Red Wine Béarnaise

While traveling through Provence one fall, I discovered that the local, aromatic herb blend was often used to coat meats in a manner that reminded me of Paul Prudhomme's blackened red-fish. This recipe is my own interpolation, falling somewhere between St. Remy and New Orleans.

6 filet mignon steaks,
  each 2 inches thick
  (6 to 8 ounces each)
Salt and freshly ground
  pepper to taste
4 tablespoons imported
  herbes de Provence
3 shallots, minced
3 tablespoons chopped
  fresh tarragon

3 tablespoons red wine
  vinegar
½ cup dry red wine
2 large egg yolks
¾ cup (1½ sticks)
  unsalted butter,
  melted, then cooled to
  lukewarm
3 tablespoons olive oil

1. One hour before serving, season the steaks generously all over with salt and pepper. Rub a generous 1 teaspoon of the herbes de Provence into each side of the filets. Let sit at room temperature.

2. In the meantime, make the red wine Béarnaise. Combine the shallots, tarragon, vinegar, and wine in a small skillet. Reduce the mixture over medium-high heat until all but 2 tablespoons of liquid remain. Turn off the heat and whisk in the egg yolks, one at a time. Gradually whisk in the melted butter, tablespoon by tablespoon, until all is absorbed and the sauce is thickened. Keep the Béarnaise warm in the top of a double boiler set over simmering water or in a warm spot near the stove. (Be careful not to overheat or the mixture will separate.)

3. Coat a large well-seasoned frying pan with the olive oil. Heat over high heat until very hot. Add the steaks and cook until the bottoms are well browned, 3 to 4 minutes. Turn the steaks and brown the other side for 2 to 3 minutes. Reduce the heat to medium and continue cooking until the meat reaches the desired doneness, 3 minutes more for rare. Transfer the steaks to serving plates and nap each with a generous amount of the red wine Béarnaise.

Makes 6 servings.

Beef Tenderloin au Poivre

When entertaining, this pepper-crusted beef tenderloin is much easier to prepare than the classic recipe for individual steak au poivre and much more opulent in presentation. During spells of hot weather, I roast the tenderloin during the cooler morning hours and serve it chilled for dinner accompanied by Tomato Bearnaise Mayonnaise, Remoulade Sauce, or Aioli (see the Index). When serving the tenderloin straight from the oven, I like to dot the rosy pink slices with Herb Garden Butter (recipe follows).

1 beef tenderloin, trimmed of fat (3½ to 4 pounds after trimming)
⅓ cup Dijon mustard

4½ teaspoons coarsely ground black peppercorns
4½ teaspoons coarsely ground white peppercorns

1. Preheat the oven to 425°F.
2. Rub the tenderloin generously all over with the mustard. Combine the peppercorns and press them evenly all over the surface of the meat. Place the meat in a roasting pan and cook for 45 minutes for rare meat, or longer for desired doneness. To serve warm, let stand for 5 minutes, then slice into ½-inch thick slices. Dot each with a dollop of Herb Garden Butter. Serve 2 to 3 slices per person. If serving the tenderloin cold, let the meat cool to room temperature, then wrap it in aluminum foil and refrigerate for several hours. Remove from the refrigerator about 15 minutes before serving and carve into ½-inch-thick slices. Arrange the slices on a platter along with a bowl of the sauce of your choice.
Makes 8 servings.

Herb Garden Butter

1 cup dry red wine
2 shallots, minced
¾ cup (1½ sticks) unsalted butter, at room temperature

1 tablespoon minced fresh tarragon
1 tablespoon minced fresh basil
1 tablespoon minced fresh parsley

1. Combine the red wine and shallots in a small saucepan and reduce over medium-high heat until only 3 tablespoons of the liquid remains.

2. Beat the butter and the herbs together in a mixing bowl until well creamed. Gradually beat in the wine reduction, tablespoon by tablespoon. Refrigerate until 30 minutes before serving. Serve the butter at room temperature.

Makes about ¾ cup.

Rainwater Chili

This recipe was created in honor of a person of boundless and contagious enthusiasm who rescued me many times from the tribulations of life in the food business, yet continues to be my most avid supporter. The friendship that began as a food summit on a widow's walk has survived everything from scandalous culinary confessions to capers with Armenian caviar purveyors in the South of France. Our unique rapport is one of the greatest rewards of my years in this business.

¼ cup olive oil
2 large Spanish onions,
    chopped
3 to 4 fresh jalapeño
    peppers, seeded and
    minced
1 yellow bell pepper,
    seeded and diced
1 green bell pepper,
    seeded and diced
5 cloves garlic, minced
¼ cup best-quality chili
    powder
2 tablespoons ground cumin
2 tablespoons dried oregano
1 tablespoon sweet
    paprika
1 tablespoon hot paprika
2 teaspoons ground
    cinnamon

1 teaspoon turmeric
1 teaspoon ground
    coriander seeds
½ teaspoon ground cardamon
3 tablespoons unsweetened
    cocoa powder
2 pounds ground beef sirloin
12 ounces hot Italian
    sausage, removed from
    casings and crumbled
12 ounces sweet Italian
    sausage, removed from
    casings and crumbled
1 can (35 ounces)
    tomatoes, undrained
½ cup golden tequila
1 bottle (12 ounces) beer
1 cup pitted Niçoise or
    Greek olives
Salt to taste

1. Heat the oil in a large pot over medium-high heat. Add the onions and cook, stirring occasionally, for 10 minutes.

2. Stir in the jalapeños, bell peppers, and garlic; cook, stirring occasionally, for 5 minutes. Add all the seasonings and the cocoa powder and cook, stirring occasionally, 5 minutes longer. Remove from the heat.

3. Brown the sirloin and sausage in a skillet, crumbling the meat with the back of a wooden spoon, over medium-high heat just until the meat is no longer pink. Add the meat to the onion mixture and return the pan to medium heat.

4. Stir in the tomatoes, tequila, beer, and olives. Season to taste with salt. Simmer the chili uncovered over low heat for about 1 hour.

5. Serve the chili hot in deep bowls, accompanied by bowls of sour cream, grated Cheddar cheese, and diced onions, tomatoes, and/or avocado. The chili is even better the next day and makes great nachos.

Makes 6 to 8 servings.

TAPAS TEXAS-STYLE

Great Guacamole
Salsa with Blue Corn Chips
Tex-Mex Turnovers
Baby Chiles Rellenos
Sausage in Brioche
Caviar Tartines
Grilled Soft-Shell Crabs
Miniature Lobster Salad
Club Sandwiches
Rainwater Chili in Pita Pockets
Que Sera Sarah Brownies

Tecate Beer, lots of Tequila, and Limes

Ossobuco

Ossobuco and I go back a long way. The story begins about fifteen years ago with my grandmother. She loved good food and adventurous eating and would always have some recipe or another she wanted us to cook together when I came to visit. Because my grandfather disdained any food that might be labeled "fancy," my grandmother would eagerly await my collaboration to satisfy her more esoteric cravings. Together we shared in gourmet extravaganzas, surreptitiously preparing steak tartare, sweetbreads, chicken fat cupcakes, and calamondin pies. One day we made ossobuco and passed it off on my grandfather as a new Perdue chicken part. It seems as if I've been making ossobuco ever since. This recipe is my thoroughly evolved version of this wonderful Italian dish. A good Italian risotto is the best accompaniment.

¾ cup all-purpose flour	6 carrots, peeled and
Salt and freshly ground	minced
pepper to taste	3 plum tomatoes, seeded
3 pounds veal shank cut	and chopped
into 8 pieces, each 1½	5 sun-dried tomatoes
to 2 inches thick	packed in oil, drained,
3 tablespoons olive oil	and minced
2 tablespoons unsalted	6 cloves garlic, minced
butter	2 cups beef stock,
3 leeks, rinsed, dried,	preferably homemade
and minced	1 cup dry white wine

GREMOLATA:

Finely grated zest of 1	½ cup minced fresh parsley
lemon	3 cloves garlic, minced

1. Season the flour with salt and pepper and dredge the veal shanks with the seasoned flour. Heat the oil and butter in a Dutch oven or large ovenproof casserole over medium-high heat. Add the veal shanks in batches and brown on all sides. Remove the browned shanks to a large plate.

2. Preheat the oven to 300°F.

3. Add the leeks and carrots to the pan and cook, stirring occasionally, for about 7 minutes. Stir

in the plum tomatoes, sun-dried tomatoes, and 6 cloves garlic; cook 5 minutes longer.

4. Add the beef stock and wine to the pan. Taste and adjust the seasoning. Return the veal shanks to the pan. Heat to boiling, then remove the pan from the heat. If you want, the dish can be refrigerated overnight at this point and finished the next day.

5. Cover the Dutch oven and place the pan the oven. Cook until the veal is very tender, about 1½ hours.

6. Meanwhile, prepare the gremolata: Combine the lemon zest, parsley, and 3 cloves garlic in a small bowl.

7. Serve the ossobuco in wide shallow bowls or plates and sprinkle each serving with a little of the gremolata.

Makes 6 to 8 servings.

Veal Marengo

For buffet entertaining this dish is a welcome variation on the now familiar *boeuf Bourguignon.*

½ cup all-purpose flour
Salt and freshly ground
*   pepper to taste*
3 pounds boneless lean
*   veal, cut into 2-inch*
*   cubes*
¼ cup olive oil
1 very large onion,
*   chopped*
1 cup dry white wine
1 cup chicken stock,
*   preferably homemade*

4 ripe tomatoes, seeded
*   and cut into ½-inch pieces*
3 cloves garlic, minced
1 tablespoon chopped
*   fresh tarragon*
1 teaspoon dried thyme
2 tablespoons fine strips
*   orange zest*
12 ounces fresh small
*   button mushrooms*
½ cup chopped fresh
*   parsley*

1. Season the flour with salt and pepper and lightly coat the veal cubes with the seasoned flour. Heat the olive oil in a Dutch oven or heavy casserole over medium-high heat. Add the veal in batches and quickly brown on all sides. Remove the browned veal to a large plate.

2. Add the onion to the pan and sauté over medium heat just until limp, 5 to 7 minutes. Pour in the wine and chicken stock and stir to scrape up any brown bits clinging to the bottom of the pan. Return the veal to the pot and add the tomatoes, garlic, tarragon, thyme, and orange zest. Simmer uncovered, stirring occasionally, until the veal is very tender, for about 1¼ hours.

3. Stir in the mushrooms and simmer 10 to 15 minutes longer. Season to taste with salt and pepper. If the sauce seems too thin at this point, remove the solids with a slotted spoon and keep warm. Reduce the sauce over high heat until thickened to the proper consistency. Return the solids and stir to combine. Sprinkle the stew with the parsley and serve with hot buttered noodles.

Makes 8 servings.

Moussaka

This is a great Mediterranean entrée perfect for summer entertaining, for it is best made ahead and will feed a summer cottage of houseguests quite sumptuously. Take advantage of summer's bountiful plump purple eggplants.

3 large eggplants
Salt
2 pounds lean ground
   lamb
¼ to ½ cup olive oil
2 medium onions,
   coarsely chopped
4 cloves garlic, minced

1½ tablespoons ground
   cinnamon
½ tablespoon grated nutmeg
2 teaspoons dried oregano
1 can (14½ ounces)
   whole tomatoes, undrained
1 cup dry red wine
Freshly ground pepper to taste

BECHAMEL:
½ cup (1 stick) unsalted
   butter
6 tablespoons all-purpose
   flour
4 cups hot milk

½ teaspoon grated
   nutmeg
Salt and freshly ground
   white pepper to taste
3 large eggs, beaten

5 cups grated (about ¾ pound) Kasseri cheese
   (or substitute Italian sharp)

1. Using a vegetable peeler, remove the peel from each eggplant in long strips, leaving a few narrow purple stripes of skin. Cut the eggplants crosswise into ½-inch-thick slices. Sprinkle the slices with salt and lay them out on paper towels to absorb the moisture.

2. Place the lamb and 1 tablespoon of the oil in a skillet. Cook, crumbling the meat with a fork, over medium-high heat just until the meat begins to lose its pink color, 3 to 4 minutes.

3. Add the onions and the garlic to the lamb and cook, stirring occasionally, for 10 minutes. Season with the cinnamon, nutmeg, and oregano and cook 1 minute. Stir in the canned tomatoes, wine, and salt and black pepper to taste. Simmer uncovered for 25 to 30 minutes, then remove from the heat.

4. Meanwhile, cook the eggplant: Pat the eggplant slices dry with paper towels. Dribble a little olive oil in a large nonstick skillet and sauté the eggplant in batches until lightly browned on both sides. Add more oil as needed, but be careful not to add too much oil, for the eggplant will absorb it all and become soggy and greasy. Place the cooked eggplant on a large plate.

5. Preheat the oven to 300°F.

6. Prepare the béchamel: Melt the butter in a medium saucepan over medium-high heat. Add the flour and whisk until smooth. Cook, stirring constantly, 1 minute. Gradually whisk in the milk; cook, stirring constantly, until smooth and thickened. Season with the nutmeg and salt and white pepper to taste. Stir ½ cup of the hot sauce into the beaten eggs in a small bowl and then stir the egg mixture into the remaining sauce. Cook several minutes longer, stirring constantly, then remove from the heat.

7. To assemble the moussaka, arrange half the eggplant in a large oval or rectangular casserole, about 17 x 12 inches. Spread all the lamb sauce over the eggplant and sprinkle with half the cheese. Top with the remaining eggplant. Pour the béchamel over all and sprinkle with the remaining cheese.

8. Bake the moussaka for 1 hour. Let cool to room temperature and refrigerate overnight.

9. Let the moussaka warm to room temperature before reheating. Bake in an oven preheated to 350°F until browned and bubbly, about 30 minutes. Serve with a big green salad and crusty rolls. (The moussaka is cooked twice because it tastes better reheated the second day.)

Makes 12 to 14 servings.

Summer Chicken Sauté

This is a colorful and light entrée for casual summer entertaining. As with all stir-fry preparations, the work is in the preliminary chopping of ingredients, and the cooking goes very quickly. Serve with it a simple risotto or buttered spinach fettuccine.

4 to 6 tablespoons fruity
   olive oil
5 whole boneless, skinless
   chicken breast halves,
   cut into 2-inch cubes
2 red bell peppers, seeded
   and cut into 1-inch
   squares
2 yellow bell peppers,
   seeded and cut into
   1-inch squares
1 large summer squash,
   cut crosswise into
   ¼-inch-thick slices,
   then halved
1 large zucchini, cut
   crosswise into
   ¼-inch-thick slices,
   then halved

½ cup sweet Marsala
2 tablespoons chopped
   fresh thyme
2 tablespoons chopped
   fresh rosemary
2 large tomatoes, seeded
   and finely diced
1 cup heavy or whipping
   cream
2 to 3 tablespoons fresh
   lemon juice
Salt and freshly ground
   pepper to taste
3 tablespoons chopped
   fresh basil

1. Heat 2 tablespoons of the oil in a wok over medium-high heat. Add as much of the chicken as will comfortably fit in the wok and stir-fry just until barely cooked through, 5 to 6 minutes. Remove with a slotted spoon to a large plate. Repeat with the remaining chicken.

2. Add 1 tablespoon or so more oil to the wok and heat. Add the bell peppers and stir-fry until crisp-tender, 3 to 4 minutes. Remove with a slotted spoon and add to the chicken.

3. Add a bit more oil to the wok and stir-fry the summer squash and zucchini just until crisp-tender, 3 to 4 minutes. Remove with a slotted spoon and toss with the chicken and peppers.

4. Add the Marsala, thyme, rosemary, and tomatoes to the wok. Heat to boiling and cook until the mixture is syrupy. Add the cream and cook until reduced by about half. Season to taste with the lemon juice, salt, and pepper.

5. Return the chicken and vegetables to the wok, stir to coat with the sauce, and heat through. Transfer to a serving platter and sprinkle with the basil.

Makes 8 servings.

Jerry's Chicken Curry

J erry is a wonderfully unique friend and a good, no-nonsense cook. Many strong bonds of friendship have been strengthened around generous meals in his charming old Nantucket home. Over the years, lingering late into the evening over Jerry's legendary candlelight curry dinners has brought much culinary contentment as well as provided many "brilliant" solutions to life's dilemmas. Serve this with rice and favorite curry condiments—cashews, banana chips, diced apples, and mango chutney, toasted coconut, chopped scallions.

½ cup unbleached
   all-purpose flour
Salt and freshly ground
   pepper to taste
3 boneless whole chicken
   breasts, halved
5 tablespoons unsalted
   butter
1 medium onion, minced
2 cloves garlic, minced
2 green bell peppers,
   seeded and diced

3 tablespoons (or more to
   taste) best-quality
   curry powder
1 can (15 ounces) stewed
   tomatoes
1 can (15 ounces) cream
   of coconut
Dash Worcestershire
   sauce
Dash Tabasco sauce
½ cup currants

1. Season the flour with salt and pepper in a shallow bowl. Lightly coat the chicken with the seasoned flour.

2. Heat 3 tablespoons of the butter in a large skillet over medium-high heat. Add the chicken and lightly brown on all sides. Remove the chicken from the skillet.

3. Preheat the oven to 350°F.

4. Add the remaining 2 tablespoons butter to the skillet and melt over medium heat. Add the onions, garlic, and bell peppers;

sauté, stirring frequently, until the vegetables are soft, 5 to 7 minutes. Stir in the curry powder and cook 2 minutes longer.

5. Stir in the tomatoes and coconut cream. Heat to simmering and season with Worcestershire, Tabasco, and salt and pepper to taste. Stir in the currants and remove from heat.

6. Arrange the chicken breasts in casserole and pour the curry sauce over the chicken. Bake covered until the chicken is tender, about 45 minutes.

Makes 4 to 6 servings.

Roasted Chicken

T here is nothing more comforting and restorative when suffering from the excesses of rich food and decadent living than a simple roasted chicken. There is, however, a good jigger of Grand Marnier added to the glaze lest the cure provide too sudden a withdrawal from all of life's vices.

1 roasting chicken, about
   7 pounds
1 orange, quartered
1 small onion, quartered

Salt and freshly ground
   pepper to taste
2 teaspoons dried rosemary
½ cup water

GLAZE:
3 tablespoons unsalted
   butter
3 tablespoons grainy
   Dijon mustard
3 tablespoons honey

1 tablespoon apricot jam
3 tablespoons Grand
   Marnier or other fine
   orange liqueur

1. Preheat the oven to 400°F.

2. Rinse the chicken inside and out and pat dry. Squeeze the juice of the orange quarters over the bird, inside and out. Place the orange and onion inside the bird and tie the legs together with kitchen string.

3. Sprinkle salt and pepper all over the outside of the bird, then sprinkle with the rosemary. Place the bird, breast side up, in a roasting pan and pour the water into the pan.

4. Roast the chicken for 20 minutes. Reduce the heat to 350°F and roast for 1 hour.

5. While the bird is roasting, prepare the glaze: Heat the butter, mustard, honey, and jam in a small saucepan until smooth and hot to the touch. Remove from the heat and stir in the Grand Marnier. Spoon the glaze over the chicken and bake until the bird is golden brown and the meat is tender, about 40 minutes longer.

Makes 4 to 6 servings.

Chicken Shoemaker

This was a frequently requested meal from my aunt's Nantucket kitchen. The name is a translation from the Italian, and in Italy the dish is regarded as spicy-hot peasant fare. The easy preparation makes this great for friends with hot pepper palates.

⅓ cup olive oil
3 tablespoons unsalted butter
10 cloves garlic, very coarsely chopped
8 to 10 hot cherry peppers, halved but not seeded (see Note)

15 chicken thighs, cut crosswise in half
½ cup dry white wine
1½ tablespoons balsamic vinegar
Salt to taste

1. Heat the oil and butter in a large skillet over medium-high heat. Add the garlic and hot peppers and sauté for 5 minutes. Add the chicken and sauté until the pieces are very lightly browned on both sides, 7 to 10 minutes. Reduce the heat to low and continue cooking, sitrring frequently, for 25 minutes.

2. Stir in the wine and vinegar. Season to taste with salt. Cook several minutes more to reduce the liquid slightly. Serve with plenty of crusty bread.

Makes 6 servings.

Note: Jars of hot cherry peppers, packed in either brine or oil, are available in most supermarkets.

Apricot-Glazed Rock Cornish Hens

A nice dinner party entrée for end-of-the-summer evenings when there is a bit of an autumn chill in the air.

6 Rock Cornish hens	1½ cups dry white wine
Salt and freshly ground	¼ cup brown sugar
pepper to taste	Finely grated zest of
2 tablespoons chopped	1 orange
fresh rosemary	½ teaspoon ground cloves
1 cup dried apricot halves	Fresh rosemary sprigs for
1 cup Rosy Applesauce	garnish
(see Index)	

1. Preheat the oven to 350°F.

2. Rinse the hens inside and out under cold running water and pat dry. Season inside and out with salt and pepper. Truss the birds and place them, breast side up, in a roasting pan. Sprinkle the hens all over with the rosemary. Roast the birds 1 hour.

At 'Sconset the morning sport is surf bathing; and when we say surf bathing, we mean surf bathing. To the east there is nothing between 'Sconset and Spain, and to the south nothing between 'Sconset and the West Indies. A wave can get a fairly good running start, and hit 'Sconset beach a tolerably, decisive wallop. Not that it always does, of course. Many a summer day the old Atlantic drowses, glassy to the mother-of pearl horizon, and only tiny breakers lay their lacework on the sand. But when it does take it into its head to kick up a row, the sea cavalry come charging in with white plumes flying, and you can hear its thunder far back on the moors. 'Sconset is so closely a part of the ocean, almost more than of the land, that it is peculiarly susceptible to the ocean's moods, and lovers of the sea find it their favorite resort.

—Guide to Nantucket 1932

3. Meanwhile, prepare the apricot glaze: Quarter the dried apricots and combine with the applesauce and wine in a saucepan. Stir in the brown sugar, orange zest, and cloves. Simmer covered, stirring occasionally, for 30 minutes.

4. Press the glaze through a sieve or food mill, then spoon over the roasting game hens. Roast the birds until tender, 25 to 30 minutes. Serve garnished with fresh rosemary.

Makes 6 servings.

Shrimp Curry

W hen I have a bit of time to play in the kitchen, I enjoy experimenting with Indian curries. This recipe may not be thoroughly traditional, but I do think it tastes quite wonderful. Serve with basmati rice and plenty of curry condiments.

*3 pounds large shrimp
(16 to 24 per pound),
peeled and deveined*
3 cloves garlic, minced
*3 cups unsweetened
coconut milk (available
in Indian food markets
or homemade from
fresh coconut, see
Index)*
*9 tablespoons clarified
butter (see box,
page 195)*
1 large onion, minced
*½ cup shredded
prosciutto*
1 tablespoon fennel seeds
*¼ cup (or more to taste)
best-quality curry
powder*

*2 Granny Smith apples,
cored and cut into
½-inch chunks*
*Finely chopped zest of
1 lime*
*½ cup preserved
kumquats, chopped*
*¼ cup unbleached
all-purpose flour*
*5 tablespoons fresh lime
juice*
Salt to taste
*Light cream (see Index),
as needed*
*Basmati Rice (recipe
follows)*

1. The day before serving, place the shrimp in a bowl and toss with the minced garlic. Pour in the coconut milk. Cover the bowl and let marinate in the refrigerator overnight.

2. The next day, drain the shrimp, reserving the milk. Heat 6 tablespoons of the clarified butter in a large sauté pan or skillet over medium-high heat. Add the onion and prosciutto and cook, stirring frequently, until the onion is very soft, 10 to 15 minutes.

3. Stir in the fennel seeds and curry powder and cook 1 to 2 minutes. Add the apple, lime zest, and kumquats; cook and stir for another 2 minutes or so. Add the flour and stir well to blend. Gradually whisk in the reserved coconut milk and the lime juice. Simmer the sauce uncovered 25 to 30 minutes and season to taste with salt. If the sauce becomes too thick, thin it with light cream.

4. While the sauce is simmering, sauté the shrimp in the remaining 3 tablespoons clarified butter in a large skillet until pink and just cooked through. Add the shrimp to the sauce and simmer 5 minutes longer. Serve immediately with basmati rice.

Makes 6 to 8 servings.

Basmati Rice

2 cups basmati rice
3 tablespoons clarified
   butter (see box,
   page 195)
1 small onion, minced

1 teaspoon crushed
   cardamom seeds
1 teaspoon saffron
   threads
3 cups water

1. Sort through the rice with your fingers, picking out and discarding any foreign objects. Soak the rice in water to cover for 30 minutes, changing the water twice. Rinse well and drain.

2. Melt the butter in a medium saucepan over medium-high heat. Add the onion, cardamom, and saffron; sauté for 5 minutes.

3. Add the rice to the pot and stir to coat with the butter and spices. Add 2 cups of the water, cover the pan, and heat to boiling. Reduce the heat, add the remaining 1 cup water, and simmer covered until all the liquid has been absorbed and the rice is tender, about 20 minutes. Serve hot.

Makes 8 servings.

Spicy Codfish Cakes Remoulade

This is my New England adaptation of Maryland's famed crabcakes. It is a fabulous use for inexpensive and readily available codfish. While these codfish cakes make a wonderful, homey supper, they are so delicious and habit forming that you may even be tempted to serve them to company.

3 pounds codfish fillets,
  poached in water just
  until tender, and
  drained
1 small red onion,
  minced
4 scallions, white bulbs
  and green stalks,
  chopped
2 ribs celery, minced
2 red bell peppers, seeded
  and diced
½ cup minced fresh
  parsley
8 cups fresh bread
  crumbs
3 tablespoons Dijon
  mustard
1 teaspoon dried thyme
1½ teaspoons cayenne
  pepper
½ teaspoon
  Worcestershire sauce

4 large eggs
1 cup Hellmann's
  mayonnaise
Salt and freshly ground
  pepper to taste
1 cup unbleached
  all-purpose flour,
  seasoned lightly with
  salt and pepper
½ cup light cream (see
  Index)
3 tablespoons unsalted
  butter, or more as
  needed
Remoulade Sauce (see
  Index)
Lemon wedges and fresh
  parsley sprigs for
  garnish

1. Flake the codfish in a large mixing bowl using a wooden spoon. Add the onion, scallions, celery, peppers, and parsley and toss to combine.

2. Add 3 cups of the bread crumbs, the mustard, thyme, cayenne, and Worcestershire sauce. Toss to combine thoroughly.

3. Beat 2 of the eggs into the codfish mixture until well blended. Fold in the mayonnaise and season the mixture with salt and pepper.

4. Place the seasoned flour in a small bowl. Beat the remaining eggs with the light cream in a second bowl. Place the

remaining bread crumbs in a third bowl (or as much as will fit, replenishing as needed).

5. Use your hands to form the codfish mixture into patties 3 inches in diameter. Dip each patty lightly but thoroughly in the flour mixture, then in the egg mixture, and finally in the bread crumbs, being sure they are coated all over. Place the patties as they are formed on a flat tray in a single layer. You should have about 16 codfish cakes.

6. Melt 3 tablespoons of butter in a large frying pan over medium heat. Add as many codfish cakes as will comfortably fit in the pan and fry, turning once, until golden brown on both sides, about 4 to 5 minutes per side. Keep the codfish cakes warm in a low oven while cooking the rest. Add more butter to the pan as needed. Serve the codfish cakes with a generous dollop of the remoulade. Garnish with lemon wedges and sprigs of parsley.

Makes 8 servings.

Scallops with Sauternes and Leek Cream

Sauternes heightens the natural sweetness of bay scallops.

5 tablespoons unsalted butter	2½ cups heavy or whipping cream
4 leeks, rinsed, dried, and minced	Salt and freshly ground pepper to taste
1 tablespoon very fine strips orange zest	1½ pounds fresh bay scallops
1½ cups Sauternes	

1. Melt the butter in a medium skillet over medium-high heat. Add the leeks and sauté, stirring constantly, 5 minutes. Stir in the orange zest and pour in the Sauternes. Raise the heat and bring to a rapid boil, then lower the heat and cover the mixture with a sheet of waxed paper. Simmer until just a few tablespoons liquid remain, 20 minutes.

2. Remove and discard the waxed paper. Pour in the cream and cook until reduced by about half. Season to taste with salt and pepper.

3. Preheat the oven to 450°F.

4. Divide the scallops among 6 individual 5- to 6-inch oval ramekins. Spoon a generous amount of the sauce over the scallops in each dish. Bake just until the scallops are cooked through and the sauce is bubbling, 7 to 10 minutes. Serve at once.

Makes 6 servings.

Swordfish Portugaise

Swordfish aficionados who swear to the pure tastes of grilling this meaty fish, might wince at the thought of baking it indoors smothered in a tomato sauce. I recommend trying this method once the grill has been stored away for the winter as I find that the slightly sweet, sherry-laced sauce is a wonderful complement to the swordfish in this authentic Portuguese dish.

3 pounds swordfish steaks	½ cup tomato paste
Salt and freshly ground pepper to taste	1 tablespoon brown sugar
¼ cup fresh lemon juice	½ cup dry sherry
3 tablespoons olive oil	¾ cup dry white wine
1 large yellow onion, chopped	½ cup chopped fresh parsley or fresh coriander leaves
4 cloves garlic, minced	1 lemon, thinly sliced
3 ripe large tomatoes, seeded and cut into ¼-inch dice	

1. Arrange the swordfish in a single layer in a lightly oiled shallow baking dish. Sprinkle with salt and pepper and rub all over with the lemon juice.

2. Heat the oil in a medium saucepan over medium-high heat. Add the onion and garlic and cook, stirring frequently, for 10 minutes. Stir in the tomatoes, tomato paste, brown sugar, sherry, and wine. Simmer uncovered for 15 minutes. Stir in the parsley and season to taste with salt and pepper.

3. Preheat the oven to 375°F.

4. Pour the sauce over the fish in the baking dish and scatter the lemon slices over the top. Cover the dish tightly with aluminum foil. Bake just until the fish is cooked through, 25 to 30 minutes.

Makes 6 servings.

Poached Salmon

This is Mrs. Nathaniel Benchley's favorite summer dinner dish. Each time a platter with the fish's head peering decoratively outward is sent off to her Nantucket home, I cannot help but wonder where her son Peter really got the story idea for *Jaws!*

1 whole salmon, 7 to 8 pounds, cleaned

POACHING STOCK:

15 cups water	2 carrots, sliced
1 bottle (750 ml) dry white wine	2 tablespoons dried thyme
1 cup dry red wine	2 tablespoons fennel seeds
3 medium onions, sliced	6 sprigs fresh parsley
3 cloves garlic, halved	2 bay leaves
2 cups coarsely chopped celery tops	1 tablespoon salt
	1 tablespoon freshly ground pepper

Aspic and Garnishings for Poached Salmon (recipe follows)	Tomato Béarnaise Mayonnaise (see Index)

THINKING PINK

Chilled Mussels with Tomato-Cognac Sauce

Whole Poached Salmon with Tomato Béarnaise Mayonnaise
Purée of Fresh Beets with Horseradish
Fresh Peas with Prosciutto
Potato Boursin Salad

Deep-Dish Rhubarb Pie

California Blush Wine

1. Rinse the salmon under cold running water and pat dry.

2. Prepare the poaching stock: Place all the ingredients in a large pot and heat to a full boil. Reduce the heat and simmer the stock for 30 minutes. Strain the stock through a sieve into a fish poacher; press hard on the vegetables with the back of a wooden spoon to extract the flavorful juices.

3. Place the fish on the poaching rack, cover, and poach the fish over the simmering stock for 10 minutes per inch of thickness.

4. Remove the fish from the pan and let cool. Reserve the liquid if you wish to coat the fish with aspic. Peel the skin from the fish, leaving the head and tail intact. Transfer to a serving platter and refrigerate until cold.

5. Coat the chilled fish with aspic and scale decorations if desired. Serve with the Béarnaise mayonnaise.

Makes 10 to 12 servings.

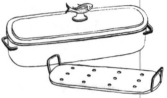

Aspic and Garnishing for Poached Salmon

3 cups salmon poaching
   liquid
2 egg whites
1 egg shell, broken into
   medium pieces
4½ teaspoons unflavored
   gelatin softened in ½
   cup cold water
1 tablespoon Pernod

Zest of 1 lemon, cut into
   2 x 2-inch strips
Zest of 1 lime, cut into
   2 x 2-inch strips
Zest of 1 orange, cut into
   2 x 2-inch strips
Fresh tarragon or dill
   sprigs

1. Clarify the salmon poaching liquid: Pour the liquid into a medium saucepan and heat over medium heat. Whisk the egg whites until they hold soft peaks and add them to the poaching liquid along with the broken egg shell. Bring to a boil, stirring occasionally. The egg white foam will rise to the top and float. Remove the pan from the heat and let it stand to allow the froth to settle to the bottom, 10 minutes. Repeat the boiling and settling process two more times.

2. Strain the liquid through a fine sieve lined with a double

thickness of dampened cheesecloth. Measure 2 cups of the clarified liquid into a clean saucepan and stir in the softened gelatin. Bring the liquid to a simmer just to dissolve the gelatin, and remove from the heat. Stir in the Pernod and refrigerate to chill the aspic, about 5 minutes.

3. When the aspic begins to thicken, spoon a thin layer over the top of the poached salmon. Using a small crescent-shaped cookie cutter, cut crescents from the citrus zests. Place these crescents decoratively over the aspic layer to resemble fish scales. Place a row of tarragon or dill sprigs down the center of the fish to look like feathery seaweed. Making sure the remaining aspic is still lightly jelled, spoon another layer over the decorations. If the aspic starts to melt and become runny, return both it and the fish to the refrigerator to set. Complete the garnishing by spooning a third layer of aspic over the fish. Refrigerate for at least 1 hour to set completely and keep chilled until serving time.

Soft-Shell Crabs with Smoked Salmon and Bacon Butter

I adore soft shell crabs. During their short summer season I invent endless ways to eat them—a crispy aside to scrambled eggs in the morning, tucked into an extravagant club sandwich at noon, on a toast point with evening cocktails. But of all the ways to enjoy this East Coast delicacy, this recipe is my very favorite.

2 shallots, minced
3 tablespoons dry white wine
1 tablespoon fresh lemon juice
¾ cup (1½ sticks) unsalted butter, cold
¼ pound smoked salmon, minced fine
8 slices bacon, cooked crisp and crumbled into small pieces

Freshly ground pepper to taste
8 soft-shell crabs, dressed
½ cup unbleached all-purpose flour seasoned with 1 teaspoon salt and 1 teaspoon freshly ground pepper
4 tablespoons clarified butter (see box, facing page)

1. Place the shallots, wine, and lemon juice in a small, non-aluminum skillet. Reduce the liquid over medium-high heat until all but 1 tablespoon remains. Reduce the heat to low and gradually whisk in the butter, tablespoon by tablespoon, until all is absorbed and the sauce is thickened. Stir in the smoked salmon and bacon. Season to taste with pepper. Remove from the heat and set aside in a warm place.

2. Dredge the crabs lightly in the flour. Melt the clarified butter in a large skillet over medium-high heat. Place the crabs topside down in the skillet and sauté until lightly browned, about 3 minutes. Turn and cook the other side until browned, 2 to 3 minutes longer.

3. Place 2 crabs on each dinner plate and spoon the smoked salmon and bacon butter generously over them. Serve at once.

Makes 4 servings.

CLARIFIED BUTTER

The reason for clarifying butter is to remove the milk solids that will burn and ruin the flavor of a dish when butter is heated over high temperatures. Clarification permits you to cook over high heat and still retain a wonderful buttery flavor.

Clarified butter keeps well in the refrigerator, so I find it worthwhile to clarify 1 pound at a time. Cut the butter into tablespoons and melt in a small saucepan over medium heat. Remove the pan from the heat and let stand for 10 minutes. Skim the white foam off the top with a slotted spoon and discard. Pour the clear yellow liquid through a fine sieve, lined with a double thickness of cheesecloth. When you get close to the bottom, avoid pouring the milky white solids that have sunk there by carefully spooning off any remaining clear butter. Discard the rest. One pound of butter yields about 1½ cups clarified butter.

Spring Seafood Pasta

When returning to the beach house for the first time in the spring, one craves something that tastes of the shore and ocean. I think this creamy scallop and smoked salmon sauce is the perfect end to a day of spring cleaning and a great welcoming dinner for old summer friends.

2 cups heavy or whipping cream
4 tablespoons vodka
Grated zest of 1 lemon
4 ounces cream cheese, at room temperature, cut into small bits
4 ounces smoked salmon, cut into thin julienne strips
4 tablespoons (½ stick) unsalted butter
½ cup finely chopped red onion

3 medium plum tomatoes, seeded and chopped
3 tablespoons chopped fresh dill
1 tablespoon chopped fresh tarragon
1 pound bay scallops
Salt and freshly ground pepper to taste
1 pound linguine or fettuccine, cooked and drained

1. Combine the cream, 3 tablespoons of the vodka, and the lemon zest in a medium saucepan. Heat to boiling and continue to cook until reduced by half. Stir in the cream cheese and smoked salmon and set aside.

2. Melt the butter in a small sauté pan or skillet over medium-high heat. Add the onion and tomatoes and cook, stirring occasionally, for 10 minutes. Stir in the dill and tarragon and cook 2 minutes longer.

3. Add the tomato mixture, bay scallops, salt and pepper to the cream mixture. Heat over medium heat until the sauce is hot and the scallops are just cooked through. Swirl in the remaining 1 tablespoon vodka and toss the sauce with the cooked pasta. Serve at once.

Makes 4 to 6 servings.

Lasagne with Red Clam Sauce

This is a good summery lasagne to make when a casual dinner for a crowd of hungry people is in order.

1 pound lasagne noodles,
  preferably homemade
3 large eggs
4 cups ricotta cheese
1 cup freshly grated
  Parmesan cheese
½ cup chopped fresh
  parsley

¼ cup chopped fresh basil
Salt and freshly ground
  pepper to taste
6 cups Red Clam Sauce
  (see Index)
1½ pounds smoked or
  regular mozzarella,
  thinly sliced

1. Heat a large pot of water to boiling. Add the lasagne noodles and cook until they are almost done but still a little chewy. (They will cook more as they bake.) Drain and rinse under cold running water.

2. Whisk the eggs and ricotta cheese together until smooth. Stir in the Parmesan, parsley, and basil. Season to taste with salt and pepper.

3. Preheat the oven to 375°F. Lightly oil a 15 x 10-inch baking pan.

4. Layer half the noodles in the prepared pan. Cover with half the clam sauce and half the ricotta filling. Arrange half the mozzarella over the ricotta. Layer the remaining noodles on top, then the remaining ricotta, clam sauce, and mozzarella.

5. Bake the lasagne until lightly browned and bubbly, 40 to 45 minutes. Let cool for 10 minutes before cutting and serving.

Makes 12 servings.

Spaghetti alla Carbonara

I am quite partial to this popular pasta dish, which I can never resist eating when in Italy and lured by the ubiquitous outdoor trattorias of the grand piazzas. I have often found that home versions skimp on the essential ingredients. This is my perfected version of the recipe created in remembrance of Trastevere days.

1 pound Italian pancetta or good-quality sliced bacon

1 medium onion, cut into thin crescent slivers

8 ounces fresh mushrooms, sliced

¼ cup dry white wine

5 large eggs, at room temperature

¾ cup heavy or whipping cream

¾ cup coarsely grated Parmesan cheese

Salt and freshly ground pepper to taste

1 pound imported spaghetti

½ cup chopped fresh parsley

1. Fry the bacon in a large skillet over medium-high heat until quite crisp. Remove from the pan, drain on paper towels, and crumble into coarse irregular pieces. Reserve 3 tablespoons of the bacon fat in the skillet.

2. Add the onion to the reserved bacon fat and cook, stirring frequently, over medium-high heat for 7 minutes. Add the mushrooms and wine and cook for 5 minutes.

3. Heat a large pot of water to boiling to cook the pasta.

4. Whisk the eggs and cream together in a mixing bowl until well blended. Stir in the Parmesan and season to taste with salt and pepper.

5. Cook the pasta in the boiling water until tender but still firm to the bite. Drain and return to the warm cooking pot. Immediately add the egg mixture, crumbled bacon, and onion mixture and toss thoroughly. Stir in the parsley. Serve at once with additional freshly grated Parmesan.

Makes 4 to 6 servings.

Penne with Tomatoes and Asparagus

This is one of my very favorite pasta recipes. I love the combination of the slowly simmered tomatoes with the crisp-tender asparagus. You can make it with fettuccine or other pasta, but I like the way the penne mirrors the shape of the asparagus.

6 tablespoons extra-virgin
  olive oil
4 cloves garlic, minced
2 carrots, peeled and
  minced
1 red bell pepper, seeded
  and minced
1 leek, rinsed, dried, and
  minced
2 ripe large tomatoes,
  seeded and diced
1½ cans (28 ounces each)
  whole tomatoes,
  drained
½ cup dry red wine
3 tablespoons chopped
  fresh fennel tops

1 tablespoon chopped
  fresh tarragon
4 tablespoons chopped
  fresh basil
Salt and freshly ground
  pepper to taste
1½ pound penne
1½ pounds fresh thin
  asparagus
2 large egg yolks
1 large egg
1 cup heavy or whipping
  cream
2 cups freshly grated
  Parmesan cheese

1. Heat 4 tablespoons of the olive oil in a large saucepan over medium-high heat. Add the garlic, carrots, bell pepper, and leek; sauté, stirring occasionally, for 10 minutes. Stir in the fresh tomatoes and cook 2 minutes.

2. Add the drained tomatoes to the sauce and mash with the back of a wooden spoon. Add the wine, fennel, tarragon, and half the basil. Season the sauce with salt and pepper to taste. Simmer uncovered, stirring occasionally, over low heat for 45 minutes.

3. Heat a large pot of water to boiling. Add the pasta and cook until tender but still firm to the bite.

4. Meanwhile, slice the tender parts of the asparagus stalks on a slight diagonal into 2-inch pieces. Heat the remaining 2 tablespoons oil in a sauté pan or skillet over high heat. Add the asparagus and stir-fry until just barely tender. Set aside.

5. When the pasta is almost ready, whisk the egg yolks, egg, and cream together in a small bowl. Add the asparagus and remaining basil to the tomato sauce and heat through.

6. Drain the pasta and toss with the tomato sauce. Quickly stir in the egg mixture and 1 cup of the Parmesan. Toss well and serve at once. Pass the remaining Parmesan.

Makes 6 servings.

Tagliolini con Caviale

This melodious-sounding Italian creation (pasta with caviar) is one of my most requested recipes and my favorite dish to serve when in a romantic mood.

2 tablespoons unsalted
    butter
3 tablespoons olive oil
2 cloves garlic, minced
1 small red onion,
    minced
Zest of 1 lemon, cut into
    very fine strips
1¼ cups Fish Stock (see
    Index), or bottled clam
    juice

¼ cup vodka
1½ cups heavy or
    whipping cream
¾ cup freshly grated
    Parmesan cheese
Salt and freshly ground
    pepper to taste
1 pound dried tagliolini,
    linguine, or fettuccine
4 ounces golden caviar

1. Heat the butter and oil in a medium skillet over medium-high heat. Add the garlic and onion and sauté, stirring frequently, for 5 minutes. Add the lemon zest, fish stock, and vodka and simmer until reduced by about half, about 15 minutes.

2. Heat a large pot of water to boiling to cook the pasta.

3. Stir the cream into the sauce and continue to simmer until thickened to the consistency of a light béchamel sauce, about 15 minutes. Stir in the cheese and heat until it melts. Season the sauce to taste with salt and pepper. Keep warm over low heat while you cook the pasta.

4. Add the pasta to the boiling water and cook until tender but still firm to the bite. Drain well.

5. Toss the warm pasta with the sauce to coat well. Divide the pasta among 4 plates. Top each serving with a heaping spoonful of caviar. Serve at once.

Makes 4 servings.

Private
Grilling

G rilling in the great outdoors is not something I do in the daily course of events at Que Sera Sarah. Rather, it is what I do during the ever scarce moments that I am not cooking for the shop or catering an island extravaganza. While I know that normal people view the all-American barbecue as an inherent part of summer living and entertaining, I personally see it as a private source of summer serenity.

When a rare interlude of uncommitted time appears in the midst of summer frenzy and I discover that I still have an appetite and friend or two who will forgive me for having been far more interested in blue corn chips, rare strains of radicchio, and escargot roe than their personal lives, I grill.

So in a weak moment of culinary confession, induced by inhaling the concentrated fumes of arcane hardwoods and vines, I am disclosing these treasured grilling recipes which have never been cooked for the public palate.

Grilled Lobster with Champagne

There is something at once extravagant and primitive about grilling lobster by the beach. The fiery red lobster shells when singed with the flames of the grill permeate the air with the most wonderful essence of ocean and seashore imaginable. I recommend preparing this dish under the full moon—the most conducive to wild feasting.

1 bottle (750 ml) dry Champagne	Salt and freshly ground pepper to taste
Leafy tops of 3 ribs celery	4 live lobsters (1½ to 2 pounds each)
3 shallots, minced	4 tablespoons olive oil
¾ cup (1½ sticks) unsalted butter, slightly softened	

1. Prepare charcoal or wood chips for grilling.

2. Place the Champagne, celery leaves, and shallots in a medium saucepan; cook over medium-high heat until just 1 cup liquid remains, about 20 minutes. Remove the celery leaves and discard. Slowly whisk in the butter, 1 tablespoon at a time, over very low heat to emulsify with the Champagne. When all the butter has been incorporated, season the mixture with salt and pepper to taste. Keep warm while grilling the lobster.

3. Kill the lobsters by inserting a sharp knife crosswise where the head meets the shell to sever the spinal cord. Turn each lobster on its back and butterfly the meaty tail. Remove the claws and crack to facilitate cooking on the grill. (If any of this makes you queasy, have your fishmonger kill and split the lobsters; just make sure it is done as close to cooking time as possible.)

4. Brush the lobsters, flesh and shells, all over with oil. Place the lobsters, flesh-side down and the claws alongside, a few inches from red-hot coals. Grill just until the flesh turns opaque, 6 to 8 minutes. Turn the lobsters over and grill just a few minutes more. Check the claws for doneness as they may take slightly longer than the tails.

5. Serve the lobsters butterflied with some of the Champagne-butter sauce spooned over the flesh. Place the claws alongside the lobsters. Serve the remaining Champagne-butter sauce in little dipping bowls.

Makes 4 servings.

Grilled Soft-Shell Crabs

O ne day I wondered why no one ever grilled soft-shells and decided to experiment. The results were sensational!

Juice of 4 limes	¼ cup chopped fresh
2 tablespoons golden	coriander
tequila	½ cup olive oil
1 clove garlic, minced	Salt and freshly ground
1 fresh jalapeño pepper,	pepper to taste
seeded and minced	8 soft-shell crabs, dressed

1. Three hours before you plan to grill the crabs, whisk the lime juice, tequila, garlic, jalapeño pepper, and coriander together in a small bowl. Gradually whisk in the oil, then season to taste with salt and pepper. Place the crabs in a single layer in a shallow bowl. Pour the marinade over the crabs. Cover the bowl and let marinate in the refrigerator for 3 hours.

2. Prepare charcoal or wood chips for grilling.

3. When the coals are quite hot, remove the crabs from the marinade and place them 3 to 4 inches from the heat. Grill just until cooked through, 2 to 3 minutes each side. Transfer the crabs to a serving platter and drizzle with some of the marinade. Serve at once.

Makes 4 servings.

Swordfish Union Street

T his recipe for my aunt's Nantucket grilled swordfish is my first memory of the very best thing I thought I had ever eaten. During my days as mother's helper on Union Street, I learned from her the secret of coating the fish with mayonnaise to keep it very moist on the grill.

To this day, grilled swordfish steaks remain the taste of

Nantucket for me. One of my favorite summer meals is grilled swordfish steaks, Summer Squash Casserole (see Index), sliced Nantucket tomatoes, and a salad of farm lettuce.

2 lemons
3 to 3½ pounds very
   fresh swordfish steaks,
   1½ to 2 inches thick
Salt and freshly ground
   pepper to taste
6 tablespoons
   mayonnaise, preferably
   homemade (if not, use
   Hellmann's)

6 tablespoons (¾ stick)
   unsalted butter, cut
   into tablespoons and at
   room temperature
3 tablespoons chopped
   fresh parsley

1. Prepare charcoal or wood chips for grilling.
2. Cut one of the lemons in half and rub the juice all over the swordfish steaks. Sprinkle the steaks on both sides with salt and pepper, then smear both sides of the steaks with the mayonnaise.
3. When the coals are hot, grill the swordfish a few inches from the heat until just cooked through, about 6 minutes each side. Remove the swordfish from the grill and spread the butter over the tops of each steak. Sprinkle with parsley and serve with the remaining lemon cut into wedges.

Makes 6 servings.

COASTAL EXUBERANCES

Scallop Ceviche

Grilled Swordfish Turkish Style
Tian of Just Picked Vegetables
Honey-Herb Rolls

Greens with Cream Dressing

Chocolate Berry Bread Pudding

Grilled Swordfish
Turkish Style

This is a simple but superb method of preparing swordfish that my sister Holly discovered on one of her many ventures through Turkey.

3 pounds fresh swordfish, cut into 1-inch chunks
¾ cup fresh lemon juice
½ cup fruity olive oil
2 cloves garlic, finely minced
1 medium red onion, cut into thin rings

Salt and freshly ground pepper to taste
36 bay leaves
2 yellow bell peppers, seeded and cut into ¾-inch pieces

1. Prepare charcoal or wood chips for grilling.

2. Place the swordfish in a shallow bowl. Whisk the lemon juice and oil together in a small bowl, then stir in the garlic and onion. Season to taste with salt and pepper. Pour the marinade over the swordfish. Cover the bowl and let marinate, tossing occasionally, in the refrigerator for 6 hours.

3. Cover the bay leaves with boiling water in a small bowl; let stand for 10 minutes to soften. Drain thoroughly.

4. Thread the swordfish chunks alternately with the bay leaves on 6 metal skewers. Every third piece or so, thread a bell pepper chunk on the skewer. Drape some of the onion slices from the fish marinade randomly in a figure-8 fashion over the fish kabobs.

5. Grill the swordfish skewers a few inches from medium-hot coals, basting occasionally with the marinade and turning the skewers every 5 minutes or so, until just cooked through, about 15 minutes.

Makes 6 servings.

Tuna Steaks with Wasabi Butter

Meaty red tuna steaks can stand up to the strong Oriental flavors of a sesame marinade. The wasabi butter transfers the Japanese influence of the raw to the cooked.

¼ cup Oriental sesame
   oil
½ cup vegetable oil
¼ cup rice wine vinegar
2 tablespoons sweet
   vermouth
1 tablespoon brown sugar
¼ cup soy sauce

2 tablespoons chopped
   fresh ginger
3 cloves garlic, minced
3 to 3½ pounds tuna
   steaks, about 1½
   inches thick

WASABI BUTTER:
½ cup (1 stick) unsalted
   butter
1½ teaspoons green
   wasabi paste (or more
   to taste if you like it
   very hot; wasabi paste
   is available at specialty
   food stores)

3 tablespoons chopped
   fresh coriander

1. At least 4 hours before you plan to grill the tuna, whisk the sesame oil, vegetable oil, vinegar, vermouth, brown sugar, and soy sauce together in a small bowl. Stir in the ginger and garlic. Pour the marinade over the tuna steaks in a shallow bowl. Cover and let marinate in the refrigerator at least 4 hours, turning the fish occasionally.

2. Meanwhile, prepare the wasabi butter: Beat the butter and wasabi paste together in a small bowl until creamy. Beat in the coriander until well blended. Store in a cool place, but let warm to room temperature before serving.

3. Prepare charcoal or wood chips for grilling.

4. When the coals are hot, remove the tuna steaks from the marinade and grill a few inches from the heat just until cooked through, 5 to 6 minutes each side. As the tuna cooks, baste it with some of the marinade to keep it moist. When the tuna is cooked, cut it into serving portions and top each serving with a heaping tablespoon of the wasabi butter.

Makes 6 servings.

Bluefish Antibes

For the past few Octobers I have been fortunate enough to spend time recuperating from my hectic summers on Nantucket lazing on the still tepid beaches of the French Riviera. I have a favorite little beach set in a cove in Antibes, which is complete with a seaside restaurant that prepares fabulous grilled local fish for lunch everyday. Longing for the R & R of the Riviera, I decided to apply the same technique to Nantucket's most common local fish—with excellent results!

3 pounds bluefish fillets	1½ tablespoons chopped
5 tablespoons extra-virgin	fresh lavender leaves
olive oil	2 teaspoons fennel seeds,
Salt and freshly ground	lightly crushed
pepper to taste	1 teaspoon ground cumin
2 tablespoons chopped	Lemon wedges
fresh rosemary	

1. Place the bluefish fillets in a shallow bowl. Brush all over with the oil and sprinkle lightly with salt and pepper.
2. Combine the rosemary, lavender, fennel, and cumin; sprinkle over the top of the fish fillets. Let marinate at room temperature for 30 minutes.
3. Prepare charcoal or wood chips for grilling.
4. When the coals are ready, grill the fish, skin-side down, a few inches from the heat for about 5 minutes. With a large spatula, flip the fillets over and grill just several minutes longer until the fish is done. Serve immediately with lemon wedges.
Makes 6 servings.

Seared Chicken Breasts with Cranberry Pecan Butter

The exquisite tenderness and moistness achieved by searing chicken breasts quickly over a hot fire is unrivaled. The brilliant pink butter adds great flavor and flair to the final presentation.

CRANBERRY PECAN BUTTER:

2 cups fresh cranberries
½ cup fresh orange juice
½ cup sugar
Grated zest of 1 orange

¾ cup (1½ sticks) unsalted
butter, at room temperature
½ cup finely chopped
toasted pecans

½ cup fruity olive oil
1 cup fresh orange juice
2 tablespoons chopped
fresh rosemary

Salt and freshly ground
pepper to taste
6 boneless, skinless whole
chicken breasts

1. Prepare the cranberry pecan butter: Combine the cranberries, the ½ cup of orange juice, the sugar, and orange zest in a small saucepan. Heat to boiling over medium-high heat. Reduce the heat and simmer, stirring occasionally, for 15 minutes. Let the cranberries cool to room temperature.

2. Purée the cooled cranberries in a blender or food processor fitted with the steel blade. Cream the butter in a medium bowl, then beat in the purée. Beat the pecans into the mixture. Store the butter in the refrigerator, but bring to room temperature when ready to serve.

3. Whisk together the olive oil and 1 cup orange juice. Stir in the rosemary and season with salt and pepper. Place the chicken breasts in a shallow dish and pour over the marinade. Let marinate at room temperature for 1 hour.

4. Prepare charcoal or wood chips for grilling.

5. Remove the chicken breasts from the marinade and grill them a few inches above the hot coals, basting continually with the leftover marinade, 3 to 4 minutes per side. Top each chicken breast with a generous rounded scoop of the cranberry pecan butter and serve.

Makes 6 servings.

Chicken Tapenade

This grilling recipe takes a little poetic license with the basic tapenade concept and stretches it into an unusual marinade for chicken. The result is very different from most barbecued chicken recipes and is probably the most succulent chicken I have ever tasted.

4 whole chicken breasts,
   halved
2 cloves garlic, minced
1 red onion, minced
6 anchovy fillets, minced
½ cup olivada (black
   olive paste, available at
   specialty food stores)

⅓ cup Cognac
⅓ cup olive oil
1½ cups dry red wine
Salt and freshly ground
   pepper to taste
½ cup chopped fresh basil

1. Place the chicken breasts in a shallow bowl. Combine the garlic, onion, anchovies, and olivada in a mixing bowl. Whisk in the Cognac and oil. Stir in the wine and season to taste with salt and pepper. Pour the marinade over the chicken and sprinkle with the basil. Let the chicken marinate for 3 hours.

2. Prepare charcoal or wood chips for grilling.

3. When the coals are ready, grill the chicken bone-side down, a few inches from the heat, basting occasionally with the marinade, about 15 minutes. Turn and continue grilling just until the chicken is cooked through but still very moist and tender, about 15 minutes more. Serve at once.

Makes 6 to 8 servings.

THE BIG ANNUAL SUMMER COCKTAIL PARTY

Scallop Puffs Que Sera
Miniature Tex-Mex Turnovers
Cornmeal Blinis with Favorite Caviars
Brie in Brioche
Country Pâté with Beer and Fennel • Mustard and
Cornichons
Vegetable Crudité • Basil Parmesan Mayonnaise and
Roasted Red Pepper Dip
Great Guacamole • Blue Corn Chips
Smoked Mussels Vinaigrette
Platter of Chicken Tapenade
(served at room temperature)

Open Bar

Duck Breasts with Grilled Radicchio and Honey Glazed Pears

A spectacular grilled dinner that heralds autumn in both flavor and color. The symphony of flavors calls for celebrating with a bottle of Burgundy or California Cabernet Sauvignon.

1 cup dry red wine
¼ cup plus 2 tablespoons
  port
3 tablespoons balsamic
  vinegar
½ cup fresh orange juice
½ cup olive oil
Zest of 1 orange, finely
  grated
1 carrot, peeled and
  sliced into thin rounds
½ cup minced fennel bulb
3 tablespoons minced
  fennel tops

2 shallots, minced
2 cloves garlic, minced
2 tablespoons minced
  fresh rosemary
Salt and freshly ground
  pepper to taste
6 boneless duck breasts
  (from 3 ducks)
6 heads radicchio, halved
3 firm pears, peeled,
  cored, and halved
3 tablespoons honey

1. Whisk together the wine, the ¼ cup of port, vinegar, orange juice, and olive oil in a small bowl. Add the orange zest, carrot, fennel and fennel tops, shallots, garlic, and rosemary. Season with salt and pepper. Place the duck breasts and radicchio flat in a large, shallow dish. Pour the marinade over all and marinate at room temperature, turning the duck breasts and radicchio occasionally, for 2 hours.

2. Prepare charcoal or wood chips for grilling.

3. Remove the radicchio from the marinade and thread onto metal skewers. Grill about 4 inches from the hot coals until wilted and lightly charred on the outside, about 5 minutes per side. Grill the duck breasts skin-side down, basting occasionally with leftover marinade, for 6 minutes. Turn and continue grilling just until the duck breasts are pink in the center, 2 to 3 minutes longer. Place the pear halves flat on the grill and brush with the 2 tablespoons port and the honey. Grill, turning once, for 3 to 4 minutes.

4. Carve the duck breasts into thin diagonal slices and fan onto a serving plate, surrounded by the radicchio and pears.

Makes 6 servings.

Lamb with Mint Salsa Verde

T he lushness of a meaty pink leg of lamb may come as a hearty surprise in the heat of a midsummer's night, but a shimmering bath of mint sauce placates the palate.

1 leg of lamb (6 to 7
    pounds), boned and
    butterflied
1½ cups Zinfandel
½ cup raspberry vinegar

½ cup fruity olive oil
1 medium red onion, minced
3 cloves garlic, minced
Salt and freshly ground
    pepper to taste

MINT SALSA VERDE:
2 bunches fresh parsley,
    chopped
4 scallions, white bulbs
    and green stalks, chopped
1 cup fresh mint leaves
4 anchovy fillets, minced
3 cloves garlic, minced

6 tablespoons fresh lemon juice
1 cup fruity olive oil
2 hard-cooked eggs,
    peeled and minced
2 tablespoons capers, drained
Salt and freshly ground
    pepper to taste

1. The morning of the day you plan to serve the lamb, place the butterflied leg of lamb in a large, shallow bowl. Whisk the Zinfandel, vinegar, and oil together in a mixing bowl. Stir in the onion and garlic and season to taste with salt and pepper. Pour the marinade over the lamb. Cover and let marinate, turning the lamb frequently, in the refrigerator at least 6 hours.

2. Meanwhile, prepare the mint salsa verde: Place the parsley, scallions, and mint in a food processor fitted with the steel blade; process to make a smooth green paste. Add the anchovies, garlic, and lemon juice and process again until smooth. With the machine running, pour the oil in a thin, steady stream through the feed tube to make a glistening green sauce. Transfer the sauce to a bowl and stir in the eggs and capers. Season to taste with salt and pepper. Store in the refrigerator but let warm to room temperature before serving.

3. Prepare charcoal or wood chips for grilling.

4. When the coals are hot, remove the lamb from marinade and place it on the grill about 4 inches from the heat. Grill, basting frequently with the marinade, about 20 minutes each side for medium rare. Cut the lamb into thin slices, spoon the mint salsa over, and serve.

Makes 10 to 12 servings.

Rosemary Lamb Chops
Provençal

In the South of France anchovies are sometimes used to impart a subtle saltiness, rather than fishiness, to the flavor of meat. This is an exquisitely simple way to cook lamb chops.

3 cloves garlic, peeled	1 teaspoon freshly ground
3 anchovy fillets	pepper
2 tablespoons fresh	3 tablespoons olive oil
rosemary leaves	2 tablespoons dry red wine
¼ cup fresh parsley leaves	8 thick lamb loin chops,
½ teaspoon dried thyme	fat trimmed
½ teaspoon salt	8 fresh rosemary sprigs

1. Place the garlic, anchovies, rosemary leaves, parsley, thyme, salt, pepper, oil, and wine in a food processor fitted with the steel blade; process until smooth.

2. Using a small sharp knife, make several shallow incisions in both sides of each lamb chop. Rub the marinade generously over both sides of the lamb chops and press it into the incisions. Place the chops on a platter and let marinate at room temperature for 1 to 1½ hours.

3. Prepare charcoal for grilling.

4. Wrap the "tail" of each lamb chop around the chop to form a circle of sorts. Wrap a fresh rosemary sprig around each chop and secure the "tail" and sprig in place by tying with kitchen string.

5. Grill the chops about 4 to 5 inches from the hot coals. They should be cooked 5 to 6 minutes each side for medium-rare meat. Serve 2 chops per person and accompany with Oil-Roasted Farm Vegetables (see Index) or Ratatouille (see Index).

Makes 4 servings.

Grilled Steak with Many Mustards

C runchy golden mustard seeds add a crisp crust to the steak, while the mustard-Cognac Béarnaise is a great variation on the classic. A dreamy grilling recipe for the lover of both mustard and steak.

3 tablespoons whole mustard seeds	1 tablespoon freshly ground pepper
2 teaspoons dry mustard	3 to 4 pounds sirloin or
1 tablespoon coarse salt (kosher)	strip steaks, 1½-inches thick

MUSTARD-COGNAC BEARNAISE:

2 shallots, minced	1 teaspoon grainy mustard
1½ tablespoons dried tarragon	Pinch cayenne pepper
¼ cup Cognac	½ cup plus 2 tablespoons
½ cup tarragon vinegar	(1¼ sticks) unsalted
4 large egg yolks	butter, melted and hot
1 tablespoon fresh lemon juice	Salt and freshly ground pepper to taste
1 tablespoon Dijon mustard	

2 tablespoons Dijon mustard	½ cup dry white wine

1. Place the mustard seeds, dry mustard, coarse salt, and pepper in a mortar. Using a pestle, grind the mixture coarsely together. Rub both sides of the steaks generously with the mustard seasoning. Let stand for 30 minutes.

2. Prepare charcoal or wood chips for grilling.

3. Meanwhile, prepare the mustard-Cognac Béarnaise: Place the shallots, tarragon, Cognac, and vinegar in a small pan. Cook over medium-high heat until almost all of the liquid has evaporated. Set aside.

4. Place the egg yolks, lemon juice, mustards, and cayenne in a blender; process for 10 seconds. With the machine running, pour the hot butter through the top; process until all is blended

and the sauce is thickened. Add the shallot reduction and blend. Season with salt and pepper to taste.

5. When the coals are hot, grill the steaks a few inches from the heat for about 5 minutes each side for rare to medium-rare meat. While the steaks are grilling, whisk the 2 tablespoons Dijon mustard and white wine together; baste the steaks with this mixture as they grill. When the steaks are done, cut into serving portions and top each serving with a generous spoonful of the Béarnaise.

Makes 6 servings.

Grilled Hamburgers au Poivre

A sumptuous version of this all-American classic. The barely cooked tomato-leek sauce adds a refreshing contrast to the peppery beef.

*2 pounds best-quality
  ground sirloin
4 shallots, minced
1½ tablespoons capers,
  drained and chopped
5 tablespoons dry red wine
1½ teaspoons salt
5 tablespoons plus 1
  teaspoon grainy Dijon
  mustard*

*5 tablespoons plus 1
  teaspoon coarsely
  ground mixed
  peppercorns (black,
  green, pink, and
  white)*

*TOMATO-LEEK SAUCE:
4 tablespoons (½ stick)
  unsalted butter
2 leeks, rinsed, dried,
  quartered, and minced
5 ripe large plum
  tomatoes, seeded and
  diced*

*3 tablespoons Cognac
2½ tablespoons minced
  fresh tarragon
3 tablespoons heavy or
  whipping cream
Salt to taste*

1. Mix the sirloin, shallots, capers, wine and salt together in a large bowl until well combined. Divide the meat mixture into 8 equal parts and shape each part into a hamburger patty.

2. Spread each side of the patties with 1 teaspoon of the mustard (2 teaspoons per patty), then press 1 teaspoon of the ground peppercorns lightly into each side of the patties (again 2 teaspoons per hamburger). Let stand at room temperature for 30 minutes.

3. Prepare charcoal or wood chips for grilling.

4. Meanwhile, prepare the tomato-leek sauce: Melt the butter in a saucepan over medium-high heat. Add the leeks and cook for 5 minutes. Stir in the tomatoes and cook 5 minutes longer. Stir in the Cognac, tarragon, cream, and salt to taste. Reduce the heat and simmer for 5 minutes and keep warm until ready to serve.

5. When the coals are hot, grill the hamburgers to desired doneness. Serve on a bed of the tomato-leek sauce or, if preferred, serve with the sauce alongside.

Makes 8 hamburgers.

Grilled Pork Tenderloin with Port, Plums, and Apricots

Great September dinner fare when the heat of the grill is as welcome for warmth as for the smoky flavor it imparts to food.

1 boneless pork loin, about 4 pounds, cut in half lengthwise	3 shallots, minced
	3 cloves garlic, halved
	½ cup dried apricots
4 tablespoons olive oil	8 fresh prune plums, cut in half and pitted
Coarse (kosher) salt	
1½ cups port	2 tablespoons chopped fresh rosemary
1 cup fresh orange juice	
3 tablespoons honey	Salt and freshly ground pepper to taste
3 tablespoons cider vinegar	

1. Rub the 2 pieces of pork loin all over with the oil and coarse salt. Place in a 5- to 6-inch-deep bowl or pan.

2. Place the remaining ingredients in a saucepan and heat to simmering. Simmer for 5 minutes, then pour the warm marinade over the pork. Let cool to room temperature. Cover the bowl and

let marinate, turning the pork occasionally, in the refrigerator at least 4 hours.

3. Prepare charcoal or wood chips for grilling.

4. When the coals are hot, remove the pork from the marinade and sear a few inches from the heat on all sides until nicely browned. Adjust the grill rack so that the pork is about 4 to 5 inches from the coals. Cover the grill and cook the pork, turning occasionally, to desired doneness, 35 to 45 minutes.

5. Boil the marinade in a saucepan for just 1 to 2 minutes. Cut the pork into ½-inch-thick slices and spoon the warm marinade over the slices.

Makes 6 to 8 servings.

Grilled Sausage Extravaganza

Sausage is one of the easiest and tastiest foods to sizzle over a grill. The accompaniments of grilled polenta and red onion all splashed with sweet red pepper butter turns this simple dish into a fabulous feast.

POLENTA:
4 cups water
1 teaspoon salt
1 cup yellow cornmeal
2 tablespoons unsalted butter
3 tablespoons chopped fresh basil
5 tablespoons freshly grated Parmesan cheese

SWEET PEPPER BUTTER:
3 red bell peppers, roasted, peeled, seeded, and coarsely chopped
6 tablespoons unsalted butter, at room temperature
½ teaspoon dried red pepper flakes
3 tablespoons chopped fresh basil
Salt and freshly ground pepper to taste

2 medium red onions, cut into thick rings
Olive oil
3 pounds smoked kielbasa sausage

1. The day before serving, prepare the polenta: Heat the water to boiling in a medium saucepan. Add the salt and gradually stir in the cornmeal with a wooden spoon. Cook over low heat until quite thick, 40 to 45 minutes, stirring occasionally and pressing out any lumps. Remove from the heat and stir in the butter, basil, and Parmesan. Transfer the polenta to a 9 x 5 x 3-inch loaf pan and refrigerate overnight to firm.

2. Prepare charcoal or wood chips for grilling.

3. Meanwhile, prepare the sweet pepper butter: Place the bell peppers and butter together in a food processor fitted with the steel blade and process until very smooth. Add the red pepper flakes and basil and blend thoroughly. Season to taste with salt and pepper. Transfer to a decorative crock and keep at room temperature.

4. When the coals are hot, cut the polenta into ½-inch-thick slices and brush both sides of each slice with olive oil. Brush the onion slices on both sides with oil as well. Cut the kielbasa into manageable grilling lengths. Place all on the grill and cook, turning as needed, until each is nicely browned on both sides. Arrange the kielbasa, polenta, and onions on a large platter. Pass the sweet pepper butter.

Makes 6 servings.

Sweet
Splurges

You never know what is enough unless you know what is more than enough.
—WILLIAM BLAKE

Personally, I am convinced that summer is the most indulgent time of all the year. While there are certainly the excesses of Thanksgiving and Christmas, or the consolations of copious amounts of comfort food in the frigid depths of winter, no season sustains an aura of continual and refreshing celebration more than summer.

It seems unfortunate that we often associate lethargy and lack of appetite with the scorch of summer. The flip side to this torrid season is the heat-inspired pursuit of temptations and healthy hedonism. As the temperature soars so does an uninhibited desire for sun-permeated outdoor activity and the consumption of perfect foods bulging with brilliant color and concentrated flavor. We really do want to have it all in the summertime! When we can't resist afternoons lazing at the beach followed by siestas, sun-stroke tennis matches, wind-surf mania, or yet another wild cocktail party, why should we pass up the tart glistening with a small fortune of raspberries or the cheesecake as comforting to the inner self as aloe to our surface sunburns?

Indeed, there is no simpler sense of gratification (or even mildly rewarding perversion) than to savor extravagantly rich confections on squelching August afternoons. An accompanying sip of steaming double espresso is all that is needed to raise the body temperature to a perfect mesh with the surrounding environs.

Espresso-Walnut Cake

Nothing heightens the intensity of chocolate more than a good jigger of espresso. This cake is assembled in the style of a European torte and it has an interior so moist and dense that it has been known to give confirmed chocolate fanatics a glimpse of heaven. It is the favorite chocolate dessert at the Que Sera Sarah.

CAKE:
- 1 cup granulated sugar
- ¼ cup water
- 1 tablespoon instant espresso powder
- 6 ounces semisweet chocolate bits
- 2 teaspoons vanilla extract
- ½ cup (1 stick) unsalted butter, at room temperature
- 8 large eggs, separated
- 1¼ cups walnuts
- 1 slice fresh white bread, crusts removed
- Pinch salt

FROSTING:
- 6 ounces semisweet chocolate bits
- ⅓ cup water
- 1 tablespoon instant espresso powder
- 1 cup (2 sticks) unsalted butter, at room temperature
- 3 large egg yolks
- ¾ cup sifted confectioners' sugar
- Ground walnuts, for garnish
- Chocolate-covered coffee beans, for garnish

1. Preheat the oven to 350°F. Butter two 9-inch round cake pans and line the bottoms with 8-inch parchment paper circles. Butter the paper and dust with flour, shaking out any excess.

2. Prepare the cake: Place the sugar, water, and espresso in a small saucepan. Bring to a boil over medium heat, stirring constantly with a wire whisk. Add the chocolate and the vanilla and heat, whisking constantly, just until the chocolate melts and the mixture is smooth. Remove from the heat and let cool.

3. Cream the butter in a large mixing bowl until light and fluffy. Beat in the egg yolks, one at a time, beating well after each addition. Gradually beat in the cooled chocolate mixture.

4. Place the walnuts and bread in a food processor fitted with the steel blade; process until ground. Stir the walnut mixture into the chocolate mixture.

5. Beat the egg whites with the salt in a mixing bowl until stiff, but not dry. Gently fold the egg whites into the chocolate mixture. Divide the batter evenly between the 2 pans.

6. Bake the cakes until the edges have pulled slightly away from the pans, 25 to 30 minutes. Cool in the pans for 15 minutes, then invert onto a wire rack to cool completely.

7. Prepare the frosting: Place the chocolate, water, and espresso in a small saucepan. Cook over low heat, stirring constantly, just until the chocolate is melted and the mixture is smooth. Refrigerate until slightly chilled.

8. Beat the butter in a large mixing bowl until light and fluffy. Beat in the egg yolks, one at a time, beating well after each addition. Gradually beat in the chilled chocolate mixture, then the confectioners' sugar, continuing to beat until the mixture is of a thick, spreading consistency.

9. Place 1 cake on a serving platter and frost the top. Top with the second cake and spread the top and sides with frosting. Place any remaining frosting in a pastry bag fitted with a decorative tip and pipe the frosting over the top of the cake. Garnish with ground walnuts and candy coffee beans, if desired. Serve the cake slightly chilled.

Makes 8 to 10 servings.

---

*T*here are pleasant drives to all parts of the island, with a never-ending variety of exquisite marine views or stretches of unfenced moorlands covered with wild flowers and overgrown with bayberry and huckleberry bushes, wild roses and sweet fern, with here and there a small pond around which and nestling among the many graceful grasses grow the beautiful pink marsh-mallows, buttercups, and violets. Many of the beauty spots lie hidden among the hills, away from the main thoroughfares and to see which it will be necessary to turn off into the old deep rutted roads which form a network over the moors or wander along the bluffs where an occasional patch of Broom or Scotch Heather blooming in all its native beauty may be found. Artists and botonists will find a wealth of material in store.

—Guide to Nantucket 1928

Honeymoon Torte

This rich nut torte recipe is another family favorite handed down from my Polish grandmother. The result is as romantic looking and tasting as its name. The chocolate and maple flavoring in the frosting have a wonderful affinity, not unlike that of honeymooners. . . .

12 large eggs, separated
1 cup granulated sugar
3½ cups ground walnuts
6 graham crackers,
   crushed to fine powder

3 tablespoons sifted
   all-purpose flour
1 teaspoon baking powder
2 teaspoons vanilla
   extract

FROSTING:
1 cup (2 sticks) unsalted
   butter, at room
   temperature
2 cups sifted
   confectioners' sugar
2 ounces unsweetened
   chocolate, melted

2 tablespoons strong
   brewed coffee
1 teaspoon maple extract
2 large eggs

1. Preheat the oven to 325°F. Butter and flour three 8-inch round cake pans.

2. Place the egg yolks and ¾ of the sugar in a large mixing bowl. Using an electric mixer, beat at high speed until the mixture is very light and fluffy, 8 to 10 minutes.

3. Mix the walnuts, graham crackers, flour, and baking powder together in a small bowl. Add to the egg yolk mixture and stir until well blended. Stir in the vanilla.

4. With clean beaters and in a clean bowl, beat the egg whites and the remaining ¼ cup sugar just until stiff peaks begin to form. Gently fold the egg whites into the nut mixture. Divide the cake batter evenly among the prepared pans.

5. Bake until the cakes pull away from the edges of the pans and the centers spring back when touched lightly in the middles, 20 to 25 minutes.

6. Cool the cakes in the pans for 30 minutes then invert onto wire racks to cool completely.

7. Meanwhile, prepare the frosting: Beat the butter and the confectioners' sugar in a mixing bowl until smooth, then beat in the melted chocolate, coffee, and maple extract. Beat in the eggs,

one at a time, beating well after each addition. Refrigerate the frosting until set but still spreadable.

8. Place 1 cake layer on a serving plate and spread the top with frosting. Top with the second layer and frost. Top with the third layer and frost the top and sides. Pipe any remaining frosting through a pastry bag fitted with a decorative tip on the top of the torte. Store the torte in the refrigerator. Let warm to room temperature 20 minutes before serving.

Makes 12 servings.

French Nut Icebox Cake

If asked to nominate a single sweet as my idea of the ultimate dessert, this icebox cake would be my choice. It is a sophisticated, rich cake that manages to be creamy, crunchy, and intensely nutty all at the same time. The unusual recipe has been handed down from my Polish grandmother and it is always served on special occasions in my family.

1 cup (2 sticks) unsalted
   butter, at room
   temperature
1¼ cups confectioners'
   sugar
3 large eggs
3 large eggs, separated
8 ounces pecans, finely
   ground

2 packages (3 ounces
   each) ladyfingers
12 chewy almond
   macaroons, 2 inches in
   diameter, from a good
   bakery
Whipped cream
   (optional)

1. Cream the butter and the sugar in a large mixing bowl until very smooth. Beat in the whole eggs, one at a time, beating well after each addition.

2. Beat the 3 egg yolks in a small bowl until lemon colored. Add to the butter mixture and beat until blended. Stir in the pecans.

3. Beat the egg whites in another mixing bowl until stiff, but not dry. Gently fold the egg whites into the batter just until blended.

4. Line a 9½-inch springform pan with waxed paper, folding the overhanging edges over the rim of the pan. Line the bottom and sides of the pan with split ladyfingers.

5. Pour half the batter into the pan. Place 6 of the macaroons gently on top. Pour in the remaining batter and top with the remaining macaroons.

6. Cover the top of the cake with a layer of waxed paper and place a plate on top to lightly weight it. Refrigerate the cake for 24 hours.

7. Unmold the cake from the springform pan and cut into thin wedges. Serve whipped cream, if desired.

Makes 12 to 16 servings.

Chocolate Macadamia Cake with Goslings Rum Crème Anglaise

A flourless cake dense with chocolate and ground macadamia nuts. Goslings is a favorite summer sipping rum that adds a nice tropical touch to the crème anglaise.

CAKE:
¾ cup unsalted
  macadamia nuts
12 ounces semisweet
  chocolate bits
2 ounces unsweetened
  chocolate

½ cup (1 stick) unsalted butter
1 cup heavy or whipping
  cream
5 large eggs
½ cup granulated sugar
1 teaspoon vanilla extract

RUM CREME ANGLAISE:
1½ cups light cream (see
  Index)
6 tablespoons brown
  sugar

6 large egg yolks
6 tablespoons Goslings or
  other dark rum

1. Preheat the oven to 325°F. Butter a 9-inch round cake pan and line the bottom with an 8½-inch parchment paper circle. Butter the paper and lightly flour the pan.

2. Toast the macadamias on a baking sheet just until lightly browned, 7 to 10 minutes.

3. Heat the semisweet chocolate, unsweetened chocolate, butter, and cream in a saucepan over medium-low heat, just until the chocolate melts and the mixture is smooth. Remove from the heat.

4. Place the eggs in a large heatproof mixing bowl and beat in the sugar and vanilla. Set the bowl in a pan of simmering water on the stove. Beat the egg mixture with a hand-held mixer just until it is warm to the touch. Remove the bowl from the water and continue beating on high speed until tripled in volume, 7 to 10 minutes.

5. Process the macadamia nuts in a food processor fitted with the steel blade until finely ground, then fold into the chocolate mixture. Gently fold the egg mixture into the chocolate mixture just until blended. Pour the batter into the prepared pan. Place the pan in a larger pan and fill the larger pan with water to come half-way up the sides of the cake pan.

6. Bake the cake until a toothpick inserted in the center comes out clean, 40 to 45 minutes. Remove the cake from the oven and waterbath. Let cool completely in the pan, then invert onto a serving plate.

7. Prepare the crème anglaise: Heat the cream and brown sugar in a small saucepan just until the sugar dissolves. Remove from the heat. Whisk the egg yolks in a mixing bowl until blended. Gradually beat in one-third of the warm cream mixture. Whisk the egg yolks back into the cream mixture and return to the stove. Cook over low heat, stirring constantly, until thick-ened to the consistency of a light custard. Remove from the heat.

8. Transfer the egg mixture to a clean bowl. Stir in the rum and set the bowl in a larger bowl filled with ice water. Cool the crème completely. Refrigerate until ready to serve.

9. To serve the cake, pool a few spoonfuls of the crème anglaise on each dessert plate. Place a small wedge of the chocolate cake in the center. Garnish with a tropical-looking flower and serve.

Makes 8 to 10 servings.

Chocolate Bombe

I believe the name says it all with this dessert!

2 packages (3 ounces
  each) ladyfingers
½ cup Grand Marnier,
  dark rum, or crème de
  cacao
3 packages (12 ounces
  each) semisweet
  chocolate bits

2 cups (1 pound)
  unsalted butter, at
  room temperature
4 cups sifted
  confectioners' sugar
16 large egg yolks
1½ tablespoons vanilla
  extract

GLAZE:
1 package (12 ounces)
  semisweet chocolate
  bits

2 tablespoons unsalted
  butter

1. Line a 2-quart mixing bowl with plastic wrap. Brush the pre-split sides of each ladyfinger with the liqueur. Line the bowl with the ladyfingers, reserving the extras for the top.

2. Melt the chocolate, stirring constantly, in the top of a double boiler over simmering water until smooth. Beat the butter, sugar, and egg yolks in a large mixing bowl at high speed until fluffy. At low speed, gradually beat in the melted chocolate and the vanilla extract.

3. Pour the chocolate mixture into the ladyfinger-lined bowl. Cover the top completely with the reserved ladyfingers. Refrigerate the bombe overnight to set.

4. The following day, invert the bombe onto a serving plate. Prepare the glaze: Melt the chocolate and butter in a small saucepan, stirring constantly, over low heat until smooth. Spread the glaze completely over the bombe. Serve the bombe slightly chilled in thin wedges.

Makes 20 to 24 servings.

Viennese Hazelnut Torte with Coffee Buttercream

A beautifully dramatic, delicious, and quintessential example of the fine art of European-style confection. The crunchy nuttiness of the cake layers are a perfect contrast to the silky smooth coffee buttercream.

CAKE:

¼ cup best-quality unsweetened cocoa powder
4½ cups hazelnuts, skinned, lightly toasted, and finely ground

12 large eggs, separated
2 cups granulated sugar
Pinch of salt

COFFEE BUTTERCREAM:

3 heaping tablespoons instant espresso powder
⅓ cup boiling water
6 large egg yolks
½ cup granulated sugar
2 cups (1 pound) unsalted butter, at room temperature

¼ cup dark sweet rum
¾ cup sifted confectioners' sugar

Additional rum for sprinkling on cakes

Chocolate-covered coffee beans, for garnish

1. Preheat the oven to 350°F. Butter three 9-inch round cake pans and line the bottoms with 8-inch parchment paper circles. Butter the paper and lightly dust each pan with flour.

2. Process the cocoa and hazelnuts in a food processor fitted with the steel blade until combined.

3. Using an electric mixer, beat the egg yolks in a mixing bowl at high speed until thick and pale yellow, 3 to 4 minutes. Gradually beat in the sugar; continue beating until the mixture is very thick, 4 to 5 minutes.

4. Beat the egg whites with the salt in a large mixing bowl until stiff but not dry.

5. Fold half the cocoa mixture into the egg yolk mixture. Lighten by gently folding in one-third of the egg whites. Fold in the remaining cocoa mixture, then gently fold in the remaining egg whites just until incorporated. Divide the batter evenly among the 3 pans.

6. Bake the cakes until the sides pull away from the pans and the centers spring back when lightly touched, 40 to 45 minutes. Let the cakes cool in the pans for 15 minutes, then invert onto wire racks to cool completely.

7. Prepare the buttercream: Dissolve the espresso in the boiling water. Whisk the egg yolks, granulated sugar, and espresso together in the top of a double boiler. Set over simmering water and cook the egg yolk mixture, whisking constantly, until it is the consistency of a medium custard, 10 to 15 minutes. Remove the pan from the water and cool to room temperature.

8. Beat the butter in a mixing bowl until creamy. Gradually beat in the coffee custard mixture and the rum. Beat in the confectioners' sugar. If the buttercream seems too runny, refrigerate it to thicken to spreading consistency.

9. Moisten each cake layer with a liberal sprinkling of rum. Spread the top and sides of each cake with a thin layer of the buttercream, stacking the layers on top of each other. Even the sides and top of the cake with more buttercream. Place any remaining buttercream in a pastry bag fitted with a decorative tip. Pipe rosettes of buttercream over the top of the torte. Decorate with the candy coffee beans. Refrigerate the torte until 15 minutes before you are ready to serve.

Makes 12 servings.

My Vision of Cheesecake

I adore cheesecakes that are dense and creamy, but I abhor them with graham cracker crumb crusts. This recipe, which I've perfected over the years, has a pastry crust with a subtle hint of citrus and a sinfully rich filling. The cheesecake can be made even more outrageous by topping it lavishly with ripe summer berries.

CRUST:

1½ cups unbleached
   all-purpose flour
⅓ cup sugar
1 teaspoon grated lemon
   zest
1 teaspoon grated orange
   zest

¾ cup (1½ sticks)
   unsalted butter, cold,
   cut into small pieces
1 large egg yolk
½ teaspoon vanilla
   extract

FILLING:

2½ pounds cream cheese,
   at room temperature
1½ cups sugar
3 tablespoons all-purpose
   flour
5 large eggs
2 large egg yolks

1 tablespoon grated
   orange zest
2 teaspoons grated lemon
   zest
1 teaspoon vanilla extract
¼ cup heavy or whipping
   cream

Ripe berries, whole or puréed (optional)

1. Prepare the crust: Place the flour, sugar, lemon and orange zests, and butter in a food processor fitted with the steel blade; process until the mixture resembles coarse meal. Add the egg yolk and vanilla and process just until the mixture starts to form a ball. Gather the dough, wrap it in plastic wrap, and refrigerate 1 hour.

2. Preheat the oven to 400°F. Butter the bottom and sides of a 9½-inch springform pan.

3. Using your fingers, press one-third of the pastry in an even layer on the bottom of the pan. Bake 10 minutes, then remove to a cool spot to cool completely.

4. Increase the heat to 475°F.

5. Prepare the filling: Beat the cream cheese and sugar in a large mixing bowl until very soft and creamy. Beat in the flour, then beat in the eggs and egg yolks, one at a time, beating well after each addition. Mix in the lemon and orange zests, vanilla, and cream.

6. Press the remaining pastry evenly around the sides of the pan. Pour the cheesecake filling into the pan.

7. Bake 10 minutes. Reduce the oven heat to 275°F and bake until the cheesecake is firm when pressed lightly in the center,

about 1 hour. Turn the oven off and let the cheesecake cool for several hours or overnight in the oven.

8. Remove the cheesecake from the side of the springform pan and refrigerate until cold. Top with lush summer berries, if desired.

Makes 12 servings.

Apricot Cheesecake

I love both the intense color and flavor of this cheesecake variation. During the summer I like to top it with a purée of fresh strawberries or raspberries for dramatic contrast. In the fall I often make a topping of simmered and sweetened cranberries.

1 cup dried apricots	1½ pounds cream cheese,
1 cup gingersnap crumbs	at room temperature
3 tablespoons unsalted	¾ cup sugar
butter, melted	4 large eggs
Grated zest of 1 orange	½ cup sour cream

1. Simmer the apricots in water to cover for 30 minutes, then drain.

2. Preheat the oven to 350°F. Butter an 8- or 9-inch springform pan.

3. Toss the gingersnap crumbs with the melted butter in a small mixing bowl. Press the crumbs over the bottom and 1 inch up the side of the prepared pan. Set aside.

4. Purée the apricots with the orange zest in a food processor fitted with the steel blade.

5. Beat the cream cheese and sugar in a large mixing bowl until very smooth and creamy. Beat in the eggs, one at a time, beating well after each addition. Using a rubber spatula, gently fold in the sour cream and apricot purée until completely blended. Pour the batter into the springform pan.

6. Bake until the center is firm when touched lightly, 50 to 60 minutes. Cool the cake on a wire rack, then refrigerate until thoroughly chilled. Top with a fruit topping, if desired, and serve.

Makes 10 to 12 servings.

Little Sarah's Shortcake

Little Sarah is one of the trusty crew of teenage girls that help me in the kitchen during Nantucket's high season frenzy. She is blond, freckled, delightfully giggly, and a real whiz in the baking department. This is the recipe for the terrific shortcake she churned out for a recent Fourth of July celebration.

2¼ cups unbleached
   all-purpose flour
½ cup plus 1 tablespoon
   sugar
1½ teaspoons baking
   powder
¾ teaspoon baking soda
½ teaspoon salt
6 tablespoons (¾ stick)
   unsalted butter, cold,
   cut into small pieces
⅔ cup buttermilk

1 large egg yolk
½ teaspoon vanilla extract
⅛ teaspoon almond
   extract
3 tablespoons heavy or
   whipping cream
⅓ cup sliced almonds
Fresh berries, and/or
   sliced peaches or
   nectarines, and
   whipped cream, for
   serving

1. Preheat the oven to 425°F. Line a baking sheet with parchment paper.

2. Place the flour, ½ cup sugar, the baking powder, baking soda, and salt in a food processor fitted with the steel blade; process briefly to combine. Add the butter and process just until the mixture is crumbly.

3. Whisk the buttermilk, egg yolk, and vanilla and almond extracts together in a small bowl. With the food processor running, pour the buttermilk mixture through the feed tube and process until the dough is somewhat sticky but still manageable. Transfer the dough to a floured sheet of waxed paper.

4. With lightly floured fingertips, gently pat the dough to an even ¾-inch thickness. Be careful not to handle the dough too much. Cut out six 3-inch circles, using a floured fluted cutter. Place the dough circles on the baking sheet.

5. Brush the tops of the cakes with the cream and arrange the almonds on top to look like the petals of a flower. Sprinkle with the remaining 1 tablespoon sugar.

6. Bake the shortcakes until lightly golden brown, 12 to 15 minutes. Cool, then split in half with a serrated knife. Fill with berries, sliced peaches or nectarines, and whipped cream.

Makes 6 shortcakes.

Blueberry-Raspberry Galette

As a young girl, I made this dessert with the blueberries and raspberries that grew wild on my grandfather's island in Maine. The recipe is still a favorite because there is something wonderfully light and summery about the combination of the barely cooked blueberries with the fresh raspberries.

CRUST:

1 cup unbleached
   all-purpose flour
1½ tablespoons sugar
6 tablespoons (¾ stick)
   unsalted butter, cold,
   cut into small pieces
½ teaspoon salt

1 teaspoon finely grated
   lemon zest
1 large egg yolk
1 tablespoon fresh lemon
   juice
1 tablespoon ice water

FILLING:

2½ cups fresh blueberries,
   preferably small wild
   ones
¼ cup sugar
2 teaspoons ground
   cinnamon

4 tablespoons (½ stick)
   unsalted butter, melted
1 tablespoon fresh lemon
   juice

1 cup fresh raspberries   Whipped cream (optional)

1. Prepare the crust: Place the flour, sugar, butter, salt, and lemon zest in a food processor fitted with the steel blade; process just until the mixture resembles coarse meal. Add the egg yolk. With the machine running, add the lemon juice and water through the feed tube and process just until the dough starts to hold together and form a ball. Gather the dough, wrap it in plastic wrap, and refrigerate at least 2 hours.

2. Roll out the dough into a 14-inch circle on a lightly floured surface. Line a 12-inch tart pan with a removable bottom with the dough; trim and crimp the edges. Freeze the shell for 30 minutes.

3. Preheat the oven to 425°F.

4. Prepare the filling: Toss the blueberries, sugar, cinnamon, butter, and lemon juice together. Spoon the filling evenly into the tart shell.

5. Bake the tart for 12 minutes. Reduce the heat to 350°F and bake until the berries are slightly soft, about 10 minutes. Let the tart cool completely.

6. Decorate the tart with 2 circles of fresh raspberries around the edge. Cut into wedges and serve with a dollop of whipped cream, if desired.

Makes 8 servings.

Double Raspberry Tart

T his tart epitomizes the best of summer. It is extravagant in its use of raspberries both in the creamy filling and clustered all over the top. The combination of colors—berry red, cloud pink, and pale green—always make me imagine that I am surrounded by a gorgeous roll of chintz fabric.

CRUST:

1¼ cups unbleached all-purpose flour

2 tablespoons sugar

½ cup (1 stick) unsalted butter, cold, cut broken into small pieces

2 teaspoons grated lemon zest

1 large egg yolk

1 to 2 tablespoons ice water

RASPBERRY CREAM:

2 cups fresh raspberries

1 tablespoon fresh lemon juice

½ cup sugar

6 tablespoons (¾ stick) unsalted butter

5 large egg yolks

1½ cups fresh raspberries

2 kiwis, peeled and sliced into thin rounds

½ cup apricot jam

¼ cup orange-flavored liqueur

1. Prepare the crust: Place the flour, sugar, butter, and lemon zest in a food processor fitted with the steel blade; process just until the mixture resembles coarse meal. Add the egg yolk and

pulse just to combine. With the machine running, add the water through the feed tube a few drops at a time, just until the dough begins to hold together. Gather the dough into a ball, wrap it in plastic wrap, and refrigerate for at least 2 hours.

2. Meanwhile, prepare the raspberry cream: Purée the raspberries, lemon juice, and sugar together in the food processor. Strain the mixture through a fine sieve to remove the seeds. Place the purée in the top of a double boiler set over simmering water. Add the butter and stir until completely melted. Whisk in the egg yolks and continue to cook over low heat, stirring constantly, until the mixture thickens to a light custard consistency. Remove from the heat and chill covered in the refrigerator at least 2 hours.

3. Roll out the dough on a lightly floured surface to a 12-inch circle. Line a 10-inch tart pan with a removable bottom with the dough; trim and crimp the edges. Freeze the shell for 30 minutes.

4. Preheat the oven to 375°F. Line the tart shell with aluminum foil and fill with lead pie weights or dried beans.

5. Bake the shell until light golden brown, about 20 to 25 minutes. Remove the foil and weights; cool the shell completely.

6. To assemble the pie, spread the raspberry cream evenly over the tart shell. Arrange concentric circles of the raspberries, interspersed with the kiwi, over the top.

7. Combine the apricot jam and orange liqueur in a small saucepan and heat over low heat just until the jam is melted and smooth. Brush all over the fruit to glaze. Serve the tart at once or refrigerate until ready to serve.

Makes 8 servings.

Deep-Dish Rhubarb Pie

My love for the color pink is absolutely inexhaustible. This pretty pie, oozing with cassis-infused spring rhubarb, is pink at its most palatable. I only lament that rhubarb has such a short growing season.

CRUST:

2½ cups unbleached all-purpose flour

5 tablespoons sugar

1 tablespoon ground cinnamon

Pinch salt

6 tablespoons unsalted butter, cold, cut into bits

6 tablespoons unsalted margarine, cold, cut into bits

4 to 5 tablespoons ice water

FILLING:

10 cups diced rhubarb

1½ cups cassis liqueur

Finely chopped zest of 2 oranges

1¾ cups sugar

⅓ cup cornstarch

1 large egg

1 tablespoon water

1. One day before you plan to serve the pie, prepare the crust: Process the flour, sugar, cinnamon, salt, butter, and margarine in a food processor fitted with the steel blade just until the mixture resembles coarse meal. With the machine running, pour the ice water through the feed tube and process just until the dough starts to form a ball. Gather the dough, wrap it in plastic wrap, and refrigerate.

2. Start the filling: Toss the rhubarb with the cassis and orange zest in a large mixing bowl. Cover the bowl with plastic wrap and let marinate at room temperature overnight.

3. Drain the liquid from the rhubarb into a small saucepan. Stir in the sugar and cornstarch. Cook, whisking constantly, over medium-high heat until thickened. Pour the sauce over the rhubarb and stir until well combined.

4. Preheat the oven to 350°F.

5. Roll out half the dough into a 12-inch circle on a lightly floured surface. Line a 10-inch pie dish with the dough; trim and crimp the edges decoratively. Mound the filling in the pie shell.

6. Roll out the remaining dough ⅛ inch thick. Cut the dough into ⅓-inch-wide strips and arrange the strips over the top of the pie in a lattice pattern. Gather the scraps and roll out ⅛ inch thick. Cut out a heart shape and place on the center of the pie.

7. Beat the egg and water together in a small bowl. Brush the egg wash over the dough. Place the dish on a baking sheet to catch any overflowing juices. Bake the pie until the crust is golden brown and the filling is bubbling, 50 to 60 minutes. Serve warm or at room temperature.

Makes 8 servings.

Lemon Chiffon Pie

A cloudlike pie that is both light and opulent.

CRUST:
½ cup (1 stick) unsalted butter, cold, cut into small pieces
4 tablespoons unsalted margarine, cold, cut into small pieces
2 cups unbleached all-purpose flour
Pinch salt
2 to 3 tablespoons ice water

FILLING:
4 large eggs, separated
6 tablespoons fresh lemon juice
¾ cup sugar
Finely grated zest of 1 lemon
1 scant tablespoon unflavored gelatin
⅓ cup cold water

TOPPING:
1 cup heavy or whipping cream
¼ cup sugar
2 teaspoons grated orange zest
½ cup ground lightly toasted almonds

1. Early in the morning or one day before you plan to serve the pie, prepare the crust: Place the butter, margarine, flour, and salt in a food processor fitted with the steel blade; process just until the mixture resembles coarse meal. With the machine running, add the ice water through the feed tube and process just until the mixture starts to form a ball. Gather the dough, wrap it in plastic wrap, and refrigerate at least 2 hours.

2. Roll out the dough into an 11-inch circle on a lightly floured surface. Line a 9-inch pie dish with the dough; trim and crimp the edges decoratively. Freeze the pie shell for 30 minutes.

3. Preheat the oven to 375°F.

4. Line the pie shell with aluminum foil and fill with pie weights or dried beans. Bake the shell until light golden brown, 20 to 25 minutes. Remove the foil and weights; cool the shell completely.

5. Prepare the filling: Beat the egg yolks, lemon juice, ½ cup of the sugar, and all but 1 teaspoon of the lemon zest in the top of a double boiler. Cook, stirring constantly, over simmering water until the mixture is the consistency of a thick custard. Remove from the heat and transfer to a medium bowl. Soften the gelatin in the cold water and stir into the lemon custard until dissolved. Let cool.

6. Beat the egg whites in a mixing bowl until stiff but not dry, then beat in the remaining ¼ cup sugar. Gently fold the egg whites into the custard. Pour the filling into the baked pie shell and refrigerate at least 2 hours.

7. When ready to serve, prepare the topping: Whip the cream, sugar, and orange zest until stiff. Transfer to a pastry bag fitted with a decorative tip and pipe the cream decoratively over the pie.

8. Dust the top of the pie with the ground toasted almonds and the reserved 1 teaspoon lemon zest. Serve at once.

Makes 8 servings.

Apple Cream-Cheese Tarts

The inspiration for these tarts comes from German fruit kuchens. However, I think the accent on the pure vanilla flavor make these tarts especially unique. Use any crisp apple or feel free to innovate with other seasonal fruits and liqueurs. I particularly like purple plums with cassis and peaches with amaretto.

CRUST:

1¼ cups unbleached all-purpose flour	⅓ cup sugar
½ cup (1 stick) unsalted butter, cold, cut into small pieces	2 teaspoons vanilla extract

APPLES:

2 large apples, peeled, cored, and cut into very thin wedges	2 tablespoons brandy
	3 tablespoons sugar
1 tablespoon fresh lemon juice	2 teaspoons ground cinnamon

CREAM-CHEESE FILLING:

8 ounces cream cheese	2 teaspoons vanilla
½ cup sugar	extract
1 large egg	

1. Prepare the crust: Place the flour, butter, and sugar in a food processor fitted with the steel blade; process until the mixture resembles coarse meal. Add the vanilla and process just until the mixture starts to hold together. Gather the dough into a ball, wrap in plastic wrap, and refrigerate 30 minutes.

2. Meanwhile, prepare the apples: Toss the apples, lemon juice, brandy, sugar, and cinnamon together in a mixing bowl. Let stand at least 20 minutes.

3. Prepare the cream-cheese filling: Break the cream cheese into small pieces and place in the food processor fitted with the steel blade. Add the sugar, egg, and vanilla and process until smooth.

4. Preheat the oven to 350°F.

5. Divide the chilled dough into 5 equal pieces. Using your fingers, press each piece of dough into a 4½-inch tart pan with a removable bottom to completely line the bottom and sides.

6. Spoon the filling into the tart shells, then arrange the apple slices overlapping in a circle on the filling in each tart shell. Pour any juices in the bowl over the tops of the tarts.

7. Place the tarts on a baking sheet and bake until the tarts are light golden brown, 35 to 45 minutes. Let cool completely, then remove the tarts from the pans. Serve at room temperature.

Makes 5 individual tarts.

Applesauce Cake with Caramel Glaze

While I dislike the very thought of carrot cake, I find that applesauce cake is an ostensibly "healthful" cake in a whole other league. This cake is the perfect treat for one of those "try-to-remember" September days when all the tourists have gone home and you can finally appreciate your summer home.

¾ cup (1½ sticks)
   unsalted butter, at
   room temperature
1½ cups (packed) brown
   sugar
2 large eggs
2½ cups Rosy
   Applesauce (see Index)
   or unsweetened
   best-quality applesauce

3 cups unbleached
   all-purpose flour
1 tablespoon baking soda
1½ tablespoons ground
   cinnamon
1 teaspoon grated nutmeg
½ teaspoon ground cloves
1¼ cups pitted dates, chopped
½ cup Calvados
1 cup coarsely chopped walnuts

GLAZE:
2 cups (packed) brown
   sugar
½ cup (1 stick) unsalted
   butter

½ cup milk

1. Preheat the oven to 350°F. Butter a 10-inch bundt or tube pan.

2. Using an electric mixer, cream the butter and sugar in a large mixing bowl until light and fluffy. Add the eggs and applesauce and beat until blended.

3. Sift the flour, baking soda, cinnamon, nutmeg, and ground cloves together and gradually stir into the butter mixture.

4. Heat the dates and Calvados in a small saucepan to boiling; boil 1 minute. Add to the cake batter. Add the walnuts and stir until combined. Pour the batter into the prepared pan.

5. Bake until a knife inserted in the center of the cake comes out clean, 50 to 60 minutes. Cool the cake in the pan for 30 minutes, then invert onto a cake rack to cool completely.

6. Meanwhile, prepare the glaze: Combine the sugar, butter, and milk in a heavy saucepan. Heat, stirring constantly, over high heat to boiling. Boil without stirring until it registers 234°F on a candy thermometer. Let cool to room temperature. Transfer the mixture to a mixing bowl and beat until fluffy. Drizzle the glaze lavishly over the cooled cake.

Makes 12 servings.

Que Sera Sarah Brownies

O ver the summers these superb brownies have achieved a sort of cult status with my customers. Many have tried in vain to duplicate them at home and others offer season-to-season guesses as to the alleged secret ingredient. The combination of sheer exasperation over failed attempts to copy them and winter withdrawal brings me several desperate phone calls a year for brownie care packages.

While all of this chocolate intrigue has been entertaining, I am at last ready to reveal my formula. Although my recipe is actually a close adaptation of Maida Heatter's widely published Palm Beach Brownies, there is a catch: the secret of the Que Sera Sarah rendition does not rest so much on mystery ingredients, but on cooking technique. To achieve the incomparable combination of wafer thin crust and dense fudge-like interior of my shop brownies, you must bake the recipe in a *convection oven* and then patiently refrigerate the brownies for several hours before devouring them. I regret to inform those chocolate lovers without state-of-the-art kitchens that the same results just cannot be achieved with a regular oven. I do suggest, however, that these brownies might be worth the investment!

8 ounces unsweetened
   chocolate
1 cup (2 sticks) unsalted
   butter
5 large eggs
1 tablespoon vanilla
   extract
2 teaspoons almond
   extract

3 tablespoons instant
   coffee powder
3¾ cups sugar
1⅔ cups unbleached
   all-purpose flour
1 cup coarsely chopped
   walnuts

1. Preheat a convection oven to 350°F. Line an 11 x 9-inch pan with aluminum foil leaving a little overhang around the edges of the pan. Butter the foil.

2. Melt the chocolate and butter in a small saucepan over low heat, watching carefully and stirring occasionally, just until smooth.

3. Using an electric mixer, beat the eggs, vanilla and almond extracts, coffee, and sugar in a large mixing bowl at the highest speed for about 10 minutes. The mixture should increase in volume and look like softened coffee ice cream. Mix in the melted

chocolate and butter on low speed just until blended. Add the flour and nuts and stir just until mixed. Turn the brownie mixture into the prepared pan.

4. Bake the brownies in the center of the convection oven just until a hard crust forms on the top and the edges are very slightly browned, 18 to 20 minutes. The batter underneath the crust will be runny and undercooked by normal baking standards. Let the brownies cool to room temperature.

5. Refrigerate the brownies at least 6 hours or overnight. Using the foil, lift the brownies from the pan. Cut into 20 to 25 squares.

Makes 20 to 25 brownies.

White Chocolate Brownies

Another rich brownie recipe, this one for lovers of white chocolate.

1 cup (2 sticks) unsalted butter	4 large eggs
10 ounces white chocolate, broken into small pieces	1 tablespoon vanilla extract
	2 cups unbleached all-purpose flour
1¼ cups sugar	½ teaspoon salt
	1 cup coarsely chopped pecans

1. Preheat the oven to 325°F. Line an 11 x 9-inch pan with aluminum foil leaving a little overhang around the edges of the pan and butter the foil.

2. Heat the butter and chocolate, stirring frequently, in a large saucepan over low heat until melted and smooth. Remove from the heat.

3. Using a wooden spoon, stir the sugar into the melted chocolate, then stir in the eggs and vanilla. (The mixture will look curdled.) Add the flour, salt, and chopped pecans and quickly stir just until mixed. Pour the batter into the pan.

4. Bake the brownies until the top is lightly golden but the center is still somewhat soft when pressed lightly, 30 to 35 minutes. Let cool to room temperature.

5. Refrigerate the brownies at least 3 hours. Using the foil, lift the brownies from the pan. Cut into 20 to 25 squares.

Makes 20 to 25 brownies.

My Grandmother's Oatmeal Cookies

I am passionate about these cookies. They are hearty, old-fashioned cookies that contain many of the special qualities of my favorite grandmother, who taught me so much about growing up, as well as a vast amount about eating well. The cookies are quite generous in size; in fact, nibbling on one throughout the day can make the very notion of breakfast and lunch disappear. I have been known to live solely on these cookies throughout my hectic summer season.

2⅔ cups unsalted margarine
3½ cups (packed) brown sugar
3 large eggs
3 tablespoons honey
1 tablespoon vanilla extract
1½ teaspoons salt

4 cups unbleached all-purpose flour
3 pounds old-fashioned rolled oats (there are a lot of oats in these cookies!)
8 ounces dark raisins
8 ounces coarsely chopped walnuts

1. Preheat the oven to 350°F. Line baking sheets with parchment paper.

2. Cream the margarine and sugar in a very large bowl until smooth. Beat in the eggs, honey, vanilla, and salt until smooth and creamy.

3. Using a large wooden spoon or your hands, work in the flour and oats until well combined. Add the raisins and walnuts and mix until evenly distributed.

4. Shape the dough into large 3-inch balls and press into 5- to 6-inch flat cookies on the baking sheets.

5. Bake the cookies 15 minutes or to desired doneness. (Some people like slightly underdone cookies and others like very well-browned cookies. We debate this every time we make these.) Let cool on wire racks.

Makes 24 cookies.

Graham Cracker Chewies

This is a favorite recipe of my mother's. These are a moist and chewy alternative to brownies and are great packed for picnics or tailgate parties.

CRUST:

1⅓ cups graham cracker crumbs

1 tablespoon sugar

½ cup (1 stick) unsalted butter, at room temperature

2 tablespoons all-purpose flour

TOPPING:

1½ cups (packed) brown sugar

½ cup chopped pecans

⅓ cup graham cracker crumbs

½ teaspoon salt

¼ teaspoon baking powder

1 teaspoon vanilla extract

2 large eggs, beaten

1. Preheat the oven to 350°F.

2. Prepare the crust: Mix the graham cracker crumbs, sugar, butter, and flour in a mixing bowl until moist and crumbly. Press the mixture firmly and evenly in the bottom of a 9-inch-square baking pan. Bake until lightly browned, about 20 minutes.

3. Prepare the topping: Stir all the ingredients together until blended. Spread the topping over the baked crust and bake for 20 minutes. Let cool completely, then cut into 16 squares.

Makes 16 bars.

Lace Cookies

This is one of the very first recipes I learned to cook on Nantucket as a young girl. The cookies are delicate, crisp, and addictive. Serve them with goblets of afternoon iced tea or savor them with a late night demitasse of lemon-scented espresso. Be sure to choose a dry day for baking and store in an airtight tin to avoid soggy or limp cookies.

½ cup (1 stick) unsalted
  butter, at room
  temperature
1 cup sugar
1 large egg
1 teaspoon vanilla extract

Pinch salt
1 cup quick-cooking oats
2 tablespoons unbleached
  all-purpose flour
¼ teaspoon baking
  powder

1. Preheat the oven to 325°F. Line baking sheets with aluminum foil and butter the foil well.

2. Using an electric mixer, cream the butter and sugar in a medium bowl until smooth. Add the egg and the vanilla and beat until well blended.

3. Combine the oats, flour, and baking powder in a small bowl. Gradually beat the oat mixture into the butter mixture.

4. Roll the cookie dough with the palms of your hands into balls the size of a nickel. Place the balls a good 2 inches apart on the baking sheets.

5. Bake the cookies until they have spread out and look like lace and the outer edges are quite brown, 8 to 10 minutes. Remove the cookies from the oven and let cool on the baking sheets a minute or so, then transfer to wire racks to cool completely.

Makes about 40 cookies

French Lace Cookies à l'Orange

Another delicate lace cookie, this one with an enticing hint of orange.

1 cup unbleached
  all-purpose flour
1 cup finely chopped
  pecans
⅓ cup light corn syrup
2 tablespoons frozen
  orange juice
  concentrate, thawed

2 teaspoons grated orange
  zest
½ cup (1 stick) unsalted
  butter
⅔ cup (packed) brown
  sugar

1. Preheat the oven to 375°F. Line baking sheets with aluminum foil and butter the foil.

2. Sift the flour into a small bowl and toss with the pecans.

3. Place the remaining ingredients in a saucepan and heat to boiling over medium heat. Using a wooden spoon, gradually stir in the flour mixture. Drop the batter by level teaspoons 2 inches apart on the prepared baking sheets.

4. Bake until the edges of the cookies are golden brown and the centers are cooked, 6 to 8 minutes. Cool on the cookie sheets a minute or so, then transfer to wire racks with a metal spatula to cool completely. Store between layers of waxed paper in an airtight container.

Makes about 48 cookies.

Date Squares

A favorite healthy and old-fashioned recipe that has been handed down from my mother's side of the family.

FILLING:
8 ounces pitted dates   *1 cup orange juice*

CRUST:
2 cups rolled oats   *1 teaspoon baking soda*
1 cup unbleached   *¾ cup (1½ sticks)*
  all-purpose flour   *unsalted butter, melted*
1 cup (packed) brown
  sugar

1. Combine the dates and orange juice in a small saucepan and simmer, stirring occasionally, until thick, 30 minutes.

2. Preheat the oven to 350°F. Butter a 9-inch-square baking pan.

3. Meanwhile, make the crust: Stir the oats, flour, brown sugar, and baking soda together in a mixing bowl. Add the melted butter and stir until moist and crumbly.

4. Press half the oat mixture evenly in the bottom of the prepared pan. Spread the date mixture on top and sprinkle with the remaining oat mixture.

5. Bake the date squares until nicely browned, 40 to 45 minutes. Let cool completely then cut into 16 squares.

Makes 16 squares.

COCONUT MILK

Although packaged unsweetened coconut milk is becoming more widely available, many cooks still prefer to make their own. There are subtle variations of technique, but the following is the method I prefer.

Choose a coconut in which you can hear the inner liquid when the nut is shaken. Pierce the three black eyes at the top of the nut with a hammer and large nail and drain and discard the liquid. Bake the coconut on a tray in a preheated 350°F oven for 20 minutes, or until the outer shell has cracked in several places. Cool the coconut, then finish cracking the shell with a couple of good whacks of a hammer. Remove the shell, then peel the thin brown skin from the coconut meat with a sharp paring knife. Grate the white flesh with a hand grater or in a food processor. You should have about 2½ cups grated coconut.

Combine 1½ cups milk with 1 cup water and bring just to a boil. Pour the liquid over the coconut and let stand for at least 1 hour. Strain the coconut through a fine sieve lined with a double thickness of dampened cheesecloth. Place the coconut in a cloth towel and wring it to extract as much of the coconut essence as possible. Discard the solids. You should now have about 3 cups fresh coconut milk. Store, covered, in the refrigerator for 3 to 5 days and use as called for in the recipes.

Coconut Cream for Summer Fruits

This smooth custard adds a delicious tropical flair to summer fruit desserts. I particularly like it spooned over a mixture of cantaloupe, pineapple, strawberries, and blackberries that have been marinated in a little lime juice.

6 large egg yolks
½ cup sugar
2 cups coconut milk (see
 box, page 247)

½ teaspoon coconut extract or
 2 tablespoons coconut liqueur
Toasted shredded coconut
 for garnish

1. In the top of a double boiler, but off the heat, beat the egg yolks and sugar together until mixture is pale yellow and thick.

2. Bring the coconut milk just to a boil in a small saucepan, then whisk it very slowly into the egg mixture. Place over simmering water and cook, stirring constantly, until the mixture thickens to a light custard, about 10 minutes. Remove from heat and stir in the coconut extract.

3. Cool the cream to room temperature, stirring occasionally. Refrigerate until cold. Spoon liberally over bowls of your favorite mixed fresh fruits and garnish with toasted coconut.

Makes about 2 cups

Coffee
Pot de Crème

A luscious yet simple-to-make dessert for the coffee lover.

3 cups heavy or whipping
 cream
½ cup sugar
1½ tablespoons instant
 coffee powder

1 teaspoon vanilla extract
5 large egg yolks
Whipped cream
Chocolate-covered coffee
 beans

1. Preheat the oven to 325°F.

2. Mix the cream, sugar, and coffee in a medium saucepan. Cook, stirring occasionally, over medium heat until the sugar is dissolved and the mixture is quite hot to the touch. Remove from the heat and stir in the vanilla.

3. Beat the egg yolks in a mixing bowl until thick and lemony. Gradually whisk in the hot cream. Strain the mixture through a sieve into a measuring cup with a pouring lip. Pour the mixture into eight ½-cup pot-de-crème cups.

4. Place the cups in a pan and fill the pan with water to come halfway up the sides of the cups. Bake until the custard is firm to the touch when pressed gently in the center, 25 to 30 minutes. Remove the cups from the water bath and let cool to room temperature.

5. Refrigerate the pots de crème for several hours. Serve with a dollop of whipped cream and a candy coffee bean on top.

Makes 8 servings.

White Chocolate and Pear Mousse

T his shimmering pearl-colored mousse is sublime in flavor combination and texture.

PEAR PURÉE:
- 3 tablespoons unsalted butter
- 3 ripe pears, cored, peeled, and sliced

- ⅓ cup granualted sugar
- 2 tablespoons Poire Williams or other pear brandy

MOUSSE:
- 10 ounces best-quality white chocolate, broken into small pieces
- 4 tablespoons (½ stick) unsalted butter
- 6 large eggs, separated
- 1 cup sifted confectioners' sugar

- ⅓ cup Poire Williams or other pear brandy
- 2 cups heavy or whipping cream
- Fresh mint sprigs, for garnish

1. Prepare the pear purée: Melt the butter in a medium skillet over medium heat. Add the pear slices and sauté until somewhat mushy, about 15 minutes. Stir in the sugar and simmer until the pears begin to caramelize, about 10 minutes longer. Remove the pears from the heat and place in a food processor

fitted with the steel blade. Add the Poire Williams and purée until smooth. Set aside.

2. Prepare the mousse: Melt the white chocolate and butter together in a small saucepan over low heat, stirring constantly until smooth. Set aside.

3. Combine the egg yolks, sugar, and Poire Williams in the top of a double boiler. Beat with a hand-held mixer until the mixture falls into ribbons when the beaters are lifted. Place the pan over simmering water and continue whisking until quite thick, 4 to 5 minutes.

4. Transfer the egg mixture to a large mixing bowl. Add the melted white chocolate, stirring until smooth. Let cool to room temperature.

5. In a chilled bowl, beat the cream until quite stiff. In a separate bowl with clean beaters, beat the egg whites until stiff, but not dry. Gently fold the egg whites into the chocolate mixture, then gently fold in the whipped cream.

6. Divide one-third of the mousse among 8 to 10 large wine goblets. Top each serving with a layer of the pear purée. Spoon another one-third of the mousse into the goblets, and top with the remaining pear purée. Fill the goblets with the remaining mousse. Chill in the refrigerator until set, at least 2 to 3 hours. Serve chilled, garnished with fresh mint sprigs.

Makes 8 to 10 servings.

Chocolate Berry Bertry Bread Pudding

With the current revival of old-fashioned desserts, bread puddings have become quite acceptable at even the poshest dinners. Still, I wanted to concoct a bread pudding that would be dazzling and refined rather than homey. The result is this show-stopping combination of a dense chocolate bread with tart raspberries and strawberries saturated with the richest and creamiest of custards. Comfort redefined!

CHOCOLATE BREAD:

½ cup (1 stick) unsalted
butter
2½ squares (1 ounce
each) unsweetened
chocolate
2 cups unbleached,
all-purpose flour

2 teaspoons baking
powder
Pinch salt
2 large eggs
¾ cup sugar
1 teaspoon vanilla extract
⅔ cup sour cream

BERRIES:

2 cups fresh or frozen
(unsweetened)
raspberries
1½ cups quartered fresh
strawberries (about 1
pint whole berries)

3 tablespoons cassis
liqueur

CUSTARD:

4 large eggs
¾ cup sugar
¼ cup unbleached
all-purpose flour

2 cups heavy or whipping
cream

1 tablespoon unsalted
butter for assembling
the pudding

1 tablespoon sugar for
assembling the
pudding

1. Prepare the chocolate bread: Early in the day or the day before serving, preheat the oven to 350°F. Heavily butter a 9 x 3-inch loaf pan.

2. Melt the butter and chocolate in a small saucepan over low heat. Set aside to cool.

3. Sift together the flour, baking powder, and salt in a small bowl. Set aside.

4. Beat the eggs and sugar together in a large bowl until light and fluffy. Beat in the vanilla, then the cooled chocolate mixture. With a wooden spoon, stir in half of the flour mixture. Stir in the sour cream, then the remaining flour. Continue stirring until the batter is smooth. Pour the batter into the loaf pan and bake until a toothpick inserted in the middle of the loaf comes out clean, 50 to 55 minutes. Cool the bread for 10 minutes, then remove it to a rack and let cool completely.

5. Prepare the berries by combining them in a medium bowl, then tossing them with the cassis. Set aside.

6. Prepare the custard: Whisk the eggs, sugar, and flour together in a medium bowl. Add the cream in a thin, steady stream, whisking constantly, until well blended and smooth.

7. Assemble the pudding: Preheat the oven to 350°F. Butter a 1½-quart soufflé dish and sprinkle with sugar.

8. Slice the chocolate bread into half-inch-thick slices and lay them out flat on a baking sheet. Toast the bread in the oven for 15 minutes, then turn and toast the other side 10 minutes more. Set aside to cool. Do not turn off the oven.

9. Place one-third of the toasted bread slices in the soufflé dish. Top with half the berries; spoon one-third of the custard over the berries. Use half the remaining bread to make a second bread layer. Top with the remaining berries and half the custard. Make a final layer with the remaining bread and top it with the remaining custard.

10. Bake the bread pudding in the oven until the custard has set and the top is lightly browned, 1½ hours. Serve slightly warm or at room temperature.

Makes 6 to 8 servings.

Purple Plum Crunch

A great use for the late August abundance of Italian prune plums, which I find better cooked than eaten out-of-hand. The concept of apple crisp soars to new heights in this recipe.

3 pounds Italian prune plums, pitted and quartered	½ cup chopped walnuts
	1 tablespoon ground cinnamon
1½ cups (packed) brown sugar	Pinch salt
6 tablespoons cassis liqueur	¾ cup (1½ sticks) unsalted butter, cold, cut into small pieces
1 cup unbleached all-purpose flour	1 large egg, lightly beaten
¾ cup old-fashioned rolled oats	Whipped cream or vanilla ice cream, for serving

1. Preheat the oven to 375°F.

2. Combine the plums, ½ cup of the sugar, and the cassis

together in a mixing bowl. Turn into a 12 x 8-inch shallow baking dish.

3. Combine the flour, oats, walnuts, remaining 1 cup sugar, the cinnamon, and salt in another mixing bowl. Cut in the butter with a pastry blender until the mixture resembles coarse meal. Add the egg and mix until moist and crumbly. Sprinkle the topping evenly over the plums.

4. Bake the plum crunch until the plums are bubbling and the top is nicely browned, 40 to 45 minutes. Serve warm or at room temperature with a dollop of whipped cream or a scoop of vanilla ice cream, if desired.

Makes 8 to 10 servings.

Apple Crisp

A dessert that says September and always brings back memories of Mother's home cooking.

14 McIntosh apples
  (about 2½ to 3
  pounds), peeled, cored,
  and cut into ½-inch
  slices
⅓ cup granulated sugar
1 tablespoon ground
  cinnamon

½ teaspoon grated
  nutmeg
2 tablespoons fresh lemon
  juice
3 tablespoons Calvados

TOPPING:
¾ cup (1½ sticks)
  unsalted margarine
2 cups unbleached
  all-purpose flour
¾ cup (packed) brown
  sugar
1 cup old-fashioned rolled
  oats

1 tablespoon ground
  cinnamon
Pinch salt
¾ cup coarsely chopped
  skinned, toasted
  hazelnuts
1 large egg, lightly beaten

Vanilla ice cream (optional)

1. Preheat the oven to 350°F.

2. Combine the apples, sugar, cinnamon, nutmeg, lemon juice, and Calvados in a large mixing bowl. Let stand at room temperature.

3. Prepare the topping: Place the margarine, flour, brown sugar, oats, cinnamon, and salt in another mixing bowl and mix with your hands until crumbly. Add the hazelnuts and egg and mix just until evenly moistened.

4. Spoon the apple mixture into a 15 x 10-inch baking dish. Crumble the topping evenly over the apples. Bake until the topping is golden brown and the apples are bubbling and tender, about 45 minutes. Serve warm or at room temperature with vanilla ice cream, if desired.

Makes 8 to 10 servings.

Cottage
Comforts

The notion of retreating to a cottage far away from the pressures of routine workaday life always conjures up an uninhibited hunger for those types of food which I consider supremely comforting. I dream of leisurely breakfasts filled with the wafting aromas of childhood delights such as crispy bacon and flapjacks, golden yellow farm eggs, bowls of wild berries, and rustic baskets of homey baked goods. The concepts of dietary discipline, meal schedules, and daily vitamin quotas cease to exist as a nostalgic lure to cuddling the self with soothing treats creeps in.

The tattered but cozy wicker chair that always catches the first rays of morning sun begs for a basket of warm, berry-speckled muffins alongside. The crunch of a buttery croissant harmonizes beautifully with the distant drone of the crashing surf. An energizing bowl of homemade granola provides just the boost to make the mid-morning tennis match seem effortless. Indulging in a sly little cornstick or two in the laze of the afternoon reveals such simple access to the complicated concept of contentment. Sinking into the soft interior of freshly baked bread is as pacifying as a shady siesta in the hammock.

While there are few guidelines to happy cottage life, comfort should always be primary and I can conceive of no better culinary metaphor than these heart-warming recipes.

Sterling's Croissants

Sterling and I first met when I was just about to become the proprietress of Que Sera Sarah. A gifted art student, she more or less came with my building as bohemian-artist-in-residence.

Sterling the artist filled her tableaus with bowls of cobalt blue mussel shells, wedges of pink cake, and platters of pompano, while Sterling the baker created ethereal croissants. Both mediums have gained her a most appreciative Nantucket following. The croissants are the best I have ever tasted either in France or this country. In order to prepare them, you will need a large butcher block or marble surface.

5 cups unbleached all-purpose flour	3 cups water
2 cups instant nonfat dried milk	2 cups cake flour
1 cup sugar	1 cup pastry flour (see Note)
2 packages (¼ ounce each) active dry yeast	2 cups (4 sticks) unsalted butter, cold
1 teaspoon salt	Favorite Croissant Filling (recipes follow)

EGG WASH
2 large eggs   2 tablespoons water

1. Combine 4 cups of the all-purpose flour, the dried milk, sugar, yeast, and salt in a large mixing bowl or the bowl of a heavy-duty mixer. With a wooden spoon or the dough-hook attachment, mix until well combined. Add the water and mix quickly, scraping down the bowl with a rubber spatula, just until combined. Add the remaining 1 cup of all-purpose flour, the cake and pastry flours, and mix again just until combined. Turn the dough out onto a flat baking sheet (it will be rather wet and sticky), cover with plastic wrap, and refrigerate for 6 to 8 hours.

2. Scrape the dough off the tray onto a large clean butcher block or marble rolling surface that has been dusted lightly with flour. Pat the dough gently into a 15 x 10-inch rectangle and flatten it slightly with a rolling pin. Slice the butter as quickly and thinly as possible and lay it evenly all over the dough.

3. Roll out the butter-covered dough until the butter is blended in. Dust lightly with flour as needed to prevent sticking. You will have a rectangle, about 2 to 3 times its original size.

4. Fold the dough over itself in thirds, just as you would a business letter. With an open end facing you, roll out the dough again. This is the first turn. Fold the dough again into thirds and turn it clockwise one-quarter turn. Roll out the dough. This is the second turn. Repeat this process two more times for 4 turns altogether. (This gives the dough the layers needed to make light pastry.) When the dough has been rolled out for the fourth time, shape the croissants. (If you do not wish to bake the full amount, divide the dough in half, fold one half into thirds, wrap it tightly in plastic wrap, and freeze for up to 2 months. When ready to use, thaw and continue with the recipe.)

5. Roll out the dough into a very large rectangle ¼ inch thick. Cut the dough into triangles about 7 x 7 x 5½ inches. Fill as desired (see the recipes that follow for amounts) or leave plain. Roll up each triangle beginning with the smaller edge. Place them 2 to 3 inches apart on baking sheets lined with parchment paper.

6. Beat the eggs and water together in a small bowl. Brush the croissants lightly with egg wash and cover with a lightly dampened cloth. Let rise in a warm spot until doubled in bulk and springy to the touch, 45 minutes.

7. Preheat the oven to 400°F.

8. Brush the croissants once more with egg wash and bake until light golden brown all over, 20 minutes. Cool for 5 minutes and serve warm or at room temperature.

Makes 25 to 30 croissants.

Note: Three cups of a cake and pastry flour blend may be substituted for the individual ingredients listed here.

Favorite Croissant Fillings

CREAM CHEESE AND POPPY SEED:

8 ounces cream cheese	3 tablespoons poppy seeds
⅓ cup confectioners' sugar	

Place cream cheese and confectioners' sugar in a food processor fitted with the steel blade. Process together until smooth, scraping down the sides of the workbowl with a spatula as necessary. Add the poppy seeds and process until thoroughly incorporated. Spread a generous 1 tablespoon across the wider edge of each croissant before rolling it up.

ORANGE ALMOND:

8 ounces almond paste

3 tablespoons unsalted
butter, softened

Finely grated zest of
1 orange

Sliced almonds, optional,
for garnish

Beat together the almond paste and butter with a hand mixer until well blended. Add the orange zest and beat to incorporate. Spread the filling in a thin snake-like line across the wider edge of each croissant before rolling it up. Top each formed croissant with a scattering of sliced almonds, if desired.

HAM AND HONEY MUSTARD:

¼ pound prosciutto or
Wesphalian ham,
thinly sliced

½ cup honey mustard

Spread a generous coating of mustard over the surface of each croissant to within ¼ inch of the edges. Top with 1 slice of ham, then roll it up.

Bran Muffins

Everyone loves a good moist bran muffin. I have friends who have spent years searching for the best bran muffin recipe. This recipe may not be the best in the whole world, but it comes fairly close.

1 cup (2 sticks) unsalted
butter, at room
temperature

1 cup (packed) brown
sugar

½ cup honey

3 large eggs

2½ cups unbleached
all-purpose flour

1 heaping tablespoon
baking soda

1 teaspoon ground
cinnamon

½ teaspoon salt

2½ cups unsweetened
bran cereal

2½ cups buttermilk

8 ounces chopped dates

½ cup coarsely chopped
walnuts (optional)

1. Preheat the oven to 375°F. Place paper liners in 24 muffin cups.

2. Cream the butter and sugar in a large mixing bowl until well blended. Add the honey and beat until smooth. Add the eggs, one at a time, beating well after each addition.

3. Sift the flour, baking soda, cinnamon, and salt into another bowl. Add the bran and toss to combine. Add the flour mixture alternately with the buttermilk to the batter, gently beating after each addition just until mixed. Stir in the dates and walnuts, if using.

4. Spoon the batter into the cups, filling each cup almost to the top. Bake until puffed and lightly crusted, about 25 minutes. Serve warm or at room temperature with butter.

Makes 24 muffins.

Cranberry Harvest Muffins

A rich, dense, and fruity muffin that is a nourishing little boost on frosty mornings and elegant enough for special holiday entertaining.

3 cups unbleached all-purpose flour	1 cup (2 sticks) unsalted butter, melted
1 tablespoon baking powder	1½ cups coarsely chopped fresh cranberries
½ teaspoon baking soda	½ cup diced Calimyrna figs
½ teaspoon salt	
1 tablespoon ground cinnamon	¾ cup coarsely chopped, toasted and skinned hazelnuts
2 teaspoons ground ginger	¾ cup (packed) brown sugar
1¼ cups milk	
2 large eggs	¾ cup granulated sugar

1. Preheat the oven to 375°F. Place paper liners in 20 muffins cups.

2. Sift the flour, baking powder, baking soda, salt, cinnamon, and ginger together in a large mixing bowl. Make a well in the

center of the mixture and add the milk, eggs, and melted butter. Stir quickly just to combine. Add the cranberries, figs, hazelnuts, and both sugars and stir just to distribute the fruits, nuts, and sugar evenly throughout the batter.

3. Spoon the batter into the cups, filling each cup almost to the top. Bake until puffed and golden brown, 20 to 25 minutes.

Makes 20 muffins.

BREAKFAST AMIDST PALE PEONIES

Pink Bellinis
Unbeatable Scrambled Eggs
Avocado on Toast
Sliced Smoked Salmon
Tri-Berry Muffins

Iced Espresso

Tri-Berry Muffins

The secret to these muffins was discovered far too early one morning after a wild night on the town. Sterling and I had drowsily mixed a big bowl of the batter and then realized—in the nick of time—that we had forgotten to add the sugar. We decided that the only viable solution was to stir in the sugar as quickly as possible and hope for the best. Once the muffins were baked we were thrilled to discover that our serendipitous technique produced muffins with an irresistibly crunchy and crackled top. Now the catch is remembering to add the sugar last.

All of one berry or fruit can be used in these muffins, but the tri-berry combination is a favorite.

3½ cups unbleached
  all-purpose flour
1 tablespoon baking
  powder
½ teaspoon baking soda
½ teaspoon salt
4½ teaspoons ground
  cinnamon
1¼ cups milk

2 large eggs
1 cup (2 sticks) unsalted
  butter or unsalted
  margarine, melted
1 cup blueberries
1 cup diced strawberries
1 cup raspberries
1½ cups sugar

1. Preheat the oven to 375°F. Place paper liners in 20 muffin cups.

2. Stir the flour, baking powder, baking soda, salt, and cinnamon together in a large bowl. Make a well in the center of the flour mixture. Add the milk, eggs, and butter to the well and stir quickly just to combine. Add the berries and sugar and stir quickly again just to combine.

3. Spoon the batter into the cups, filling each cup almost to the top. Bake until brown and crusty, about 20 minutes.

Makes 20 muffins.

Pumpkin Muffins with Crystallized Ginger

A moist and dense, autumn-hued muffin that delights the ever-increasing contingent of ginger lovers. This recipe makes quite a few muffins, but they do freeze well.

1 can (15 ounces)
  unsweetened pumpkin
  purée
2 cups (packed) brown
  sugar
1 cup (2 sticks) unsalted
  margarine, melted
4 large eggs
½ cup apple cider
3½ cups unbleached
  all-purpose flour
2 teaspoons baking soda

2 teaspoons baking
  powder
1 teaspoon salt
4½ teaspoons ground
  cinnamon
4½ teaspoons ground
  ginger
1 teaspoon grated nutmeg
½ teaspoon ground cloves
1 cup finely chopped
  crystallized ginger

1. Preheat the oven to 350°F. Place paper liners in 28 muffin cups.

2. Stir the pumpkin, sugar, and margarine together in a large mixing bowl. Add the eggs and beat until the mixture is smooth. Stir in the cider.

3. Sift the flour, baking soda, baking powder, salt, cinnamon, ground ginger, nutmeg, and cloves into another bowl. Gradually stir the flour mixture into the pumpkin mixture until thoroughly mixed. Fold in the crystallized ginger until evenly distributed.

4. Spoon the batter into the cups, filling each cup almost to the top. Bake until puffed and golden, 20 to 25 minutes. Serve warm with butter.

Makes 26 to 28 muffins.

Crunchy Cornsticks with Chiles and Cheddar

These cornsticks are filled with flavors Texans adore. However, if you prefer a milder and more traditional cornstick, you can simply omit the chile pepper, chili powder, and cumin. The creamed corn makes these cornsticks extra rich and the grated Cheddar adds a golden crunch.

Melted lard or bacon fat
   for the molds
1 cup yellow cornmeal
1 cup plus 2 tablespoons
   unbleached all-purpose
   flour
2 teaspoons baking
   powder
1 teaspoon baking soda
2 teaspoons cumin
1 teaspoon best-quality
   chili powder
1 teaspoon salt
1 can (17 ounces)
   creamed corn
1 cup buttermilk

4 tablespoons (½ stick)
   unsalted butter, melted
2 large eggs
1¼ cups grated sharp
   Cheddar cheese
1 fresh long red chile,
   seeded and minced, or
   1 can (4 ounces)
   minced green chiles

1. Preheat the oven to 350°F. Lightly coat cornstick molds with the melted lard or bacon fat.

2. Stir the cornmeal, flour, baking powder, baking soda, cumin, chili powder, and salt together in a mixing bowl.

3. Whisk the corn, buttermilk, butter, and eggs together in a large mixing bowl. Add the cornmeal mixture to the corn mixture and stir just until combined. Add the Cheddar and chile and fold just until they are evenly distributed.

4. Spoon the batter into the prepared molds, filling each two-thirds full. Bake until the cornsticks are crusty golden brown, 10 to 12 minutes. Let cool slightly then turn out onto a wire rack to cool completely. If necessary, repeat with the remaining batter, lightly coating the molds with melted fat after each batch.

Makes 28 cornsticks.

Currant and Caraway Scones

A winning combination that is great for nibbling any time of the day.

4½ cups unbleached
   all-purpose flour
2 teaspoons baking
   powder
1 teaspoon baking soda
3 tablespoons sugar
1 cup (2 sticks) unsalted
   butter, cold, cut into
   small pieces

1¼ cups heavy or
   whipping cream
1 cup currants
¼ cup sweet Marsala
1 tablespoon caraway
   seeds
1 large egg
1 tablespoon water

1. Stir the flour, baking powder, baking soda, and sugar together in a large mixing bowl. Cut the butter into the flour mixture with a pastry blender until it resembles coarse meal. Add the cream and mix with your hands until the dough comes together.

2. Place the currants and Marsala in a small pan and heat to boiling. Reduce the heat and simmer for 2 minutes. Remove from the heat and cool 10 minutes. Mix the currants with liquid and the caraway seeds into the dough. Wrap the dough in plastic wrap and refrigerate at least 1 hour.

3. Preheat the oven to 350°F. Line baking sheets with parchment paper.

4. Divide the scone dough in half. Roll out each half ¾ inch thick on a floured surface. Cut into hearts, using a 2- to 3-inch heart-shaped cutter. Place the hearts 1 inch apart on the baking sheets. Mix the egg and water in a small bowl. Brush the egg wash over the top of each scone.

5. Bake the scones until light golden brown, about 15 minutes. Serve warm or at room temperature with whipped butter.

Makes about 36 scones.

Marbled Apricot Bread

The swirl of cream cheese in this moist tea bread adds a special flair. The bread keeps well in the refrigerator and is wonderful to have on hand for houseguests.

1 cup dried apricots, cut
   into thin strips
½ cup golden raisins
4 tablespoons (½ stick)
   unsalted butter, at
   room temperature
½ cup (packed) brown
   sugar
½ cup granulated sugar

1 large egg
2 cups unbleached
   all-purpose flour
2 teaspoons baking
   powder
½ teaspoon baking soda
½ teaspoon salt
¾ cup orange juice
½ cup chopped walnuts

CREAM CHEESE FILLING:
6 ounces cream cheese
⅓ cup granulated sugar
1 large egg

1 tablespoon grated
   orange zest

1. Combine the apricots and raisins in a small bowl. Add boiling water to cover and let stand for 30 minutes. Drain.

2. Preheat the oven to 350°F. Grease a 9 x 5-inch loaf pan and lightly dust with flour.

3. Beat the butter, brown sugar, and granulated sugar in a medium mixing bowl until creamy. Beat in the egg.

4. Sift the flour, baking powder, baking soda, and salt together in a medium bowl. Add the flour mixture alternately with the orange juice to the butter mixture to make a fairly thick batter. Stir in the apricots, raisins, and walnuts.

5. Prepare the filling: Place all the ingredients in a food processor fitted with the steel blade; process until smooth.

6. Pour two-thirds of the batter into the prepared pan. Top with all the filling, then top with the remaining batter. Lightly swirl with a knife.

7. Bake until the bread is golden brown and firm to the touch, 55 to 60 minutes. Let cool in the pan 10 minutes, then turn out onto a wire rack to cool completely. Store, wrapped in foil or plastic wrap, in the refrigerator. Cut into thick slices to serve.

Makes 1 loaf.

Portuguese Beer Bread

Nantucket's Portuguese heritage has encouraged a keen curiosity about Portuguese food. While Portuguese white bread is daily fare, even today, on the island, I particularly like the malty heartiness of this crusty Portuguese beer bread. Enjoy it on a blustery autumn day while gazing at the ocean—perhaps in the direction of Portugal.

2 packages (¼ ounce each) active dry yeast
2 tablespoons dark molasses
2 cups strong beer or imported dark beer, warmed to 105°F to 115°F

1½ cups whole-wheat flour
2 teaspoons salt
¼ cup fruity olive oil
4½ to 5 cups unbleached all-purpose flour

1. Place the yeast and molasses in a large mixing bowl. Add the warm beer and let the mixture stand until doubled in bulk and quite spongy, 10 to 15 minutes.

2. Using a wooden spoon, stir in the whole-wheat flour, salt, and olive oil. Gradually work in the all-purpose flour, 1 cup at a time, to make a stiff but elastic dough. Turn out onto a lightly floured surface and knead the dough until smooth and elastic, 5 to 10 minutes.

3. Lightly coat a large bowl with olive oil. Place the dough in the bowl and turn once to coat with oil. Cover the bowl with plastic wrap. Let rise in a warm place until doubled in bulk, about 1½ hours.

4. Punch the dough down, shape into a ball, and let rise again until doubled in bulk, about 1 hour.

5. Punch the dough down again and turn it out onto a lightly floured work surface. Divide the dough into 6 equal pieces. Roll each part into a rope, 12 to 14 inches long. Braid 3 ropes together and coil the braid into a circle. Repeat with the remaining 3 ropes.

6. Place the braided circles on lightly greased baking sheets and cover with dampened towels. Let rise again until doubled in bulk, about 45 minutes.

7. Meanwhile, preheat the oven to 475°F. When the oven is hot, place a large baking pan of boiling water in the bottom of the oven to create steam while the bread bakes.

8. When the bread has risen, mist it all over with water and place it in the hot oven. Bake, misting the bread 3 times during the first 15 minutes, until the bread is crusty and golden brown, 25 to 30 minutes. Serve warm with a frothy mug of beer and a steaming bowl of Kale Soup (see Index).

Makes 2 braided loaves.

Saffron and Pistachio Bread

Serve this rustic, sunny yellow bread with an assortment of ripened cheeses.

1½ packages (¼ ounce each) active dry yeast	½ cup freshly grated Parmesan cheese
2 teaspoons sugar	¼ cup shelled pistachio nuts
2 teaspoons saffron threads	6 to 6½ cups unbleached all-purpose flour
2½ cups warm water (105°F to 115°F)	1 tablespoon water
	2 tablespoons fruity olive oil
2 teaspoons salt	1 tablespoon coarsely
2 large eggs	chopped fresh rosemary

1. Combine the yeast, sugar, and 1½ teaspoons of the saffron in a large mixing bowl. Pour in the warm water and let stand for 5 minutes.

2. Stir in the salt, 1 egg, the cheese, and pistachios. Stir in the flour, ½ cup at a time, until the dough is somewhat stiff. Turn the dough out onto a floured surface and knead until smooth and elastic, about 10 minutes.

3. Lightly coat a large bowl with olive oil. Place the dough in the bowl and turn once to coat with oil. Cover the bowl with plastic wrap or a dampened towel and let the dough rise in a warm place until doubled in bulk, about 1¼ hours.

4. Punch the dough down and turn out onto a floured surface. Roll the dough into a thick rope, then shape into a large ring with a center opening about 5 inches in diameter. Place the ring on a baking sheet lined with parchment paper. Beat the remaining egg with 1 tablespoon water and brush it all over the top and sides of the bread. Sprinkle the top of the loaf with the remaining ½ teaspoon saffron and the rosemary. Let rise covered in a warm spot for another 30 to 40 minutes.

5. Preheat the oven to 350°F.

6. Bake the bread until light golden brown and it sounds hollow when tapped on the bottom, 50 to 60 minutes. Let the bread cool completely on a wire rack before serving.

Makes 1 large ring (at least 12 servings).

Honey-Herb Rolls

Sterling began making these rolls one summer, and we fell instantly in love with their rustic look and fabulous sweet-and-savory flavor combination. They are tasty rolls for a summer dinner bread basket, and the leftovers make great sandwich beginnings.

7 to 8 cups unbleached all-purpose flour	1 tablespoon salt
1½ packages (¼ ounce each) active dry yeast	1 cup honey
	3 cups warm water (105°F to 115°F)

HERB MIX:

¼ cup olive oil	1 bunch dill, minced
1 large red onion, minced	3 tablespoons fines herbes
3 cloves garlic, minced	
1 bunch parsley, minced	

Egg Wash:
2 large eggs   *2 tablespoons water*

1. Combine 4 cups of the flour, the yeast, and salt in a large mixing bowl. Using a wooden spoon, stir in the honey and warm water until smooth. Gradually stir in the remaining flour to make a soft dough. Knead the dough on a floured surface until smooth and satiny, about 10 minutes. Transfer the dough to a clean bowl. Cover and let rise until doubled in bulk, about 2 hours.

2. Meanwhile, prepare the herb mix: Heat the oil in a small skillet over medium-high heat. Add the onion and garlic and sauté, stirring occasionally, for 10 minutes. Add the parsley, dill, and *fines herbes* and sauté several minutes. Remove from the heat.

3. Punch the dough down and cut into 24 equal pieces. Place a little bit of the herb mixture in the center of each piece of dough and shape into round roll on a lightly floured surface. Make sure the herb mixture is completely enclosed. Place the rolls about 2 inches apart on baking sheets lined with parchment paper. Brush some of the herb mixture over the outside of the rolls. Let the rolls rise covered in a warm spot until doubled in bulk, about 45 minutes.

4. Preheat the oven to 350°F.

5. Mix the eggs with the water in a small bowl. Brush each roll with the egg wash. Bake until the rolls are light golden brown, 15 to 20 minutes. Serve warm or cooled.

Makes 24 three-inch rolls.

Avocado on Toast

When our family used to visit my grandparents in Florida, my grandmother would invite each one of her grandchildren in turn to share in his or her favorite breakfast. My special request was always my grandmother's invention of avocado on toast. To this day, it would still be what I would order if I had the indulgent luxury of savoring breakfast in bed.

1 perfectly ripe large   *Salt and freshly ground*
*   Florida avocado*   *   pepper to taste*
4 slices rye bread, lightly
*   toasted and buttered*

Quarter, pit, and peel the avocado. Place 1 avocado quarter on each slice of rye toast and mash the avocado lightly with a fork. Sprinkle with salt and pepper to taste. Serve at once. (You can further embellish the avocado with crisp, crumbled bacon or a scattering of finely minced smoked salmon.)

Makes 2 servings.

Foggy Morning Flapjacks

Thick fogs and misty mornings are an inevitable part of coastal living. These oversize hearty pancakes provide wonderful consolation during those damp and gloomy spells without sunshine. Top with seasonal fruits or your favorite homemade preserves.

⅔ cup old-fashioned
  rolled oats
1⅓ cups whole-wheat
  flour
⅔ cup unbleached
  all-purpose flour
⅔ cup yellow cornmeal
4 teaspoons baking
  powder
2 teaspoons baking soda

2 teaspoons salt
¾ cup (1½ sticks)
  unsalted butter, cold,
  cut into bits
4 cups buttermilk
4 large eggs
⅓ cup maple syrup
Melted butter for the
  griddle

BRUNCH UNDER THE EIDERDOWN

Foggy Morning Flapjacks
with
Whipped Butter and Beach Plum Jam
Sautéed Sausages

Rich Hot Chocolate

The Sunday New York Times

1. Process the oats in a blender or food processor fitted with the steel blade to a coarse powder. Mix the oats, whole-wheat flour, unbleached flour, cornmeal, baking powder, baking soda, and salt together in a large mixing bowl.

2. Using a pastry blender or your hands, work the butter into the dry ingredients until well blended.

3. Whisk the buttermilk, eggs, and maple syrup together in another bowl. Add to the flour mixture and stir until well blended. Let the batter stand for 5 minutes.

4. Heat a large griddle over medium heat. When hot, brush the surface with some of the melted butter.

5. Drop large spoonfuls of the batter onto the griddle to make pancakes 4 to 5 inches in diameter. When bubbles form on the top and the bottoms are light brown, flip them over and continue to cook until cooked through, about 2 minutes. Serve at once or keep them warm in a 275°F oven until all of the pancakes are cooked. (Leftover batter may be stored in the refrigerator in a covered plastic container for 2 to 3 days or frozen for up to 2 months.)

Makes 8 to 10 servings or about 24 pancakes.

Homemade Granola

When the granola craze first struck in the late sixties, my mother started to make her own, and it was better than any granola that I had ever tasted. I still believe it to be the best. I always have a huge bowl of freshly toasted granola in the store, and it sells well at any time of year. In the summer it is wonderful mixed with plain yogurt and fresh berries. In the chillier months a hearty bowl mixed with milk is a delicious and fortifying start to the day. Don't think that you have to be a "nuts-and-berries" health freak to enjoy this; the blend of ingredients makes this granola truly indulgent.

9 cups old-fashioned
*   rolled oats*
4 cups shredded coconut
1½ cups whole hazelnuts
1½ cups slivered or sliced
*   almonds*

¾ cup honey
1½ cups vegetable oil
1 cup golden raisins
1 cup dark raisins
½ cup chopped dates
*   (optional)*

1. Preheat the oven to 375°F.

2. Toss the oats, coconut, hazelnuts, and almonds together in a 13 x 9-inch baking pan.

3. Whisk the honey and oil together in a small bowl. Pour over the oat mixture and stir with a wooden spoon until all the oats and nuts are coated.

4. Bake, stirring occasionally with the wooden spoon, until the mixture turns a nice even golden brown, 35 to 45 minutes.

5. Remove the granola from the oven and stir constantly to aerate the mixture and keep it from sticking together, until the granola is cool. Stir in the golden and dark raisins and the dates, if using. Other diced fruits, such as apricots, figs, and prunes, can be added or substituted if you want. Store the granola in an airtight glass canister or tightly wrapped earthenware bowl.

Makes about 18 cups.

Savory Potato Pancakes

These crispy golden pancakes with subtle hints of onion and rosemary are delicious country fare when served with Rosy Applesauce and grilled sweet Italian sausage.

6 large boiling potatoes, peeled
2 shallots, minced
2 tablespoons minced fresh rosemary
2 tablespoons unbleached all-purpose flour
1 large egg, lightly beaten
4 tablespoons heavy or whipping cream
Salt and freshly ground pepper to taste
Vegetable oil for frying
Rosy Applesauce (recipe follows)

1. Grate the potatoes with a hand grater or in a food processor fitted with the large shredding disk. Place them in the center of a clean dish cloth and squeeze tightly to extract as much liquid as possible.

2. Place the potatoes in a large mixing bowl and toss with the shallots, rosemary, and flour. With a large spoon beat in the egg, cream, salt and pepper until well blended. Cook this mixture as quickly as possible or the potatoes will begin to discolor.

3. Preheat the oven to 300°F.

4. Brush a large flat skillet all over with a few tablespoons of oil and heat over medium-high heat. Using your hands, form the potato mixture into patties 3 inches in diameter and ½ inch thick.

5. Place as many pancakes as will comfortably fit in the skillet and fry until crusty and golden brown, 3 to 4 minutes per side. Repeat with the remaining batter, adding more oil to the skillet as needed.

6. Keep the pancakes warm in the oven until all are cooked. Serve 2 to 3 pancakes per person accompanied by the applesauce and sausage.

Makes 16 to 18 pancakes.

Rosy Applesauce

Homemade applesauce, especially served warm, is real security food for me. I like to make my applesauce from a blend of freshly picked orchard apples—McIntosh, Macoun, and Jonathan, for example. I also leave the skins on the apples while simmering because I love the rich rosy hue they bring to the finished product.

3 pounds of your favorite
   apples, cored,
   unpeeled, and cut into
   chunks
1½ cups water
3 tablespoons Calvados
   or other brandy

1 tablespoon fresh lemon
   juice
½ cup (packed) brown sugar
1 tablespoon ground
   cinnamon
½ teaspoon grated
   nutmeg

1. Combine the apples, water, Calvados, and lemon juice in a large heavy soup kettle. Bring just to a boil over medium-high heat, then reduce to a simmer. Cook uncovered until the apples are quite soft, about 40 minutes. Stir in the brown sugar, cinnamon, and nutmeg. Remove from heat.

2. Press the mixture through a food mill to purée and remove the skins. Taste for flavor and adjust the sugar and spices if necessary. Serve at once or store covered in the refrigerator until ready to use.

Makes about 2 quarts.

Chicken and Apple Hash with Cider Cream

A fancy and updated version of hash with a woodsy flavor that makes it the perfect dish for an autumn brunch.

4 tablespoons (½ stick)
  unsalted butter
1 large red onion, chopped
½ cup diced (½-inch
  pieces) fennel or celery
2 Granny Smith apples,
  cored, unpeeled, and·
  thinly sliced

4 whole boneless, skinless
  chicken breasts,
  poached just until
  barely cooked (see
  Index)
2 cups cooked wild rice

CIDER CREAM:
4 tablespoons (½ stick)
  unsalted butter
2 tablespoons unbleached
  all-purpose flour
2 cups apple cider
3 tablespoons heavy or
  whipping cream

1 teaspoon ground coriander
½ teaspoon grated nutmeg
Salt and freshly ground
  pepper to taste

1. Preheat the oven to 350°F. Butter a 12 x 9-inch casserole.

2. Melt the butter in a medium skillet over medium-high heat. Add the onion, fennel or celery, and apple slices and sauté, stirring occasionally, for 10 minutes. Remove from the heat and transfer to a medium mixing bowl.

3. Cut the chicken into irregular chunks, about ½ to 1 inch in size. Add them to the mixing bowl. Stir in the wild rice to blend.

4. Prepare the cider cream: Melt the butter in a medium saucepan over medium heat. Whisk in the flour and cook, stirring constantly, for 1 minute. Gradually whisk in the cider ½ cup at a time, whisking until smooth and thickened after each addition. When all of the cider has been added, whisk in the cream. Reduce the heat to low and continue to cook, stirring occasionally, for 10 minutes more. The sauce should be the consistency of a medium béchamel. Season with the coriander, nutmeg, salt and pepper. Remove from the heat.

5. Combine the cider cream with the chicken mixture, blending well. Transfer the mixture to the casserole. Bake just until the

hash is heated throughout, 20 to 25 minutes. Serve at once accompanied by a basket of your favorite breakfast breads.
Makes 8 servings.

Breakfast Scallops

This dish is assembled the night before, so that you can wake up to an indulgent breakfast treat that tastes like a rich seafood quiche without the crust.

Butter for the baking pan
3 cups stale French bread
   cubes
1 pound fresh bay
   scallops
12 large eggs
½ cup heavy or whipping
   cream

2 teaspoons dried
   tarragon
Salt and freshly ground
   pepper to taste
10 ounces Cheddar
   cheese, shredded
2 teaspoons paprika

1. Coat an 11 x 8-inch baking pan with butter. Spread the cubed bread in the pan, then sprinkle the scallops evenly among the bread cubes.

2. Beat the eggs, cream, tarragon, salt, and pepper together in a large bowl and pour over the bread and scallops. Sprinkle the Cheddar over the top, then sprinkle with the paprika. Cover the pan with plastic wrap and refrigerate overnight.

Mistletoe Mornings

Fresh Clemetines
Breakfast Scallops
Avocado on Toast with Crumbled Bacon
Festive Fruit Bread
Raspberry Hearts

Grapefruit Mimosas
Coffee

3. The next morning, preheat the oven to 350°F.

4. Bake the scallop casserole for 30 minutes. Heat the broiler and broil the casserole 6 inches from the heat for 5 minutes. Serve hot.

Makes 6 to 8 servings.

Unbeatable Scrambled Eggs

Late one morning I was sitting in Harry's Bar in Venice. While I knew that in the true spirit of culinary adventure I should have been ordering cuttlefish in its own ink, I really craved the basic comfort of scrambled eggs. Their eggs were absolutely the most memorable I have ever eaten. The following recipe is my attempt to approximate Harry's eggs.

8 large eggs
3 ounces Montrachet
  goat cheese without
  ash, at room
  temperature
Salt and freshly ground
  pepper to taste

6 tablespoons (¾ stick)
  unsalted butter
2 tablespoons snipped
  fresh chives

1. Place a strainer over a medium mixing bowl. Break the eggs into the strainer and push them through, using the back of a wooden spoon. Add the goat cheese and push it through the strainer in the same manner. Whisk the eggs and cheese together and season to taste with salt and pepper.

2. The secret to making ever-so-creamy eggs is to cook them in a double boiler. Melt the butter in the top of a double boiler over simmering water.

3. When the butter is completely melted, add the egg mixture. Cook slowly over the simmering (not boiling) water, stirring constantly, especially around the sides, with a rubber spatula. Cook until the eggs are set as desired, 10 to 15 minutes. Stir in the chives.

4. Spoon the eggs onto 4 warmed plates and serve at once. If yo wish to be a touch more decadent, top each serving with a dollop of crème fraîche and a spoonful of good caviar.

Makes 4 servings.

Thanksgiving
by the Sea

Savoring Thanksgiving on Nantucket is almost like going back in time to the Pilgrims' first Thanksgiving celebration at Plymouth Rock. Faded along with the autumn foliage and crimson moors are the sophisticated flourishes of the summer tourists as the island returns to the somber but cozy gray of its Quaker heritage. The raw, damp chill of the ocean is everywhere—piercing with a reminding shiver of what it must have been like in settlement days and sending the islanders scurrying back to their old sea-captain's houses to snuggle around eighteenth-century fireplaces.

Local scallopers fill the harbor at dawn every day as perfect testimony to Nantucket's ongoing reliance upon the bounty of the sea, while, at the stand on Main Street, salt-misted Brussels sprouts still on the stalk, turnips, kale, and cranberries signal the end of the farm season. A few of the more rugged summer residents return to brave one last family weekend in their unheated cottages and mingle summer memories of easy living with struggles of contracting the local plumber and carpenter to drain the pipes and batten the shutters for winter. Yet, for all those that share in the experience of Thanksgiving on Nantucket, there is an overwhelming sense of appreciation for the island's preservation of the best of Americana and its endowment of natural beauty. Indeed, the Thanksgiving meal is just one small token of all there is to be thankful for on the Atlantic-splashed shores of this special community.

Nantucket Scallop Bisque

This soup fulfills the platonic ideal of a perfect shellfish bisque. It is soothing, rich, and creamy and just a bit extravagant with its plentiful scallops and frail little wisps of saffron.

STOCK:

4 cups water
2 cups dry white wine
1 medium onion, sliced
2 carrots, sliced
2 cloves garlic, crushed
6 black peppercorns

2 sprigs parsley
1 teaspoon best-quality
  curry powder
1 teaspoon dried thyme
1 teaspoon fennel seeds

1¼ pounds fresh bay
  scallops
4 tablespoons (½ stick)
  unsalted butter
¼ cup unbleached
  all-purpose flour
2½ cups milk
½ cup dry white wine

1 cup heavy or whipping
  cream
1 teaspoon saffron
  threads
3 tablespoons Pernod
2 large egg yolks
Salt and freshly ground
  white pepper to taste

1. Place all the stock ingredients in a small stockpot and simmer uncovered for 20 minutes. Strain the stock, pressing the vegetables with the back of a spoon to extract as much liquid as possible. Discard the solids.

2. Return the stock to the pot and heat to a low boil. Add the bay scallops and poach just for 1 minute. Remove the scallops from the stock and reserve the scallops and the stock separately.

3. Melt the butter in a large pot over medium-high heat. Whisk in the flour and cook, stirring constantly, for 1 minute. Gradually add the stock, whisking until perfectly smooth. Whisk in the milk, wine, and ½ cup of the cream. Simmer uncovered, stirring occasionally, for 10 minutes.

4. Stir the saffron and Pernod into the soup. Whisk the remaining ½ cup cream and 2 egg yolks together in a small bowl. Gradually whisk ¾ cup of the hot soup into the egg yolk mixture. Whisk the mixture back into the soup. Be careful not to let the soup come to a boil from this point on, or it will curdle. Season the soup to taste with salt and white pepper. Return the scallops to the soup and heat through. Serve hot in small portions.

Makes 2 quarts.

Broiled Oysters with Cider Sabayon

When celebrating Thanksgiving in a seaside community, I believe one should pay homage to the bounty of the ocean in some form or another. These oysters are a rich and elegant way to begin the Thanksgiving festivities. I suggest serving each guest only one or two by a roaring fire just to tempt the appetite.

1 small white onion, minced

1 tablespoon cider vinegar

¾ cup plus 2 tablespoons apple cider

6 tablespoons (¾ stick) unsalted butter, cut into small pieces

3 tablespoons heavy or whipping cream

Salt and freshly ground pepper to taste

2 large egg yolks

18 fresh oysters on the half-shell

Sliced apples, for garnish

1. First, make the cider sabayon: Place the onion, vinegar, and ¾ cup cider in a small saucepan. Heat to boiling and continue to boil until just 1 tablespoon liquid remains. Whisk in the butter, 1 piece at a time, over the lowest possible heat. (The butter must emulsify the mixture rather than melt into it.) When all the butter has been added, whisk in the cream and season to taste with salt and pepper.

2. Whisk the egg yolks and remaining 2 tablespoons cider together in the top of a double boiler. Set the pan over simmering water and whisk constantly until the mixture is light, frothy, and doubled in volume, 3 to 4 minutes. Gently whisk into the butter mixture.

3. Preheat the broiler and arrange the rack or broiler pan 6 inches from the heat.

4. Place the oysters on a sturdy baking sheet. Spoon about 1½ tablespoons of the cider sabayon over each oyster. Broil the oysters until puffed and lightly browned, 3 to 4 minutes. Serve on small plates, garnished with a few apple slices, with cocktail forks.

Makes 18 oysters.

THE THANKSGIVING MENU

At Que Sera Sarah, we prepare everything for Thanksgiving except the turkey. Roast turkey just doesn't travel well, and the real pleasure of Thanksgiving is filling your own home for an entire day with the aroma of the bird as it cooks. The following is typical of the turkey accessories that the shop offers each year.

THANKSGIVING BY THE SEA

Nantucket Scallop Bisque
Broiled Oysters with Cider Sabayon
Harvest Crudités
Bay Scallop Gougère
Pumpkin Biscuits with Smoked Pheasant
and Beach Plum Jam

Cranberry-Orange Anadama Rolls
Savory Sausage-Apricot Stuffing

Shredded Brussels Sprouts with Prosciutto and Parmesan
Casserole of Sweet Potatoes and Pears
Classic Creamed Onions
Baked Julienne of Potatoes and Celeriac
Glazed Parsnips and Carrots
Whipped Turnips with Bacon and Caraway

Cranberry-Kumquat Relish
Confit of Cranberries, Figs, and Baby Onions

Deep-Dish Cranberry-Cassis Pie
Southern Pecan Pie
Golden Delicious Apple Tart
Pear and Parsnip Pie
Pumpkin Mousse

Harvest Crudités

I t is traditional for many to serve celery sticks, carrot sticks, and olives before the big Thanksgiving feast. This recipe refines that notion with the inclusion of the warm Italian dipping sauce known as bagna cauda—my version is enriched with nutty ground hazelnuts.

HAZELNUT BAGNA CAUDA:

1 cup heavy or whipping cream
2 slices white bread, crusts removed
6 cloves garlic, peeled
8 anchovy fillets, drained
2 teaspoons grated lemon zest

⅔ cup hazelnuts, lightly toasted and skinned
½ cup light olive oil or hazelnut oil
4 tablespoons (½ stick) unsalted butter
1 cup light cream (see Index)

A pleasing assortment of autumn vegetables, cut for crudités, such as baby carrots, blanched Brussels sprouts, thinly sliced purple turnips, parsnip sticks, radicchio leaves, fresh wild mushrooms, and red and yellow bell pepper strips

1. Prepare the bagna cauda: Pour ¼ cup of the heavy cream over the bread in a small bowl. Let stand for 5 minutes, then wring out any excess liquid by squeezing the bread with your hands.

2. Place the bread, garlic, anchovies, lemon zest, and hazelnuts in a food processor fitted with the steel blade; process to a *very* smooth paste. With the machine running, pour the oil in a thin, steady stream through the feed tube; continue to process until well blended.

3. Melt the butter in a medium saucepan over low heat. Gradually whisk in the hazelnut purée. Cook, stirring constantly, over low heat for 5 minutes. Gradually whisk in the remaining ¾ cup heavy cream and the light cream. Be careful not to let the mixture boil or it will curdle. When the mixture is creamy and thick, transfer it to a heatproof serving bowl or chafing dish. Serve warm surrounded by the crudités.

Makes about 2½ cups dipping sauce.

Bay Scallop Gougère

This dramatic appetizer is a happy blending of the classic French gougère and some New England ingenuity.

GOUGERE DOUGH:

½ cup (1 stick) unsalted butter

2 cups milk

2 cups unbleached all-purpose flour

8 large eggs

2 cups Gruyère or Italian Fontina, cut into ¼-inch dice

1 tablespoon grainy mustard

1 teaspoon salt

1 teaspoon freshly ground pepper

FILLING:

4 tablespoons (½ stick) unsalted butter

1½ pounds bay scallops

1 medium red onion, chopped

½ cup tarragon vinegar

1 cup heavy or whipping cream

2 tablespoons Dijon mustard

1 tablespoon grainy mustard

2 tablespoons medium-dry sherry

Salt and freshly ground pepper to taste

1 cup grated Gruyère or Italian Fontina

1. The day before serving, prepare the gougère dough: Heat the butter and milk in a medium saucepan to boiling. Remove from the heat. Add the flour and stir until the mixture is smooth and cleans the side of the pan. Add the eggs, one at a time, beating well after each addition. Stir in the cheese, mustard, salt, and pepper. Cook, stirring constantly, over low heat just until the cheese melts.

2. Butter a 15 x 10-inch baking sheet. Spread the dough over the entire sheet, building up the sides and leaving just a thin layer of dough in the middle. Cover tightly with plastic wrap and refrigerate overnight.

3. The next day, prepare the filling: Melt the butter in a large skillet over medium-high heat. Add the scallops and sauté for just 1 minute. Remove the scallops with a slotted spoon and set aside.

4. Add the onion to the skillet and sauté for 2 minutes. Pour in the vinegar and heat until just 1 tablespoon remains. Pour in the cream, then stir in the mustards and sherry. Season with salt and pepper to taste. Continue to cook until the mixture is quite thick and reduced by about half. Remove from the heat and stir in the scallops.

5. Preheat the oven to 400°F.

6. Remove the gougère dough from the refrigerator. Spread the scallop mixture evenly over the dough. Sprinkle the grated cheese evenly over all. Bake the scallop gougère until puffed and golden brown, 40 to 45 minutes.

7. Let cool several minutes, then cut into bite-size squares and pass with cocktails.

Makes 10 to 12 servings.

Pumpkin Biscuits

W hen I make these biscuits for Thanksgiving, I like to cut them out with a pineapple-shaped cookie cutter. I then split them in half and fill them with a dab of the local Beach Plum Jam (see Index) and slivers of smoked pheasant. Both the jam and the pheasant celebrate Nantucket's native bounty, but feel free to make substitutions. The unadorned biscuits also make a nice addition to the Thanksgiving bread basket.

2½ cups unbleached all-purpose flour	1 can (15 ounces) unsweetened pumpkin purée
1 tablespoon baking powder	2 teaspoons grated orange zest
1 teaspoon salt	2 tablespoons heavy or whipping cream
2½ tablespoons brown sugar	
½ cup (1 stick) unsalted butter, cold, cut into small bits	

1. Preheat the oven to 400°F. Butter baking sheets.

2. Sift the flour, baking powder, salt, and brown sugar into a mixing bowl. Using a pastry blender, cut in the butter until the mixture resembles very coarse meal.

3. Stir in the pumpkin and orange zest to make a soft dough.

4. With floured hands and working on a well-floured surface, pat the biscuit dough ½ inch thick. Cut out using a floured decorative 2-inch cutter. Place the biscuits on the prepared baking sheets. Gather the scraps of dough, pat out ½ inch thick, and cut out as many biscuits as possible.

5. Using a pastry brush, brush the tops of the biscuits lightly with cream. Bake just until lightly browned, about 15 minutes.

Makes about 36 biscuits.

Cranberry-Orange Anadama Rolls

A few delicious liberties have been taken with this favorite old New England recipe. Lush ruby-colored cranberries abound in the bogs of Cape Cod and Nantucket throughout the fall and I can never resist tucking the berries into as many recipes as possible.

1½ cups cranberry juice
½ cup yellow cornmeal, plus additional for sprinkling the rolls
4 tablespoons (½ stick) unsalted butter, at room temperature
⅓ cup plus 2 tablespoons dark molasses
1 teaspoon salt
1 package (¼ ounce) active dry yeast

½ cup warm water
1 cup whole-wheat flour
2½ cups fresh cranberries
Finely chopped zest of 1 orange
4 to 5 cups unbleached all-purpose flour
1 large egg
1 tablespoon water

1. Heat the cranberry juice in a small saucepan to just below boiling and gradually stir in ½ cup cornmeal. Reduce the heat to low and stir the mixture constantly with a wooden spoon until the mixture is as thick and smooth as porridge, 5 to 7 minutes. Remove from the heat.

2. Immediately add the butter and stir until melted. Stir in ⅓ cup molasses and the salt. Let cool to room temperature.

3. Meanwhile, sprinkle the yeast over the warm water in a large bowl and let stand for 10 minutes. Stir in the whole-wheat flour and the cooled cornmeal mixture.

4. Place the cranberries, orange zest, and remaining 2 tablespoons molasses in a food processor fitted with the steel blade; process with on/off pulses just until the cranberries are coarsely chopped. Add the cranberry mixture to the dough and stir until thoroughly mixed.

5. If you have a heavy-duty mixer with a dough hook, place the dough in the mixer bowl and mix in the all-purpose flour. Or you may mix in the all-purpose flour, 1 cup at a time, using a wooden spoon and later your hands when the dough is too stiff to stir. The dough should be soft and pliable. Knead the dough on a lightly floured surface until smooth and elastic, about 10 minutes by hand. Shape the dough into a ball, place it in a buttered bowl, and turn the buttered side up. Cover loosely with plastic wrap and let rise in a warm spot until doubled in bulk, about 1½ hours.

6. Punch the dough down and turn out onto a lightly floured surface. Shape the dough into round rolls, about 3 inches in diameter. Place 2 inches apart on lightly greased baking sheets.

7. Cover the rolls loosely with dampened towels and let rise again until doubled in bulk, 30 to 45 minutes.

8. Preheat the oven to 375°F.

9. Beat the egg and water together and brush over the rolls. Sprinkle the tops lightly with cornmeal. Bake the rolls until golden brown, about 20 minutes. Serve warm with butter.

Makes 20 rolls.

Savory Apricot-Sausage Stuffing

Stuffing is my very favorite part of Thanksgiving. I love to make it and adore eating it even more. I have been known to sneak a little home a few days before Thanksgiving to relish in a dinner composed entirely of baked stuffing and a few flutes of chilled Champagne. You'll find that this recipe makes plenty of delectable stuffing for both a bit of private indulgence and the main event.

3 cups diced dried
  apricots
½ cup amaretto liqueur
1 cup Cognac or brandy
1½ cups (3 sticks)
  unsalted butter
1 very large yellow onion,
  chopped
1 bunch scallions, white
  bulbs and green stalks,
  sliced
6 ribs celery, coarsely
  chopped
1½ pounds Pepperidge
  Farm's herb stuffing
  crumbs

1 pound sweet Italian
  sausage, casings
  removed
12 ounces bulk pork
  sausage
2 cups chestnuts, peeled
  and coarsely chopped
1 ripe pear, cored and
  diced
3 tablespoons chopped
  fresh rosemary or 1
  tablespoon dried
3½ cups chicken stock,
  preferably homemade
Salt and freshly ground
  pepper to taste

1. Soak the apricots in the amaretto and ½ cup of the Cognac for 2 hours.

2. Melt ¾ cup of the butter in a large sauté pan or skillet over medium-high heat. Add the onion, scallions, and celery and cook, stirring occasionally, for 10 minutes. Transfer to a large mixing bowl and toss with the stuffing crumbs.

3. Add the Italian and bulk sausage to the same pan and cook, crumbling the meat with a fork or the back of a large spoon, over medium-high heat until the meat is no longer pink. Add the meat to the stuffing mixture and stir to combine.

4. Add the chestnuts, pear, and rosemary to the stuffing and toss to combine. Stir in the apricots with the liquid.

5. Heat the remaining ¾ cup butter with the chicken stock in a saucepan just until the butter is completely melted. Pour the butter mixture and the remaining ½ cup Cognac over the stuffing mixture. Mix the stuffing well and season to taste with salt and pepper.

6. Store the stuffing in the refrigerator until ready to cook the turkey. Any stuffing that won't fit in the bird can be placed in a buttered casserole and baked at 350°F for 40 minutes.

Makes enough to stuff a 22- to 24-pound turkey.

Shredded Brussels Sprouts with Prosciutto and Parmesan

This is an outrageously rich preparation for Brussels sprouts that can also be served solo as a luncheon entrée.

½ cup (1 stick) unsalted
  butter
6 cloves garlic, minced
4 ounces thinly sliced
  prosciutto, cut into
  thin slivers
2 pounds Brussels
  sprouts, trimmed and
  shredded by cutting
  each into several thin
  slices
3 tablespoons all-purpose
  flour

1½ cups heavy or
  whipping cream
1 cup light cream (see
  Index)
¼ cup sweet Marsala
1 teaspoon grated nutmeg
Salt and freshly ground
  pepper to taste
1½ cups freshly grated
  Parmesan cheese

1. Preheat the oven to 350°F.

2. Melt the butter in a large sauté pan or skillet over medium-high heat. Add the garlic and the prosciutto and cook, tossing with a spoon, for 4 minutes.

3. Add the Brussels sprouts and continue to cook, tossing constantly, for another 4 minutes. Stir in the flour and toss to coat the Brussels sprouts.

4. Gradually stir in the heavy cream, light cream, and Marsala. Reduce the heat and simmer until the Brussels sprouts are just barely tender, about 5 minutes. Add the nutmeg and season to taste with salt and pepper. Stir in 1 cup of the Parmesan and cook just until the cheese is melted. Remove from the heat. (You can prepare the gratin to this point the day before you are serving it and refrigerate covered overnight. Bring the gratin to room temperature before baking.)

5. Transfer the mixture to a shallow 9-inch-square gratin dish. Top with the remaining ½ cup Parmesan. Bake the gratin until bubbly and the top is slightly browned, about 20 minutes. Serve hot.

Makes 10 to 12 servings.

Casserole of Sweet Potatoes and Pears

A successful combination that celebrates autumn in color and flavor.

6 large sweet potatoes, peeled and sliced ½ inch thick	½ cup orange juice
	¾ cup (packed) brown sugar
6 ripe pears, peeled, cored, and cut into 8 wedges each	4 tablespoons (½ stick) unsalted butter
	½ cup golden raisins
⅓ cup pear brandy	Salt to taste

1. Place the sweet potato slices in a pot and add water to cover. Heat to boiling. Reduce the heat and simmer uncovered just until barely tender, 12 to 15 minutes. Drain well.

2. Preheat the oven to 375°F.

3. Arrange the sweet potatoes and pears in alternate layers in a medium-size casserole.

4. Combine the pear brandy, orange juice, brown sugar, butter, and raisins in a small saucepan. Heat over medium heat until the sugar is dissolved and the butter melted. Season with a little salt. Pour the sauce over the sweet potatoes and pears, stirring to distribute evenly.

5. Bake the casserole until lightly browned and bubbly, about 30 minutes. Serve hot.

Makes 10 to 12 servings.

Classic Creamed Onions

Creamed onions are definitely one of the more time-consuming dishes to make at Thanksgiving, but I think the results are well worth the somewhat tearful labor.

3 pounds small white   1 cup dry white wine
  onions, peeled   4 tablespoons (½ stick)
1½ cups water, plus   unsalted butter
  additional if needed

BECHAMEL:
4 tablespoons (½ stick)   1 tablespoon chopped
  unsalted butter   fresh tarragon or
¼ cup unbleached   2 teaspoons dried
  all-purpose flour   Pinch grated nutmeg
1 cup cooking liquid from   Salt and freshly ground
  the onions   pepper to taste
1 cup milk
½ cup heavy or whipping cream

½ cup corn-bread crumbs
3 tablespoons unsalted butter, melted

1. Drop the onions into a large pot of boiling water and blanch for 1 minute. Drain, cool, and slip off the skins.

2. Place the onions in a medium saucepan and add the water, wine, and butter. Heat to boiling. Reduce the heat and simmer uncovered, stirring occasionally, until just barely tender, 15 to 20 minutes. Add more water if needed during cooking. Drain the onions, reserving 1 cup of the cooking liquid.

3. Prepare the béchamel: Melt the butter in a small saucepan over medium heat. Whisk in the flour and cook, stirring constantly, until the mixture turns light golden, about 2 minutes. Gradually whisk in the cooking liquid to make a thick and smooth sauce. Then gradually whisk in the milk and cream to make a smooth sauce. Season with the tarragon, nutmeg, salt, and pepper. Simmer, stirring occasionally, over low heat to allow the flavors to blend, 10 to 15 minutes.

4. Preheat the oven to 350°F.

5. Combine the béchamel and onions and transfer to a buttered gratin dish large enough to hold the onions in a single layer. Mix the corn-bread crumbs with the melted butter and sprinkle evenly over the dish. (You can prepare the creamed onions to this point the day before you are serving them and refrigerate covered overnight. Bring the onions to room temperature before baking.)

6. Bake the onions until the sauce begins to bubble and the onions are heated through, 20 to 25 minutes. Serve hot.

Makes 12 servings.

Baked Julienne of Potatoes and Celeriac

This is one of my favorite vegetable combinations baked into an irresistible looking and tasting gratin. The dish contrasts nicely with the traditional Thanksgiving vegetable purées.

4 large boiling potatoes,
  peeled and cut into
  thin julienne strips
3½ cups julienned
  celeriac, canned or
  fresh
1 medium onion, chopped
3 large eggs
1 cup heavy or whipping
  cream

1 cup milk
5 ounces St. André
  cheese
1 teaspoon celery seeds
Salt and freshly ground
  pepper to taste
4 tablespoons (½ stick)
  unsalted butter, melted

1. Preheat the oven to 375°F.

2. Place the julienned potatoes and celeriac in a clean kitchen towel and squeeze out as much moisture as possible. Toss the potatoes, celeriac and onion together in a mixing bowl.

3. Beat the eggs, cream, milk, and cheese in a small bowl until smooth. Season with the celery seeds, salt, and pepper.

4. Coat the bottom of a large gratin dish with the melted butter. Spread the potato, celeriac, and onion mixture evenly in the dish and pour the egg mixture evenly over all.

5. Bake the gratin until the vegetables are tender and the top is crusty and brown, 55 to 60 minutes. Let cool several minutes, then serve.

Makes 10 to 12 servings.

Glazed Parsnips and Carrots

This simple vegetable preparation exudes the colors and flavors of autumn harvest. I like to make it with a choice friend's native Nantucket honey.

1 pound thin parsnips,
  peeled and cut
  lengthwise in half
12 ounces baby carrots,
  peeled and trimmed
3 tablespoons unsalted
  butter

2 tablespoons fresh orange
  juice
3 tablespoons honey
1 teaspoon best-quality
  curry powder
Salt and freshly ground
  pepper to taste

1. Preheat the oven to 400°F.

2. Cook the parsnips and carrots separately in boiling water to cover just until barely tender, about 8 minutes for the parsnips and 10 to 12 minutes for the carrots. Drain the vegetables well and combine them in a shallow gratin dish.

3. Melt the butter in a small saucepan. Stir in the orange juice, honey, and curry powder. Heat to boiling, then pour the mixture over the parsnips and carrots. Sprinkle with salt and pepper to taste.

4. Bake the vegetables until lightly glazed, 15 to 20 minutes. Serve hot.

Makes 8 to 10 servings.

Whipped Turnips with Bacon and Caraway

Of the many aromas of Thanksgiving, the smell of turnips cooking is my very favorite. My aunt invented this savory turnip combination and has served it at every one of the splendid Thanskgiving dinners I have shared in at her old sea-captain's house on Nantucket.

4 pounds yellow turnips
  (rutabagas), peeled
  and cut into 2-inch
  chunks
4 tablespoons (½ stick)
  unsalted butter
½ cup sour cream
2 teaspoons caraway seeds

1 teaspoon sugar
Salt and freshly ground
  pepper to taste
8 slices bacon, cooked
  crisp and drained
Paprika

1. Preheat the oven to 350°F. Butter a 13 x 11-inch gratin dish.

2. Place the turnips in a pot and add water to cover. Heat to boiling over high heat. Reduce the heat and simmer until very tender, 25 to 30 minutes. Drain the turnips well and place in a mixing bowl.

3. Beat the turnips with an electric mixer. Add the butter and sour cream and beat until the mixture is fluffy but still retains some texture. Beat in the caraway seeds and sugar, then season to taste with salt and pepper.

4. Transfer the mixture to the prepared dish. Chop the bacon into small pieces and sprinkle over the top of the casserole. Sprinkle lightly with paprika. (The casserole can be stored in the refrigerator at this point. Warm to room temperature before baking.) Bake the casserole until heated through, about 20 minutes. Serve hot.

Makes 10 to 12 servings.

Cranberry-Kumquat Relish

This unusual rendition of Thanksgiving relish keeps in the refrigerator for at least two weeks. Once the turkey has disappeared, the relish makes for a refreshing surprise tucked into sandwiches or served as a condiment with roast pork, lamb, or turkey.

2 packages (12 ounces each) fresh cranberries
1 orange
1 lemon
½ cup granulated sugar
½ cup (packed) brown sugar

10 bottled or fresh kumquats, seeded and diced
⅓ cup pine nuts, lightly toasted
⅓ cup cranberry liqueur

1. Place the cranberries in a food processor fitted with the steel blade; process with on/off pulses just until very coarsely chopped. Be careful not to overprocess the cranberries. Transfer to a mixing bowl.

2. Seed both the lemon and orange and cut into small chunks. Process in the food processor until finely diced. Add to the cranberries. Add both sugars and stir until thoroughly mixed.

3. Return about one-third of the cranberry mixture to the food processor and process until finely minced. Stir into the remaining mixture in the bowl.

4. Stir in the kumquats, pine nuts, and liqueur. Refrigerate the relish several hours to allow the flavors to mellow and blend.

Makes about 2 quarts.

Confit of Cranberries, Figs, and Baby Onions

A delicious and unusual mélange to serve in place of or, better yet, in addition to traditional cranberry relish.

8 ounces dried figs, quartered
1 cup boiling water
5 tablespoons unsalted butter
2 dozen small white onions (about 1 inch in diameter), blanched in boiling water 1 minute, trimmed, and peeled

¼ cup sugar
4 tablespoons balsamic vinegar
2 cups dry white wine
1 package (12 ounces) fresh cranberries

1. Soak the figs in boiling water in a small bowl for 15 minutes.

2. Melt the butter in a heavy saucepan over medium-high heat. Add the onions and stir to coat with butter. Stir in the sugar and 1 tablespoon of the vinegar. Cook, stirring constantly, just until the sugar caramelizes, about 2 minutes.

3. Stir in the remaining 3 tablespoons vinegar, 1 cup of the wine, and the figs with liquid. Heat to boiling. Reduce the heat to low and simmer, stirring occasionally, for 30 minutes. Stir in another ½ cup wine and cook 15 minutes longer.

4. Stir in the cranberries and the remaining ½ cup wine. Simmer, stirring occasionally, for 25 minutes. Let cool to room temperature before serving. The confit can be stored in the refrigerator; let warm to room temperature before serving.

Makes about 1 quart.

Deep-Dish Cranberry-Cassis Pie

The affinity of flavors in this pie makes it a most fitting conclusion to a day of Thanksgiving delights.

CRUST:
2½ cups unbleached
   all-purpose flour
5 tablespoons (packed)
   brown sugar
1 tablespoon ground
   ginger
Pinch salt
6 tablespoons (¾ stick)
   unsalted butter, cold,
   cut into small pieces

6 tablespoons unsalted
   margarine, cold, cut
   into small pieces
4 to 5 tablespoons apple
   cider, cold

FILLING:
8 cups fresh cranberries
Grated zest of 2 oranges
1 cup cassis liqueur
½ cup Grand Marnier
1¾ cups granulated
   sugar

⅓ cup cornstarch
½ cup minced candied
   ginger
1 large egg
1 tablespoon water

1. One day before you plan to serve the pie, make the crust and marinate the filling. For the crust: Place the flour, brown sugar, ginger, salt, butter, and margarine in a food processor fitted with the steel blade; process until the mixture resembles coarse meal. With the machine running, pour the cider through the feed tube and process just until the mixture begins to form a ball. Wrap in plastic wrap and refrigerate overnight.

2. Marinate the filling: Place the cranberries in a large bowl. Add the orange zest, cassis, and Grand Marnier and toss to combine. Cover and let marinate at room temperature overnight.

3. The next day, drain the liquid from the cranberries into a medium saucepan. Stir in the sugar and cornstarch. Heat, stirring constantly, over medium-high heat until thick and translucent. Pour the sauce over the cranberries and stir in the candied ginger.

4. Preheat the oven to 350°F.

5. Divide the dough in half. Roll out one-half into an 11-inch circle on a lightly floured surface. Line a 9-inch pie pan with the

dough; trim and crimp the edges decoratively. Pour the cranberry filling into the pie shell.

6. Roll out the remaining dough ⅛ inch thick. Cut into ½-inch-wide strips and arrange in a lattice pattern on the top of the pie. Trim the edges. Beat the egg and water in a small bowl and brush over the pastry. Place the pan on a baking sheet to catch any drips.

7. Bake the pie until the crust is golden brown and the filling is bubbling, 50 to 60 minutes. Let cool to room temperature before serving.

Makes 8 servings.

Southern Pecan Pie

My family recipe for this traditional American dessert.

Pastry for 9-inch pie shell (see Lemon Chiffon Pie in Index)
½ cup unsalted butter, at room temperature
½ cup sugar
¾ cup light corn syrup
¼ cup honey

3 large eggs, lightly beaten
1 teaspoon vanilla extract
1 cup coarsely chopped pecans
1 cup pecan halves
Whipped cream for serving

1. Line a 9-inch pie plate with the pastry; trim and crimp the edges decoratively. Refrigerate the pie shell while preparing the filling.

2. Preheat the oven to 350°F.

3. Using an electric mixer, cream the butter and sugar in a mixing bowl. Beat in the corn syrup and honey, then beat in the eggs and vanilla. Stir in the pecan pieces.

4. Pour the mixture into the pie shell. Arrange the pecan halves in concentric circles over the filling.

5. Bake the pie until the top is golden brown and firm when lightly pressed in the center, about 55 minutes. Serve accompanied by a bowl of whipped cream.

Makes 8 to 10 servings.

Golden Delicious
Apple Tart

This tart always wins rave reviews. It has the look of the most exquisite of French pastries and the homey flavor of old-fashioned American pie. I like to serve it for dessert after the sumptuous Thanksgiving repast because it is lighter than most traditional desserts.

CRUST:
6 tablespoons (¾ stick)
   unsalted butter, cold,
   cut into small pieces
1 cup unbleached
   all-purpose flour

2 tablespoons sugar
2 tablespoons (or as
   needed) cold water

FILLING:
5 Golden Delicious
   apples
5 tablespoons sugar
4 tablespoons (½ stick)
   unsalted butter

Pinch ground cinnamon
1½ tablespoons Calvados

GLAZE:
3 tablespoons apricot jam   1 tablespoon water

1. Prepare the crust: Place the butter, flour, and sugar in a food processor fitted with the steel blade; process just until the mixture resembles coarse meal. With the machine running, pour enough cold water through the feed tube to form a dough. Wrap in plastic wrap and refrigerate at least 1 hour.

2. Roll out the dough into a 10½-inch circle on a lightly floured surface. Line a 9-inch tart pan with a removable bottom with the dough; trim and crimp the edges decoratively. Place the tart pan in the freezer while making the filling.

3. Prepare the filling: Peel the apples, then cut them in half from top to bottom. Core the apple halves. Place 1 half flat on a cutting board and cut into thin slices without separating the slices. Maintain the shape of the apple half as best you can. Repeat with the remaining apples.

4. Preheat the oven to 375°F.

5. Remove the tart shell from the freezer and arrange the apples inside by fanning each half from the outer edge of the shell toward the center. Fill any gaps with extra apple slices. The tart should look like one big flower blossom.

6. Sprinkle the sugar evenly over the apple slices and dot with the butter. Sprinkle with cinnamon and the Calvados.

7. Bake the tart until light golden brown, about 45 minutes.

8. While the tart is baking, heat the apricot jam and the water in a small pan until the jam is melted. Brush the glaze evenly over the baked warm apple tart. Serve the tart warm or at room temperature.

Makes 6 to 8 servings.

Pear and Parsnip Pie

I prefer the delicate flavor of this custardy pie to the more traditional pumpkin pie.

Pastry for 9-inch pie shell
   (see Lemon Chiffon Pie
   in Index)
5 cups sliced peeled
   parsnips
2 tablespoons unsalted
   butter
2 ripe large Anjou pears,
   peeled and diced
3 tablespoons Calvados
4 large eggs
½ cup honey
½ cup (packed) brown
   sugar

⅔ cup heavy or whipping
   cream
1 tablespoon ground
   ginger
2 teaspoons ground
   cinnamon
½ teaspoon grated
   nutmeg
Whipped cream flavored
   with several
   tablespoons Poire
   Williams or other pear
   brandy (optional)

1. Line a 9-inch pie plate with the pastry; trim and crimp the edges decoratively. Refrigerate the pie shell while preparing the filling.

2. Place the parsnips in a medium saucepan and add water to

cover. Cook uncovered over medium heat until very tender, about 20 minutes. Drain.

3. While the parsnips are cooking, melt the butter in a skillet over medium-high heat. Add the pears and sauté for several minutes. Stir in 2 tablespoons of the Calvados and simmer the pears, stirring occasionally, until they are quite soft, 12 to 15 minutes.

4. Preheat the oven to 375°F.

5. Place the parsnips and pears in a food processor fitted with the steel blade; process until very smooth. Let cool to room temperature.

6. Beat the eggs, honey, sugar, and cream together in a mixing bowl. Add the cooled parsnip purée and whisk until well blended. Whisk in the ginger, cinnamon, and nutmeg. Pour the filling into the pie shell.

7. Bake the pie until the top is golden and the center is set, 50 to 60 minutes. Serve at room temperature with flavored whipped cream, if desired.

Makes 6 to 8 servings.

Pumpkin Mousse

Since I have never been a fan of pumpkin pie, I prefer to fill my Thanksgiving pumpkin quota with this lighter and more glamorous mousse.

1 envelope unflavored
  gelatin
¼ cup amber-colored rum
4 large eggs
⅔ cup sugar
1 cup canned
  unsweetened pumpkin
  purée
2 teaspoons ground
  cinnamon
2 teaspoons ground
  ginger

½ teaspoon grated
  nutmeg
½ teaspoon ground cloves
2 teaspoons grated orange
  zest
1 cup heavy or whipping
  cream, cold
Toasted slivered almonds
  and whipped cream
  (optional)

1. Sprinkle the gelatin over the rum in a heatproof small bowl. Place the bowl in a pan and pour in simmering water to come half-way up the side of the bowl. Stir to dissolve the gelatin. Remove from the heat and let cool to room temperature.

2. Beat the eggs in a large mixing bowl until thick. Gradually beat in the sugar and continue beating until the mixture is very light and lemon colored, about 5 minutes. Stir in the pumpkin, spices, and orange zest thoroughly, then stir in the cooled gelatin.

3. Using clean beaters, whip the cream in another mixing bowl until stiff. Gently fold the cream into the pumpkin mixture. Spoon the mousse into individual glasses and refrigerate at least 3 hours before serving. Garnish with toasted almonds and dollop of whipped cream, if desired.

Makes 8 servings.

A
Christmas
Stroll

December on Nantucket brings a flurry of holiday activity and the denouement of the island's prolific entertaining season. While there is one last inundation of tourists arranged by the Chamber of Commerce and known as Nantucket's Christmas Stroll, those who truly love the island celebrate the season with quieter parties that revolve around the warm and welcoming hospitality of an open house.

The treasured historic demeanor of the town takes on a special glow with doorways and window sashes garlanded in a mix of evergreen and island-inspired decorations. As the first snowflakes mingle with the froth of the winter waves at the ocean's edge, Christmas shopping among locals tends to mellow into a pleasant gathering with neighbors and friends. Those who have lingered long enough to flirt with a winter's hibernation on the island develop a natural sense of camaraderie that is also evident in the relaxed style of entertaining.

The recipes that make up this final chapter are an assortment of end-of-the-season inspirations and traditional family recipes. They are foods that are at once festive and flexible—one last splurge of savories and sugarplums before the quiet, cozy, and contemplative months commence with a long-awaited island lullaby.

Lobster Fritters with Rouille

The extravagance of these puffy little fritters is well suited to the festive glitter of holiday entertaining. The lobster-colored rouille—a spicy provençal sauce of roasted red peppers, garlic, and olive oil—adds just the right splash of contrast to the cheese and seafood-rich flavor of the fritters.

ROUILLE:

½ cup fresh bread crumbs
1 large egg yolk
4 cloves garlic, minced
1 roasted red pepper (see Index), seeded and chopped
2 tablespoons fresh lemon juice
½ teaspoon hot red pepper flakes, or to taste
1 cup fruity olive oil
Salt to taste

4 large boiling potatoes, peeled
6 tablespoons (¾ stick) unsalted butter
1 bunch scallions, white bulbs and green stalks, minced
2 cloves garlic, minced
3 large eggs yolks
3 tablespoons heavy or whipping cream
1¼ pounds fresh cooked lobster meat, finely diced
2 cups shredded sharp white Cheddar cheese
3 tablespoons chopped fresh parsley
1 tablespoon crumbled dried tarragon
Salt and freshly ground pepper to taste
½ cup unbleached all-purpose flour
2 large eggs, beaten
3 cups fresh bread crumbs
Vegetable oil for frying
Fresh parsley sprigs and lime slices, for garnish

1. Prepare the rouille: Place the bread crumbs, egg yolk, garlic, roasted pepper, lemon juice, and red pepper flakes in a food processor fitted with the steel blade. Process until smooth. With the machine running, pour in the olive oil in a thin, steady stream through the feed tube. Process until thick. Season to taste with salt. Refrigerate the rouille until ready to use.

2. Place the potatoes in a medium saucepan, add water to cover, and boil until tender, 20 to 25 minutes.

3. Melt 2 tablespoons of the butter in a small skillet, add the scallions and garlic, and sauté over medium high heat, stirring constantly, for 5 minutes.

4. Drain the potatoes and place in a large bowl. Add the remaining 4 tablespoons butter, the scallion mixture, egg yolks, and heavy cream and mash together with a hand mixer.

5. Add the lobster, cheese, parsley, and tarragon to the mashed potatoes and stir to combine. Season to taste with salt and pepper.

6. Form the mixture into small patties. Dip each patty first in flour, then in beaten egg, and finally in the bread crumbs to coat. (The fritters may be made in advance to this point and stored in a single layer in the refrigerator.)

7. Heat oil in a deep-fat fryer to 375°F or, pour oil to ½ inch depth in a large skillet and heat over medium-high heat. Fry the fritters in batches until golden brown all over and drain on paper towels. Keep warm in a low oven while cooking the rest.

8. Top each fritter with a dollop of the rouille and a small sprig of parsley. Arrange on a serving platter garnished with lime slices and serve at once.

Makes 4 dozen fritters.

Oysters with Bacon and Balsamic Beurre Blanc

While balsamic vinegar may be the greatest food discovery of the past decade, the affinity that the vinegar has with oysters has got to be the second greatest discovery. Just the aroma of this oyster preparation makes me swoon.

½ cup balsamic vinegar
⅓ cup dry red wine
2 shallots, minced
1¼ cups (2½ sticks) unsalted butter, cold, cut into tablespoons
Salt and freshly ground pepper to taste

36 fresh oysters, on the half-shell
¾ pound bacon, partially cooked, but browned
Parsley and lemon wedges, for garnish

1. Combine ¼ cup of the vinegar, the red wine, and the shallots in a small, non-aluminum skillet. Reduce over medium heat until only 2 tablespoons of liquid remain. Whisk in the butter, tablespoon by tablespoon, over very low heat so it blends rather than melts into the vinegar mixture. When all the butter has been incorporated, remove the skillet from the heat and season to taste with salt and pepper.

2. Preheat the broiler.

3. Spoon a scant 2 teaspoons of the balsamic beurre blanc on top of each oyster. Top with a strip of bacon cut 1½ to 2 inches long. Place the oysters on a baking sheet. Drizzle the remaining ¼ cup of vinegar over the oysters.

4. Place the oysters 6 inches from the heat and broil for 2 minutes. Raise the broiler tray 2 inches and cook just until the bacon is well crisped, about 30 seconds more. Spoon any juices that have accumulated on the baking sheet over the oysters and garnish with parsley sprigs and lemon wedges. Serve at once with cocktail forks.

Makes 3 dozen.

Christmas Sushi Roll

Nantucket bay scallops are at their most plump and best throughout the holiday season. They are so sweet raw that it often seems a shame to cook them.

2 pounds very fresh bay
  scallops
1½ cups fresh lemon juice
2 tablespoons chopped
  fresh ginger
3 unwaxed medium
  cucumbers, as straight
  as possible

1 jar (4 ounces) Japanese
  pickled ginger, cut into
  thin strips
1 cup soy sauce
Wasabi paste (Japanese
  horseradish)

1. Place the bay scallops in a shallow dish and cover with the lemon juice. Stir in the ginger. Cover and let marinate in the refrigerator for 3 hours.

2. Drain the scallops thoroughly. Slice the cucumbers lengthwise as thinly as possible. (A meat slicer is ideal for this task; otherwise a very sharp knife and steady hand are recommended.) Cut each of the strips lengthwise in half, so that you end up with strips about 6 inches long, ½ inch wide, and ⅛ inch thick.

3. Wrap each scallop in a cucumber strip and secure with a toothpick. Place the rolls on serving platters and place a little strip of the pickled ginger on the center of each scallop. Refrigerate until ready to serve.

4. Serve the scallops with a bowl of soy sauce and a mound of wasabi paste on a small plate for dipping.

Makes about 100 rolls.

Phyllo Flowers

These delicious little hors d'oeuvres look like miniature pink poinsettias. The garnish of glistening salmon caviar adds just the right sparkle to the seasonal festivities.

8 ounces Montrachet goat cheese without the ash, at room temperature

8 ounces cream cheese, at room temperature

2 large eggs

½ cup heavy or whipping cream

8 ounces smoked salmon, finely minced

3 tablespoons chopped fresh dill

Salt and freshly ground pepper to taste

8 ounces phyllo dough

Melted unsalted butter, as needed

1 jar (¾ ounce) salmon caviar, for garnish

1. Beat the goat cheese and cream cheese together in a mixing bowl until fluffy. Beat in the eggs, one at a time, beating well after each addition. Stir in the cream until well blended. Stir in the smoked salmon and dill and season with salt and pepper.

2. Lay out the phyllo dough on a clean work surface and cut into 3-inch squares. Keep the phyllo covered with a dampened towel to prevent it from drying out.

3. Preheat the oven to 350°F. Lightly brush 1½-inch miniature muffin cups with butter.

4. Lightly brush 2 phyllo squares with melted butter and lay, overlapping, on a muffin cup. Brush 2 more squares and arrange

overlapping the first 2 squares at a 90° angle. Gently ease the dough into the muffin cup. It should resemble the cup of a flower. Spoon the salmon mixture into the phyllo, filling it to the top. Repeat with the remaining phyllo and filling.

5. Bake the filled phyllo cups until the filling is lightly puffed and the phyllo is golden, about 20 minutes. Let cool slightly and gently remove from the pans. Top each cup with a little spoonful of salmon caviar and serve hot. (These can be baked in advance, removed from the pans, and reheated on a baking sheet for 10 to 15 minutes in a 350°F oven.)

Makes about 72 hors d'oeuvres.

THE ANNUAL HOLIDAY GATHERING

Savory Baby Strudels
Phyllo Flowers
Chile Con Queso Dip
Chicken Honey Drums
Smoked Bluefish Pâté
I'm Dreaming of a White Chicken Salad
Radishes with Sweet Butter and Caviar
Winter Moons
Poppy-seed Sand Dollars
Baby Fruitcakes

Homemade Eggnog and Mixed Drinks

Sausages with Warm Cranberry Cumberland Sauce

Ruby-colored cranberries blend wonderfully with the classic cumberland sauce to make a tart, Christmas-colored condiment for dipping favorite sausages.

2 cups fresh cranberries
¾ cup red currant jelly
½ cup sugar
2 tablespoons fresh lemon
   juice
3 tablespoons port
1 tablespoon Dijon
   mustard
1 shallot, finely minced

Finely grated zest of
   1 lemon
Finely grated zest of
   1 orange
2½ pounds kielbasa or
   sweet Italian sausage,
   cut into bite-size pieces
   and cooked until well
   browned

1. Place the cranberries, currant jelly, and sugar in a small saucepan and simmer over medium heat until the cranberry skins pop and the jelly melts, 15 minutes.

2. Place the cranberry mixture in a blender and add the lemon juice, port, mustard, shallot, and lemon and orange zest; blend until smooth. Transfer the mixture to a small chafing dish to keep warm.

3. Arrange the sausages on a platter and spear with toothpicks, so guests can dip them into the warm cumberland sauce.

Makes 10 to 12 hors d'oeuvre servings; about 2½ cups cumberland sauce.

Radishes with Sweet Butter and Caviar

A miniature Christmas-colored hors d'oeuvre that is crunchy and sophisticated.

48 red radishes
1 cup (2 sticks) unsalted
   butter, at room
   temperature, whipped

1 jar (4 ounces) salmon
   or sturgeon caviar
Fresh dill sprigs

1. Several hours before serving, trim the radish bottoms so they can stand upright. Scoop out some of the top center portion of each radish and cut the top of the shell into a zigzag flower shape. Refrigerate in a bowl of ice water for several hours to crisp.

2. Drain the radishes and pat dry. Spoon the butter into a pastry bag fitted with a star tip and pipe about 1 teaspoon butter into the center of each radish flower. Arrange the radishes on a serving tray.

3. Spoon a little cluster of caviar eggs on top of the butter on each radish flower. Garnish with a tiny sprig of dill and serve.

Makes 48 hors d'oeuvres.

Savory Baby Strudels

These are a unique variation on the rather commonplace phyllo triangle party hors d'oeuvre. Smoky sausage blended with fruity apples, raisins, and crunchy caraway seeds give these the condensed flavor of an Alsatian Choucroute Garni.

4 tablespoons (½ stick) unsalted butter

3 medium leeks (including two-thirds of green tops), rinsed, dried, and minced

3 cloves garlic, minced

½ cup diced hard Italian sausage

2 medium apples, peeled, cored, and cut into ½-inch dice

3 tablespoons golden raisins

3 tablespoons dry white wine

1 tablespoon caraway seeds

6 ounces shredded sage Cheddar cheese (see Note)

Salt and freshly ground pepper to taste

8 ounces phyllo dough

Melted unsalted butter, as needed

1. Make the strudel filling: Melt the butter in a medium skillet over medium-high heat. Add the leeks and garlic and sauté, stirring constantly, for 10 minutes.

2. Stir in the diced sausage, apples, raisins, wine, and caraway seeds. Reduce the heat to medium and simmer, stirring occasionally, for 10 minutes. Remove from the heat and let cool for 15 minutes.

3. Stir in the Cheddar. Season to taste with salt and pepper.

4. Lay out the phyllo dough on a clean work surface and cut crosswise into 2½-inch-wide strips. Keep the dough covered with a dampened towel to prevent it from drying out.

5. Preheat the oven to 350°F. Butter 2 baking sheets.

6. Lightly brush 2 strips with melted butter and place exactly on top of one another. Place a heaping teaspoon of filling at the end of the doubled strip and roll up tightly like a scroll. Repeat with the remaining phyllo and filling. Place the baby strudels, seam-sides down, 1 inch apart on the prepared baking sheets.

7. Brush the tops and sides of the strudels lightly with more butter. Bake until golden brown, 20 to 25 minutes. Let cool slightly and transfer to a serving platter. (The strudels can also be slightly underbaked and refrigerated or frozen until needed. Bake in a 350°F oven until golden brown.)

Makes about 36 baby strudels.

Note: If you can't find sage Cheddar cheese, use regular Cheddar and add ½ teaspoon ground sage

I'm Dreaming of a White Chicken Salad

As yet another example of quintessential blond food, this is a great chicken salad to make during the winter months when the usual fruit and vegetable mix-ins for chicken salad are not at their peak. This makes a sensational holiday hors d'oeuvre when spooned into the hollow of a radicchio leaf or endive spear.

3 pounds boneless, skinless chicken breasts, poached and cooled (see Index)
1 can (8 ounces) water chestnuts, rinsed, drained, and cut into 3 slices each

2½ cups canned or fresh thin celeriac strips
1 can (14 ounces) hearts of palm, drained and sliced ½ inch thick
½ cup sliced almonds, lightly toasted

GINGER MAYONNAISE:
2 large egg yolks
2 teaspoons Dijon mustard
1 tablespoon fresh lemon juice

2½ tablespoons finely minced fresh ginger
2 cups vegetable oil
2 teaspoons ground ginger
Salt to taste

1. Cut the chicken into ¾-inch chunks. Combine the chicken, water chestnuts, celeriac, hearts of palm, and toasted almonds in a large mixing bowl.

2. Prepare the ginger mayonnaise: Process the egg yolks, mustard, lemon juice, and fresh ginger in a food processor fitted with the metal blade. With the motor running, add the oil in a thin, steady stream. Add the ground ginger and salt and continue processing until the mayonnaise is thick and smooth.

3. Add the mayonnaise to the chicken salad and toss to coat. Refrigerate the salad for several hours to allow the flavors to blend.

Makes about 2 quarts.

Chicken Honey Drums

The crunchy pecans, sharp mustard, and sweet honey coating on these chubby little chicken legs make them festive finger food for buffet nibbling.

16 chicken drumsticks
4 tablespoons (½ stick)
   unsalted butter
¼ cup honey
2 tablespoons Dijon
   mustard

½ cup fresh bread crumbs
½ cup pecans, finely
   chopped
Salt and freshly ground
   pepper to taste

1. Preheat the oven to 350°F. Arrange the chicken drumsticks in rows on a baking sheet lined with parchment paper or aluminum foil.

2. Melt the butter in a small saucepan over medium heat. Stir in the honey and the mustard and simmer, stirring occasionally, for 5 minutes. Remove from the heat.

3. Using a pastry brush, brush each drumstick generously and all over with the honey mixture. If there is any remaining, reserve it. Combine the bread crumbs and pecans and sprinkle generously all over the drumsticks.

4. Bake the drumsticks until the meat is tender and the coating is nicely browned, 50 to 60 minutes. Drizzle with the remaining honey mixture. Arrange the drumsticks on a platter and serve warm.

Makes 16 drumsticks.

Que Sera Christmas Torta

I**f** you are a devotee of the incredibly sensuous Italian cheese tortas as I am, you have probably experienced extended periods of deprivation due solely to the inherently capricious nature of Italian cheese makers and shippers. I decided to try making my own after one particularly long spell without a single mouthful of my favorite Peck's Basil Torta. Modesty aside, I thought the result was stunning and the red, white, and green colors are most suited to holiday festivities.

1¼ pounds cream cheese, at room temperature
¾ cup (1½ sticks) unsalted butter, at room temperature
5 ounces Montrachet goat cheese without ash, at room temperature

1 pound sliced Italian Fontina or Provolone
1 cup good-quality pesto
12 sun-dried tomatoes packed in oil, drained
⅓ cup pine nuts, lightly toasted

1. One day before serving, line a 9 x 5-inch loaf pan with a double thickness of slightly dampened cheesecloth.

2. Beat the cream cheese, butter, and goat cheese together in a mixing bowl until very smooth.

3. To assemble the torta, arrange a layer of the sliced cheese on the bottom of the lined loaf pan. Trim the edges of the cheese to fit if necessary. Spread a layer of the cheese mixture evenly on top with a rubber spatula. Top with a thin layer of pesto and top the pesto with another layer of the sliced cheese. Spread a layer of the cheese mixture on top of the sliced cheese. Top with a layer of sun-dried tomatoes and a sprinkling of the pine nuts. Continue to layer the ingredients in the pan, alternating the pesto and sun-dried tomatoes.

4. Cover the top with a layer of lightly dampened cheese-cloth and press the torta gently with the palm of your hand to compress the layers. Refrigerate overnight.

5. When you are ready to serve, remove the cheesecloth from the top and unmold the torta onto a serving platter. Remove the cheesecloth liner. Arrange crackers or sliced fresh French bread around the torta. Garnish the top with a few sprigs of holly leaves, if desired.

Makes 25 to 30 servings.

Chile Con Queso Dip

This warm dipping sauce is a sort of Mexican fondue. The creamy pink color flecked with the red and green of the minced peppers is well suited to Christmastime. I like to offer with it a variety of dippers—nacho chips, sautéed chorizo sausage, corn bread, and an assortment of raw vegetables.

3 tablespoons olive oil
2 bunches scallions, white bulbs and green stalks, minced
3 fresh jalapeño peppers, or to taste, seeded and minced
1 red bell pepper, seeded and minced
1 can (17 ounces) plum tomatoes, drained and chopped

2 cups light cream (see Index)
6 ounces cream cheese
8 ounces Monterey Jack cheese, shredded
8 ounces sharp Cheddar cheese, shredded
2 tablespoons all-purpose flour
1 tablespoon cumin
Salt and freshly ground pepper to taste

1. Heat the oil in a medium saucepan over medium-high heat. Add the scallions, jalapeños, and bell pepper; sauté, stirring frequently, until the vegetables are softened, 5 to 7 minutes.

2. Stir in the tomatoes and simmer 5 minutes. Stir in the cream and heat the mixture just to boiling, then remove from the heat.

3. Break the cream cheese into small pieces and add to the hot cream mixture. Stir until completely melted. Toss the shredded cheeses with the flour and stir into the hot mixture, one handful at a time, until all is completely melted.

4. Return the mixture to low heat and stir until heated through. Season with the cumin, salt, and pepper. Transfer the mixture to a chafing dish and serve warm with a selection of the suggested dippers.

Makes about 1 quart.

Festive Fruit Bread

In my opinion, there should always be some extravagant fruit bread to make the holiday table complete. This recipe yields a generous four loaves, so you may want to tuck extras in holiday gift baskets and share them with friends.

1 cup diced dried apricots
1 cup diced mixed
    candied fruits
1 cup diced dried figs
½ cup golden raisins
¾ cup amaretto liqueur
3 packages (¼ ounce
    each) active dry yeast
½ cup warm water
2 cups milk
1 cup (2 sticks) unsalted
    butter
¾ cup granulated sugar
1 teaspoon saffron
    threads

1 teaspoon almond
    extract
Grated zest of 1 lemon
Grated zest of 1 orange
1 teaspoon salt
9½ to 10 cups
    unbleached all-purpose
    flour
4 large eggs
¾ cup pine nuts
1 tablespoon water
Confectioners' sugar,
    optional, for garnish

1. The night before making the bread, combine the apricots, candied fruit, figs, raisins, and amaretto in a mixing bowl. Let marinate overnight.

2. Sprinkle the yeast over the warm water in a large mixing bowl; let stand 5 to 10 minutes to dissolve. Place the milk, butter, sugar, saffron, almond extract, lemon and orange zests, and salt in a medium saucepan. Heat over low heat, stirring occasionally, just until the butter is melted (this mixture should get no warmer than 115°F).

3. Add the milk mixture to the yeast and stir to blend. Stir in 4 cups of the flour and 3 of the eggs. Beat vigorously with a wooden spoon until smooth. Mix in enough of the remaining flour to make a moderately stiff dough. Turn the dough out onto a floured surface and knead until smooth and satiny, 10 to 15 minutes. Transfer to a buttered very large bowl. Turn the dough so that it is buttered-side up. Cover with a dampened towel and let rise in a warm place until doubled in bulk, about 1½ hours.

4. Stir the pine nuts into the marinated fruit

mixture. Punch the dough down and turn out onto a floured work surface. Very gently knead the marinated fruit and nuts into the dough until all are well distributed in the dough. Return the dough to the buttered bowl. Cover with a dampened towel and let rise again until doubled in bulk, about 1½ hours.

5. Punch the dough down and divide it into 4 equal parts. Roll out each piece into a 18 x 12-inch rectangle and roll up each from a short side into a baguette-shaped loaf. Place the loaves at least 4 inches apart on greased large baking sheets. Cover with dampened towels and let rise once again until doubled in size, about 1 hour.

6. Preheat the oven to 375°F.

7. Beat the remaining egg and 1 tablespoon water together in a small bowl. Brush the tops of the loaves with the egg wash. Bake the bread until golden brown, 40 to 45 minutes. Let cool completely. Sift confectioners' sugar over the tops just before serving, if desired.

Makes 4 long loaves.

Tahitian Vanilla Nuts

With Tahitian vanilla beans a current flavoring rage, these exotic sounding nuts make a fashionable fireside nibble or midnight snack certain to ensure dreamy visions of sugarplums. If you can resist hoarding all the nuts for yourself, they make a welcome Christmas gift for a host or hostess.

¾ pound shelled brazil or macadamia nuts
2 tablespoons vegetable oil
2 tablespoons Cointreau
¼ cup sugar
1 whole vanilla bean (preferably Tahitian), pulverized in a blender or minced as finely as possible by hand

2 teaspoons ground cinnamon
½ teaspoon ground nutmeg
½ teaspoon ground cloves
Salt to taste

1. Preheat the oven to 350°F.

2. Blanch the nuts in boiling water for 1 minute and drain thoroughly.

3. Whisk the oil, Cointreau, and sugar together in a bowl. Add the nuts, stir to coat, and let marinate for 15 minutes.

4. Spread the nuts into a 9-inch-square baking pan and toast in the oven until light golden brown, 25 to 30 minutes.

5. In a clean bowl, mix the vanilla, cinnamon, nutmeg, and cloves together. Toss the hot nuts in the spice mixture to coat well. Sprinkle with salt. Lay the nuts out on a double thickness of paper towels to absorb any excess oil and cool completely. Store in an airtight tin until serving time.

Makes about 2½ cups.

Polish Poppy-Seed Bread

This bread is my personal favorite of the traditional holiday foods my family makes at Christmas.

2 packages (¼ ounce each) active dry yeast	2 teaspoons ground cardamom
5 to 6 cups unbleached all-purpose flour	2 teaspoons grated lemon zest
1½ cups milk	1 teaspoon salt
½ cup (1 stick) unsalted butter	3 large eggs
⅓ cup sugar	1 can (12 ounces) poppy-seed filling

1. Combine the yeast and 2 cups of the flour in a large mixing bowl. Heat the milk, butter, sugar, cardamom, lemon zest, and salt in a saucepan just until warm, stirring to melt the butter. Add the milk mixture and the eggs to the yeast and flour. Beat at low speed 30 seconds, scraping the bowl constantly. Increase the speed to high and beat 3 minutes longer.

2. Stir in enough of the remaining flour by hand, to make a moderately stiff dough. Turn the dough onto a floured surface and knead until smooth and satiny, 5 to 10 minutes. Transfer the dough to a lightly buttered large bowl and turn the buttered-side up. Cover with a dampened towel and let rise in a warm place until doubled in bulk, about 1½ hours.

3. Punch the dough down and divide in half. Let rest 10 minutes. Roll out half the dough into a 24 x 8-inch rectangle on a lightly floured surface. Leaving a 1-inch border on all sides, spread half the poppy-seed filling over the dough. Roll up, starting at one short side; seal the ends and place seam-side down in a butterd 9 x 5 x 3-inch loaf pan. Repeat with the remaining dough. Cover the loaf pans with dampened towels and let rise in a warm place until doubled in bulk, about 45 minutes.

4. Preheat the oven to 350°F.

5. Bake the loaves until nicely browned, 40 to 45 minutes. Cool in the pans for 10 minutes, then turn out onto a wire rack to cool completely. Slice and serve with whipped butter.

Makes 2 loaves.

Baby Fruitcakes

These are the ideal accompaniment to steaming cups of tea or after-dinner snifters of Cognac.

½ cup (1 stick) unsalted
   butter, at room
   temperature
½ cup granulated sugar
2 large eggs
1¼ cups finely diced
   mixed candied fruit

2 tablespoons
   orange-flavored liqueur
1¾ cups unbleached
   all-purpose flour
1 teaspoon baking powder
½ teaspoon ground
   cardamom

GLAZE:
1 cup sifted confectioners'
   sugar
3 tablespoons
   orange-flavored liqueur

1 teaspoon grated orange
   zest
¼ cup sliced almonds,
   toasted, for garnish

1. Preheat the oven to 350°F. Lightly butter 1½-inch miniature muffin cups.

2. Cream the butter and granulated sugar in a mixing bowl until light and fluffy. Beat in the eggs, one at a time, beating well after each addition. Stir in the candied fruit and liqueur.

3. Sift the flour, baking powder, and cardamom together into a medium bowl, then gently stir into the batter until well blended.

4. Fill each cup two-thirds full with batter. Bake until the fruitcakes spring back when pressed lightly in the center, 15 to 20 minutes. Cool slightly, then turn out onto wire racks to cool completely.

5. Prepare the glaze: Stir the confectioners' sugar, liqueur, and orange zest in a small bowl until smooth. Dip the top of each baby fruitcake in the glaze and top with 1 almond slice each. Return to the wire racks to let the glaze set. Store the fruitcakes in airtight containers up to 1 week.

Makes about 40 cakes.

Orange Shortbread

This is the cookie I look forward to most each holiday season.

2 cups (4 sticks) unsalted butter, at room temperature	Pinch salt
	Finely grated zest of 2 oranges
1½ cups (packed) brown sugar	2 large eggs
4 cups unbleached all-purpose flour	2 tablespoons water

1. Cream the butter and brown sugar in a mixing bowl. Gradually beat in the flour and salt to make a fairly stiff dough. Stir in the orange zest. Wrap the dough in plastic wrap and refrigerate at least 2 hours.

2. Preheat the oven to 350°F. Line baking sheets with parchment paper.

3. Roll out the dough ½ inch thick on a lightly floured surface. Cut out the dough with an assortment of 1½- to 2-inch cookie cutters. Place the cookies on the prepared baking sheets.

4. Beat the eggs and water together in a small bowl and brush lightly over the cookies. Bake until light golden brown, 15 to 20 minutes. Let cool on wire racks, then store in airtight containers until ready to serve.

Makes about 60 cookies.

THE FIRE IS SO DELIGHTFUL. . . .

Que Sera Christmas Torta
Tahitian Vanilla Nuts
Oysters with Bacon and Balsamic Beurre Blanc
Lobster Fritters with Rouille
Sausages with Warm Cranberry Cumberland Sauce
Polish Cream Cheese Cookies
Orange Shortbread

Rosé Champagne

Polish Cream Cheese Cookies

One final Christmas recipe from my polish grandmother. The delicate cream cheese crust and tart little mouthful of apricot filling make these cookies an ideal conclusion to a day of feasting.

½ pound cream cheese, cold, cut into small bits
1 cup (2 sticks) unsalted butter, cold, cut into tablespoons
2 cups unbleached all-purpose flour

1 cup dried apricots
3 cups water
¼ cup granulated sugar
1 tablespoon fresh lemon juice
Confectioners' sugar for dusting

1. Prepare the dough at least 3 hours in advance or the day before: Place the cream cheese, butter, and flour in a food processor fitted with the steel blade. Process just until the ingredients begin to form a ball. Wrap the dough in plastic wrap and refrigerate.

2. One hour before you are ready to bake the cookies, place the apricots in a heavy saucepan and cover with the water. Bring to a boil, then lower the heat and simmer uncovered until the

apricots are very tender, about 45 minutes. Add more water as needed to keep the apricots covered. Drain and purée the apricots with the sugar and lemon juice in a food processor until smooth.

3. Preheat the oven to 350°F. Line baking sheets with parchment paper.

4. Roll the cream cheese pastry out to ⅛-inch thickness on a lightly floured surface. With a pastry wheel, cut the dough into 2-inch squares.

5. Place a dab of apricot filling near one corner of each dough square. Fold the dough over to make a triangle and seal the edges together by pressing lightly with the tines of a fork. Place the cookies 1 inch apart on the lined baking sheets.

6. Bake the cookies just until light golden brown, 12 to 15 minutes. Cool on wire racks and store the cookies in an airtight container in the refrigerator. Just before serving, sprinkle each cookie with a light dusting of confectioners' sugar.

Makes about 36 cookies.

Poppy-Seed Sand Dollars

I love creating food around themes; these tasty little cookies are the result of once creating a whole shoreline of Christmas cookies.

8 ounces cream cheese, cold, broken into small pieces
1 cup (2 sticks) unsalted butter, cold, cut into small pieces
½ cup granulated sugar
3 cups unbleached all-purpose flour
1 teaspoon almond extract
1 can (12½ ounces) poppy-seed filling
Confectioners' sugar

1. Place the cream cheese, butter, granulated sugar, flour, and almond extract in a food processor fitted with the steel blade; process just until the dough starts to gather into a ball. Wrap the dough in plastic wrap and refrigerate several hours or overnight.

2. Preheat the oven to 350°F. Line baking sheets with parchment paper.

3. Divide the dough into 4 equal pieces. Roll out one piece at a time ⅛ inch thick on a lightly floured surface. Cut out with a 2-inch-round cookie cutter.

4. Place half the dough circles ½ inch apart on the lined baking sheets. Place 1 teaspoon of the poppy-seed filling in the center of each circle. Top each cookie with another dough circle and press the edges together with your fingers. Cut a small X in the center of each cookie with a sharp knife. Repeat until all the dough and scraps have been used.

5. Bake the cookies just until very slightly browned, about 8 minutes. Cool on wire racks, then dust heavily with sifted confectioners' sugar. Store in airtight containers up to 1 week.

Makes about 80 cookies.

Raspberry Hearts

Luxurious raspberry jam sparkles like Christmas tree ornaments in the center of this linzer-type cookie.

2 cups unbleached
  all-purpose flour
¼ cup (packed) brown
  sugar
¾ cup (1½ sticks)
  unsalted butter, at
  room temperature, cut
  into small pieces
2 large egg yolks
2 hard-cooked egg yolks,
  pressed through fine
  sieve

Finely grated zest of 1
  lemon
2 teaspoons ground
  cinnamon
Pinch salt
8 ounces best-quality
  raspberry jam
2 large eggs
2 tablespoons water

1. Place the flour, sugar, butter, egg yolks, lemon zest, cinnamon, and salt in a mixing bowl. Mix with your hands until the dough holds together and all the ingredients are well blended. Wrap the dough in plastic wrap and refrigerate at least 2 hours.

2. Roll out the dough ¼ inch thick on a lightly floured surface. Using a 2½- to 3-inch heart-shaped cookie cutter, cut out as many hearts as possible. Gather the dough scraps, reroll, and cut out more hearts. Using a smaller heart-shaped cookie cutter, cut out the centers of half the cookies.

3. Preheat the oven to 350°F. Line baking sheets with parchment paper.

4. Spread each whole heart with a thin coating of raspberry jam. Top with a heart frame. Repeat until all the dough has been used. Place the hearts 1 inch apart on the lined baking sheets. Beat the 2 eggs with water in a small bowl and brush lightly over the cookie frames.

5. Bake the cookies just until light golden brown, 12 to 15 minutes. Cool on wire racks and store in the freezer or in an airtight container until ready to serve.

Makes about 24 cookies.

Winter Moons

Crisp and crunchy hazelnut crescent cookies dusted lightly with snowy confectioners' sugar.

1 cup (2 sticks) unsalted butter, at room temperature	1 teaspoon grated lemon zest
1½ cups hazelnuts, lightly toasted, skinned, and finely ground	⅔ cup granulated sugar
	2½ cups unbleached all-purpose flour, sifted
2 teaspoons vanilla extract	Confectioners' sugar

1. Preheat the oven to 325°F.

2. Beat the butter in a large mixing bowl until fluffy. Gradually beat in the hazelnuts, vanilla, and lemon zest. Beat in the granulated sugar.

3. Using a wooden spoon, gradually stir in the flour until all is well blended.

4. Roll out the dough ¼ inch thick on a lightly floured surface. Cut out the dough with a 2½-inch crescent-shaped

cookie cutter. Bake the cookies on ungreased baking sheets until lightly browned, 12 to 15 minutes. Let cool on wire racks.

5. When the cookies are cooled, sift confectioners' sugar over them.

Makes about 48 cookies.

Grapefruit Curd Tarts

Grapefruit is at its peak during the winter months and I love to experiment with its tart and slightly bitter flavor. This curd recipe is a delicious variation on the traditional lemon flavor and it makes a good, light finale to rich holiday feasting. The combination of the sunny yellow grapefruit curd set against the crisp and snowy white meringue tart shells dissipates all of winter's bleakness.

MERINGUE TARTS:

8 large egg whites, at
   room temperature
½ teaspoon cream of
   tartar

1½ cups superfine sugar
1½ tablespoons
   orange-flavored liqueur

GRAPEFRUIT CURD:

1½ cups fresh grapefruit
   juice
8 large egg yolks
1¼ cups granulated
   sugar

½ cup plus 2 tablespoons
   (1¼ sticks) unsalted
   butter, cut into tablespoons
Finely shredded zest of 1
   grapefruit

Pink grapefruit sections or fresh mint sprigs, for garnish

1. Beat the egg whites with an electric mixer in a large bowl until foamy. Add the cream of tartar and continue beating until the whites form soft peaks. Beat in the superfine sugar, tablespoon by tablespoon, until all is added and the mixture holds very stiff peaks.

2. Preheat the oven to 225°F. Line two 15 x 12-inch baking sheets with parchment paper.

3. Spoon the meringue into a pastry bag fitted with a star tip. Pipe onto the lined baking sheets in 3-inch circles that are ½ inch

thick. Place 8 tarts on each baking sheet. Pipe a ring of meringue, 1½ inches high around the edge of each circle to form the side of the tarts.

4. Bake in the oven until the meringues are firm and dry, about 2 hours. Cool, then remove the meringues from the baking sheets with a metal spatula. If not filling the shells immediately, store in an airtight container in a cool, dry spot.

5. While the meringue bakes prepare the grapefruit curd: Place the grapefruit juice in a small saucepan and reduce over high heat to ¾ cup. Cool to room temperature.

6. In a heavy saucepan, beat the egg yolks, sugar, and reduced grapefruit juice together. Place over medium-low heat and whisk constantly until the mixture thickens to custard consistency, 12 to 15 minutes. (Do not allow the mixture to boil or it may curdle.) Remove from the heat and whisk in the butter, 1 tablespoon at a time, until each is melted and the mixture is smooth. Stir in the grapefruit zest and store in the refrigerator until ready to serve.

7. Just before serving, spoon or pipe the grapefruit curd into the center of each meringue tart. Garnish with pink grapefruit sections or mint sprigs.

Makes sixteen 3-inch tarts.

Bûche de Noël

A rich chocolate and coffee version of this traditional French Christmas specialty.

CAKE:

1 cup sifted cake flour	3 large eggs
¼ cup unsweetened cocoa powder	1 cup granulated sugar
	½ cup water
1 teaspoon baking powder	1 teaspoon vanilla extract
¼ teaspoon salt	Confectioners' sugar

COFFEE CREAM FILLING:

1 cup heavy or whipping cream, very cold	½ cup sifted confectioners' sugar
1½ tablespoons instant coffee powder	

CHOCOLATE ICING:

4 tablespoons (½ stick)
  unsalted butter
2 ounces unsweetened
  chocolate
2½ cups sifted
  confectioners' sugar

¼ cup sour cream
2 tablespoons
  coffee-flavored liqueur
¼ cup chopped, shelled
  pistachio nuts

1. Preheat the oven to 375°F. Butter a 15 x 10-inch jelly-roll pan. Line with a piece of waxed paper ½ inch smaller than the pan; butter the paper.

2. Prepare the cake: Sift the cake flour, cocoa, baking powder, and salt together onto a large sheet of waxed paper. Set aside.

3. Beat the eggs in a medium mixing bowl until thick and creamy. Beat in the sugar, 1 tablespoon at a time; continue beating until the mixture is very thick. Stir in the water and vanilla. Using a large rubber spatula, quickly fold in the flour mixture just until thoroughly combined. Pour the batter into the prepared pan and spread evenly. Bake until the cake pulls away from the sides of the pan and springs back when touched lightly in the center, 12 to 15 minutes.

4. Using a sharp knife, trim ¼ inch cake from all sides. Invert the cake onto a clean kitchen towel dusted lightly with confectioners' sugar. Peel off the waxed paper and starting with a short side, roll up the cake in the towel like a jelly roll. Let cool completely on a wire rack.

5. Prepare the coffee cream filling: Beat the cream, coffee, and confectioners' sugar in a cold mixing bowl until quite stiff. Carefully unroll the cake and spread evenly with the filling. Roll up the cake and place on a serving plate. Refrigerate while making the icing.

6. Prepare the icing: Melt the butter and chocolate in the top of a double boiler over simmering water. Cool slightly. Beat the confectioners' sugar, sour cream, and liqueur together in a mixing bowl. Gradually beat in the melted chocolate to make a smooth, spreadable frosting.

7. To finish the *bûche*, cut a diagonal slice, 1½ inches deep, from one end of the cake roll. Place the slice about one-third of the way down the roll to resemble a knot on a log. Spread the top and sides of the cake with the chocolate icing. Using the tines of a fork, draw lines in the icing to resemble the bark on a tree. Sprinkle with the pistachios and sift confectioners' sugar very lightly over the top. Store in the refrigerator until ready to serve.

Makes 8 to 10 servings.

COLD
WEATHER
COOKING

The Long Simmer

"In the writing process, the more a story cooks,
the better."
— Doris Lessing

"My candle burns at both ends;
   It will not last the night;
But ah, my foes, and oh, my friends —
   It gives a lovely light!"
— Edna St. Vincent Millay

I have always been fascinated by the nuances of temperature. When I reflect upon the things that made me feel the most secure as a child, the memory of cozying up against the warm doors of my mother's double-decker oven as the evening's meal simmered comes instantly to mind. This must have instilled within me a first unconscious sense of the special interplay that exists between a sense of nourishment and degrees of temperature.

Years later, when I was to open my Que Sera Sarah food shop on Nantucket, the role of temperature again surfaced, but in a very conscious and different way. The preparations in my shop were specifically created to taste best when served cold or at room temperature. This was a calculated effort on my part to use food as both an expression and a reflection of the carefree coolness of the summer lifestyle on Nantucket. The challenge to chill became so much of a consuming passion for me that over time, both my customers and curious passers-by began to wonder what I did with myself when the days became crisper than my summer soups and salads.

In many ways this book is born out of the summer tourist's queried refrain to every seasonal island shopkeeper: What do you do during the winter on *that* island? After a near decade of exhausting my potpourri of respondent quips such as "I maintain the cutting edge on my chopping knives through my other profession as a neurosurgeon," I've decided to be less evasive and more revealing about the warmth of my autumn-to-spring culinary existence. Besides, now that I've recently come to my senses and left behind life in the public and perishable lane of running a daily food business (I sold my Que Sera Sarah shop in 1989), I find myself growing a little nostalgic for an audience to entertain with a more truthful answer.

For me cold-weather cooking commences neither with the first frost nor the winter solstice, but rather with the late August and early September exodus of summer vacationers from Nantucket. Then sunlight hours are already waning, beach time is becoming less predictable and more precarious, and the nights seem cooler and blacker as they become streaked with the seasonal splurge of silvery shooting stars. The humid days that had been spent mercilessly chopping and dicing ingredients for refrigerator cuisine in order to avoid firing the oven are now happily traded for dewy mornings that begin with the harmonized click of switches for both oven and coffee brewer. When I wrote about summertime in my *Nantucket Open-House Cookbook*, quoting a line from Seneca ("When shall we live if not now?") seemed like a natural. Yet, as soon as Labor Day passes and a September morning dawns with a thermometer reading of sixty degrees or less, I become inspired by a different sort of Seneca-like notion: I think, "When shall I, or anyone for that matter, *cook* if not now?"

Cravings for the bounty of prime farm vegetables are not diminished but rather augmented by the influx of a new crop of heartier, season-end recipes. Sliced beefsteak tomatoes cast off summer's simple vinaigrettes to slip into nourishing garden soups and cheesy pies. Eggplant eases away from its ratatouille companions to spiral solo into a toasty pizza roulade, while the ever-plentiful zucchini finds palatable new life in Italian based risottos and zuppas. Picnics take place on thick blankets in sheltered alcoves of sand dunes, beach-plum heath, and filigreed woodland. Cocktail and dinner parties sustain their warmth as much from assertive foods as from colorful company. Pork loins prefer the oven to the outdoor barbecue and shrimp forgo their glacial cocktail beds for the singe of the au gratin dish. The secret design of nature never ceases to fascinate as summer's last fertile hurrah lingers to launch the initial kickoff to cold-weather cooking with intense and indelible flavors.

As the colors of the landscape turn from summer brights to autumn golds and russets, so too does the produce palette shift to hues of butternut squash, pumpkin, parsnip, rutabaga, and red cabbage. The air takes on the crispness of an orchard apple and the tingle of a tart cranberry. Thoughts turn to Thanksgiving and serious feasting on — not only the turkey — but all the accoutrements from savory dressings, ruby relishes, sweet potatoes, and creamed onions to flaky pies, soothing puddings, and old-fashioned brown betties. It's hard to pay enough culinary homage to such a harvest cornucopia, particularly with the breathless activities of the Christmas season fast approaching.

For many, the December holiday season is associated with the hustle and bustle of shopping, decorating, and well-wishing to friends and family either next door or scattered halfway around the globe. For me silver bells and decked halls fuel my unique brand of "gastro-romanticism" and spur me into a frenzy of flamboyant entertaining. Caviar is my catalyst as the dinner table becomes my oyster as well as my foie gras, lobster, rack of lamb, truffle, and trifle. The choice between wrapping escargots in prosciutto or gifts in fancy yuletide paper becomes a tough one. Champagne toasts flow, mulled libations simmer and spice the home, while Christmas cookies of all flavors and nations adorn coffee tables, gift baskets, and guest room bedsides. The notion of cold-weather cooking as bleak and functional finds no audience in the sugarplum fairyland of my December kitchen.

The whipped-up winds of January nor'easters, however, bring on a whole new shifting of "cuisinary" gears. Herein lies the real meat in the vast spectrum of cold-weather cooking. With the twinkling lights and glittery decorations of the previous month packed away for another year, winter becomes a reality. It is at last time to turn attention to serious tasks, inward inflections, and outdoor combat with the wicked elements of weather. The angst of income-tax preparation and the frostbite of snow shoveling require specific sorts of foods — namely straightforward soups, stews, and casseroles.

The need to nurture is at its peak in January and February when the notion of spending all day slaving over a hot stove seems preferable to most other activities. Cooking takes on the aura of a pleasurable and fulfilling winter project akin to knitting a sweater, studying a Wagnerian opera, reading the collected works of Tolstoy, or viewing a selection of movie classics on the VCR. Low mercury readings and 4 P.M. sunsets signal the best time for baking breads, slow-cooking beef stews to rib-sticking richness, learning how to make a Mexican mole from scratch, or harnessing the patience to stuff squid sacs and cabbage leaves.

For outdoor enthusiasts, winter serves up a paradise of alliterative activities from skiing to sledding, skating, snowshoeing, and snowsculpting. But whether one has a sporting streak or not, I'm convinced that the pristine aftermath of a fresh snowfall energizes the explorer latent in all of us. As the landscape is cleansed, altered, and strangely silenced by iced-over ponds and puddles, snow cover and curvaceous drifts play tricks on normally perceived boundaries, urban and rural alike. The urge to stroll through such a becalmed and enchanted winter wonderland is infectious. Equally infectious is the appetite engendered by all snow-spiked activities. Grilling over an open fireplace and twirling heartily sauced strands of pasta are splendid winter ways of sating hungers invigorated by life in a cold climate.

The downside to winter is that it rarely knows when to give way to the regenerative forces of spring. If only March could truly be counted on to "come in like a lion and go out like a lamb!" I personally feel especially sorry that March is so universally despised since I was born close to the Ides and like to keep my birthday a rosy occasion. So, when the weather lets me down by stubbornly clinging to winter, I lift myself up by escaping into a culinary world of inventive fish dishes and poetic spring feasts. The ability to view spring as a state of mind rather than an actual change of seasons is at the very heart of the Pisces personality, after all. . . .

The sort of cooking that mediates the chill of a blustery, kite-flying, daffodilish day becomes a distant cousin to the dishes that imparted warmth during those first nippy nights back in September. Spring cuisine favors lamb, veal, and chicken over autumn's pork, while warmed vegetables continue to play a vital role — only they are now much more delicate than their sun-drenched counterparts from late summer harvests. Grassy green asparagus bundles, fiddlehead ferns, and crunchy shelled peas reawaken our palates to freshness and pave a delicious finale to the long and varied array of warming foods that sustain the sweep of chilly times.

Although I have written this cookbook from the perspective of my own New England seasons, my general sensitivity to temperature makes me aware that the sensation of cold weather is a relative experience. While I used to be amused by my Southern cousins' donning of woolen coats and calfskin boots in the very type of weather that would encourage me to pack away such winter wear, I now appreciate the insight those actions add to my fascination with when and why we eat the foods we do. Just as a calendar is never a totally predictable guide to the course of the seasons, longitude and latitude don't necessarily define how cold is perceived and reacted to by a given individual.

A final note about my cold-weather recipes is that they are often not as simple as my summer recipes. Dishes from the dark depths of winter, in particular, require extra creative coaxing, and thus time, to bring flavors alive. The cookbook field has grown considerably since I first co-authored the *Silver Palate Good Times Cookbook* in 1984. There are now cookbooks to cover almost any dietary need, predilection, and/or restriction. I continue to write my books for people who look to cooking as a pleasurable pastime, cultural exploration, and artistically fulfilling outlet. Many of my recipes are better suited to entertaining and special occasions than to the pressures and constraints of workaday living. In fact, a vast portion are unabashedly created to leave a glowing impression, so you'll probably want to share them with your nearest and dearest unless, of course, you prefer to beam alone. While the media tells us that nesting and family life are back in vogue, my recipes parallel that trend by leaning toward a highly domestic, hands-on approach to food preparation and serving. If you have become as suspicious of plastic pouched, processed, and fast foods as I have, you'll probably enjoy the sense of returning to a monogamous relationship with your meals — single-handedly taking foods all the way from market to chopping block to oven to table.

Still wondering what I do in the winter? I burn my culinary candle, if not others, at both ends!

Sarah Leah Chase

SO LONG, SUMMER

$\mathbf{T}$he waning of summer's long, steamy days stirs up mixed emotions. The first sign of a day too chilly to go to the beach or sport about unencumbered in sleeveless splendor definitely makes me melancholy. Yet, at the same time, I find myself welcoming the post-Labor-Day nip and zip to the air as it reinvigorates artistic juices parched dangerously dry by the heat and hedonism of a Nantucket summer. As the fall approaches, my inventive fire seems to run a course parallel to the crescendo of color change that sets the September and October landscape ablaze.

As a cook, I no longer want the lazy August ease of dressing a garden-ripe tomato with merely a drizzle of olive oil and smattering of shredded basil leaves. No, September makes me wish to savor the prime harvest of deep red tomatoes with searing, simmering, stewing, and scalloping in warm pies, soups, and side dishes. Since salad making is my foremost culinary passion, the rustle of a crimson leaf underfoot fails to deter me from inventing yet another fresh chicken, potato, or crunchy vegetable blend. I warm up my new creations by intensifying flavors with dried apricots and figs, smoky ham, vibrant roasted peppers, piquant capers, and musty, dark olives.

Nor does the autumnal equinox signal the end of my alfresco picnic afternoons. Rather, it announces tailgate time, when the bikini, bicycle, and beach towel are traded in for a sweater, rusty station wagon, and tattered wool blanket. There are pizza roulades oozing eggplant and goat cheese, cornmeal-crusted empanadas and applesauce cakes begging to be packed into baskets destined for fall foliage outings.

Much to my regret, the one thing that does come to an end with Labor Day on Nantucket is the social smorgasbord of summer friendships. To deflect the sorrows of such partings, I send cherished pals off with memorable farewell feasts that straddle the seasons of both summer and fall. The grilled fish and tangles of angel hair that greeted my island companions in June become, in the span of a few months, crackling roast pork loins and pumpkin-and-prosciutto-layered lasagnes that honor the generosity of rich harvests and camaraderie alike.

Sicilian Eggplant Caponata

— ❖ —

The intrigue of this lusty relish comes from the interplay of oven-roasted vegetables with sweet (raisins and chocolate) and pungent (anchovies, olives, capers, balsamic vinegar) ingredients. Caponata makes a great hors d'oeuvre simply spread on crackers or pita toasts, an extraordinary condiment for beef or lamb burgers, and a toothsome accompaniment to the roasted meats that warm up autumn menus.

½ cup golden raisins
¾ cup dry red wine
2 ounces bittersweet
  chocolate, shaved or
  chopped into bits
3 medium eggplants, peeled
  and cut into ½-inch slices
2 large onions, cut into
  ½-inch slices
½ cup olive oil
1 can (28 ounces) plum
  tomatoes
3 tablespoons drained capers
5 anchovy fillets, minced

1 cup Calamata olives,
  pitted and sliced
1 jar (5½ ounces) pitted
  Spanish olives, drained
  and sliced
1 jalapeño chile, stemmed,
  seeded, and minced, or
  more to taste
¼ cup balsamic vinegar
½ cup shredded fresh basil
  leaves
Salt and freshly ground
  black pepper to taste

1. The day before serving, place the raisins in a small saucepan and cover with the wine. Bring to a simmer over medium heat, add the chocolate, and stir until just melted. Set the mixture aside.

2. Preheat the oven to 400°F.

3. Brush the eggplant and onion slices with the olive oil and place in separate large roasting pans. It is all right if the vegetables overlap a little bit. Roast the vegetables in the oven, turning once, until they are soft and lightly blistered, 25 to 30 minutes. Cool until easy to handle.

4. Meanwhile, drain the juice from the tomatoes into a large mixing bowl. Stir the raisin mixture into the juice. Chop the tomatoes and add along with the capers, anchovies, olives, and jalapeño chile.

5. Chop the roasted eggplant and onion into coarse chunks and add them to the tomato mixture. Finally add the vinegar and basil and season the mixture with salt and pepper. Cover and let the mixture mellow overnight in the refrigerator. Serve at room temperature or slightly warmed. The relish will keep up to 2 weeks in the refrigerator.

Makes 12 cups

Peperonata

— ❖ —

A colorful and intense condiment to have on hand to enrich many end-of-the-summer foods. While this pepper relish is frequently paired with scrambled eggs or grilled fish steaks, I'm most partial to it spooned lavishly into a warm crusty roll with a few thin slices of hard sausage and a glaze of melted mozzarella — my idea of a heavenly sandwich to eat while tucked into a beach dune on a blustery September afternoon.

¼ cup olive oil
1 large onion, sliced into thin crescent slivers
3 cloves garlic, minced
2 red bell peppers, stemmed, seeded, and cut into ½-inch-wide strips
2 yellow bell peppers, stemmed, seeded, and cut into ½-inch-wide strips

1 green bell pepper, stemmed, seeded, and cut into ½-inch-wide strips
2 ripe large tomatoes, seeded and cut into ½-inch-wide wedges
¼ cup slivered fresh basil leaves
Salt and freshly ground black pepper to taste

Heat the olive oil in a large skillet over medium-high heat. Add the onion and garlic and sauté until the onion is a light golden brown, about 10 minutes. Add the pepper strips and sauté 5 minutes more. Add the tomatoes, reduce the heat to medium-low, and cook uncovered until the tomato juices have evaporated, 10 to 15 minutes more. Stir in the basil, salt, and pepper. Remove from the heat and serve either warm or at room temperature. Peperonata will keep in the refrigerator for up to 1 week.

Makes 2½ to 3 cups

Ribollita

— ✤ —

Ribollita, a thick Tuscan porridge of vegetables, is a type of minestrone that is ladled over slices of stale bread and grated Parmesan. When the soup is reheated (ribollita means "reboiled"), the bread disintegrates, making a deliciously hearty soup.

¼ cup plus 2 tablespoons olive oil
1 large onion, minced
3 cloves garlic, minced
4 carrots, peeled and minced
4 ribs celery, minced
1 cup minced fresh parsley
2 teaspoons dried thyme
2 large potatoes, peeled and cut into ½-inch chunks
3 small zucchini, thinly sliced
1 small head green cabbage, shredded
1 can (28 ounces) plum tomatoes, undrained
8 ounces beet greens or Swiss chard, trimmed and coarsely chopped

10 ounces fresh or thawed frozen spinach, coarsely chopped
2½ quarts chicken broth, preferably homemade
2 cups dry red wine
1 cup canned cannellini (white kidney) beans, drained
Salt and freshly ground black pepper to taste
8 slices (each 1 inch thick) stale French or Italian bread
1½ cups freshly grated Parmesan cheese

GARNISHES
½ cup extra virgin olive oil
½ cup freshly grated Parmesan cheese

4 scallions, trimmed and minced

1. The day before serving, heat the olive oil over medium-high heat in a large stockpot. Add the onion, garlic, carrots, celery, parsley, and thyme. Sauté 15 minutes, stirring frequently.

2. Add the potatoes, zucchini, cabbage, tomatoes, beet greens, and spinach; toss to combine with the other vegetables. Stir in the chicken broth and red wine. Simmer the soup uncovered until the vegetables are very tender, 1¼ to 1½ hours. Fifteen minutes before the soup is done, stir in the cannellini beans and season to taste with salt and pepper.

3. Ladle one-third of the soup into a clean stockpot. Cover with 4 slices of the bread and ¾ cup Parmesan. Cover the bread layer with another third of the soup. Make a layer of the remaining bread and ¾ cup Parmesan. Cover with the remaining soup. Refrigerate overnight.

4. About 30 minutes before serving, reheat the soup over medium heat, stirring frequently, until hot. Ladle the soup into large soup bowls and garnish each serving with a drizzle of extra virgin olive oil and a sprinkle of Parmesan and scallions. Serve at once.

Makes 10 to 12 servings

Nantucket Tomato Soup

— ❖ —

I have always been an incredible fan of tomato soup, and there is none better than a batch concocted from the sunny September harvest of local farm tomatoes. So rich and nourishing is the flavor that I become fleetingly convinced that life would be perfect if such a tomato soup could be replicated 365 days a year. Paradise reigns at least one month each year as my rosy stockpot simmers to aromatize both kitchen and soul.

3 tablespoons unsalted
  butter
3 tablespoons olive oil
2 large onions, chopped
3 cloves garlic, minced
3 carrots, peeled and minced
3 ribs celery, minced
12 vine-ripened large beefsteak
  tomatoes, seeded and diced

1 cup dry white wine
4 to 5 cups chicken broth,
  preferably homemade
Salt and freshly ground
  black pepper to taste
¾ cup heavy or whipping
  cream (optional)
½ cup shredded fresh basil
  leaves

1. Heat the butter and oil in a large stockpot over medium-high heat. Add the onions and garlic and cook, stirring occasionally, 5 minutes. Add the carrots and celery and cook uncovered until the vegetables are soft and translucent, 15 minutes more.

2. Add the tomatoes to the pot and toss to combine with the vegetables. Add the white wine and enough chicken broth to make a thick soup consistency. Let simmer uncovered 40 minutes. Season to taste with salt and pepper.

3. Purée half the soup in a blender or food processor and combine with the original mixture. If using cream, add it when puréeing the soup. Reheat the soup and stir in the basil just before serving. Serve the soup hot; although if it is Indian Summer weather, the soup is quite delicious at room temperature.

Makes 8 to 10 servings

Orzo and
Roasted Vegetable Salad

— ❖ —

One late-September day when a catering client of mine had been anticipating a hefty platter of risotto at a wedding rehearsal buffet and the entire island of Nantucket was uncharacteristically devoid of Arborio rice, I summoned a handy box of orzo to the rescue. It so happened that visiting in-laws, guests, and even the apologetic chef liked the makeshift alternative enough to name it a favorite.

2 medium eggplants, peeled
  and cut into ½-inch chunks
2 red bell peppers, stemmed,
  seeded, and cut into ½-
  inch dice
2 yellow bell peppers,
  stemmed, seeded, and cut
  into ½-inch dice
2 cloves garlic, minced
1 to 1¼ cups fruity olive
  oil
Salt and freshly ground
  black pepper to taste

1 pound orzo (rice-shaped
  pasta), cooked according
  to package directions and
  drained
1 bunch scallions, trimmed
  and minced
12 ounces feta cheese,
  crumbled
½ cup fresh mint leaves,
  chopped
⅓ cup pine nuts, lightly
  toasted
⅓ cup fresh lemon juice

1. Preheat the oven to 375°F.

2. Toss the eggplant, peppers, and garlic together in a roasting pan. Drizzle with ½ cup of the olive oil and season with salt and pepper. Roast the vegetables in the oven, stirring occasionally, until soft and lightly blistered, about 45 minutes.

3. In a large mixing bowl combine the cooked orzo with the roasted vegetables. Stir in the scallions, feta, mint, and pine nuts. Dress the salad with the lemon juice and enough of the remaining oil to moisten thoroughly. Taste and adjust the seasonings. Transfer to an attractive bowl and serve slightly warm or at room temperature.

Makes 8 to 10 servings

TOASTING NUTS

— ⸭ —

Many of my recipes call for nuts that are lightly toasted because toasting releases oils which produces a nuttier-tasting nut. A general axiom to remember when toasting nuts is: A watched nut never burns! Thus, if the doorbell or phone rings, don't answer it!

Preheat the oven, or even a toaster oven for smaller amounts, to 350°F. Spread the nuts in a single layer on a baking sheet and place them in the oven. Cook, watching carefully, until the nuts have taken on the next shade deeper in brown, 10 to 12 minutes maximum. Let cool and use as directed in the recipes. This method not only produces perfect nuts but also happy cooks given that burning a batch of pine nuts can inflict severe economic woe.

Panzanella

— ✥ —

Panzanella, a Tuscan peasant salad, was often featured as an autumn specialty in my shop because it is hearty, and autumn was the only time when I was lucky enough to find a leftover loaf or two of my own homemade bread. If you love to sop up the last bit of delicious sauce with a crusty heel of bread, you will love this salad.

3 ripe large beefsteak tomatoes, seeded and cut into ½-inch dice

2 cucumbers, peeled, halved, seeded, and cut on a sharp diagonal into ¼-inch slices

1 yellow bell pepper, stemmed, seeded, and cut into thin julienne strips

1 red onion, cut into thin rings

2 tablespoons drained capers

½ cup imported black olives, pitted and coarsely chopped

⅔ cup (or as needed) best-quality extra virgin olive oil

¼ cup balsamic vinegar

Kosher (coarse) salt and freshly ground black pepper to taste

5 cups coarsely cubed day-old crusty bread, such as semolina, French, or peasant

½ cup shredded fresh basil leaves

1. In a large mixing bowl combine the tomatoes, cucumbers, pepper, red onion, capers, and olives. Toss with the olive oil and vinegar, then season with salt and pepper. Let sit for 30 minutes to marinate.

2. Toss the bread and basil with the vegetables and let sit another hour so the bread can absorb the dressing and vegetable juices. If the salad seems dry, drizzle with a bit more olive oil. Serve at room temperature.

Makes 6 to 8 servings

Curried Chicken Salad with Autumn Fruits

— ❖ —

Life never seems quite normal if I am not working on a new chicken salad recipe. This one is a real winner! Plump strips of white chicken are contrasted with pan-roasted almonds and a julienne of figs, dates, and dried apricots. All is bathed in an exotic blend of mango chutney, curry, and cream.

3½ pounds boneless,
skinless chicken breasts,
poached just until tender
and cooled to room
temperature
½ cup dried figs, cut into
julienne strips
½ cup pitted dates, cut
into julienne strips
½ cup dried apricot halves,
cut into julienne strips
¾ cup plus 1 tablespoon
vegetable oil

1 large clove garlic finely
minced
¾ cup blanched whole
almonds
½ teaspoon kosher (coarse)
salt
¾ cup mango chutney
1 large egg
1½ tablespoons good-
quality curry powder
½ cup heavy or whipping
cream
Salt to taste

1. Cut the poached chicken breasts into 2 × ¾-inch strips and mix with the figs, dates, and apricots in a large mixing bowl.

2. Heat 1 tablespoon oil over medium-heat in a medium-size skillet. Stir in the garlic and almonds and cook, stirring constantly, until the almonds are lightly toasted, 3 to 4 minutes. Sprinkle with the kosher salt and toss with the chicken and fruit.

3. Place the chutney, egg, and curry powder in a food processor and process until smooth. With the machine running, pour the remaining ¾ cup oil through the feed tube in a thin, steady stream. Then pour in the heavy cream with the machine still running to make a thick cream sauce. Season to taste with salt. Bind the salad together with the dressing.

4. Transfer the salad to a serving bowl and refrigerate a couple hours before serving.

Makes 6 to 8 servings

Bistro Carrot Salad

— ✤ —

This is an uncomplicated yet alluring carrot salad. If you own a mandoline (a fancy French slicing device), it will make the julienne preparation go much more quickly, but I've always found a certain satisfaction in doing the cutting by hand. Like the other popular French bistro salad — *céleri rémoulade* — this salad pairs perfectly with an autumn charcuterie plate.

1½ pounds carrots, peeled
and trimmed
3 tablespoons fresh lemon
juice
2 teaspoons Dijon mustard
1 teaspoon sugar

½ cup fruity olive oil
Salt and freshly ground
black pepper to taste
5 scallions, trimmed and
minced
⅓ cup minced fresh parsley

1. Cut the carrots by hand or with a mandoline into thin julienne strips 2 to 2½ inches long. Blanch the carrots in a large pot of boiling water until just barely tender, 3 to 4 minutes. Drain well and set aside.

2. Whisk together the lemon juice, mustard, and sugar in a large mixing bowl. Gradually whisk in the olive oil, then season to taste with salt and pepper. Toss the warm carrots with the dressing and mix in the scallions and parsley. Transfer to a serving bowl. The salad may be served slightly warm, at room temperature, or chilled.

Makes 6 servings

Country Potato Salad with Prosciutto and Chopped Egg

—✧—

This hearty and colorful potato salad is the after-Labor-Day version that I used to love to make at my specialty food shop, Que Sera Sarah.

3 pounds small red
potatoes, scrubbed but
not peeled
½ cup dry white wine
2 tablespoons fresh lemon
juice
⅓ cup olive oil
Salt and freshly ground
black pepper to taste
1 bunch scallions, trimmed
and minced
1 jar (4 ounces) pimientos,
drained and chopped

½ cup chopped fresh dill,
plus additional for
garnish
⅓ pound thinly sliced
prosciutto, cut into thick
slivers
5 hard-cooked large eggs,
peeled and coarsely
chopped
2 tablespoons Dijon
mustard
1 cup sour cream

1. Place the potatoes in a large pot and add water to cover. Heat to a boil, then lower the heat and simmer uncovered until fork-tender, 25 to 30 minutes. Drain in a colander.

2. While the potatoes are cooking, whisk together the wine, lemon juice, and olive oil in a large mixing bowl. Season with salt and pepper. Stir in the scallions, pimientos, dill, and prosciutto. Cut the hot potatoes into large uneven chunks, add to the bowl, and toss to combine. Mix in the chopped eggs.

3. In a small bowl, whisk together the mustard and sour cream; add it to the salad to bind. Transfer to a serving bowl, garnish with a little additional dill, and serve slightly warm or at room temperature.

Makes 6 to 8 servings

Potato Caesar Salad

— ❖ —

When the nights get a little nippy and I want something more substantial than romaine leaves with my favorite Caesar salad dressing, I make this simple, yet soul-satisfying, warm potato salad. It's great with a nice rosy steak or steamed lobster.

4 pound small red potatoes,
   scrubbed but not peeled
5 anchovy fillets, drained
   and minced
2 cloves garlic, minced
1 tablespoon grainy Dijon
   mustard
2 teaspoons dried thyme
1 large egg yolk
3 tablespoons balsamic
   vinegar
2 tablespoons fresh lemon
   juice

½ cup vegetable oil
1 cup olive oil
8 sun-dried tomatoes,
   packed in oil, drained
   and finely chopped
Salt and freshly ground
   black pepper to taste
1 bunch parsley, stems
   discarded, leaves
   minced
1 cup freshly grated
   Parmesan cheese

1. Place the potatoes in a large pot and add water to cover. Heat to a boil, then lower the heat and simmer uncovered until fork-tender, about 25 minutes. Drain in a colander and let cool a few minutes.

2. While the potatoes are cooking, make the Caesar dressing. Place the anchovies, garlic, mustard, thyme, egg yolk, vinegar, and lemon juice in a food processor and process just to combine. With the machine running, pour the oils through the feed tube in a thin, steady

stream to make a thick mayonnaise. Add the sun-dried tomatoes and pulse just to combine. Season the dressing to taste with salt and pepper.

3. Cut the warm potatoes into large uneven chunks. Toss with a generous amount of Caesar dressing to bind, then mix in the parsley and Parmesan. Serve at once or at room temperature.

Makes 10 to 12 servings

Calabrian Cauliflower Salad

— ❖ —

Infusing vegetables with the strong flavors of Southern Italian cooking adds a warmth and complexity to the taste of a dish. Mild cauliflower serves as a good vehicle for a lusty combination of Calabrian ingredients. This dish may be served as an antipasto, a glamorous relish, or vegetable accompaniment to roasted poultry.

2 medium heads
    cauliflower, trimmed and
    broken into florets
1½ cups chicken broth,
    preferably homemade
⅓ cup golden raisins
6 anchovy fillets, minced
2 cloves garlic, minced
3 tablespoons drained
    capers
½ cup diced pitted
    imported black olives

½ cup chopped pimiento
2 tablespoons balsamic
    vinegar
½ cup fruity olive oil
Dried red pepper flakes to
    taste
2 teaspoons dried oregano
Salt and freshly ground
    black pepper to taste
½ cup chopped fresh
    parsley

1. Steam the cauliflower over simmering chicken broth just until crisp-tender. Remove the cauliflower to cool and reserve the broth.

2. Add the raisins to the broth and boil over medium-high heat until the stock is reduced to ½ cup and the raisins are quite plump, 12 to 15 minutes. Set aside.

3. In a mixing bowl combine the anchovies, garlic, capers, olives, pimiento, and vinegar. Whisk in the olive oil, then add the reduced stock and raisins. Season with the red pepper flakes, oregano, salt, and pepper. Add the cauliflower and toss to coat and combine. Add the parsley just before serving. Serve slightly chilled or at room temperature. The salad improves a bit with time and will keep in the refrigerator for up to 1 week.

Makes 6 to 8 servings

Fruity Olive Oil and Friends

— ✦ —

I am frequently asked what I mean when I call for fruity olive oil in a recipe. Since a search for a bottle of olive oil labeled "fruity" will be in vain, let me offer a clarification. There are four main types of olive oil as well as numerous color variations ranging from pale straw to rich golden green. Extra virgin olive oil is the best, purest, and most expensive of the lot. Extra virgin signifies that the olives were hand picked and then pressed by the timeless method of stone wheels without the use of heat. In general extra virgin olive oil should not be used for frying and sautéing since heat can destroy its taste, but rather drizzled sparingly as a flavoring condiment over vegetables or splashed atop soups and stews in a delicious and authentically Italian manner.

Virgin olive oil comes from the second pressing of the olives. Pure olive oil results when the olive pulp remaining from the second pressing is treated with chemicals to extract flavor. It usually has the palest color and is the best choice either to use in quantity or to subject to the heat of frying and sautéing. The fourth type of olive oil is denoted by the term fine. Since it is the result of further chemical treatment of the pulp to extract the final drop of flavor, I think that the highly acidic and often bitter end product is better suited to fueling a car (preferably Italian) than use in gastronomic endeavors.

Now depending on the integrity of the olive oil maker and the region in the Mediterranean where the olives are grown, all of the first three grades of olive oil may yield the blessed fruitiness, in that they will bear a deep, rich color and a pronounced olive flavor. I look for moderately priced virgin olive oils for those recipes of mine calling for fruity olive oil. Determining whether an oil tastes fruity is more personal than scientific. I suggest shopping around for a variety of olive oils from different regions and in different price ranges. Set up a comparative tasting by pouring the oils into little bowls and then dunking a fresh chunk of bread into each to taste the oil in an unadulterated form. Let your palate, rather than price, lead you to a personal favorite.

Warm Mushroom and Arugula Salad

— ❖ —

As salad making has always been my greatest food passion, I don't stop with the onset of colder weather. I simply heat everything up. This is a wonderfully woodsy, warm salad for chilly autumn evenings.

7 tablespoons fruity olive oil

8 ounces shiitake mushrooms, stems discarded, caps thinly sliced

8 ounces domestic white mushrooms, stems discarded, caps thinly sliced

2 cloves garlic, minced

2 anchovy fillets, minced

¼ cup pitted Niçoise olives, finely minced

2 tablespoons capers

2 tablespoons fresh lemon juice

1 tablespoon balsamic vinegar

2 bunches arugula, trimmed, rinsed, and patted dry

Salt and freshly ground black pepper

4 ounces crumbled Gorgonzola cheese

1. Heat 3 tablespoons of the oil in a skillet over medium-high heat. Add the mushrooms and sauté, stirring frequently, 5 minutes. Reduce the heat to medium and stir in the garlic, anchovies, olives, capers, lemon juice, and balsamic vinegar. Simmer 5 minutes or so to blend the flavors.

2. Meanwhile, toss the arugula with the remaining olive oil in a large salad bowl. Season to taste with salt and pepper. Add the warm mushroom mixture to the arugula and toss until thoroughly blended. Mix in the Gorgonzola and divide the salad among 6 plates. Serve at once.

Makes 6 servings

Mixed Greens with Spiced Pecans, Chèvre, and Hot Cider Dressing

— ✛ —

At first glance this salad may appear to be a lot of work; but the spiced pecans can be made up to 2 weeks in advance, leaving only the salad ingredients and dressing until the final preparation. The salad has such an exquisite array of contrasting flavors and textures that I am very content devouring it as an entire meal rather than relegating it to a daintier accompaniment portion.

SPICED PECANS

2 cups pecan halves
2½ tablespoons vegetable
   oil
¼ cup sugar
1 teaspoon salt
1 teaspoon ground
   cinnamon

¼ teaspoon grated nutmeg
¼ teaspoon ground cloves
½ teaspoon ground ginger
½ teaspoon dry mustard

HOT CIDER DRESSING

2 cups apple cider
8 slices bacon, cut into
   1-inch pieces
3 shallots, minced
1 teaspoon ground
   cinnamon

1 tablespoon honey mustard
½ cup olive oil
Salt and freshly ground
   black pepper to taste.

SALAD

12 cups torn mixed salad
   greens, such as leaf
   lettuce, radicchio, endive,
   and watercress
1 cup thinly sliced fennel
   bulb

1½ large McIntosh apples,
   cored and thinly sliced
4 ounces crumbled chèvre,
   such as Montrachet

1. Prepare the spiced pecans: Place the nuts in a small bowl, cover with boiling water, and let soak for 15 minutes. Drain well and pat dry on paper towels.
2. Preheat the oven to 300°F.

3. Spread the nuts on an ungreased baking sheet and toast stirring occasionally, for 45 minutes. Remove the nuts and increase the oven temperature to 350°F.

4. Whisk together the vegetable oil, sugar, salt, cinnamon, nutmeg, cloves, ginger, and mustard in a medium-size bowl. Add the hot nuts and toss to coat thoroughly. Spread the nuts in a single layer on the baking sheet and roast 15 minutes. Let cool, then store in an airtight container up to 2 weeks.

5. When ready to prepare the salad, place the cider in a small saucepan and boil until reduced to ½ cup, 20 to 25 minutes. Set aside. Sauté the bacon in a medium-size skillet over medium-high heat until crisp. Drain on paper towels and discard all but 3 tablespoons of the fat remaining in the skillet. Add the shallots to the skillet and sauté over medium heat until softened, about 3 minutes. Whisk in the cinnamon and mustard and cook 1 minute more. Add the reduced cider and the olive oil; season to taste with salt and pepper. Keep the dressing hot over medium-low heat.

6. Toss the salad greens, 1 cup of the spiced pecans, the reserved bacon, the fennel, apples, and chèvre together in a large salad bowl. Toss with the hot cider dressing and serve at once.

Makes 6 servings

Scalloped Tomatoes

— ❖ —

Scalloped tomatoes, when made with fresh, rather than canned, tomatoes, are the most comforting hot vegetable dish I know.

3 tablespoons bacon fat
2 cups cubed French bread
(½-inch cubes)
16 ripe plum tomatoes, cut
into ½-inch cubes
2 cloves garlic, minced
2 tablespoons sugar
Salt and freshly ground
black pepper to taste

½ cup shredded fresh basil
leaves
1 cup freshly grated
Parmesan cheese
2 tablespoons fruity olive
oil

1. Preheat the oven to 350°F.
2. Heat the bacon fat in a large skillet over medium heat. Add

the bread cubes and stir to coat evenly with the fat. Sauté until lightly browned all over, 5 to 7 minutes. Add the tomatoes, garlic, and sugar to the pan. Cook, stirring frequently, 5 minutes. Season with salt and pepper, then stir in the basil and remove from the heat.

3. Transfer the tomato mixture to a shallow 1½-quart casserole. Sprinkle the Parmesan over the top and drizzle with the olive oil. Bake until bubbling and lightly browned, 35 to 40 minutes. Serve at once.

Makes 6 servings

Farewell-to-Friends Fettuccine

— ✤ —

Columbus Day weekend signals the final exodus of summer friends off Nantucket and back to urban realities. I invented this sauce, a cross between Roman Amatriciana and saffron-laced Sardinian sausage ragout to bid a group of special island cronies a delicious farewell.

2 pounds sweet Italian
   sausage, casings removed
   and crumbled
4 ounces sliced pancetta or
   bacon, finely diced
1 large onion, coarsely
   chopped
3 cloves garlic, minced
1 teaspoon fennel seeds
1 teaspoon saffron threads
3½ pounds ripe fresh
   tomatoes, coarsely chopped

½ cup dry red wine
2 tablespoons tomato paste
½ cup heavy or whipping cream
½ cup shredded fresh basil leaves
Salt and freshly ground
   black pepper to taste
2 pounds fettuccine, cooked
   according to package
   directions just before
   serving and drained
Freshly grated Parmesan
   cheese

1. Place the sausage and pancetta in a large skillet and sauté over medium-high heat, crumbling the sausage with the back of a wooden spoon, until it loses its pink color, 10 to 15 minutes.

2. Stir in the onion, garlic, fennel, and saffron; cook uncovered, stirring occasionally, 15 minutes. Add the tomatoes, red wine, and tomato paste; cook over medium heat another 20 minutes. The to-matoes should be soft but still retain some of their shape. Stir in the cream, basil, salt, and pepper and cook just 1 minute more.

3. Toss the hot cooked fettuccine with the sauce in a large serv-ing bowl. Serve at once accompanied with freshly grated Parmesan.

Makes 10 to 12 servings

Pumpkin, Prosciutto, and Parmesan Lasagne

— ❖ —

Though we often think of pumpkin as quintessentially American, the Italians are the most innovative in the ways which they combine *zucca*, or pumpkin, with pasta. While I have often savored pumpkin-filled tortellini, it wasn't until recently that layering pumpkin with compatible flavors in a lasagne began to intrigue me. Toasted walnuts and fresh sage leaves round out this alliterative pasta creation. The resulting dish is rich, soothing, unusual, and perfect for a dinner party on the first frosty night in October or for a sophisticated Halloween soirée.

PUMPKIN FILLING
½ cup (1 stick) unsalted butter
6 leeks, trimmed, rinsed well, and minced
4 cups pumpkin purée, fresh or canned
½ cup dry white wine
Salt and freshly ground black pepper to taste

BECHAMEL
½ cup (1 stick) unsalted butter
6 tablespoons unbleached all-purpose flour
2 cups chicken broth, preferably homemade, at room temperature
2 cups light cream, at room temperature
1 cup freshly grated Parmesan cheese
½ teaspoon grated nutmeg
Salt and freshly ground white pepper to taste
3 large eggs, at room temperature, lightly beaten

FOR ASSEMBLY
1¼ pounds lasagne noodles, cooked al dente and drained
8 ounces thinly sliced prosciutto
¼ cup fresh sage leaves, torn into irregular pieces
1½ cups freshly grated Parmesan cheese
2 cups walnut pieces, lightly toasted

1. Preheat the oven to 350°F. Butter a 15 × 10-inch casserole or baking pan.

2. Prepare the pumpkin filling: Melt the butter in a large skillet over medium heat. Add the leeks and sauté, stirring occasionally, until very tender, about 15 minutes. Stir in the pumpkin and the white wine and cook, stirring constantly 2 minutes. Remove from the heat and season with salt and pepper. Set aside.

3. Prepare the béchamel: Melt the butter in a medium saucepan over medium-high heat. Add the flour and whisk until smooth. Cook, stirring constantly, 1 minute. Gradually whisk in the chicken broth, then the light cream; cook, stirring constantly, until smooth and thickened. Stir in the Parmesan and season with the nutmeg, salt, and white pepper. Stir ½ cup of the hot sauce into the beaten eggs in a small bowl, then stir the egg mixture into the remaining sauce. Cook a couple minutes longer, stirring constantly, then remove from the heat.

4. To assemble the lasagne, make a layer of the lasagne noodles in the prepared casserole and top with half the sliced prosciutto and one-third of the béchamel. Scatter half the sage leaves evenly over the top. Cover with another layer of noodles, then all the pumpkin filling, 1 cup of the Parmesan, and 1 cup of the walnuts. Make another layer of the lasagne noodles and top with the rest of the prosciutto, another third of the béchamel, and the remaining sage. Make a final layer of noodles and top with the remaining béchamel, walnuts, and Parmesan.

5. Bake the lasagne in the oven until lightly browned and bubbling, 50 to 60 minutes. Let cool 10 minutes before cutting and serving.

Makes 12 servings

A HARVEST NIGHT TO REMEMBER

— ❖ —

Roasted Pepper and Artichoke Puffs

— ❖ —

Pumpkin, Prosciutto, and Parmesan Lasagne
Warm Mushroom and Arugula Salad
Italian Bread

— ❖ —

Ruby Poached Pears

Perciatelli with Shiitake Mushrooms and Fresh Ginger

— ✦ —

W hile most pasta salads tend to be summery, this unusual creation, a sort of Italo-Oriental merger, fills an autumnal gap. Perciatelli
is a big, fat spaghetti-shaped strand, and a pasta I simply adore. It
provides a perfect foil for the assertive flavors and textures of the
sauce. This dish would be fabulous as the centerpiece of a football
tailgate picnic when the food matters more than the final outcome of
the game!

¾ cup olive oil
3 tablespoons Oriental
   sesame oil
3 large onions, cut into
   ¼-inch crescent slivers
3 tablespoons light brown
   sugar
5 cups seeded diced, fresh
   or canned tomatoes
3 cloves garlic, minced
2 tablespoons tomato paste
¼ cup balsamic
   vinegar
1 teaspoon ground
   coriander
Salt and freshly ground
   black pepper to taste

2 pounds shiitake
   mushrooms, stems
   discarded caps thinly
   sliced
12 ounces domestic white
   mushrooms, thinly sliced
1½ pounds perciatelli,
   cooked according to
   package directions and
   drained
1 bunch scallions, trimmed
   and sliced on a diagonal
3 tablespoons finely minced
   fresh ginger
3 tablespoons soy sauce

1. Heat ¼ cup of the olive oil with 1 teaspoon of the sesame oil
in a large saucepan over medium-high heat. Add the onions and cook,
stirring frequently, 15 minutes. Stir in the brown sugar and cook a
few minutes more to caramelize the onions.

2. Stir in the tomatoes, garlic, tomato paste, and vinegar. Season
with the coriander, salt, and pepper. Simmer uncovered over medium
heat 30 minutes.

3. Meanwhile, sauté both kinds of mushrooms in the remaining
½ cup olive oil with a little dash of sesame oil. This is best done in
a large skillet in batches over medium-high heat. Ration the oils between 2 to 3 batches of mushrooms and cook each batch until the
mushrooms are lightly browned and crisp, rather than moist, 7 to 10

minutes. Add each batch to the tomato sauce as it is completed.

4. In a large mixing bowl toss the cooked perciatelli with the scallions, ginger, soy sauce, and remaining sesame oil. Add the tomato-mushroom sauce to the pasta and toss thoroughly to combine. Transfer the pasta to a large serving bowl and serve at room temperature.

Makes 8 to 10 servings

Warm Tomato Pie

Since I cannot conceive of a summer day without at least one vine-ripened tomato on the menu, this is the best way I know to satisfy those same cravings when September sweater weather urges a little warming of the farmstand bounty. The Parmesan-laced crust and filling rich with onions, mustard, and mozzarella play a splendid supporting role to the year's reddest and plumpest beefsteak tomatoes.

CRUST

1¾ cups unbleached all-purpose flour
1 tablespoon sugar
½ cup (1 stick) unsalted butter, chilled, cut into small pieces

½ cup freshly grated Parmesan cheese
1 tablespoon fresh lemon juice
2 to 3 tablespoons ice water

FILLING

2 tablespoons unsalted butter
1 tablespoon olive oil
1 large onion, chopped
3 tablespoons Dijon mustard
8 ounces mozzarella cheese, thinly sliced

2 large egg yolks
1 large egg
1 cup half-and-half
Salt and freshly ground black pepper to taste

TOPPING

3 very large beefsteak tomatoes, sliced
2 tablespoons extra virgin olive oil

2 cloves garlic, minced
1 tablespoon dried Italian herb blend

1. Prepare the crust: Place the flour, sugar, butter, and Parmesan in a food processor and process just until the mixture resembles coarse meal. With the machine running, add the lemon juice and 2 tablespoons of the ice water through the feed tube; process just until the mixture starts to gather into a ball. (You may have to add up to 1 tablespoon more of the water.) Shape the dough into a thick disk, wrap in plastic wrap, and refrigerate 1 hour.

2. Roll out the dough on a lightly floured surface into a 12-inch circle. Line a 10 to 11- inch pie plate with the dough; trim and crimp the edges decoratively. Refrigerate while working on the rest of the recipe.

3. Preheat the oven to 400°F.

4. Prepare the filling: Heat the butter and olive oil in a skillet over medium-high heat. Add the onion and sauté 5 minutes. Reduce the heat to medium and continue cooking until the onion is very soft, about 10 minutes longer. Brush the mustard evenly over the bottom of the pie shell, then top with the onion mixture. Lay the slices of mozzarella on top.

5. Whisk together the egg yolks, egg, and half-and-half. Season with salt and pepper and pour over the cheese in the pie shell.

6. Arrange the sliced tomatoes in circles to cover the top of the pie. Drizzle with the olive oil, then sprinkle with the garlic and dried herbs. Bake until cooked through and lightly browned, 45 to 50 minutes. Let cool 15 minutes, then cut into wedges and serve.

Makes 8 servings.

Season's End Pizza Roulade

— ❖ —

This literal (and figurative) twist on pizza is stunning to look at and fabulous to eat. While I love serving it at a fall luncheon or picnic, the roulade is also a welcome savory at evening cocktail parties.

1 double recipe Pizza
   Dough (see page 47)
2 large eggplants, cut
   lengthwise into thin slices
5 tablespoons extra virgin
   olive oil
1 pound ricotta cheese
4 ounces soft chèvre cheese
2 cloves garlic, minced
¼ cup shredded fresh basil
   leaves
¼ cup minced fresh parsley

½ cup freshly grated
   Parmesan cheese
⅓ cup pine nuts, lightly
   toasted
Salt and freshly ground
   black pepper to taste
8 ounces thinly sliced
   prosciutto
8 ripe plum tomatoes,
   thinly sliced
1 pound mozzarella cheese,
   thinly sliced

1. Have ready the pizza dough, risen until double in bulk.
2. Preheat the oven to 400°F.
3. Lay the eggplant slices out on baking sheets and brush both sides lightly with 4 tablespoons of the olive oil. Roast the eggplant slices in the oven until soft, slightly browned, and blistered, 20 to 25 minutes. Do not turn off the oven.
4. While the eggplant is cooking, beat the ricotta and chèvre together until light and fluffy. Stir in the garlic, basil, parsley, Parmesan, and pine nuts. Season the mixture with salt and pepper.
5. On a lightly floured large surface, roll the pizza dough out to a 24 × 16-inch rectangle. Spread the dough evenly with all the ricotta mixture. Layer the prosciutto over the ricotta and top with the tomatoes and then the eggplant slices. Make a final layer of the sliced mozzarella.
6. Starting from a long side, roll up the dough jelly-roll fashion to make a large log. If you don't have have a baking sheet or oven large enough for the whole roulade, cut it in half and bake it on 2 separate baking sheets. Seal the cut ends by stretching and pinching together a little pizza dough over the exposed filling. Brush the top of the pizza roulade lightly with the remaining tablespoon olive oil.
7. Bake until golden brown, 45 to 50 minutes. Let cool to room temperature. Cut into 1 to 1½-inch-thick slices to serve.
Makes 10 to 12 servings

Shrimp with Tomatoes and Feta Cheese

— ❖ —

This is a real nostalgic recipe for me, for it is the dish I ordered on one of my first unchaperoned dinner dates at a then-trendy restaurant in Cambridge, Massachusetts. It is simple to prepare, and I particularly enjoy cooking it at the end of the summer when both red and yellow tomatoes are in their prime. The adolescent associations enrich the culinary pleasure with a sort of Ponce de León, fountain-of-youth flavor.

4 tablespoons (½ stick) unsalted butter

3 tablespoons olive oil

3 large garlic cloves, minced

36 large shrimp, peeled and deveined, with the tails left on

1 cup dry white wine

8 ounces ripe red tomatoes, seeded and cut into ½-inch dice

8 ounces ripe yellow tomatoes, seeded and cut into ½-inch dice

1½ tablespoons chopped fresh oregano or 2 teaspoons dried

3 tablespoons shredded fresh basil leaves

Pinch dried red pepper flakes

Salt to taste

6 ounces feta cheese, crumbled

1. Preheat the oven to 400°F.

2. Heat the butter and olive oil in a large heavy skillet over medium-high heat. Add the garlic and shrimp and cook, turning the shrimp, until they are just barely pink, 2½ to 3 minutes. Divide the shrimp among six 6-inch round gratin dishes.

3. Add the wine to the skillet and cook over high heat until reduced by half. Stir in the tomatoes and simmer 2 minutes. Add the oregano, basil, red pepper flakes, and salt; cook 30 seconds more.

4. Spoon the tomato mixture evenly over the shrimp in the gratin dishes, then scatter a generous amount of feta cheese over each. Place the dishes on a baking sheet and bake until the cheese is melted and bubbling, 8 to 10 minutes. Serve at once.

Makes 6 servings

Pork and Apricot Empanadas

— ✛ —

This autumn flavored empanada is the sort of recipe that really excites me. The empanadas are colorful, portable, attractive, and the unusually delectable combination of ingredients makes tasters stand up and cheer for something other than a football team at a tailgate picnic. For Mexican food aficionados, these golden turnovers smack of south-of-the-border savor.

CORNMEAL-CREAM CHEESE CRUST

2 cups unbleached all-purpose flour
1 cup yellow cornmeal
1 cup (2 sticks) unsalted butter, chilled, cut into small pieces

8 ounces cream cheese, chilled, cut into small pieces
Pinch salt

EMPANADA FILLING

1 pound lean pork, cut into ½-inch cubes
1 medium onion, minced
4 cloves garlic, minced
2 jalapeño chiles, stemmed, seeded, and minced
1 bay leaf
1 teaspoon ground cinnamon
1 bottle (12 ounces) beer
⅔ cup dried apricots, cut into slivers

8 ounces cream cheese, at room temperature
½ red bell pepper, seeded and diced
¼ cup pine nuts, lightly toasted
4 scallions, trimmed and minced
½ cup minced cilantro (fresh coriander)
Salt and freshly ground black pepper to taste

EGG WASH

1 large egg

1 tablespoon water

1. Prepare the crust: Place the flour, cornmeal, butter, cream cheese, and salt in a food processor. Process just until the mixture begins to gather into a ball. Shape the dough into a thick disk, wrap in a plastic wrap, and refrigerate at least 1 hour.

2. Meanwhile prepare the filling: Combine the pork, onion, garlic, jalapeño chiles, bay leaf, cinnamon, and beer in a saucepan. Bring to a boil over medium-high heat. Reduce the heat and simmer uncovered 15 minutes. Stir in the apricots and continue simmering another 15 minutes.

3. Transfer the pork mixture to a food processor and remove the bay leaf. Process just until coarsely chopped and set aside.

4. In a medium-size mixing bowl, beat the cream cheese with an electric mixer until light and fluffy. Stir in the bell pepper, pine nuts, scallions, and cilantro. Add the reserved pork mixture and stir well to combine. Season the mixture with salt and pepper.

5. Preheat the oven to 375°F. Line 2 large baking sheets with parchment paper.

6. Remove the dough from the refrigerator and divide it in half. On a lightly floured surface, roll out half the dough ⅛ inch thick. Cut out as many 5-inch squares as possible, reserving the dough scraps.

7. Place about ¼ cup filling on half of each square. Fold each square neatly in half to form a triangle. Seal by pressing the edges with the tines of a fork. Arrange the turnovers ½ inch apart on a prepared baking sheet. Repeat the process with the remaining dough and filling to make about 18 turnovers.

8. For the egg wash, beat the egg and water together and brush over the empanadas. Roll out any remaining dough scraps and cut into small stars or other shapes with cookie cutters. Place the small shapes decoratively on top of the empanadas and brush again with egg wash.

9. Bake the empanadas until lightly browned all over, 25 to 30 minutes. Serve warm or at room temperature.

Makes 18 empanadas

TAILGATE TIME

— ✧ —

Nantucket Tomato Soup

— ✧ —

Pork and Apricot Empanadas
Orzo and Roasted Vegetable Salad
Bistro Carrot Salad

— ✧ —

Ivy League Chocolate Chunk Cookies

Autumn Pork Roast

— ✛ —

To my mind there is no greater embodiment of the coming of autumn than a dinner in which a crackling pork roast holds center stage. This recipe is inspired by the Tuscan *arista*, or pork loin, scented with wild fennel gathered nearby in the Chianti hills. Accompany with Mashed Potatoes with Garlic and Olive Oil and Braised Red Cabbage with Apple and Mustard Seeds (see Index for page numbers).

3 tablespoons olive oil
1 bunch scallions, trimmed
  and minced
1 medium onion, chopped
3 cloves garlic, minced
3 thick slices fresh French
  bread, crumbled
8 ounces bulk pork sausage,
  crumbled
1 bulb fennel, trimmed and
  minced
1 cup finely chopped fresh
  parsley
2 tablespoons minced fresh
  rosemary

2 tablespoons minced fresh
  thyme
Grated zest of 1 lemon
3 tablespoons fresh lemon
  juice
2 ounces sliced prosciutto,
  minced
Salt and freshly ground
  black pepper to taste
1 tied rolled shoulder pork
  (about 4 pounds)
2 cups dry white wine

1. Preheat the oven to 425°F.

2. Heat the oil in a large skillet over medium-high heat. Add the scallions, onion, and garlic; sauté for 5 minutes. Stir in the bread, sausage, fennel, parsley, rosemary, and thyme. Cook uncovered until the sausage loses its pink color and the fennel is tender, about 15 minutes. Add the lemon zest and juice, prosciutto, salt, and pepper; cook a few minutes more.

3. Unroll the pork roast and pat the stuffing evenly over the surface. Reroll and tie the roast, then place it in a roasting pan. Pour the wine around the roast and rub the surface with salt and pepper. Roast 30 minutes. Reduce the heat to 350°F and continue roasting until the internal temperature reads between 160 and 170°F on a meat thermometer, about 1½ to 2 hours more.

4. Transfer the roast to a serving platter, remove the string, and let sit for 10 minutes before carving. Cut the roast into thick slices and serve with a spoonful of the pan juices, if desired.

Makes 8 servings

Purple Plum Brûlée

— ❖ —

A delightfully simple yet stylish fruit dessert to make with early autumn's Italian prune plums.

1½ pounds ripe prune
  plums, pitted and
  quartered
3 tablespoons cassis liqueur
1 tablespoon fresh lemon
  juice
2 teaspoons ground
  cinnamon

1 cup heavy or whipping
  cream
1 cup sour cream
¼ cup (packed) light
  brown sugar

1. Preheat the broiler.
2. Toss the plums with the cassis, lemon juice, and cinnamon in a mixing bowl. Spread in a shallow 1½-quart baking dish. Whisk together the cream and sour cream and pour over the plums. Sift the brown sugar over the top.
3. Place the dish underneath the broiler 3 inches from the heat and broil until browned and bubbling about 5 minutes. Serve at once spooned into shallow compote dishes.

Makes 6 servings

Walnut-Rum-Raisin-Applesauce Cake

— ❖ —

I packed as many delicious autumnal delights as I could into this wonderfully moist bundt cake. Great as a homey dessert or as a special morning treat with freshly brewed coffee.

1 cup golden raisins
½ cup dark rum
2 cups walnut pieces
2½ cups unbleached all-
   purpose flour
2 teaspoons baking powder
1 teaspoon baking soda
1 tablespoon ground
   cinnamon
½ teaspoon grated nutmeg

1 cup (2 sticks) unsalted
   butter
1 teaspoon vanilla extract
1 cup (packed) light brown
   sugar
2 large eggs
½ cup sour cream
½ cup applesauce,
   preferably homemade
Finely grated zest of 1 lemon

RUM SYRUP
½ cup (packed) light
   brown sugar
½ cup sweet apple cider

¼ cup dark rum
Confectioners' sugar for
   garnish

1. Place the raisins and ½ cup rum in a small saucepan. Bring to a boil over high heat, then simmer 10 minutes. Remove from the heat and set aside.

2. Preheat the oven to 350°F. Butter a 9-cup bundt or tube pan.

3. Place 1 cup of the walnuts in a food processor and process until finely chopped, but not powdered. Coat the bottom and sides of the bundt pan with the nuts. It is all right if a few extra nuts fall to the bottom of the pan. Set aside.

4. Toss together all the dry indredients in a small bowl and set aside. In a large mixing bowl cream together the butter, vanilla, and brown sugar. Beat in the eggs, one at a time, beating well after each addition. Add the dry ingredients alternately with the sour cream and applesauce, mixing until all is thoroughly blended.

5. Fold the lemon zest, rum-soaked raisins, and remaining 1 cup walnuts into the batter. Pour the batter into the prepared bundt pan and smooth the top with a rubber spatula.

6. Bake the cake until a cake tester inserted in the middle of the cake comes out clean, 1 hour. Let the cake cool in the pan 15 minutes.

7. In the meantime, prepare the rum syrup: Place the brown sugar, cider, and ¼ cup rum in a small saucepan. Simmer for a few minutes, stirring to dissolve the sugar. Remove from the heat. Invert the cake onto a rack and remove the pan. Using a pastry brush, brush the warm syrup all over the warm cake until all has been absorbed. Let the cake cool completely. Sift confectioners' sugar over the top before serving.

Makes 10 to 12 servings

Scotch Irish Cake

— ❖ —

This caramelized sheet cake has been a speciality of Nantucket bake shops for years. Its homey flavors make it a popular cake to bake for a crowd. My version uses generous amounts of coconut and pecans.

1 cup (2 sticks) unsalted
   margarine
2 cups (packed) light brown
   sugar
½ cup granulated sugar
4 large eggs
3 tablespoons dark molasses

1 cup water
3 cups unbleached all-
   purpose flour
1 tablespoon baking soda
1½ tablespoons ground cinnamon
½ teaspoon salt
2½ cups quick-cooking oats

CARAMEL TOPPING
½ cup (1 stick) unsalted
   butter
1 cup (packed) light brown
   sugar

½ cup light cream
1½ cups shredded coconut
1¼ cups coarsely chopped
   pecans

1. Preheat the oven to 350°F. Butter and lightly flour a 15 × 10 × 2-inch baking pan.

2. Cream together the margarine and both sugars in a large mixing bowl. Beat in the eggs and molasses until well blended, then beat in the water. (The batter may separate a little at this point, but the dry ingredients will soon bind it back together.)

3. Sift the flour, baking soda, cinnamon, and salt together over the batter and stir until smooth and well blended. Stir in the oats. Pour the batter evenly into the prepared pan. Bake until lightly browned and cooked through in the center, 40 to 45 minutes.

4. While the cake is baking, prepare the caramel topping: Melt

the butter in a saucepan over low heat. Add the brown sugar and cream and stir until smooth. Stir in the coconut and pecans. Remove from the heat.

5. Preheat the broiler. Spread the topping evenly over the warm cake. Broil 3 inches from the heat until the topping is golden and bubbling, 4 to 5 minutes. Let the cake cool to room temperature and cut into 20 squares.

Makes 20 servings

Ivy League Chocolate Chunk Cookies

— ✛ —

The inspiration for these scrumptious cookies comes from an inn in Princeton, New Jersey. The subtle hints of lemon, cinnamon, and oats added to a basic Toll House cookie batter put these cookies in a league by themselves.

1 cup (2 sticks) unsalted
    butter
1¼ cups granulated sugar
¾ cup (packed) light
    brown sugar
4 large eggs
1½ tablespoons vanilla
    extract
1 tablespoon fresh lemon
    juice

2½ cups unbleached all-
    purpose flour
2 teaspoons baking powder
2 teaspoons ground cinnamon
½ teaspoon salt
¾ cup old-fashioned rolled oats
10 ounces semisweet or
    bittersweet chocolate chunks
1½ cups coarsely chopped
    walnuts

1. Preheat the oven to 350°F. Line baking sheets with parchment paper.

2. Cream the butter and both sugars together in a large mixing bowl. Beat the eggs one by one, beating well after each addition. Beat in the vanilla and lemon juice.

3. Sift together the flour, baking powder, cinnamon, and salt. Gradually stir it into the creamed mixture to make a smooth batter. Stir in the oats, chocolate, and walnuts until thoroughly incorporated.

4. Drop the batter by 2 tablespoonsful 2 inches apart on the lined baking sheets. Bake until cooked through in the center and light golden brown, 12 to 15 minutes. Transfer to a wire rack to cool.

Makes 3 dozen

FINGER FOODS FOR FROSTY WEATHER

Novelist Graham Greene once remarked that "There is a charm in improvised eating which a regular meal lacks ... a glamour never to be recaptured. ..." Personally, I couldn't agree more and such has made me into a grand connoisseur of appetizers and hors d'oeuvres that go beyond merely tickling the palate to sating hidden hungers in new and unexpected ways. My enthusiasm for the recipes in this chapter—Roasted Pepper and Artichoke Puffs, Pacific Flavor Shrimp, White Clam and Bacon Pizza, Saucisson Paysanne and Black Bean Hummus to name a few—is boundless. These are the informal yet often sophisticated morsels that I am happiest eating morning (!), noon, and night, the creations that I love most to invent, teach to students, and garnish for presentation.

While I certainly enjoy orchestrating a perfectly balanced meal of traditional courses, I'm at my most innovative when given free rein to pamper guests with many small appetizers that share no rhyme or reason except to lead one on an exotic taste voyage around the globe. Inclement weather on the homefront matters little when Mexico, the Orient, Normandy, New England, Canada, and the Caribbean are but a few of the destinations that are fair game for ingredient inspiration and a cold-weather cocktail party that sizzles. Eclectic palates and snowbound souls take heart, for these are recipes designed to be mixed and matched in an impromptu fashion for the pleasure of warming and waking up hibernating tastebuds.

❖

Roasted Pepper and Artichoke Puffs

— ✥ —

Once in a rare while, I perfect an hors d'oeuvre that is so successful and addictive that I end up serving it at every party without ever tiring of it. The Scallop Puffs Que Sera, from my *Nantucket Open House* cookbook, have become one such signature morsel and these, I wager, are destined to serve as co-stars.

2 tablespoons unsalted
  butter
1 bunch scallions, trimmed
  and minced
2 cloves garlic, minced
1 can (13¾ ounces)
  artichoke bottoms,
  drained and cut into ¼-
  inch dice
3 ounces thinly sliced
  prosciutto, minced
3 tablespoons finely
  shredded fresh basil
  leaves
2 ounces Parmesan cheese,
  grated (about ½ cup)

2 ounces Jarlsberg
  or Gruyère cheese,
  grated (about ½ cup)
1 tablespoon fresh lemon
  juice
Freshly ground black pepper
  to taste
½ cup Hellmann's
  mayonnaise
3 red bell peppers
3 yellow bell peppers
¼ cup olive oil
2 tablespoons balsamic
  vinegar
Salt to taste

1. Melt the butter in a small skillet over medium-high heat. Add the scallions and garlic and cook, stirring frequently, just until softened, 2 to 3 minutes. Transfer to a medium-size mixing bowl.

2. Add the artichoke bottoms, prosciutto, basil, Parmesan, and Jarlsberg to the scallions and toss to combine. Sprinkle with the lemon juice and pepper. Bind the mixture with the mayonnaise and refrigerate at least 1 hour.

3. Meanwhile prepare the peppers: Preheat the oven to 400°F. Stem and seed each pepper, then cut into chunks about 2 × 1½ inches. Place the peppers in a single layer in a large, shallow baking dish. Drizzle with the olive oil and vinegar and sprinkle with salt and pepper. Roast the peppers 15 minutes, stirring once halfway through the cooking time. Remove from the oven and let cool.

4. When ready to serve the hors d'oeuvres, preheat the broiler. Mound about 2 teaspoons of the artichoke mixture onto each pepper

wedge. Arrange in rows on baking sheets and broil 3 to 4 inches from the heat until puffed and bubbly, about 2 minutes. Let cool a few minutes, then transfer to a serving tray and pass with plenty of cocktail napkins.

Makes about 4 dozen

Tortilla
Spirals

— ❖ —

These versatile, Mexican morsels are fun to make and great to nibble. Once made, they can be stored in the refrigerator up to a week or even frozen. Omit the chicken if a vegetarian version is preferred, and adjust the hotness to your taste with the cayenne pepper. These are celebrated party fare, though I often toast a few spirals at noontime to accompany a steaming bowl of soup.

6 ounces cream cheese, at room temperature
4 ounces mild chèvre, such as Montrachet
1 clove garlic, minced
3 scallions, trimmed and minced
1 can (4 ounces) chopped green chiles
6 sun-dried tomatoes, packed in oil, drained but oil reserved, thinly slivered
⅓ cup pitted black olives, minced
4 ounces Monterey Jack cheese, shredded
1 cup finely diced cooked white chicken meat
3 tablespoons minced cilantro (fresh coriander)
2 teaspoons best-quality chili powder
Cayenne pepper to taste
Salt to taste
14 large (10-inch) flour tortillas

1. Beat the cream cheese and chèvre together in a mixing bowl until smooth. Beat in all the remaining ingredients except the tortillas and oil from the sun-dried tomatoes.

2. Spread 1 tortilla with a generous 2 tablespoons of the cheese mixture. Top with a second tortilla and spread in the same fashion with the cheese mixture. Roll up the 2 tortillas tightly like a jelly roll

and wrap in plastic wrap. Repeat the process with the remaining tortillas and cheese mixture. Refrigerate at least 2 hours.

3. Preheat the oven to 400°F.

4. Cut each tortilla roll into ½-inch slices and place cut sides up
on a nonstick baking sheet. Brush the top of each with a little oil
from the sun-dried tomatoes. Bake in the oven until puffed and lightly
browned, 12 to 15 minutes. Let cool a minute or two and serve.

Makes 9 dozen

Polenta for Crostini

— ✤ —

Most of the crostini I ate in Italy were made with rounds of stale
Tuscan bread brushed with olive oil and toasted, but I personally
prefer little squares of fried polenta as the base of my crostini.

2 quarts water	*2 teaspoons salt*
3 tablespoons unsalted	*3 cups fine yellow cornmeal*
butter	*Olive oil for sautéing*

1. In a large heavy saucepan combine the water, butter, and salt.
Bring to a boil over medium-high heat. Very, very gradually pour in
the cornmeal, stirring constantly with a wooden spoon. When all the
cornmeal has been added, reduce the heat to medium-low. Continue
cooking and stirring until the mixture is thick, smooth, and pulls away
from the side of the pan, about 15 to 20 minutes.

2. Spread the polenta evenly in a buttered 15 × 10-inch baking
sheet. Cool, then cover with plastic wrap and refrigerate until ready
to use.

3. To make the crostini, turn the chilled polenta out of the pan
and cut into 1½-inch squares. In a large heavy skillet heat a few
tablespoons of olive oil over medium heat. Sauté the polenta squares
in batches, flipping once with a spatula, until lightly browned on both
sides and heated through, about 5 minutes. Add more olive oil to the
skillet as needed. Keep the sautéed polenta squares warm on a baking
sheet in a low oven. Use as directed with the various toppings that
follow.

Makes about 4 dozen squares

ITALIAN CROSTINI

— ❖ —

Crostini are little rounds or squares of fried bread or polenta which sport a variety of savory toppings. They appear on antipasto menus everywhere in Tuscany. I know because I recently sampled innumerable disappointing examples of crostini during an otherwise engaging vacation pedaling a bicycle predominantly up to the medieval hilltowns which dot the Chianti countryside. While I can confidently report that the renaissance landscapes of da Vinci are very much alive, the typical Tuscan toast — whether chicken liver or porcini — has not fared as well. In the hope of returning to the American hors d'oeuvre scene armed with the quintessential crostini recipe, I crunched this ubiquitous canape in every little trattoria from the banks of the Arno to the formidable towers of San Gimignano, all much to the exasperation of my traveling companion who couldn't fathom why anyone would repeatedly order something that looked like cat food on toast.

In order to save face, I finally declared that upon my return to North America I would reinvent the crostini so that it tasted as wonderfully Italian as it sounded. Arrogance not withstanding, I think that the recipes here are worthy of starting a crostini renaissance. They are created especially for you, Richard, in an attempt to redeem your suffering as my crostini companion in Tuscany.

Chicken Liver Spread for Crostini

— ❖ —

When chicken livers are seasoned and blended properly, they make a wonderful savory spread. However, because most chicken liver preparations tend to end up looking like therapeutic mud from a fancy Italian spa, care must be taken with garnishing and the final presentation. I suggest topping each crostini with a healthy sprig of parsley or silvery sage leaf and sprinkling with a few toasted pine nuts.

2 tablespoons unsalted
  butter
1 medium onion, minced
2 cloves garlic, minced
8 ounces cream cheese, at
  room temperature
2½ tablespoons olive oil
1 pound chicken livers,
  rinsed, membranes
  removed, and cut into
  ½-inch pieces
3 thin slices prosciutto
  (about 1 ounce), minced
2 tablespoons chopped fresh
  sage
4 juniper berries, crushed to
  a powder

3 tablespoons sweet
  Marsala
1 tablespoon fresh lemon
  juice
Salt and freshly ground
  black pepper to taste
2 tablespoons drained
  capers
¼ cup pine nuts, lightly
  toasted
½ cup chopped fresh
  parsley
Polenta for Crostini (see
  page 37)
Small parsley sprigs or sage
  leaves for garnish

1. Melt the butter in a medium-size skillet over medium heat. Add the onion and garlic and cook 10 minutes, stirring occasionally. Transfer the mixture to a food processor, add the cream cheese, and process until combined but not perfectly smooth. Set aside.

2. Heat the olive oil in the same skillet over medium-high heat. Add the chicken livers, prosciutto, sage, and juniper. Cook, stirring occasionally, just until the livers are cooked through, 7 to 8 minutes. Stir in the Marsala and lemon juice, season with salt and pepper, and cook 2 minutes more.

3. Add the chicken liver mixture to the cream cheese mixture in the processor and process until well combined. (The mixture may seem a bit liquidy at this point, but it will firm up once refrigerated.) Add the capers, pine nuts, and parsley; process quickly just to combine.

4. Transfer the mixture to a bowl and refrigerate covered at least 6 hours to let the flavors blend and mellow. Let warm to room temperature before serving. Spread a generous amount of the spread on each warm polenta crostini, garnish, and serve.

Makes about 3 cups, enough for 48 crostini

ARRIVEDERCI ISOLA

— ❖ —

Chicken Liver Crostini
Sicilian Eggplant Caponata

— ❖ —

Farewell-to-Friends Fettucine
Mixed salad greens
Flasks of Chianti

— ❖ —

Purple Plum Brûlée
Espresso

Olive Spread for Crostini

— ❖ —

This spread is inspired by the flavors of Southern Italian cooking. The combination of coarsely chopped olives, lots of simmered garlic, sweet raisins, and zesty citrus lends a rustic appeal.

16 cloves garlic, peeled and
    each clove quartered
    lengthwise
¼ cup plus 2 tablespoons
    olive oil
½ cup raisins
⅓ cup dry white wine
1¼ cups chopped pitted
    Calamata olives
1 cup chopped pitted green
    olives

1 teaspoon fennel seeds
1 tablespoon grated orange
    zest
1 teaspoon grated lemon
    zest
2 tablespoons fresh orange
    juice
Polenta for Crostini (see
    page 37)

1. Put the garlic and 2 tablespoons of the olive oil in a small skillet. Simmer the garlic over medium-low heat until it is sweet and tender but not mushy, about 15 minutes.

2. Meanwhile put the raisins in a small saucepan, add the wine, and simmer over low heat 7 to 10 minutes to plump the raisins.

3. In a mixing bowl combine the garlic and raisins with the chopped olives. Season the mixture with the fennel seeds and citrus zests, then toss with the remaining ¼ cup olive oil and orange juice. Let the mixture sit at room temperature for a few hours to mellow the flavors. Spoon the mixture on warm polenta crostini.

Makes about 2½ cups, enough for 48 crostini

Quattro Formaggi Spread for Crostini

— ⬥ —

Forever the cheese lover, I like this crostini topping the best.

6 ounces cream cheese, at
  room temperature
6 ounces Gorgonzola cheese,
  at room temperature
2 cloves garlic, finely minced
8 ounces mozzarella cheese,
  shredded
3 ounces freshly grated
  Parmesan cheese

3 tablespoons chopped fresh
  basil leaves
Freshly ground black pepper
  to taste
Polenta for Crostini (see
  page 37)
4 sun-dried tomatoes
  packed in oil, drained
  and cut into thin slivers

1. In a small mixing bowl mash together the cream cheese and Gorgonzola until thoroughly combined. Mix in the garlic. Add the mozzarella and Parmesan and fold until all the cheeses are well mixed. Season with the basil and pepper.

2. Preheat the broiler.

3. Spread a generous tablespoon of the cheese mixture evenly over each polenta square, then press a sliver of sun-dried tomato on top. Place in rows on a baking sheet and broil 3 to 4 inches from the heat until the cheese is melting and bubbly, 1 to 2 minutes. Transfer to a serving tray and serve at once.

Makes about 2½ cups, enough for 48 crostini

Paterson Pasties

— ✣ —

These plump little pocket hors d'oeuvres remind me of the pies and savories served in British pubs. When I first made these I had a charming Scottish fellow, unwinding from a three-year stint in the English Army, assisting me in my shop. I loved the way his army training surfaced in the kitchen as he assured me that he committed each and every one of my recipe commands to memory so I would not have to repeat them again. To honor such dedication, I gave his name to these tasty little Cheddar, apple, and sausage morsels. Here's to you, Tim!

PASTRY

3½ cups unbleached all-purpose flour
1¼ cups (2½ sticks) unsalted butter, chilled, cut into bits

2½ cups shredded sharp Cheddar cheese
Pinch salt
2 large eggs

FILLING

4 tablespoons (½ stick) unsalted butter
2 leeks (white and light green parts), rinsed well and minced
⅓ pound shiitake mushrooms, stems discarded, caps minced
12 ounces bulk pork sausage
3 tablespoons Calvados or brandy

2 apples, peeled, cored, and diced
2 tablespoons chopped fresh sage or 1 teaspoon dried
¾ cup shredded sharp Cheddar cheese
Salt and freshly ground black pepper to taste

EGG WASH

2 large eggs

2 tablespoons water

1. Prepare the pastry: Place the flour, butter, Cheddar, and salt in a food processor and process until the mixture resembles coarse meal. Add the eggs and process just until the dough comes together. Wrap in plastic wrap and refrigerate several hours or overnight.

2. Prepare the filling: Melt the butter in a large skillet over medium-high heat. Stir in the leeks and shiitake mushrooms and sauté until softened, 5 minutes. Add the sausage and Calvados and cook, crumbling the sausage with the back of a spoon, until the sausage is cooked through, about 15 minutes. Stir in the apples, sage, and Cheddar and cook a couple of minutes more. Remove from the heat and season to taste with salt and pepper.

3. Preheat the oven to 375°F. Line baking sheets with parchment paper.

4. Divide the pastry dough in half and roll out each half ⅛-inch thick on a lightly floured surface. With a round cookie cutter about 2½ inches in diameter, cut out as many circles as possible from the dough. Save the scraps to make decorative garnishes.

5. To make the pasties, put a teaspoon of filling in the center of a dough circle, cover with another circle, and seal by pressing the edges together with the tines of a fork. Repeat the process and transfer the pasties to lined baking sheets.

6. For the egg wash, beat the eggs and water together and brush over each pasty. If you want, roll out the dough scraps and cut with a small decorative cookie cutter (star, heart, crescent moon). Place the shape on the center of each pasty and brush again with egg wash.

7. Bake the pasties in the oven until light golden brown, about 20 minutes. Let cool a minute or two and serve hot. The pasties also can be stored in the refrigerator for a few hours before baking or baked ahead and then reheated.

Makes about 4 dozen

NOVEMBER NIBBLES

— ✧ —

Paterson Pasties
Winter Guacamole
Mushrooms Bordeaux
Camembert Normande
Lamb Sâté

— ✧ —

Cranberry Curd Tartlets
Pear and Biscotti Strudel

Curled Spinach Crêpes with Smoked Salmon and Cream Cheese

— ❖ —

Crêpes laced with spinach, scallions, and dill are smeared with lemony cream cheese and sliced smoked salmon, rolled into logs, and then sliced into delectable bite-size morsels. The spiral effect of the pink and green is stunning and makes this hors d'oeuvre look like a very Western sushi roll.

SPINACH CREPES

3 large eggs
1½ cups milk
1 cup unbleached all-purpose flour
1 package (10 ounces) frozen chopped spinach, cooked and drained well
1 bunch scallions, trimmed and minced

3 tablespoons chopped fresh dill
Pinch of cayenne pepper
Salt and freshly ground black pepper to taste
½ cup water
1 to 2 tablespoons vegetable oil

SALMON FILLING

1 pound cream cheese, at room temperature
1 tablespoon grated lemon zest
1 tablespoon fresh lemon juice
2 shallots, finely minced

3 tablespoons minced fresh dill
2 tablespoons drained capers
2 teaspoons best-quality Hungarian sweet paprika
12 ounces thinly sliced smoked salmon

1. Prepare the crêpes: Place the eggs and milk in a mixing bowl and beat with an electric mixer at high speed 1 minute. Add the flour and beat until smooth and light, about 1 minute more. Stir in the spinach, scallions, dill, cayenne, salt, and pepper. Stir in the water and let the batter sit 15 minutes.

2. Heat a 7 or 8-inch crêpe pan over medium-high heat. Brush lightly with vegetable oil. Ladle about ⅓ cup batter into the hot pan, tilting to coat the bottom evenly. Cook until lightly browned on the bottom, about 2 minutes. Flip the crêpe over carefully and continue

cooking until light brown spots appear on the bottom, about 30 seconds more. Remove and let cool. Repeat the process with the remaining batter and oil to make 10 crêpes. (The crêpes can be made ahead and refrigerated, wrapped in plastic, 2 days before the final assembly.)

3. Prepare the filling: Beat the cream cheese with an electric mixer until light and fluffy. Beat in the lemon zest, juice, shallots, dill, capers, and paprika.

4. Lay the crêpes spotted side up on a flat surface. Spread each with a generous 2 tablespoons of the cream cheese mixture, then cover with a layer of the salmon slices. Roll each crêpe tightly, jelly-roll fashion, then wrap each roll in plastic wrap. Refrigerate at least 2 hours.

5. Trim the uneven ends off the rolls and cut into ½-inch-thick slices. Arrange on a platter and serve slightly chilled.

Makes about 60

Smoked Salmon with Ginger Butter

— ✦ —

These canapés are one of the most simple, sophisticated, and appreciated appetizers I know.

2½ tablespoons minced fresh ginger
1 cup (2 sticks) unsalted butter, at room temperature
1 pound square-loaf European-style whole-grain, rye, or pumpernickel bread

12 ounces thinly sliced best-quality smoked salmon
Freshly ground black pepper

1. Place the ginger and butter in a food processor and process until smooth and fluffy. Or beat the mixture using an electric mixer.

2. Cut each slice of bread into 4 triangles. Toast lightly and let cool. Spread each triangle generously with the ginger butter and top with a slice of salmon. Sprinkle the top of each canapé with a little freshly ground pepper. Arrange on serving trays and pass.

Makes 60 canapés

Scallops with Bacon and Maple Cream

— ❖ —

The idea for this winning recipe comes from the White Barn Inn in Kennebunkport, Maine. A while ago family members returned from a spirited birthday celebration for my uncle at the inn raving about the scallop appetizer. Though I have tried to check the appetizer out for myself, I just never seem to be there at the right moment. In the meantime lucky family members have continued to torment me with conflicting reports about how this exquisite concoction is made. Living on Nantucket within a stone's throw of some of the world's best scallops, I content myself and guests with this irresistible rendition.

2½ cups heavy or whipping
   cream
⅓ cup pure maple syrup
1½ tablespoons Dijon
   mustard
½ teaspoon grated nutmeg
Salt and freshly ground
   white pepper to taste

1½ pounds fresh bay scallops
1 pound sliced maple-cured
   bacon
2 tablespoons snipped fresh
   chives or minced fresh
   parsley

1. Combine the cream and maple syrup in a medium saucepan. Bring just to a boil, then simmer until reduced almost by half, 15 to 20 minutes. Stir in the mustard, nutmeg, salt, and pepper; simmer a few minutes more and remove from the heat.

2. Cut the bacon slices so that they wrap once around the scallops. Wrap each scallop in a piece of bacon. Place the scallops in rows on a broiling tray. (The recipe can be prepared in advance to this point. Refrigerate the sauce and scallops up to 8 hours.)

3. When ready to serve, preheat the broiler.

4. Warm the cream sauce over medium-low heat. Broil the scallops 4 to 5 inches from the heat until the bacon is browned and crisp, 4 to 5 minutes. Transfer the hot scallops with toothpicks to a shallow serving dish that will just hold them in a single layer. Pour the maple cream over all, sprinkle with chives, and serve at once.

Makes 8 to 10 appetizer servings

Note: For a more formal first course, place 5 or 6 scallops, without toothpicks, on a plate and nap with the maple cream sauce. Serve with knife and fork and perhaps bread for savoring every last drop of sauce.

White Clam and Bacon Pizza

— ✦ —

For years I have been intrigued by stories about a scrumptious white clam pizza made at a pizza parlor in New Haven, Connecticut. As I am very fond of pasta with white clam sauce, I found the thought of the pizza most appealing. After playing around with the idea in my kitchen, the recipe has evolved into one of my very favorites. I have added bacon to the original concept — a fabulous smoky and crisp contrast to the chewiness of the clams. Serve cut into small squares for a cocktail party or be piggy and make it a satisfying Sunday supper.

PIZZA DOUGH
1 package active dry yeast
1 cup warm water
3 tablespoons olive oil
1¼ teaspoons salt

3 to 3½ cups unbleached
  all-purpose flour
Yellow cornmeal

CLAM AND BACON TOPPING
4 ounces sliced bacon, cut
  into ½-inch dice
3 tablespoons olive oil
2 large cloves garlic, minced
2 teaspoons dried oregano
Pinch of dried red pepper
  flakes

1½ cups minced clams,
  fresh or thawed frozen
3 tablespoons minced fresh
  parsley
¼ cup freshly grated
  Parmesan cheese

1. Prepare the pizza dough: Sprinkle the yeast over the warm water in a large mixing bowl and let dissolve for 4 to 5 minutes. Whisk in the oil and the salt. Using a wooden spoon, mix in the flour, ½ cup at a time, to make a soft and sticky dough. Turn the dough out onto a floured surface and knead until smooth and satiny, 8 to 10 minutes. Transfer the dough to a clean mixing bowl, cover, and let rise in a warm, draft-free place until doubled, 1½ to 2 hours.

2. In the meantime, prepare the clam topping: Sauté the bacon in a skillet over medium-high heat until cooked through but not quite crisp. (The bacon will finish crisping as it bakes on the pizza.) Remove the bacon from the skillet with a slotted spoon and let drain on paper towels. Add the olive oil to the bacon fat in the skillet. Stir in the garlic, oregano, and red pepper flakes and sauté 2 minutes. Add the clams and simmer over medium heat 5 minutes. Remove from the heat

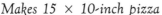

and stir in the parsley and bacon.

    3. Preheat the oven to 375°F. Sprinkle a 15 × 10-inch baking sheet lightly with cornmeal.

    4. Punch down the pizza dough and roll it out to fit into the pan. Stretch the dough in the pan and crimp the edges decoratively. Spread the clam topping evenly over the dough and scatter the Parmesan over all.

    5. Bake the pizza until puffed and golden brown around the edges, 30 to 40 minutes. Let cool slightly, then cut into small or large squares.

    Makes 15 × 10-inch pizza

Shrimp and Orange Pot Stickers

— ❖ —

My favorite food in the panoply of Chinese cooking is dumplings. Pot stickers are pan-fried dumplings that get their crunch and their name by literally sticking to the bottom of the pot. Most recipes call for a combination of seafood and meat in the filling, but I prefer the more extravagant use of all shrimp. Packaged wonton skins are remarkably easy to work with, and these dumplings make an exotic and stellar party hors d'oeuvre.

1 ounce dried mushrooms,
   preferably Chinese black
   mushrooms
1½ tablespoons minced
   fresh ginger
4 scallions, trimmed and
   minced
1 small carrot, peeled and
   minced
½ cup canned whole water
   chestnuts, drained and
   minced
1 tablespoon grated orange
   zest
2 tablespoons minced
   cilantro (fresh coriander)

1 large egg white
1 pound raw shrimp, peeled
   and deveined
1½ tablespoons soy sauce
2 tablespoons dry sherry
1 teaspoon sugar
1 teaspoon Oriental sesame
   oil
Dash of hot chile oil
Cornstarch
40 prepared wonton skins
3 tablespoons vegetable oil

SAUCE

1 cup fresh orange juice
2 tablespoons dry sherry
2 tablespoons soy sauce
1 tablespoon chopped fresh
   ginger
2 tablespoons toasted sesame
   seeds
1 tablespoon chopped
   orange zest

1 teaspoon Oriental sesame
   oil
1 tablespoon light brown
   sugar
1 tablespoon hoisin sauce
Several drops hot chile oil

1. Soak the mushrooms in hot water to cover until softened, about 30 minutes. Drain and finely mince.

2. Combine the mushrooms, ginger, scallions, carrot, water chestnuts, orange zest, and cilantro in a large mixing bowl. Set aside.

3. Beat the egg white in a small bowl just until foamy. Place the shrimp in a food processor, add the egg white, and process until the shrimp is very finely minced. Add the mushroom mixture and process to combine. Add the soy sauce, sherry, sugar, sesame oil, and chile oil; process just to combine. Transfer the mixture to a mixing bowl and set aside.

4. Line a couple of baking sheets with waxed paper and sift cornstarch lightly over the paper. Place a scant tablespoon of the shrimp filling on the center of each wonton skin. With your finger moisten the edges of the skin with water, fold the skin in half into a triangle, and pinch the edges together to seal. Moisten the 2 opposite points of the triangle with another drop of water and pinch the points together. Place the dumplings on the prepared trays as you work. (The dumplings can be prepared ahead up to this point; cover with a

clean, dry kitchen towel and refrigerate up to 4 hours.)

5. Prepare the sauce by combining all the ingredients in a small bowl.

6. Coat 2 heavy 12-inch skillets each with 1½ tablespoons vegetable oil. Heat the skillets over high heat. When sizzling, add half the dumplings to each pan. Brown the bottoms evenly, lifting carefully every now and again with a spatula to prevent burning. The dumplings will brown in 5 to 7 minutes. Divide the sauce equally between the skillets and continue cooking until the dumplings are cooked through and translucent and the sauce is reduced to a glaze, about 5 minutes more.

7. Transfer the dumplings to a serving platter and pass with either toothpicks or, more authentically, chopsticks.

Makes 40 dumplings

CHOPPING SCALLIONS AND LEEKS

—❖—

I never realized what a scallion and leek fiend I was until my recipes were copy edited for this book. Many came back with the dreaded yellow flag, indicating that a clarification was in order—just how much of the scallion or leek green do I use when chopping or slicing? Now, since I like these onion cousins especially for their green accent, I use all the white bulb and as much of the green stalk as is tender and fresh looking. Depending on the time of year and local quality control, this can amount to almost the entire stalk or as little as a half or third of the green. So when recipes in this book call for scallions and leeks to be trimmed, discard only tough, blemished, or wilted tops from the bunches.

Pacific Flavor Shrimp

— ❖ —

Shrimp's popularity never ceases to amaze me. Even in this time of newfangled hors d'oeuvres, "having shrimp" and plenty of it still sets the standard for what makes a good party. Since my catering conscience won't allow me to send a mound of shrimp accompanied by cocktail sauce off to a party, I devised this dish after being inspired by Hugh Carpenter's *Pacific Flavors* cookbook. The shrimp are cooked, tossed in sesame oil, and then mixed in a very provocative tomato-based sauce. Arrange in a shallow serving bowl and have guests spear the shrimp with toothpicks.

1½ cups tomato purée
2½ tablespoons light brown sugar
2 cloves garlic, minced
Chopped zest of 1 lime
¼ cup fresh lime juice
1½ tablespoons Oriental chile paste
¾ cup shredded fresh basil leaves
2 tablespoons cornstarch
2 tablespoons water

3 pounds medium to large shrimp, peeled, deveined, cooked, and drained
2 tablespoons Oriental sesame oil
Dried red pepper flakes to taste
Lime wedges for garnish

1. Combine the tomato purée, sugar, garlic, lime juice, lime zest, chile paste, and ½ cup of the basil in a saucepan. Dissolve the cornstarch in the water and set aside. Bring the sauce ingredients to a low boil over medium heat and cook a few minutes. Stir in the cornstarch and cook just until the sauce is thick and glossy. Remove from the heat and let cool to room temperature.

2. Toss the cooked shrimp with the sesame oil in a mixing bowl. Sprinkle with red pepper flakes to taste. Add the cooled tomato sauce and toss to combine. Transfer to a shallow serving bowl and sprinkle with the remaining ¼ cup basil. Garnish with lime wedges. Serve chilled or at room temperature.

Makes 12 to 15 appetizer servings

My Brother's Brandade de Morue

— ❖ —

While salt cod is often cast a dubious glance in the current sea of sushi and rare tuna, the Europeans have long known many magical transformations for these ugly crusted and leathery slabs of dried fish. It is thought that sixteenth-century Portuguese sailors were the first to salt and sun-dry the fresh cod they caught as a means of preserving it during voyages of many months at sea. In fact the great French epicure Escoffier later credited the Portuguese with bringing "the gas-tronomic values of this precious fish to Europe."

The warm French dip known as brandade is one of my favorite salt cod preparations. I think of it as a cold-weather cousin to lusty aioli. The following version is the one my brother serves as an appetizer at his restaurant, Jonathan's, snuggled in the little town of Blue Hill, along the midcoast of Maine.

1 pound salt cod	¼ cup heavy or whipping
2 large baking potatoes,	cream
peeled	Freshly ground white
8 cloves garlic, minced	pepper to taste
⅓ cup fruity olive oil	French bread rounds, toasted

1. Soak the salt cod in cold water to cover overnight, changing the water several times. Rinse the fish and drain. Cut into 1-inch squares and lay the pieces out on a kitchen towel; place another towel on top and gently squeeze out any excess water. Set aside.

2. Place the potatoes in a saucepan, cover with water, and boil until tender. Drain and set aside.

3. Place the salt cod and garlic in a food processor and process with quick pulses until the fish is finely ground. With the machine running, pour the olive oil slowly through the feed tube and process until incorporated.

4. Cut the warm potatoes into coarse chunks, add to the proces-sor, and process just until incorporated. Be careful at this point not to overprocess or the potatoes will become gluey. Add the cream and pulse quickly just to blend. Season to taste with white pepper. (At this point the brandade may be refrigerated until ready to serve but no longer than 5 days.)

5. When ready to serve, preheat the oven to 425°F.

6. Spoon the brandade into a 9-inch gratin dish or several (8 to

10) smaller gratin dishes if serving individually. Heat until warmed through and slightly browned and crusted on top, 12 to 15 minutes. Serve with plenty of toast rounds for dipping.

Makes 8 to 10 servings

AVOCADO MAGIC

— ❖ —

I used to plan ahead for recipes requiring avocados to allow ample time for ripening. Then I picked up a great rapid ripening tip one day from the Kentucky hostess of a baby shower. She swore that the perfectly ripened avocados that we were enjoying in our salad had been rock hard the day before. Her secret sounded strange to me — she buried the whole avocados in a canister of all-purpose flour for twenty-four hours and they emerged soft and ready to use. So I went home and tried it myself. The trick does indeed work!

Winter Guacamole

— ❖ —

Many of my happiest summer memories include a spicy bowl of guacamole and an icy salt-rimmed Margarita. Since winter still provides terrific avocados but not great guacamole mix-ins, I devised this hearty and unconventional cold-weather variation to inspire rhapsodic winter memories as well.

3 ripe avocados, preferably Hass

3 tablespoons fresh lime juice

3 scallions, trimmed and finely minced

2 small jalapeño chiles, stemmed, seeded, and minced

4 sun-dried tomatoes, packed in oil, drained and minced

1 cup shredded sharp Cheddar cheese

5 slices bacon, cooked crisp and coarsely crumbled

3 tablespoons minced cilantro (fresh coriander)

Salt to taste

Pit and peel the avocados and mash the pulp in a medium-size mixing bowl to a chunky consistency (a large wooden spoon or potato masher works well). Add the lime juice, scallions, jalapeño chiles, and sun-dried tomatoes, then fold in the cheese, bacon, and cilantro. Season to taste with salt. Serve the guacamole as soon as possible to keep the bacon crisp. Accompany with your favorite chips for dipping.

Makes 3 to 4 cups

Late Harvest Salsa

— ❖ —

When the last of summer's vegetables are salvaged from the vines before the first frost, I make this smoky salsa and serve it warm with blue and yellow corn chips. Oven roasting the vegetables intensifies the garden-ripe flavor and helps disguise the little surface imperfections that can afflict end-of-season produce. This is a simple yet sensational addition to the ever-expanding salsa craze.

6 ripe beefsteak tomatoes
1 yellow bell pepper
¼ cup fruity olive oil
Salt and freshly ground
  black pepper to taste
1 bunch scallions, trimmed
  and minced

2 jalapeño chiles,
  stemmed, seeded,
  and minced
½ cup fresh lime
  juice
⅓ cup minced cilantro
  (fresh coriander)

1. Preheat the broiler.
2. Place the tomatoes and yellow pepper in a roasting pan and coat generously with the olive oil. Sprinkle with salt and pepper. Broil the vegetables 4 to 5 inches from the heat, turning frequently, until blistered and lightly charred all over, 20 to 25 minutes. Let cool for a few minutes.
3. Remove the blistered skin from the tomatoes and bell pepper; remove the stem and seeds from the pepper. Place the vegetables along with any accumulated pan juices in a food processor and purée until smooth. Transfer the purée to a mixing bowl.
4. Stir the scallions, jalapeño chiles, lime juice, and cilantro into the tomato mixture. Season with salt and pepper. Serve the salsa warm with your favorite corn chips.

Makes about 3 cups

Black Bean Hummus

— ❖ —

This is my ingenious and tasty entry into the current trend of serving black-hued foods. In this hummus, black beans take the place of the chick-peas and peanut butter the place of sesame tahini. Lime juice, hot peppers, and cilantro add a Caribbean twist, which may be accented further by using sweet potato and banana chips as dippers instead of the traditional pita triangles.

8 ounces of dried black
beans, soaked overnight,
then cooked in fresh
water until tender
⅓ cup fresh lime juice
3 large cloves garlic, minced
½ cup freshly ground
smooth peanut butter
½ to ¾ cup water

2 jalapeño chiles, stemmed,
seeded, and minced
½ cup minced cilantro
(fresh coriander)
Salt to taste
2 tablespoons olive oil
Lime wedges for garnish
Black olives for garnish

1. Drain and rinse the cooked black beans. Let cool to room temperature.

2. Place the lime juice, garlic, and peanut butter in a food processor and process to a smooth paste.

3. Add the black beans and process until the mixture is very smooth, thinning it to spreading consistency with the water while processing. Add the jalapeño chiles and cilantro and pulse the machine just to incorporate. Season to taste with salt.

4. Transfer the black bean hummus to a serving bowl. Drizzle the top with olive oil to make it glisten. Garnish with lime wedges and black olives. Serve at room temperature accompanied by the dippers of your choice.

Makes about 4 cups

THE
LONG AND SHORT
OF EGGPLANT

— ❖ —

Culinary historians trace the origins of eggplant to Southeast Asia where, curiously enough, it was prized for its bitterness. The vegetable later entered India via Bengal and continued from there to spread throughout the rest of the world. Initially, though, the Asian's love of the eggplant's bitter flavor and spongy texture didn't migrate with it. Excerpts from ancient literatures recorded the skin's ominous purple hue as that of a scorpion's belly and the taste as that of a scorpion's sting. Other sources attributed both madness and melancholy to the ingestion of eggplant. When it was discovered in the ninth century that the bitter juices could be extracted by salting the vegetable for an hour or so before cooking, eggplant began its slow ascent to universal popularity. By the sixteenth century, Arabs referred to eggplant as "lord of the vegetables," and the Ottoman Empire in Turkey began a great and everlasting love affair with the vegetable by creating a truly staggering array of different eggplant delights.

Eggplant, as we know it today, comes in many different shapes, sizes, and colors, which I find breeds a lot of confusion and controversy. Most Mediterranean and Asian cooks recommend small and/or thin eggplants for they believe they have the least bitter flavor and fewest seeds. I disagree. Small may be chic and adorable but big and plump is better in my book. Since many of my recipes call for roasted eggplant pulp, I appreciate the ample yield of the larger varieties and have never detected any compromise in flavor. In addition, my many years of baba ghanouj, ratatouille, and moussaka making have convinced me that the brutish-looking larger eggplants actually have fewer seeds than their miniature counterparts. In conclusion, may only the debates over size, and not your eggplants, be bitter.

Strange Flavor Eggplant

— ✥ —

I first sampled the Chinese vegetable creation, Strange Flavor Eggplant, a few years ago at Barbara Tropp's poetic China Moon Café in San Francisco. Tastebuds titillated and transformed, I could scarcely wait to return to my own East Coast kitchen to concoct a batch with my own personal stamp. When the food savvy staff of my Que Sera Sarah store unabashedly devoured my experiment, I realized that from here on in, it would be bye, bye baba ghanouj as the favorite ethnic eggplant dip on the fashionable cocktail party circuit.

Serve this spicy-sweet spread either warm, at room temperature, or chilled, with homemade Sesame Sippets.

1½ pounds eggplant (about 2 medium)
3 tablespoons vegetable oil
2 teaspoons Oriental sesame oil
3 cloves garlic, minced
2 tablespoons chopped fresh ginger
3 scallions, trimmed and minced
¼ teaspoon dried red pepper flakes
3½ tablespoons soy sauce
3 tablespoons light brown sugar
1 tablespoon rice wine vinegar
1 tablespoon fresh lemon juice
2 tablespoons chopped cilantro (fresh coriander)
Sesame Sippets (recipe follows)

1. Preheat the oven to 425°F.
2. Place the whole eggplants on a baking sheet and prick in several places with a fork to allow steam to escape. Coat the eggplants with 1 tablespoon of the vegetable oil. Roast, turning once halfway through cooking, until the pulp is quite soft, 30 to 40 minutes. Let stand until cool enough to handle.
3. Cut off the stems and peel the skin from the eggplants. Place the pulp in a food processor and process until smooth. Set aside.
4. Heat the remaining 2 tablespoons vegetable oil along with the sesame oil in a medium-size skillet over medium-high heat. Add the garlic, ginger, scallions, and red pepper flakes; quickly cook, stirring constantly, for 1 minute.
5. Whisk together the soy sauce, brown sugar, and vinegar just until the sugar is dissolved. Add at once to the skillet and bring to a boil. Stir in the puréed eggplant and simmer for 3 minutes. Remove from the heat and stir in the lemon juice and cilantro. Transfer to a serving bowl and serve accompanied by Sesame Sippets.

Makes about 2½ cups

Sesame Sippets

— ❖ —

These are simple to make and taste so much more special than those store-bought crackers.

4 large (7 to 8 inches in
  diameter) pita breads,
  each separated horizontally
  into 2 rounds
½ cup vegetable oil

1 tablespoon Oriental
  sesame oil
¼ cup sesame seeds

1. Preheat the oven to 350°F.
2. Mix the vegetable and sesame oils in a small bowl. With a pastry brush, coat the exposed side of each pita half lightly with oil. Sprinkle generously with sesame seeds. With a sharp knife, cut the pita halves into irregular, bite-size triangles. Place on baking trays.
3. Toast the triangles in the oven until lightly browned and crisp, 7 to 9 minutes. Let cool and store in an airtight container.
Makes about 5 dozen

Red Sauce
Rapson

— ❖ —

A cigar-chomping, Calvados-swilling Texan named Bill Rapson, a member of my recent cycling expedition through Normandy, told me about this unusual seafood sauce of his while we shared a bottle of Beaujolais at the Brasserie les Vapeurs in fashionable Trouville-sur-Mer. The notion of mixing tomatoes with jalapeño chiles and almond extract as a condiment for raw oysters sounded just whacky enough to be exceptional. As promised, upon return he sent up a copy of the recipe from Houston. I interpreted it and tested it on a mixed group of conservative New Englanders and worldly Nantucket travelers. While all actually admitted to enjoying it dolloped over oysters on the half-shell, most thought that it would be even more spectacular tossed with poached mussels or shrimp. In enthusiastic agreement, I now share Red Sauce Rapson with the hope that it infuses new rapture and adventure into many a shellfish feast!

3 tablespoons olive oil
4 ripe large tomatoes,
 seeded and finely diced
2 jalapeño or serrano chiles,
 stemmed, seeded, and
 minced
1 small red bell pepper,
 stemmed, seeded, and
 diced

½ cup coarsely ground
 almonds
1 teaspoon pure almond
 extract
3 tablespoons minced fresh
 tarragon or 1 tablespoon
 dried
Salt and freshly ground
 black pepper to taste

Heat the olive oil over medium heat in a large skillet. Add the tomatoes, jalapeño chiles, bell pepper, almonds, and almond extract. Simmer uncovered, stirring occasionally, 15 minutes. Remove from the heat and stir in the fresh tarragon. (If using dried tarragon, add it initially to the skillet with the other ingredients.) Season to taste with salt and pepper. Chill the sauce several hours in the refrigerator. Serve as a sauce on raw oysters or clams or as a dip for cooked mussels, shrimp, lobster, or crab.

Makes about 3 cups

Cashew Chicken with Lime Marmalade Dipping Sauce

— ✦ —

Many of my most creative hors d'oeuvres have evolved out of unbearably harried times in the kitchen. In this particular instance, I had promised a customer during a very busy weekend that I would invent some sort of tropical chicken tidbit for her Saturday night cocktail party. Just as the sands of the hourglass started to run a mite thin, I was saved by a miraculous surge of culinary adrenaline. I only regret that it took a crisis to give birth to this fabulous combination of textures and flavors.

¼ cup dry sherry
¼ cup soy sauce
1 tablespoon Oriental
  sesame oil
2 tablespoons fresh lime
  juice
Finely grated zest of 1 lime
2 cloves garlic, minced
1½ tablespoons minced
  fresh ginger

2 pounds boneless, skinless
  chicken breasts, cut into
  1-inch cubes
1½ cups cashews, lightly
  toasted
½ cup sesame seeds
½ cup cornstarch

LIME MARMALADE DIPPING SAUCE

1 jar (16 ounces) lime
  marmalade
1 jar (5 ounces) prepared
  white horseradish

3 tablespoons chopped
  cilantro (fresh coriander)

1. At least 2 hours ahead of time, marinate the chicken: In a small bowl whisk together the sherry, soy sauce, sesame oil, and lime juice. Stir in the lime zest, garlic, and ginger. Place the chicken cubes in a large bowl and toss with the marinade. Refrigerate covered at least 2 hours.

2. Preheat the oven to 375°F. Lightly oil a baking sheet.

3. Place the cashews, sesame seeds, and cornstarch in a food processor and process until the mixture looks like small, powdery pebbles. Transfer to a shallow dish, such as a pie plate.

4. Remove the chicken from the marinade, reserving any left over. Dredge each chicken cube with the cashew mixture to coat evenly. Place the cubes slightly apart on the prepared baking sheet. Bake in the oven, drizzling with the reserved marinade, until the chicken is just cooked through, about 10 minutes.

5. In the meantime, heat the lime marmalade in a saucepan over medium-low heat just until melted. Remove from the heat and stir in the horseradish and cilantro. Transfer to a small serving bowl. Spear each chicken cube with a toothpick, arrange on a serving platter, and pass with the sauce.

Makes about 5 dozen pieces

Saucisson Paysanne

— ✥ —

This is my elaboration on a recipe from a great friend and bon vivant, Canadian publisher Al Cummings. Though Al and I have indulged in many extravagant feasts at renowned restaurants, both of us secretly share insatiable cravings for hearty and peasanty sausage cookery. While the rewards of kielbasa kinship are many, the sharing of this rustic hors d'oeuvre recipe is among the most coveted.

1 smoked kielbasa, about
   1 pound
1 cup dry white wine
1 heaping tablespoon light
   brown sugar
2 tablespoons strong Dijon
   mustard

2 tablespoons Calvados or
   brandy
3 tablespoons chopped fresh
   parsley
Freshly ground black pepper
   to taste

1. Cut the kielbasa into 1-inch slices, then cut each slice into quarters. Put the meat in a heavy skillet just large enough to hold all the pieces in a single layer and pour in the wine.

2. Bring the wine to a boil and cook uncovered until the wine has almost evaporated and looks syrupy, about 12 minutes. Stir in the brown sugar, mustard, and Calvados; cook 1 minute more.

3. Toss the sausage with the parsley and pepper to taste. Serve hot or at room temperature with toothpicks for spearing and thin rounds of crusty Fresh bread for dipping in the juices.

Makes 6 to 8 appetizer servings

Lamb Sâté

— ✥ —

This flavorful, Indonesian-inspired skewer can be made with almost any sort of seafood, poultry, or meat. However I personally feel that the highly seasoned sâté sauce best complements heartier meats such as lamb and pork. My version is a favorite developed after many tries.

LAMB AND MARINADE

3 tablespoons vegetable oil
1 tablespoon Oriental
  sesame oil
3 tablespoons soy sauce
½ cup cream sherry

Finely grated zest of 1 lime
1 clove garlic, minced
3 pounds lean lamb, cut
  into ¾-inch cubes

SATE SAUCE

3 tablespoons vegetable oil
1 tablespoon Oriental
  sesame oil
1 bunch scallions, trimmed
  and minced
3 cloves garlic, minced
2 tablespoons minced fresh
  ginger
2 jalapeño or serrano chiles,
  stemmed, seeded, and
  minced
2 tablespoons rice wine
  vinegar
2 tablespoons light brown
  sugar

3 tablespoons soy
  sauce
3 tablespoons tomato
  paste
½ cup chunky peanut
  butter
3 tablespoons fresh lime
  juice
1 teaspoon ground
  coriander
⅓ cup chopped cilantro
  (fresh coriander)

1. Prepare the lamb marinade: Whisk together the vegetable oil, sesame oil, soy sauce, and sherry. Stir in the lime zest and garlic. Place the lamb in a large shallow dish and coat with the marinade. Marinate covered in the refrigerator, stirring once in a while, at least 3 hours or up to 24 hours.

2. Meanwhile, prepare the sâté sauce: Heat the vegetable and sesame oils together in a large skillet over medium-high heat. Add the scallions, garlic, ginger, and jalapeño chiles; sauté until softened, 3 to 4 minutes. Blend in the vinegar, sugar, and soy sauce, stirring to dissolve the sugar. Add the tomato paste, peanut butter, lime juice, and coriander; stir until smooth. Thin the sauce to the consistency of sour cream with water. Let simmer over medium heat 10 minutes. Remove from the heat and stir in the cilantro.

3. When ready to cook the sâtés, preheat the broiler. Soak about 24 thin wooden skewers in water for a few minutes to prevent them from burning under the broiler.

4. Thread 3 or 4 pieces of the marinated lamb on the skewers. Place the skewers on a broiling rack and brush liberally with the sâté sauce. Broil 4 to 5 inches from the heat, turning once, about 3 minutes each side. Pass the sâté skewers at once on a platter with a little bowl of extra sâté sauce for dipping.

Makes about 2 dozen skewers

Autumn Pâté with Mushrooms and Hazelnuts

— ❖ —

Many pâtés achieve their characteristic complexity of flavor by using game forcemeats. Since game is often expensive and difficult to come by, I could never stand the thought of grinding it up into a pâté. I had a hunch that the ground turkey meat that I had been seeing with increasing frequency in the supermarket would make a great and economical substitute. I followed my instincts and added textural variety with sautéed shiitake mushrooms and crunchy hazelnuts to end up with a pâté whose flavor I felt embodied the essence of autumn.

Pâté will keep in the refrigerator, well wrapped, for two weeks or it can be frozen up to a couple months. It is excellent for entertaining and also makes a welcome hostess gift. In addition to mustard and cornichons, I often accompany my cold-weather pâtés with a side dish of homemade cranberry relish.

2 pounds ground lean turkey meat
8 ounces pork fatback, diced
12 ounces bulk pork sausage
1 medium onion, minced
5 cloves garlic, minced
3 tablespoons chopped fresh rosemary
2 tablespoons chopped fresh thyme
1 teaspoon ground coriander
2 teaspoons salt
2 teaspoons freshly ground black pepper

1 pound lean pork, cut into 2 × ⅓-inch strips
4 ounces thinly sliced prosciutto, minced
2 large eggs, lightly beaten
¾ cup Calvados or brandy
6 bay leaves
1 pound sliced bacon
3 tablespoons unsalted butter
1 pound shiitake mushrooms, stems discarded, caps thinly sliced
¾ cup lightly toasted skinned hazelnuts, coarsely chopped

1. The day before baking the pâté, combine the turkey, pork fatback, sausage, onion, and garlic. Put the mixture through a meat grinder or process in a food processor until it is well blended.

2. Place the mixture in a large mixing bowl and mix in the rosemary, thyme, coriander, salt, pepper, pork strips, and prosciutto. Beat in the eggs and the Calvados to bind. Cover the mixture and let sit overnight in the refrigerator.

3. Preheat the oven to 350°F.

4. Place a row of 3 bay leaves down the center of each of two 6 to 8 cup terrines or loaf pans. Line each with bacon slices arranged crosswise to line both the sides and bottom. Let the ends of the slices hang over the edges of the pan.

5. Melt the butter in a skillet over medium-high heat. Add the mushrooms and sauté, stirring frequently until lightly browned and any liquid has evaporated, about 10 minutes. Remove from the heat.

6. Layer one-third of the pâté mixture into the prepared terrines. Top with half the sautéed mushrooms and half the hazelnuts. Top with another third of the meat mixture, then the remaining mush-rooms and hazelnuts. Make a final layer with the rest of the meat and pack the mixture compactly with your hands or the back of a wooden spoon. Fold the overhanging bacon slices over the top of each pâté.

7. Completely wrap each pan tightly with aluminum foil. Place the pans in a larger baking pan and pour in enough hot water to come halfway up the sides of the pâté pans. Bake the pâtés 1½ hours. Remove from the oven and let cool under a weight (such as a large can of tomatoes or juice), 2 hours. Chill the pâtés several hours before unmolding and serving.

Makes two 8 × 3-inch pâtés

Camembert Normande

— ❖ —

A recent fall bicycle jaunt through the cow- and cathedral-laden countryside of Normandy awakened new respect for the native Camembert and Calvados. While I certainly savored and sipped my share of both to fuel my pedaling, I soon felt the urge to pay some sort of homage to remembered flavors once back at home. This elegantly soused and dressed wheel of oozing Camembert can almost make me mistake Nantucket for the quaint Norman seaport of Honfleur.

1 wheel (8 ounces)
   Camembert or Brie
3 tablespoons Calvados
1 cup skinned hazelnuts,
   very lightly toasted
1 tablespoon unsalted
   butter, at room
   temperature

2 crisp Granny Smith
   apples, thinly sliced
Sliced French bread

1. The day before you plan to serve the Camembert, gently scrape the thick white parts of the skin from the cheese but do not remove the rind. Poke the surface of the cheese lightly all over with the tines of a fork. Place the cheese on a plate and pour the Calvados over it. Marinate at room temperature for 24 hours, turning the cheese over occasionally.

2. The following day, finely chop the hazelnuts in a food processor. Add the butter and process just to combine. Pat the hazelnut mixture evenly all over the top and sides of the cheese. Transfer to a baking dish and refrigerate covered 1 hour.

3. Preheat the oven to 400°F.

4. Bake the cheese until the nuts are golden brown, about 12 to 15 minutes. Serve at once with apple wedges and French bread.

Serves 1 to 8

Winter Fruit Stuffed with Chutney Cream Cheese

— ❖ —

A hollowed-out pineapple half is the traditional vessel for this exotic sweet-and-savory cheese spread. However, I'm fond of spooning it onto little kumquat halves, garnishing them with a dusting of toasted coconut, and passing them as a bite-size hors d'oeuvre. Use your imagination as the curry flavors blend beautifully with most winter fruits.

1½ pounds cream cheese, at room temperature
3 tablespoons medium dry sherry
3 tablespoons light brown sugar
1 tablespoon best-quality curry powder
1 tablespoon ground ginger
1 teaspoon dry mustard
1 bunch scallions, trimmed and finely minced
⅔ cup mango chutney, finely chopped

6 ounces shredded sharp Cheddar cheese
Grated zest of 1 lime
6 ounces hickory-smoked almonds, coarsely chopped
Garnishes of winter fruits (grapes, oranges, apples, pears, and kumquats) in bite-size pieces, toasted coconut, or wheatmeal crackers, if serving as a spread

Using an electric mixer, cream together the cream cheese, sherry, brown sugar, curry, ginger, and mustard in a large mixing bowl. Stir in the scallions, chutney, Cheddar, lime zest, and almonds. Let the flavors mellow for a few hours in the refrigerator. Serve slightly chilled or at room temperature as a dip in a hollowed-out pineapple half or piped onto individual, bite-size pieces of fruit. Garnish with toasted coconut.

Makes 6 cups

Spanakopita

— ❖ —

I had mixed feelings about including this Greek spinach-and-cheese pie recipe in the book, because I think it is a rather dated hors d'oeuvre. Yet it was a very popular item at my shop, and customers always commented that the Que Sera Sarah version was the best they had ever tasted. A big tray of spanakopita is a relatively easy way to provide a lot of bite-size nibbles for a crowd, and I'll take cutting this pie into little squares any day over folding dozens of individual phyllo triangles! In that time-saving spirit, I present the tried-and-true recipe from my shop files.

1 to 1½ cups (2 to 3
   sticks) unsalted butter,
   melted
6 large eggs, beaten
3 pounds ricotta cheese
2½ tablespoons unsalted
   butter
2 bunches scallions,
   trimmed and minced
3 packages (10 ounces each)
   frozen spinach, cooked
   and drained

8 ounces feta cheese,
   crumbled
1½ cups shredded
   mozzarella cheese
½ cup minced fresh
   dill
Salt and freshly ground
   black pepper to taste
1 pound phyllo dough,
   thawed
2 tablespoons sesame
   seeds

1. Preheat the oven to 375°F. Brush an 18 × 12 × 2-inch baking pan with a thin coating of melted butter.

2. In a large mixing bowl whisk together the eggs and ricotta until smooth. Melt the 2½ tablespoons butter in a medium skillet over medium-high heat. Add the scallions and sauté just until softened, about 3 minutes. Add to the ricotta mixture along with the spinach, feta, mozzarella, and dill. Mix until well combined and season with salt and pepper.

   3. Unwrap the phyllo dough, lay it out flat on a clean surface, and cover the top with a slightly damp kitchen towel to keep the dough from drying out while working.

   4. Cover the bottom of the prepared baking pan with 1 sheet of phyllo dough. Brush with a thin coating of the melted butter, then continue layering and buttering the dough in the same manner for 8 sheets. Cover with an unbuttered ninth sheet and spread half the ricotta-spinach filling evenly over the top. Layer 5 more buttered sheets of dough on top of the filling. Top with a sixth unbuttered sheet of dough and spread with the remaining filling. Layer and butter all the remaining sheets of dough on top of the filling. Brush the top sheet generously with butter and sprinkle with the sesame seeds.

   5. Bake the spanakopita in the oven until it is puffed and golden brown on top, 1 to 1¼ hours. Cool for 10 minutes, then cut into serving pieces. If you wish to make miniature hors d'oeuvre squares, the spanakopita will cut farm more easily if cooled, refrigerated, and then cut. Heat the individual squares on a baking sheet in a preheated 350°F oven for 10 to 15 minutes. Pass at once.

   Makes 16 large squares or about 150 miniature squares

Mushrooms Bordeaux

— ❖ —

I used to make this hors d'oeuvre quite frequently during my early years on Nantucket. I had sort of forgotten about it until recently when I was trying to conjure up something warm, wonderful, and innovative to do with mushrooms. The dish is an intriguing upside-down version of stuffed mushrooms — sautéed mushroom caps float on a bed of minced stems, bread crumbs, garlic, parsley, and pine nuts. Perfect for tapas-style cocktail parties where the food requires more forks than fingers.

3 pounds large domestic
white mushrooms
6 tablespoons (¾ stick)
unsalted butter
6 tablespoons olive oil
6 cloves garlic, minced
½ cup dry red wine
2½ cups bread crumbs,
made from day-old
French bread

1 cup minced fresh parsley
⅓ cup freshly grated
Parmesan cheese
2 tablespoons pine nuts,
lightly toasted
3 tablespoons heavy or
whipping cream
Salt and freshly ground
black pepper to taste

1. Separate all the mushroom caps from the stems. Reserve 30 of the biggest, best-looking caps. Finely chop the remaining caps along with stems. Wrap the chopped mushrooms in a clean kitchen towel and squeeze to extract as much moisture as possible. Set aside.

2. Heat 1 tablespoon each butter and oil in a large skillet over medium-high heat. Sauté a third of the mushroom caps, light golden brown, 4 to 5 minutes. Turn the caps over and cook another 2 minutes; remove to a platter. Repeat the process, adding another tablespoon each butter and oil to the skillet for each batch.

3. When all the mushroom caps have been cooked, heat the remaining 3 tablespoons each butter and oil in the same skillet over medium-high heat. Add all the chopped mushrooms and sauté until softened and lightly browned, 5 minutes. Add the red wine and simmer uncovered over medium-low heat until almost all of the liquid has evaporated, 15 to 20 minutes. Stir in the bread crumbs and cook 5 minutes more. Add the Parmesan, pine nuts, and cream; cook 1 minute more. Season to taste with salt and pepper.

4. Preheat the oven to 350°F.

5. Spread the chopped mushroom mixture in a shallow, 12 to 14-inch round baking dish. Arrange the mushroom caps right side up decoratively over the filling. Bake in the oven just until heated through, 12 to 15 minutes. Serve at once, letting each guest scoop a few whole mushrooms with filling onto a small plate.

Makes 10 to 12 servings

THINKING THANKS-GIVING

◆

PART I

SAVORIES

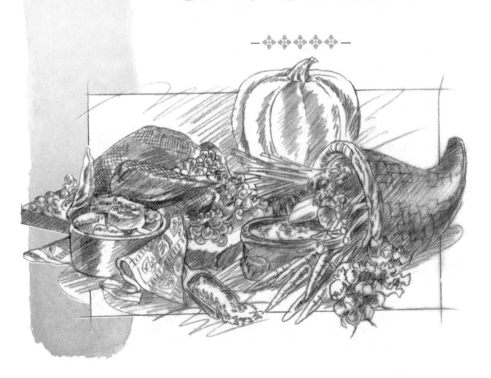

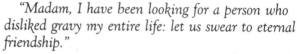

"Madam, I have been looking for a person who disliked gravy my entire life: let us swear to eternal friendship."

—Sydney Smith

"A thankful heart is not only the greatest virtue, but the parent of all other virtues."

—Cicero

We have been conditioned to think of Thanksgiving as the quintessential American holiday, but the fact is that celebrations of thanksgiving—as a repast or cere-mony to honor the bountiful harvest—date back to ancient times. The Chinese partook of a three-day-long lunar feast at the time of the harvest moon; the Greeks and Romans created gods, goddesses, and myths to explain yearly growing cycles; over 3,000 years ago the ancient Hebrews celebrated the autumn festival of *Succot* to thank God for making plants; and the Egyptians held an annual parade and banquet in worship of Min, their god of vegetation and fertility.

While the turkey is deservedly the great symbol of our American Thanksgiving, my greatest culinary stimulus con-tinues to stem from nature's miracle gift of vegetation that yields an odyssey of inspirational side dishes.

Back in the 1860s, a women's magazine editor by the name of Sarah Josepha Hale led a successful crusade to convince Abraham Lincoln to declare Thanksgiving an annual national holiday. Ms. Hale also believed that Thanksgiving should be treated as a special time for women to display their culinary prowess. In this post-feminist age, such an anachronistic con-cept is one that I simply adore and do, in fact, practice. The one problem is that with an overflowing harvest palette—broccoli, Brussels sprouts, carrots, cabbage, cauliflower, celeriac, fennel, parsnips, pumpkins, squash, turnips, and as-sorted other tubers—I can confine neither all my thanks nor prowess to one grand meal on Thankgiving day! Thus this chapter contains recipes aplenty for the accoutrements of

Thanksgiving indulgence (gravy excepted), to inspire the holiday menu as well as cooking during the entire month of November and even through the whole frigid stretch of winter right up to the first signs of new spring crops. If this seems a mite zealous, keep in mind that the austere Pilgrims had a first Thanksgiving that spanned nearly an entire week. Truly there always has been and, hopefully, always will be a surfeit for which to be extremely thankful.

Belmont Inn Thanksgiving Dressing

Nantucket friends Jerry Clare and John Mancarella — two of my best and most diehard summer beach buddies — sadly abandoned me a few seasons back in order to revamp a bed-and-breakfast inn and restaurant in Camden, Maine. While I miss their sunny companionship, I have since coveted my brief stays at the charming and cozy Belmont as it is resplendent with many of my favorite colors and chintz fabrics. The team served their first Thanksgiving dinner at the inn's restaurant this past November, and the following is John's highly original recipe for an ambrosial turkey dressing.

1 loaf day-old Sambuca Corn Bread (see page 233)
½ cup (1 stick) unsalted butter
1 large onion, minced
4 large ribs celery, cut into ¼-inch slices
1½ pounds sweet Italian sausage, casings removed
1½ cups chicken broth, preferably homemade

2 tablespoons Sambuca liqueur
½ cup squash or pumpkin seeds, toasted and ground in a blender or food processor
1½ tablespoons ground coriander
Salt and freshly ground black pepper to taste
1 large egg, slightly beaten

1. The day before you plan to make the dressing, crumble the Sambuca Corn Bread into small pieces and let it dry in the open air overnight.

2. The next day melt the butter in a large skillet over medium-high heat. Add the onion and celery and sauté until softened, about 10 minutes. Transfer to a large mixing bowl and combine with the corn bread crumbs.

3. Add the sausage to the same skillet and cook over medium-high heat, crumbling into small pieces with the back of a wooden spoon, until the meat loses its pink color and begins to brown, about 15 minutes. Add to the stuffing mix. Add the chicken broth and Sambuca to the skillet and heat, scraping up any brown bits clinging to the bottom, until slightly reduced. Add the liquid to the stuffing mixture and stir well to combine.

4. Stir in the ground squash seeds and season with the coriander, salt, and pepper. Bind the dressing together with the beaten egg.

5. If using the stuffing for a turkey, store it in the refrigerator until the turkey is ready to be roasted. If baking it as a side dish, place it in a buttered casserole and bake at 350°F until browned and crisp, about 45 minutes.

Makes enough to stuff a 16 to 20 pound turkey or 12 to 15 side-dish servings

Corn Bread Stuffing with Linguiça and Kale

— ❖ —

One of my great culinary thrills is in inventing new stuffing combinations. The inspiration for this recipe comes from the reading of recipes for Southern ways with greens overlapping with a vacation through linguiça land, better known as the Portuguese section of Fall River, Massachusetts. The end result is like *caldo verde* translated from soup to stuffing. While the recipe makes an ample amount for stuffing a big Thanksgiving bird, I enjoy baking smaller amounts of it in a casserole as a starchy accompaniment to sautéed scallops, broiled lobster, or baked cod. Stuffing freezes well if packed securely in sturdy plastic bags. It will keep up to three months and bring enjoyment long after the last of the turkey carcass has disappeared.

1 pound kale, tough center ribs removed, torn into 1-inch pieces
1 cup (2 sticks) unsalted butter
1 large onion, chopped
1 medium bulb fennel, coarsely chopped
2 medium-size red bell peppers, stemmed, seeded, and diced
4 cloves garlic, minced
1½ pounds Pepperidge Farm corn-bread stuffing crumbs

2 pounds linguiça sausage, cut on a diagonal into ¼-inch slices
1 can (16½ ounces) creamed corn
1½ cups shredded sharp Cheddar cheese
½ cup pine nuts, lightly toasted
2½ cups chicken broth, preferably homemade
1 tablespoon dried oregano
Salt and freshly ground black pepper to taste

1. Bring a large pot of water to a boil and add the kale. Blanch until the kale is cooked and tender, about 5 minutes. Drain in a colander and cool slightly. Squeeze out as much excess water as possible by wringing it with your hands. Set aside.

2. Melt ¾ cup of the butter in a large skillet over medium-high heat. Stir in the onion, fennel, red peppers, and garlic. Cook, stirring frequently, until the vegetables are softened, about 10 minutes. Transfer to a large mixing bowl and toss with the stuffing crumbs.

3. In the same skillet sauté the linguiça in batches, stirring frequently, until browned all over. Add to the stuffing along with any accumulated drippings.

4. Add the creamed corn, Cheddar, and pine nuts and stir to combine. Heat the remaining ¼ cup butter with the chicken broth in a saucepan just until the butter is melted. Pour over the stuffing and stir to moisten completely. (If the stuffing seems too dry, you may have to add a little more chicken broth and melted butter, this will depend on the fattiness and moisture content of the linguiça.) Season the stuffing with the oregano and salt and pepper to taste.

5. If using the stuffing for a turkey, store it in the refrigerator until the turkey is ready to be roasted. If baking it as a side dish, place the desired amount in a buttered casserole and bake at 350°F for 35 to 40 minutes.

Makes enough to stuff a 22 to 24 pound turkey or 15 to 20 side-dish servings

TURKEY TALK AND TREPEDATION

— ❖ —

Throughout my years as a commercial caterer, I spent umpteen hours experimenting with and preparing every traditional Thanksgiving food except, oddly enough, the turkey! I firmly believed a whole roasted turkey could not and should not be take-out fare. I maintained no moral qualms about grinding quarts of cranberry relishes, mashing pounds and pounds of buttery potatoes, scoring bushels of Brussels sprouts, peeling bags of thick-skinned rutabagas and yams, or crimping flaky ring upon ring of homemade pies for my hungry customers. But I adamantly insisted that each and every one fill the home with the paramount aroma of Thanksgiving, the smell of the big bird roasting in one's own oven.

Upon my recent retirement from life in the perishable lane of a day-to-day food shop, I have had to pay my dues for having escaped ever roasting my own or anyone else's turkey. Indeed, my goose finally got cooked when I became a spokesperson for the consumer hot-line of a national turkey company. Now fondly known as Ms. Butterball, I have had to confront and combat not only my own but thousands of the people's trepidations about cooking this symbol of Americana.

There is no doubt in my mind, my previous mastery of much more ornate forms of gastronomy aside, that the cooking of a turkey — weighing anywhere from 12 to 24 pounds — in the confines of most home ovens is plainly intimidating. Really now, what comparable experience do most nonprofessional cooks have with preparing such a beastly mass of meat, which then serves as the focal point of a family celebration geared soley to feasting! The psychological implications alone are enough to make the designated cook think of trading platters with the turkey.

Fortunately I now possess the equivalent of a Ph.D. in the esoteric field of turkey trivia and can faithfully assure frightened turkey ingenues that a little knowledge goes a long way. In the course of my reign as Ms. Butterball, I have observed and tasted turkeys cooked by all of the oldest, newest, and whackiest methods at a huge turkey test kitchen outside Chicago staffed by dedicated home economists. As a result, I now am thoroughly convinced of one surefire way of preparing the holiday bird, Moreover as a veteran pie baker, I can declare that this method is not as easy as but easier than pie! It is what the congenial phone operators who answer callers' queries on the tur-

key talk-line refer to as *Open Pan Roasting*. Instructions are as follows:

- Thaw the turkey in the refrigerator or in cold water. When ready to cook, remove the wrapper and preheat the oven to 325°F.
- Remove the neck and giblets from the body cavities. Rinse the turkey and pat dry.
- Stuff the neck and body cavities lightly, if desired. Turn the wings back to secure the neck skin in place. Truss the legs together if necessary.
- Place the turkey, breast side up, on a flat rack in an open pan about 2 inches deep. Insert a meat thermometer deep into the thickest part of the thigh next to the body but not touching the bone.
- Rub the turkey skin with 2 tablespoons vegetable or olive oil to prevent drying. Further basting (unless you are a type-A personality) is unnecessary. When the skin is golden brown, shield the breast loosely with foil to prevent over browning.
- The turkey is done when the internal thigh temperature registers between 180° to 185°F. When the thigh is pierced with a fork, the juices should run clear, not pink. A 16 pound bird takes an average of 3½ to 4 hours when roasted at 325°F. Let the turkey stand uncovered for 15 to 20 minutes before serving to ensure easier carving.

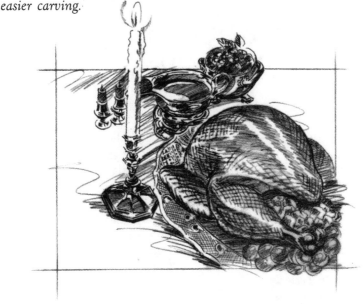

Parsnip and Parmesan Sticks

— ✥ —

A simple and elegant way to prepare this often misunderstood root vegetable.

4 tablespoons (½ stick)
  unsalted butter
1½ pounds parsnips, peeled
  and cut into slender 3 x
  ½-inch sticks
½ cup freshly grated
  Parmesan cheese

Salt and freshly ground
  black pepper to taste
3 tablespoons minced fresh
  parsley

In a large skillet melt the butter over medium-high heat. Add the parsnip sticks and sauté until lightly browned and tender, 10 to 12 minutes. Sprinkle with the Parmesan and toss to coat, then season with salt, pepper, and parsley. Serve at once.

Makes 4 to 6 Servings

Roasted Celeriac and Shallot Purée

— ✥ —

The names for this foreboding root vegetable tend to be fickle— celeriac, celery root, celery knobs—but my love for its intense flavor is unequivocal. The technique of oven roasting places this recipe in the category of kitchen aromas to make you swoon.

2 medium knobs celeriac
  (celery root), peeled
  and cut into coarse
  1-inch chunks
8 shallots, peeled
3 tablespoons unsalted
  butter, melted

½ cups dry white vermouth
¼ cup heavy or whipping
  cream
Salt and freshly ground
  white pepper to taste

1. Preheat the oven to 375°F.

2. Toss the celeriac, shallots, and the melted butter together in a roasting pan. Sprinkle the vermouth over all. Roast the vegetables in the oven, stirring occasionally, until tender and browned, about 1 hour.

3. Place the vegetables and any pan juices in a food processor, add the cream, and process until very smooth. Season to taste with salt and white pepper. Serve at once or reheat later in the top of a double boiler or in a microwave oven.

Makes 6 to 8 servings

Oven-Roasted Fall Vegetables

— ❖ —

One of the most popular recipes in my *Nantucket Open House* cookbook was a simple but colorful and flavorful mélange called Oil-Roasted Farm Vegetables. While working on this book, I woke up in the middle of one night with the idea of applying the concept to root vegetables. I set to work the very next day and I'm happy to report that my middle-of-the-night culinary inspirations are quite trustworthy.

4 medium parsnips, peeled and cut on a diagonal into ½-inch slices
1 medium rutabaga, peeled and cut into ¾-inch chunks
1 knob celeriac (celery root), peeled and cut into ½-inch chunks
2 large red potatoes, scrubbed and sliced ½-inch thick

8 ounces baby carrots, peeled and trimmed
1 fennel bulb, trimmed and cut crosswise into ¼-inch-thick slices
10 shallots, peeled
½ cup (1 stick) unsalted butter, melted
⅔ cup dry white vermouth
Kosher (coarse) salt and freshly ground black pepper to taste

1. Preheat the oven to 325°F.

2. Toss all the vegetables together in a large roasting pan. Drizzle with the melted butter and vermouth; then season with salt and pepper. Cover the pan tightly with aluminum foil and cook 30 minutes.

3. Uncover the vegetables and continue cooking, stirring occasionally, until the vegetables are tender and lightly browned, 45 to 60 minutes more. Serve at once.

Makes 8 to 10 servings

Fennel Purée

— ❖ —

A fennel aficionado, I find this is my very favorite way to prepare the vegetable. I've even thought of eating this particular dish for breakfast in place of hot cereal! The more conventional may find it better suited to accompanying poultry, game, and pork. The rice in the recipe adds necessary body to the fennel without diluting its flavor in the way that a potato thickener would.

½ cup (1 stick) unsalted
   butter
10 cups minced fennel bulb
   (about 3 fennel bulbs)
2 leeks (white and light
   green parts), trimmed,
   rinsed well, and
   minced

½ cup dry white wine
1½ cups cooked Arborio or
   long-grain rice
Salt and freshly ground
   black pepper to taste
Feathery fennel tops for
   garnish

1. Melt the butter in a large skillet over medium heat and add the fennel and leeks, stirring to coat with the butter. Sauté 5 minutes, add the wine, and cover the surface of the fennel with a sheet of waxed paper. Reduce the heat slightly and sweat the vegetables until very tender, about 30 minutes.

2. Transfer the vegetables to a food processor, add the rice, and process until very smooth. For the silkiest texture, pass the purée through a food mill to remove any stringy fibers. Season the purée with salt and pepper to taste. Reheat in the top of a double boiler over simmering water before serving. Garnish each serving with a sprig of fennel top if desired.

Makes 6 to 8 servings

Braised Fennel, Parma Style

— ❖ —

A nother enticing way to cook this anise-flavored vegetable based on an Italian recipe from the beautiful, pink-cast city of Parma.

5 fennel bulbs, trimmed
  and quartered
⅓ cup olive oil
2 cups dry white wine
4 sweet Italian sausages,
  casings removed
Salt and freshly ground
  black pepper to taste

1 cup freshly grated
  Parmesan cheese
2 tablespoons minced
  feathery fennel tops
2 tablespoons extra virgin
  olive oil

1. Combine the fennel with ⅓ cup olive oil and the wine in a large, deep skillet. Bring to a boil, then reduce to a simmer. Cover the pan and braise the fennel until tender, about 40 minutes.

2. While the fennel is cooking, brown the sausage in a small skillet over medium-high heat, crumbling it into small pieces with the back of a wooden spoon. When the sausage is cooked through and crispy, remove it from the heat.

3. Preheat the oven to 375°F.

4. Remove the fennel from the skillet with a slotted spoon and arrange in a 10 to 12-inch round or oval gratin dish. Boil the liquid remaining in the skillet until reduced to ⅓ cup. Season with salt and pepper and pour over the fennel. Scatter the sausage over the fennel, then top with the Parmesan. Sprinkle with the fennel tops and drizzle with the extra virgin olive oil.

5. Bake until browned and bubbling, 20 minutes. Serve hot.

Makes 6 to 8 servings

Creamed Spinach

— ❖ —

Good creamed spinach is one of the most soothing dishes ever invented. To capture the delicate essence of spinach, the time-consuming labor of washing, stemming, sorting, and chopping fresh leaves is a must.

2 pounds fresh spinach,
  rinsed well and stemmed
3 tablespoons unsalted
  butter
1 bunch scallions, trimmed
  and minced
8 ounces cream cheese, at
  room temperature

2 tablespoons heavy or
  whipping cream
2 tablespoons fresh lemon
  juice
Salt and freshly ground
  black pepper to taste
½ teaspoon freshly grated
  nutmeg

1. Place the spinach leaves in a steamer and cook over simmering water just until wilted, 5 to 10 minutes. Drain well, cool slightly, and chop.

2. Melt the butter in a medium-size heavy skillet over medium heat. Add the scallions, and sauté for 5 minutes. Break the cream cheese into small pieces, add it to the skillet, and stir until melted and smooth. Add the spinach to the skillet, and stir well to combine. Stir in the cream and lemon juice, then season with the salt, pepper, and nutmeg. Cook just until heated through, 5 to 7 minutes. Serve at once.

Makes 6 to 8 servings

Mustard Creamed Onions

— ❖ —

T hese are a tangy, golden-hued twist on the classic version of pale white creamed onions. The standard cream sauce is laced with both grainy and strong Dijon mustards and the dish is topped with a whisper of freshly grated Parmesan cheese and warm sprinkling of russet-colored paprika.

2 pounds small white onions, peeled
3 cups water
3 tablespoons unsalted butter
3 tablespoons unbleached all-purpose flour
1 cup milk
3 tablespoons medium-dry or cream Sherry
1 tablespoon grainy Dijon mustard
1 tablespoon smooth Dijon mustard
Pinch grated nutmeg
Salt and freshly ground white pepper to taste
3 tablespoons snipped fresh chives
3 tablespoons freshly grated Parmesan cheese
2 teaspoons sweet Hungarian paprika

1. Place the onions in a medium-size saucepan, cover with the water, and bring to a boil. Reduce the heat and simmer uncovered until the onions are just barely tender, 15 to 20 minutes. Drain, reserving 1 cup of the cooking liquid.

2. Prepare the cream sauce: Melt the butter in a small saucepan

over medium heat. Whisk in the flour and cook, stirring constantly, 2 minutes. Gradually whisk in first the reserved cooking liquid, then the milk and Sherry to make a smooth sauce. Swirl in both mustards and season with the nutmeg, salt, and pepper. Simmer stirring occasionally, over low heat to allow the flavors to blend, 7 to 10 minutes. Stir in the chives and remove from the heat.

3. Preheat the oven to 350°F. Butter a gratin dish large enough to hold the onions in a single layer.

4. Combine the mustard cream sauce with the onions and transfer to the prepared dish. Sprinkle the top with the Parmesan and paprika. (The dish may be prepared up to this point 2 days in advance and refrigerated until baking time. Bring the dish to room temperature prior to baking.)

5. Bake the creamed onions until the sauce is bubbling and the top is golden brown, about 30 minutes. Serve hot.

Makes 8 to 10 servings

Baby Carrots with Brown Sugar and Mustard

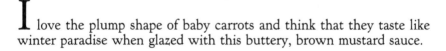

I love the plump shape of baby carrots and think that they taste like winter paradise when glazed with this buttery, brown mustard sauce.

1 pound baby carrots, trimmed and peeled	2½ tablespoons light brown sugar
3 tablespoons unsalted butter	1 tablespoon grainy Dijon mustard

1. Blanch, steam, or microwave the carrots until crisp-tender, 6 to 8 minutes.

2. Melt the butter in a medium-size skillet over medium heat. Stir in the brown sugar and mustard to make a smooth sauce. Add the cooked carrots to the skillet and toss to coat with the sauce. Cook 1 minute more, then serve at once.

Makes 6 servings

Grand Marnier-Glazed Carrots

— ❖ —

It's a shame that the staple bag of carrots is often overlooked among the more fashionable produce at the supermarket. Carrots and oranges have both a color and flavor affinity. So, the Grand Marnier in this recipe guarantees a boost in reputation for the friendly common carrot. Serve with a crispy roasted chicken or a succulent cut of pork.

3 tablespoons unsalted butter	⅓ cup Grand Marnier or other orange liqueur
1 pound carrots, peeled and cut on a sharp diagonal into ⅓-inch-thick slices	2 tablespoons chopped fresh parsley
3 tablespoons orange marmalade	

1. Melt the butter in a heavy skillet over medium-high heat. Add the carrots and toss to coat with the butter. Stir in the marmalade and heat until melted. Add the Grand Marnier and bring to a boil. Lower the heat and simmer covered 5 minutes.

2. Uncover the carrots and continue to cook until tender and the liquid has been reduced to a glaze, 4 to 5 minutes more. Sprinkle with the parsley and serve at once.

Makes 6 servings

Braised Belgian Endive

— ❖ —

I've always thought of pearly and pale green Belgian endive as epitomizing aristocracy in a vegetable. While it most often appears as a crisp spoke in a variety of tossed salads, I am quite fond of it in its most extravagant role as a wonderfully warm and silky oven-braised vegetable. The subtle bitter flavor of endive makes it both a delicious accompaniment and contrast to the richness of a rib roast or a crispy duckling.

5 tablespoons unsalted
   butter
12 Belgian endives
3 tablespoons sugar
¼ cup fresh lemon juice

2 teaspoons crumbled dried
   tarragon
Salt and freshly ground
   white pepper to taste

1. Preheat the oven to 350°F.

2. Melt the butter in an ovenproof casserole just large enough to hold the endives in a single layer over medium heat. Arrange the endives in the casserole and brown in the butter, turning with tongs, 5 to 7 minutes. Sprinkle with the sugar and cook a few minutes more until lightly caramelized. Remove from the heat.

3. Pour the lemon juice over the endives and sprinkle with the tarragon, salt, and white pepper. Cover the casserole tightly with a lid or piece of aluminum foil and bake in the oven until the endives are very soft and tender, about 1 hour. Serve 2 whole endives per person.

Makes 6 servings

Broccoli with Toasted Hazelnuts and Pancetta

— ❖ —

Italian ingenuity with simple vegetables never ceases to amaze me. This recipe adaptation will make you understand why vegetables are accorded the status of a separate course in many Italian restaurants.

2 large heads broccoli,
   trimmed and broken into
   large florets
6 tablespoons fruity
   olive oil
3 cloves garlic, peeled
½ cup lightly toasted, finely
   chopped hazelnuts

2 teaspoons finely grated
   lemon zest
⅓ pound sliced pancetta
   or bacon, cooked
   until crisp and
   coarsely crumbled
Salt and freshly ground
   black pepper to taste

1. Blanch the broccoli in boiling salted water or steam in a vegetable steamer just until crisp-tender. Drain and set aside.

2. Heat the olive oil in a large skillet over medium heat. Add the garlic and cook for 5 minutes to infuse the oil with the flavor.

Remove and discard the garlic cloves.

3. Add the broccoli to the skillet and toss to coat with the hot oil. Stir in the hazelnuts, lemon zest, and crumbled pancetta, then season with salt and pepper. Serve at once.

Makes 6 to 8 servings

Braised Red Cabbage with Apple and Mustard Seeds

— ❖ —

When summer's vegetables dwindle, keep in mind that cooked cabbage makes a welcome addition to the autumn and winter repertoire. Red cabbage, in particular, always adds a deep burst of color to the often muted shades of cold-weather cooking. This preparation pairs beautifully with pork and game dishes.

4 slices bacon
1 tablespoon golden
  mustard seeds
1 medium onion, cut into
  crescent slivers
2 Granny Smith apples,
  peeled, cored, and cut
  into ¼-inch-thick slices
2 tablespoons light brown
  sugar

2 tablespoons balsamic
  vinegar
1 medium head red
  cabbage, cored and thinly
  shredded
½ cup dry white wine
1 tablespoon Dijon mustard
Salt and freshly ground
  black pepper to taste

1. Cook the bacon in a large heavy skillet over medium-high heat until crisp. Remove the bacon to drain on paper towels.

2. Add the mustard seeds to the bacon fat in the skillet. As soon as you begin to hear them pop, add the onion and apples to the pan. Sauté 5 minutes, stirring frequently. Stir in the brown sugar and vinegar and cook a minute or so to dissolve the sugar.

3. Add the cabbage to the skillet and stir to combine with the onion-apple mixture. Stir in the wine and the mustard. Simmer uncovered over medium heat, stirring occasionally, just until the cabbage is tender, 10 to 15 minutes. Add the bacon to the cabbage, season to taste with salt and pepper, then serve at once.

Makes 6 to 8 servings

Frizzled Radicchio with Pancetta and Rosemary

— ✤ —

In Italy, radicchio frequently is eaten cooked or grilled rather than raw in salads. Since radicchio's popularity has soared in North America, it has become almost as ubiquitous in its raw state as iceberg lettuce once was. I personally find this recipe a delicious antidote to the use and abuse of this beautiful imported chicory.

4 medium heads radicchio
⅓ to ½ cup fruity olive oil
2 ounces pancetta, thinly
   sliced
3 tablespoons coarsely
   chopped fresh rosemary

Kosher (coarse) salt and
   freshly ground black
   pepper to taste

1. Preheat the broiler.
2. Discard any wilted outer leaves from the radicchio. Cut each head into 4 to 6 wedges and arrange snugly in an ovenproof dish. Drizzle evenly with the olive oil and scatter the pancetta and rosemary over the top. Season with salt and pepper.
3. Place the radicchio 7 to 8 inches from the heat. Broil until the radicchio is tender when pierced with a fork in the center and the edges of the leaves are curled and slightly charred, 12 to 15 minutes. Serve as a vegetable, hot, warm, or at room temperature.
Makes 4 to 6 servings

Maple-Glazed Brussels Sprouts and Chestnuts

— ✠ —

I am a Brussels sprouts fiend. What asparagus is to springtime and vibrant vine-ripened tomatoes to summer, Brussels sprouts are to me in the winter months. They are the original baby vegetable and often remind me more of furled peony blossoms than miniature cabbages. The vegetable's variant hues of green and grace of structure make it an elegant accompaniment. This particular smoky and sweet preparation goes well with roasts of drama such as a standing rib, crown roast of pork, or the Thanksgiving turkey.

24 whole chestnuts, peeled
   (see box, facing page)
2 cups chicken broth
   preferably homemade
6 slices bacon, cut into
   small dice
1½ pounds Brussels sprouts,
   trimmed and cut with an
   X on the bottom

2½ tablespoons maple syrup
Salt and freshly ground
   black pepper to taste

1. Steam the Brussels sprouts in a vegetable steamer over boiling water just until crisp-tender, 8 to 10 minutes. Drain and set aside to cool slightly.

2. Place the chestnuts and chicken broth in a small saucepan and simmer over medium heat until the chestnuts are tender, about 25 minutes.

3. In the meantime, sauté the bacon in a medium-size skillet until crisp. Remove and drain on paper towels. Pour off all but 2 tablespoons of the fat remaining in the skillet.

4. Cut the Brussels sprouts lengthwise in half and place in the skillet. Add the chestnuts to the skillet along with 3 tablespoons of the cooking broth, then stir in the maple syrup. Heat over medium-high heat, stirring frequently, until the liquid is reduced to a glaze, about 5 minutes. Add the cooked bacon and season with salt and pepper. Serve at once.

Makes 6 to 8 servings

CHESTNUTS NOT ROASTING ON AN OPEN FIRE

— ❖ —

The microwave oven and I have never exactly been bosom buddies. The main reason for our differences is that I prefer knowing the doneness of cooked foods by the usual tactile and visual techniques to the alerting sound of an electronic beep. Nonetheless my microwave and I recently reached a peaceful accord over fresh chestnuts. The microwave makes removing those nasty brown shells enclosing the chestnuts a breeze. Follow these simple instructions: Cut an X with a sharp knife across the flat side of each chestnut and place them in a single layer in a shallow microwave-safe baking dish. Do not cover. Cook on high power for 8 minutes in a large oven or 10 minutes in a compact oven. Cool slightly. The outer shell and inner skin should peel away easily.

If you do not own a microwave, preheat the oven to 350°F. Cut the X on the flat side of each chestnut. Bake the nuts in a roasting pan until the outer shell and inner skin can be easily removed, 20 to 30 minutes.

Braised Beets with Sherry Vinegar

— ❖ —

Those who know my predilection for any color or flavor in the pink family will not be surprised to learn that beets are one of my very favorite vegetables. I particularly love the warm hue and musky sherry essence this recipe brings to plates of hearty coldweather food.

2 bunches medium-large beets, greens trimmed
12 large shallots, peeled
3 tablespoons olive oil
½ cup dry red wine
Salt and freshly ground black pepper to taste
3 tablespoons light brown sugar
3 tablespoons sherry vinegar

1. Preheat the oven to 375°F.

2. Peel the beets and cut each one into 8 chunks or wedges. Mix the beets and shallots together in a 12 × 9-inch baking dish. Toss with the olive oil and red wine and season with salt and pepper. Cover the dish tightly with aluminum foil and bake until the beets are just barely tender, 1 to 1¼ hours.

3. Stir in the brown sugar and sherry vinegar. Bake uncovered, stirring occasionally, until the vegetables are tender and glazed with the sauce, 15 to 20 minutes more. Serve at once.

Makes 6 to 8 servings

Rutabagas Anna

— ❖ —

This spectacular yet simple vegetable torte takes its inspiration from the classic French preparation *pommes Anna* — a pie of sliced potatoes lavished in butter and promiscuously named after a cocotte of the Napoleonic era. My substitution of rutabagas imparts a lovely autumnal hue. While the dish is traditionally made by brushing each layer of thinly sliced vegetables with clarified butter, I am partial to using either rendered duck fat or bacon drippings. As the moment of triumph in this recipe hinges on a perfect unmolding, it is essential to begin with a proper baking dish — either a 12-inch cast-iron or copper ovenproof skillet or, in a pinch, a similarly sized springform pan or deep cake pan. Rutabagas Anna are a perfect accompaniment to roasted game birds or pork.

2 medium rutabagas (2½ to
    3 pounds total), peeled,
    cut in half, and then
    into thin ⅛-inch slices
1 cup rendered duck fat,
    bacon fat, or clarified
    butter (see box, facing
    page)

2 tablespoons caraway
    seeds
Salt and freshly ground
    black pepper to taste

1. Preheat the oven to 425°F.

2. Keep the duck fat, bacon fat, or clarified butter warm in small saucepan over low heat. Using a pastry brush, coat a 12-inch skillet or baking pan with a generous amount of the fat. Make a layer of the rutabagas by slightly overlapping the slices in concentric circles. You

want to put some thought into the first layer for, once unmolded, it's the one you will see.

3. Brush the layer of rutabagas lightly with the fat and sprinkle lightly with a few caraway seeds, salt, and pepper. Continue the process of layering the rutabaga slices, brushing with fat, and seasoning. Press down on the rutabagas occasionally to ensure a compact cake and to make room for all the layers. When the layering has been completed, cover the baking dish tightly with a double thickness of aluminum foil. Place an ovenproof weight, such as a slightly smaller frying pan, on top of the rutabagas and press down.

4. Bake the rutabagas with the weight 30 minutes. Remove the weight, uncover the rutabagas, and bake until the rutabagas are crisp and brown on top and tender throughout, about 30 minutes more.

5. Using pot holders and being careful not to burn yourself, invert the pan onto a warm large serving plate. Blot up any excess fat with paper towels. Present the rutabagas Anna whole at the table and serve by slicing into pie-shaped wedges.

Makes 6 to 8 servings

CLARIFYING
CLARIFIED BUTTER

— ❖ —

Clarified butter is butter that has had the milk solids removed to yield a butter of delicious purity. It is essential for lending the best flavor to delicate pastries as well as savory dishes that require searing meat in butter heated to a high temperature.

In a heavy saucepan melt a pound of butter over low heat. Remove the pan from the heat, let stand 3 minutes, then skim and discard any froth from the top. Strain the butter by slowly pouring it through a fine sieve lined with a double thickness of cheesecloth. When you get close to the end of the butter avoid the milky white solids that have sunk to the bottom by carefully spooning off any remaining clear liquid butter. Discard the milk solids. Store the clarified butter in the refrigerator. It will keep indefinitely. One pound of butter yields about 1½ cups clarified butter.

Cauliflower with Balsamic Vinegar

— ✦ —

From time to time, I get inexplicable cauliflower cravings. When I can restrain myself from devouring the whole head raw, this is a favorite hot preparation.

2 tablespoons olive oil
4 ounces pancetta or bacon,
  cut into small dice
1 large cauliflower, trimmed
  and cut into large florets
2 cloves garlic, minced
5 ripe plum tomatoes, cut
  into eighths
⅓ cup balsamic vinegar

½ cup chicken broth,
  preferably homemade
1 teaspoon sugar
1 teaspoon anchovy
  paste
Salt and freshly ground
  black pepper to taste
3 tablespoons minced fresh
  parsley

1. Heat the oil in a large skillet over medium-high heat. Add the pancetta and cook until softened but not browned, about 3 minutes. Add the cauliflower and sauté, stirring frequently, until lightly browned, 5 to 7 minutes.

2. Add the garlic and tomatoes to the skillet and cook 2 minutes more. Stir in the vinegar, broth, sugar, and anchovy paste. Cover, reduce the heat to low, and simmer until the cauliflower is crisp-tender, 5 minutes.

3. Uncover, increase the heat again, and cook until the liquid is reduced to a glaze. Season with salt and pepper. Sprinkle with parsley and serve at once.

Makes 6 to 8 servings

Mixed Winter Squash Provençal

— ❖ —

After several attempts at trying to do something graceful and personally riveting with acorn squash, using typical sweet flavor accents, I concluded that it was an unruly vegetable. In a final moment of vexation, I went to the market and selected one of every tumorous-looking winter squash available. Instead of employing the vegetables as a concave container for some syrupy assemblage, I applied a little summer strategy and mixed three different types of squash with savory ingredients. While I'm certain that this recipe would be successful using all acorn or butternut squash, I prefer the subtle contrast of colors and flavors in the medley and the fact that a lot of winter-squash guilt is assuaged with one fell swoop. Finally I must confess that while this concoction slowly baked for 2½ hours, I became quite the lover of this pumpkin-colored pulp.

8 cups cubed (½ inch)
  peeled winter squash,
  such as butternut, acorn
  and turban
¼ cup instant flour, such
  as Wondra
2 teaspoons ground ginger
6 cloves garlic, minced
½ cup minced fresh parsley
2 tablespoons minced fresh
  rosemary

Salt and freshly ground
  black pepper to taste
⅓ cup plus 2 tablespoons
  fruity olive oil

1. Preheat the oven to 325°F.
2. Combine all the cubed squash in a large mixing bowl, add the flour and ginger, and toss to coat. Mix in the garlic, parsley, and rosemary, then season with salt and pepper. Pour in ⅓ cup of olive oil and stir to coat the vegetables evenly. Transfer to a shallow 2-quart baking dish and drizzle the top with the remaining 2 tablespoons olive oil. Cover with aluminum foil.
3. Bake covered 1½ hours. Uncover and bake until the top is crusty brown, 45 to 60 minutes more. The long baking allows the bottom layer of squash to almost melt while the top layer forms an enticing crust. Let cool a few minutes and serve.
Makes 6 to 8 servings

Rosti with Bacon and Onions

— ❖ —

During my first year away at boarding school I had an outgoing roommate with a flamboyant French father, an elegant Canadian mother and a ski chalet in Vermont. During my first ski weekend with her, Mother Boyer treated us to the spectacular Swiss potato pancake known as *rosti*. I have never forgotten how delicious it tasted and am delighted to give a recipe in this book. While there are several variations of *rosti*, this one — with bacon and onions — is the version popular in the Swiss capital of Bern.

6 medium russet potatoes,
  unpeeled
1 pound sliced bacon
1 medium-size red onion,
  minced

Salt and freshly ground
  black pepper to taste
4 tablespoons (½ stick)
  unsalted butter
2 tablespoons vegetable oil

1. Bring a pot of salted water to a boil. Add the potatoes and cook over medium heat 15 minutes. (The potatoes will still be quite firm in the centers.) Drain the potatoes and rinse under cold water. Drain again and refrigerate at least 3 hours or overnight.

2. Place the bacon in a large skillet and cook over medium heat until crisp, 15 to 20 minutes. Drain on paper towels, then crumble the bacon.

3. Peel the chilled potatoes. In a food processor fitted with the shredding disk or on the large holes of a hand-held grater, shred the potatoes. In a mixing bowl, toss the potatoes with the bacon, onion, salt, and pepper.

4. Heat 2 tablespoons of the butter and 1 tablespoon of the oil in a 12-inch nonstick skillet over medium-high heat. Add the potato mixture, spread it evenly over the pan, and press it down firmly with a metal spatula. Cook over medium heat until the underside is golden brown, 12 to 15 minutes.

5. To flip the pancakes, remove the skillet from the heat, invert a large heatproof plate over the skillet, and using potholders, unmold it onto the plate. Add the remaining butter and oil to the skillet and heat over medium-high heat. Slide the pancake back into the skillet, uncooked side down. Continue cooking and pressing down with the spatula until the underside is golden, 10 to 12 minutes more.

6. Slide the pancake onto a heated platter. Cut it into wedges and serve at once.

Makes 6 to 8 side-dish servings.

A New England Thanksgiving

— ✦ —

Cotuit Oysters with Apple Cider Mignonette

— ✦ —

Smoked Mussel and Pumpkin Bisque
Cheddar and Mustard Cornsticks

— ✦ —

Roast turkey with Belmont Inn Thanksgiving Dressing
Potato Gratin
Rutabagas Anna
Maple-Glazed Brussels Sprouts and Chestnuts
Grand Marnier-Glazed Carrots
Nantucket Cranberry Relish

— ✦ —

Apple Dumplings
Bûche de Thanksgiving

Potato Gratin

— ✦ —

There is no more sinful, simple, and satisfying combination in the world than a good gratin of sliced potatoes and nutty Gruyère cheese. With a dish of this in the oven or on the table, it will be of little concern how frightful the weather is outside. Let it snow!

2 tablespoons unsalted butter	8 ounces Gruyère cheese, shredded
2 cloves garlic, minced	1 large egg
2½ pounds (8 to 10) russet potatoes, peeled and very thinly sliced	1 cup milk
Salt and freshly ground black pepper to taste	1 cup heavy or whipping cream

1. Preheat the oven to 375°F.
2. Butter the bottom and sides of a 13 × 9 × 2-inch gratin dish.

Then, scatter the minced garlic over the bottom.

3. Make a single layer of potato slices in the dish, season with salt and pepper, and sprinkle with a few tablespoons of cheese. Repeat the layers until all the potatoes are used.

4. Whisk together the egg, milk, and cream; pour this mixture over the potatoes. Sprinkle all the remaining cheese on top.

5. Bake until the potatoes are tender and the top is bubbling and golden brown, about 1 hour. Serve piping hot.

Makes 6 to 8 servings

Potato, Onion, and Cheddar Gratin

— ⬩ —

Every once in a while and much to my amazement, an odd lot of Yukon Gold potatoes finds its way to the normally pathetic produce shelves of Nantucket's winter markets. I instantly snatch them up because their buttery flavor and golden hue make this recipe superior.

3 tablespoons unsalted
  butter
1 large onion, thinly sliced
2 pounds Yukon Gold or
  russet potatoes, peeled
  and thinly sliced
2 cups shredded sharp
  Cheddar cheese

Salt and freshly ground
  black pepper to taste
Grated nutmeg to taste
1¼ cups chicken broth,
  preferably homemade

1. Preheat the oven to 350°F. Butter a shallow 1½-quart casserole.

2. Melt the butter in a skillet over medium heat. Add the onion and sauté until very soft, about 15 minutes.

3. Alternate layers of the onion, potatoes, and cheese in the prepared dish, seasoning with salt, pepper, and nutmeg as you go. Pour the broth over the layers and cover the casserole with the lid or aluminum foil.

4. Bake 45 minutes. Uncover and continue baking until the top is lightly browned and the potatoes are tender, 15 to 20 minutes more. Serve piping hot.

Makes 6 servings

Mashed Potatoes with Garlic and Olive Oil

— ❖ —

A fashionable restaurant in Paris by the name of *La Maison Blanche* started the trend of mashing potatoes with olive oil rather than cream and butter. The results are utterly satisfying. My version has great rustic appeal as I use unpeeled red-skinned potatoes and lots of garlic. This is the perfect accompaniment to that splurging feast with a prime cut of red meat.

3 pounds medium-size red-	*½ cup extra virgin olive oil,*
skinned potatoes	*plus additional if desired*
6 large cloves garlic,	*Salt and freshly ground*
unpeeled	*black pepper to taste*

1. Place the potatoes and garlic in a pot and cover amply with water. Bring to a boil over high heat, reduce to a simmer, and cook uncovered until the potatoes are tender, 35 to 45 minutes. Drain the potatoes and garlic. Return the potatoes to the pot, reserving the garlic, and cook over medium heat for a minute or two to evaporate any excess liquid.

2. Place the potatoes in a large mixing bowl. Squeeze the garlic pulp from the skins and add to the potatoes. Beat the potatoes with a hand-held electric mixer until fluffy. With the mixer running, slowly beat in the olive oil. Season the potatoes with salt and pepper and serve at once. It is nice to drizzle each serving with a little additional olive oil.

Makes 6 to 8 servings

Italian
Rosemary Potatoes

— ✥ —

These sensationally simple and crusty potato spears conjure up the best memories of Italian-grandmother-style cooking. While the potatoes are perfect with all sorts of roasts and grilled foods, I often skip the meat and opt for a purely potato plate.

8 large russet potatoes, scrubbed	Kosher (coarse) salt and freshly ground black pepper to taste
½ cup fruity olive oil	
4 large cloves garlic, peeled and cut into thin slivers	3 tablespoons chopped fresh rosemary or 1 tablespoon dried

1. Cut each potato lengthwise into 8 wedges or spears. Place in a mixing bowl and toss with the olive oil, garlic, salt, and pepper. Let marinate at room temperature 30 minutes.

2. Preheat the oven to 350°F.

3. Spread the potatoes in a roasting pan and bake 45 minutes, tossing them occasionally with a spoon. Sprinkle with the rosemary and continue roasting until the potatoes are crusty golden brown on the outside and tender inside, another 15 to 20 minutes. Let cool for a few minutes before serving.

Makes 8 servings

Baked Stuffed
Sweet Potatoes

— ✥ —

One of the great things about sweet potatoes is that you rarely hear anything bad about them. Nutritionists adore them for they are rich in vitamin A, potassium, and calcium. Creative winter cooks delight in the vibrant color and buttery flavor they bring to monotone plates. In this tasty and slightly Southwestern side dish, sweet potatoes discover a natural companion in mashed avocados.

4 large sweet potatoes
1 tablespoon olive oil
1 teaspoon kosher (coarse)
    salt
2 tablespoons unsalted
    butter
½ cup sour cream
2 small or 1 large ripe
    avocado, peeled, pitted,
    and mashed
2 tablespoons fresh lime
    juice

½ teaspoon dry mustard
1 jalapeño chile, seeded and
    minced
4 scallions, minced
2 tablespoons minced
    cilantro (fresh coriander)
1 cup shredded sharp
    Cheddar cheese
Salt and freshly ground
    black pepper to taste

1. Preheat oven to 375°F.

2. Scrub, then dry the potatoes. Rub them with the olive oil, sprinkle with the salt, and prick with a fork in several places. Bake in a small roasting pan until done, 45 to 60 minutes.

3. Cut the potatoes lengthwise in half. Scoop out the pulp without tearing the skin into a mixing bowl. Add the butter and sour cream and beat until smooth. Mix in the avocado, lime juice, mustard, jalapeño chile, scallions, and cilantro. Fold in half of the Cheddar and season the mixture with salt and pepper.

4. Fill the potato skins generously with the mixture. Sprinkle the remaining Cheddar over the tops. The potatoes may be prepared ahead up to this point and refrigerated until ready to bake.

5. When ready to bake, preheat the oven to 350°F.

6. Arrange the potatoes on a baking sheet and bake until the cheese is melted and the stuffing is heated through, about 25 minutes. Serve at once.

Makes 8 stuffed potato halves

Sweet Potato Pancakes

— ✣ —

These crisp, lacy pancakes take their inspiration from Jewish potato latkes, which are a popular part of traditional Hanukkah celebrations. The sweet potato flavor is enhanced with ginger in three different forms — powdered, gingersnap cookie crumbs, and crystallized. They make a nice textural contrast to the Thanksgiving vegetable purées and are also a pleasant surprise as an accompaniment to hearty winter stews.

5 medium-large sweet
potatoes, peeled
1 bunch scallions, trimmed
and minced
½ cup crushed gingersnap
cookie crumbs
3 tablespoons unbleached
all-purpose flour

3 large eggs
½ cup light cream
2 teaspoons ground ginger
Salt and freshly ground
black pepper to taste
3 tablespoons finely minced
crystallized ginger
Vegetable oil for frying

1. Grate the potatoes with a hand grater or in a food processor fitted with the large shredding disk. Place them in the center of a clean cotton kitchen towel and squeeze tightly to extract as much liquid as possible.

2. Place the potatoes in a large mixing bowl, add the scallions, gingersnap crumbs, and flour, and toss to combine. In a separate small bowl whisk together the eggs, cream, ground ginger, salt, and pepper. Add to the potatoes and stir until well blended. Stir in the crystallized ginger.

3. Brush a large flat skillet all over with a few tablespoons vegetable oil and heat over medium-high heat. Using your hands, shape the potato mixture into plump patties about 2½ inches in diameter. Place as many pancakes as will comfortably fit in the skillet and fry, turning once, until crusty golden brown on both sides, 6 to 8 minutes. Repeat with the remaining potato mixture, adding more vegetable oil to the pan if necessary.

4. If not serving the potato pancakes immediately, they may be kept warm on a tray in a 300°F oven. Or they can be refrigerated up to 3 days, then reheated on a baking sheet in a 350°F oven until warmed through, about 20 minutes.

Makes 20 to 24 pancakes

Sweet Potato and Pineapple Pudding Praline

— ❖ —

A terrific recipe that manages to be sweet, citrusy, fluffy, and crunchy all at the same time. Serve as a contrast to more savory vegetable preparations or let it star alongside a pork roast, baked ham, or glazed spareribs.

2 pounds sweet potatoes,
peeled and cubed
4 tablespoons (½ stick)
unsalted butter, at room
temperature
4 large egg yolks
3 tablespoons light brown
sugar
1 can (20 ounces) crushed
unsweetened pineapple,
undrained

Finely chopped zest of 1
orange
3 tablespoons golden
rum
¼ teaspoon grated
nutmeg
½ teaspoon ground
ginger
Salt and freshly ground
black pepper to taste

PRALINE TOPPING
10 tablespoons (1¼ sticks)
unsalted butter, melted
1 cup (packed) light brown
sugar
1 cup shredded coconut

1½ cups coarsely chopped
pecans
1½ tablespoons golden rum
¼ cup light cream

1. Preheat the oven to 350°F. Butter a 2½ to 3-quart shallow
baking dish.
2. Place the sweet potatoes in a large saucepan, cover with
water, and boil until very tender, 25 to 30 minutes. Drain well and
place in a large mixing bowl.
3. Using an electric mixer, beat the warm sweet potatoes with
the butter, egg yolks, and brown sugar until smooth. Add the pineapple, orange zest, and rum and mix until incorporated. Season with
the nutmeg, ginger, salt, and pepper. Transfer the mixture to the prepared baking dish.
4. Prepare the praline topping: In a small bowl stir the melted
butter and brown sugar together until smooth. Fold in the coconut
and pecans; then stir in the rum and cream. Spread the mixture
evenly over the top of the sweet potatoes.
5. Bake the pudding until golden brown, 30 to 35 minutes. Preheat the broiler and broil the pudding 6 inches from the heat just
until the top begins to bubble madly, 45 to 60 seconds. Let cool a few
minutes, then serve.
Makes 10 to 12 servings

Wild Rice and Cider Pilaf

— ✤ —

I have always found parboiling and then baking the best way to cook wild rice. Apple cider replaces the traditional stock in this recipe and complements the woodsy taste of the rice with a subtle sweetness. Diced apples added in the last five minutes add color and crunch.

2 cups wild rice
4 tablespoons (½ stick) unsalted butter
3 carrots, peeled and minced
1 medium-size red onion, chopped
⅓ cup golden raisins

5 cups sweet apple cider
1 cup dry white wine
1 teaspoon dried thyme
Salt and freshly ground black pepper to taste
2 Cortland, Macoun or McIntosh apples, (with peel), cored and diced

1. Place the rice in a bowl, cover generously with cold water, and let soak for 1 hour. Drain. Heat a 2-quart pot of salted water to boiling. Add the rice and blanch 5 minutes. Drain again and set aside.
2. Preheat the oven to 350°F.
3. Melt the butter in a large skillet over medium-high heat. Add the carrots and onion and sauté, stirring frequently, until the vegetables have softened, 5 to 7 minutes. Stir in the raisins and the rice and cook 1 minute more.
4. Transfer the rice to a rectangular baking pan, about 13 × 9 inches. Blend in the cider, wine, thyme, salt, and pepper. Cover the pan tightly with aluminum foil and bake until the liquid is absorbed and the rice is tender, about 1 hour. Uncover the rice, stir in the apples, and bake 5 minutes more. Serve at once.

Makes 8 servings

THINKING THANKS- GIVING

PART II

SWEETS

"Comfort me with apples, for I am sick of love."
— *King Solomon*

As a member of the new breed of chefs during the megatrend eighties, ivy-educated and food-fad fed in every hot new restaurant between Nantucket, New York, and the Napa Valley, it is absolutely amazing that I have emerged with nary a kiwi, carambola, nor passion fruit in my repertoire. There must be something inexpungible in my Yankee roots that makes me favor a hefty wedge of my mother's apple pie to the most haute couture sliver of Tiramisù. Indeed, if truth be told, I would opt for a crate of cranberries from the swampy bogs of Cape Cod over the most precious half-pint of raspberries any day of the week. Come November, I not only love but also need the uncomplicated comfort of a just-baked Apple Brown Betty harboring an ovenful of warmth. Ruby Poached Pears proffer the most innocent sort of seduction, while pumpkin puddings, oatmeal cookies, and maple mousses remind one that pleasure can be a very simple affair. This collection of homey and nostalgic special relishes and desserts is rooted for the most part in the straightforward traditions of old-fashioned New England cookery. These are pies, puddings, and custards that render a sweet finale to the Thanksgiving feast and then continue to entice with the most reassuring antidote I know to blustery winds and icy drafts during cold-weather months.

Whole Cranberry Sauce

— ❖ —

A preference for cooked cranberry sauce or raw cranberry relish seems to have more to do with family traditions than taste. For those reared in the "cooked" mode, this version laced with port and crunchy toasted pecan halves is bound to please.

> 1 pound fresh cranberries
> ½ cup port
> ½ cup fresh orange juice
> 1 cup diced dried apricots
> ½ cup (packed) light
>   brown sugar
>
> ¾ cup granulated sugar
> ¾ cup pecan halves, lightly
>   toasted

Place the cranberries, port, orange juice, apricots, and sugars in a saucepan. Cook the mixture over medium heat, stirring occasionally, until the cranberries are cooked and the sauce is thick, 25 to 30 minutes. Remove from the heat, cool, and stir in the pecan halves. Store covered in the refrigerator. The mixture will keep for several weeks and is best brought to room temperature before serving.

Makes about 4 cups

Nantucket Cranberry Relish

— ❖ —

This raw relish is so named because it is the recipe I am most eager to make when the island's first cranberries of the season are harvested. The citrus of lime and tangerine complements the tang of the cranberries and I've always found the unique flavor of pine nuts to have a natural affinity with cranberries. I think a dollop of this relish perks up any plate or palate, be it breakfast, lunch or dinner.

> 1½ pounds fresh cranberries
> 1 lime
> 1 tangerine
> ¾ cup (packed) light
>   brown sugar
>
> ¾ cup granulated sugar
> 3 tablespoons orange liqueur
> Scant pinch ground cloves
> ¼ cup pine nuts, lightly
>   toasted

1. Place the cranberries in a food processor and process just until the cranberries are coarsely chopped. Transfer to a mixing bowl.

2. Cut the lime and tangerine (peel and all) into ½-inch pieces. Remove any tangerine seeds and place the fruits in the food processor. Process until the fruit is finely chopped. Add to the cranberries.

3. Add the sugars, orange liqueur, and cloves to the cranberries and stir well to combine. Taste for sweetness and adjust if it seems too tart. Fold in the pine nuts and let the flavors of the relish mellow overnight in the refrigerator. This relish will keep for several weeks stored in the refrigerator.

Makes about 6 cups

Canadian Cranberry Confit

— ❖ —

My friend Al Cummings prevailed upon me from his office in Toronto to include this recipe in my cookbook. When I told him that I already had a surfeit of wonderful cranberry recipes, he pleaded with me to make room for just one more since this confit always leaves fellow Torontonians "crying for more!" Since I know far better than to question any of Al's epicurean passions, I concocted a batch of this tart and tangy cranberry confit in my kitchen posthaste. Al, of course, did not lead me astray, and I am delighted to present my adaptation of the recipe as an alluring alternative to sweet cranberry relishes.

1½ pounds white pearl onions	½ cup sugar
⅔ cup golden raisins	½ cup balsamic vinegar
⅔ cup dark raisins	1½ cups dry red wine
2 cups boiling water	3 cloves garlic, minced
6 tablespoons (¾ stick) unsalted butter	½ teaspoon dried thyme
	½ teaspoon salt
	12 ounces fresh cranberries

1. Trim the onions, leaving the skins on. Drop the onions into a large pot of boiling water and cook 30 seconds. Drain and slip the onions out of their skins as soon as they are cool enough to handle.

2. Combine the raisins in a small bowl, cover with the 2 cups of boiling water, and let stand 10 minutes.

3. Melt the butter in a large heavy saucepan over medium heat

and stir in the onions. Add the sugar and 1 tablespoon of the vinegar. Cook, stirring constantly, until the sugar is dissolved and beginning to caramelize, about 5 minutes. Add the remaining vinegar and the wine; bring to a boil and continue to boil 2 minutes. Add the raisins with soaking liquid, the garlic, thyme, and salt. Simmer the mixture covered until the onions are tender, about 45 minutes.

4. Add the cranberries to the pan. Simmer uncovered, stirring occasionally, until the cranberries are cooked and the confit has thickened, 20 to 25 minutes. Let the confit cool and serve at room temperature. Store any leftover confit in the refrigerator but be sure to bring it back to room temperature before serving.

Makes about 4 cups

Pumpkin Crème Caramel

— ❖ —

For some reason I have an adversity to pumpkin pie, so I am forever conjuring up alternatives. This one is quite elegant, even though I have never had much luck getting all of the caramel coating to come out when I invert the dessert. Inevitably, there is a nice hard coating of caramel glued to the bottom of the mold. Rather than wrestle with the stuff with a soapy scouring pad, I stab it hard with a blunt knife to loosen it and break it up into praline-like shards. This is an excellent form of stress release, and the shards look stunning sprinkled all over and around the crème caramel.

1 cup granulated sugar	1 teaspoon ground ginger
¼ cup water	2 teaspoons ground
¾ cup chopped lightly	cinnamon
toasted macadamia nuts	6 large eggs
½ cup (packed) light	8 ounces cream cheese, at
brown sugar	room temperature
1 cup pumpkin purée, fresh	3 cups half-and-half,
or canned	scalded
⅓ cup orange-flavored	1 can (14 ounces)
liqueur	sweetened condensed
1 teaspoon grated nutmeg	milk

1. Preheat the oven to 350°F.
2. In a small saucepan combine the granulated sugar and the

water. Bring to a boil over high heat, stirring to dissolve the sugar. Continue to boil, without stirring, until the mixture turns golden brown, about 5 minutes. Watch carefully to avoid burning. Pour the hot caramel immediately into a 2-quart ring mold. Sprinkle with the macadamia nuts and tilt to coat the sides of the mold. Set aside.

3. Using an electric mixer, beat together the brown sugar, pumpkin, liqueur, nutmeg, ginger, and cinnamon in a large bowl. Gradually beat in the eggs, cream cheese, scalded half-and-half, and condensed milk. Beat until very smooth, 4 to 5 minutes. Pour the mixture into the ring mold.

4. Place the mold in a larger baking pan and pour in enough hot water to come 1 inch up the side of the mold. Bake until firm and set, 50 to 60 minutes. Cool 1 hour, then refrigerate overnight.

5. Run the tip of a small knife around the side of the custard to loosen it. Dip the bottom part of the mold briefly in a shallow dish of very hot water to loosen the caramel. Invert quickly onto a serving plate. Pry any caramel remaining in the mold loose by jabbing it forcefully with a blunt knife. (Beware of flying shards.) Sprinkle the pieces of caramel over the custard. Serve the custard in slices. For an even richer dessert, the slices may be placed on top of a smooth fruit sauce, such as raspberry or cranberry, or served in a pool of liqueur-spiked crème anglaise.

Makes 8 to 10 servings

Pumpkin-and-Pear Bread Pudding

— ⬦ —

This is another one of my alternative-to-pumpkin-pie desserts. As it was not conceived as a quick dessert using up stale bread, it should not be undertaken unless you are in the mood to do some serious cooking and have the time to devote to an elaborate but ultimately satisfying and tasty creation. The bread in the dessert is a homemade yeast-based pumpkin bread, which is worth making in its own right to use as a fabulous enclosure for that day-after-Thanksgiving sandwich. The custard is also pumpkin and all is crowned lavishly with cider-simmered pears. The Caramelized Amaretto Cream adds the final embellishment. Allow two days for the work and to build up adequate anticipation for enjoying the final masterpiece.

PUMPKIN BREAD

1½ tablespoons active dry
   yeast
⅓ cup warm water
4 tablespoons (½ stick)
   unsalted butter, melted
1 cup pumpkin purée, fresh
   or canned

3 tablespoons honey
2 teaspoons salt
2 large eggs
⅓ cup milk
5 to 5½ cups unbleached
   all-purpose flour

PEARS

2 cups sweet apple cider
3 tablespoons amaretto
   liqueur
½ cup (packed) light
   brown sugar

1 tablespoon ground
   cinnamon
1 teaspoon grated nutmeg
6 pears, peeled, cored, and
   thinly sliced

PUMPKIN CUSTARD

2½ cups milk
¾ cups heavy or whipping
   cream
6 large eggs
2 cups pumpkin purée,
   fresh or canned

¾ cup granulated sugar
1 tablespoon ground
   cinnamon
1 teaspoon grated nutmeg
3 tablespoons amaretto
   liqueur

Caramelized Amaretto
   Cream (recipe follows)

1. Two days before you plan to serve the pudding, prepare the bread: Place the yeast and water in a large mixing bowl and let stand until dissolved, 5 to 10 minutes. Meanwhile, whisk together the butter, pumpkin, honey, salt, eggs, and milk. Whisk this mixture into the yeast. Using a wooden spoon, gradually stir in enough flour to make a soft, pliable dough. Knead on a lightly floured surface until smooth and satiny, about 5 minutes.

2. Transfer the dough to a clean bowl, cover, and let rise in a warm, draft-free place until doubled, 1 to 1½ hours.

3. Butter a 9 × 5-inch loaf pan. Punch the dough down and transfer it to to a lightly floured surface. Roll out into a 15 × 9-inch rectangle. Starting at one short side, roll the dough into a loaf and place in the prepared loaf pan. Cover and let rise again until doubled, about 1 hour.

4. Preheat the oven to 375°F.

5. Bake the pumpkin bread until crusty and brown on top, 45 to 50 minutes. Cool slightly, remove from the pan, and cool completely. Let the bread sit uncovered for at least a day before cutting into ½-inch cubes for the pudding. You will need 9 cups of loosely packed cubes for the pudding; save the remaining bread for another use.

6. Prepare the pears: Place the cider, liqueur, brown sugar, cinnamon, and nutmeg in a medium-size saucepan. Bring to a simmer over medium heat, stirring to dissolve the sugar. Add the sliced pears and cook 5 minutes. Remove the pears with a slotted spoon and set aside in a bowl. Simmer the remaining liquid until reduced to a thin syrup, about 30 minutes. Return the pears to the pan and cook a few minutes more, turning the pears to coat with the syrup. Set aside.

7. Preheat the oven to 350°F. Butter a 15 × 10-inch baking dish.

8. Place the 9 cups cubed pumpkin bread in the prepared baking dish.

9. Prepare the pumpkin custard: Scald the milk and cream together in a saucepan over medium heat. In a mixing bowl whisk together the eggs, pumpkin, sugar, cinnamon, and nutmeg until well blended. Whisk in the scalded milk and cream, then the liqueur. Pour the custard evenly over the bread in the baking dish.

10. Set the baking dish in a larger baking pan and add enough water to come 1 inch up the side of the dish. Bake the pudding 40 minutes. Spoon the pears and syrup over the top and bake until the custard is set, 20 to 25 minutes longer. Serve the pudding warm or at room temperature, drizzling each serving with Caramelized Amaretto Cream.

Makes 12 servings

Caramelized Amaretto Cream

— ❖ —

1 cup sugar
¾ cup water
1 teaspoon vanilla extract

1 cup heavy or whipping
    cream, at room temperature
¼ cup amaretto liqueur

1. Place the sugar, water, and vanilla in a small heavy saucepan. Stir over low heat to dissolve the sugar. Increase the heat to medium-high and boil, without stirring, until the mixture turns golden brown, 5 to 7 minutes. Remove from the heat.

2. Gradually whisk in the cream, being careful to stand back as the mixture will sputter and bubble. Return the mixture to low heat and stir until thickened to the consistency of thick whipping cream, 5 to 7 minutes. Remove from the heat and stir in the liqueur. Serve warm.

Makes about 2 cups

Apple Brown Betty

— ⬩ —

I've always thought of Apple Brown Betty, a casserole of sliced apples and sweetened and buttered crumbs, as the quintessential Yankee, cold-weather dessert. Using day-old doughnuts for the crumbs makes for an extra good rendition of this homey apple pudding.

8 apples, peeled, cored, and
   coarsely sliced
½ cup (packed) light
   brown sugar
¼ cup granulated sugar
1 tablespoon ground
   cinnamon
1 teaspoon grated nutmeg
1 tablespoon fresh lemon juice

½ cup apple cider
4 day-old plain doughnuts
½ cup old-fashioned rolled
   oats
½ cup walnuts, coarsely
   chopped
6 tablespoons (¾ stick)
   unsalted butter, melted
2 tablespoons unsalted butter

1. Preheat the oven to 350°F.
2. Toss the apples with the sugars, spices, lemon juice, and cider in a large mixing bowl.
3. Process the doughnuts into crumbs in a food processor and toss with the oatmeal and walnuts. Drizzle with the melted butter and toss to moisten the crumbs evenly.
4. Sprinkle one-third of the crumbs over the bottom of a deep 2-quart casserole. Top with half the apple mixture. Sprinkle with another third of the crumbs and top with the rest of the apples. Sprinkle the remaining crumbs over the top and dot with 2 tablespoons butter.
5. Bake until the top is crusty brown and the apples are bubbly, about 1 hour. Serve warm with whipped cream or vanilla ice cream.
Makes 8 to 10 servings

Maple Mousse

— ⬩ —

This mousse is a welcome light sweet in the post-harvest repertoire of desserts. I make it with dark amber maple syrup rather than the more expensive grade A because I feel the less refined syrup imparts a richer and more complex flavor to the mousse.

1 envelope unflavored
   gelatin
⅓ cup cold water
3 large eggs, separated
⅓ cup (packed) light
   brown sugar
1 cup dark amber maple
   syrup

2 tablespoons dark rum
¼ cup granulated sugar
2 cups heavy or whipping
   cream
Small maple sugar candies
   for garnish

1. Sprinkle the gelatin over the cold water and set aside to soften, 5 minutes.

2. Place the egg yolks, brown sugar, and maple syrup in the top of a double boiler and stir to combine. Cook over simmering water, stirring constantly, until slightly thickened, 7 to 8 minutes. Remove from the heat, add the gelatin, and stir to dissolve. Cool completely, then refrigerate until the mixture just begins to set, 15 to 20 minutes. (Do not allow it to gel.) Stir in the rum.

3. Beat the egg whites until soft peaks form. Beat in the granulated sugar, 1 tablespoon at a time, and continue to beat until stiff and shiny. Gently fold half the egg whites into the maple mixture to lighten, then fold in the remaining whites.

4. Beat the cream until soft peaks form. Fold into the maple mixture. Spoon the mousse into a serving bowl or individual stemmed goblets. Refrigerate several hours or overnight. Garnish the top of each serving with a small maple sugar candy.

Makes 6 to 8 servings

Cranberry-Oatmeal Cookies

— ✦ —

These are a holiday variation on My Grandmother's Oatmeal Cookies published in my last cookbook. The original recipe is not only one of my very favorites but also the most controversial recipe in the *Nantucket Open-House* collection. Most home cooks had difficulty incorporating the 4 pounds of oats into the batter that the commercial mixer in my catering kitchen accomplished quite effortlessly. I received numerous calls, at all hours of the day and night, from would-be cookie makers exasperated and exhausted by the culinary aerobics of making the batter. To appease all weary oatmeal-cookie lovers, I have scaled down the recipe and can confidently guarantee delicious home results. Cranberry fiend that I am, I might add that I prefer this pretty, ruby-speckled version to the original recipe. Bake plenty, the cookies make an especially welcome Thanksgiving or Christmas hostess gift.

1½ cups (3 sticks) unsalted margarine
1¾ cups (packed) light brown sugar
2 large eggs
1½ tablespoons honey
2 teaspoons vanilla extract
½ teaspoon salt
2 cups unbleached all-purpose flour

1 box (18 ounces) old-fashioned rolled oats
12 ounces fresh cranberries, coarsely chopped
½ cup golden raisins
Finely chopped zest of 1 orange
1¼ cups coarsely chopped walnuts

1. Preheat the oven to 350°F. Line baking sheets with parchment paper.
2. Cream the margarine and sugar in a large bowl until smooth. Add the eggs, honey, vanilla, and salt and beat until smooth and creamy.
3. Using a large wooden spoon or your hands, work in the flour and oats until well combined. Add the cranberries, raisins, orange zest, and walnuts; mix until evenly incorporated.
4. With your hands, form the dough on the baking sheets into patties ½ inch thick and 2½ to 3 inches in diameter.
5. Bake the cookies until lightly browned but still a little soft at the center, 15 to 20 minutes. Cool on wire racks.
Makes about 25 cookies

Ruby Poached Pears

— ❖ —

The voluptuous simplicity of these sparkling red pears makes them a stunning fruit dessert. An accompanying blue-veined cheese and a plate of biscotti would enhance the presentation beautifully.

5 cups fruity red wine, such as Beaujolais or Zinfandel	8 whole cloves
¾ cup sugar	Zest of 1 lemon removed in a wide spiral strip
¼ cup cassis liqueur	10 medium-ripe pears, peeled
2 cinnamon sticks (2 inches each)	2 tablespoons cornstarch

1. Combine the wine, sugar, liqueur, cinnamon sticks, cloves, and lemon zest in a wide, deep saucepan. Bring to a boil, stirring to dissolve the sugar.

2. Carefully add the pears to the pan, stem end up, making sure all are immersed in the liquid, and simmer uncovered until tender but not mushy, about 20 minutes. Let cool to room temperature in the poaching liquid.

3. Remove the pears from the pan and place upright on a tray or platter. Bring the poaching liquid to a full boil and continue to boil until reduced to 2 cups, 15 to 20 minutes. Strain into a clean small saucepan. Add the cornstarch and cook over medium heat, stirring constantly, until thickened and shiny. Remove from the heat.

4. Using a pastry brush, coat the poached pears generously with the glaze. Transfer the pears to a serving platter. Serve at room temperature within 3 to 4 hours of glazing.

Makes 10 servings

Apple Dumplings

— ❖ —

The old-fashioned flavor of this great, homey dessert is not obtained without some serious time and effort in the kitchen. However, the dumplings are more fun than fussy to assemble, and the rave reviews of dessert lovers are sure to make the domestic endeavor most worthwhile.

DUMPLING PASTRY

2½ cups unbleached all-
  purpose flour
Pinch of salt
1 cup (2 sticks) unsalted
  butter, chilled, cut into
  small pieces

8 ounces cream cheese,
  chilled, cut into small
  pieces
1 teaspoon vanilla extract

FILLING

½ cup golden raisins
⅓ cup Calvados or
  applejack
3 tablespoons unsalted
  butter, chilled, cut into
  small cubes
½ cup (packed) light
  brown sugar

½ cup walnuts, coarsely
  chopped
1 teaspoon ground
  cinnamon
¼ teaspoon grated
  nutmeg

6 large Golden Delicious
  apples
2 large eggs, lightly beaten
8 cinnamon graham cracker
  squares, crushed into fine
  crumbs

6 cinnamon sticks (2 inches
  each)

1. Prepare the pastry: Place the flour, salt, butter, and cream cheese in a food processor and process until the mixture resembles coarse crumbs. Add the vanilla and continue processing until the dough forms a ball. Shape the dough into a flat disk, wrap in plastic, and refrigerate at least 1 hour.

2. In the meantime, prepare the filling: Place the raisins and Calvados in a small saucepan, bring to a boil, then simmer 10 minutes. Remove from the heat and cool slightly. In a small bowl blend the butter and sugar together with a fork until crumbly. Stir in the walnuts, cinnamon, and nutmeg, then blend in the raisins and set aside.

3. Preheat the oven to 375°F. Line a baking sheet with parchment paper.

4. Using a small paring knife, core each apple without piercing through the bottom of the apple. Peel the apples.

5. Place the graham cracker crumbs in a shallow bowl. Brush each apple with some of the beaten egg, then roll in the crumbs to coat thoroughly. Fill the center of each apple compactly with the raisin filling.

6. Divide the chilled pastry into 6 equal pieces. Roll out each piece ⅛ inch thick, then trim to a 9-inch circle, reserving the scraps. Set an apple in the center of each pastry circle. Bring up all sides of

the pastry to enclose the apple and meet on top at the center. Poke a cinnamon stick in the center of each apple to serve as a mock stem. Seal the pastry around the cinnamon stick, trimming the excess.

7. Arrange the dumplings on the baking sheet and brush the pastry all over with the beaten egg. Roll out the pastry scraps and cut out free-form leaves to place around the "stems" on each dumpling. Brush again with egg.

8. Bake until the apples are tender and the crust is golden brown, about 40 minutes. Serve warm or at room temperature.

Makes 6 servings

Chocolate, Date, and Pecan Pie

I've never been too wild about the layer of custard that forms in the middle of most pecan pies, so I decided to experiment with a chewier, date-laced filling. I was crazy about the results and must add that the chocolate, coffee, and bourbon all conspire to make this one of the best pecan pies ever!

CRUST
1½ cups unbleached all-purpose flour
¼ teaspoon salt
½ cup (1 stick) unsalted butter, chilled, cut into small pieces

2 to 3 tablespoons ice water

FILLING
6 ounces semisweet chocolate chips
1 tablespoon instant coffee granules
3 tablespoons bourbon
½ cup (1 stick) unsalted butter, at room temperature

½ cup (packed) light brown sugar
½ cup light corn syrup
2 teaspoons vanilla extract
3 large eggs
1¼ cups coarsely chopped pitted dates
1⅔ cups pecan halves

1. Prepare the crust: Place the flour, salt, and butter in a food processor and process just until the mixture resembles coarse crumbs. With the machine running, add the water through the feed tube and process just until the dough begins to form into a ball. Wrap the dough in plastic wrap and refrigerate 1 hour.

2. Preheat the oven to 350°F.

3. Roll the dough out into a 12-inch circle on a lightly floured surface. Transfer to a 10-inch pie plate; trim and crimp the edge decoratively. Place the pie shell in the freezer while preparing the filling.

4. Place the chocolate chips, coffee, and bourbon in a small saucepan. Heat over low heat, stirring frequently until the chocolate is melted. Remove from the heat and set aside.

5. Using an electric mixer, cream the butter and sugar together in a medium-size bowl. Beat in the corn syrup, vanilla, and eggs, one at a time. Stir in the melted chocolate mixture and the dates. Coarsely chop ⅔ cup of the pecans and stir into the filling. Pour the filling evenly into the prepared pie shell. Arrange the whole pecan halves in circles over the top of the pie.

6. Bake the pie until the filling is set, 45 to 50 minutes. Cool to room temperature and serve in slices with a dollop of whipped cream if desired.

Makes 8 to 10 servings

Toby Greenberg's Cranberry Pie

— ⸎ —

As a cook and cookbook author, I'm always delighted by the bonus of receiving a wonderful recipe from a friend. Although the sharing of tried and true recipes certainly makes my professional job easier, it is really the rich friendships born of culinary connections that make my private life truly meaningful.

Toby is a great and enthusiastic lady from Baltimore whom I befriended as a favored customer when I was starting out in the catering business. Throughout the years of entertainment highs and culinary woes, she has become an avid supporter and cherished confidante. While this fabulous crustless pie recipe reveals something of Toby's impeccable taste, it cannot begin to communicate and capture the extraordinary warmth and caring of her personality.

12 ounces fresh cranberries
½ cup (packed) light
   brown sugar
1 tablespoon grated orange
   zest
1 teaspoon ground
   cinnamon
¾ cup coarsely chopped
   walnuts
2 large eggs

½ cup (1 stick) unsalted
   butter, melted
1 cup granulated sugar
1 teaspoon vanilla
   extract
¼ cup sour cream
1 cup unbleached all-
   purpose flour

1. Preheat the oven to 325°F. Butter a 10-inch pie plate.

2. Place the cranberries in the prepared pie plate and toss them with the brown sugar, orange zest, cinnamon, and walnuts so all is evenly mixed. Spread the mixture out evenly in the plate.

3. Whisk the eggs together in a mixing bowl. Beat in the butter, sugar, vanilla, and sour cream until blended. Gradually stir in the flour and mix until smooth. Pour evenly over the cranberries in the pie plate.

4. Bake the pie until the fruit is bubbling and it is browned on top, 55 to 60 minutes. Serve warm or at room temperature with a scoop of vanilla ice cream if desired.

Makes 6 to 8 servings

Neiman Marcus Apple Pie

— ❖ —

This is my mother's elaboration on a recipe clipped out of a ladies' magazine years ago. The pie should be made with tart apples, and it is at my father's insistence that we use Rhode Island Greenings. Depending on her mood, my mother will flavor the apples with either cinnamon, Scandinavian cardamom, or angostura bitters. Unlike most pies, this one tastes better a day or two after it is baked. For many years now, it has been my favorite way to both end the Thanksgiving splendor and begin the day the morning after.

CRUST
2 cups unbleached all-
   purpose flour
½ (1 stick) unsalted butter,
   chilled, cut into small
   pieces

½ cup vegetable shortening
¼ teaspoon salt
3 to 4 tablespoons ice
   water

FILLING

11 cups quartered, cored, peeled Rhode Island Greening apples (about 12)

¾ cup sugar

¼ cup unbleached all-purpose flour

1 teaspoon salt

⅔ cup heavy or whipping cream

1 tablespoon ground cinnamon, 1 teaspoon ground cardamom, or dash of angostura bitters

Milk for brushing the top crust

1. Prepare the crust: Place the flour, butter, shortening and salt in a food processor and process just until the mixture resembles coarse crumbs. With the machine running, add enough ice water through the feed tube for the dough to begin to form into a ball. Wrap the dough in plastic wrap and refrigerate.

2. Preheat the oven to 375°F.

3. Divide the pastry dough in half. Roll out one half into a 12-inch circle on a lightly floured surface. Line a 10-inch pie plate with the dough and trim the edge.

4. Prepare the filling: Place the apples in a large mixing bowl and toss with the sugar, flour, salt, cream, and seasoning of choice. Mound the filling in the pie shell.

5. Roll out the remaining dough ⅛ inch thick. Cover the pie with the top crust, pressing firmly to seal the edge, and crimp the edge decoratively. Make several small steam vent slashes in the top crust, then brush it with a little milk to ensure a shiny crust. Place the pie on a baking sheet to catch any drips while baking.

6. Bake the pie until the crust is golden brown and the filling is bubbling, 1¼ to 1½ hours. If the crust seems to be getting too brown, cover it loosely with foil and continue baking. Cool the pie overnight. Serve at room temperature with whipped cream or vanilla ice cream if desired.

Makes 8 to 10 servings

Bartlett Pear Tart

— ✥ —

This sublime tart requires some time and concentration to prepare, but it is well worth the effort, for the dessert is one of the most exquisite finales I know to a stylish dinner. I first created this tart while visiting my parents in Maine to pay homage to the delicious pear wine that Bob and Cathe Bartlett make at their Down East winery, so the Bartlett in the title of the recipe is really a double entendre. As the Bartlett's pear wine is hard to come by outside of Maine, I've also tested the recipe with a dry white wine; the results are fine, although the pear flavor in the custard will be more subtle.

HAZELNUT CRUST
1 cup skinned hazelnuts,
  lightly toasted
¼ cup granulated sugar
1¼ cups unbleached all-
  purpose flour
½ teaspoon ground
  cinnamon

Pinch of salt
½ cup (1 stick) unsalted
  butter, chilled, cut into
  small pieces
1 large egg yolk

POACHED PEARS
5 ripe Bartlett pears,
  peeled, halved lengthwise,
  and cored
2 cups pear or dry white
  wine

3 tablespoons granulated
  sugar
4 whole cloves

CUSTARD FILLING
1½ cups half-and-half
6 large egg yolks
¼ cup unbleached all-
  purpose flour

½ cup (packed) light
  brown sugar
1 teaspoon almond extract
1 tablespoon unsalted butter

GLAZE
½ cup apricot jam, melted
3 tablespoons skinned
  toasted hazelnuts,
  coarsely chopped

1. Prepare the crust: Place the hazelnuts and sugar in a food processor and process until the nuts are finely ground. Add the flour, cinnamon, and salt; process to combine. Add the butter and egg yolk; process just until the dough forms a ball. Press the dough over the bottom and up the side of a fluted 10-inch tart pan. Place the tart shell in the freezer for 15 minutes.

2. Preheat the oven to 375°F.

3. Prick the chilled tart shell on the bottom with a fork in several places. Bake just until the shell begins to brown lightly, 12 to 15 minutes. Remove from the oven and set aside to cool.

4. Prepare the poached pears: Place the pears, wine, sugar, and cloves in a shallow wide saucepan. Bring to a boil, then simmer the pears uncovered until they are just crisp-tender, 12 to 15 minutes.

Remove the pears with a slotted spoon and let drain on a large plate. Boil the poaching liquid over high heat until reduced to ⅓ cup; it will be thick and syrupy. Discard the cloves and set aside.

5. Prepare the custard: Bring the half-and-half to a simmer in a small saucepan. In a mixing bowl whisk the egg yolks, flour, and brown sugar until smooth. Gradually whisk in about half the simmering cream to warm the egg mixture, then whisk it back into the remaining cream. Bring just to a boil over medium heat, stirring constantly. Reduce the heat and simmer, stirring constantly, until the custard is thick and smooth, a few minutes more. Transfer the hot custard to a clean bowl and whisk in the almond extract, butter, and reduced poaching liquid. Set aside.

6. When ready to assemble the tart, preheat the oven again to 375°F.

7. Spread the custard evenly in the partially baked tart shell. Lay the pear halves cut side down on a clean work surface. Carefully slice the halves crosswise at ⅛-inch intervals, cutting almost but not quite all the way through to the bottom. (The pear halves should remain intact on the cut side.) Arrange the pears on top of the custard in a circle with the narrow points to the center and a half pear set in the center of the tart. Fan the pear slices slightly by pressing them gently into the custard.

8. Bake the tart until the custard is set and lightly browned, 30 to 40 minutes.

9. Brush the warm tart evenly with the melted apricot jam to glaze, then sprinkle with the chopped hazelnuts. Serve the tart slightly warm or at room temperature.

Makes 8 servings

Apple Streusel Tart

— ✤ —

The food processor makes this sensational tart a breeze to assemble. The crunch of three different nuts with the crispness of just-harvested apples makes this dessert the culinary equivalent to an invigorating stroll through the countryside on a clear and chilly day.

CRUST

1¼ cups unbleached all-
  purpose flour
⅓ cup confectioners' sugar
1½ teaspoons ground
  cinnamon

5½ tablespoons unsalted
  butter, chilled, cut into
  small pieces
1 large egg
2 tablespoons cold water

NUT CREAM

¾ cup blanched almonds
¾ cup skinned hazelnuts
¾ cup granulated sugar
½ cup (1 stick) unsalted
  butter at room temperature

1 large egg
½ teaspoon almond extract
½ teaspoon vanilla extract

APPLES AND STREUSEL TOPPING

4 apples such as Golden
  Delicious or McIntosh,
  peeled, cored, and thinly
  sliced
1 tablespoon fresh lemon
  juice
1 tablespoon brandy
3 tablespoons unbleached
  all-purpose flour
3 tablespoons light brown
  sugar

3 tablespoons unsalted
  butter
1 tablespoon ground
  cinnamon
3 tablespoons walnuts,
  coarsely chopped
3 tablespoons old-fashioned
  rolled oats

1. Prepare the crust: Place the flour, sugar, cinnamon, and butter in a food processor and process just until the mixture forms coarse crumbs. Beat the egg and water together, add to the flour mixture, and process just until the mixture begins to form into a ball. Dust the dough lightly with flour, wrap in plastic wrap, and refrigerate 30 minutes.

2. Roll out the dough into a 12-inch circle on a lightly floured surface. Transfer to a 10 to 11-inch tart pan with a removable bottom; trim and crimp the edge. Place the tart shell in the freezer while proceeding with the recipe.

3. Preheat the oven to 400°F.

4. Prepare the nut cream: Place the almonds, hazelnuts, and sugar in a food processor and process until the nuts are finely ground. Add the butter, egg, and extracts and process until smooth. Set aside briefly.

5. Prepare the topping: Toss the sliced apples with the lemon juice and brandy in a mixing bowl. Spread the nut cream evenly over the bottom of the chilled tart shell. Arrange the apple slices in con-centric circles over the nut cream.

6. Place the 3 tablespoons flour, brown sugar, and butter in the food processor and process until crumbly. Add the cinnamon, walnuts, and oatmeal; process quickly just to incorporate. Sprinkle the streusel topping over the apples.

7. Bake the tart until the streusel is golden brown and the filling is set, 45 to 50 minutes. Serve warm or at room temperature with rich vanilla ice cream.

Makes 8 servings

Cranberry Curd Tartlets

— ✤ —

These make a light and gentle ending to a rich Thanksgiving dinner. They are so dainty and delicious that I am also prone to making them at Christmastime, when a little sprig of holly serves as a smashing garnish.

ALMOND CRUST
½ cup blanched almonds, lightly toasted
1½ cups unbleached all-purpose flour
½ cup (1 stick) unsalted butter, chilled, cut into small pieces

2 tablespoons sugar
Pinch of salt
1 large egg
1 teaspoon almond extract

CRANBERRY CURD
4 cups fresh cranberries (about 1½ packages)
½ cup fresh orange juice
1 to 1¼ cups sugar
6 large egg yolks
½ cup (1 stick) unsalted butter

2 tablespoons Grand Marnier or other orange liqueur
1 tablespoon grated orange zest
Whole cranberries or tiny holly sprigs for garnish

1. Prepare the almond crust: Place the almonds and flour in a food processor and process until the nuts are finely ground. Add the butter, sugar, and salt; process until the mixture resembles coarse

meal. Add the egg and almond extract and continue processing just until the dough holds together. Wrap the dough in plastic wrap and refrigerate at least 1 hour.

2. Preheat the oven to 425°F.

3. Roll the dough out ⅛ inch thick on a lightly floured surface. Cut the dough into circles to fit into ten 3 to 3½-inch round tartlet tins. Trim and crimp the edges decoratively. Line each pastry shell with aluminum foil and fill with pie weights or dried beans. Bake until beginning to brown lightly, 10 to 15 minutes. Remove the foil and pie weights, reduce the oven temperature to 350°F, and continue baking until the shells are golden brown, about 5 minutes more. Let cool completely.

4. Prepare the cranberry curd: Place the cranberries, orange juice, and 1 cup sugar in a medium saucepan. Bring to a simmer over medium heat and continue cooking, stirring frequently, until the berries have popped and are very soft, 15 to 20 minutes. Press the berries through a food mill to purée and discard the skins and seeds.

5. Place the cranberry purée in a clean saucepan. Taste for sweetness and add up to ¼ cup sugar if the mixture seems too tart. Whisk in the egg yolks and cook over low heat, stirring constantly, until very thick, 10 to 15 minutes. Remove the heat and stir in the butter, 1 tablespoon at a time, waiting for each tablespoon to melt before adding another. Stir in the Grand Marnier and orange zest. Let the mixture cool, then refrigerate for several hours.

6. Just before serving, pipe the cranberry curd through a pastry bag fitted with a decorative tip into the baked pastry shells. Garnish each tartlet in the center with a whole cranberry or a holly sprig.

Makes 10 tartlets

German Apple Torte

— ❖ —

This stunning apple creation is baked in a springform pan with a lovely marzipan pastry. The filling is rich with buttery, Calvados-laced apples which are further embellished with a topping of almond streusel. The result is a unique harvest dessert with the appeal of apple pie and the finesse of European confectionary art.

MARZIPAN CRUST

3 cups unbleached all-
  purpose flour
1 teaspoon baking powder
1 teaspoon ground
  cinnamon
½ cup granulated sugar
3 ounces almond paste,
  broken into small pieces

1 cup (2 sticks) unsalted
  butter, chilled, cut into
  small pieces
1 large egg, lightly beaten
½ teaspoon almond
  extract
1 tablespoon fresh lemon
  juice

APPLE FILLING

4 tablespoons (½ stick)
  unsalted butter
½ cup (packed) light
  brown sugar
1 tablespoon fresh lemon
  juice
Grated zest of 1 lemon
1 tablespoon ground
  cinnamon

½ teaspoon grated nutmeg
12 cups coarsely sliced
  cored peeled cooking
  apples, such as Rhode
  Island Greenings (about
  12 apples)
1 tablespoon cornstarch
¼ cup Calvados or
  applejack

STREUSEL TOPPING

4 tablespoons (½ stick)
  unsalted butter, chilled,
  cut into small pieces
½ cup granulated sugar

½ cup unbleached all-
  purpose flour
½ cup slivered
  almonds

1. Preheat the oven to 350°F.
2. Prepare the marzipan crust: Place the flour, baking powder, cinnamon, and granulated sugar in a food processor and process just to combine. Add the almond paste and butter; process until the mixture resembles coarse crumbs. Add the egg, extract, and lemon juice; process until the mixture just begins to form into a ball.
3. Press two-thirds of the pastry over the bottom and 2½ inches up the side of a 9-inch springform pan. Refrigerate the remaining dough while preparing the apple filling.
4. To prepare the filling, melt the butter in a large pot over medium heat. Stir in the brown sugar, lemon juice and zest, cinnamon, and nutmeg. Add the apples and stir to coat. Simmer uncovered, stirring occasionally, until the apples are tender, 8 to 10 minutes.
5. In a small bowl dissolve the cornstarch in the Calvados. Stir into the apple mixture and cook, stirring constantly, until thickened, 1 to 2 minutes. Remove from the heat and pour the filling into the crust in the springform pan.
6. Prepare the streusel topping: Place the butter, granulated sugar, and flour in a food processor and process just until the mixture

resembles coarse crumbs. Add the almonds and pulse the machine just to combine. Sprinkle the streusel over the top of the apples in the pan.

7. Roll out the remaining pastry into a 9½-inch circle and transfer to the top of the torte. Press the edges together to seal and trim and crimp them decoratively. Cut a few slits in the top to allow steam to escape.

8. Bake until the pastry is golden brown, 50 to 60 minutes. Cool to room temperature, remove the side of the pan, and serve cut into wedges.

Makes 10 to 12 servings

Bûche de Thanksgiving

— ❖ —

*B*ûche is the French word for log and a *Bûche de Noël* is a chocolate cake made to look like a tree log and served as a traditional French Christmas dessert. I decided to borrow the concept for an American log cake using the flavors of Thanksgiving. A pumpkin-and-spice genoise cake is rolled with a cream cheese and candied ginger filling, while a generous sprinkling of buttery nut brickle imparts a delightful praline crunch.

PUMPKIN SPICE GENOISE

1 cup cake flour
1 teaspoon baking powder
1 tablespoon ground
  cinnamon
2 teaspoons ground ginger
½ teaspoon grated nutmeg
¼ teaspoon salt
3 large eggs

1 cup (packed) light brown
  sugar
1 cup pumpkin purée,
  canned or fresh
1 cup Heath Bar Bits 'O
  Brickle or other nut
  brickle (about 6 ounces)
Confectioners' sugar

GINGER CREAM-CHEESE FILLING

8 ounces cream cheese, at
  room temperature
2 tablespoons unsalted
  butter, at room
  temperature
1 cup confectioners' sugar
⅓ cup crystallized ginger,
  finely chopped

1 cup Heath Bar Bits 'O
  Brickle or other nut
  brickle
½ cup confectioners' sugar
  for garnish

1. Preheat the oven to 375°F. Butter a 15 × 10-inch jelly-roll pan. Line with a piece of waxed or parchment paper cut ½ inch smaller than the pan, then butter the paper.

2. Prepare the genoise: Sift the cake flour, baking powder, cinnamon, ginger, nutmeg, and salt together into a bowl; set aside.

3. Using an electric mixer, beat the eggs in a medium-size bowl until thick and creamy, 4 to 5 minutes. Beat in the brown sugar, 1 tablespoon at a time, and continue beating until the mixture is very thick. Beat in the pumpkin purée. Using a large rubber spatula, quickly fold in the sifted flour mixture just until thoroughly combined. Spread the batter evenly in the prepared pan. Sprinkle the top evenly with the butter brickle. Bake until the cake springs back when touched lightly in the center, about 15 minutes. Let cool 5 minutes.

4. Using a sharp knife, trim ¼ inch cake from all sides. Invert the cake onto a clean kitchen towel that has been dusted generously with confectioners' sugar. Peel off the paper. Starting with one short side, roll up the cake in the towel jelly-roll fashion. Let cool completely on a wire rack.

5. Prepare the ginger cream-cheese filling: Beat together the cream cheese and butter until light and fluffy. Add 1 cup confectioners' sugar and beat until smooth. Stir in the crystallized ginger and butter brickle.

6. Carefully unroll the cooled cake and spread evenly with the filling. Reroll the cake and transfer to a serving platter. Cover and refrigerate for a few hours to allow the cake to set and the flavors to blend. Just before serving, sift ¼ cup confectioners' sugar over the entire cake. Cut into 1-inch slices to serve.

Makes 8 servings

Pear and Biscotti Strudel

Biscotti are nutty, nonsweet Italian biscuits meant for dunking in dessert wines at the end of a meal. They have recently become fashionable in this country, and there are several good packaged brands available in specialty food stores. When biscotti are ground up, they make an excellent replacement for dried bread or cake crumbs in traditional strudel recipes. Packaged phyllo dough makes this recipe a breeze to prepare. In order to use the entire package of phyllo dough, this recipe makes two strudels, each feeding 5 or 6 people. If you haven't the need for two, the extra strudel will freeze quite nicely.

6 ripe pears, peeled, cored,
  and thickly sliced
1 tablespoon fresh lemon
  juice
Finely grated zest of 1
  lemon
⅔ cup (packed) light
  brown sugar
½ cup golden raisins
2 teaspoons ground
  cinnamon

1 teaspoon ground ginger
2 tablespoons brandy
1 package (1 pound) phyllo
  dough, thawed if frozen
1½ cups clarified butter,
  melted (see page 89)
1½ cups finely ground
  biscotti crumbs
Confectioners' sugar for
  garnish

1. For the filling, toss the pears with the lemon juice and zest in a mixing bowl. Stir in the brown sugar, raisins, cinnamon, ginger, and brandy. Let marinate at least 15 minutes.

2. Preheat the oven to 375°F. Butter 2 baking sheets.

3. Using a large work surface, unroll the phyllo dough into a stack of flat sheets and cover with a damp kitchen towel to keep them from drying out while working. Assemble each strudel on a large sheet of parchment or waxed paper to aid in rolling them up. Place 1 sheet of phyllo dough on the paper and brush lightly with the butter. Lay another sheet on top, brush it with the butter, then sprinkle with a fine layer of the biscotti crumbs. Repeat the process, sprinkling every other sheet with crumbs, until you have 9 sheets layered and the top one is buttered but not sprinkled with crumbs. On top of the ninth sheet make a compact row of half the filling, spacing it 2 inches from one long end of the dough. Layer 2 more sheets of phyllo dough over the filling, brushing each with butter and sprinkling the second with biscotti crumbs.

4. Using the paper as an aid, roll up the strudel, jelly-roll fashion, starting at the edge closest to the filling. Slip the strudel onto a prepared baking sheet, making sure the seam side is down. Brush the top and sides of the strudel generously with butter. Repeat the process to make the second strudel.

5. Bake the strudels until golden brown, about 40 minutes. Serve warm, dusted with sifted confectioners' sugar.

Makes 2 strudels, 10 to 12 servings

SOUPS
FOR THE
SOLSTICE

"Onion Soup sustains. The process of making it is somewhat like the process of learning to love. It requires commitment, extraordinary effort, time, and will make you cry."

— Ronni Lundy
Esquire

Every year, just around the time the clocks are reluctantly turned back one hour and afternoon darkens to night at the ungodly hour of 4 P.M., a bowl of hot and hearty soup becomes my best friend in the entire world. Seriously, I have learned after many long off-seasons weathered on a desolate island where the local electric company can't be counted on to be generating heat through the home radiators, and moths have munched major cavities into once-toasty woolens, and a man-of-the-moment is not quite within cuddling range, a thick and nourishing cauldron of soup is a mighty fine thermal surrogate to have handy on the back burner. Furthermore, a mug of minestrone has never talked back to me nor has a cup of chowder ever made rude inquiries about the state of my income taxes or whether the color of my blonde locks is real. What a friend! More congenial than many a mate and almost as consoling as a doting mother.

Soups simmered with the winter solstice in mind make versatile cold-weather fare. Fish soups from Provence and chunky chowders and cheesy onion soups from New England steal center stage at homespun suppers while unusual Spanish Garlic Soup or Pumpkin and Smoked Mussel Bisque exude a subtle air of sophistication as a first course at a more elaborate meal. Spicy Black Bean Soup, stick-to-your-ribs Polish Potato and Mushroom Soup, and tradition-steeped Italian Pasta e Fagioli percolate warmth, if not sunshine, into even the bleakest of winter days. Whoever penned the proverb, "Of soup and love, the first is best," may just have been onto something...

Smoked Haddock and Celeriac Chowder

— ❖ —

This soup is made in the fashion of a hearty New England clam chowder except that I have substituted smoked haddock for the clams and intensely flavored celery root for the potatoes. I suspect most chowder aficionados will love the arresting flavors in this innovation.

8 ounces sliced bacon, cut into ½-inch dice
1 large onion, chopped
2 cloves garlic, minced
2 teaspoons dried thyme
1 teaspoon dried chervil
2 medium knobs celeriac (celery root), peeled and cut into ½-inch cubes
5 cups fish broth or bottled clam juice
1 cup dry white wine
1¼ pounds smoked haddock (finnan haddie)
2 cups milk
1 cup heavy or whipping cream
Salt and freshly ground black pepper to taste
Chopped fresh parsley for garnish
Paprika for garnish

1. Fry the bacon in a large stockpot over medium-high heat, stirring frequently, until crisp. Drain the bacon on paper towels.

2. Pour all but 3 tablespoons of the fat from the pot. Add the onion, garlic, thyme, and chervil; cook, stirring occasionally, 5 minutes. Reduce the heat to low, cover the pot, and sweat the vegetables for 10 minutes.

3. Add the celeriac to the pot and toss to combine with the vegetables. Pour in the fish broth and the white wine. Bring to a boil, then simmer until the celeriac is very tender, 25 to 30 minutes.

4. In the meantime, place the smoked haddock in a saucepan and pour the milk over it. Heat to boiling, then simmer until the fish flakes easily with a fork, about 15 minutes. Remove the fish from the pan, reserving the milk, and set aside to cool slightly.

5. Purée half the soup in a blender or food processor; return to the pot and mix with the remaining soup. Flake the haddock into bite-size pieces and stir into the soup with the reserved milk. Stir in the cream and season to taste with salt and pepper.

6. Simmer the soup over low heat about 15 minutes to blend the flavors. Just before serving, stir in the reserved bacon. Ladle the soup into bowls and sprinkle each portion with parsley and paprika.

Makes 6 to 8 servings

Fish Soup with Saffron and Orange Aioli

— ❖ —

This is my New England winter version of Southern France's famous bouillabaisse. While there is controversy even in France over
how to make the best and most authentic version of this Provençal
soup (Fernand Point claimed that *la bouillabaisse* could only be made
within sight of the Mediterranean), I believe that the magic of Mar-
seilles marries perfectly with the frosty bounty of Cape Cod waters. I
shy away from the traditional inclusion of lobster and shrimp as I
believe the elegance of these upper-crust crustaceans is lost when
submerged in broth, and instead favor meaty fresh cod, sweet local
scallops, and briny mussels and clams. I also have substituted a sensational Saffron and Orange Aioli for the usual accompaniment of rust-
colored rouille, because I love the bright yellow contrast of the sauce
with the red of the tomato-tinged fish broth. Make this soup meal
when you really feel like spending a weekend afternoon in the kitchen
cooking and then treating special friends to the labor of your love.
Serve it with a green salad and plenty of toasted French bread.

FISH BROTH

⅓ cup fruity olive oil
1 bunch leeks (white and tender green parts), rinsed well, trimmed, and minced
1 large onion, minced
5 cloves garlic, minced
1 can (28 ounces) crushed tomatoes
2 cups fresh orange juice
2½ quarts water

2 bay leaves
1 tablespoon dried thyme
2 teaspoons dried tarragon
½ teaspoon fennel seeds
1 teaspoon saffron threads
1 strip (2 inches) fresh orange zest
4 to 5 pounds non-oily–fish frames, heads, and scraps

SEAFOOD

2 pounds cod, cut into 1½ to 2-inch chunks
1 pound bay scallops
3 tablespoons extra virgin olive oil
3 tablespoons dry white wine
2 cloves garlic, minced

½ teaspoon fennel seeds, ground in a mortar and pestle or finely chopped
½ teaspoon saffron threads
2 dozen clams, such as littleneck or top neck
2 dozen mussels

FINISHING THE SOUP

Salt and freshly ground black pepper to taste
1 red bell pepper, stemmed, seeded, and cut into fine julienne strips about 2 inches long
1 small bulb fennel, cut into fine julienne strips about 2 inches long

3 tablespoons Pernod (anise liqueur)
16 slices (each ½ inch thick) French bread, toasted
Saffron and Orange Aioli (recipe follows)
½ cup chopped fresh parsley

1. Prepare the fish broth: Heat the olive oil over medium-high heat in a large stockpot, then add the leeks and onion. Cook, stirring frequently 5 minutes. Add the garlic and cook 3 minutes more.

2. Stir in the tomatoes, orange juice, water, bay leaves, thyme, tarragon, fennel, saffron, orange zest, and fish trimmings. Bring to a boil, then reduce the heat and simmer uncovered, stirring occasionally, 45 to 50 minutes.

3. In the meantime, prepare the seafood: Mix the cod and scallops together and toss with the olive oil, wine, garlic, fennel seeds,

and saffron. Let marinate at least 1 hour.

4. Scrub the clams and mussels well and soak 1 hour in cold water. Just before cooking, drain well and remove the beards from the mussels.

5. Strain the fish broth into a large, wide, shallow stockpot, pressing hard to extract all the juices from the ingredients. Season the stock with salt and pepper to taste and return to medium heat. Add the julienne of red pepper and fennel and simmer 15 minutes.

6. About 10 minutes before serving, bring the broth to a boil and add the clams and mussels. When the shells just begin to open, add the cod and scallops with their marinade and simmer just until all the fish is cooked, about 5 minutes. Stir in the Pernod.

7. Ladle the soup into large, shallow soup bowls. Float a couple rounds of toasted French bread on top and spoon a generous dollop of Saffron and Orange Aioli over the toast. Sprinkle with parsley.

Makes 6 to 8 servings

Saffron and Orange Aioli

1 slice (½ inch thick) day-old French bread	1 teaspoon saffron threads
3 tablespoons half-and-half	2 large egg yolks
3 cloves garlic, minced	1¼ cups fruity olive oil
2 teaspoons grated orange zest	3 tablespoons extra virgin olive oil
2 tablespoons fresh orange juice	Salt to taste

1. Trim the crust from the bread and tear the bread into irregular pieces. Combine the bread and half-and-half in a small bowl and let stand 5 minutes. Gather the bread in a ball and squeeze out as much liquid as possible.

2. Place the bread, garlic, orange zest, orange juice, saffron, and egg yolks in a food processor and process until blended. With the machine running, pour the oils in a thin, steady stream through the feed tube to make a thick emulsion. Season the aioli to taste with salt and refrigerate covered until ready to serve.

Makes 2 cups

Smoked Mussel
and Pumpkin Bisque

— ❖ —

I am a big fan of the mussels that are smoked at Ducktrap Farm in Maine. After coming across several French recipes that combined pumpkin with shellfish, I became inspired to experiment with this smoked mussel and pumpkin combination. The subtle color nuances among the pumpkin, mussels, and saffron could be taken from a van Gogh *Sunflowers* palette, while the rich flavors also hint of the South of France. Be sure to mince the leeks, carrots, and red pepper in a uniform manner, as the soup is not puréed and the vegetables impart a lovely confetti effect to the finished soup.

STOCK
12 cups water
3 cups dry white wine
1 red onion, sliced
2 carrots, scrubbed and sliced
2 cloves garlic, coarsely chopped

1½ cups sliced fennel or celery tops
1 piece (2 inches) fresh ginger, sliced
2 teaspoons curry powder
Pinch dried red pepper flakes
1 teaspoon salt

BISQUE
½ cup (1 stick) unsalted butter
1 bunch leeks (white and tender green parts), rinsed well, trimmed, and finely minced
2 carrots, peeled and finely minced
1 red bell pepper, stemmed, seeded, and finely minced
2 teaspoons saffron threads
¼ cup unbleached all-purpose flour

4 cups pumpkin purée, canned or fresh
1½ cups milk
2 cups heavy or whipping cream
Salt and freshly ground black pepper to taste
1½ pounds good-quality smoked mussels (not tinned), drained if oily

1. Place all the stock ingredients in a stockpot and simmer uncovered 45 minutes. Strain the stock, pressing the vegetables with the back of a spoon to extract the liquid. Discard the solids.
2. Melt the butter in a large pot over medium-high heat. Add

the leeks, carrots, red pepper, and saffron; sauté, stirring frequently, 5 minutes. Reduce the heat to low and cook the vegetables slowly, uncovered, 25 minutes longer.

3. Stir in the flour and cook, stirring constantly, 2 minutes. Gradually whisk in the stock and pumpkin purée. Simmer for 15 minutes to blend flavors.

4. Stir in the milk and heavy cream. Adjust the seasonings with salt and pepper. Finally stir in the mussels and heat a few minutes more just to get the soup hot throughout. Serve.

Makes 8 to 10 servings

Polish Mushroom and Potato Soup

— ⚜ —

This intensely flavored, soul-satisfying soup from Poland was a unanimous favorite among those who helped with the task of tasting my latest recipe creations. I would certainly second the motion!

1 cup dried porcini mushrooms	1 tablespoon caraway seeds
4 cups water	4 cups beef broth, preferably homemade, or water if a vegetarian soup is desired
½ cup (1 stick) unsalted butter	
3 leeks (white and light green parts), rinsed well, trimmed, and finely minced	5 large potatoes, peeled and cut into ½-inch chunks
	4 cups milk
1 medium onion, finely minced	Salt and freshly ground black pepper to taste
3 ribs celery, finely minced	1 cup sour cream
1 large carrot, peeled and finely minced	¼ cup unbleached, all-purpose flour
1 pound domestic white mushrooms, thinly sliced	2 teaspoons sweet Hungarian paprika

1. Place the dried mushrooms and water in a saucepan. Bring to a boil, then simmer uncovered 30 minutes. Strain the mushrooms, reserving the cooking liquid. Coarsely chop the mushrooms and set aside.

2. Melt the butter in a large stockpot over medium-high heat. Add the leeks, onion, celery, and carrot. Sauté 5 minutes. Reduce the heat to medium and add the fresh mushrooms, dried mushrooms, and caraway seeds; continue cooking until the vegetables are very tender, 15 to 20 minutes.

3. Meanwhile, combine the reserved mushroom cooking liquid, the beef broth and potatoes in a pot. Simmer until the potatoes are tender, 20 to 25 minutes. Add the potatoes and liquid to the sautéed vegetables and mash about half the potatoes against the side of the pot with the back of a large spoon to help thicken the soup.

4. Add the milk to the soup and heat through. Season with salt and pepper. Whisk the sour cream, flour, and paprika together in a small bowl until smooth. Stir into the hot soup to blend. Cook the soup a few minutes more over low heat. (It is important not to let the soup boil at this point or it will curdle.) Serve the soup hot ladled into wide bowls.

Makes 10 to 12 servings

Pasta e Fagioli alla Clementina

My very special and vibrant friend Elena Latici, who shared her Grandfather's Peasant Sauce recipe in my last book, came to visit one foggy, raw winter week on Nantucket. She once again warmed my kitchen with her humor and an exceptional old-world Italian recipe. This one comes from her feisty and independent ninety-year-old grandmother, Clementina. Though Pasta e Fagioli is a very popular soup throughout Italy, this rendition is from Clementina's native Emilia-Romagna, and I wouldn't trade it for any other variation.

2 cups dried red kidney
    beans, soaked in water
    overnight
1 chunk (2 inches square)
    salt pork
1 medium onion, peeled
1 can (28 ounces) tomatoes,
    drained and finely
    chopped

¾ cup acini pepe or other
    pastina (miniature pasta)
Salt and freshly ground
    black pepper to taste
Extra virgin olive oil for
    garnish
Freshly grated Parmesan
    cheese for garnish

1. Drain the soaked kidney beans and place in a large saucepan. Cover generously with fresh water and bring to a boil over medium-high heat. Reduce the heat to a simmer and cook until very tender, about 1¼ hours.

2. In the meantime, place the salt pork on a chopping block and finely mince. Slice the onion, place it on top of the salt pork, and continue chopping until the onion is finely minced. (Clementina insists that the two be chopped one on top of the other, and I have the greatest respect for the time-honored wisdom of her technique.)

3. Place the salt pork and onion in a stockpot and sauté slowly over medium-low heat until nicely browned, about 30 minutes. Set aside until the beans are cooked.

4. Drain the beans, reserving the cooking liquid. Purée the beans by passing them through a food mill. (Do not use a food processor as the objective is to remove the bean skins as well. Moistening the beans with some of the cooking liquid will make the puréeing process easier.

5. Add the beans to the stockpot along with the tomatoes, 3 cups of the reserved cooking liquid, and the *acini pepe*. Season to taste with salt and pepper. Bring the soup to a simmer and cook uncovered, stirring occasionally, until the pasta is tender, 30 to 40 minutes.

6. Ladle the soup into deep bowls and pass a cruet of extra virgin olive oil and a bowl of freshly grated Parmesan to sprinkle over the soup.

Makes 6 servings

Quick Tortellini and Spinach Soup

— ❖ —

This soup tastes like something a lucky traveler might happen upon in a rustic kitchen in the Italian hills. However, if you have some good chicken broth on hand and access to quality commercial tortellini, you can whip up this romantic, rib-sticking soup in 30 to 40 minutes. While I often use canned chicken broth in a pinch, the success of this recipe really depends on the richness of homemade chicken stock. Once you have that as a base, the rest is a breeze.

2 tablespoons olive oil
2 ounces pancetta, finely diced
3 cloves garlic, minced
1 medium onion, finely chopped
9 cups homemade chicken broth
2 teaspoons dried Italian herb blend
9 ounces best-quality commercial spinach or cheese tortellini

1 can (28 ounces) crushed tomatoes packed in purée
8 ounces fresh spinach, rinsed well, stemmed, and coarsely chopped
Salt and freshly ground black pepper to taste
1 cup freshly grated Parmesan cheese

1. Heat the olive oil in a stockpot over medium-high heat. Add the pancetta, garlic, and onion; cook, stirring frequently, until lightly browned, 10 to 15 minutes.

2. Add the chicken broth and Italian herbs. Bring to a boil and stir in the tortellini. Simmer uncovered until the tortellini is cooked, 10 to 12 minutes. Stir in the crushed tomatoes and simmer another 5 minutes. Add the spinach and cook just until wilted, about 3 minutes. Season to taste with salt and pepper.

3. Ladle the hot soup into bowls and top with a liberal sprinkling of grated Parmesan.

Makes 6 to 8 servings

Curried Lentil Soup
with Chutney Butter

—✦—

In India, *dahl* is a porridge of spiced legumes that is basic to many meals. Here I have thinned the mixture to a soup consistency and enhanced it with a dollop of chutney butter. It is one of the most intoxicatingly aromatic soups I have ever concocted, and I highly recommend it to lovers of exotic seasonings and Indian cooking.

3 tablespoons unsalted butter at room temperature.
1 large onion, minced
2 cloves garlic, minced
2 tablespoons chopped fresh ginger
2 serrano chiles, stemmed, seeded, and minced
3 cinnamon sticks (2 inches each)
2 bay leaves

1 generous tablespoon Madras curry powder
1½ cups yellow lentils or yellow split peas
2 to 2½ quarts chicken broth, preferably homemade
2 lemons
¼ cup minced cilantro (fresh coriander)
Salt to taste

CHUTNEY BUTTER
½ cup (1 stick) unsalted butter, at room temperature

½ cup mango or peach chutney

1. Melt the butter over medium-high heat in a heavy soup pot. Add the onion, garlic, ginger, chiles, cinnamon sticks, and bay leaves. Sauté, stirring occasionally, until the vegetables are soft and translucent, 5 to 7 minutes. Add the curry powder and cook 2 minutes more.

2. Add the lentils and 2 quarts chicken broth to the pot. Bring to a boil, then simmer 15 minutes. Halve the lemons, squeeze the juice, and add both the juice and the remaining lemon rinds to the soup. Continue to simmer uncovered, stirring occasionally, until the lentils are tender, about 40 minutes. If the soup seems to be too thick, thin with additional chicken broth.

3. Remove the bay leaves, cinnamon sticks, and lemon rinds from the soup. Season lightly with salt. Purée half the soup in a food processor or blender, and return it to the unpuréed soup, and stir to combine. Add the cilantro and keep the soup warm over low heat.

4. Make the chutney butter by processing the butter and chutney together until smooth in a food processor. Ladle the hot soup into bowls and top with a generous dollop of the chutney butter. Serve at once.

Makes 6 servings

Lamb and Lentil Soup

—❖—

Lamb and lemon infuse this hearty lentil soup with a Mediterranean flavor. The swirl of rich walnut and Roquefort butter that garnishes each serving takes the soup from homey to refined.

1 pound lean ground lamb	1 cup dry red wine
1 tablespoon olive oil	1 pound lentils, soaked in
1 large onion, minced	water overnight and
1 bunch scallions, trimmed	drained
and minced	1 teaspoon dried thyme
3 cloves garlic, minced	2 bay leaves
3 carrots, peeled and	Salt and freshly ground
minced	black pepper to taste
2 tablespoons tomato paste	Finely grated zest of 1
½ cup minced fresh parsley	lemon
2½ quarts beef broth	
preferably homemade, or	
water	

WALNUT AND ROQUEFORT BUTTER

½ cup (1 stick) unsalted	3 ounces Roquefort
butter, at room	cheese
temperature	2 tablespoons minced fresh
¼ cup walnuts, lightly	parsley
toasted	

1. Heat a large heavy stockpot over medium-high heat, add the lamb and brown it, crumbling it into small pieces with the back of a wooden spoon. When no pink color remains, remove it from the pot and set aside. Drain all but 2 tablespoons fat from the pot.

2. Add the olive oil to the fat. Add the onion, scallions, garlic, and carrots and sauté 5 minutes. Reduce the heat to medium and cook uncovered until the vegetables are quite soft, about 10 minutes. Stir in the tomato paste and parsley and cook 1 minute more.

3. Gradually stir in the beef broth and red wine. Add the lentils, reserved lamb, the thyme, bay leaves, salt, and pepper. Bring the soup to a boil, then simmer uncovered 1 hour, stirring occasionally and skimming off any foam that rises to the top of the soup. Add the lemon zest and continue simmering until the lentils are very tender, about 30 minutes more.

4. Purée half the soup in a food processor. Return it to the un-puréed soup and stir well to combine. Reheat the soup over medium heat.

5. Meanwhile make the walnut and Roquefort butter. Place all the ingredients in a food processor and process, pulsing the machine on and off, until smooth and creamy. Ladle the hot soup into serving bowls and garnish each portion with a heaping tablespoon of the but-ter. Swirl with a spoon or knife tip to create a marbelized effect. Serve at once.

Makes 8 to 10 servings

Southwestern Corn and Cheese Chowder

— ❖ —

This spectacular and nourishing chowder is chock-full of Southwest-ern and Mexican color, flavor, and texture. I'm particularly fond of the sweet potato cubes in the soup and the contrast between the melted and partially melted cheese.

2 extra large sweet
  potatoes, peeled and cut
  into ½-inch cubes
6 cups chicken broth,
  preferably homemade
1 bottle (12 ounces)
  Mexican beer
2 teaspoons ground cumin
1 bay leaf
4 ounces thick bacon slices,
  finely diced
1 large onion, chopped
2 cloves garlic, minced

1 can (16 ounces) creamed
  corn
1 can (4 ounces) diced
  green chiles
2 teaspoons best-quality
  chili powder
Cayenne pepper to taste
2 cups milk
½ cup heavy or whipping cream
1 pound Monterey Jack cheese
Salt to taste
½ cup chopped cilantro
  (fresh coriander)

1. Place the sweet potatoes, 3 cups of the chicken broth, the beer, cumin, and bay leaf in a medium saucepan. Bring to a boil then simmer until the pota-toes are crisp-tender, 12 to 15 minutes. Discard the bay leaf.

2. Meanwhile cook the bacon until crisp in a large stockpot. Remove the bacon and drain on paper towels. Add the onion and garlic to the fat remain-ing in the pot; sauté over medium-high heat until quite soft, about 10 minutes. Add the sweet potatoes with the cooking liquid to the onion and stir in the remaining 3 cups broth as well.

3. Add the creamed corn and green chiles to the soup and season with the chili powder and cayenne. Gradually stir in the milk and cream. Simmer the soup uncovered 10 minutes.

4. Shred 12 ounces of the cheese and cut the remaining 4 ounces cheese into small dice. Reduce the heat under the soup to low and add the shredded cheese, stirring just until melted. Season the soup with salt and stir in the reserved bacon and the cilantro. Ladle the hot chowder into deep bowls, stir-ring a generous tablespoon of diced cheese into each serving. Serve at once.

Makes 10 to 12 servings.

Black Bean
Soup

—❖—

My idea of a perfect lunch on a snowy afternoon is a big bowl of spicy black bean soup accompanied by a couple thick slices of banana bread.

8 ounces sliced bacon,
  diced
1 large onion, minced
3 cloves garlic, minced
6 carrots, peeled and
  minced
4 ribs celery, minced
3 jalapeño chiles, stemmed,
  seeded, and diced
¼ cup ground cumin
¼ cup dried oregano
1 pound black turtle beans,
  soaked overnight in water

3½ to 4 quarts chicken
  broth, preferably
  homemade
½ cup fresh lime juice
½ cup cream sherry
Salt and freshly ground
  black pepper to taste
½ cup minced cilantro
  (fresh coriander)
Sour cream for garnish

1. Cook the bacon in a large stockpot over medium-high heat until it begins to crisp. Remove it with a slotted spoon and set aside to drain on paper towels.

2. Add the onion, garlic, carrots, and celery to the bacon fat in the pot; sauté, stirring occasionally, 10 minutes. Stir in the jalapeños and cook 5 minutes more. Stir in the cumin and oregano.

3. Rinse and drain the black beans and add to the stockpot. Cover with 3½ quarts chicken broth. Simmer uncovered until the beans are very tender and beginning to fall apart, about 2 hours. Thin with additional broth if the mixture seems to be getting too thick.

4. Stir in the lime juice, and sherry, and reserved bacon. Season to taste with salt and pepper. Just before serving, swirl in the cilantro. Serve piping hot in bowls garnished with a dollop of sour cream.

Makes 8 to 10 servings

Tortilla Soup

— ❖ —

Scrutinizing the ingredients and methodology of making tortilla soup is the best introduction to philosophy, Texas-style, that I know. A lot of research, reading, and debate went into the development of this master recipe, and I must confess that I now prefer being with a bowl of tortilla soup to the obtuse ontological study of "What is being."

8 small onions, peeled and
  halved
8 ripe medium tomatoes
4 tablespoons olive oil
6 corn tortillas
4 cloves garlic, minced
2 jalapeño chiles, stemmed,
  seeded, and minced
1 tablespoon chili powder
1 teaspoon dried oregano
2 teaspoons ground cumin
7 cups chicken broth,
  preferably homemade
2 cups beef broth,
  preferably homemade

3 tablespoons fresh lime juice
Salt to taste
2 tablespoons vegetable oil
5 tablespoons finely grated
  Parmesan or Pecorino
  Romano cheese
2 boneless, skinless chicken
  breasts, poached, cooled,
  and cut into julienne
  strips
1 ripe avocado, diced and
  tossed with a little lime
  juice to prevent
  discoloration
Cilantro leaves (fresh coriander)

1. Preheat the broiler.
2. Rub the onions and tomatoes with 2 tablespoons of the olive

oil and place in a single layer in a 12 × 9-inch roasting pan. Broil the vegetables 4 inches from the heat, turning frequently until charred all over, 20 to 25 minutes. Purée the vegetables with accumulated pan juices in a food processor and set aside.

3. Heat the remaining 2 tablespoons olive oil in a stockpot over medium-high heat. Tear 2 of the tortillas into small pieces and sauté them in the oil along with the garlic and jalapeños just until softened, 3 to 4 minutes. Stir in the chili powder, oregano, and cumin; cook 1 minute more.

4. Add the chicken and beef broths to the pot and bring just to a boil. Stir in the reserved tomato-onion purée and the lime juice. Season to taste with salt. Simmer uncovered, stirring occasionally, 30 minutes.

5. Preheat the oven to 375°F.

6. Meanwhile, cut the remaining 4 tortillas into ½-inch-wide strips. Place in the same pan used for roasting the tomatoes and onions and toss with the vegetable oil to lightly coat. Bake the tortilla strips until lightly browned and crisped, about 10 minutes. Toss with the grated Parmesan and return to the oven 2 to 3 minutes more just to lightly bake and melt the cheese. Set aside to cool.

7. Strain the broth through a sieve, pushing hard against the vegetables with the back of a spoon to extract all the juices and flavor. Ladle the hot broth into soup bowls and garnish each serving with a generous amount of chicken, avocado, cilantro, and baked tortilla strips. Serve at once.

Makes 6 servings

Pilgrim's Porridge

— ❖ —

This garlicky oatmeal soup is a night-before-Thanksgiving tradition in my family. Members of the family now travel from all over New England to celebrate Thanksgiving on Cape Cod at my aunt and uncle's antique-filled home. All weary journeyers who arrive on Wednesday evening are greeted first by the heady and hale aroma of this soup simmering on my aunt's twelve-burner range and then treated to a soul-restoring soup supper. In the course of many Thanksgivings, my aunt's soup has gone through several evolutions and name changes, but when my quick-witted mother came up with the title Pilgrim's Porridge after a long drive from the coast of Maine, we all agreed it was most befitting. Garnish the soup with either Parmesan-dusted croutons or my Chèvre Soup Croutons.

4 cups old-fashioned rolled
oats
6 tablespoons peanut
oil
2 large onions, chopped
12 large cloves garlic,
minced
12 ripe large plum
tomatoes, cut into
eighths
1 bottle (12 ounces)
Heineken or other
imported beer

2 cups dry white wine
6 to 8 cups chicken broth,
preferably homemade
1 teaspoon dried red pepper
flakes
1 cup chopped cilantro
(fresh coriander)
Salt to taste
1 cup chopped fresh parsley
or watercress
Chèvre Soup Croutons
(recipe follows)

1. The day before serving, preheat the oven to 300°F.

2. Put the oats in a roasting pan and toast in the oven, stirring frequently, until light brown, 10 to 15 minutes. Remove and set aside.

3. Heat the oil in a large stockpot over medium-high heat. Add the onions and sauté until soft and translucent, about 10 minutes. Add the garlic and tomatoes and sauté 5 minutes more.

4. Stir in the oats, beer, wine, and chicken broth. Season with the red pepper flakes, cilantro, and salt. Reduce the heat to medium-low and bring the soup to a very slow boil. It is important to stir the soup frequently as it has a tendency to stick to the bottom of the pot. Once the soup comes to a boil, remove it from the heat and let cool to room temperature, still stirring frequently. Cover the soup and refrigerate overnight.

5. The next day, reheat the soup over low heat. If the soup seems too thick, thin it with either more chicken broth, beer, wine, or even water. Five minutes before serving, stir in the chopped parsley or watercress. Serve piping hot in deep soup bowls, garnished with croutons.

Makes 10 to 12 servings

Chèvre
Soup Croutons

— ❖ —

These unique cheese croutons add a special flourish to a bowl of vegetable soup and are quite the addictive nibble solely by themselves.

¾ cup unbleached all-
  purpose flour
5 ounces fresh mild chèvre,
  such as Montrachet,
  crumbled
3 tablespoons unsalted
  butter, chilled, cut into
  small pieces
3 tablespoons sour cream

½ teaspoon dried thyme
½ teaspoon salt
½ teaspoon freshly ground
  black pepper
1 large egg
2 tablespoons water
½ cup freshly grated
  Parmesan cheese

1. Place the flour, chèvre, butter, sour cream, thyme, salt, and pepper in a food processor and process just until the dough begins to form into a ball. Dust lightly with flour, wrap in plastic, and refrigerate at least 1 hour.

2. Preheat the oven to 350°F. Line a baking sheet with parchment paper.

3. Roll the dough out ⅓ inch thick on a lightly floured surface. Cut into ½-inch cubes and place in rows on the lined baking sheet. Beat the egg and water together and coat the croutons with the mixture using a pastry brush, then sprinkle each with a little Parmesan.

4. Bake until light golden brown, 10 to 12 minutes. Cool and store in an airtight container.

Makes about 4 dozen

Spanish Garlic Soup

— ❖ —

Despite the robust-sounding title of this soup, I find it delicate and elegant. I like to serve it as a first course at somewhat formal occasions when lamb or beef are featured as a main course.

⅓ cup extra virgin olive oil
9 cloves garlic, peeled and
  slightly bruised
8 slices (each ⅓ inch thick)
  day-old French bread
2½ quarts chicken broth,
  preferably homemade
½ cup dry (fino) Spanish
  sherry
2 bay leaves

Salt and freshly ground
  black pepper to taste
4 large egg yolks, at room
  temperature
⅓ cup heavy or whipping
  cream, at room
  temperature
¼ cup minced fresh parsley
  or basil

1. Heat the olive oil over medium-low heat in a medium-size stockpot. Add the garlic and sauté slowly until golden brown all over, and very, very soft, 30 to 40 minutes. Remove from the pot to a small bowl with a slotted spoon and mash coarsely with a fork. Set aside.

2. Sauté the bread slices in batches over low heat in the olive oil remaining in the pot. When one side becomes golden, flip and continue cooking until the other side is crusty and golden as well, 15 to 20 minutes in all. Remove from the pot and set aside to drain on a plate lined with a double thickness of paper towels.

3. Add the chicken broth to the pot along with the crushed garlic, the sherry, and bay leaves. Season to taste with salt and pepper. Cook the soup uncovered over very low heat 1 hour. Pour the soup through a strainer, pressing hard with a wooden spoon to extract the essence of the garlic.

4. When ready to serve, whisk together the egg yolks and cream in a large bowl until light and frothy. Bring the garlic-scented chicken broth just to a boil. Whisking constantly, gradually beat the hot broth into the egg-cream mixture. Serve immediately, garnished with a bread crouton and a sprinkling of parsley or basil. A chilled glass of the *fino* sherry used in the soup is a typical accompaniment.

Makes 8 servings

Flemish Endive Soup

This soup is simple to make yet very, very sophisticated. The flavor of the endive is subtle and alluring, while the thinly shredded prosciutto adds complementary color and a peppery accent.

4 tablespoons (½ stick)
  unsalted butter
1 medium-size red onion,
  minced
1 fat leek (white and light
  green parts), rinsed well,
  washed, trimmed, and
  minced
2 teaspoons dried tarragon
1 pound Belgian endive,
  rinsed and thinly sliced
  crosswise
1 cup dry white wine

6 cups chicken broth,
  preferably homemade
1 teaspoon sugar
1 cup heavy or whipping
  cream
1¼ cups milk
4 ounces thinly sliced
  prosciutto, cut into thin
  julienne strips
Salt and freshly ground
  white pepper to taste
1 large egg yolk, at room
  temperature

1. Melt the butter in a stockpot over medium heat. Add the onion, leek, and tarragon; sauté 10 minutes. Stir in the sliced endive, stir to combine with the vegetables, and sauté 5 minutes.

2. Add the wine and chicken broth to the pot and simmer uncovered, stirring occasionally, 10 minutes. Blend in the sugar, cream, 1 cup of the milk, the prosciutto, salt, and white pepper. Simmer another 10 minutes.

3. In a small bowl whisk the egg yolk with the remaining ¼ cup milk, then add to the soup in a thin stream, stirring constantly. Serve the soup at once.

Makes 6 servings

Potage Crécy

— ❖ —

This soup takes its name from a town in France known for its particularly tasty carrots. I first learned to make it from a French teacher when I was away at boarding school. I recently revived my tattered copy of that original recipe, for this purée of carrot soup, for all its simplicity and purity, remains a cherished favorite.

4 tablespoons (½ stick) unsalted butter
1 large onion, minced
3 tablespoons tomato paste
¼ cup raw white rice
2½ quarts chicken broth, preferably homemade
1½ pounds carrots, peeled and cut into ½ to 1-inch pieces

1 cup heavy or whipping cream
Salt and freshly ground black pepper to taste
Carrot curls for garnish

1. Melt the butter in a large stockpot over medium-high heat. Add the onion and sauté 5 minutes. Blend in the tomato paste, then add the rice and stir to coat with the butter.

2. Gradually whisk in the chicken broth. Add the carrots and simmer uncovered until the carrots are very tender, about 40 minutes. Purée the soup in batches in a blender until very smooth. Return to a clean stockpot, season with salt and pepper, and swirl in the cream. Reheat the soup and serve it hot, garnished with a fresh carrot curl.

Makes 10 to 12 servings

Onion Soup with Cider and Cheddar Gratin

— ❖ —

A bit of cross-inspirational liberty from both Normandy and New England has been taken with this popular French classic. The cider heightens the natural sweetness of caramelized onions, while the cheese gratin capitalizes on the unbeatable Yankee combo of apples and Cheddar. Serve with frosty mugs of sparkling hard cider and enjoy an apple quota sure to keep the doctor away.

4 tablespoons (½ stick) unsalted butter
2 tablespoons olive oil
5 giant onions, peeled and thinly sliced
1 tablespoon light brown sugar
⅓ cup Calvados
¼ cup unbleached all-purpose flour
4 cups orchard-pressed sweet apple cider

2½ quarts chicken broth, preferably homemade
Salt and freshly ground black pepper to taste
8 slices (each 1 inch thick) French bread, lightly toasted
1 pound sharp Cheddar cheese, grated
1 cup freshly grated Parmesan cheese

1. Heat the butter and olive oil in a large stockpot over medium-high heat. Add the onions and cook, stirring occasionally, 30 minutes. Stir in the sugar and cook 10 minutes more to caramelize the onions.

2. Pour in the Calvados and flame it with a match, being careful to stand back from the pot. When the flames have subsided, stir in the flour and cook 3 minutes, stirring constantly. (For more on flambé techniques, see page 186.)

3. Gradually stir in the cider, then the chicken broth. Season to taste with salt and pepper. Simmer uncovered over medium heat 45 minutes.

4. Preheat the broiler.

5. Ladle the hot soup into 8 ovenproof soup bowls. Top each with one of the toasted slices of French bread. Combine the grated Cheddar and Parmesan and sprinkle generously over the soup and bread. Place the soup bowls on a baking sheet and broil 6 inches from the heat until the cheese is bubbling and lighly browned on top, about 5 minutes. Let cool slightly, then serve with big spoons and napkins.
Makes 8 servings

Winter Asparagus Soup

— ❖ —

Although available winter produce is improving beyond the limp and boring stage of the pre-radicchio age, the exotica traveling from warmer corners of the globe often has lost its essence by the time it arrives at markets stateside. Truthfully no one is more cheered than I by the notion of year-round asparagus, but I often find the spears that depart Mexico in December lack the youthful complexion and silkiness of seasonal spring asparagus. Yet these woody stalks make a much better candidate for this rich soup than those plucked in May.

5 tablespoons unsalted butter
1 medium onion, minced
2 leeks (white and tender
    green parts), rinsed well,
    trimmed, and minced
3 cloves garlic, minced
2 carrots, peeled and cut
    into ¼-inch dice
1 tablespoon dried tarragon
    leaves
Pinch of cayenne pepper
½ cup chopped fresh parsley

1½ pounds asparagus,
    trimmed and cut into
    1-inch pieces
1 cup dry white wine
5 cups chicken broth,
    preferably homemade
3 tablespoons finely
    chopped fresh dill
1 cup heavy or whipping
    cream
Salt and freshly ground
    white pepper to taste

1. Melt the butter in a soup pot over medium heat. Add the onion, leeks, garlic, and carrots; cook uncovered, stirring occasionally, until the vegetables are quite soft, about 20 minutes.

2. Stir in the tarragon, cayenne, parsley, and asparagus; cook 2 minutes more. Add the wine and chicken broth. Bring the soup to a boil, then simmer uncovered until all the vegetables are very tender, 40 to 45 minutes. Stir in the dill and remove from the heat.

3. Add the cream to the soup and process it in batches in a

blender until very smooth. Season the soup to taste with salt and white pepper. Serve at once or refrigerate and reheat over medium-low heat when ready to serve.

Makes 6 servings

Mr. Powers's Broccoli and Mustard Seed Soup

— ❖ —

No cookbook of mine can ever be complete without at least one contribution from that crazed family of cooks in Weston, Connecticut, the Powers clan. Father P. revived my spirits with this deliciously original soup one noontime after a seemingly endless Amtrak trip from New York. Fortunately I managed to convince him to part with the recipe by promising new and illustrious stardom in my forthcoming cookbook.

6 tablespoons (¾ stick) unsalted butter

2 medium onions, minced

2 large potatoes, peeled and diced

1 large bunch broccoli, trimmed and chopped (including tender stems)

6 cups chicken broth, preferably homemade

Salt and freshly ground black pepper to taste

1 cup heavy or whipping cream

¼ cup golden mustard seeds

1 cup freshly grated Parmesan cheese

1. Melt the butter in a stockpot over medium-high heat. Add the onion and sauté until soft and translucent, about 10 minutes. Stir in the potatoes and broccoli, cover with chicken broth, and season with salt and pepper. Simmer uncovered until the vegetables are very tender, 30 to 40 minutes.

2. Add the cream and purée the soup in a food processor. Return the soup to the pot and stir in the mustard seeds and Parmesan. (If the soup seems too thick, thin it with some milk.) Reheat the soup if needed and serve hot.

Note: The mustard seed flavor becomes more pronounced as the soup sits, so you may want to make the soup a day or so in advance.

Makes 6 servings

DECEMBER
DAZZLE

Incurable mistletoed romantic that I am, I adore all the holiday hoopla and merrymaking that culminate in the celebration of Christmas Day. I get swept up in the selection of the most artistic or charming card to send season's greetings to faraway friends. I become elated by the local search for this year's fullest tree, most original ornaments, splashiest gift wrap, fancy fireside stockings, fragrant wreaths, berried holly boughs, and healthiest pots of blooming poinsettias. The smells of Christmas—evergreen, eucalyptus, frankincense, pomanders, cinnamon sticks, and sugar and spice cookies baking—are among my very favorites. The sounds of the Yuletide—sleigh bells, silver bells, the Nutcracker Suite, Handel's Messiah, Gregorian chants, and just good old carols sung by Bing Crosby or conducted by Mitch Miller—add to my sentimentality during this most joyous season.

From an entertainment standpoint, I relish the contagion and festive incentive to splurge with lavish foods and formal parties. If revelers are willing to defy the encroaching cold and hostile climate by donning black tie, tails, velveteen, silks, satins, and taffeta rather than down and long johns, I say greet them with oysters, caviar, foie gras, and white truffles—not dips, chips, and canapés. Indulge cherished family members and guests with crown roasts, standing ribs of beef, racks of lamb, and save the homey stews and casseroles for the nesting instincts that emerge with the New Year. Take momentary leave of the comforts of puddings and pies to savor elaborate trifles and slivers of dense chocolate tortes. 'Tis the season, if ever there was one, for feasts of grandiloquence.

Prosciutto-Wrapped Escargot

— ✣ —

The shells, tongs, and special dishes that traditionally accompany the ritual of escargot eating once seemed like an epicurean novelty but now strike me as more of an unnecessary affectation. These pros-ciutto-enrobed snails are my no-paraphernalia remedy. Naturally, the irresistible garlic butter has been preserved and even further enhanced with a subtle addition of Parmesan cheese. Serve these as an hors d'oeuvre set out for guests to help themselves or as a pre-theater or after-theater main course.

1 cup (2 sticks) unsalted
   butter, at room
   temperature
3 large cloves garlic,
   minced
2 shallots, minced
½ cup minced fresh
   parsley
½ cup freshly grated
   Parmesan cheese
1 tablespoon dry vermouth
1 teaspoon Pernod or other
   anise liqueur (optional)

2 teaspoons fresh lemon
   juice
½ teaspoon salt
1 teaspoon freshly ground
   black pepper
36 paper-thin slices
   prosciutto (about 1
   pound)
36 canned Burgundy snails,
   rinsed and drained
Minced fresh parsley for
   garnish
Sliced fresh French bread

1. Using an electric mixer, beat the butter until light and fluffy. Beat in the garlic, shallots, parsley, and Parmesan. On low speed blend in the vermouth, Pernod, and lemon juice. Season with salt and pepper.

2. Spread each slice of prosciutto with a generous tablespoon of the garlic butter. Place a snail in the center of each buttered slice and roll up tightly around each snail. Arrange the wrapped snails close together and seam side down in a baking dish. (The snails may also be placed in individual gratin dishes allowing 6 per serving.)

3. When ready to cook the escargot, preheat the oven to 400°F. Bake the escargot for 10 minutes. Turn on the broiler and broil the dish a few inches from the heat until the butter is sizzling, about 1 minute. Sprinkle with a smattering of fresh parsley, insert a toothpick in each snail if serving from one dish, and serve at once with plenty of bread to soak up the garlic butter that has oozed into the dish.

Makes 36 snails, 12 to 18 hors-d'oeuvre or 6 first-course or light supper servings

Mashed Potato Swirls with Caviar

— ❖ —

These light, little potato puffs prove to be the perfect vehicle for indulging in a mouthful of your favorite caviar. Pass on a sterling silver tray to set the tone of the season's most extravagant party.

6 medium baking
  potatoes
3 tablespoons unsalted
  butter, at room
  temperature
½ cup milk
1 large egg, lightly
  beaten
1 large egg white, lightly
  beaten
1 shallot, finely minced

2 teaspoons finely grated
  lemon zest
Salt to taste
Pinch of grated nutmeg
1 cup sour cream or crème
  fraîche
4 ounces caviar (whatever
  taste and budget permit)

1. Preheat the oven to 425°F.

2. Prick the potatoes and bake until tender, 50 to 60 minutes. Let the potatoes cool for 15 minutes, then scoop out the pulp, discarding the skins. Press the pulp through a food mill or ricer into a mixing bowl. Beat in the butter, milk, egg, and egg white. Stir in the shallot and lemon zest; season with salt and nutmeg.

3. Reduce the oven temperature to 400°F. Line a large baking sheet with parchment paper.

4. Transfer the potato mixture to a pastry tube fitted with a large star tip. Pipe twenty 2-inch round swirls (coils) in rows on the baking sheet. Use a small spoon to press a round indentation in the center of each swirl (large enough to hold a teaspoon of sour cream and a teaspoon of caviar).

5. Bake the potato swirls until crisp and lightly browned, 10 to 12 minutes. Transfer the hot swirls to a serving platter. Fill the hollow of each with a teaspoon of sour cream topped with a teaspoon of caviar. Serve at once.

Makes 20 swirls

Note: The potato swirls may be baked ahead and reheated in a 350°F oven 7 to 10 minutes before serving. They also make a stunning sit-down first course; allow 2 swirls per person.

Baby Buckwheat Popovers
with
Pressed Caviar

These miniature popovers are a nifty twist on Russian blini. The buckwheat flour imparts distinctive flavor while the instant flour gives an ethereal lightness. The one trick to this recipe is to serve the popovers the moment they emerge from the oven. Thus I suggest making the batter in advance and giving it a final whizz in the blender just before filling the popover cups. Pressed caviar, by the way, is the broken eggs of Beluga, Sevruga, and Ossetra caviars pressed together into a dense and flavorful paste with the taste, but not the cost, of the world's best sturgeon roes.

1 cup milk
3 tablespoons heavy or
   whipping cream
½ cup buckwheat
   flour
¾ cup instant flour, such
   as Wondra
½ teaspoon salt
4 large eggs
1 tablespoon finely grated
   lemon zest

2 tablespoons unsalted
   butter, melted
1 cup crème fraîche or
   sour cream
4 ounces pressed caviar

1. Preheat the oven to 375°F.

2. Place the milk, cream, flours, salt, eggs, and lemon zest in a blender container. Blend the mixture, stopping occasionally to scrape the sides with a rubber spatula, until very smooth.

3. Brush miniature muffin cups with melted butter. Pour the popover batter into the cups, filling each one three-quarters full. Bake until puffed and golden brown, about 20 minutes.

4. Immediately split open the steaming popovers and fill with a teaspoonful each of crème fraîche and pressed caviar. Pop whole into your mouth and savor a truly celestial moment!

Makes 50 baby popovers

Oysters Rockefeller

— ❖ —

This famed oyster creation was invented in 1899 in New Orleans at Antoine's restaurant and named for the richness of its green sauce. The original version had eighteen ingredients in the sauce and has remained a trade secret to this day. Nonetheless, I maintain a very definite opinion on what the perfect Oysters Rockefeller should be and this is my private formula.

½ cup (1 stick) unsalted
    butter
2 shallots, minced
1 bunch scallions, trimmed
    and minced
½ cup minced fennel
    bulb
1 bunch watercress,
    stemmed and coarsely
    chopped
1 package (10 ounces)
    frozen chopped spinach,
    thawed and squeezed dry
3 tablespoons chopped fresh
    parsley

2 tablespoons Pernod or
    Herbsaint (an anise-
    flavored Southern cordial)
Tabasco sauce to taste
1½ tablespoons fresh lemon
    juice
½ cup fresh bread crumbs
1 cup heavy or whipping
    cream
1 cup grated Swiss cheese
Salt and freshly ground
    black pepper to taste
1½ pounds kosher (coarse) salt
36 fresh oysters on the
    half-shell

1. Melt the butter in a large skillet over medium heat. Add the shallots, scallions, and fennel; sauté until the vegetables are quite soft, 5 to 7 minutes. Stir in the watercress, spinach, and parsley; cook until the watercress is wilted, 2 to 3 minutes longer.

2. Stir in the Pernod, Tabasco, lemon juice, bread crumbs, cream, and ½ cup of the cheese. Season with salt and pepper. Let the sauce simmer 5 minutes to blend flavors and thicken slightly. Cool to room temperature.

3. Spread a ½-inch layer of the salt on each of 2 baking sheets. Cover each oyster with a generous tablespoon of the green sauce and arrange the oysters securely on top of the salt. Sprinkle a little of the remaining Swiss cheese on top of each. (The oysters may be prepared up to this point and refrigerated for a few hours before cooking.)

4. Preheat the oven to 450°F.

5. Bake the oysters until the cheese and sauce are bubbling, 5 to 8 minutes. Serve at once.

Makes 36 oysters, 6 to 9 servings

Don We Now Our Gay Apparel

— ❖ —

Oyster Croustades

— ❖ —

Roast Rack of Lamb with a Cilantro Crust
Roasted Cleriac and Shallot Pureé
Grand Marnier-Glazed Carrots
Braised Beets with Sherry Vinegar
California Merlot

— ❖ —

Chocolate and Apricot Linzertorte

Oyster Croustades

— ❖ —

These baked oyster cups make a substantial nibble and are perfect for open-house cocktail parties where guests expect to make a meal of the hors d'oeuvres.

24 slices rye bread, crusts removed

4 tablespoons (½ stick) unsalted butter, melted

⅓ pound thick bacon slices, finely diced

1 bunch scallions, trimmed and minced

1½ cups sliced domestic white mushrooms

⅓ cup cream sherry

1¼ cups heavy or whipping cream

24 shucked oysters, coarsely chopped

1 tablespoon fresh lemon juice

1 cup shredded Swiss cheese

Salt and freshly ground black pepper to taste

Paprika

1. Preheat the oven to 350°F.

2. Roll the bread slices flat with a rolling pin and cut out one 3-inch circle from each slice. Brush one side of each circle with melted butter, then press each, buttered side down, into a muffin cup. Bake

just until lightly toasted, 5 to 7 minutes. Set aside, but keep the oven on.

3. Fry the bacon in a large skillet over medium-high heat until crisp. Remove with a slotted spoon and drain on paper towels. Discard all but 2 tablespoons fat from the pan. Add the scallions and mushrooms; sauté 5 minutes. Add the sherry and cook until most of the liquid has evaporated. Stir in the cream and simmer 5 minutes longer.

4. Add the oysters, lemon juice, cheese, and reserved bacon to the pan. Cook just until the cheese is melted, 1 to 2 minutes. Season with salt and pepper and remove from the heat.

5. Fill each bread cup three-quarters full with the oyster mixture. Sprinkle the tops lightly with paprika. Bake until set and lightly browned, 12 to 15 minutes. Let cool a few minutes, then carefully remove from the muffin tins and serve at once. (The croustades may also be baked in advance, refrigerated, and reheated in a 350°F oven until warmed through.)

Makes 24 cups

Two Raw Sauces for Raw Oysters

— ❖ —

Entire books have been devoted to cooking oysters, yet, when it comes right down to it, real oyster aficionados swear they enjoy the bivalves most raw, aquiver on the half-shell. The Frenchman Alexandre Dumas wrote back in the nineteenth century in his *Grand Dictionnaire de Cuisine* that "Oysters are usually eaten in the simplest way in the world. One opens them, extracts them, sprinkles a few drops of lemon juice on them and swallows them. The most refined gourmands prepare a kind of sauce with vinegar, pepper, and shallot and dip the oysters in this before swallowing them." I have always been fond of the sauce Dumas describes, which is more commonly known today as *mignonette*. I offer here two New England variations on the classic French *mignonette*, which I feel are particularly jolly for December entertaining.

Apple Cider Mignonette

— ✤ —

2 shallots, trimmed and
  finely minced
½ Granny Smith apple,
  peeled, cored, and finely
  diced

½ cup apple cider
½ cup cider vinegar
2 teaspoons coarsely cracked
  black pepper

Mix together all the ingredients and let sit for 1 hour to mellow. Spoon over freshly chilled raw oysters on the half-shell.
Makes 1½ cups sauce

Cranberry Balsamic Mignonette

— ✤ —

½ cup fresh cranberries,
  coarsely chopped
1 bunch scallions, trimmed
  and finely minced

½ cup dry red wine
½ cup balsamic vinegar
2 teaspoons coarsely cracked
  black pepper

Mix together all the ingredients and let sit for 1 hour to mellow. Spoon over freshly opened chilled raw oysters on the half-shell.
Makes 1½ cups sauce

Note: For a party a large platter of oysters alternating the apple
cider and cranberry mignonette sauces is stunning.

Foie Gras with Capers and Late-Harvest Riesling

— ❖ —

I am one who finds ecstasy easily in an unadorned morsel of seared foie gras, so any further saucing becomes a perfect illustration of my aunt's favorite philosophy: "If you are going to do, you might as well overdo." In this particular gilded rendition, the salty piquancy of the capers harmonizes smoothly with the silkiness of the liver and the musty sweetness of the wine. Serve and savor, naturally, with more of the late-harvest Riesling, well chilled.

1 small lobe fresh domestic
    foie gras, grade A or B
Salt and freshly ground
    black pepper
1 shallot, minced
½ cup late-harvest Riesling

1 teaspoon light brown
    sugar
1 tablespoon capers, drained
2 tablespoons unsalted
    butter, at room
    temperature

1. Cut the foie gras into 6 slices, about ⅓ inch thick. Season the slices on both sides with salt and pepper.

2. Heat a large heavy skillet over high heat until very hot. Reduce the heat to medium-high, add the foie gras, and quickly sauté just until lightly browned, 30 to 40 seconds each side. Remove from the pan and keep warm.

3. Discard all but a thin coating of the foie gras fat from the pan. Return to medium-high heat and add the shallot. Cook 1 minute. Stir in the wine and the sugar and cook until reduced by half. Add the capers and remove from the heat. Gradually whisk in the butter to emulsify with the sauce. Pour over the foie gras and serve at once.

Makes 2 servings

Foie Gras Venetian Style

— ❖ —

Sautéed calf's liver smothered with onions, or *fegato alla veneziana*, is a classic northern Italian dish. It occurred to me one day, when I just happened to have a foie gras lobe resting in my refrigerator, that the ultimate rendition of the recipe had yet to be made. I simmered the onions very slowly with Sauternes and combined them with quickly seared slivers of foie gras. Soar to a great Venetian zenith with this sophisticated twist on liver and onions, then follow with a bowl of grains the morning after to realign the cholesterol count.

¼ cup extra virgin olive oil	Salt and freshly ground
3 large white onions, cut	black pepper to taste
into thin crescent slivers	1 large lobe fresh domestic
1¼ cups Sauternes or other	foie gras, grade A or B
late-harvest wine	3 tablespoons minced fresh parsley

.1 Heat the olive oil in a large skillet over medium heat. Add the onions and cook, stirring frequently, until softened and wilted, about 15 minutes.

2. Add the Sauternes to the onions and simmer uncovered over low heat until the onions are very sweet and caramelized and most of the liquid has evaporated, about 1 hour. Season the onions with salt and pepper.

3. Cut the foie gras into thin slices, about ¼ inch thick. Season the slices on both sides with salt and pepper. Heat a large heavy skillet over high heat until very hot. Reduce the heat to medium-high, add the foie gras, and quickly sauté the slices on both sides just until lightly browned, 30 to 40 seconds each side. Work in batches, if necessary, and drain the fat from the skillet as you go along.

4. When all of the foie gras has been sautéed, spoon a mound of the simmered onions on each serving plate. Arrange the foie gras slices over the top. Garnish with parsley and serve at once.

Makes 3 to 4 servings

Whole Roasted Foie Gras with Orange and Ginger

— ❖ —

Having read on more than one occasion about roasting foie gras whole, I became curious but approached this recipe only after great procrastination and lengthy discussion with my friendly foie gras purveyor. Since I had been anointed many a time with the sputtering fat that is released when even the littlest slices of this delicacy are seared, I feared roasting would reduce this very expensive gastronomic investment to a pool of elite but worthless cholesterol.

Fortunately, the recipe worked perfectly and brought my appreciation and understanding of foie gras to new heights. One word of advice: Most foie gras preparations call for deveining the liver before cooking, but unless you are a brilliant brain surgeon, it is almost impossible to devein a foie gras without causing gross mutilation of the liver. Because it is essential that foie gras for roasting be intact, I didn't devein it but found that I could remove the major veins quite easily after cooking as I sliced the liver for serving.

1 large lobe fresh domestic foie gras, grade A	1/3 cup Grand Marnier
1 teaspoon Chinese five-spice powder	2 tablespoons balsamic vinegar
Salt and freshly ground black pepper to taste	2 teaspoons apricot jam
1 shallot, minced	3/4 cup fresh orange juice
2 tablespoons minced fresh ginger	1 teaspoon cornstarch
	1 tablespoon cold water
	1 tablespoon finely julienned orange zest

1. Soak the foie gras in ice water to cover for 2 hours. Drain, pat dry, and let warm to room temperature.

2. Preheat the oven to 425°F.

3. Sprinkle the five-spice powder evenly over the foie gras, then season with salt and pepper. Place the liver in a medium-size round or oval enamel casserole with a lid.

4. Roast the foie gras in the oven 5 minutes. Reduce the oven temperature to 300°F and continue roasting another 15 minutes, basting occasionally with some of the rendered fat in the casserole.

5. Transfer the foie gras to a plate and cover with foil to keep warm while preparing the sauce.

6. Discard all but the thinnest coating of rendered fat from the casserole and heat over medium-high heat. Add the shallot and ginger and sauté until softened, about 1 minute. Pour in the Grand Marnier and vinegar; heat, stirring to scrape up any browned bits, 1 minute. Add the apricot jam and stir just until melted. Add the orange juice and bring to a boil. Simmer until reduced by about half. Dissolve the cornstarch in the water, stir into the sauce, and cook just until the sauce thickens slightly and becomes shiny. Stir in the orange zest and remove from the heat.

7. Cut the liver on a slight diagonal into 1/3-inch-thick slices. Overlap 2 or 3 slices on a warmed serving plate and nap with the orange ginger sauce. Serve at once with a glass of chilled Sauternes.

Makes 3 to 4 servings

Wild Rice, Mushroom, and Oyster Bisque

— ❖ —

I have frequently seen recipes for soups that combine both wild rice and mushrooms or mushrooms and oysters, but I never heard of one that made a natural merger of all three. If you can imagine a taste even more alluring than any one of the component parts, then you may have a faint idea of how decadently sublime this creation really is.

¾ cup dried porcini
  mushrooms
2 cups boiling water
6 tablespoons (¾ stick)
  unsalted butter)
1 large onion, minced
½ cup minced celery
1½ teaspoons dried thyme
Pinch of grated nutmeg
¼ cup unbleached all-
  purpose flour
4 cups fish stock or bottled
  clam juice, plus any
  accumulated juices from
  the shucked oysters
½ cup cream sherry
6 ounces fresh oyster
  mushrooms, sliced ¼ inch
  thick

8 ounces domestic white
  mushrooms, sliced ¼ inch
  thick
¾ cup heavy or whipping
  cream
Salt and freshly ground
  black pepper to taste
1½ cups cooked wild rice
1 pound fresh shucked
  oysters, cut in half if
  they are particularly large
Chopped fresh parsley or
  small sprigs thyme for
  garnish

1. Place the porcini in a small bowl and cover with the boiling water. Let stand 30 minutes. Remove the porcini from the liquid, reserving the liquid. If the mushrooms are sandy, pour the liquid through a strainer lined with a double thickness of cheesecloth and massage any dirt out of the mushrooms with your hands. Chop the mushrooms fine.

2. Melt 4 tablespoons of the butter in a large soup pot over medium-high heat. Add the onion, celery, porcini, thyme, and nutmeg. Sauté, stirring frequently, until the vegetables are soft and translucent, about 10 minutes. Stir in the flour and cook 2 minutes more, stirring constantly.

3. Gradually stir in the reserved mushroom liquid, the fish stock

and oyster juices, and sherry. Simmer uncovered 45 minutes, stirring occasionally.

4. While the soup is simmering, sauté the oyster mushrooms. Melt the remaining 2 tablespoons butter in a medium-size skillet over medium heat. Add the oyster and domestic white mushrooms and cook, stirring frequently until the liquid has evaporated and the mushrooms are cooked through but not browned, about 10 minutes. Set aside.

5. Purée the soup in a blender along with the cream until very smooth. Season to taste with salt and pepper. Pour the soup into a clean pot and return to the stove over medium heat.

6. Add the sautéed mushrooms, wild rice, and oysters to the soup. Cook 10 minutes to heat through and blend the flavors. Serve at once garnished with a little parsley or thyme.

Makes 6 servings

Risotto with White Truffles

— ✛ —

To say that white truffles have an intoxicating aroma is an understatement. I once traveled for three days through Europe in a Peugeot with a fresh white truffle from Alba and I can attest to a real intoxication/repulsion relationship with the tuber's earthiness. In the case of white truffles, there can, indeed, be too much of a good thing. My advice is to make an exquisite and rare occasion of indulging in this exorbitantly expensive fungus, but never, never travel with one!

I believe that the simpler the preparation the better with white truffles. They should not be cooked but rather shaved whisper thin over a dish at the last minute. This creamy white risotto, lightened with a splash of sparkling wine, is the ultimate truffle vehicle and a wildly elegant first course for extravagant holiday entertaining.

4 tablespoons (½ stick)
   unsalted butter
2 tablespoons extra virgin
   olive oil
2 shallots, minced
2 cups Arborio rice
5 cups chicken broth,
   preferably homemade

2 cups Prosecco (Italian sparkling
   wine) or other semi-dry
   sparkling wine
Salt and freshly ground white
   pepper to taste
¾ cup freshly grated Parmesan
   cheese
3 to 4 ounces fresh white truffles

1. Heat the butter and olive oil together in a heavy skillet over medium-high heat. Add the shallots and cook until softened 4 to 5 minutes.

2. Add the rice and stir to coat well with the butter and oil. Cook, stirring constantly, until the rice becomes translucent, about 3 minutes.

3. Begin adding the chicken broth, 1 cup at a time, stirring and allowing the broth to be fully absorbed before adding the next cup, 5 to 7 minutes.

4. When all the chicken broth has been absorbed, add the Prosecco in the same manner. The rice should be al dente and the overall consistency of the dish moist. Total cooking time will be between 20 and 25 minutes.

5. Season the rice with salt and white pepper. Remove from the heat and stir in the Parmesan cheese. Divide the rice among 6 shallow seving dishes. Garnish each serving with several ultrathin shavings of white truffle. Serve at once.

Makes 6 servings

Standing Rib Roast

— ❖ —

We always have roast beef for Christmas dinner in my family and I never cease to be overwhelmed by how purely fabulous the meat smells as it cooks in the oven. For me it is as much a part of the smell of Christmas as is pine and balsam. While many cook this cut of beef slowly, I prefer to roast it like a tenderloin — quickly with intense heat to sear in the flavor. Be sure to save the fat trimmings so that they may be rendered and used to make the other two delights of a roast beef dinner — potatoes roasted in beef fat and Yorkshire pudding.

1 rib roast (about 4 ribs, 9 pounds), trimmed of chine bone and excess fat, and tied	3 tablespoons Dijon mustard
	1 tablespoon dried rosemary
3 large cloves garlic, cut into slivers	Kosher (coarse) salt and freshly ground black pepper to taste

1. Preheat the oven to 500°F. Have the beef at room temperature.

2. With the tip of a small sharp knife, cut several ½-inch-deep slits all over the meat and insert the garlic slivers. Rub the meat all

over with the mustard and sprinkle with the rosemary, salt, and pepper.

3. Place the meat, rib side down, in a roasting pan. Roast the beef 1 hour (15 minutes per rib) for a rare roast or 16 minutes longer for a medium-rare roast. Turn the oven off but do not open the door. Let the roast sit in the oven for another hour to finish cooking. Remove from the oven and let rest 10 to 15 minutes before carving.

Makes 8 to 10 servings

A CHRISTMAS FEAST

— ❖ —

Wild Rice, Mushroom, and Oyster Bisque

— ❖ —

Standing Rib Roast
Rich Yorkshire Pudding with Boursin
Maple-Glazed Brussel Sprouts and Chestnuts
Baked Cherry Tomatoes Provençal
Baby Carrots with Brown Sugar and Mustard

— ❖ —

Christmas Trifle

Rich Yorkshire Pudding with Boursin

— ❖ —

As a young girl, I found the dramatic transformation of Yorkshire pudding as it baked as magical as Santa Claus. Today it is still a source of great fascination. This is my sophisticated, grown-up version of the recipe.

6 large eggs
1½ cups unbleached all-
 purpose flour
1 teaspoon salt
Pinch of grated nutmeg

2½ cups milk
3 tablespoons minced fresh
 parsley
⅓ cup hot roast beef fat
6 ounces Boursin cheese

1. Preheat the oven to 400°F.

2. Place the eggs, flour, salt, and nutmeg in a blender container. Blend until well combined stopping to scrape down the sides of the container as necessary. With the blender running, slowly pour in the milk and blend until smooth. Stir in the parsley.

3. Coat a 13 × 9-inch glass baking dish with the roast beef fat and place it in the oven a few minutes to get hot. Pour the pudding mixture evenly over the hot fat. Crumble the Boursin cheese over all. Bake until very puffed and golden brown, about 45 minutes. Serve at once.

Makes 8 to 10 servings

Roast Rack of Lamb with a Cilantro Crust

— ✛ —

The sophistication yet ease of preparing a rack of lamb makes it a perfect choice for a small intimate Christmas dinner. Both cilantro and garlic share a fabulous affinity for the flavor of lamb.

4 cloves garlic, peeled
½ cup walnuts, lightly
   toasted
1½ cups cilantro leaves
   (fresh coriander)
¼ cup fresh lemon juice
¼ cup olive oil

½ cup freshly grated
   Parmesan cheese
¼ teaspoon cayenne pepper
Salt and freshly ground
   black pepper to taste
2 trimmed racks of lamb,
   about 1½ pounds each

1. Place the garlic, walnuts, and cilantro in a food processor and process to a coarse paste. Add the lemon juice, olive oil, and Parmesan; process until smooth. Season with cayenne, salt, and pepper.

2. Preheat the oven to 450°F.

3. Coat the racks of lamb generously on both sides with the cilantro pesto. (If there is extra pesto, save it to serve with the cooked lamb.) Place the racks of lamb, meat side down, on a rack in a roasting pan. Roast 15 to 20 minutes for medium-rare meat.

4. Let the lamb rest 5 to 10 minutes before carving. Using a long, thin knife, cut the racks between the bones into chops. Serve 3 to 4 chops per person.

Makes 4 servings

Crown Roast of Pork

— ✥ —

Acrown roast of pork is the most dramatic cut of meat I know, which makes it the perfect pièce de résistance at a Christmas dinner celebration. The lavishness of the recipe is supported by the stuffing of wild rice, oysters, and hazelnuts. A feast fit for both kings and loved family members and friends.

WILD RICE STUFFING

6 ounces wild rice, cooked and drained

2 cups freshly shucked oysters

8 ounces bulk pork sausage

½ cup (1 stick) unsalted butter

5 ribs celery, diced

3 carrots, peeled and minced

1 large onion, chopped

8 ounces domestic white mushrooms, sliced

⅓ cup brandy

1 cup hazelnuts, lightly toasted and coarsely chopped

1 package (8 ounces) Pepperidge Farm corn-bread stuffing crumbs

1 large egg, lightly beaten

Salt and freshly ground black pepper to taste

PORK ROAST

2 tablespoons olive oil

2 teaspoons Dijon mustard

3 tablespoons cassis liqueur

Salt and freshly ground black pepper to taste

1 crown roast of pork (16 ribs, 7 to 8 pounds)

1. Prepare the stuffing: Place the cooked wild rice in a large mixing bowl. Drain the oysters, reserving ½ cup of the liquor. Coarsely chop the oysters and combine with the rice.

2. Brown the sausage in a large heavy skillet over medium-high heat, crumbling the meat into small pieces with the back of a wooden spoon. Add to the rice mixture. Melt the butter in the same skillet and stir in the celery, carrots, and onion. Sauté over medium-high heat until the vegetables are softened, 5 to 7 minutes. Add the mushrooms, brandy, and reserved oyster juices. Continue cooking, stirring frequently, until the liquid has evaporated, about 10 minutes more. Add to the rice and stir well to combine.

3. Add the hazelnuts and stuffing crumbs and toss to combine. Bind the stuffing with the beaten egg and season to taste with salt

and pepper. Refrigerate the stuffing until ready to roast the pork.

4. Preheat the oven to 450°F.

5. Prepare the roast: Whisk together the oil, mustard, cassis, salt, and pepper. Place the crown roast in a roasting pan and brush the outside with the oil mixture. Spoon the stuffing into the center of the roast (any extra stuffing can be baked separately), then cover the stuffing with a piece of buttered aluminum foil. Individually wrap each rib end with a small piece of foil to prevent it from charring.

6. Roast the pork for 20 minutes. Reduce the heat to 325°F and continue roasting until a meat thermometer inserted in the meat away from the bone registers 160°F, about 1¾ hours more.

7. Transfer the roast to a heated serving platter. Discard the foil tips and replace with paper or metallic papillotes if desired. Let the roast rest 15 minutes before carving.

Makes 8 to 12 servings

Herbed Lobster Sauté

— ❖ —

I have long harbored the romantic notion of breaking with family tradition for one Christmas dinner and serving an intimate red and green lobster feast. If I ever find myself in lobster country with a passionate friend or two on December 25th, this will be the extravagantly delicious entrée I'll prepare.

3 live lobsters (1½ pounds each)	1 can (8 ounces) tomato purée
6 tablespoons (¾ stick) unsalted butter	1 teaspoon saffron threads
2 tablespoons fruity olive oil	1 teaspoon best-quality curry powder
1 medium-size red onion, minced	½ teaspoon fennel seeds
2 carrots, peeled and minced	Pinch cayenne pepper
2 cloves garlic, minced	Salt and freshly ground black pepper to taste
1¼ cups dry white wine	½ cup shredded fresh basil
	½ cup minced fresh parsley

1. Have a fishmonger or a non-squeamish companion kill the lobsters and cut the meaty sections of each (the claws and tail) into

large 3-inch chunks. Discard the head and legs for purposes of this recipe.

2. Heat the butter and oil together in a large skillet over medium-high heat. Add the lobster pieces and sauté, stirring frequently, until the shells turn bright red, about 5 minutes. Stir in the onion, carrots, and garlic; cook until the vegetables are softened, 5 to 7 minutes.

3. Add the wine, tomato purée, saffron, curry, fennel, and cayenne. Simmer until the sauce has reduced by about a third and the lobster meat is tender, 15 to 20 minutes. Season with salt and pepper. Add the parsley and basil and cook 1 minute more. Serve at once accompanied with small forks and picks to help extract the meat from the shells. Be sure to have plenty of chilled French Champagne on hand.

Makes 3 to 4 servings

Christmas Truffle Tart

— ❖ —

This dessert is simply luxurious. A crunchy chocolate and hazelnut crust offsets a velvety smooth, two-tone filling of coffee and orange-chocolate truffle cream. A sweet worthy of serving as the grand finale to all the holiday festivities.

CRUST
1½ cups chocolate wafer crumbs
½ cup ground lightly toasted skinned hazelnuts

2 tablespoons sugar
6 tablespoons (¾ stick) unsalted butter, melted

FILLING
1 cup (2 sticks) unsalted butter
2 tablespoons instant coffee granules
12 ounces bittersweet chocolate, cut into small pieces
¾ cup sugar

6 large egg yolks
3 tablespoons Grand Marnier or other orange liqueur
1 cup heavy or whipping cream, whipped
Cocoa powder for garnish

1. Prepare the crust: Toss together the chocolate crumbs, hazel-nuts, and sugar. With a fork mix in the melted butter until the mixture is thoroughly moistened. Using your fingers, press the mixture evenly over the bottom and up the side of a 10-inch tart pan with a removable bottom. Refrigerate while preparing the filling.

2. In a saucepan heat the butter, coffee, and chocolate over low heat just until smooth. Cool for a few minutes.

3. Meanwhile beat the sugar and egg yolks together with an electric mixer until light and lemon colored, 4 to 5 minutes. Beat in the chocolate mixture and Grand Marnier. Measure and reserve ½ cup of this mixture for garnishing.

4. Divide the remaining chocolate mixture in half. Spread half over the bottom of the tart shell. Fold the whipped cream into the remaining half and spread on top of the first layer in the tart. Refrigerate the tart at least 1 hour to set.

5. If the chocolate mixture reserved for garnishing is too runny to be piped through a pastry bag, refrigerate it until thickened to the proper consistency. Put the mixture in a pastry bag fitted with a decorative star tip. Make a border of chocolate stars around the rim of the tart and place one star in the center. Sieve cocoa powder lightly over the entire tart. Keep the tart refrigerated until 10 minutes before serving. Serve in rather small wedges as it is exceedingly rich.

Makes 10 to 12 servings

Chocolate Raspberry Cake

— ✣ —

I invented this cake for a customer who had requested an extrava-gant chocolate and raspberry birthday cake when there was nary a fresh raspberry to be found on the island of Nantucket. I cheated by baking frozen unsweetened raspberries into the chocolate batter. The results were so astonishingly wonderful that I decided that the cake would be ideal at holiday time, when fresh raspberries are also out of season. My mother made the cake this past Christmas with the frozen raspberries from the family garden, and we all delighted in savoring a little taste of August in the midst of the subzero temperatures of a Down East yuletide.

CAKE

8 ounces bittersweet
  chocolate
½ cup (1 stick) unsalted
  butter
3 tablespoons framboise,
  Chambord, or other
  raspberry liqueur

4 large eggs, separated
¾ cup sugar
1 cup sifted cake flour
1 cup individually frozen
  unsweetened raspberries

FROSTING

⅔ cup sugar
1 tablespoon instant coffee
  granules
½ cup heavy or whipping
  cream
3 ounces unsweetened
  chocolate, finely chopped

4 tablespoons (½ stick)
  unsalted butter, room
  temperature
1 teaspoon vanilla
  extract

1. Preheat the oven to 325°F. Butter a 9-inch round cake pan, line the bottom with waxed or parchment paper, butter the paper and side of the pan, then lightly flour both.

2. Prepare the cake: Melt the chocolate and butter together in a saucepan over low heat, stirring constantly, until smooth. Stir in the raspberry liqueur and remove from the heat.

3. Using an electric mixer, beat the egg yolks with ¼ cup of the sugar until the batter forms a slowly dissolving ribbon when the beater is lifted. Fold in the chocolate mixture. Beat the egg whites gradually adding the remaining ½ cup sugar until the peaks hold their shape. Fold the beaten egg whites and flour alternately and a third at a time, into the chocolate mixture. Mix gently just until combined. Quickly and gently fold in the frozen raspberries.

4. Transfer the batter to the prepared pan and bake until a toothpick inserted in the middle of the cake comes out clean, 30 to 35 minutes. Cool a few minutes in the pan, then carefully invert onto a rack and peel off the paper. Let cool completely.

5. Prepare the frosting: Combine the sugar, coffee, and cream in a small saucepan. Bring to a boil over medium-high heat, stirring constantly. Reduce the heat to low and simmer 5 minutes without stirring. Remove from the heat, add the chocolate, and stir until melted. Whisk in the butter and vanilla to make a smooth mixture. Refrigerate the frosting for several minutes to thicken it to spreading consistency but do not allow it to become firm.

6. Frost the top and side of the cake generously. Serve the cake at room temperature. If you wish, serve the cake with a dollop of whipped cream or on a pool of raspberry sauce or crème anglaise.

Makes 8 servings

Chocolate Chestnut Mousse Cake

— ❖ —

I used to be terrified of tackling dessert recipes that called for technical devices like candy thermometers. But my love for European-style chestnut desserts encouraged me to address my fear of science in order to indulge in the intense emotional gratification of this luscious cake. I discovered that candy thermometers were actually nifty little gadgets, and that a meltingly rich chestnut confection makes a quintessential cap to Christmas dinner.

CHESTNUT MOUSSE

1 can (15½ ounces) chestnut purée
2 tablespoons crème de cacao
1 teaspoon maple extract
½ cup (packed) light brown sugar
¼ cup water
3 large egg yolks
1 cup (2 sticks) unsalted butter, at room temperature

CHOCOLATE MOUSSE

10 ounces bittersweet chocolate
½ cup granulated sugar
¼ cup water
3 large egg yolks
1 cup (2 sticks) unsalted butter, at room temperature

6 large egg whites

1. One day before serving, lightly oil a 9 x 5-inch loaf pan. Line the bottom and sides with waxed paper and lightly oil the paper. Set aside.

2. Prepare the chestnut mousse: Using an electric mixer, in a medium-size mixing bowl beat together the chestnut purée, crème de cacao, and maple extract until very smooth. Set aside.

3. Bring the brown sugar and water to a boil in a small saucepan. Cook until the mixture registers 220°F on a candy thermometer, about 5 minutes.

4. Meanwhile beat the 3 egg yolks at high speed with an electric mixer until pale yellow. Continue beating while slowly pouring the hot sugar syrup over the egg yolks. Beat until the mixture is thick and cool, about 5 minutes. Continue beating while adding the butter, 1 tablespoon at a time, until all is incorporated and smooth, then beat in the chestnut mixture. Set aside while preparing the chocolate mousse.

5. Melt the chocolate in the top of a double boiler over simmer-ing water. Cool slightly. Bring the granulated sugar and water to a boil in a small saucepan and continue to boil until the mixture regis-ters 220°F on a candy thermometer. Beat the 3 egg yolks and beat in the sugar syrup and butter as directed in Step 4. Add the melted chocolate and beat until smooth.

6. Beat the egg whites in a large mixing bowl until stiff but not dry. Gently fold half the egg whites into the chestnut mousse and the other half into the chocolate mousse.

7. Spread about one-third of the chestnut mousse evenly in the prepared pan. Cover with half the chocolate mousse, then another third of the chestnut mixture. Repeat, ending with the last third of the chestnut mousse on top. Cover the loaf with plastic wrap and refrigerate overnight.

8. Just before serving, run a sharp knife around the inside of the pan and invert the cake onto a serving platter. Cut the cake into ½-inch slices. It may be further embellished with a dollop of whipped cream or a pool of crème anglaise.

Makes 12 to 15 servings

Florian Fruitcake

— ✣ —

Lots of people are fond of making leaden-fruitcake jokes, but I per-sonally don't feel that any Christmas is complete without the ritual of baking the cake, brushing it with spirits for at least a month, and then finally nibbling on the masterpiece on Christmas Eve, Christmas Day, and probably throughout all of January. This recipe came from my mother's mother, my greatly adored Grandmother Florian. The finished product looks like a stained glass window when sliced and held up to the light. In addition to holiday indulgence, the cake has been used on at least one occasion as the wedding cake base for the nuptials of a Florian grandchild. My grandmother noted on the original recipe that it was "odd to mix but really excellent."

1½ pounds pitted dates,
coarsely chopped
1 pound candied pineapple,
coarsely chopped
1 pound candied whole red
cherries
2 cups unbleached all-
purpose flour

2 teaspoons baking powder
½ teaspoon salt
4 large eggs, at room
temperature
1 cup sugar
2 pounds pecan halves
½ cup brandy, rum, or
spirit of choice

1. Preheat the oven to 275°F. Grease either two 9-inch spring-form pans or two 9 x 5-inch loaf pans. Line with parchment or waxed paper and grease the paper.

2. Mix together the dates, pineapples, and cherries in a large mixing bowl. Sift together the flour, baking powder, and salt, then resift the mixture over the fruit. Mix well with your hands to ensure that each piece of fruit is well coated with flour.

3. Beat the eggs in a small bowl until frothy. Gradually beat in the sugar and continue beating until the mixture is thick and lemon colored. Add to the fruit mixture and combine well.

4. Add the nuts to the batter and mix with your hands until everything is evenly distributed and well coated with the batter.

5. Pack the batter into the prepared pans, pressing down lightly. Bake until a cake tester inserted in the center of the cake comes out clean, 1½ to 1¾ hours. Cool to room temperature.

6. Unmold the cakes from the pans. Place each in the center of a large, doubled piece of cheesecloth. Sprinkle the cakes with some of the brandy or rum. Wrap in the cloth, then wrap again in aluminum foil. Store the cakes at room temperature, sprinkling with some more of the brandy or rum every week or so, for 2 to 4 weeks before serving.

Makes 2 large fruitcakes

Chocolate and Apricot Linzertorte

— ✦ —

This rendition of the classic Austrian dessert borrows its flavors from another famous Viennese confection, the sacher torte.

CHOCOLATE-HAZELNUT CRUST

1 cup skinned hazelnuts,
  lightly toasted
¼ cup confectioners' sugar
1½ cups unbleached all-
  purpose flour
½ cup granulated sugar
⅓ cup unsweetened cocoa
  powder
2 teaspoons ground
  cinnamon

¼ teaspoon ground cloves
Pinch of salt
1 cup (2 sticks) unsalted
  butter, chilled, cut into
  small pieces
2 large egg yolks
2 teaspoons finely grated
  orange zest
1 teaspoon finely grated
  lemon zest

APRICOT FILLING

½ cup dried apricots, cut
  into quarters
¼ cup Grand Marnier or
  other orange liqueur
¼ cup fresh orange juice
1 jar (16 ounces) apricot
  preserves

2 large egg whites
2 tablespoons slivered
  almonds
Confectioners' sugar for
  garnish

1. Preheat the oven to 350°F.
2. Prepare the crust: Place the hazelnuts and confectioners' sugar in a food processor and process until the nuts are finely ground. Add the flour, granulated sugar, cocoa, cinnamon, cloves, and salt; process to blend. Add the butter and process until the mixture resembles coarse crumbs. Add the egg yolks and the citrus zests; process until dough forms into a ball.
3. Press a little bit more than half the dough into an 11-inch tart pan with a removable bottom. Make sure the dough covers the bottom and the side of the pan. Wrap the remaining dough in plastic and refrigerate.
4. Bake the tart shell until just beginning to brown, 15 to 20 minutes. Remove from the oven and let cool.
5. Meanwhile prepare the filling: Combine the apricots, liqueur,

and orange juice in a small saucepan. Bring to a boil, then simmer uncovered 10 minutes. Add the apricot preserves and simmer until melted, about 5 minutes more. Remove from the heat and spread over the bottom of the cooled tart shell.

6. Roll out the remaining dough ¼ inch thick. Cut into ½-inch-wide strips and arrange in a lattice pattern over the top of the torte. Use any scraps to finish off the edges. Beat the egg whites until frothy, then brush all over the torte. Sprinkle the top with the slivered almonds and brush once more with the egg whites.

7. Bake the linzertorte until the almonds are browned and the jam filling is bubbling, 30 to 40 minutes. Cool the torte completely, remove the side of the pan, and dust the top with sifted confectioners' sugar just before serving.

Makes 8 servings

Christmas Trifle

— ❖ —

Trifle is an English pudding that became popular as a Christmas dessert during the Victorian era. The standard trifle consists of lady-fingers or sponge cake spread with jam and then layered with custard, fruit, whipped cream, and sherry. A clear glass bowl is the preferred serving dish so that the lovely layers may be admired. My recipe takes a few liberties: A fluffy apricot mousse replaces the custard and the layers are interlaced with crumbled almond macaroons and raspberries. Trifle makes a spirited and decorative finale to Christmas dinner and has the added bonus of advance assembly.

APRICOT MOUSSE
8 ounces dried apricots
2½ cups water
½ cup cream sherry
1 envelope unflavored
   gelatin
¼ cup cold water
5 large eggs, separated

1 cup milk
¾ cup sugar
Pinch of cream of tartar
¾ cup heavy or whipping
   cream, whipped to hold a
   stiff peak

TRIFLE ASSEMBLY

2 dozen ladyfingers
¾ cup red currant jam
½ cup cream sherry
12 chewy almond macaroons,
  each 2 inches in diameter

1½ cups frozen
  unsweetened whole
  raspberries

GARNISH

¾ cup heavy or whipping
  cream, whipped to hold a
  stiff peak

½ cup slivered almonds,
  lightly toasted

1. Prepare the apricot mousse: In a small saucepan combine the apricots and water. Bring the water to a boil, then simmer, stirring occasionally, until the apricots are very soft and most of the water has evaporated, 25 to 30 minutes. Add the sherry and continue to simmer, stirring occasionally, 5 minutes.

2. Purée the apricots with the liquid in a food processor. Transfer the purée to a large mixing bowl and set aside to cool to room temperature.

3. Meanwhile sprinkle the gelatin over the cold water in a small bowl; let sit to soften for 10 minutes. Whisk together the egg yolks, milk, and ½ cup of the sugar in a small heavy saucepan stirring constantly, over medium-low heat until just thick enough to coat a spoon, 5 to 7 minutes. Be careful not to let the custard boil. Remove the custard from the heat, add the softened gelatin, and stir until the gelatin is dissolved. Stir the custard mixture into the apricot purée until well combined. Continue cooling the mixture to room temperature.

4. When the mixture has cooled, beat the egg whites until frothy. Beat in the cream of tartar and remaining ¼ cup sugar, a little at a time, and continue to beat until the whites hold soft, glossy peaks. Have the cream whipped and ready at this point as well. Stir one-quarter of the whites into the apricot mixture, then fold in the remaining whites. Just before the whites are completely incorporated, fold in the whipped cream gently but thoroughly.

5. Assemble the trifle: Spread half the ladyfingers on the split side with half the jam. Line the bottom of a 2½ to 3-quart glass bowl with the ladyfingers, jam side up. Drizzle with half the sherry and sprinkle with half the macaroons. Top with half the raspberries, then spread half the apricot mousse over the top. Repeat the layers ending with the final half of the apricot mousse.

6. Cover the trifle and refrigerate at least 6 hours or up to 3 days. Just before serving, decorate the trifle by piping rosettes of whipped cream around the edge and sprinkling the top with the toasted almonds. Spoon the trifle into shallow glass serving bowls.

Makes 10 to 12 servings

HOLIDAY
CHEER

The Christmas season is the most nostalgic time of the entire year, but there are many of us who possess neither the spare time nor plumped pocketbook to sustain the tradition-laden, sumptuous spreads of the preceding "December Dazzle" chapter. Yet only a real scrooge would not set aside a little time to prepare for greeting visiting friends and family with a wee bit of personalized hospitality.

This chapter is filled with those thoughts—a warming mug of hot cocoa or mulled cider or a plate of crisp and buttery cookies—that bring lingering contentment to those who pop by to say a quick "merry, merry" or convey prosperous tidings for the New Year.

Smart cocktails like the Raspberry and Champagne Aperitif or French 75 are perfect for clinking together in wishful toasts for the coming year, while hot toddies such as an old-fashioned Wassail Bowl or spiced brew of Swedish Glögg can steam consolation to friends who may be in need of a little cheering or sympathy during this sometimes difficult season.

Whether you prefer your winter libation as hot as the fireplace blaze or as chilled as the outside snow, a sweet assortment of homemade cookies is a welcome accompaniment. I have found it rewarding to allocate an afternoon or evening in early December to cookie cutting and making. Selecting three or four different recipes to bake and then inhaling the aromas is not only guaranteed to bring on gleeful spirits but also ensures ample tins or freezers full of cookies to share when the Christmas crunch comes at the end of the month.

Raspberry and Champagne Aperitif

— ❖ —

While I love Champagne in its purest form—poured directly from a frosty bottle (preferably French) into my ever refillable flute—I also enjoy a gala Champagne concoction from time to time, most particularly during mirthful holiday times.

¼ cup frozen unsweetened
   whole raspberries
2 tablespoons Grand
   Marnier or other orange
   liqueur

2 teaspoons cassis liqueur
¾ cup chilled Champagne

Place the raspberries, Grand Marnier, cassis, and Champagne in a blender and whizz until well combined and smooth. Pour into a tall flute and serve at once. If you wish to be fastidiously elegant, you may strain the drink through a small tea strainer to remove the raspberry seeds, but personally I am rarely that patient.
   Makes 1 aperitif

French 75

— ❖ —

I have always thought the French 75 the smartest of Champagne cocktails. It was named after a powerful 75-millimeter cannon used during World War I. Since then, there have been many disagreements over which potent alcohol to combine with the Champagne, but to my taste Cognac is the firewater of choice. Numbers aside, this libation is a spirited way to toast the last decade of the twentieth century.

1 sugar cube
2 tablespoons Cognac

¾ cup chilled Champagne
Dash angostura bitters

Place the sugar cube in the bottom of a glass flute, add the Cognac and Champagne, sprinkle with the dash of bitters, and serve at once.
   Makes 1 aperitif

Winter
Bloody Mary

— ❖ —

This is the sequel to Hammie Heard's Bloody Mary in my *Nantucket Open-House Cookbook*. I ran into Hammie and his wife, Ginger, recently during a Christmas-time crossing on the *Nantucket* steamship. They related that they had an unusual new Bloody Mary recipe for me that had come to them via London, and I immediately knew, considering the expert source, that it would be wonderful. Ginger and Hammie spent a giddy winter's evening perfecting the formula and then handed the recipe to me with the precautionary note — if you enjoy more than one, be sure to have a designated driver in tow!

2 ounces regular or pepper-
  flavored vodka
1 ounce Shooting Sherry or
  Harvey's Bristol Cream

½ ounce fresh orange juice
Ice cubes
6 ounces Clamato juice
Orange slices for garnish

Pour the vodka, sherry, and orange juice into a highball glass. Fill the glass with ice cubes, then pour in the Clamato juice. Stir very well. Garnish the side of the glass with an orange slice and serve at once.
  Makes 1 drink

Nantucket Sleigh Ride

— ❖ —

The phrase *Nantucket Sleigh Ride* is an idiom from the heyday of the island's whaling era. When the whale rather than the harpooner gained the upper hand in this beastly yet prosperous pursuit, the whale often ended up taking the whaler's ship on a rollicking spin over the high seas. This unexpected and terrorizing jaunt became quaintly known as a *Nantucket Sleigh Ride*. Since the days of burning whale oil have long since past, I thought the phrase might enjoy a clever revival as a name for a potent hot toddy to dispel the ever prevailing raw chill that blows off Nantucket's winter waters.

4 orange spice tea bags
6 cups boiling water
2 cups orange juice
1 quart cranberry juice
2 tablespoons honey

1 cinnamon stick
   (about 2 inches)
½ cup fresh cranberries
1½ cups Grand Marnier or
   other orange liqueur

1. Place the tea bags in the bottom of a large pot or kettle. Cover with the boiling water and let steep 5 minutes. Remove and discard the tea bags.

2. Add the orange juice, cranberry juice, honey, cinnamon stick, and whole cranberries to the pot. Bring just to a boil, then simmer 15 minutes. Stir in the Grand Marnier and serve at once ladled into mugs.

Makes 8 servings

Mocha-Coconut Eggnog

— ❖ —

Eggnog is an outrageous creation, and anyone who ever stopped to think about the calories in a little glass cup of the elixir could never stay jolly. So it is best not to think but to *drink,* keeping in mind that January's sole redeeming feature may be the time for penance that it affords. This is not a traditional recipe for eggnog but a creative rendition that combines one of my favorite flavor trios — coffee, chocolate, and coconut.

6 large eggs, separated
½ cup sugar
1 cup rum
1 cup bittersweet chocolate
   liqueur
1 cup strong brewed coffee,
   cold
1 can (15 ounces) cream of
   coconut

6 cups half-and-half
2 cups heavy or whipping
   cream
Freshly grated nutmeg for
   garnish
Shaved bittersweet chocolate
   for garnish

1. Using an electric mixer, beat the egg yolks in a large bowl at high speed until light and frothy. Gradually beat in the sugar and

continue to beat until pale yellow and fluffy. With the mixer at low speed, beat in the rum, chocolate liqueur, coffee, cream of coconut, half-and-half, and 1 cup of the cream. (This mixture may be made ahead up to this point and refrigerated covered until ready to serve.)

2. To serve, pour the mixture into a 4-quart punch bowl. Beat the egg whites until stiff but not dry and fold into the eggnog. Beat the remaining 1 cup of cream until stiff and fold into the eggnog as well. Ladle the eggnog into punch glasses and top each serving with a little nutmeg and shaved chocolate.

Makes about 24 servings

Hot Mulled Beaujolais Nouveau

— ❖ —

The plentiful year-end supply, reasonable price, and light, fruity quality of Beaujolais Nouveau make it a perfect choice for mulling in quantity. This recipe eliminates the large amounts of sugar called for in most spiced wine brews and uses instead a healthy splash of French cassis liqueur.

2 bottles (750 ml each) Beaujolais Nouveau
½ cup cassis liqueur
Zest of 1 orange, peeled in continuous spiral if possible
Zest of 1 lemon, peeled in continuous spiral if possible
2 cinnamon sticks (about 2 inches each)

6 whole cardamom pods
6 whole cloves
6 allspice berries
1 teaspoon freshly grated nutmeg
Cinnamon sticks for garnish

1. Place the wine, cassis, citrus zests, and cinnamon sticks in a medium-size pan. Make a cheesecloth spice bag with the cardamom, cloves, allspice, and nutmeg and add to the wine.

2. Bring the wine just to a boil, then simmer uncovered 20 to 25 minutes. Ladle the hot wine into mugs or cut-glass punch cups with an additional cinnamon stick as a stirrer.

Makes 6 to 8 servings

Swedish Glögg

— ❖ —

One sip of this potent, warm brew will bring instant insight into how Northern peoples cope with the cold in the land of the midnight sun. Glögg, with its rich blend of spices, nuts, dried fruits and three types of alcohol, is quite the elaborate libation and guaranteed to cure almost anyone who is chilled or ailing.

4 cups fresh orange juice
½ cup slivered almonds
1½ cups golden raisins
1 cup pitted whole prunes,
   cut in half
10 whole cloves
2 cinnamon sticks
   (about 2 inches each),
   broken in half

1 piece (1 inch) fresh
   ginger
8 whole cardamom
   pods
2 bottles (750 ml each)
   ruby port
1½ cups brandy
1½ cups vodka or
   aquavit

1. Pour the orange juice into a large pan. Add the almonds, raisins, and prunes. Make a cheesecloth spice bag with the cloves, cinnamon sticks, ginger, and cardamom and add to the pan. Bring the mixture to a boil, then simmer covered 45 minutes.

2. Discard the spice bag. Add the port to the pan and heat until just beginning to simmer. Add the brandy and vodka and heat through. Carefully ignite the mixture with a match (see box, page 186). Cover the pan to smother the flames. Ladle the hot glögg into cups or mugs and serve at once.

Makes 8 to 10 servings

Christmas Wassail Bowl

— ❖ —

The original English wassail bowl was a mixture of hot spiced ale and toasted apples. The word itself comes from the Anglo-Saxon *weshal*, signifying good health or wholeness. The ingredients in wassail have evolved with time, but the original sentiment of affirming good friendships with a cup of wassail lingers on today.

3 McIntosh apples,
unpeeled, cored, and cut
into ½-inch slices
1 tablespoon fresh lemon
juice
2 tablespoons unsalted
butter
½ cup (packed) light
brown sugar
4 cups sweet apple cider
2 cups fresh orange juice
Grated zest of 1 lemon
Grated zest of 1 orange

2 tablespoons finely chopped
crystallized ginger
12 whole cloves
2 cinnamon sticks (about 2
inches each), broken in half
6 whole cardamom pods
½ cup dark rum
½ cup Calvados
2 cans (12 ounces each)
light-colored beer or ale
Thin orange slices for garnish
Freshly grated nutmeg for
garnish

1. Toss the apple slices with the lemon juice. Melt the butter in a medium-size skillet over medium heat. Add the apples and ¼ cup of the brown sugar; stir to coat with the butter. Cook the apples, stirring frequently, until tender but not mushy, 10 to 15 minutes. Set aside.

2. In a large pot bring the cider, remaining ¼ cup sugar, the orange juice, zests, and crystallized ginger to a boil. Make a cheesecloth spice bag with the cloves, cinnamon, and cardamom and add to the cider mixture. Simmer uncovered, stirring occasionally, 30 minutes.

3. Add the rum, Calvados, and beer; continue to simmer a few minutes more. Discard the spice bag and transfer the wassail to a heat-proof punch bowl. Add the sautéed apples. Garnish the rim of the punch bowl with the orange slices. Ladle the hot punch into mugs or cups and garnish each serving with a fresh grating of nutmeg.

Makes 12 to 15 servings

How Not To Feel The Burn

— ❖ —

*F*lambéing is a dramatic cooking technique, however caution must be exercised. Ignite the alcohol as soon as possible after adding it to the skillet. If cooking on a gas range, you can simply tilt the skillet toward the burner flame. Otherwise, strike a wooden match, throw it into the skillet, and immediately step several feet back. When the flames have subsided, approach the skillet and wave a hand back and forth above it to hasten the extinguishing of lingering flames. When all has returned to normal, discreetly fish out the match (if used) from the skillet and proceed with the recipe.

Warm White Wine with Pear Brandy Flambé

— ✧ —

Most hot mulled wine mixtures start with a base of red wine, but there is no reason not to heat up a little white wine in the winter months to warm those friends and guests who prefer white wine to red. The pale straw color of this brew looks very smart in a clear glass mug, and the pear brandy flambé is not only fortifying but also quite dramatic.

2 bottles (750 ml each) dry
   white wine
½ cup honey
Zest of lemon, peeled in
   continuous spiral if
   possible
1 cinnamon stick
   (about 2 inches)

8 whole cloves
¾ cup Poire Williams or
   other pear brandy
Very thin fresh pear slices
   for garnish

1. Place the wine, honey, lemon zest, cinnamon stick, and cloves in a medium-size pan. Bring to a simmer over medium heat, stirring to dissolve the honey, and simmer 15 minutes.

2. In a small saucepan heat the Poire Williams just until hot to the touch. Add to the white wine mixture and ignite with a match (see box, facing page). When the flames subside, ladle the drink into mugs and garnish each serving with a pear slice.

Makes 6 to 8 servings

Homemade Hot Cocoa

— ✧ —

Making hot cocoa from scratch, while quite simple, is one of winter's more decadent pastimes. No mix can ever compare with the luxury and richness of this home blend. A cup may be made even more potable by lacing it with a jigger of any number of cordials — Grand Marnier, amaretto, Vandermint, and raspberry Chambord, to name a few—but I personally find the intensity of the chocolate indulgence enough. Serve to rosy-cheeked pals after a skiing or skating outing, or to ensure the sweetest of dreams by sipping just before bedtime.

> ⅓ cup brewed coffee
> 1 ounce (1 square)
>   unsweetened chocolate
> 1 tablespoon unsweetened
>   cocoa powder
>
> 5 tablespoons sugar
> 1½ cups milk
> 1 cup half-and-half
> ¼ teaspoon almond
>   extract

Combine the coffee, chocolate, cocoa, and sugar in a small saucepan. Heat over medium heat, stirring frequently, until the chocolate is melted and the sugar dissolved. Stir in the milk, half-and-half, and almond extract; heat until piping hot, but not boiling. Pour the mixture into a blender container and whizz until light and frothy. Pour into mugs and serve at once.

Makes 3 or 4 servings

Hot White Chocolate

— ❖ —

After becoming enthralled with regular hot cocoa, I couldn't resist the temptation to try a variation that indulged my love for white chocolate. I was by no means disappointed with the result and now take great delight in its silky and subtle flavors and particularly enjoy its creamy look, which seems as pure as the driven snow. If a more potent and less pure cup is desired, a splash of Grand Marnier or Tia Maria would perform the trick perfectly.

> 2 ounces best-quality white
>   chocolate, chopped
> ⅓ cup brewed coffee
> ½ teaspoon vanilla extract
>
> 1½ cups milk or half-and-
>   half
> Grated nutmeg for garnish

Melt the chocolate in a small heavy saucepan over very low heat, stirring frequently. Stir in the coffee and vanilla until smooth. Add the milk, increase the heat to medium, and heat until the mixture is quite hot but not boiling. Pour the mixture into a blender container and whizz until frothy. Pour the chocolate into 2 cups and sprinkle each with a light dusting of nutmeg. Serve at once.

Makes 2 servings

Drink Divine

— ✦ —

"Wine is man's most successful effort to translate the perishable into the permanent."
— H.E. Armstrong

"Drink wine in Winter for Cold, and in Summer for Heat."
— H.G. Bohn
Handbook of Proverbs,
1855

"If God forbade drinking, would He have made wine so good?"
— Armand, Cardinal Richelieu
Miramé, c. 1625

"A hot drink is as good as an overcoat."
— Gaius Petronius
Satyricon 70

"Excellent wine generates enthusiasm. And whatever you do with enthusiasm is generally successful."
— Phillippe de Rothschild

"Champagne, if you are seeking the truth, is better than a lie detector. It encourages a man to be expansive, even reckless, while lie detectors are only a challenge to tell lies successfully."
— Graham Greene
Travels with My Aunt

"I should have drunk more Champagne."
— John Maynard Keynes
(alleged last words)

Mulled Cider

— ✦ —

Good New England apple cider from a roadside mill is one of my very favorite beverages in the world. Mulling cider with a select mixture of spices perfumes the house with wonderful aromas and makes for the most comforting warm winter drink I know. Children love the cider "as is" from the pot, while adults often enjoy the added kick of a jigger of rum, brandy, or Calvados. When pulling out all the stops, float a pat of spiced butter on top of a steaming mug, spiked or unspiked, of the golden brew.

2 quarts fresh apple
   cider
1/4 cup (packed) light
   brown sugar
2 bay leaves
2 cinnamon sticks
   (about 2 inches each)
1/2 teaspoon whole
   cloves
1/2 teaspoon ground
   cardamom

1/2 teaspoon grated
   nutmeg
Zest of 1 orange, peeled
   in continuous spiral
   if possible
1 ounce per serving of rum,
   brandy, or Calvados
   (optional)

SPICED BUTTER (optional)
1/2 cup (1 stick) unsalted
   butter, at room
   temperature
2 cups (packed) dark brown
   sugar

1 tablespoon ground
   cinnamon
1/2 teaspoon grated nutmeg
1/2 teaspoon ground cloves

1. Combine the cider, light brown sugar, bay leaves, cinnamon sticks, cloves, cardamom, nutmeg, and orange zest in a large pan. Bring to a boil, then simmer uncovered 30 minutes. Strain the spices from the mixture and discard. Return the cider to pan and keep warm. The cider is ready to be served as is. If spiking it, pour 1 ounce of the preferred liquor into each serving mug and fill with the hot cider.

2. If the cider is to be embellished with the spiced butter, cream the butter and dark brown sugar together with an electric mixer until light and fluffy. Add the spices and continue beating 1 minute more. Float a heaping teaspoon of the butter on top of each serving of hot cider. Store any leftover butter in the refrigerator for future batches of mulled cider.

Makes 8 servings

Cranberry-Nut Rugelach

— ❖ —

There are many variations of this super-flaky Jewish pastry. I decided to make mine with a decidedly Nantucket and holiday flavor by adding sparkling ruby cranberries to the traditional dried fruit filling. An exquisite experiment, if I do say so myself.

SOUR CREAM PASTRY

2 cups unbleached all-
    purpose flour
1 cup (2 sticks) unsalted
    butter, chilled, cut into
    small pieces

1 large egg yolk
¾ cup sour cream
Pinch of salt

CRANBERRY-NUT FILLING

¾ cup dried figs, minced
½ cup dried apricots,
    minced
½ cup golden raisins
2 cups fresh cranberries
1 tablespoon honey

½ cup (packed) light
    brown sugar
2 tablespoons Grand
    Marnier or orange liqueur
½ cup walnuts, finely
    chopped but not ground

TOPPING

3 tablespoons unsalted
    butter, melted
¼ cup granulated sugar

2 teaspoons ground
    cinnamon

1. Prepare the pastry: Place all the ingredients in a food processor and process just until the dough resembles coarse meal. Do not let the dough begin to form a ball or it will not be as flaky as it should be. Instead turn the dough out onto a smooth surface and loosely bring it together with your hands. Wrap securely in plastic wrap and refrigerate at least 3 hours or overnight.

2. Prepare the cranberry filling: Place the figs, apricots, raisins, cranberries, honey, brown sugar, and Grand Marnier in a medium-size saucepan. Cook, stirring frequently, over medium heat until the cranberries have popped and released their juices, 10 to 15 minutes. Transfer the mixture to a food processor and process to make a more homogenized mixture (it will not get completely smooth). Add the walnuts and pulse just to incorporate. Transfer the mixture to a bowl and let cool to room temperature.

3. When ready to bake, preheat the oven to 350°F.

4. Divide the pastry dough equally into 4 pieces. Work with 1

piece at a time and keep the others refrigerated. On a lightly floured surface, roll each piece into an approximate 9-inch circle. Spread one-quarter of the filling mixture evenly over the surface of the dough.

5. With a sharp knife or pastry cutter, cut the circle into 12 equal wedges as if you were cutting a pizza or a pie. Beginning with the outside edge of each wedge, roll tightly to the center to make a crescent. Place the rugelach 1 inch apart and pointed end down on an ungreased baking sheet. Repeat the process with the remaining dough and filling, keeping the assembled pastries refrigerated while working.

6. For the topping, brush the rugelach with the melted butter. Combine the sugar and cinnamon and sprinkle generously over the pastries. Bake until light golden brown, 20 to 25 minutes. Serve slightly warm or at room temperature. As rugelach tend to be best when freshly baked, store any extras in plastic bags in the freezer and thaw as the craving strikes.

Makes 4 dozen pastries

Florentines

— ❖ —

Florentines are a traditional Italian cookie that have a taste of Oriental sweetmeats similar to that found in the Sienese spice cake *panforte.* While they look quite a bit like lace cookies, the taste is more complex and mysterious and, therefore, often an acquired one. My version replaces the traditional drizzle of dark chocolate with white chocolate as I find the snowy color more appropriate to the holiday season.

½ cup (packed) light
   brown sugar
½ cup honey
½ cup heavy or whipping
   cream
Pinch of salt
1½ cups slivered almonds

½ cup finely minced
   candied orange peel
½ cup unbleached all-
   purpose flour
6 ounces white chocolate
1 tablespoon vegetable
   oil

1. Preheat the oven to 350°F. Line baking sheets with aluminum foil and butter lightly.

2. Combine the sugar, honey, cream, and salt in a medium-size saucepan. Bring to a boil, stirring constantly, and continue to boil until the mixture reads 238°F on a candy thermometer (soft-ball stage).

3. Remove the pan from the heat, add the almonds, orange peel,

and flour, and stir until thoroughly combined.

4. Drop the batter on the prepared baking sheets by the table-spoonful, spacing about 2½ to 3 inches apart as the cookies will spread. Flatten each cookie slightly with the back of a spoon.

5. Bake the cookies until they are browned around the edges and cooked in the centers, 10 to 12 minutes.

6. Let the cookies cool completely on the foil. Using a metal spatula, carefully peel the foil away from the cookies.

7. Melt the chocolate in the top of a double boiler over simmering water. Stir in the vegetable oil. With a spoon and using quick motions, drizzle the chocolate in a zigzag pattern over the top of each cookie. When the chocolate has set, store the cookies in an airtight container up to 1 week.

Makes 2 to 2½ dozen cookies

Maple and Molasses Spice Cookies

— ❖ —

B aking and decorating cutout cookies is one of the great pleasures and pastimes of an old-fashioned Christmas. Too often, however, recipes for cutout cookies end up tasting like cardboard because their dough must be firm enough to roll out very thin yet maintain a shape when baked. This recipe is my flavorful antidote to the blandness of decorated Christmas cookies. Maple syrup, molasses, brown sugar, mixed spices, and lemon zest impart assertive flavors, while ground almonds replace some of the flour to add interesting texture.

1 cup (2 sticks) unsalted butter	1½ tablespoons ground ginger
½ cup maple syrup	1 tablespoon ground cinnamon
½ cup dark molasses	½ teaspoon ground cloves
¾ cup light brown sugar	½ teaspoon grated nutmeg
2 large eggs	Grated zest of 1 lemon
5½ to 6 cups unbleached all-purpose flour	Ornamental Icing (recipe follows)
1 cup finely ground almonds	
1½ teaspoons baking soda	

1. In a large saucepan heat the butter, syrup, molasses, and brown sugar over medium heat, stirring frequently, just until the butter is melted and the mixture is smooth. Remove from the heat and transfer

the mixture to a mixing bowl. Whisk in the eggs.

2. Stir together 5 cups of the flour, the ground almonds, baking soda, spices, and lemon zest. Gradually incorporate the dry ingredients into the batter, stirring with a sturdy wooden spoon. Add enough of the remaining flour to make a fairly stiff dough.

3. With lightly floured hands, shape the dough into a thick disk, wrap securely in plastic wrap, and refrigerate at least 3 hours or overnight.

4. When ready to bake the cookies, preheat the oven to 350°F. Prepare the baking sheets by buttering them lightly or lining them with parchment paper.

5. Divide the dough equally into 4 pieces. Work with 1 piece at a time and keep the others refrigerated. Roll the dough out ⅛ inch thick on a lightly floured surface. Cut into your favorite shapes with lightly floured cookie cutters and transfer to the prepared baking sheets. Repeat the process with the remaining dough.

6. Bake the cookies until lightly browned and set, about 10 minutes. Let cool slightly, then transfer with a spatula to wire racks to cool completely.

7. Decorate the cookies with ornamental icing using unbridled artistic flair. Let the icing set until dry. Arrange the cookies on decorative trays so friends may exclaim that they are too pretty to eat; but share anyway.

Makes about 6 dozen cookies

Ornamental Icing

—❖—

This is a good all-purpose icing for decorating sugar or spice cookies. If you are into elaborate decorating schemes, make several batches of the icing in small bowls and color each with a few drops of food color. My mother, who has a steady and very creative hand, always applies her icing with toothpicks. If this method proves too great a challenge, pipe the icing onto the cookies using a pastry bag fitted with a very small decorating tip. This is the basic recipe for one batch of icing.

1 large egg white
1½ cups confectioners' sugar
½ teaspoon cream of tartar

1 scant drop almond extract
Cream or milk as needed
Food colors if desired

Whisk together the egg white, confectioners' sugar, cream of tartar, and almond extract until smooth and thick. Thin to spreading or piping consistency with cream or milk. Blend in a few drops of food color if you want. Any leftover icing can be stored, tightly covered, in the refrigerator. Bring to room temperature when ready to use.
Makes about 1½ cups

STARRY, STARRY NIGHT

— ✣ —

Roasted Pepper and Artichoke Puffs
Winter Guacamole
Pacific Flavor Shrimp
Curled Spinach Crêpes with Smoked Salmon and
Cream Sauce
White Clam and Bacon Pizza
Saucisson Paysanne
Winter Fruit Stuffed with Chutney Cream Cheese

— ✣ —

Espresso-Grand Marnier Balls
Pine Nut Macaroons

Pine Nut Macaroons

— ✣ —

These cookies, a moist and chewy Roman Christmas treat, are the ultimate in sophistication. The dusting of confectioners' sugar makes each cookie look like a snow-covered porcupine. Savor with thick espresso and dream of a *Bianco Natale!*

1 pound almond paste   4 large egg whites
1 cup granulated sugar   ¾ cup pine nuts
1 teaspoon vanilla extract   ½ cup confectioners' sugar

1. Preheat the oven to 300°F. Line baking sheets with parchment or waxed paper.
2. Using an electric mixer, cream together the almond paste and granulated sugar in a mixing bowl until smooth. Beat in the vanilla.

Gradually beat in the egg whites to make a smooth and somewhat fluffy mixture.

3. Drop the batter by the heaping teaspoonful 1 inch apart on the prepared baking sheets. By hand, stud each cookie generously with pine nuts, then liberally sift the confectioners' sugar over the tops.

4. Bake the macaroons until light golden brown, 18 to 20 minutes. Let cool slightly, then transfer with a metal spatula to a wire rack to cool completely. Store in an airtight container up to 1 week.

Makes 4 to 4½ dozen cookies

Coffee and Chocolate Chip Shortbread

— ❖ —

These are a merger between two irresistibly popular cookies — Toll House and buttery shortbread. The coffee tempers the sweetness and makes these a natural nibble with a rich, pick-me-up cup of espresso.

½ cup plus 2 tablespoons (1¼ sticks) unsalted butter, at room temperature
1¼ cups unbleached all-purpose flour

1 tablespoon instant coffee granules
½ cup confectioners' sugar, sifted
½ teaspoon vanilla extract
1 cup semisweet chocolate chips

1. Preheat the oven to 325°F.

2. Place the butter, flour, coffee, sugar, and vanilla in a mixing bowl. Work the mixture together with a large wooden spoon until smooth. Add the chocolate chips and stir just to incorporate.

3. Lightly flour your fingers and press the dough evenly over the bottom of an ungreased 9-inch square pan. Using the tip of a sharp paring knife, score the dough into 16 squares. Prick each square a few times with the tines of a fork.

4. Bake just until the dough is set and beginning to color, about 20 minutes. Let cool a few minutes, then retrace the scored lines with the tip of the knife. Cool completely in the pan. Remove from the pan and store in an airtight container up to 1 week.

Makes 16 cookies

Oatmeal Shortbread

— ❖ —

I adore most foods made with oatmeal, and these toasty shortbread cookies are no exception — just what the doctor ordered to brighten a steaming pot of tea on an inclement afternoon.

¾ cup (1½ sticks) unsalted
  butter, at room
  temperature
½ cup (packed) light
  brown sugar
1¼ cups unbleached all-
  purpose flour

1⅔ cups old-fashioned
  rolled oats
½ teaspoon salt
1 teaspoon ground
  cinnamon

1. Preheat the oven to 350°F. Line a large baking sheet with parchment paper.

2. Using an electric mixer, cream together the butter and sugar in a mixing bowl until light and fluffy. In another bowl combine the flour, 1 cup of the oats, the salt, and cinnamon. Add to the butter mixture, stirring with a wooden spoon just until combined.

3. Finely grind the remaining ⅔ cup oats in a blender or food processor. Dust a pastry cloth or other flat rolling surface with some of the ground oats. Divide the shortbread dough in half. Roll out each half into a circle about 8 inches in diameter and ⅜ inch thick. Sprinkle the remaining oatmeal over the top of the dough and press it into the surface with the rolling pin.

4. Using a sharp knife, cut each circle into 8 wedges. Prick each wedge all over with the tines of a fork. Transfer to the prepared baking sheet. Bake until golden brown, 18 to 20 minutes. Cool on a wire rack, then store in an airtight container up to 1 week.

Makes 16 cookies

Christmas Wreath Cookies

— ❖ —

The cream cheese in this pastry yields an extraordinary light and flaky cookie, and the jam center adds just the right sparkle of holiday merriment. These are truly one of my favorite Christmas cookies.

2 cups unbleached all-
purpose flour
1 cup (2 sticks) unsalted
butter, chilled, cut into
small pieces
8 ounces cream cheese,
chilled, cut into small
cubes

1 cup currant, seedless
raspberry, or other red
jam
1 large egg
1 tablespoon water

1. Place the flour, butter, and cream cheese in a food processor and process until the dough begins to form into a ball. Wrap in plastic wrap and refrigerate several hours or overnight.

2. Preheat the oven to 400°F. Line baking sheets with parchment paper.

3. Divide the dough in half. Roll out each half ⅛ inch thick on a lightly floured surface. Cut out 2½-inch circles with a round cookie cutter. Place half the rounds in rows ½ inch apart on the prepared baking sheets and spread each one with a scant teaspoon of the jam.

4. Cut a smaller round out of the center of each of the remaining rounds to make an O or doughnut shape. Place on top of the rounds with the jam. Make more cookies in the same fashion with any pastry scraps. Beat the egg together with the water. Brush the edges of the cookies lightly with this egg wash.

5. Bake until puffed and light golden brown, 7 to 8 minutes. Cool on wire racks and store in an airtight container up to 3 days.

Makes about 4 dozen cookies

TIS THE SEASON OPEN HOUSE

— ✦ —

Mocha-Coconut Eggnog
Hot Mulled Beaujolais Nouveau

— ✦ —

Camembert Normande
Chicken Liver Crostini
Spanakopita

— ✦ —

Florian Fruitcake
Cranberry-Nut Rugelach
Christmas Wreath Cookies
Chocolate Mint Sticks

Polish Butter Cookies

— ❖ —

This is yet another elegant recipe from my Polish grandmother's recipe file. A shortbread-type cookie made even richer with eggs, they were my father's favorite Christmas cookie when he was a boy. My mother and I think they make a rather sweet treat on Valentine's Day, too.

1 cup (2 sticks) unsalted butter, at room temperature
Scant ½ cup sugar
2 hard-cooked large egg yolks, pressed through a sieve

1 large egg yolk, lightly beaten
1 teaspoon almond extract
1 teaspoon vanilla extract
2 cups unbleached all-purpose flour

1. Using an electric mixer, cream together the butter and sugar in a mixing bowl until light and fluffy. Beat in the cooked and raw egg yolks and both extracts. Using a wooden spoon, gradually incorporate the flour to make a smooth, somewhat stiff dough. Wrap the dough in plastic wrap and refrigerate 2 hours.

2. Preheat the oven to 350°F.

3. Roll out the dough ⅔ inch thick on a lightly floured surface. (The cookies are supposed to be plump.) Cut into shapes with small 1 to 1½-inch cookie cutters — hearts and stars work nicely. Gather up the scraps, reroll, and cut out more cookies. Place ½ inch apart on ungreased baking sheets.

4. Bake the cookies until they just begin to take on the slightest tinge of color, about 10 minutes. Cool on wire racks and store in an airtight container up to 1 week.

Makes about 6 dozen small cookies

Jan Hagels

— ❖ —

These traditional Dutch cookies used to be commercially made when I was a young girl, and they were a family favorite. This home-baked version is even more delectable.

2½ cups unbleached all-
   purpose flour
1 cup sugar
2 teaspoons ground
   cinnamon

1 cup (2 sticks) unsalted
   butter, chilled, cut into
   small pieces
2 large eggs, separated
1½ cups sliced almonds

1. Preheat the oven to 350°F. Line a 17 × 11-inch jelly-roll pan with aluminum foil and butter the foil lightly.

2. Place the flour, ½ cup of the sugar, 1 teaspoon of the cinnamon, and the butter in a food processor and process until crumbly. Add the egg yolks and continue processing until the mixture forms into a ball. Press the dough evenly into the prepared jelly-roll pan.

3. Beat the egg whites lightly and brush over the dough. Sprinkle the almonds generously over the top. Combine the remaining ½ cup sugar and 1 teaspoon cinnamon and sprinkle over the almonds.

4. Bake until firm and lightly browned, 20 to 25 minutes. Cool 5 minutes; transfer to a flat cutting surface by lifting the foil ends. Using a sharp knife, cut into 2-inch squares. Cool completely and store in an airtight container up to 1 week.

Makes about 4 dozen cookies

Black Forest Christmas Cookies

— ✤ —

A moist and rich chocolate dough encloses the delightful surprise of a cherry center.

2 cups unbleached all-
   purpose flour
2 teaspoons baking powder
Pinch of salt
½ cup (1 stick) unsalted
   butter
¾ cup (packed) light
   brown sugar

1 cup granulated sugar
3 large eggs
1 teaspoon almond extract
4 ounces unsweetened
   chocolate, melted and
   cooled
1 cup canned pitted sweet
   cherries, drained

1. Sift together the flour, baking powder, and salt; set aside.

2. Using an electric mixer, cream the butter and both sugars together in a mixing bowl until light and fluffy. Beat in the eggs and

almond extract and continue to beat until the mixture is light and lemon colored, about 3 minutes. Beat in the melted chocolate. Gradually stir in the flour mixture, mixing just to blend. Refrigerate the dough 1 hour to firm up.

3. Preheat the oven to 350°F. Line baking sheets with parchment paper.

4. To form each cookie, take a heaping tablespoon of dough, make an indentation in the center, insert a cherry, then shape the dough into a ball around the cherry center. Place the cookies in rows 1 inch apart on the prepared baking sheets.

5. Bake the cookies until the tops are puffed and just beginning to crack, 10 to 12 minutes. Remove to a wire rack to cool, then store in an airtight container up to 1 week.

Makes 36 to 40 cookies

Coconut Snowballs

— ❖ —

Three favorite flavors of Christmas abound in these buttery morsels — lemon, orange, and coconut. The glistening sugar coating recalls one of the most poetic lines from *'Twas the Night Before Christmas:* "The moon on the breast of the new fallen snow gave the luster of midday to objects below."

1 cup (2 sticks) unsalted
   butter, at room
   temperature
½ cup sugar, plus
   additional for coating
1 teaspoon vanilla
   extract
Pinch of salt

2½ cups unbleached all-
   purpose flour
1½ cups flaked coconut,
   lightly toasted
1 tablespoon grated lemon
   zest
1 tablespoon grated orange
   zest

1. Preheat the oven to 375°F. Line baking sheets with parchment paper.

2. Using an electric mixer, cream the butter and ½ cup sugar together in a mixing bowl until light and fluffy. Beat in the vanilla and salt. Gradually stir in the flour to make a fairly stiff dough. Work in the coconut and citrus zests until evenly distributed.

3. Shape the dough into small balls about 1 inch in diameter. Place in rows about ½ inch apart on the prepared baking sheets.

4. Bake until the bottoms of the cookies just begin to take on a hint of color, about 10 minutes. Let the cookies cool a minute or two, then roll in a shallow dish of sugar to coat. Cool completely and store in an airtight container up to 1 week.

Makes about 4½ dozen cookies

Espresso-
Grand Marnier Balls

— ❖ —

I must confess that I have always adored these uncooked, boozy little Christmas balls, a sort of mock truffle, made from ground cookie crumbs, nuts, liqueur, and corn syrup. This recipe is the ultimate version after many holiday seasons of experimenting. They require at least a week of aging, tucked away in a tin out of sight and out of mind. Once unveiled they are the perfect sweet to end a gala evening.

1 package (9 ounces) chocolate wafers
1 cup skinned toasted hazelnuts
1½ cups confectioners' sugar
1 tablespoon instant espresso powder

½ cup Grand Marnier or other orange liqueur
2½ tablespoons light corn syrup
½ cup granulated sugar

1. Pulverize the chocolate wafers and hazelnuts together in a food processor. Add the confectioners' sugar and process to combine.

2. Dissolve the espresso in the Grand Marnier and add to the chocolate crumbs along with the corn syrup. Process until the mixture forms a moist mass.

3. Break off small pieces of the dough and roll them into 1-inch

balls. Place the granulated sugar in a shallow bowl and roll each ball in the sugar to coat. Store loosely packed between layers of waxed paper in a cookie tin. Let age 1 week before serving.

Makes 4 to 4½ dozen cookies

Lemon Squares

—✣—

Lemon-scented cookies, candies, and cakes always are a welcome change from the plethora of cloying holiday sweets. These are made extra dressy with a frangipane crust and crunchy dusting of sliced almonds over the lemony filling.

FRANGIPANE CRUST
1 cup unbleached all-purpose flour
2 tablespoons almond paste
½ cup (1 stick) unsalted butter, chilled, cut into small pieces

¼ cup confectioners' sugar
Pinch of salt
1 teaspoon grated lemon zest

LEMON FILLING
2 large eggs
¾ cup granulated sugar
2 tablespoons grated lemon zest
5 tablespoons fresh lemon juice

2½ tablespoons unbleached all-purpose flour
½ teaspoon baking powder

TOPPING
½ cup sliced almonds

Confectioners' sugar

1. Preheat the oven to 375°F. Lightly butter a 9-inch square pan.
2. Prepare the crust: Place all the crust ingredients in a food processor and process just until the mixture begins to form into a ball. Pat evenly into the prepared pan and bake until lightly browned, about 15 minutes. Remove from the oven and reduce the heat to 350°F.
3. Prepare the filling: Place all the filling ingredients in a food processor and process until the mixture is very smooth, about 1 minute. Pour the filling over the crust. Sprinkle the almonds for topping evenly over the filling.

4. Return to the oven and bake until the filling is set and the nuts are lightly toasted, about 20 minutes. Cool completely. Sift a dusting of confectioners' sugar over the top and cut into 24 squares.

Makes 2 dozen cookies

Springerle

— ❖ —

Springerle are German Christmas cookies dating from midwinter pagan celebrations and requiring special embossing rolling pins or molds. Because the poor could not afford the tribal sacrifice of live animals to the gods, they offered tokens in the form of cookies stamped with animal shapes. My mother used to make springerle when I was a little girl. They are not terribly sweet and remind me a bit of Italian biscotti.

2 large eggs
1¼ cups sugar
1 tablespoon grated
   lemon zest
2 tablespoons anise seeds

2½ cups unbleached all-
   purpose flour
½ teaspoon baking
   powder
½ teaspoon salt

1. The day before baking these cookies, prepare the dough: Using an electric mixer beat the eggs in a medium mixing bowl until thick and lemon colored. Gradually beat in the sugar and continue to beat until the mixture is very thick and forms a ribbon when the beater is lifted, about 10 minutes. Beat in the lemon zest and anise seeds.

2. Combine the flour, baking powder, and salt; gradually work it into the batter to make a stiff dough.

3. Butter 2 large baking sheets well. Roll out the dough ½ inch thick on a lightly floured surface. Dust the springerle molds or rolling pin lightly with flour to prevent sticking. Emboss the dough with the designs and cut into individual cookies with a sharp knife. Place the cookies on the prepared baking sheets and store the unbaked cookies overnight in a dry place.

4. The next day, preheat the oven to 300°F.

5. Bake the cookies until they just begin to take on a hint of color, about 20 minutes. Let cool and store in an airtight container with a thick slice of apple (replace the apple slice from time to time) to maintain moistness.

Makes about 3 dozen cookies

Chocolate Mint Sticks

— ⊹ —

When I was in ninth grade, I listed my passions in my school yearbook as "pink and peppermint." This recipe for these refreshing Christmas sweets is testimony that little has changed over the course of twenty years.

BROWNIE BASE

2 ounces (2 squares) semisweet chocolate

½ cup (1 stick) unsalted butter

¾ cup granulated sugar

2 large eggs

½ teaspoon peppermint extract

½ cup unbleached all-purpose flour

Pinch of salt

PINK FILLING

2 tablespoons unsalted butter, melted

1½ cups confectioners' sugar, sifted

1 tablespoon white crème de menthe

1 tablespoon milk or light cream

1 or 2 drops red food color

CHOCOLATE GLAZE AND TOPPING

2 ounces (2 squares) semisweet chocolate

2 tablespoons unsalted butter

3 tablespoons pistachio nuts, coarsely chopped

1. Preheat the oven to 325°F. Butter an 8-inch square pan.
2. Prepare the brownie base: Melt the chocolate and butter together in a small saucepan over low heat, stirring constantly. Remove from the heat and whisk in the sugar, eggs, and peppermint extract until smooth. Gently fold in the flour and salt just until combined. Spread the batter in the prepared pan. Bake just until the center springs back when lightly touched in the center, 20 to 25 minutes. Remove from the oven and cool to room temperature.
3. Prepare the filling: Blend together the melted butter and confectioners' sugar until smooth. Thin with the crème de menthe and milk and tint pale pink with the red food color. Spread the filling

evenly over the cooled brownie layer and refrigerate until set, at least 2 hours.

4. Prepare the glaze: Melt the chocolate and butter together in a small saucepan over low heat, stirring until smooth. Spread evenly over the pink filling layer and sprinkle with the pistachio nuts. Cut into sticks 4 × ½ inch. Store in the refrigerator up to 3 days. Serve at room temperature with after-dinner coffee. These are really quite elegant.

Make 14 cookies

Iced Almonds

— ✥ —

I had a grandfather who was both a nut and a nut lover. As a young girl, I made this special confection for him as a Christmas present. These are sweet, salty, buttery, and filled with nostalgia.

*1 cup blanched whole
  almonds
½ cup sugar
2 tablespoons unsalted
  butter*

*½ teaspoon vanilla
  extract
Salt to taste*

1. Heat the almonds, sugar, and butter together in a heavy skillet over medium heat, stirring constantly, until the almonds and sugar are toasted to a golden brown, about 15 minutes. Stand back and quickly stir in the vanilla — it will splatter a bit. Remove from the heat.

2. Immediately spread the almonds out on a large sheet of heavy aluminum foil and sprinkle with salt. Let cool completely, and then break into small bite-size clusters. Store in an airtight container.

Makes 1½ cups almonds

COLD-
WEATHER
COMFORTS

A groundhog must be either extremely brave or absolutely idiotic to interrupt a winter's hibernation for an icy blast of fresh air in the beginning of February; but I certainly have to admire the creature's curiosity, for I personally find it difficult to pop my head out from underneath my cozy down comforter to assess just how bleak any given winter day is. Cold weather makes it easy to figure out how Nantucket got its nickname—The Grey Lady of the Sea—as many a morning is a monotone landscape of overcast skies, drab seas, and scrubby moorland covered with bare and brittle branches. A natural inclination is to stay tucked securely in bed unless, of course, there is some wonderful wake-up food to lure a reluctant body to rise 'n' shine.

This chapter offers a combination of just such jump-start breakfast fare along with an assortment of leavened bread-stuffs to ensure at least some rising action in an icicle-eaved house. No matter how low the outside temperature dips or how high the snow drifts, the workday or weekend can be faced more cheerfully when the stomach is comforted by salubrious morning foods. Treats such as Soft Scrambled Eggs with Lobster, Finnan Haddie Hash, Poppy-Seed Noodle Pudding, and golden Flannel Cakes make it a cinch to trade the warmth of the covers for that of the kitchen and table. And baked goods like Banana Streusel Muffins, Cranberry Orange Scones, and wholesome Oatmeal Bread provide toasty gratifications during this chilliest time of year.

❖

WINTRY WEEKEND BRUNCH

— ⋄ —

Citrus Terrine

— ⋄ —

Cornmeal Crêpes with Chèvre and Hot Pepper Jelly
Assorted savory sausages
Cranberry Streusal Coffee Cake

— ⋄ —

Jamaican Blue Mountain coffee

Citrus Terrine

— ⋄ —

This unusual and beautiful fruit terrine makes a stunning opener for a winter breakfast or brunch party. Segments of oranges and pink grapefruit are suspended in a mixture of gelatin-laced juices and then frozen into a loaf that looks like a spectacular tropical sunset. The sliced terrine may be served plain or further embellished by a contrasting fruit sauce—cranberries, frozen raspberries, and even spring rhubarb are particularly complementary.

8 large navel oranges
4 large pink grapefruit
½ cup frozen unsweetened
  whole raspberries
Fresh orange or grapefruit
  juice, if needed

⅓ cup sugar
1½ tablespoons unflavored
  gelatin
½ cup orange-flavored
  liqueur

1. One day before serving, line a 9 × 5-inch loaf pan with a large piece of plastic wrap that overhangs the edges of the pan by 3 or 4 inches. Set aside.

2. Carefully peel the oranges and grapefruit, scraping away all of the white pith with a sharp paring knife. Cut into segments discarding the seeds, if any, and the membranes that separate the sections, but reserve the juices. Combine the frozen raspberries with the fruit.

3. Drain off and measure the citrus juices. If necessary, add additional fresh juice to make 2½ cups. Pour it into a saucepan and add the sugar.

4. Stir the gelatin into the orange-flavored liqueur. Set aside.

5. Bring the juices to a boil, then simmer until reduced by a third, 10 minutes. Immediately whisk in the softened gelatin, stirring until dissolved.

6. Mix together the juice mixture and the fruit sections. Transfer to the prepared loaf pan. Fold the excess plastic wrap over the top of the terrine. Freeze the terrine overnight.

7. When ready to serve the terrine, unmold it by running a knife around the edges of the loaf pan. Pull on the plastic wrap and invert the terrine onto a flat cutting surface. Remove and discard the plastic. Cut the terrine into ½-inch slices and arrange on a platter to defrost. Serve cold but not frozen, as is, or accompanied by a contrasting sauce.

Makes 12 to 15 servings

Banana-Citrus Compote

— ❖ —

A simple fruit compote which highlights the surprisingly delicious affinity between citrus and bananas. Serve in clear glass bowls as the kick-off to a winter brunch.

¾ cup water
¾ cup sugar
2 tablespoons finely julienned lime zest
1 tablespoon finely julienned lemon zest
1 tablespoon finely julienned orange zest
8 ripe bananas
Juice of 1 lime

1. Combine the water and sugar in a small heavy saucepan. Bring to a boil and stir in the zests. Boil, stirring occasionally, 3 minutes. Remove from the heat and let cool 10 minutes.

2. Peel the bananas and cut diagonally into ½-inch-thick slices. Toss with the lime juice. Pour the warm syrup over the bananas, stir to coat, and let macerate at room temperature 30 minutes. Serve at once or chill for a couple of hours and serve cold. The compote must be used within 24 hours for optimum flavor and color.

Makes 6 to 8 servings

A FRENCH FIND

— ❖ —

One fall, after completing my guiding duties on a bicycle trip through Normandy, I had to return the group's cycles to headquarters in Burgundy. The errand completed, I rented a car and set off to savor some of my favorite spots in the lush Burgundy countryside. As I headed south over the Côte d'Or, I sadly discovered that several of my former haunts were booked solid. With darkness approaching, a kind concierge in Tournus phoned ahead and secured me the last room in a formidable château in the little village of Saint-Germain-du-Plain. When I arrived, huge gates opened by electronic magic to let my little red Renault into the inner sanctum. I was promptly welcomed, whisked up to a high-ceilinged suite of baronial splendor, and asked to join the seven other international guests for an apéritif maison by the roaring fire in the downstairs salon.

Next, we were all led graciously into a small, elegant dining room illuminated entirely by candles. As I was still quite plumped by the excesses of wining and dining in Normandy, I tried to dissuade my lovely hosts (a vain exercise in Burgundy) from plying me with yet another five-course feast. I managed to negotiate the meal down to three truly remarkable courses and was especially delighted to find a simple yet exquisite banana compote among the glistening rich pastries on the dessert cart. I immediately thought how splendid the fruit mélange would taste as a morning eye-opener and alternate to the usual winter grapefruit half. The next day over café au lait, croissants, and pots of the most delicious homemade jams I have ever tasted, I coyly cajoled the recipe from the jovial chef-owner of the charming château. Voilà! Here it is! (see facing page)

Mexican Scrambled Eggs

— ❖ —

In the vast spectrum of egg creations, I believe I hold those with a Mexican bent the most dear. South of the border, in *huevos rancheros* country, this particular blend of creamy eggs with crisp, fried tortilla strips and colorful tomatoes and peppers is known as *migas*. It is a spectacularly satisfying scramble of flavors and textures — a great weekend wake-up!

¼ cup vegetable oil
10 corn tortillas, cut into
   3 × ½-inch strips
1 bunch scallions, trimmed
   and minced
1 red bell pepper, stemmed,
   seeded, and cut into thin
   julienne strips
2 jalapeño chiles, stemmed,
   seeded, and minced
3 cloves garlic, minced
4 plum tomatoes, coarsely
   chopped
1 teaspoon ground cumin

3 tablespoons chopped
   cilantro (fresh coriander)
2 tablespoons unsalted
   butter
10 large eggs, lightly
   beaten
Salt and freshly ground
   black pepper to taste
Sour cream or grated
   Cheddar cheese for
   garnish

1. Heat the oil in a large skillet over medium-high heat. Add the tortilla strips and fry, turning frequently, until crisp and golden, about 5 minutes. Remove from the skillet and drain on paper towels.

2. Add the scallions, bell pepper, and jalapeño chiles to the skillet; sauté until softened, about 3 minutes. Add the garlic and tomatoes and cook over medium heat 5 minutes. Sprinkle with the cumin and cook 1 minute more. Remove from the heat and stir in the cilantro. Set aside.

3. In a clean large skillet, melt the butter over medium heat. Season the beaten eggs with salt and pepper and pour into the skillet. Cook, stirring the eggs constantly with a rubber spatula, until they begin to set. Stir in the tortilla strips and vegetable mixture and continue cookings the eggs to desired doneness. Serve at once, garnishing each serving with a dollop of sour cream or sprinkling of Cheddar cheese.

Makes 6 servings

Soft Scrambled Eggs with Lobster

— ❖ —

If I had to name one recipe that could ensure my rising from the sleepy down comfort of my bed on the cruelest of winter mornings, this would be it.

6 tablespoons (¾ stick) unsalted butter
½ red bell pepper, stemmed, seeded, and minced
12 ounces freshly cooked lobster meat, torn into ½-inch chunks

2 tablespoons snipped fresh chives
9 large eggs, beaten just until blended
5 tablespoons heavy or whipping cream
Salt and freshly ground black pepper to taste

1. In a small skillet melt 2 tablespoons of the butter over medium heat. Add the bell pepper and sauté 2 minutes. Add the lobster and cook a few minutes just until warmed through. Stir in the chives, cook 30 seconds more, and remove from the heat.

2. In a medium-size heavy skillet melt 2 tablespoons more of the butter over low heat. Swirl in the eggs and half the cream. Gently scramble the eggs, stirring with a rubber spatula, until thickened, about 5 minutes.

3. Add the remaining cream and 2 tablespoons butter to the eggs and continue stirring until the mixture is very thick and creamy. Season with salt and pepper. Quickly fold in the warmed lobster mixture just until evenly distributed. Spoon the scrambled eggs onto 4 warmed plates and serve at once with your favorite toast or bagels.

Makes 4 servings

Corn and Chorizo Cazuela

— ❖ —

Another rich and delicious Mexican breakfast dish. This one resembles a frittata and can be made ahead and reheated. *Cazuela* is the Spanish word for the type of casserole dish in which the custard is baked. In Mexico the dish is sometimes lined with corn husks.

1 pound chorizo sausage
4 cups corn kernels, fresh or
   thawed frozen
8 ounces cream cheese
½ cup yellow cornmeal
6 large eggs
¼ cup sugar
4 ounces sharp Cheddar
   cheese, shredded
2 teaspoons salt

2 teaspoons dried oregano
Pinch cayenne pepper
1 cup milk
2 tablespoons vegetable oil
1 bunch scallions, trimmed
   and minced
3 fresh Anaheim chiles,
   stemmed, seeded and diced
8 ounces Monterey Jack
   cheese, shredded

1. Place the chorizo in a pan and cover with water. Bring to a boil, then simmer uncovered 15 minutes. Drain and set aside to cool.

2. Preheat the oven to 375°F. Lightly butter a shallow 2-quart casserole.

3. Place 2 cups of the corn, the cream cheese, and the cornmeal in a food processor and purée until very smooth. Beat the eggs with the sugar in a large mixing bowl until well blended, then whisk in the corn purée until smooth. Stir in the remaining 2 cups corn and the shredded Cheddar. Season with salt, oregano, and cayenne pepper. Thin the mixture by stirring in the milk. Set aside briefly.

4. Heat the oil in a small skillet over medium-high heat. Add the scallions and chiles; sauté until softened, about 3 minutes.

5. Pour half the corn custard into the prepared casserole. Sprinkle the shredded Monterey Jack over the top. Scatter the sautéed scallions and chiles over the cheese. Top with the rest of the corn custard. Slice the chorizo thin and lay the slices evenly over the top of the custard.

6. Bake until the custard is set and the top is lightly browned, 45 to 55 minutes. Serve hot or at room temperature cut into wedges. (The custard may be baked ahead and stored in the refrigerator. Cover the casserole with aluminum foil and reheat at 350°F 20 to 25 minutes.)

Makes 8 to 10 servings

Cornmeal Crêpes with Chèvre and Hot Pepper Jelly

— ✦ —

This recipe began as an hors d'œuvre experiment and ended up as a fabulous brunch dish. Think of a blintz that's migrated south of the border, then heat up your crêpe pan and start churning these out as fast as you can. There are a couple secrets to success. Substituting club soda for water in the crêpe recipe yields a lightness that balances out the heartiness of the cornmeal. Secondly, the fresh chèvre should be very light and mild; domestic works better than imported in this instance. I used fresh chèvre from York Hill Farm in central Maine, which has an incredible ricottalike fluffiness. Serve these crêpes with grilled sausages alongside.

CREPES
1½ cups unbleached all-
  purpose flour
½ cup yellow cornmeal
½ teaspoon salt
½ teaspoon ground cumin
¼ teaspoon garlic powder
Pinch of cayenne pepper
1 cup milk

1 cup club soda
4 large eggs
3 tablespoons unsalted
  butter, melted
Unsalted butter or
  vegetable oil for cooking
  the crêpes

FILLING AND FINISHING
1 log (12 ounces) fresh
  chèvre, sliced ½ inch
  thick
1 jar (8 ounces) red or
  green hot pepper jelly

1 bunch long chives,
  blanched in boiling water
  30 seconds and drained
6 tablespoons (¾ stick)
  unsalted butter, melted

1. Prepare the crêpes: Mix the flour, cornmeal, salt, cumin, garlic powder, and cayenne in a medium-size mixing bowl. Make a well in the center and pour in the milk, club soda, eggs, and melted butter. Whisk until blended and smooth. Let the batter sit 30 minutes.

2. Heat a 6- or 7-inch nonstick crêpe pan over medium-high heat and coat it lightly with butter or oil. Ladle just enough of the batter into the pan to coat evenly and thinly. Cook until the bottom is lightly browned, 30 to 45 seconds. Flip the crêpe and cook a few seconds more. Continue the process until all the batter is used, stacking the crêpes on top of one another.

3. Preheat the oven to 350°F.

4. To assemble the crêpes, turn the crêpes browned side down. Place a slice of chèvre on the center of each crêpe and top with a scant teaspoon of hot pepper jelly. Fold the sides of the crêpe over the cheese to make a rectangular bundle. Secure by tying each crêpe with a blanched chive. Arrange the crêpes in a single layer in a shallow casserole. Drizzle evenly with the melted butter. (The crêpes may be prepared ahead to this point and refrigerated for a day or so before baking.)

5. Bake the crêpes just long enough to warm through and begin to melt the chèvre, 15 to 20 minutes. Serve at once, accompanied by grilled sausages if desired.

Makes 6 servings

Twice-Baked Cheese Soufflés

— ❖ —

The timing involved in whisking together soufflés when entertaining can intimidate even the most seasoned cooks. This recipe dispels the angst of the rise and fall and yields a soufflé that is not only twice-baked but also twice as tasty and light.

1½ cups milk
½ cup dry white wine
1 small onion, peeled and sliced
3 tablespoons unsalted butter
¼ cup unbleached all-purpose flour
6 ounces mild chèvre, such as Montrachet, crumbled
2 ounces blue cheese, crumbled
3 large eggs, separated, at room temperature

2 tablespoons coarsely chopped fresh rosemary
Pinch of grated nutmeg
Salt and freshly ground black pepper to taste
1 cup heavy or whipping cream
2 tablespoons tomato paste
2 ounces freshly grated Parmesan cheese, about ½ cup
2 ounces shredded Jarlsberg or Swiss cheese, about ½ cup

1. Place the milk, wine, and onion in a small heavy saucepan. Scald over medium-high heat, then strain, discarding the onion.

2. Melt the butter in a medium-size saucepan over medium heat. Whisk in the flour and cook 2 minutes, stirring constantly. Gradually

whisk in the scalded milk mixture. Cook, stirring constantly, until smooth and thick, about 4 minutes. Add the chèvre and blue cheese; continue cooking and stirring until the cheese is melted.

3. Whisk the egg yolks together in a small bowl. Whisk in a little of the hot cheese mixture, then whisk back into the remaining cheese mixture. Stir in the rosemary, nutmeg, salt, and pepper. Remove from the heat and let cool to lukewarm.

4. Preheat the oven to 350°F. Butter six 1-cup soufflé dishes.

5. Using an electric mixer, beat the egg whites until stiff but not dry. Gently fold into the cooled cheese base. Divide the mixture evenly between the prepared dishes. Place the dishes in a large baking pan and add enough hot water to come halfway up the sides of the dishes. Bake until the soufflés are lightly browned and firm in the center, about 25 minutes. Remove from the water bath and cool.

6. In the meantime, whisk together the heavy cream and tomato paste in a small saucepan. Bring to a boil over medium-high heat, then simmer until reduced and slightly thickened, about 10 minutes. (Everything may be prepared in advance up to this point and covered and refrigerated up to 24 hours before the final baking. Bring everything back to room temperature and reheat the oven to 350°F.)

7. Run a small knife around the edges of the soufflés and invert onto individual gratin dishes or ovenproof plates. Spoon the tomato cream evenly around the soufflés and sprinkle the cream and soufflés with a mixture of the Parmesan and Jarlsberg. Bake until the soufflés are repuffed and the sauce is bubbling, 10 to 15 minutes. Serve at once.

Makes 6 servings

VERY VANILLA, VERY VALENTINE

— ❖ —

Raspberry and Champagne Aperitif
Banana Citrus Compote

— ❖ —

Twice-Baked Cheese Soufflés
Chicken Livers with Mustard Seeds
Cranberry-Vanilla Muffins

— ❖ —

Vanilla infused coffee

Smoky Ham Hash

— ✦ —

Hash is gratifying both as a hearty brunch dish and the humble star of a simple Sunday night supper. My remodeled version of this homey hodgepodge is laced with coppery rutabaga and radiant red pepper and then accented with the staccatolike crunch of caraway seeds. Serve solo or, more traditionally, with scrambled, fried, or poached eggs.

1 small rutabaga, peeled and cut into ½-inch cubes

3 large red-skinned potatoes (unpeeled) scrubbed and cut into ½-inch cubes

1 large red onion, coarsely chopped

3 cloves garlic, minced

3 tablespoons bacon fat

1 red bell pepper, stemmed, seeded, and cut into ¼-inch dice

1 pound good-quality baked lean ham, thinly sliced and cut into ½-inch squares

2 tablespoons unsalted butter

⅓ cup dry white wine

1½ teaspoons caraway seeds

1 teaspoon white wine Worcestershire sauce

Salt and freshly ground black pepper to taste

½ cup chopped fresh parsley

1 tablespoon grainy Dijon mustard

1. Cook the rutabagas and potatoes in separate pans of boiling water until crisp-tender, 10 to 15 minutes. Drain both.

2. In a large skillet, sauté the onion and garlic in the bacon fat over medium-high heat 3 minutes. Add the bell pepper and cook 2 minutes more.

3. Stir in the rutabaga, potatoes, ham, butter, and white wine. Season with the caraway seeds, Worcestershire, salt if needed, and pepper. Cook the hash, stirring frequently, over medium heat until all the liquid has evaporated and the mixture is lightly browned and crisp, 20 to 25 minutes.

4. Stir in the parsley and mustard, and cook 2 minutes more. Serve at once.

Makes 6 to 8 servings

Finnan Haddie Hash

— ❖ —

This is a variation on traditional red flannel hash, which is made with chopped beets, potatoes, and corned beef. I have replaced the corned beef with plump flakes of smoked haddock, and I believe the results are sensational. In my book, any day that starts off with a plate of beet-pink food has got to be a terrific one!

1½ pounds finnan haddie (smoked haddock)
3 cups milk
2 tablespoons vegetable oil
4 tablespoons (½ stick) unsalted butter
1 medium onion, minced
2 cups diced (½ inch) peeled cooked beets
4 cups diced (½ inch) cooked potatoes
2 tablespoons fresh lemon juice
Salt and freshly ground black pepper to taste
2 hard-cooked eggs, chopped
¼ cup minced fresh parsley

1. Cut the finnan haddie in half, place in a saucepan, and cover with the milk. Heat to boiling, then reduce the heat and simmer 20 minutes. Pour off the poaching liquid, reserving ½ cup. When the fish is cool enough to handle, flake it into small pieces, discarding any bones as you go along. Set aside.

2. Heat the oil and 2 tablespoons of the butter in a large skillet over medium-high heat. Add the onion and sauté until very soft, about 10 minutes.

3. Meanwhile mix together the fish, beets, and potatoes. Add to the skillet with the lemon juice, reserved poaching milk, and remaining 2 tablespoons butter. Season with salt and lots of pepper. Cook, turning with a spatula from time to time, until the hash is cooked through and slightly crusted, about 15 minutes. Sprinkle each serving with a garnish of chopped egg and parsley.

Makes 6 servings

Chicken Livers with Mustard Seeds

— ❖ —

Sautéed whole chicken livers make both an economical and elegant weekend brunch. In this recipe the mustard seeds lend a tangy and crunchy contrast to the creamy pink livers. Optional accompaniments include scrambled eggs, thickly sliced homemade toast, and the crossword puzzle from the Sunday *New York Times*.

1 pound chicken livers, trimmed and separated into lobes
¾ cup unbleached all-purpose flour
Salt and freshly ground black pepper to taste
2 tablespoons unsalted butter
2 tablespoons bacon fat or vegetable oil
1 small onion, minced
4 ounces domestic white mushrooms, sliced
1½ tablespoons golden mustard seeds

⅓ cup cream sherry
¾ cup chicken broth, preferably homemade
1½ teaspoons Dijon mustard
2 tablespoons heavy or whipping cream
¼ cup chopped fresh parsley

1. Rinse and pat dry the livers. Mix the flour, salt, and pepper in a shallow dish. Coat the livers in the flour, shaking off any excess.

2. Heat the butter and bacon fat together in a large skillet over medium-high heat. Add the livers and sauté, turning frequently, until browned on the outside but still slightly pink within, 3 to 4 minutes. Transfer the livers to a side plate.

3. Add the onion, mushrooms, and mustard seeds to the skillet; sauté until the vegetables just begin to soften, about 2 minutes. Add the sherry and stir to deglaze the skillet, scraping up any brown bits clinging to the bottom. Add the chicken broth and mustard and simmer 5 minutes. Blend in the cream and simmer 3 minutes more. Taste and adjust seasonings with salt and pepper.

4. Return the chicken livers to the skillet and cook just until heated through. Sprinkle with parsley and serve at once.

Makes 4 servings

Poppy-Seed Noodle Pudding

— ❖ —

A while ago I participated in a cookbook and food extravaganza in Providence, Rhode Island. Lora Brody was promoting her new book, *Cooking with Memories*, in the booth across from me and dishing out a fabulous sweet noodle pudding known as kugel. Treats from Julia Child and Jacques Pepin notwithstanding, this custardy and comforting pudding was my favorite new flavor discovery of the evening. I have infused my version with a bit of my Polish heritage by sweetening the noodles with a poppy-seed filling, but I have pretty much borrowed the great apricot and almond topping from Lora Brody's original recipe.

1 pound wide egg noodles
2 tablespoons unsalted
   butter
4 large eggs
1 cup sour cream

2 cups cottage cheese
1 can (12½ ounces) poppy-
   seed filling
1½ cups milk
2 teaspoons grated lemon zest

TOPPING

3 tablespoons unsalted
   butter
1 jar (12 ounces) apricot
   preserves

¼ cup (packed) light
   brown sugar
1 cup sliced almonds

1. Preheat the oven to 350°F. Butter a 15 × 12-inch glass or ceramic baking dish.

2. Cook the noodles in a large pot of boiling salted water until al dente. Drain and toss the warm noodles with the butter in a large mixing bowl.

3. In a medium-size mixing bowl whisk together the eggs, sour cream, and cottage cheese until well blended. Stir in the poppy-seed filling until thoroughly incorporated. Thin with the milk and add the lemon zest. Combine the dairy mixture with the noodles, mixing well. Turn the mixture into the prepared dish and bake 30 minutes.

4. Meanwhile prepare the topping: Melt the butter in a saucepan over medium heat. Stir in the preserves and brown sugar; cook until melted and smooth. Stir in the almonds and remove from the heat. Spread the topping in a thin layer evenly over the top of the pudding. Return to the oven and continue baking until the pudding is firm and the top is lightly browned and bubbling, about 45 minutes longer. Let sit 10 minutes, then cut into serving squares and serve at once.

Makes 10 to 12 servings

Flannel Cakes
with Canadian Bacon and
Mushroom Compote

— ❖ —

The mere name of these pancakes from early American cooking is warming. Yeast and beaten egg whites lighten the hearty cornmeal base. While the pancakes are delicious served with syrup, I'm partial to a more modern pairing with the following nutty, woodsy, smoky, and slightly sweet compote.

2 cups milk
3 tablespoons unsalted
    butter
1 package active dry
    yeast
¼ cup warm water (110 to
    115°F)
2 large eggs, separated
½ teaspoon salt
1 cup yellow cornmeal

1½ cups unbleached all-
    purpose flour
1 to 2 tablespoons vegetable
    oil
Canadian Bacon and
    Mushroom Compote
    (recipe follows)

1. At least an hour before you plan to cook the pancakes, heat the milk and butter together in a small saucepan until the butter melts. Remove from the heat and set aside to cool.

2. Combine the yeast and water in a medium-size mixing bowl. Let stand 5 to 10 minutes to dissolve. Whisk in the cooled milk mixture, the egg yolks, salt, cornmeal, and 1 cup of the flour. Cover with plastic wrap and let rise in a warm place 45 to 60 minutes.

3. When ready to cook, stir down the batter and add the remaining ½ cup flour. Beat the egg whites until stiff but not dry; gently fold them into the batter just until incorporated.

4. Heat a griddle until medium-hot and brush with vegetable oil. Spoon about ¼ cup batter onto the griddle for each pancake. Cook until bubbles form on the top, flip, and cook a minute or so more to lightly brown the bottoms. Transfer to a warm serving platter while cooking the rest of the pancakes. Serve warm with either butter and syrup or the following Canadian Bacon and Mushroom Compote.

Makes 20 to 24 flannel cakes

Canadian Bacon and Mushroom Compote

4 tablespoons (½ stick)
   unsalted butter
1 small onion, minced
4 ounces Canadian bacon,
   thinly sliced and diced
8 ounces sliced shiitake or
   cremini mushrooms
2 tablespoons cream sherry

2 tablespoons maple syrup
½ cup heavy or whipping
   cream
1 cup skinned hazelnuts,
   lightly toasted and
   coarsely chopped
Freshly ground black pepper
   to taste

1. Melt the butter in a medium-size skillet over medium heat. Add the onion and bacon and sauté 5 minutes. Stir in the mushrooms and sherry; cook 5 minutes more.

2. Pour the maple syrup and cream into the skillet. Bring to a boil, then simmer uncovered until slightly thickened, 5 to 7 minutes. Stir in the hazelnuts and season to taste with pepper. Serve warm spooned over hot flannel cakes.

Makes about 4 cups

Raised Waffles

This recipe has been circulating in my mother's Tuesday needlework group in Blue Hill, Maine. One member, a colorful child psychiatrist, discovered it in an old Fannie Farmer cookbook and raved about the wonderfully light and crisp waffles. When my mother made these for me during a December visit, the intoxicating, yeasty aroma lured me up from the steady warmth of my electric blanket.

½ cup warm water (110 to
   115°F)
1 package active dry yeast
1 teaspoon sugar
2 cups lukewarm milk
½ cup (1 stick) unsalted
   butter, melted and cooled

1 teaspoon salt
2 cups unbleached all-
   purpose flour
2 large eggs, lightly
   beaten
Pinch of baking soda

1. The night before, combine the water, yeast, and sugar in a large mixing bowl. Let stand 5 minutes for the yeast to dissolve.

2. Add the milk, butter, salt, and flour and stir until completely smooth. Cover the bowl with plastic wrap and let sit overnight at room temperature.

3. The next morning heat a waffle iron according to the manufacturer's instructions. Beat the eggs with the baking soda and add to the batter, stirring until well mixed. Pour enough of the batter onto the hot waffle iron to cover it and cook until crisp and golden. Repeat the process until all the batter is used. Serve the waffles hot with favorite toppings.

Makes 6 large waffles

Buckwheat-Date Muffins

— ⸙ —

Having discovered the joys of cooking with buckwheat flour has tempted me to kiss bran muffins goodbye forever. Whereas bran is dense and hearty, buckwheat is crunchy and light, making for one of the best muffins I've ever tasted. Buckwheat has no gluten, so it must be mixed with regular flour and leavened with a bit extra baking powder. Since buckwheat hasn't become trendy yet, the flour may have to be sought out in the local health food store.

1 cup buckwheat flour	2 large eggs
1¼ cups unbleached all-purpose flour	⅔ cup sour cream
¾ cup (packed) light brown sugar	1 tablespoon maple syrup or honey
1½ tablespoons baking powder	½ cup (1 stick) unsalted butter or margarine, melted and cooled
½ teaspoon baking soda	1½ cups chopped pitted dates
½ teaspoon salt	

1. Preheat the oven to 375°F. Line 12 to 14 muffin cups with paper liners.

2. Place the flours, brown sugar, baking powder, soda, and salt in a mixing bowl and stir to combine.

3. Make a well in the center and add the eggs, sour cream, syrup, and butter to the well. Mix quickly just until thoroughly combined. Quickly stir in the dates.

4. Divide the batter between the muffin cups, filling each one almost almost full. Bake until light golden brown and a toothpick inserted in the center of a muffin comes out clean. Serve the muffins warm or at room temperature.

Makes 12 to 14 muffins

Banana Streusel Muffins

— ✣ —

Because bananas are always available, their comforting texture and flavor are often taken for granted. The fruit adds creamy moistness to the morning muffin and shines in the company of tropical ginger and coconut. One bite of these rich and crunchy muffins provides instant transport on the Chiquita Express to memories of warmer times and climes.

STREUSEL TOPPING
¼ cup unbleached all-
   purpose flour
½ cup coarsely chopped
   pecans
¼ cup shredded coconut

3 tablespoons light brown
   sugar
¼ teaspoon grated nutmeg
2½ tablespoons unsalted
   butter, melted

BATTER
1½ cups unbleached all-
   purpose flour
2 teaspoons baking powder
¼ teaspoon baking soda
Pinch of salt
1 tablespoon ground ginger
¼ teaspoon grated nutmeg
½ cup (packed) light
   brown sugar

2 large eggs
1 cup sour cream
1 tablespoon unsalted
   butter, melted
3 ripe medium bananas,
   cut into ¼-inch dice

1. Preheat the oven to 350°F. Line 12 muffin cups with paper liners.

2. Prepare the streusel topping: In a small bowl toss together the flour, pecans, coconut, brown sugar, and nutmeg until well combined. Pour in the melted butter and stir until the mixture is moistened and crumbly. Set aside.

3. Prepare the batter: Sift the flour, baking powder, soda, salt, ginger, nutmeg, and brown sugar into a medium-size mixing bowl. Make a well in the center.

4. In another bowl, beat together the eggs, sour cream, and melted butter just until blended and pour into the well in the dry ingredients. Mix together quickly with a wooden spoon just until combined. Stir in the diced bananas, mashing them slightly with the back of the spoon, just until incorporated. Do not overmix the batter.

5. Divide the batter between the muffin cups, filling each one about seven-eighths full. Sprinkle the streusel topping evenly over the tops. Bake the muffins until the tops are lightly browned and a tooth-pick inserted in the center of a muffin comes out clean, 25 to 30 minutes. Serve the muffins warm or at room temperature.

Makes 12 muffins

Cranberry-Vanilla Muffins

Iam such a great believer in the aphrodisiacal powers of vanilla that my favorite fragrance is a French *parfumier's* essence of vanilla. If I wear vanilla, one can only imagine how I love to cook with it! In this recipe half a vanilla bean is ground right into the sugar to dominate the flavor of the muffin. Scarlet-colored cranberries suggest even more romance — try these on Valentine's Day.

BATTER
½ vanilla bean, cut into
  small pieces
1 cup sugar
½ cup (1 stick) unsalted
  butter
2 large eggs
2 cups unbleached all-
  purpose flour

2 teaspoons baking
  powder
¼ teaspoon salt
½ cup milk
2½ cups fresh cranberries,
  coarsely chopped

TOPPING
2 tablespoons sugar

½ teaspoon grated nutmeg

1. Preheat the oven to 375°F. Line 12 to 14 muffin cups with paper liners.

2. Prepare the batter: Place the vanilla bean and sugar in a blen-

der or food processor and process until the vanilla bean is ground into tiny flecks.

3. Using an electric mixer, cream the vanilla sugar with the butter in a mixing bowl until smooth. Add the eggs one at a time, beating well after each addition.

4. Mix together the flour, baking powder, and salt. Add the dry ingredients to the creamed mixture alternately with the milk, mixing until smooth and fluffy. Fold in the cranberries.

5. Divide the batter between the muffin cups, filling each one almost full. Mix together the sugar and nutmeg for the topping and sprinkle generously over the muffins. Bake until puffed, light golden brown, and a toothpick inserted in the center of a muffin comes out clean, about 25 minutes. Serve the muffins warm or at room temperature.

Makes 12 to 14 muffins

Cranberry-Orange Scones

— ❖ —

Feathery light yet rich scones with an attractive tart contrast of cranberries and orange zest. Cut into heart shapes for a Valentine's Day treat.

2 cups unbleached all-
   purpose flour
	1 cup fresh cranberries,
	   coarsely chopped

1/3 cup plus 2 tablespoons
   sugar
	1 tablespoon grated orange
	   zest

1 tablespoon baking powder	1 large egg
1/2 teaspoon salt	1 large egg, separated

4 tablespoons (1/2 stick)
   unsalted butter, chilled,
   cut into small pieces
	3/4 cup heavy or whipping
	   cream

1. Preheat the oven to 400°F. Grease a baking sheet or line it with parchment paper.

2. Place the flour, 1/3 cup sugar, the baking powder, salt, and butter in a food processor and process until the mixture resembles coarse crumbs. Transfer to a large mixing bowl. Stir in the cranberries and orange zest.

3. Lightly beat the whole egg and egg yolk together in a small bowl. Whisk in the cream until blended. Add to the flour mixture and stir until the dough begins to hold together.

4. Turn the dough out onto a lightly floured surface and knead gently until smooth. Roll out the dough 1 inch thick. Cut out with a 3-inch round or heart-shaped cookie cutter. Place 1 inch apart on the prepared baking sheet.

5. Beat the egg white just until foamy and brush over the top of each scone with a pastry brush. Sprinkle the scones lightly with remaining 2 tablespoons sugar. Bake until puffed and light golden brown, 15 to 20 minutes. Serve warm or at room temperature.

Makes 9 or 10 scones

Apricot and Ginger Cream Scones

— ❖ —

The good news is that these scones contain no butter. The bad news is that they contain a lot of heavy cream instead. However, if one is to sin in the Nutrispeak Nineties, these scones are definitely worth the forbidden fat and cholesterol. Besides, an extra fifteen minutes on the StairMaster or LifeCycle just may assuage the guilt.

DOUGH
2 cups unbleached all-
   purpose flour
¼ cup (packed) light
   brown sugar
1 tablespoon baking powder
½ teaspoon salt

½ cup dried apricots,
   slivered
¼ cup crystallized ginger,
   finely minced
1¼ cups heavy or whipping
   cream

GLAZE
2 tablespoons heavy or
   whipping cream

2 tablespoons granulated
   sugar

1. Preheat the oven to 425°F. Line a baking sheet with parchment paper.

2. Prepare the dough: In a mixing bowl stir together the flour, brown sugar, baking powder, and salt. Mix in the apricots and ginger. Using a wooden spoon, gradually stir in the cream to form a sticky dough.

3. Turn the dough out onto a well-floured surface and shape into

a circle about 10 inches in diameter. Sprinkle with a little more flour if the dough seems too sticky. Cut the circle into 12 pie-shaped wedges and arrange about 1 inch apart on the prepared baking sheet.

4. For the glaze, brush a thin coating of cream over each scone and sprinkle with the granulated sugar. Bake until puffed and golden brown, 12 to 15 minutes. Serve warm or at room temperature.

Makes 12 scones

MID-DAY CARIBBEAN CRAVINGS

— ❖ —

Cashew Chicken with Lime Marmalade Dipping Sauce
Black Bean Soup
Banana Bread

— ❖ —

Carib Beer

— ❖ —

Coconut Snowballs

Banana Bread

— ❖ —

I suppose I could wax eloquent for paragraphs on the delights of this recipe, but, quite simply, I believe it is the most exquisite banana bread in the whole world.

½ cup golden raisins
⅓ cup Jamaican rum
½ cup (1 stick) unsalted butter
½ cup (packed) light brown sugar
1 large egg
2 teaspoons vanilla extract
2 cups unbleached all-purpose flour
1 teaspoon baking powder

½ teaspoon baking soda
½ teaspoon salt
1 teaspoon grated nutmeg
1 teaspoon ground ginger
3 very ripe bananas, mashed
⅔ cup macadamia nuts, lightly toasted and coarsely chopped
½ cup shredded coconut

1. Preheat the oven to 350°F. Grease and lightly flour a 9 x 5-inch loaf pan and set aside.

2. Place the raisins and rum together in a small saucepan. Bring to a boil, then simmer 10 minutes. Set aside to cool.

3. Using an electric mixer, cream the butter and sugar together in a mixing bowl. Add the egg and beat until light and fluffy. Beat in the vanilla.

4. Sift all the dry ingredients and spices together and add to the butter mixture alternately with the mashed banana, stirring well after each addition.

5. Gently fold in the macadamia nuts, coconut, and raisins with rum. Pour evenly into the prepared pan.

6. Bake the bread until a toothpick inserted in the middle of the loaf comes out clean, about 1 hour. Cool in the pan 30 minutes, then invert onto a wire rack to cool completely. Serve at room temperature in thick slices.

Makes one 9 x 5-inch loaf

Irish
Soda Bread

— ❖ —

I'm a great fan of Irish Soda bread because it is relatively easy to make and always delicious to eat. Since it requires no yeast and thus no rising time, it can be assembled shortly before guests arrive for soup or stew suppers. The aroma of baking bread will fill the air and diners will feel especially warmed by the privilege of breaking apart a hot mound of homemade bread.

1 cup golden raisins
3 tablespoons Scotch whiskey
2 cups unbleached all-purpose flour
2 cups whole-wheat flour
⅓ cup (packed) light brown sugar
1 tablespoon baking powder
1 teaspoon baking soda
1¼ teaspoons salt
2 large eggs
1¾ cups buttermilk
3 tablespoons unsalted butter, melted
1 tablespoon caraway seeds

1. At least 1 hour before making the bread, toss the raisins with the Scotch and let sit to plump and soften them.

2. Preheat the oven to 375°F. Grease a baking sheet or line it with parchment paper.

3. In a large bowl mix together the flours, sugar, baking powder, soda, and salt. In a smaller bowl whisk together the eggs, buttermilk, and melted butter. Add the wet ingredients to the dry and stir with a wooden spoon until moistened. Stir in the raisins and the caraway seeds.

4. Shape the dough into a large round loaf on the prepared baking sheet. Slash a deep X across the top of the bread with a sharp knife or razor. Bake until brown and crusty, 45 to 50 minutes. Serve hot from the oven or at room temperature.

Makes 1 large loaf

Cheddar and Mustard Corn Sticks

— ❖ —

Yellow cornmeal always delivers a special crunchiness to baked goods. Here that quality is balanced by the creaminess of melted cheddar and the subtle crackle of mustard seeds. Serve these corn sticks as a homey accompaniment to winter brunch egg dishes and save some for later-in-the-day soups and stews.

1½ cups unbleached all-purpose flour
1¼ cups yellow cornmeal
2 tablespoons sugar
2 teaspoons baking powder
½ teaspoon baking soda
½ teaspoon salt
1¼ cups grated sharp Cheddar cheese
2 tablespoons finely chopped chives or scallions
2 large eggs

1¼ cups buttermilk
4 tablespoons (½ stick) unsalted butter, melted
3 tablespoons grainy Dijon mustard
1 tablespoon mustard seeds
Melted lard, bacon fat, or butter for the molds

1. Preheat the oven to 350°F.

2. Stir the flour, cornmeal, sugar, baking powder, soda, salt, Cheddar, and chives together in a mixing bowl.

3. Whisk the eggs, buttermilk, butter, mustard, and mustard seeds together in a large mixing bowl. Add the cornmeal mixture and stir just until combined.

4. Brush corn stick molds lightly with melted lard and spoon the batter into the molds, filling each three-quarters full.

5. Bake until the corn sticks are crusty golden brown, 15 to 20 minutes. Let cool slightly, then turn out onto a wire rack to cool completely. If necessary, repeat the process with any remaining batter, brushing the molds with lard before adding the batter.

Makes 14 to 16 corn sticks

Corn Bread with Carrots and Pecans

— ❖ —

This moist and colorful bread is easy to make and is a festive accompaniment to both Mexican-style egg dishes and soup-based lunches and suppers.

1 cup unbleached all-
   purpose flour
1 cup yellow cornmeal
¼ cup sugar
1 tablespoon baking powder
½ teaspoon salt
1 cup buttermilk
2 large eggs

4 tablespoons (½ stick)
   unsalted butter, melted
   and cooled
1½ cups finely shredded
   carrots
1 cup finely chopped pecans

1. Preheat the oven to 400°F. Butter a 10-inch pie plate and set aside.

2. Combine the flour, cornmeal, sugar, baking powder, and salt in a large mixing bowl. Make a well in the center and add the buttermilk, eggs, and melted butter. Stir together quickly with a wooden spoon just until blended. Fold in the shredded carrots and pecans. Be careful not to overmix the batter.

3. Spread the batter evenly in the prepared dish. Bake until light golden brown and a toothpick inserted in the center of the bread comes out clean, 25 to 30 minutes. Let cool a few minutes. Serve either warm or at room temperature cut into wedges.

Makes 6 to 8 servings

Sambuca Corn Bread

— ✢ —

I first heard about this recipe when my friend John told me he had used it as the base for Thanksgiving turkey dressing at his inn in Camden, Maine. John's descriptions of the dressing were so fabulously appetizing that I immediately looked up the recipe for this unusual sweet corn bread in Carol Field's masterful *The Italian Baker*. I set about proofing and kneading a slightly revised version and became gastronomically delirious over the final results. The first loaf disappeared before it could become stale enough to use in John's recipe. Henceforth, the voice of experience recommends: Make the bread to enjoy in its own right, but make extra because both of the recipes in this book that call for it are superb.

1 package active dry yeast
¼ cup warm water
2 tablespoons milk
1 cup unbleached all-
purpose flour, plus
additional as needed
1¼ cups yellow cornmeal
¾ cup sugar

½ teaspoon salt
3 large eggs
3 tablespoons Sambuca
liqueur
6 tablespoons (¾ stick)
unsalted butter, at room
temperature

1. Sprinkle the yeast over the water and milk in a mixing bowl; let sit until foamy, about 5 minutes. Add 1 cup flour and stir until smooth. Cover with plastic wrap and let rise in a warm, draft-free spot 2 hours.

2. Into the yeast sponge, stir the cornmeal, sugar, salt, eggs, and 2 tablespoons of the Sambuca. Work in the butter. If the dough still seems sticky, work in enough flour to make an elastic, but not stiff, dough. Turn out onto a lightly floured surface and knead until smooth and satiny, 5 to 7 minutes.

3. Generously grease a 6-cup baking dish, such as a ceramic soufflé dish. Transfer the dough to the prepared dish. Cover with a clean kitchen towel and let rise in a warm, draft-free spot until doubled in bulk, 2 to 3 hours.

4. Preheat the oven to 375°F.

5. Brush the top of the loaf with the remaining tablespoon Sambuca. Bake until lightly browned and a toothpick inserted in the center of the loaf comes out clean, 50 to 60 minutes. Cool completely, then turn out of the baking dish.

Makes 1 loaf

Oatmeal Bread

— ❖ —

A stout loaf of home-baked oatmeal bread is a good winter staple. Fortunately this recipe yields two loaves since one is likely to be consumed hot from the oven. Oatmeal bread makes excellent breakfast toast, a good lunch box sandwich, and a real treat with a bowl of thick soup or stew.

DOUGH

1½ cups old-fashioned
   rolled oats
2 cups boiling water
4 tablespoons (½ stick)
   unsalted butter, cut into
   small pieces
½ cup honey

1 tablespoon salt
2 packages active dry yeast
⅓ cup warm cider or apple
   juice (110 to 115°F)
2 cups whole-wheat flour
2½ to 3 cups unbleached
   all-purpose flour

TOPPING

1 large egg
2 tablespoons water

4 tablespoons old-fashioned
   rolled oats

   1. Prepare the dough: Place the oatmeal in a mixing bowl and cover with the boiling water. Add the butter and stir until melted. Stir in the honey and salt. Let cool to lukewarm.
   2. Meanwhile dissolve the yeast in the warm cider in a large mixing bowl. Stir in the cooled oatmeal mixture, then the wholewheat flour. Gradually work in enough all-purpose flour to make a smooth dough. Turn out onto a lightly floured surface and knead until satiny, about 5 minutes. Place in a clean large bowl, cover with a kitchen towel, and let rise in a warm, draft-free place until doubled in bulk, about 1 hour.
   3. Preheat the oven to 350°F. Grease two 9 x 5-inch loaf pans.
   4. Punch the dough down and divide it in half. Knead briefly, then shape into loaves and place in the prepared pans. Cover the loaf pans with a kitchen towel and let the bread rise to the tops of the pans in a warm place 30 minutes.
   5. For the topping, beat the egg with 2 tablespoons water and brush over the tops of the loaves. Sprinkle each loaf with 2 tablespoons oatmeal. Bake until golden and a toothpick inserted in the center of a loaf comes out clean, about 40 minutes. Let cool in the pans 10 minutes, then turn out onto a wire rack to cool completely. Serve the bread warm or at room temperature.
   Makes 2 loaves

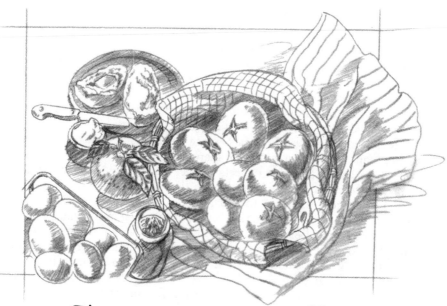

Tangerine Rye Rolls

— ❖ —

These dense, plump rolls are filled with flavors bold enough to team with many of winter's hearty egg dishes and stews. The fennel seeds and tangerine peel are a zesty enhancement to the rich rye base.

1 bottle (12 ounces) dark
   beer
⅓ cup (packed) light
   brown sugar
¼ cup molasses
2 tablespoons unsalted
   butter
2 packages active dry yeast
3 to 3½ cups unbleached
   all-purpose flour

2 teaspoons salt
1 tablespoon fennel seeds
1 tablespoon finely chopped
   tangerine zest
2½ cups rye flour
1 large egg
1 tablespoon water

1. In a small saucepan heat the beer, brown sugar, molasses, and butter together over low heat, stirring frequently, until the butter is melted and the mixture is warm to the touch (about 115°F). Pour this mixture over the yeast in a large mixing bowl and let sit until quite foamy, about 10 minutes.

2. Using a wooden spoon, stir in 1½ cups of the all-purpose flour, the salt, fennel seeds, and tangerine zest. Stir until smooth.

Gradually stir in the rye flour and enough of the remaining all-purpose flour to make a soft dough. Knead the dough on a lightly floured surface, until smooth and elastic, 7 to 8 minutes. Transfer the dough to a buttered large bowl. Cover and let rise in a warm, draft-free place until doubled in bulk, 1 to 1½ hours.

3. Line 2 baking sheets with parchment paper. Punch the dough down and turn it out onto a lightly floured surface. Cut the dough into 24 equal pieces. Roll each piece several times with the palm of your hand to form a nice roll shape. Place the rolls about 2 inches apart on the lined baking sheets. Cover and let rise in a warm place until doubled in bulk, 45 to 60 minutes.

4. Preheat the oven to 375°F.

5. Using a razor blade or scissors, cut or snip a small X on the top of each roll. Beat the egg and water together in a small bowl and brush over each roll. Bake until light golden brown and hollow sounding when a roll is tapped on the bottom, 20 to 25 minutes. Serve warm or cooled with a crock of sweet butter. These rolls will freeze well and are great to keep on hand for unexpected entertaining throughout the winter months. They also make a nice base for turkey sandwiches.

Makes 2 dozen rolls

Rye Bread with Applesauce and Cheddar

— ❖ —

This hearty bread is made moist with applesauce and rich and tangy with sharp Cheddar cheese. Perfect with a steaming bowl of soup or sliced for a terrific grilled cheese sandwich.

2 cups rye flour	1½ cups applesauce,
3 to 4 cups unbleached all-	preferably homemade
purpose flour	¼ cup dark molasses
2 packages active dry	4 tablespoons (½ stick)
yeast	unsalted butter
2 cups shredded sharp	1 large egg
Cheddar cheese	2 tablespoons water
2 tablespoons caraway seeds	
2 teaspoons salt	

1. Combine the rye flour, 2 cups all-purpose flour, the yeast, Cheddar cheese, caraway, and salt in a large mixing bowl.

2. Heat the applesauce, molasses, and butter together in a small saucepan over low heat, stirring frequently, just until the butter melts. Add this mixture to the dry ingredients and stir to form a sticky ball. Gradually work in enough of the remaining flour to make a moderately stiff dough. Turn the dough out onto a floured work surface and knead until smooth and elastic, 7 to 10 minutes.

3. Grease a large bowl, add the dough and turn it once to grease the top. Cover and let rise in a warm, draft-free place until doubled in bulk, 1 to 1½ hours.

4. Grease 2 baking sheets or line with parchment paper. Punch the dough down, divide it in half, and let it rest a few minutes. Shape each half into a free-form oval loaf and place on a prepared baking sheet. Cover and let rise again until doubled in bulk, 45 to 60 minutes.

5. Meanwhile preheat the oven to 375°F.

6. When the bread has doubled, beat the egg and 2 tablespoons water together and brush over the top and sides of the loaves. Make a couple of diagonal slashes across the top of each loaf with a sharp knife or razor blade. Bake the loaves until browned and hollow sounding when tapped on the bottom, 45 to 55 minutes. Cool on wire racks.

Makes 2 loaves

Some islands are undeniably more insular than others: Few seem more absolutely surrounded by water than Nantucket on a gusty night of the fall, when the wind blows wild off the open Atlantic, and a whiplash rain assaults the waterfront. Then, as the big car ferry from Hyannis cautiously eases itself alongside Steamboat Wharf, and the lights of Nantucket town gleam wetly through the downpour, it feels as if you are arriving somewhere infinitely remote and oceanic, barricaded against all the world by the stormy sea itself.

—Jan Morris
Islands Magazine

Cranberry Streusel Coffee Cake

— ⊰⊱ —

This winter coffee cake is relatively easy to make and absolutely luscious to consume.

COFFEE CAKE
½ cup (1 stick) unsalted butter, at room temperature
1 cup granulated sugar
2 large eggs
1 teaspoon vanilla extract
1 tablespoon grated orange zest

2 cups unbleached all-purpose flour
1 teaspoon baking powder
1 teaspoon baking soda
½ teaspoon salt
1 cup sour cream
2½ cups whole fresh cranberries

STREUSEL TOPPING
¾ cup (packed) light brown sugar
½ cup unbleached all-purpose flour
2 teaspoons ground cinnamon

4 tablespoons (½ stick) unsalted butter
½ cup walnuts, coarsely chopped

1. Preheat the oven to 350°F. Butter and lightly flour a 13 × 9-inch baking pan.

2. Prepare the coffee cake: Using an electric mixer, cream the butter and sugar together until light and fluffy. Beat in the eggs one at a time, then the vanilla and orange zest.

3. Mix the flour, baking powder, soda, and salt together. Add the flour mixture to the creamed mixture alternately with the sour cream to make a smooth, thick batter. Spread the batter evenly in the prepared pan. Sprinkle the cranberries over the top.

4. Prepare the topping: Toss the sugar, flour, and cinnamon together in a small mixing bowl. Cut in the butter with 2 knives or pastry blender until the mixture is crumbly. Stir in the walnuts. Sprinkle the streusel evenly over the cranberries on the coffee cake.

5. Bake until a cake tester inserted in the center comes out clean, about 45 minutes. Serve warm or at room temperature, cut into squares.

Makes 10 to 12 servings

STORMY
WEATHER
AND
MAGIC
MOUNTAINS

*"You better come on in my kitchen
'Cause it's going to be raining outdoors."*
— Robert Johnson

*"On days when warmth is the most important
need of the human heart, the kitchen is the place
you can find it; it dries the wet sock, it cools the
hot little brain."*
— E. B. White

When the weather outside is frightful—
skies unleashing torrents of rain, snow, hail, and sleet and
winds exercising fiercely cathartic howls—the kitchen needs
to be filled with the antidotal aromas of slowly simmering stews,
substantial pastas, and the steady crackle of roasting meats.
There is something about a storm which prompts the instinct to
fortify the body with warm and restorative dishes. Inclement
cold weather makes us crave sustaining foods, such as lamb
shanks, short ribs, red-sauced spaghetti, and hearty sausage
ragouts—fare that often seems too heavy at any other time of
year. Indeed, now is the season that Carême's famous declara-
tion "Beef is the soul of cookery" seems most appropriate.

This chapter is resplendent with recipes that harbor the
hidden bounty of winter. When the days aren't bright, it is
hard to expect the foods to be, but keep in mind that the rich
brown hue of beef stew, pot roast, and meat loaf is the very
color of deep and rewarding flavor. I'll grant that cooking
within the limitations of stormy winter weather is a creative
challenge, but it is one made all the easier by the sharing of
recipes for clove- and cinnamon-scented Greek Stifado and
treasured family heirlooms like paprika-laced Hungarian
Chicken and plump Stuffed Cabbage Leaves. These are not
main courses on the cutting edge of fashionable cuisine but
rather steaming pots of nostalgia that ladle forth primal satisfaction without making any complicated demands.

Hungarian Chicken

— ❖ —

This is one of the most cherished and controversial recipes in my family. The original recipe comes from a small book of recipes that my Polish grandmother recorded for my grandfather so that he could cook easy and hearty food when he was off on sporting trips with other male friends. My father whispers that my mother's version doesn't taste like his mother's; my mother fumes silently, and I yearn to create the perfect rendition of Hungarian Chicken and thereby restore family harmony. Hopefully, this recipe rests a mere notch below memories of my grandmother's mastery.

4 ounces salt pork, cut into very fine dice
2 large onions, cut into thin crescent slivers
1 large red bell pepper, stemmed, seeded, and diced
2 heaping tablespoons best-quality sweet Hungarian paprika, or more if desired
1 tablespoon tomato paste

1 cup chicken broth, preferably homemade
½ cup celery leaves, coarsely chopped
5 whole chicken breasts, halved
¼ cup unbleached all-purpose flour
1 cup sour cream
Salt to taste
Chopped fresh parsley for garnish

1. In a large skillet fry the salt pork over medium-high heat until lightly browned and crisp, 7 to 10 minutes.

2. Add the onions and bell pepper to the salt pork and sauté until the onion is soft and lightly browned, about 10 minutes. Remove the pan from the heat and stir in the paprika and tomato paste. When the mixture is bright red, stir in the chicken broth and celery leaves.

3. Add the chicken to the skillet, cover, and simmer slowly over medium-low heat, basting the meat occasionally with the vegetable mixture. After 30 minutes, turn the chicken pieces over, cover again, and simmer until the chicken is very tender, about 45 minutes more.

4. Using a large slotted spoon, remove the chicken from the skillet and keep warm. Whisk together the flour and sour cream until smooth, then slowly whisk it into the pan juices and vegetables. Heat through but do not boil, stirring constantly. Season to taste with salt.

5. Return the chicken to the skillet and coat with the sauce. Serve over wide egg noodles, rice, or spaetzle.

Makes 8 to 10 servings.

Indian Chicken Ragout

— ✦ —

Spicy yogurt-marinated chicken quarters are simmered with a cashew and saffron paste to create a sunny-colored and exotic-tasting winter dish. Accompany with white or basmati rice and crispy pappadams.

2 cups plain yogurt
6 cloves garlic, minced
3 tablespoons chopped fresh ginger
2 teaspoons ground cardamom
2 teaspoons fennel seeds
1½ tablespoons best-quality curry powder
¼ teaspoon cayenne pepper
2 chickens, 2½ to 3 pounds each, quartered

2 teaspoons saffron threads
¼ cup boiling water
¾ cup roasted cashews
6 tablespoons vegetable oil
2 cinnamon sticks (2 inches each)
1 large onion, finely chopped
Salt to taste
Minced scallions or chopped cilantro (fresh coriander) for garnish

1. Early in the day, whisk together the yogurt, garlic, ginger, and spices. Rinse the chickens, pat dry, place in a shallow dish, and cover with the yogurt marinade. Cover with plastic wrap and let marinate in the refrigerator at least 4 hours, turning occasionally.

2. Soak the saffron in the boiling water 2 minutes. Process the cashews in a food processor to a paste. Add the hot saffron water and process until smooth. Set aside.

3. Heat the oil in a large heavy skillet over medium-high heat. Stir in the cinnamon sticks and cook 1 minute. Add the onions and cook, stirring occasionally, until quite soft, about 10 minutes. Reduce the heat to medium, stir in the cashew mixture, and simmer 5 minutes.

4. Scrape the marinade off the chicken pieces and reserve. Add the chicken to the skillet and brown on all sides, basting frequently with the onion-cashew mixture.

5. Add the reserved marinade to the skillet, cover, and simmer until the chicken is tender, 35 to 40 minutes. Garnish with scallions or cilantro and serve at once.

Makes 6 to 8 servings.

Country Captain with a Coconut Crust

— ✥ —

Country Captain is a Southern chicken dish that I'm crazy about. According to rumor, the recipe originated back in the late 1700s or early 1800s during the era of trading between the East Indies and various American ports. Apparently one Southern galley chef grew so tired of cooking the same bland food that he dipped into the cargo of exotic spices to enliven the evening's chicken. The chef then prepared the same recipe in port at Savannah, Georgia, to great acclaim. To this day the inventive concoction continues to enjoy local popularity. My recipe takes a few modern liberties by employing an array of beautifully colored bell peppers and by embellishing with an extravagant coconut crust.

1 cup unbleached all-
    purpose flour
2 tablespoons best-quality
    sweet Hungarian paprika
Salt and freshly ground
    black pepper to taste
6 chicken thighs
3 whole chicken breasts,
    halved
2 tablespoons bacon fat
3 tablespoons vegetable oil
2 large onions, coarsely
    chopped
3 cloves garlic, minced

4 bell peppers of assorted
    colors, stemmed, seeded,
    and coarsely chopped
1½ tablespoons best-quality
    curry powder
½ cup dry red wine
1 can (16 ounces) stewed
    tomatoes
½ cup dried currants
3 tablespoons mango
    chutney

COCONUT CRUST
4 tablespoons (½ stick)
    unsalted butter, melted
3 tablespoons fresh lime
    juice

1 cup shredded coconut
1 cup sliced almonds

1. Preheat the oven to 350°F.

2. Combine the flour, paprika, salt, and pepper in a shallow dish. Coat the chicken pieces in the flour mixture, shaking off any excess. Heat the bacon fat and vegetable oil together in a large heavy skillet over medium-high heat. Brown the chicken in batches on all sides.

Arrange the chicken pieces in a large casserole or Dutch oven.

3. Add the onions and garlic to the fat remaining in the skillet. Sauté 3 minutes, then stir in the peppers and curry powder; cook, stirring constantly, 5 minutes. Add the wine, tomatoes, currants, and chutney; simmer 5 minutes.

4. Cover the chicken with the sauce. Cover the casserole and bake 1¼ hours.

5. In the meantime, prepare the coconut crust: Blend the butter, lime juice, coconut, and almonds together in a small bowl. Uncover the chicken and sprinkle the top evenly with the coconut mixture. Return to the oven and bake until the topping is lightly browned, 15 to 20 minutes. Serve hot accompanied with rice.

Makes 8 to 10 servings.

NORTHERN CLIMES, SOUTHERN ACCENTS

— ❖ —

Oysters Rockefeller

— ❖ —

Country Captain with a Coconut Crust
Rice pilaf
Spinach salad

— ❖ —

Chocolate Date and Pecan Pie

Turkey Mole

— ❖ —

Making *mole* is to immerse oneself in Mexican cooking at its finest and most complex. Anyone who is transfixed, as I am, by the culinary alchemy that transpires when such diverse ingredients as dried chiles, chocolate, and pumpkin seeds are blended cannot help but be lured into at least one *mole* experience. As cooking a *mole* requires a long time, it's a challenge to undertake during bleak winter months. (What did you do this winter? . . . I made *mole*!)

A nun is credited with inventing *mole* back in the seventeenth century to impress a Spanish bishop visiting the Santa Rosa Convent in Puebla. A modern Mexican by the name of Paco Ignacio Taibo has recently written an entire book on the history of mole. He speculated on the inception of the recipe as follows: "Sister Andrea decided to go in by the terribly complex ways of gastronomic baroque and summed up in one dish all the luxury of the American country; it was a great moment, above all a valiant moment, very valiant. To fry an egg is a serious thing, as anyone *well* knows who can fry one *well*, but to make a *mole* before anyone else is an imaginative thing and one that only fearless souls can bring to pass."

MEAT AND STOCK
1 turkey, 10 to 12 pounds
3 ribs celery

1 large onion, quartered

MOLE SAUCE
2 large dried ancho chiles
1½ cups boiling water
1½ cups canned diced or
   crushed tomatoes packed
   in purée
1 can (4 ounces) chopped
   green chiles
½ cup dried currants
2 heaping tablespoons
   unsweetened cocoa
   powder
¼ teaspoon ground cloves
¼ cup sesame seeds
½ cup hulled pumpkin seeds

¼ cup slivered almonds
1½ teaspoons coriander seeds
1½ teaspoons anise seeds
1½ teaspoons cumin seeds
3 tablespoons vegetable oil
1 large onion, chopped
3 cloves garlic, minced
2 small hot fresh chiles,
   seeded and minced
2 cinnamon sticks (about 2
   inches each)
¼ cup sugar
Salt to taste
Toasted sesame seeds for garnish

1. Using a sharp boning knife, remove the meat and skin from the turkey, reserving the bones and carcass. Cut the meat into 2-inch cubes and refrigerate. Place all the scraps and bones in a large stockpot, cover with water, and add the celery and onion. Bring to a boil, then reduce the heat and simmer uncovered 1 hour. Strain, discarding the bones and vegetables and reserving the stock.

2. Preheat the oven to 350°F.

3. Prepare the *mole* sauce: Stem and seed the ancho chiles, then chop into small irregular pieces. Toast in the oven 3 to 4 minutes, turning once. Transfer to a small bowl, cover with the boiling water, and let steep 30 minutes.

4. Place the tomatoes and green chiles in a food processor and purée until smooth. Drain the ancho chiles, reserving the liquid, and add them to the processor. Purée again until smooth. Transfer to a mixing bowl and stir in the currants, cocoa, and cloves.

5. Place the sesame seeds, pumpkin seeds, and almonds in a small skillet. Cook, stirring frequently, over medium heat until toasted, 5 to 7 minutes. Transfer to the food processor. Add the coriander, anise, and cumin seeds to the skillet and cook, stirring frequently, until toasted, 3 to 4 minutes. Add to the food processor. Purée the nuts and seeds, adding a little of the chile soaking liquid, to make a thick, smooth paste. Combine with the tomato mixture.

6. Heat the vegetable oil in a large skillet over medium-high heat. Add the onion, garlic, and fresh chiles; sauté until quite soft, 7 to 9 minutes. Add to the tomato mixture. Purée everything once again, in batches, until smooth. Thin the sauce to the consistency of heavy cream with the reserved turkey stock.

7. Transfer the sauce to a saucepan and add the cinnamon sticks. Simmer the sauce uncovered over medium heat 45 minutes. Add turkey stock as needed to keep the sauce the consistency of cream. Season the sauce with the sugar and salt to taste. Remove from the heat.

8. Bring the remaining turkey stock to a boil in a large saucepan. Add the turkey meat and poach over low heat just until tender, 15 to 20 minutes. Let cool to room temperature in the stock.

9. About 30 minutes before serving, preheat the oven to 350°F.

10. Drain the turkey and arrange in a large casserole dish. Cover with the mole sauce and bake until heated through, 25 to 30 minutes. Garnish with a sprinkling of toasted sesame seeds. Serve hot with plain rice or boiled corn pasta.

Makes 8 to 10 servings.

Roast Duck with Blood Oranges

— ✜ —

Researching duck recipes and reading Proust have always induced within me an overwhelming urge to take a long shower to metaphorically cleanse my mind of convoluted excesses. Then it occurred to me one day that a duck recipe needn't read like an elaborate treasure hunt to be wonderfully tasty. Why not simply roast a duck like a chicken! This flash of Hemingwayesque clarity coincided with the arrival of sweet blood oranges from Spain, which in turn led me to think of complementary Spanish flavorings. The resulting dish is immensely appealing for its ease of preparation and sensational flavor.

2 Long Island ducks, 4 to
   4½ pounds each
2 teaspoons ground cloves
1 tablespoon saffron threads

Salt and freshly ground
   black pepper to taste
2 cloves garlic, minced
5 blood oranges

1. Remove the neck, liver, and gizzards from the ducks' cavities and set aside for another use or discard. Rinse the ducks under cold water and pat dry. Cut each duck through the breastbone to open it up, then flatten it out (do not cut through the backbone). Remove all the visible fat from the duck by cutting it away with a sharp knife. There should be quite a bit, and it may be saved and rendered for cooking potatoes or Rutabagas Anna.

2. Place the flattened ducks in a large roasting pan without overlapping them. Rub the ground cloves all over the skin. Sprinkle with saffron threads and season liberally with salt and pepper. Scatter the minced garlic over all.

3. Slice the oranges in half and using your hands, squeeze the juice over the ducks. Tuck the orange halves in around the ducks. Let marinate at room temperature 1 hour.

4. Preheat the oven to 400°F

5. Roast the ducks about 1 hour, basting occasionally with the accumulated pan juices. The ducks are done when the skin is browned and crisp and the meat is quite tender. Carve the ducks into serving pieces and serve with a couple of the orange halves.

Makes 4 to 6 servings.

Rabbit
Terra-Cotta

— ❖ —

This recipe combines a Polish marinade for rabbit with an Italian method of cooking chicken, and it is a heavenly culinary marriage. One of the secrets of the recipe is to resist the temptation to lift the lid off the terra-cotta casserole as the rabbit cooks, for the tenderness and flavor intensity of the dish depend on the sealed cooking process in combination with high heat. Unlike Pandora's box, the contents, when unveiled, will make you and your lucky dinner guests swoon with delight.

1½ cups balsamic vinegar
3 tablespoons Dijon
　　mustard
10 juniper berries
10 whole black peppercorns
2 rabbits, 2 to 2½ pounds
　　each, cut into 2- to 3-
　　inch pieces (the butcher
　　should do this for you)

½ cup (1 stick) unsalted
　　butter, melted
3 tablespoons chopped fresh
　　rosemary
Salt and freshly ground
　　black pepper to taste
12 ounces thinly sliced
　　prosciutto

1. One day before serving, whisk together the vinegar and mustard in a small saucepan. Stir in the juniper and peppercorns. Bring the mixture to a boil, then simmer 10 minutes. Cool to room temperature. Place the rabbits in a shallow dish and cover with the marinade. Marinate overnight in the refrigerator, turning occasionally.

2. Drain the rabbits and reserve the marinade. Combine the melted butter and rosemary. Using a pastry brush, brush each piece of rabbit generously with the herb butter. Sprinkle each with salt and pepper. Wrap each piece of rabbit securely with a slice of prosciutto, cutting the prosciutto to fit.

3. Arrange the rabbit pieces, seam side down, compactly in a terra-cotta casserole. It is all right to make more than one layer if need be. Strain the reserved marinade and pour ¾ cup of it into the casserole. Seal the top of the casserole securely with aluminum foil and cover with the lid.

4. Place the casserole in a cold oven, then turn the oven temperature to 450°F. Bake 1¾ hours without opening the casserole. Remove from the oven and let sit for 5 minutes. Remove the lid and foil, pausing to savor one of the most incredible aromas in the entire world. Serve 4 to 5 pieces per person.

Makes 6 servings.

Roast Pheasant with Champagne Cabbage and Noodles

— ❖ —

Pheasant served on a bed of braised cabbage or sauerkraut is a classic European game dish. In my recipe the cabbage gets an added kick from being slowly simmered in Champagne and then tossed with silky egg noodles. I believe this dish should be enjoyed in some windswept abode tucked away high in the mountains.

CABBAGE AND NOODLES

3 tablespoons unsalted
  butter
1 large onion, thinly sliced
1 tablespoon sugar
1 small head green cabbage,
  cored and shredded
1 cup fresh sauerkraut,
  rinsed and drained
2 Granny Smith apples,
  peeled, cored, and thinly
  sliced

1 piece (1 inch) fresh
  ginger
2 cups Champagne or
  sparkling white wine
Salt and freshly ground
  black pepper to taste
12 ounces spinach or
  regular egg noodles

ROAST PHEASANT

1 small onion, thinly sliced
1 carrot, coarsely chopped
1 rib celery, coarsely
  chopped
2 cloves garlic, cut in half
2 pheasants, 2 to 2½
  pounds each, rinsed well
  and patted dry

4 tablespoons vegetable oil
Salt and freshly ground
  black pepper to taste

1. Prepare the cabbage and noodles: Melt the butter in a large pot over medium-high heat. Add the onion and sugar and sauté until the onion is soft and lightly caramelized, 7 to 8 minutes. Stir in the cabbage and sauté 3 minutes more. Add the sauerkraut, apples, ginger, and Champagne. Simmer uncovered over medium-low heat, stirring occasionally, 1 hour. About 10 minutes before serving, remove the ginger and discard. Cook the noodles in a large pot of boiling salted

water just until al dente; drain. Toss the hot noodles with the cabbage mixture and season to taste with salt and pepper.

2. Preheat the oven to 400°F.

3. While the cabbage is cooking, prepare the pheasants: mix together the onion, carrot, celery, and garlic. Stuff each pheasant cavity
with the mixture and truss the birds. Rub each with 2 tablespoons of
the oil and sprinkle with salt and pepper.

4. Place the birds on their sides in a large roasting pan; roast 15
minutes. Turn each bird onto its other side and roast another 15
minutes, basting occasionally with pan drippings. Turn the birds
breast side up and continue roasting until a meat thermometer inserted in the thickest part of the thigh registers 150 to 160°F, 20 to
25 minutes longer.

5. Transfer the pheasants to a carving board. Remove the trus-
sing strings and cut into serving quarters, discarding the vegetable
stuffing from the cavities.

6. Place the cabbage and noodles on a large serving platter. Arrange the pheasant quarters over the top. Serve at once, buffet style.
Makes 6 to 8 servings.

Pan-Fried Steak with Balsamic Glaze

To my mind a pan-fried rib-eye steak is the essence of satisfying
bistro cooking. The balsamic vinegar glaze is something I picked up
while traveling through Modena, the Italian birthplace of this sweet-
and-sour and incredibly noble vinegar. Accompany the steaks with a
sinful potato gratin, and you might just begin speaking in a dialect of
some romance language!

Kosher (coarse) salt
4 rib-eye steaks, about ½
    inch thick
1 large shallot, minced
½ cup balsamic vinegar

3 tablespoons unsalted
    butter
Freshly ground black pepper
    to taste

1. Sprinkle a large cast-iron skillet generously with kosher salt
and heat over high heat. When the salt begins to jump up off the
bottom of the skillet, add the steaks. Sear until the bottom is crusted

brown, 2 to 3 minutes, and turn to the other side. Sear 2 to 3 minutes more for rare steak, or longer to desired doneness. Remove the steaks from the pan and place on warmed serving plates

2. Add the shallot to the skillet and cook 30 seconds. Pour in the vinegar and boil until reduced to 2 tablespoons. Remove the pan from the heat, swirl in the butter, and season the sauce with pepper to taste. Drizzle the sauce over the steaks and serve at once.

Makes 4 servings.

BEEF INTERLUDE

— ✣ —

Winter Asparagus Soup

— ✣ —

Pan-Fried Steak with Balsamic Glaze
Mashed Potatoes with Garlic and Olive Oil
Broccoli with Toasted Hazelnuts and Pancetta

— ✣ —

Chocolate-Chestnut Mousse Cake

Deviled Beef Ribs

— ✤ —

I'm normally a rather dainty eater, but in the chilliest depths of winter I get great primeval gratification gnawing on a meaty and mustardy bone. I simply adore this way of preparing beef short ribs and think it not such a bad idea to indulge our hidden Neanderthal urges every once in a great while.

¼ cup olive oil
1 clove garlic, minced
1 tablespoon dried Italian herb blend
2 bay leaves, coarsely chopped
1 teaspoon salt
1 teaspoon freshly ground black pepper

12 meaty beef short ribs, cut into 3-inch lengths
3 tablespoons coarse mustard
½ cup Dijon mustard
⅓ cup dry white wine
2½ cups fresh bread crumbs
½ cup minced fresh parsley

1. Preheat the oven to 375°F.

2. In a small bowl whisk together the oil, garlic, Italian herbs, bay leaves, salt, and pepper. Arrange the beef ribs in a single layer in a large roasting pan and drizzle with the oil mixture. Roast, turning the ribs once, until nicely browned all over, about 1¼ hours. Remove from the oven and let cool 30 minutes.

3. Whisk together both mustards and the wine until smooth. Combine the bread crumbs and parsley in a shallow bowl. Brush each rib generously with the mustard mixture, then roll it in the bread crumbs, coating all sides. Place the ribs in a clean roasting pan and drizzle with any pan drippings from the first roasting pan.

4. Return the ribs to the oven and bake until the crumbs are golden, 30 to 35 minutes longer. Serve at once with plenty of napkins.

Makes 6 to 8 servings

Slow-Cooked Beef Stew

— ❖ —

I came across this method of cooking beef stew in a spiral-bound community cookbook. Exasperated by many of my other attempts at stew making, I decided that it was worth trying my recipe cooked their way. Perhaps, I reasoned, an unwatched and unstirred pot would yield the best stew. I tested the stew while viewing *Gone With the Wind*, which proved the perfect diversion since the stew must bake slowly for five hours. The result, I believe, could have been served with pride during the best of times at Tara.

2½ pounds lean beef stew meat, cut into 1- to 1½-inch cubes

12 ounces baby carrots, peeled and trimmed

3 large potatoes, peeled and cut into 1-inch cubes

2 medium turnips, peeled and cut into ¾-inch cubes

4 small onions (about 2 inches in diameter), peeled and quartered

3 cloves garlic, minced

1 teaspoon celery seeds

1 teaspoon dried thyme

2 teaspoons salt

2 teaspoons freshly ground black pepper

2½ cups V-8 juice

½ cup dry red wine

1 tablespoon Dijon mustard

2 tablespoons light brown sugar

3½ tablespoons tapioca

1. Preheat the oven to 275°F.

2. In a large mixing bowl combine the beef with all the vegetables. Season with the garlic, celery seeds, thyme, salt, and pepper.

3. In a small bowl whisk together the V-8 juice, wine, mustard, brown sugar, and tapioca, making sure to dissolve the sugar and tapioca. Add this mixture to the meat and vegetables; stir well to blend.

4. Transfer the stew to a Dutch oven or large casserole. Cover lightly and cook 5 hours without peeking or disturbing. Serve at once, or refrigerate overnight and reheat the next day.

Makes 6 servings

Freda's Beef Stew

— ❖ —

Freda lives in Fitchburg, Massachusetts, and is the mother of my best girl friend, Olga. One day when I was relating my stew-making saga to Olga, she called home to her mother for advice. Freda was horrified that I would make stew with lowly chuck rather than bottom round or sirloin and that, furthermore, I marinated the meat. Freda says that searing the meat is essential to making good stew and marinated meat retains too much liquid to ever sear. Olga never liked beef stew, but the rest of the family adored Freda's rendition. To set Olga's friend straight, Freda generously offered to share the recipe and her Greek wisdom for this homey stew. Here is the recipe that Olga (fool!) would never eat.

2 tablespoons olive oil
1 large onion, finely chopped
2 cloves garlic, minced
1 bay leaf
2 pounds beef bottom round or sirloin, cut into 1-inch cubes
1 can (8 ounces) tomato sauce
2 to 3 cups beef broth, preferably homemade
1 teaspoon Worcestershire sauce

Salt and freshly ground black pepper to taste
8 ounces carrots, peeled and cut diagonally into 1-inch chunks
6 ribs celery, cut diagonally into 1-inch chunks
6 small onions, 1 to 1½ inches in diameter, peeled but left whole
2 large potatoes, peeled and cut into ½-inch cubes
1 box (10 ounces) frozen peas

1. Heat the olive oil in a large stew pot or Dutch oven over medium-high heat. Add the large onion, the garlic, and bay leaf; sauté until soft and translucent, 7 to 10 minutes. Remove from the pot and set aside.

2. Add the beef to the pot in two batches and sear until browned on all sides, 7 to 8 minutes per batch. Return the sautéed onion mixture to the pot along with the tomato sauce and just enough broth to cover the meat. Season with Worcestershire, salt, and pepper. Reduce the heat to a simmer, cover the pot, and cook 30 minutes, stirring occasionally.

3. Add the carrots, celery, small onions, and potatoes to the pot. Add enough beef broth to cover the vegetables. Cover and continue to simmer, stirring occasionally, until the vegetables are tender, 1¼ to 1½ hours. If the stew seems dry at any point, add more beef broth or even a splash of wine. Add the peas 5 minutes before serving and stir to incorporate and heat through.

4. Serve the stew ladled into shallow soup bowls. Freda likes to serve Bisquick-style biscuits as an accompaniment.

Makes 4 servings

West Indian Beef Stew

— ❖ —

This is the retaliatory "quick stew" I invented after my initial attempts at more traditional stew making had left me disappointed. It is not a true stew since the usual method of long, slow cooking to develop flavor is replaced by using bold ingredients that cook quickly and yield instant flavor enhancement. Rosy chunks of sirloin are seared rare and then combined with a colorful and potent melange of peppers, ginger, rum, and cilantro. The tropical intrigue of this spicy winter entrée is completed by an accompanying side of mashed yams.

½ cup unbleached all-purpose flour
1 teaspoon ground ginger
2 teaspoons salt, plus additional to taste
1 teaspoon freshly ground black pepper, plus additional to taste
2½ pounds boneless beef sirloin, cut into 1-inch chunks
5 tablespoons vegetable oil
1 large onion, cut into ¼-inch-wide crescent slivers
1 red bell pepper, stemmed, seeded, and cut into ½-inch squares
1 green bell pepper, stemmed, seeded, and cut into ½-inch squares
1 yellow bell pepper, stemmed, seeded, and cut into ½-inch squares

3 serrano or jalapeño chiles, seeded and minced
3 cloves garlic, minced
2 tablespoons minced fresh ginger
3 tablespoons tomato paste
1 tablespoon molasses
1 can (13¾ ounces) beef broth
¼ cup pimiento-stuffed olives, sliced
3 medium tomatoes, seeded and cut into ¾-inch chunks
2 tablespoons fresh lime juice
3 tablespoons dark rum
½ cup chopped cilantro (fresh coriander)
½ cup coarsely chopped toasted macadamia nuts

1. Mix together the flour, ground ginger, 2 teaspoons salt, and 1 teaspoon pepper. Lightly coat the sirloin with the flour mixture.

2. Heat the oil in a wide, squat stew pot over medium-high heat. Sear the beef in batches until browned on all sides, about 5 minutes per batch. Remove from the pot and set aside.

3. Add the onion to the pot and sauté, stirring frequently, 3 minutes. Add the bell peppers, chiles, garlic, and fresh ginger; continue to sauté, stirring occasionally, over medium-high heat 5 minutes more.

4. Stir in the tomato paste, molasses, and beef broth. Bring just to a boil, then simmer 30 minutes, stirring occasionally.

5. Return the seared beef to the pot and simmer 10 minutes. Add the olives and tomatoes and cook 5 minutes more. The meat should be medium rare. Just before serving stir in the lime juice and rum and season to taste with salt and pepper. Ladle the stew onto plates and sprinkle generously with the chopped cilantro and macadamia nuts.

Makes 6 servings

SARAH'S STEW-MAKING SAGA

— ✦ —

After conceiving the idea for a book about cold-weather cooking, the very first recipe I set out to perfect was for a rib-sticking, homey beef stew. I spent nearly a week researching in books how fellow chefs had approached stew making in the hopes of gaining some insight into the ingredients and methods to employ in my own stew pot.

Research completed, for my first ill-fated attempt, I marinated humble chunks of stew meat in a not-so-humble bottle of red Burgundy wine for a good 24-hour period. The following morning, I stumbled wearily onto stew-making mistake number 1: There is no way that liquid-saturated meat will ever sear properly. Wine, if it is to be included should be added as a part of the cooking liquid, after the meat has been browned.

I proceeded with the recipe, nonetheless, and compounded my errors by unnecessarily adding precious ingredients such as dried wild mushrooms and cute but flavorless baby vegetables. A borrowing of the Mies van der Rohe architectural axiom, "less is more," would have been most helpful. The ensuing three hours of attentive simmering and stirring kindled great anticipation yet yielded extreme disappointment. When I sat down to taste the steaming stew of my labor, I had to confess that an uncooked plate of carpaccio or steak tartare would have provided infinitely greater joy.

Frustrated by so much effort and so little satisfaction, I related my tale of trial and error to others, and was overwhelmed by a responsive barrage of resolute stew-making rules. I had no idea that the subject of stew elicited such strong opinions and now have come to realize that strong opinions rarely distill to general accord. Thus, I have decided to include three different variations of beef stew in this book to encompass many of the preferences and prejudices that my research uncovered. While much of the controversy seems to center on whether the best beef stew comes from sirloin or chuck, there is rather universal agreement that the flavor of a slow-simmered stew improves with a day or two of age. In fact, the same could also be said of my own approach to stewing these days—it certainly has benefited from a little age!

Stifado

— ❖ —

Stifado is a Greek meat stew cooked with wine and small white onions. My Greek girl friends tell me that their mothers always make the stew with beef, but I decided to try it with lamb instead. I found that the normally distinctive flavor of lamb tends to pale in the company of such strong seasonings as vinegar, cumin, and clove. I've since concluded that either beef or lamb will produce a memorable feast.

¼ cup olive oil
3 pounds lean lamb or beef,
   cut into 1½-inch cubes
1 medium onion, chopped
3 cloves garlic, minced
1½ cups dry red wine
3 tablespoons balsamic
   vinegar
2 tablespoons light brown
   sugar
1 can (6 ounces) tomato
   paste
1 teaspoon ground cumin
1 teaspoon ground cloves
2 bay leaves

2 cinnamon sticks (about 2
   inches each)
½ cup dried currants
2 strips (3 x 1 inch each)
   orange zest
Salt and freshly ground
   black pepper to taste
2 pounds small white onions
8 ounces feta cheese,
   crumbled
¾ cup pine nuts, lightly
   toasted
Barley and Grape Leaf
   Dumplings (recipe
   follows)

1. Heat the olive oil in a large stew pot or Dutch oven over medium-high heat. Sear the lamb in batches until browned all over. Remove from the pot with a slotted spoon and set aside.

2. Add the onion and garlic to the pot and cook, stirring frequently, until softened, about 5 minutes. Add the wine, vinegar, brown sugar, and tomato paste; stir together until smooth. Season with the cumin, cloves, bay leaves, and cinnamon sticks. Return the meat along with the currants and orange zest to the pot. Add salt and pepper to taste. Bring the stew to a simmer, cover, and let cook over medium-low heat 1 hour.

3. Meanwhile blanch the white onions in boiling water to cover, 5 minutes. Drain, let cool slightly, and peel. After the stew has cooked 1 hour, add the onions and simmer covered 1 hour more. (The stew may be prepared up to this point and refrigerated 1 to 2 days before serving, if desired.)

4. Serve the stew hot accompanied by the feta and pine nuts in individual small bowls and the dumplings.

Makes 6 to 8 servings

Barley and Grape Leaf Dumplings

— ⚜ —

My mother and I collaborated on the invention of these homey and delicious dumplings for a dinner party featuring Greek Stifado.

¾ cup pearl barley
1 extra large egg yolk
¾ cup grated Monterey
  Jack cheese
½ cup freshly grated
  Parmesan cheese
1⅓ cups unbleached all-
  purpose flour
½ cup brine-packed grape
  leaves, rinsed, drained,
  and cut into fine
  julienne strips

Salt and freshly ground
  black pepper to taste
2 extra large egg whites
4 tablespoons (½ stick)
  unsalted butter,
  melted
2 tablespoons minced
  fresh parsley

1. Cook the barley according to package directions until very tender. Drain and chill in the refrigerator at least 3 hours.

2. Put the chilled barley in a food processor and process until smooth. Add the egg yolk, Monterey Jack, ¼ cup of the Parmesan, and ⅓ cup of the flour; process just until mixed. Transfer the mixture to a bowl and stir in the grape leaves, salt, and pepper.

3. Beat the egg whites until stiff, but not dry. Gently fold into the barley mixture along with another ⅓ cup of flour.

4. Line a baking sheet with waxed paper. Place the remaining flour in a shallow dish. Using 2 spoons, shape about 2 heaping table-spoons of the barley dough into a small football shape, drop it into the flour, and coat it lightly. Transfer to the lined baking sheet and repeat the process until all the dough has been used.

5. Bring a large pot of salted water to a boil. Drop 6 to 8 dump-lings at a time into the water and cook until they float to the top, about 1 minute. Remove the dumplings from the pot with a slotted spoon and drain on paper towels. When all the dumplings have been cooked, arrange them in a single layer in an ovenproof baking dish. Drizzle with the melted butter and sprinkle with the remaining Parmesan cheese. (The dumplings may be prepared up to this point and refrigerated 1 to 2 days before baking.)

6. Preheat the oven to 375°F.

7. Bake the dumplings until they are puffed and light golden brown, 25 to 30 minutes. Sprinkle with the parsley and serve at once.

Makes 6 to 8 servings

Ropa Vieja

— ✦ —

R opa Vieja is a spicy Cuban beef dish which gets it name, "old clothes" in translation, from the long cooking of the meat which ends up resembling a pile of rags. Shredded beef to me is the ultimate in comfort food, and I believe adventuresome cooks will find the flavors in this dish new and enticing. Rice, black beans, and fried bananas are traditional and delicious accompaniments.

2 pounds flank steak
1 carrot, coarsely chopped
2 ribs celery, coarsely chopped
1 medium onion, quartered
5 tablespoons olive oil
2 tablespoons fresh lime juice
3 tablespoons fresh orange juice
4 cloves garlic, minced
Salt and freshly ground black pepper to taste
1 large onion, chopped
½ green bell pepper, stemmed, seeded, and cut into thin strips

½ red bell pepper, stemmed, seeded, and cut into thin strips
2 small hot fresh chiles, seeded and minced
3 plum tomatoes, seeded and diced
1 cup tomato sauce, preferably homemade
1 teaspoon ground cinnamon
1 teaspoon ground cumin
Pinch ground cloves
2 tablespoons capers, drained
3 tablespoons chopped cilantro (fresh coriander)

1. Put the steak, carrot, celery, and quartered onion in a pot and add water to cover. Bring to a boil, then simmer uncovered until the meat is very tender, about 1½ hours. Let the meat sit in the cooking liquid until cool enough to handle. Remove the meat and reserve the stock.

2. Using your fingers, shred the beef into thin strips and place in a mixing bowl. Whisk together 2 tablespoons of the olive oil, the lime juice, orange juice, one-quarter of the minced garlic, the salt, and pepper. Toss with the beef and let marinate at room temperature 1 hour.

3. Meanwhile heat the remaining 3 tablespoons oil in a large skillet over medium-high heat. Add the chopped onion, remaining garlic, the pepper strips, and chiles. Sauté until the vegetables are softened, about 5 minutes. Add the plum tomatoes and cook 1 minute more. Add the tomato sauce, 1 cup of the reserved stock, the cinnamon, cumin, and cloves. Simmer uncovered 15 minutes. Stir in the

shredded beef with the marinade and the capers; simmer 15 minutes longer. Season to taste with salt and pepper. Stir in the cilantro just before serving.

Makes 6 servings

Note: This recipe may be made ahead and reheated the following day, which seems to intensify the flavors.

Winter Pot Roast

— ✥ —

This homey winter standby is transformed into company fare by cooking the meat in a rich sauce of olives, lemon, dried fruits, and red wine. The dish is better when prepared ahead and allowed to mellow overnight in the refrigerator, so be sure to plan your entertaining schedule accordingly.

¼ cup olive oil
1 beef rump roast, 4 to 4½ pounds
Salt and freshly ground black pepper to taste
2 large onions, minced
4 large cloves garlic, minced
2 teaspoons anchovy paste
¼ cup (packed) light brown sugar
2½ cups beef broth, preferably homemade
1 cup fruity red wine, such as Zinfandel or Beaujolais
½ cup imported black olives, pitted and coarsely chopped
½ cup pimiento-stuffed green olives, halved
2 tablespoons capers, drained
½ cup dried apricots
½ cup whole pitted prunes
½ cup Calimyrna figs, cut lengthwise in half
Grated zest of 1 lemon
2 tablespoons fresh lemon juice
1 tablespoon dried oregano

1. Heat the olive oil in a large pot or Dutch oven over medium-high heat. Season the rump roast by rubbing it all over with salt and pepper. Brown the roast on all sides in the hot oil, 15 minutes. Remove the roast from the pot and set aside on a platter.

2. Add the onions to the pot and sauté until softened, about 5 minutes. Stir in the garlic and cook another 5 minutes. Blend in the anchovy paste and brown sugar until smooth. Pour in the beef broth and red wine, then mix in the olives, capers, dried fruits, and lemon

zest and juice. Season with the oregano and additional salt and pepper if necessary.

3. Return the seared roast to the pot. Bring the mixture just to a simmer over medium heat. Cover the pot, reduce the heat to low, and simmer, turning the meat occasionally, until it is very tender, about 3 hours. Let the pot roast cool to room temperature, then refrigerate overnight.

4. Before serving the following day, preheat the oven to 350°F.

5. Remove the pot roast from the pot and slice thin. Overlap the slices in a large baking dish. Skin the fat from the sauce and spoon the sauce generously over the meat slices. Cover the baking dish with aluminum foil and bake until the meat is heated through, about 30 minutes. Serve with buttered noodles, mashed potatoes, or rice.

Makes 6 to 8 servings

Auntie's Meat Loaf

— ❖ —

Some of my fondest memories of my Aunt De's Nantucket kitchen center around this fabulous meat loaf. I knew it had to be special when my uncle requested it year after year for his birthday dinner. The recipe yields two ample loaves because my aunt never does anything in moderation! Tips from the inventor include removing all rings and precious wrist ornaments before attacking the nitty-gritty hand mixing of five pounds of meat. De insists on serving the meat loaf with the bourbon-spiked Tomato Relish published in my *Nantucket Open House Cookbook*. Other favored accompaniments include baked sweet potatoes and almond-buttered green beans.

1 tablespoon olive oil
1 large onion, diced
1 pound (⅔ loaf)
   Pepperidge Farm wheat
   bread
2 cans (28 ounces each)
   crushed tomatoes in purée
1½ to 2 cups whole milk
1 cup minced fresh parsley
½ cup freshly grated
   Parmesan cheese
1 teaspoon dried oregano

2 tablespoons dried
   marjoram
1 teaspoon celery salt
1 tablespoon Worcestershire
   sauce
1 teaspoon dried red pepper
   flakes (optional)
Salt and freshly ground
   black pepper to taste
5 pounds lean ground
   beef
1 pound sliced bacon

1. Preheat the oven to 325°F.

2. Heat the olive oil in a small skillet over medium heat. Add the onion and sauté 5 minutes. Remove from the heat.

3. Cut the bread into ½-inch cubes and place in a very large mixing bowl. Add 1⅓ cans of the crushed tomatoes and stir to blend. Pour in enough milk to just cover the mixture. Add the sautéed onion, ½ cup of the parsley, the Parmesan, and all the seasonings. With "ringless fingers and freshly washed hands," mix in the meat until thoroughly blended.

4. Divide the mixture in half and shape each half into a loaf. Place them in a large nonstick roasting pan. Arrange the bacon slices diagonally, across each loaf and tuck the ends under the loaves. Spread the meat loaves with the remaining ⅔ can crushed tomatoes and sprinkle with the remaining ½ cup parsley.

5. Bake 1½ hours. After 1 hour, drain off any fat that has accumulated in the pans. Let the meat loaves rest at least 5 minutes before cutting into thick slices.

Makes 2 large meat loaves

Braised Lamb Shanks with Bourbon Barbecue Sauce

— ❖ —

This slowly simmered feast of hearty and flavorful lamb shanks lures salty Down Easters into the cozy comfort of my brother Jonathan's restaurant in Blue Hill, Maine.

¾ cup unbleached all-purpose flour

2 teaspoons salt

1 teaspoon freshly ground black pepper

6 lamb shanks, 12 to 16 ounces each

3 tablespoons olive oil

2 tablespoons dried rosemary

1 jar (18 ounces) barbecue sauce, preferably K.C. Masterpiece Barbecue Sauce

2 cups bourbon

2 tablespoons light brown sugar

4 cloves garlic, minced

1 large red onion, halved and thinly sliced

1 teaspoon cayenne pepper

2 tablespoons dried mustard

1 bottle (12 ounces) beer

1 to 2 cups beef broth, preferably homemade

1. Preheat the oven to 325°F.

2. Mix together the flour, salt, and pepper in a wide shallow dish and coat the lamb shanks with the flour mixture.

3. Pour the olive oil into a large heavy pot and heat over medium-high heat. Add the lamb shanks and brown on all sides, 15 to 20 minutes. Add the rosemary to the pot and cook a few minutes more to lightly toast it. Transfer the lamb shanks and accumulated pan drippings to a deep roasting pan.

4. Combine all the remaining ingredients, including 1 cup of the beef stock, in a mixing bowl and pour over the lamb shanks. Cover the pan tightly with aluminum foil.

5. Braise the lamb shanks in the oven for 2½ hours. Check every now and again to make sure there is enough braising liquid. If the mixture becomes too dry or thick, add more beef broth. The meat is done when it is tender and practically falling off the bone.

Makes 6 servings

Braised Lamb Shanks with White Beans and Goat Cheese Crust

— ❖ —

This is a satisfying and hearty peasant dish that takes its inspiration from the more elaborate French cassoulet. While there are several steps that go into the preparation of this earthy meal, none are terribly complicated and all will keep the cook toasty warm by the stove on a discouraging sub-zero day. The dish would even benefit from being prepared a day in advance and reheated for the comfort and nourishment of a few close friends.

4 cloves garlic, finely
minced
¼ cup Dijon mustard
4 meaty lamb shanks, 3½
to 4 pounds total
1 tablespoon fresh whole
rosemary leaves, or 1
teaspoon dried
1 tablespoon herbes de
Provence
Salt and freshly ground
black pepper to taste
1½ cups beef broth,
preferably homemade
1 cup dry red wine
4 bay leaves
4 tablespoons olive oil
3 carrots, peeled and cut
into ¼-inch dice

1 large onion, coarsely
chopped
1 pound small white beans,
soaked overnight, then
drained
6 cups water
¼ cup tomato paste
1 large head garlic, cloves
peeled and cut lengthwise
in half
1½ cups coarse fresh white
bread crumbs
½ cup chopped fresh
parsley
4 ounces soft chèvre,
crumbled

1. Preheat the oven to 450°F.

2. Make a paste of the minced garlic and the mustard and smear generously all over each lamb shank. Place the lamb shanks in a roasting pan just large enough to hold them in a single layer (12 × 9 inches or thereabouts). Sprinkle the shanks with half the rosemary, all the *herbes de Provence*, and salt and pepper to taste. Pour ½ cup each beef broth and wine into the pan. Scatter the bay leaves in the liquid. Roast the lamb shanks uncovered until lightly crusted and browned, about 25 minutes.

3. Reduce the oven temperature to 300°F. Cover the pan tightly with a double layer of aluminum foil. Continue to cook the lamb shanks for 1¾ hours. Remove the foil and cook 15 minutes longer.

4. Meanwhile prepare the beans: Heat 2 tablespoons of the olive oil in an 8-quart heatproof enamel casserole or Dutch oven over medium-high heat. Add the carrots and onion and sauté 5 minutes. Add the beans and stir to coat with the vegetables and oil. Cover with the water and bring to a boil. Simmer the beans uncovered 30 minutes; they will still be somewhat undercooked at this point but will finish cooking later. Drain the beans and return them to the casserole. Stir in the tomato paste, garlic cloves, and remaining rosemary.

5. When the lamb shanks are finished cooking, remove them from the pan and set aside. Degrease the liquid in the pan and pour it into a small saucepan. Add the remaining 1 cup beef broth and ½ cup wine. Bring to a boil, then simmer until reduced by about half, 15 to 20 minutes. Pour this liquid into the casserole with the beans.

Bring the beans to a simmer and cook until tender, about 30 minutes more. Season to taste with salt and pepper.

6. Arrange the lamb shanks in the pot with the beans, making sure the entire top of the casserole is covered with a layer of beans.

7. For the crumb crust, toss the bread crumbs and parsley with the remaining 2 tablespoons olive oil just until moistened. Sprinkle this mixture evenly over the top of the beans. Crumble the chèvre evenly over all.

8. Preheat the oven to 350°F.

9. Bake the stew uncovered until the beans are bubbling and the top is nicely crusted, 40 to 45 minutes. Remove from the oven and let sit 5 minutes. Serve 1 lamb shank per person with plenty of beans and an ample portion of crust. Accompany with a hearty red wine and a simple green salad.

Makes 4 hearty servings

Pork with Bourbon-Soaked Prunes and Apricots

— ❖ —

I'm the sort of person who can walk into a meat market and fall in love with a pork roast. I have actually rearranged my suitcase in the middle of Balducci's, a popular specialty foods market in New York City, in order to bring a pork loin back to Nantucket. Dried fruits are a natural winter combination with pork, and I believe this to be the ultimate rendition of a popular recipe. This is a stunning entrée that is likely to transform privileged dinner guests into lifelong friends.

½ cup pitted prunes
½ cup dried apricots
1 cup bourbon
1½ cups fresh bread crumbs
¾ cup walnuts, diced small
2 shallots, minced
1 teaspoon dried sage
2 tablespoons chopped fresh rosemary, or 1 tablespoon dried
Salt and freshly ground black pepper to taste

1 large egg, lightly beaten
1 boned and tied pork loin roast, 4 to 5 pounds
¼ cup Dijon mustard
½ cup (packed) light brown sugar
1 cup dry white wine
2 to 3 cups beef broth, preferably homemade
2 bay leaves

1. Place the prunes and apricots in a small saucepan, cover with ½ cup of the bourbon, and bring to a simmer over medium heat. Simmer 10 minutes and remove from the heat. In a large mixing bowl combine the fruit and liquid with the bread crumbs, walnuts, and shallots. Season with the sage, rosemary, salt, and pepper. Bind the stuffing together with the beaten egg. (Depending on how moist the bread crumbs are and how much bourbon the fruit absorbs, you may not need the whole egg to bind. The mixture should just stick together, but not be soggy.)

2. Preheat the oven to 425°F.

3. Untie the pork roast and gently pack the stuffing evenly over the center of the roast. Tie the roast back together and place it in a roasting pan. Smear the mustard liberally all over the surface of the roast, then gently pat the brown sugar over the mustard. Season with salt and pepper. Pour the wine, remaining ½ cup bourbon, and 2 cups broth around the roast. Add the bay leaves to the liquid.

4. Cover the roasting pan and cook 45 minutes. Uncover the pan and cook until a meat thermometer registers 160°F, 45 to 60 minutes more. Baste the roast occasionally with the pan juices, adding more broth if the liquid evaporates too rapidly.

5. Discard the strings from the roast and cut into thick slices. Spoon some of the degreased pan juices over the pork if desired.

Makes 8 servings

JANUARY ENTHRALL

— ❖ —

Strange Flavor Eggplant with
Sesame Sippets

— ❖ —

Pork with Bourbon-Soaked Prunes
and Apricots

— ❖ —

Wild Rice and Cider Pilaf
Rutabagas Anna
Nantucket Cranberry Relish

— ❖ —

Gigondas

— ❖ —

Bartlett Pear Tart

— ❖ —

Chestnut Stuffed
Breast of Veal

— ❖ —

Recently my great pal Olga kissed the slumping world of Boston real estate goodbye and went off for an autumn jaunt through Italy. She returned raving about the chestnut cookery that she had enjoyed, which inspired me to go into a culinary phase best described as my chestnut period. Here is one of the winning results from that time.

1 veal breast, 5 to 6
    pounds, boned
Salt and freshly ground
    black pepper to taste
1 teaspoon grated nutmeg
1½ pounds ground veal
1 cup soft fresh bread
    crumbs
4 ounces thinly sliced
    prosciutto, minced
1 bunch scallions, trimmed
    and minced
½ cup brandy
½ cup heavy or whipping
    cream

2 large eggs
¼ minced fresh parsley, plus
    additional for garnish
1 teaspoon dried marjoram
1 teaspoon dried thyme
24 shelled cooked fresh
    chestnuts (see box, page
    87)
6 tablespoons (¾ stick)
    unsalted butter
3 carrots, peeled and
    minced
3 ribs celery, minced
3 cloves garlic, minced
1½ cups dry white wine

1. Place the veal breast top side down on a large chopping block; pound with a meat mallet to ½ inch thickness. Sprinkle all over with salt, pepper, and ½ teaspoon of the nutmeg.

2. In a large mixing bowl combine the ground veal, bread crumbs, prosciutto, scallions, brandy, cream, eggs, parsley, marjoram, and thyme. Mix with a large wooden spoon until smooth. Season with salt, pepper, and the remaining ½ teaspoon nutmeg.

3. Pat half the stuffing over the inside surface of the veal breast, leaving a 1-inch border all around. Scatter the chestnuts over the stuffing, then pat the remaining stuffing on top. Starting with the long edge, roll up the veal breast and tie securely with kitchen string.

4. Melt the butter in a Dutch oven over medium heat. Add the veal and brown on all sides, 10 to 15 minutes. Add the carrots, celery, garlic, and 1 cup of the wine to the pan. Bring to a boil, then reduce the heat to a simmer. Cover and cook until the meat is tender, about 3 hours. Turn the meat several times during cooking and add the

remaining ½ cup wine to the pan as needed.

5. Remove the veal to a warmed platter. Skim the fat from the pan juices and taste for seasoning. Slice the veal and sprinkle with a little fresh parsley. Serve with the pan vegetables and juices.

Makes 6 to 8 servings

Veal Stew with Peppers and Olives

—❖—

To my mind, this stew embodies the quintessence of good Italian cooking. It is simple and straightforward, yet concentrated with rich flavor and color. Serve as a comforting Sunday night supper with a tangle of unembellished pasta.

¼ cup olive oil
3 pounds boneless veal stew
   meat, cut into 1-inch
   cubes
3 cloves garlic, minced
½ cup minced fresh parsley,
   plus additional for garnish
1 large red bell pepper,
   stemmed, seeded, and cut
   into 1-inch squares
1 large green bell pepper,
   stemmed, seeded, and cut
   into 1-inch squares
1 large yellow bell pepper,
   stemmed, seeded, and cut
   into 1-inch squares

3 tablespoons unbleached
   all-purpose flour
1 tablespoon tomato paste
¾ to 1 cup dry white wine
1 can (35 ounces) plum
   tomatoes, drained and
   coarsely chopped
1 heaping tablespoon dried
   Italian herb blend
½ cup imported green olives,
   pitted and coarsely chopped
½ cup imported black
   olives, pitted and coarsely
   chopped
Salt and freshly ground
   black pepper to taste

1. Heat the olive oil in a large heavy pot or Dutch oven over medium-high heat. Add the veal cubes in batches and brown on all sides. Remove and set aside.

2. Add the garlic and parsley to the pot and sauté until softened, 2 to 3 minutes. Stir in the bell peppers and sauté, stirring frequently, 5 minutes more.

3. Stir in the flour and tomato paste and cook 1 minute. Gradually stir in the wine and tomatoes. Return the veal to the pot and add the Italian herbs and olives. Season the stew to taste with salt and pepper. Simmer uncovered over medium-low heat until the meat is very tender, about 1 hour. Garnish each serving with a sprinkling of fresh parsley.

Makes 6 to 8 servings

Mixed Sausage Ragout

— ✤ —

I've fallen into the very peculiar habit of purchasing sausages wherever I travel. When I can successfully manage to transport my sausage heist back home, this is the sort of rewarding mélange I like to create. Loukanika, by the way, is a terrific Greek sausage flavored with orange zest and fennel.

3 tablespoons olive oil
1 pound hot Italian
   sausages, cut into 2-inch
   pieces
1 pound bratwurst, cut into
   2-inch pieces
1 pound kielbasa, sliced
   diagonally into 1-inch
   chunks
1 pound loukanika, sliced
   diagonally into 1-inch
   chunks
3 large onions, peeled and
   sliced into rings

6 cloves garlic, minced
2 teaspoons ground cumin
1½ tablespoons dried
   oregano
1 can (28 ounces) whole
   tomatoes, undrained
1 cup dry red wine
1 jar (7¼ ounces) roasted
   peppers, drained and
   coarsely chopped
1 cup large Spanish olives,
   halved and pitted
Salt and freshly ground
   black pepper to taste

TOPPING (optional)
6 ounces crumbled feta
   cheese

½ cup minced fresh parsley
2 cups fresh bread crumbs

1. Heat the olive oil in a large stockpot over medium-high heat. Add the sausages in batches and brown on all sides. Remove them from the pot and drain on paper towels. Discard all but 3 tablespoons fat from the pot.

2. Add the onions to the pot and cook over medium heat, stirring frequently, until quite soft and tender, about 15 minutes. Add the garlic, cumin, and oregano and cook 2 minutes more. Add the tomatoes, wine, roasted peppers, and olives. Simmer 10 minutes. Return

the sausages to the pot and continue simmering uncovered for 15 minutes. Season to taste with salt and pepper. The ragout may be served
as is or baked with the bread crumb topping.

3. For the topping, preheat the oven to 350°F.

4. Transfer the sausage ragout to a large casserole. Mix together
the feta, parsley, and bread crumbs, mashing the cheese slightly with
a fork. Sprinkle over the top of the ragout. Bake until the casserole is
bubbling and the crumbs are crusted and light brown, 25 to 30 minutes. Serve at once.

Makes 8 to 10 servings

Oxtail Stew

— ❖ —

Oxtails are both incredibly flavorful and inexpensive. They make
a great base for hearty winter soups and stews and offer an interesting
change of pace. Yucca is a root vegetable available at Spanish, Latin
American, or African specialty markets that adds a nice hint of exoticism to this recipe. However, if it is impossible to locate, two large
russet potatoes may be substituted without lessening the unusual and
colorful allure of this soulful ragout.

½ cup unbleached all-
  purpose flour
1 teaspoon ground ginger
1 teaspoon salt, plus
  additional to taste
1 teaspoon freshly ground
  black pepper, plus
  additional to taste
3½ pounds oxtails, cut into
  2-inch lengths
4 tablespoons olive oil
1 large onion, chopped
6 cloves garlic, minced
2 jalapeños chiles, seeded
  and minced
1 green bell pepper,
  stemmed, seeded, and
  coarsely chopped
1 yellow bell pepper,
  stemmed, seeded, and
  coarsely chopped

1 tablespoon dried oregano
½ cup fresh orange juice
¼ cup fresh lime juice
2 quarts beef broth,
  preferably homemade
2 yams, peeled, halved
  lengthwise, and sliced ½
  inch thick
2 yucca roots, peeled,
  halved lengthwise, and
  sliced ½ inch thick
1 medium rutabaga, peeled
  and cut into ¾-inch
  chunks
3 large carrots, peeled and
  cut into thick 3-inch-long
  sticks
½ cup chopped cilantro
  (fresh coriander)
4 ounces banana chips

1. In a shallow bowl mix together the flour, ginger, and 1 tea-spoon each salt and pepper. Coat the oxtails in the flour mixture.

2. Heat 3 tablespoons of the olive oil in a Dutch oven over medium-high heat. Brown the oxtails in batches in the hot oil, turning frequently, 15 to 20 minutes per batch. Remove the oxtails from the pan and set aside.

3. Add the remaining 1 tablespoon oil to the pan and stir in the onion, garlic, jalapeños, and bell peppers. Cook for 10 minutes, stirring frequently and scraping up any browned bits sticking to the bottom of the pan. Add the oregano and cook 1 minute more.

4. Pour in the orange juice, lime juice, and beef broth. Stir to blend with the vegetables. Return the oxtails to the pan and bring the mixture just to a boil. Reduce the heat to a simmer, cover the pan, and simmer 2 hours, stirring every once in awhile.

5. Add all the vegetables to the stew and simmer until the vege-tables are tender, about 1 hour more. Season the stew with salt and pepper to taste. Serve the stew in wide shallow bowls topped with a liberal sprinkling of cilantro and banana chips (a wonderful tropical touch!).

Makes 6 servings

Stuffed Cabbage Leaves

— ✥ —

Cabbage leaves rolled and baked with a stuffing of ground meat and rice is one of the great rib-sticking dishes of European peasant cuisines. In my particular Polish heritage, the dish is known as *golum-kis,* and it is from Poland that I take my inspiration for this hearty, winter one-dish meal.

FILLING

1 head (3 pounds) green
   cabbage
3 tablespoons unsalted
   butter
1 large onion, minced
3 cloves garlic, minced
8 ounces smoked kielbasa,
   cut into ¼-inch dice
2 cups cooked white rice

1½ pounds lean ground
   pork
½ cup minced fresh parsley
1 tablespoon caraway seeds
1 tablespoon sweet
   Hungarian paprika
Salt and freshly ground
   black pepper to taste
1 large egg, beaten

SAUCE

3 tablespoons unsalted
   butter
1 large onion, minced
3 cups beef broth,
   preferably homemade
1 cup dry white wine
¼ cup (packed) light
   brown sugar

1½ cups fresh sauerkraut,
   rinsed and drained
   (see Note)
1 cup unsweetened
   applesauce
4 slices bacon

1. Bring a large pot of salted water to a boil. Remove the core from the cabbage with a sharp knife and discard it along with any wilted outer leaves. Immerse the cabbage in the pot of boiling water. Using a fork or tongs, gently remove the outer leaves from the cabbage as they become cooked and tender, after about 3 minutes. When all the large leaves have been removed, let the remaining small head of cabbage continue to cook until tender, about 5 minutes longer. Drain all well and set aside.

2. Prepare the filling: Melt the butter in a large skillet over medium-high heat. Add the onion and garlic and sauté 10 minutes. Stir in the kielbasa and cook 5 minutes more. In a large mixing bowl combine the cooked mixture, the rice, ground pork, parsley, caraway, and paprika. Season the mixture with salt and pepper and bind it together with the beaten egg.

3. To stuff the cabbage leaves, lay one cabbage leaf flat and place ¼ cup filling in a log shape near the base of the leaf. Fold the bottom of the leaf over filling, then fold the sides toward the center and roll it tightly into a plump log shape. Arrange the stuffed cabbage roll, seam side down, in a large casserole. Repeat with the remaining leaves and filling.

4. Preheat the oven to 325°F.

5. Prepare the sauce: Melt the butter in a large skillet over medium-high heat. Add the onion and sauté until softened, about 5 minutes. Shred the cooked small head of cabbage, add it to the skillet, and sauté 5 minutes more. Combine the vegetables with the beef broth, wine, brown sugar, sauerkraut, and applesauce. Pour the sauce evenly around and over the cabbage rolls in the casserole. Lay the bacon slices diagonally over the top.

6. Cover the casserole with a lid or aluminum foil. Bake 1½ hours, then remove the lid and bake another 30 minutes. Serve hot.
Makes 10 to 12 servings

Note: If you can't find fresh sauerkraut, the variety sold in bags will do. Don't substitute canned in this recipe.

BROWNING SAUSAGE MEAT

— ⋄ —

*M*ost *store-bought sausages contain enough fat to allow for browning without adding extra butter or oil to the skillet. To prepare sausage meat for cooking, remove the casings by splitting them lengthwise down the center with a sharp knife. Open the sausages outward like a butterfly and remove the meat with a spoon or your fingers. Heat a large, heavy skillet over medium-high heat; add the sausage meat and crumble into small pieces using the back of a wooden spoon. Cook, stirring occasionally, until the meat loses all of its pink color, about 10 minutes. To brown, continue cooking and stirring the sausage meat an additional 7 to 10 minutes. Remove the sausage meat from the skillet with a slotted spoon and drain on paper towels. Discard fat remaining in the skillet.*

Four-Bean Chili

— ❖ —

*A*s a kid, the thing I despised most about chili were the red kidney beans. Now that I've matured into a bean fiend, I've discovered that I love the look of a multitude of different beans, glistening like precious stones, in a steaming crock of chili. Chili is not a dainty dish, and I believe that it should be made in quantity and served to a boisterous crowd. I make chili evenings into festive gatherings by offering an array of garnishes in earthenware bowls so that each guest may doctor a portion to individual liking. Some of my favorite additions are shredded sharp Cheddar, lime-marinated diced avocado, pitted black olives, and minced fresh scallions and cilantro. A basket of warmed blue corn chips is also a welcome accompaniment.

½ pound each dried black, red kidney, garbanzo (chick-peas), and white navy beans, picked over for pebbles and soaked in water overnight

12 ounces sliced bacon, diced

3 large onions, minced

1 bunch scallions, trimmed and minced

½ cup minced garlic (about 1 head)

6 jalapeño chiles, seeded and minced

3 tablespoons ground cumin

1 tablespoon whole cumin seeds

3 tablespoons ground coriander

3 tablespoons paprika

3 tablespoons good-quality chili powder

¼ cup dried oregano

¼ teaspoon cayenne pepper

4 cans (28 ounces each) tomatoes packed in purée, about 12 cups

2 bottles (12 ounces each) dark beer

3 pounds lean ground beef

1 pound hot Italian sausage, casings removed (see box, page 273)

Salt to taste

1. Rinse and drain the soaked beans. Place in a large pot and cover with fresh water. Bring to a boil over medium-high heat and skim off any foam that rises to the surface. Simmer the beans just until tender, 1 to 1½ hours.

2. While the beans are cooking, fry the bacon in a large pot or Dutch oven over medium-high heat just until crisp. Remove with a slotted spoon and drain on paper towels. Add the onions, scallions, and garlic to the bacon fat; sauté, stirring occasionally, until soft and translucent, about 10 minutes. Stir in the jalapeños and cook 5 minutes more.

3. Place all the seasonings in a dry skillet and toast them over medium-low heat, swirling the mixture in the pan continuously and being careful not to burn, 2 to 3 minutes. When the mixture is quite fragrant, add it to the onions and cook 5 minutes.

4. Add the tomatoes and beer; simmer over medium heat about 30 minutes.

5. In the meantime, sauté the beef and sausage together in a large skillet over medium-high heat. Crumble the meat with the back

of a wooden spoon and cook just until the meat is no longer pink. Drain the fat and add the meat to the tomato mixture in the pot.

6. When the beans have cooked, drain them and add them to the chili. Season to taste with salt and stir in the reserved bacon. If the mixture seems too thick, thin with water or more dark beer. Serve now or simmer the chili over low heat up to 1 hour to blend the flavors a bit more. The chili may also be chilled and reheated.

Makes at least 20 servings

MAGIC MOUNTAINS

— ❖ —

Svelte and slippery-tailed mermaids rather than bellowing abominable snowmen have always made up my world of fantasy in living along the shores of coastal New England. Seaside aficionado that I am, luring me away to snowcapped peaks, where the oxygen is thin rather than salty, is a tough sell. Yet when I do indulge my childhood passion for schussing down powdery slopes or cross-country skiing deep in the silence of evergreen forests, I find that mountains fill my senses with many a new and fresh revelation. There is a secret hidden in the icy white purity and immutability of mountain vistas that is mentally cleansing and cathartic, but another wonderful force aloft in the frosty and crisp air is the mysterious stimulation of appetite.

Mountains impose certitude, and I am positive that I like mine with starch. Starch that is, not as in collars, but as in carbohydrates — platters of pasta and polenta, and pots of bubbling baked beans. After going through the inevitable four-wheel-drive machinations to get to the mountains, I'm not one to cozy up to a fire for the day. No, I prefer to be bundled to the nines, communing with nature, and partaking of winter sports so that sheer exhilaration overcomes the numbness in my toes and burns enough calories to earn me guiltless enjoyment in all the warming recipes I've created. The pleasant nutritional truth is that our bodies need carbohydrates, not only as a fuel for combating a frigid climate but also for the nutrients, proteins, and fiber. An enticing mountain motto of mine is: Reward simple winter pleasures with complex carbohydrates!

Poverty Casserole

— ❖ —

This dish takes its name more from the original intention of the recipe than the actual cost. The winter after I first opened Que Sera Sarah, I lived in a drafty apartment above my shop and though rich in culinary energy and surplus gourmet ingredients, I was monetarily poor. After resisting the temptation to run the furnace on my plentiful larder of extra virgin olive oil instead of going out to buy costly crude oil, I devoted myself to devising a series of resourceful meals, which, ironically, found their economy by using up my wealth of fancy specialty foods.

Poverty Casserole began as a sincere attempt to make a quick and humble supper of baked hamburger and macaroni. It just so happened that the pasta I had on hand was tricolor imported ziti . . . and then there were sun-dried tomatoes and always the good Italian olive oil. Rumors began to circulate around the sleepy little island, and former summer customers began to call and place orders for Poverty Casserole. Suddenly my survival tactics began to bring in a nice little kitty to finance a winter escape.

3 tablespoons extra virgin olive oil
1 medium onion, minced
2 cloves garlic, minced
1 pound lean ground beef
8 whole sun-dried tomatoes packed in oil, drained and minced
1 can (28 ounces) crushed tomatoes in purée
2 tablespoons dried oregano

2 teaspoons dried marjoram
Salt and freshly ground black pepper to taste
1 bag (14 ounces) imported ziti
2 large eggs
⅔ cup heavy or whipping cream
2 cups shredded mozzarella
3 tablespoons freshly grated Parmesan cheese

1. Preheat the oven to 350°F.

2. Heat the oil in a large skillet over medium-high heat. Add the onion and garlic and sauté 5 minutes. Stir in the ground beef and cook, crumbling it with the back of a wooden spoon, until it loses its pink color. Add the sun-dried tomatoes, crushed tomatoes, and seasonings. Let the mixture simmer uncovered 15 minutes.

3. Meanwhile cook the ziti in a large pot of salted boiling water until al dente, then drain.

4. Whisk the eggs and cream together in the bottom of a 3-quart

Dutch oven or other ovenproof casserole. Quickly toss the drained ziti with the eggs and cream. Add the meat mixture and stir to combine thoroughly. Fold in 1½ cups of the shredded mozzarella. Top the pasta mixture with the remaining ½ cup mozzarella and the Parmesan.

5. Bake uncovered until the cheese is melted and the casserole is bubbling, 30 to 40 minutes. Serve at once with a green salad and crusty bread.

Makes 4 to 6 servings

SKATING ON THIN ICE

— ❖ —

Warm Dandelion Salad

— ❖ —

Spaghetti with Meatballs
Italian bread

— ❖ —

Zinfandel
Ivy League Chocolate Chunk Cookies

Spaghetti with Meatballs

— ❖ —

A supper of spaghetti and meatballs is quintessential homey fare. So homey, in fact, that I had cooked my way through gastronomic tomes before ever attempting this American family staple. But I undertook the creation of my version with as much fervor as I had once applied perfecting *coq au vin* and *ossobuco*. While making a decent tomato sauce is second nature to me, I put a lot of thought and research into blending a terrific meatball. Mine are filled with cheesy secrets — the meat itself is blended with both ricotta and Parmesan, and a healthy nugget of mozzarella is then tucked into the center of each ball to ooze out upon cutting into the finished product.

TOMATO SAUCE

¼ cup olive oil
1 large onion, minced
3 large cloves garlic, minced
1 carrot, peeled and minced
1 bell pepper, any color,
    stemmed, seeded, and diced
1 tablespoon dried Italian
    herb blend

1 teaspoon fennel seeds
2 cans (28 ounces each)
    whole tomatoes, undrained
1 can (6 ounces) tomato paste
1 cup dry red wine
2 teaspoons sugar
Salt and freshly ground
    black pepper to taste

MEATBALLS

2 pounds lean ground beef
1 pound lean ground pork
4 ounces prosciutto, ground
    or finely minced
1 medium onion, finely
    minced
3 large cloves garlic, finely
    minced
½ cup minced fresh parsley
¼ teaspoon grated nutmeg
1 tablespoon dried oregano

½ cup freshly grated
    Parmesan cheese
¾ cup ricotta cheese
½ cup fresh bread crumbs
3 large eggs, lightly beaten
Salt and freshly ground
    black pepper to taste
8 ounces mozzarella cheese,
    cut into ½-inch cubes
¼ cup olive oil
2 pounds spaghetti

1. Prepare the tomato sauce: Heat the olive oil in a large heavy pot over medium-high heat. Add the onion, garlic, carrot, and bell pepper and sauté 10 minutes. Stir in the herbs and fennel seeds. Add the tomatoes, tomato paste, wine, sugar, salt, and pepper. Bring to a simmer, cover, and continue to simmer 1 hour, stirring occasionally.

2. While the sauce is simmering, prepare the meatballs: Combine the beef, pork, and prosciutto in a large mixing bowl. With your hands or a large wooden spoon, mix in all the remaining ingredients through the eggs. Season with salt and pepper. Grease a baking sheet or line it with parchment paper.

3. Preheat the oven to 375°F.

4. To form each meatball, take a generous scoop of the meat mixture, flatten it into a patty, place a cube of mozzarella in the center, then roll into a ball about 3 inches in diameter. Place the meatballs ½ inch apart on the prepared baking sheet. (The mixture should make about 24 meatballs.) Brush each meatball lightly all over with the olive oil. Bake until cooked through and lightly browned, about 40 minutes. Using a slotted spoon, transfer the meatballs to the tomato sauce. Simmer uncovered 30 minutes longer.

5. Fifteen minutes before serving, cook the spaghetti in a large pot of salted boiling water until al dente. Drain and transfer to a pasta bowl. Top with the sauce and meatballs.

Makes 10 to 12 servings

Pastitsio

— ✛ —

Pastitsio is a robust Greek casserole of pasta baked with a lamb meat sauce and a rich custard. It is a great buffet dish to feed a hungry crowd. While it is traditionally made with elbow macaroni, I prefer to use a more exciting shape of small pasta, such as shells, rotini, or orechiette (little ears). I also lace the custard sauce with saffron to bring out a sunnier flavor.

LAMB SAUCE

2 tablespoons olive oil
2 large onions, chopped
2 cloves garlic, minced
2½ pounds lean ground
 lamb
1 tablespoon dried oregano
1 tablespoon ground
 cinnamon

Pinch of ground cloves
1 can (28 ounces) diced
 tomatoes in tomato purée
½ cup dry red wine
Salt and freshly ground
 black pepper to taste
½ cup minced fresh parsley

PASTA LAYER

1 large eggplant, about 1
 pound, peeled and cut
 into ½-inch cubes
2 cloves garlic, minced
½ cup olive oil

Salt and freshly ground
 black pepper to taste
1 pound small shaped pasta
2 cups shredded Kasseri
 cheese

SAFFRON CUSTARD

4 tablespoons (½ stick)
 unsalted butter
¼ cup unbleached all-
 purpose flour
1 teaspoon saffron threads
2¼ cups milk
½ teaspoon grated nutmeg

Salt and freshly ground
 white pepper to taste
1½ cups ricotta cheese
2 large eggs
1 tablespoon grated lemon zest
1½ cups shredded Kasseri
 cheese

1. Prepare the lamb sauce: Heat the olive oil in a large heavy pot over medium-high heat. Add the onions and garlic and sauté 5 minutes. Stir in the lamb, crumbling it with the back of a wooden spoon, and cook until the lamb loses its pink color and starts to brown, 12 to 15 minutes. Stir in the oregano, cinnamon, cloves, tomatoes, wine, salt, and pepper; simmer uncovered, stirring occasionally 15 minutes. Stir in the parsley and remove from the heat. Set aside.

2. Preheat the oven to 400°F.

3. Prepare the pasta layer: Toss the eggplant and garlic together

in a roasting pan. Drizzle with ¼ cup of the olive oil and sprinkle with salt and pepper. Roast the eggplant, stirring occasionally, until soft and lightly browned, about 20 minutes. Reduce the oven temperature to 350°F.

4. Meanwhile cook the pasta in a large pot of salted boiling water until al dente, then drain. Mix the roasted eggplant with the cooked pasta. Stir in the remaining ¼ cup olive oil and the 2 cups Kasseri cheese. Set aside while preparing the custard.

5. For the custard, melt the butter in a medium saucepan over medium heat. Add the flour and whisk until smooth. Cook, stirring constantly, 1 minute. Add the saffron and gradually whisk in the milk; cook, stirring constantly, until smooth and thickened, 5 to 7 minutes. Lower the heat and season the custard with nutmeg, salt, and white pepper; cook 5 minutes more. Whisk together the ricotta, eggs, and lemon zest, then whisk this mixture into the hot custard sauce until smooth.

6. To assemble the pastitsio, have ready a large 4-quart round, oval, or square casserole. Cover the bottom of the casserole with half of the lamb sauce. Top with all the pasta and then the remaining lamb sauce. Spread the saffron custard over the top and sprinkle with the 1½ cups Kasseri cheese. (The pastitsio may be made ahead up to this point and refrigerated for a day before baking. When ready to bake, have the casserole at room temperature.)

7. Bake the casserole until lightly browned and bubbly, 45 to 50 minutes. Let cool 10 minutes before serving.

Makes 12 to 15 servings

Good cooking is the result of a balance struck between frugality and liberality. . . . It is born out in communities where the supply of food is conditioned by the seasons.

Once we lose touch with the spendthrift aspect of nature's provisions epitomized in the raising of a crop, we are in danger of losing touch with life itself. When Providence supplies the means, the preparation and sharing of food takes on a sacred aspect. The fact that every crop is of short duration promotes a spirit of making the best of it while it lasts and conserving part of it for future use . . . .

Poverty rather than wealth gives the good things of life their true significance.

— Patience Gray
Honey from a Weed

Bolognese Sauce

— ✤ —

This basic Italian meat sauce has withstood the test of time and many a newfangled pasta innovation. I have always been a fan of this *ragù* and like it best dolloped generously over thick strands of spaghetti or plump tubes of mostaccioli. Serve on an icy sub-zero night when food provides primal satisfaction.

½ cup dried mushrooms
1 cup boiling water
3 tablespoons unsalted
   butter
4 ounces pancetta or bacon,
   cut into ¼-inch dice
3 thin slices prosciutto,
   minced
2 large onions, chopped
3 cloves garlic, minced
3 carrots, peeled and minced
2 ribs celery, minced
8 ounces lean ground beef

8 ounces ground veal
8 ounces lean ground pork
2 cups dry white wine
2 cans (35 ounces each)
   plum tomatoes,
   undrained
1 teaspoon grated nutmeg
Salt and freshly ground
   black pepper to taste
4 raw chicken livers, cut
   into ½-inch dice
1 cup heavy or whipping
   cream

1. Place the dried mushrooms in a small bowl, cover with the boiling water, and let soak while the sauce is being prepared.

2. Melt the butter in a large heavy pot over medium heat. Add the pancetta and cook until lightly browned, 5 to 7 minutes. Stir in the prosciutto and cook 1 minute more.

3. Stir in the onions, garlic, carrots, and celery; sauté, stirring occasionally, until softened, about 10 minutes.

4. Stir in the beef, veal, and pork. Cook, crumbling the meat with a wooden spoon, just until the meat begins to lose its pink color. Add the wine, bring to a boil, and cook until the liquid is almost completely reduced.

5. Drain the soaked mushrooms, reserving the liquid (strain it if it's sandy). Coarsely chop the mushrooms and add them to the sauce along with the soaking liquid. Coarsely chop the tomatoes and add with their liquid to the sauce.

6. Season the sauce with the nutmeg, salt, and pepper. Simmer uncovered over low heat, stirring occasionally 1¼ hours. Add the chicken livers. Increase the heat to bring the sauce just to a boil and simmer 5 minutes. Just before serving, stir in the cream.

Makes about 2 quarts (enough for 2 pounds pasta)

Artist's Arrabbiata

— ❖ —

My artist friend Sterling, former croissant baker and fortune-teller at Que Sera Sarah, learned to make this magnificent yet simple pasta dish when living and painting in Florence. In Italian, *arrabbiata* means "angered" or "enraged" and refers to the infusion of hot red pepper flakes in olive oil.

When Sterling paid an off-season visit to Nantucket to personally teach me how to enrage my own kitchen, she surprised me with an after-dinner gift of an unusual, three-dimensional painting of a piece of cake. Since the painting was neither titled nor signed we both agreed that the scrawling of "After the Arrabbiata" across the back of the canvas would serve as sufficient historic documentation.

Sterling notes that the recipe is quick to assemble and thereby ideally suited to the spontaneity of feeding starving artist friends.

⅓ cup plus 2 tablespoons fruity olive oil
6 large cloves garlic, peeled and cut into coarse slivers
½ to 1 teaspoon dried red pepper flakes (according to mood)
12 ripe plum tomatoes, cut into quarters
Salt to taste
4 ounces pancetta (optional)
12 ounces penne
1 cup freshly grated Parmesan or Pecorino Romano cheese

1. Heat ⅓ cup olive oil in a skillet over medium-high heat. Add the garlic and sauté until golden, 3 to 5 minutes. Stir in the red pepper flakes and cook 1 minute more. Add the tomatoes and simmer over medium heat, stirring occasionally, until the tomatoes cook down and the sauce has thickened, about 15 minutes. Season to taste (rather generously) with salt.

2. Meanwhile, if you are adding pancetta, cook it in a skillet over medium heat until crisp, 10 to 12 minutes. Drain, then crumble the pancetta.

3. Cook the penne in a large pot of salted boiling water until al dente. Drain and toss with the remaining 2 tablespoons olive oil. Divide among 4 serving plates. Top each portion with an ample amount of sauce, a generous sprinkling of Parmesan, and some crumbled pancetta if using. Serve at once with crusty bread and a green salad.

Makes 4 servings.

Pasta with Gorgonzola and Spinach

— ❖ —

This recipe pays homage to one of my fondest food memories from youthful travels in Italy. Rome has always been my favorite Italian city and on my first trip there, I wandered off one evening in search of a reasonable meal and found a little family-run restaurant tucked into a narrow alley. The menu did not have the extensive array of pasta dishes of other more fashionable restaurants and offered but one pasta selection — the house specialty of pasta with Gorgonzola cream. I have never forgotten how delicious it tasted and my quest to re-create it recently ended in my own kitchen.

4 tablespoons (½ stick)
  unsalted butter
8 ounces sweet Gorgonzola
  cheese, crumbled into
  small pieces
1¼ cups heavy or whipping
  cream
8 ounces fresh spinach,
  stemmed, rinsed well, and
  coarsely chopped

1 cup freshly grated
  Parmesan cheese
Salt and freshly ground
  black pepper to taste
1 pound spaghetti or penne
3 tablespoons pine nuts,
  lightly toasted

1. Melt the butter in a heatproof casserole large enough to hold the cooked pasta over medium heat. Gradually add the Gorgonzola and stir until melted and smooth. Add the cream and cook, stirring frequently, until the sauce has thickened, about 10 minutes. Reduce the heat to very low.

2. In the meantime, cook the pasta in a large pot of boiling salted water until al dente. Drain.

3. Add the spinach and ½ cup of the Parmesan to the sauce, stirring just until the spinach begins to wilt. Quickly add the hot pasta and toss to coat. Serve at once garnished with the pine nuts and the remaining Parmesan.

Makes 4 to 6 servings

Fusilli with Broccoli, Sicilian Style

— ✢ —

It is often difficult to impart depth of flavor into pasta dishes based on vegetables without the addition of meat or a thick tomato sauce. This recipe borrows from the seemingly incongruous ingredients of Sicilian cuisine, like the combination of anchovies with golden raisins, to achieve a rich, complex, and hauntingly delicious result. I would be happy making and eating this fusilli at least once a week during the winter months.

*1 large bunch broccoli,
  trimmed and cut into
  florets and 1-inch stem
  pieces*
½ cup fruity olive oil
*1 bunch (3 to 4) leeks
  (white and tender
  green parts), trimmed,
  rinsed well, and minced*
4 cloves garlic, minced
*1 heaping tablespoon
  anchovy paste*
*Pinch of saffron
  threads*

*8 sun-dried tomatoes
  packed in oil, drained
  and minced*
½ cup golden raisins
⅓ cup pine nuts
12 ounces dried fusilli
*4 ounces Pecorino Romano
  cheese, freshly grated,
  about 1 cup*
*Salt and freshly ground
  black pepper to taste*

1. Blanch, steam, or microwave the broccoli just until slightly undercooked. Drain and set aside.

2. Heat ¼ cup of the olive oil in a large skillet over medium-high heat. Add the leeks and sauté until quite soft, about 10 minutes. Add the garlic and sauté 1 minute more. Stir in the anchovy paste, saffron, sun-dried tomatoes, raisins, and pine nuts. Cook over low heat to blend the flavors, 5 to 6 minutes. Stir in the reserved broccoli.

3. In the meantime, cook the pasta in a large pot of salted boiling water until al dente. Just before draining, ladle ¾ cup of the pasta cooking water into the vegetable sauce. Drain the pasta thoroughly.

4. Toss the hot pasta with the sauce, mixing in the remaining ¼ cup olive oil and the grated Romano cheese. Season to taste with salt and pepper. (The dish may not need salt since both the anchovies and cheese are salty.) Serve at once.

Makes 4 servings

> *U*sually, at this hour, the snowfall stopped, as though to have a look at what it had done; a like effect was produced by the rare days when the storm ceased, and the uninterrupted power of the sun sought to thaw away the pure and lovely surface from the new-fallen masses. The sight was at once fairylike and comic, an infantine fantasy. The thick light cushions plumped up on the boughs of trees, the humps and mounds of snow-covered rock cropping or undergrowth, the droll, dwarfish, crouching disguise all ordinary objects wore, made of the scene a landscape in gnome-land, an illustration for a fairytale. Such was the immediate view — wearisome to move in, quaintly, roguishly stimulating to the fancy. But when one looked across the intervening space, at the towering marble statuary of the high Alps in full snow, one felt quite a different emotion, and that was awe of their majestic sublimity.
> — Thomas Mann
> The Magic Mountain

Baked Beans with an Apple Rum Crust

— ❖ —

Since I was born and raised in the heart of Yankee baked-bean country, I researched long and hard before undertaking this recipe. People who harbor strong opinions about the proper way to bake beans will often object to either sweetening with too much molasses, adding chopped onions to the bean mixture, or the seemingly unhealthy burial of a juicy slab of salt pork in the center of the pot. In my quest for perfection, I discovered that I not only liked all of the above, but also enjoyed the added embellishment of topping the bean pot with a crust of sliced apples, rum, and brown sugar.

Making baked beans epitomizes old-fashioned slow cooking. After a long Friday night and Saturday day of soaking and simmering, the beans make a satisfying weekend supper accompanied by grilled sausages and brown bread.

1 pound navy or white pea
  beans
1 large onion, minced
2 cloves garlic, minced
2 tablespoons minced fresh
  ginger
2 tablespoons tomato paste
2 tablespoons balsamic
  vinegar
⅔ cup dark molasses

1 tablespoon dry mustard
1½ teaspoons salt
1 bottle (12 ounces) beer
8 ounces salt pork (in one
  chunk)
8 whole cloves

APPLE RUM CRUST

2 large Granny Smith
  apples, peeled, cored, and
  thinly sliced
4 tablespoons (½ stick)
  unsalted butter,
  melted

¼ cup (packed) light
  brown sugar
¼ cup dark rum

1. At least one day before serving the beans, pick over the beans for pebbles, place them in a large bowl, cover with cold water, and let soak overnight.

2. The next day rinse and drain the beans. Place them in a pot and cover with fresh water. Bring to a boil, then simmer uncovered until the beans are barely tender and the skins begin to pop, about 45 minutes. Drain the beans, reserving the cooking liquid.

3. Preheat the oven to 300°F.

4. Place the cooked beans in a 2-quart casserole. Add the onion, garlic, ginger, tomato paste, vinegar, molasses, dry mustard, and salt; stir to mix well. Add the beer and enough of the reserved cooking liquid to cover the beans generously. Score the salt pork in a grid pattern with a sharp knife. Stick the whole cloves at random into the salt pork and bury it in the center of the beans.

5. Cover the casserole and bake 5 hours, giving the beans a stir every now and again. Add more of the reserved cooking liquid if necessary to keep the beans just covered with liquid.

6. Uncover the beans. Arrange the apple slices in concentric circles (as if you were making an apple tart) over the top of the beans. In a small bowl stir together the melted butter, brown sugar, and rum until smooth. Pour over the apple slices. Bake the beans uncovered for another hour. Serve hot. (The beans are also excellent reheated in the days to follow.)

Makes 6 servings

Dolly Parton Polenta

— ✤ —

If you have ever gone through the culinary exercise of making polenta from scratch, you will immediately understand the name of this recipe. It just so happens that the intensive and relentless stirring of this cornmeal mush seems to do wonders for the pectorals. I limit myself to making no more than one batch of polenta every two months thereby lessening my chances of competing with the singer herself for any titles.

4 ounces pancetta, finely
   diced
2 tablespoons olive oil
3 cloves garlic, minced
1½ pounds kale, stemmed
   and coarsely chopped
Salt and freshly ground
   black pepper to taste
1½ cups fine yellow
   cornmeal

1 cup water
4 cups chicken broth,
   preferably homemade
2 tablespoons unsalted
   butter
⅔ cup freshly grated
   Parmesan cheese
2 cups shredded Gruyère or
   Italian Fontina cheese

    1. Cook the pancetta in a large heavy skillet over medium heat, stirring frequently, until browned and crisp. Remove from the skillet and drain on paper towels. Discard the fat.

    2. Add the olive oil and garlic to the skillet and cook over medium heat 1 minute. Add the kale. Cook, stirring frequently, just until the leaves are tender, 5 to 7 minutes. Toss the kale with the pancetta in a mixing bowl. Season to taste with salt and pepper. Set aside.

    3. In a heavy 2-quart saucepan, stir together the cornmeal and water to make a smooth, thick paste. Very slowly add the broth, stirring constantly with a wooden spoon, so that there are no lumps and the mixture is smooth.

4. Cook the polenta over medium-low heat, stirring constantly, until the mixture is quite thick and begins to pull away from the side of the pan, about 25 minutes. Stir in the butter and Parmesan. Remove from the heat.

5. While the polenta is cooling, preheat the oven to 350°F. Generously butter a 2-quart gratin dish.

6. Spoon one-third of the polenta into the prepared dish. Top with half the kale mixture and one-third of the shredded cheese. Make another layer in the same fashion, then top with the remaining polenta and cheese.

7. Bake until the cheese is lightly browned and bubbling, 30 to 40 minutes. Let cool a few minutes, then serve.

Makes 6 to 8 servings

THE BRUMAL FIRE of the VIANDS

"Cooking is an art, not a science. You perform it by doing it, living it, not by reading about it in a book. It is sculpture of the soul. A good cook works by the fire of imagination, not merely by the oak fire or beech fire in the stove."
— Robert P. Tristram Coffin
Mainstays of Maine

Searing viands over a fire is the oldest cooking technique known to mankind, and grilling over the glowing embers in a winter fireplace approximates methods of prehistoric cuisine better than any other form of cookery. While the recent grilling craze has produced a truly mind-boggling array of all-weather equipment from portable hibachis and futuristic-looking kettles to motorized rotisseries and electric and gas grills, I prefer the romance and communal fun of gathering indoors around an open fire on a crisp and starry winter evening. Fireplace cookery lures the cook from exile in the kitchen into the living room and creates the entertaining aura of a relaxed picnic, with the added bonus of being surrounded by all the creature comforts of home.

A once frustrated Girl Scout, I have started many a blazing fire by cheating with a prefabricated log or stack of old newspapers; but this is a real no-no when building an indoor fire for cooking. For hearth cookery it is important both to have a fireplace that draws well and to burn hardwoods, such as hickory, oak, birch, maple, and fruitwoods. Packaged hardwood lump charcoals may be used, but under no circumstances should chemical-laden charcoal briquettes be burned indoors. While dancing flames are great for throwing off heat or providing dramatic reading light, they must subside into the steady sunset glow of coals before indoor grilling may commence.

My fireplace grilling equipment is makeshift to say the least, but it conspires to heighten the primitive elements of the experience. Once the coals are burned down and hot, I place a few bricks or cement slabs on either side of the embers to act as a support for a wire grilling rack—usually the one borrowed from my outdoor summer grill. The proximity of the rack to the coals is adjusted simply by adding or subtracting support blocks. Other useful equipment worth mentioning includes padded asbestos oven mitts, metal spatulas, basting brushes, and long stainless-steel tongs for the easy turning of steaks, chops, and brochettes.

Cooking over an indoor fire is not an exact art, but it is a creative one that carries with it a maximum of warmth and cheer. Modesty aside, I find the recipes in this chapter magnificent as well as distinctly endowed with a hearty winter quality. Modern chefs and homemakers just may be tempted to revert to the Colonial practice of always keeping the home fires burning.

Jamaican Jerked Chicken

Jerking is a uniquely Jamaican cooking technique in which meat or fish is marinated in a spicy paste of scallions, allspice berries, cinnamon, nutmeg, and chiles and then cooked very slowly over a low fire, often made from the native allspice, or pimento wood as it is known in the Caribbean. As the meat grills, it is frequently turned over—or jerked—a motion which many say gave the dish its odd name.

One March my friend Toby from Baltimore and I took off to a spa in Jamaica to unwind from life's stresses and excesses. As we became bronzed, relaxed, and aerobically fit, we began to hunger for the native street food that the spa staff spoke of. So one day Toby and I snuck away to the town of Ocho Rios for a jerked feast. We were not disappointed as we sat devouring our jerked half chicken to the bone and soothing the fiery flavor with cool Red Stripe beer. As for ruining our calorie-conscious spa diet for the day, we quickly adopted the Jamaican attitude of "Don't worry, be happy!" Concocting a batch of my very own jerked chicken now makes me very happy, indeed.

2½ tablespoons whole
   allspice berries
1 bunch scallions, trimmed
   and finely minced
2 cloves garlic, minced
1 teaspoon ground
   cinnamon
½ teaspoon grated nutmeg
4 bay leaves, coarsely
   chopped

3 small serrano chiles,
   seeded and finely minced
3 tablespoons white wine
   vinegar
½ cup olive oil
1½ teaspoons salt
½ teaspoon freshly ground
   black pepper
2 frying chickens, cut into
   quarters

1. To make the jerk marinade, toast the allspice berries in a small heavy skillet over medium heat until aromatic and heated through, about 3 minutes. Crush the allspice berries in a mortar and pestle until all are coarsely cracked.

2. In a medium-size bowl combine the crushed berries with the scallions, garlic, cinnamon, nutmeg, bay leaves, and serrano chiles. Stir in the vinegar and olive oil, then season with the salt and pepper.

3. Place the chicken in a single layer in a shallow glass dish and cover with the marinade. Let marinate in the refrigerator, turning the pieces occasionally, at least 4 hours or as long as overnight.

4. Prepare the fireplace or grill for cooking.

5. Grill the chicken at least 6 inches above the hot coals, turning the pieces every 10 minutes, until done, 1 to 1¼ hours. If you want, add 1 tablespoon whole allspice berries to the fire halfway through the cooking time to approximate the flavor of the Jamaican wood. Serve the chicken hot off the grill with mugs of icy beer.

Makes 6 to 8 servings

DON'T WORRY, BE HAPPY

— ⋄ —

Black Bean Soup

— ⋄ —

Jamaican Jerked Chicken
Baked Stuffed Sweet Potatoes
Asparagus with Mustard Bread Crumbs

— ⋄ —

Pumpkin Crème Caramel

Grilled Chicken Breasts with Lemon and Rosemary

— ❖ —

This easy and succulently delicious recipe for chicken breasts is a year-round favorite of mine, but I find it offers a particularly cleansing break from hearty stews and casseroles in the middle of the winter. Accompany with Canadian Cranberry Confit (see Index) and steamed broccoli florets to feel healthy yet sated.

4 boneless, skinless whole chicken breasts
Salt and freshly ground black pepper to taste
½ cup fresh lemon juice

½ cup fruity olive oil
2 large cloves garlic, minced
3 tablespoons fresh rosemary, coarsely chopped

1. Arrange the chicken breasts in a single layer in a shallow glass or ceramic dish. Sprinkle with salt and pepper. Whisk the lemon juice, olive oil, garlic, and rosemary together in a small bowl and pour over the chicken breasts. Let marinate in the refrigerator, turning once or twice, at least 4 hours.
2. Prepare the fireplace or grill for cooking.
3. Grill the chicken breasts 5 to 6 inches above the hot coals 4 to 6 minutes per side, brushing with any marinade remaining in the dish. Serve at once.

Makes 4 servings

Chicken Liver Kabobs with Dried Fruit, Bacon, and Bay Leaves

— ❖ —

This preparation makes chicken livers simply irresistible and provides a scrumptious and unusual winter grill.

¾ cup dried pitted prunes
¾ cup dried apricots
18 whole bay leaves
12 ounces sliced bacon
1½ pounds chicken livers,
   trimmed and halved
1 tablespoon Dijon mustard

2 teaspoons anchovy paste
2 tablespoons cream sherry
3 tablespoons balsamic
   vinegar
½ cup olive oil
Salt and freshly ground
   black pepper to taste

1. Place the prunes and apricots in a small saucepan and add water to cover. Bring to a boil, then reduce the heat and simmer until softened, about 5 minutes. Drain and set aside.

2. Place the bay leaves in a small bowl and cover with boiling water. Let soak 5 minutes to soften; drain and set aside.

3. Prepare the fireplace or grill for cooking

4. Cut the bacon slices into lengths just long enough to wrap around each prune and apricot. Wrap all the prunes and apricots in bacon. Have ready 6 metal skewers. Thread one skewer first with a bacon-wrapped apricot, then a chicken liver half, then a bacon-wrapped prune, and finally a bay leaf. Repeat the process for 3 sets on each skewer.

5. In a small bowl whisk together the mustard, anchovy paste, sherry, and vinegar until smooth. Gradually whisk in the oil, then season to taste with salt and pepper. Brush the kabobs lightly with some of the vinaigrette.

6. Grill the kabobs about 4 inches above the hot coals, basting with the vinaigrette, until the bacon is crisp, 3 to 4 minutes on each side. Serve at once accompanied by rice pilaf.

Makes 6 servings

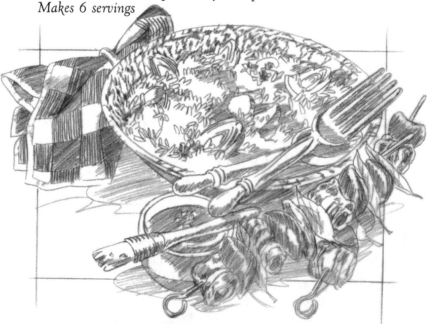

Butterflied Quail with Winter Citrus

— ❖ —

In the South, these pint-size game birds are often served for brunch to folks who have anything but birds' appetites.

CITRUS MARINADE
¼ cup fresh lemon juice
¼ cup fresh orange juice
3 tablespoons Dijon
   mustard
½ cup olive oil
½ cup Grand Marnier or
   other orange liqueur
2 cloves garlic, minced

1 tablespoon grated lemon zest
1 tablespoon grated orange
   zest
1 tablespoon dried Italian
   herb blend
Salt and freshly ground
   black pepper to taste

QUAIL
12 quail, 4 to 6 ounces each
3 navel oranges, peeled and
   sliced crosswise

2 limes, cut into wedges

1. Prepare the citrus marinade: In a small bowl whisk together the lemon juice, orange juice, and mustard until smooth. Gradually whisk in the olive oil, then stir in the Grand Marnier, garlic, lemon and orange zests, and Italian herb blend. Season with salt and pepper.

2. Using poultry shears, cut out the backbone of each quail and discard. Open up the birds and press down hard on the breastbones so the quail will lie flat. Rinse and pat dry.

3. Place the quail in a large dish or bowl and toss with the citrus marinade. Cover and marinate in the refrigerator, turning occasionally, at least 2 hours or as long as overnight.

4. Prepare the fireplace or grill for cooking.

5. Lift the quail from the marinade, reserving the liquid. Grill the quail 4 to 6 inches above the hot coals, turning and basting often with the marinade, until the juices run clear when the thigh is poked with a fork, 12 to 15 minutes.

6. Transfer the birds to a warmed serving platter. Arrange the orange slices in between the birds. Squeeze the juice from 1 of the limes over the quail; arrange the remaining lime wedges around the platter. Serve at once.

Makes 6 main-course or 12 first-course servings

SAME OLD FLAME

— ❖ —

Spanish Garlic Soup

— ❖ —

Loin Lamb Chops in a Rosy Marinade
Italian Rosemary Potatoes
Creamed Spinach
Braised Beets with Sherry Vinegar

— ❖ —

Nuits-Saint-Georges

— ❖ —

Bartlett Pear Tart

Loin Lamb Chops in a Rosy Marinade

— ❖ —

This recipe was inspired by a newspaper article on Mediterranean cooking with pomegranates. Though lured by the idea of adding exotic pomegranates to my winter cooking palette, I was deterred by the seemingly arduous task of extracting the juice called for in the recipes from the many-seeded fruit. Then I hit upon the idea of substituting Cape Cod cranberry juice for the pomegranate juice in this lamb chop marinade. The merger between native and Middle Eastern flavors proved to be a tasty one with the pomegranates still getting their play in the garnish.

1 cup cranberry juice
3 tablespoons fresh lemon
   juice
1/3 cup olive oil
2 teaspoons freshly ground
   black pepper
1 teaspoon salt
3 tablespoons fresh
   rosemary, coarsely chopped

2 cloves garlic, minced
1 tablespoon grated lemon
   zest
8 thick loin lamb chops, fat
   trimmed
3 tablespoons fresh
   pomegranate seeds for
   garnish

1. Make the marinade by combining the cranberry juice, lemon juice, olive oil, pepper, salt, rosemary, garlic, and lemon zest. Place the chops in a shallow glass dish and pour the marinade over them. Let marinade at room temperature, turning occasionally, 1 to 1½ hours.

2. Prepare the fireplace or grill for cooking.

3. Remove the chops from the marinade. Grill 4 to 5 inches above the hot coals, basting with the marinade and turning once, 10 to 12 minutes for medium-rare meat. Remove the lamb chops to a warmed serving platter and sprinkle with the pomegranate seeds. Serve at once.

Makes 4 to 6 servings

Lamb Burgers

— ❖ —

When I was a little girl my very favorite food was a cheeseburger. Now, I have a great weakness for lamb burgers. These are two different and delicious recipes that I find especially tasty when the extra effort is taken to grill them over a fire. Long live the lamb burger!

Middle Eastern Lamb Burgers

— ❖ —

½ cup dried apricots,
  coarsely slivered
1 cup boiling water
2 pounds lean ground lamb
1 bunch scallions, trimmed
  and minced
¼ cup pine nuts, lightly
  toasted

1 tablespoon ground
  cinnamon
½ teaspoon grated nutmeg
Salt and freshly ground
  black pepper to taste

1. Prepare the fireplace or grill for cooking.

2. Place the apricots in a small bowl and cover with the boiling water. Let soak 5 minutes to soften, then drain.

3. Combine the apricots with the ground lamb, scallions, and pine nuts. Season the mixture with the cinnamon, nutmeg, salt, and pepper. Form into 8 patties.

4. Grill the lamb burgers about 4 inches above the hot coals, to desired doneness. Serve the burgers plain or tucked into a pocket of pita bread.

Makes 8 lamb burgers

Lamb Burgers with Cilantro and Chèvre

2 pounds lean ground lamb	Salt and freshly ground
2 cloves garlic, minced	black pepper to taste
1 teaspoon dry mustard	4 ounces mild chèvre
½ cup cilantro leaves, (fresh coriander), minced	

1. Prepare the fireplace or grill for cooking.

2. Mix together the lamb, garlic, mustard, and cilantro until well combined. Season with salt and pepper. Divide the meat into 8 equal parts and divide the goat cheese into 8 equal nuggets.

3. Shape 1 part lamb mixture around each nugget of goat cheese, enclosing it completely, then shape it into a thick patty.

4. Grill the lamb burgers about 4 inches above the hot coals, to desired doneness. Serve the burgers plain or tucked into a bun with your favorite condiments.

Makes 8 lamb burgers

Pork Chops Italiano

A wonderfully aromatic yet straightforward recipe for marinated and grilled pork chops, which are especially tasty when cooked over hickory wood or chips. The combination of wood smoke with savory juniper, rosemary, and fennel is sure to evoke ravenous appetites in all who encounter a whiff of this Tuscan-inspired grill.

6 large center-cut pork
  chops, at least 1 inch
  thick
1 cup apple cider
¼ cup olive oil
20 juniper berries, crushed
2 large cloves garlic, peeled
3 tablespoons fresh
  rosemary, coarsely
  chopped

½ cup chopped fresh
  fennel, combination bulb
  and feathery tops
Salt and freshly ground
  black pepper to taste

1. Early in the day place the pork chops in a shallow glass dish large enough to hold them in a single layer. Pour the cider and olive oil over them and sprinkle evenly with the juniper. Mince 1 clove of the garlic and sprinkle over the meat. Cut the remaining garlic clove into 6 slivers and insert a sliver into the meat near the bone of each pork chop. Sprinkle with the rosemary and fennel; season with salt and pepper. Let marinate covered in the refrigerator several hours, turning the chops occasionally.

2. Prepare the fireplace or grill for cooking. Bring the pork chops to room temperature.

3. Grill the chops about 4 inches above the hot coals, basting occasionally with the marinade and turning once, until cooked through, 25 minutes. Serve at once.

Makes 6 servings

Strip Steaks with Bacon Lattice and Sun-Dried Tomato Butter

— ❖ —

This beef, bacon, and sun-dried tomato combination is a real winner. When I'm in a midwinter mood for an indulgent and satisfying steak dinner, this is the dish I crave. Serve it around the glow of the fire with a sizzling potato gratin, steamed Brussels sprouts, and a rich and assertive bottle of red wine, the sort that encourages philosophical reflection.

SUN-DRIED TOMATO BUTTER

¾ cup (1½ sticks) butter,
   at room temperature
1 tablespoon Dijon mustard
7 whole sun-dried tomatoes
   packed in oil, drained
   and minced

1 large clove garlic, minced
¼ cup minced fresh parsley
¼ cup freshly grated
   Parmesan cheese

STEAKS

6 strip steaks, 12 to 14
   ounces each and 1 inch
   thick
⅓ pound sliced bacon

1 tablespoon dry mustard
2 teaspoons salt
2 tablespoons coarsely
   cracked black pepper

1. Up to 1 week in advance of serving, prepare the sun-dried tomato butter: Process the butter and mustard in a food processor until smooth. Add the sun-dried tomatoes, garlic, parsley, and Parmesan. Pulse the machine on and off until the ingredients are just incorporated. Lay a large piece of plastic wrap out on a flat surface. Shape the butter into a 1-inch-thick log down the center of the wrap. Roll the plastic around the butter to enclose it completely and store in the refrigerator until ready to use.

2. Prepare the fireplace or grill for cooking.

3. To make the bacon lattice on the steaks, cut 3 deep diagonal slashes lengthwise and 2 slashes crosswise on the top of each steak with a sharp knife. Take care not to cut all the way through to the other side of the steaks. Cut the bacon into thin strips and insert them into the slashes to form a lattice. Mix together the dry mustard, salt, and pepper, and rub this mixture over both sides of the steaks.

4. Grill the steaks 3 to 4 inches above the hot coals, starting with the bacon side up and turning once, 10 to 12 minutes for medium-rare meat. As the steaks come off the grill, top each one with a 1-inch-thick slice of the tomato butter. Serve at once.

Makes 6 hearty servings.

Grilled Flank Steak with Ginger Béarnaise

— ❖ —

Lean and flavorful flank steak makes a great grilling choice for a cozy and informal fireside supper. The ginger béarnaise attests to how delectably inspired the blending of Eastern flavors with classic techniques of Western cuisine can be.

½ cup tamari soy sauce
¼ cup vegetable oil
1 tablespoon Oriental
  sesame oil
1 clove garlic, minced
2 tablespoons minced fresh
  ginger

3 scallions, trimmed and
  minced
1 flank steak, about 2
  pounds
Salt and freshly ground
  black pepper to taste

GINGER BEARNAISE
1 shallot, minced
2 tablespoons minced fresh
  ginger
3 tablespoons dry vermouth
2 tablespoons rice wine
  vinegar
½ teaspoon freshly ground
  black pepper

4 large egg yolks, at room
  temperature
¾ cup (1½ sticks) unsalted
  butter
¼ cup cilantro leaves (fresh
  coriander), minced
Salt to taste

1. In a small bowl whisk together the tamari and vegetable and sesame oils. Stir in the garlic, ginger, and scallions. Rub the steak lightly all over with salt and pepper. Place in a shallow glass dish and cover with the marinade. Let marinate at room temperature 1½ to 2 hours or covered in the refrigerator overnight.

2. Prepare the fireplace or grill for cooking.

3. Meanwhile prepare the ginger béarnaise: Bring the shallot, ginger, vermouth, vinegar, and pepper to a boil in a small saucepan; continue boiling until almost all the liquid has evaporated, 3 to 4 minutes. Place the egg yolks in a food processor and process quickly just to blend. Add the reduced mixture and pulse the machine just to combine.

4. Melt the butter in a small saucepan over medium heat until it is hot but not browned. With the food processor running, add a few

drops of the butter through the feed tube, then pour in the rest in a thin, steady stream. Season the béarnaise with the cilantro and salt. Transfer to a small bowl and keep warm near the stove.

5. Grill the flank steak 4 to 5 inches above the hot coals, basting occasionally with the marinade and turning once, 8 to 10 minutes for rare meat. Cut the steak against the grain into thin slices and serve with the béarnaise drizzled over the slices.

Makes 4 to 6 servings

Grilled Sweetbreads with Mustard-Champagne Sauce

— ❖ —

I adore sweetbreads, and grilling them over a winter fire makes an enticing home preparation for those who usually confine their passion for this organ meat to restaurant dining. Sweetbreads have an affinity for smoky flavors, so they take naturally to the grill and the bacon which shares the skewer with them. The mustard-Champagne sauce completes the recipe with just the right amount of cream and contrast.

2 pairs of sweetbreads, about 1 pound each	1 tablespoon (or to taste) grainy mustard
8 slices lean bacon	Salt and freshly ground black pepper to taste
2 shallots, minced	¼ cup olive oil
¾ cup Champagne or other sparkling dry wine	2 tablespoons fresh lemon juice
1¼ cups heavy or whipping cream	

1. The day before serving, soak the sweetbreads in a bowl of cold water for 1 hour, changing the water 3 times. Drain, then place the sweetbreads in a saucepan and cover with fresh water. Bring just to a boil, then simmer the sweetbreads until they are firm to the touch, 10 to 12 minutes. Drain and cool. Place the sweetbreads flat on a tray or plate, cover with plastic wrap or waxed paper, and refrigerate overnight with a 2-pound weight on top. (A brick or a couple of wine bottles works well.)

2. The following day, prepare the fireplace or grill for cooking. Lightly oil a grilling rack.

3. Remove and discard the membranes and connective tissues from the sweetbreads; separate them into bite-size globules. Fry the bacon in a heavy skillet over medium-low heat until it turns translucent but not brown, 2 to 3 minutes. Drain on paper towels. Thread 2 slices bacon and 8 to 10 pieces of sweetbreads onto each of 4 metal skewers, looping the bacon strips loosely around the sweetbread pieces.

4. To make the mustard-Champagne sauce, combine the shallots and Champagne in small saucepan. Bring to a boil and continue to boil until the Champagne is reduced to 2 tablespoons, 5 to 7 minutes. Add the cream and slowly boil the mixture until the cream is reduced by half and the sauce is thickened, about 10 minutes. Swirl in the mustard and season with salt and pepper. Keep warm over low heat while the sweetbreads are grilling.

5. Whisk together the olive oil and lemon juice and brush lightly over the sweetbread skewers. Grill the skewers 4 to 5 inches above the hot coals, turning frequently, until crisp and golden brown, 8 to 10 minutes.

6. Arrange the skewers on a serving platter and drizzle with the mustard sauce. Serve at once.

Makes 4 servings

Sardinian Mixed Grill

— ❖ —

A delicious combination of shrimp, chicken, and sausage threaded on bamboo skewers and then grilled, will satisfy those eaters who can't quite decide if it is poultry, pork, or seafood that strikes their fancy. Be sure to soak the bamboo skewers in water for 15 minutes prior to assembling the kabobs to prevent them from burning on the grill.

12 ounces sweet Italian
   sausage links
12 ounces hot Italian
   sausage links
1½ pounds boneless,
   skinless chicken breasts,
   cut into 1-inch chunks
1 pound medium shrimp,
   shelled and deveined

⅓ cup fresh lemon juice
½ cup olive oil
2 cloves garlic, minced
1 tablespoon dried oregano
Salt and freshly ground
   black pepper to taste

1. Place the sweet and hot Italian sausages together in a large skillet and cover with water. Bring to a boil, then simmer over medium heat until the sausages are no longer pink, 8 to 10 minutes. Drain the sausages and cut into ¾-inch slices.

2. Thread 2 each chicken chunks, sausage, and shrimp alternately on each of 16 to 18 bamboo skewers. Arrange in a single layer in a large shallow glass dish.

3. In a small bowl whisk together the lemon juice, olive oil, garlic, and oregano. Season with salt and pepper. Pour the marinade over the skewers and let marinate at room temperature, turning occasionally, 45 minutes.

4. Meanwhile prepare the fireplace or grill for cooking.

5. Grill the skewers 4 inches above the hot coals, basting occasionally and turning once, until the meat and shrimp are browned on the outside and just cooked through inside, 6 to 8 minutes. Serve hot as an appetizer or light dinner.

Makes 16 to 18 skewers

Swordfish au Poivre

— ✠ —

This fantastic swordfish recipe is a cross between the cast-iron cookery of our Colonial ancestors and the blackening techniques of Cajun cooking. A large well-seasoned cast-iron skillet that can be heated over glowing coals to the point of being red-hot is essential to the success of this recipe.

½ cup (1 stick) unsalted
  butter, at room
  temperature
Grated zest of 1 lemon
½ cup minced fresh chives
2 tablespoons capers,
  drained

2 tablespoons dry mustard
2 tablespoons coarsely
  cracked black pepper
2 pounds swordfish steaks,
  cut into eight ½-inch-
  thick scaloppine pieces
Lemon wedges for serving

1. Prepare the fireplace or grill for cooking.

2. In a small bowl blend together the butter, lemon zest, chives, and capers. Set aside.

3. Combine the dry mustard and pepper and rub generously over both sides of the swordfish pieces.

4. When the coals are hot, place a 12-inch cast-iron skillet on a

rack placed 2 to 3 inches above the coals. Heat the skillet until red-hot. Add half the lemon butter to the skillet and then half the fish. Fry quickly to blacken it, about 1 minute per side. Keep the first batch of fish warm in a low oven and cook the remaining fish in the same manner with the remaining butter. Pour any blackened butter in the skillet over all the fish. Serve at once accompanied by lemon wedges.

Makes 4 servings

Grilled Tuna with Florida Avocado Butter

— ❖ —

Smooth-skinned Florida avocados are at their peak during chilly winter months and become all the more silky and rich when blended with sweet butter in this flavorful and unusual topping for grilled fish. While the avocado butter is great with tuna, it would also offer striking contrast to grilled pink salmon steaks for a fanciful early spring dinner.

5 tablespoons French Lillet
  or other dry white
  vermouth
5 tablespoons soy sauce
3 tablespoons light brown
  sugar

1 tablespoon Oriental
  sesame oil
6 tuna steaks, 6 to 8
  ounces each and about 1
  inch thick

AVOCADO BUTTER
¾ cup (1½ sticks) unsalted
  butter, at room
  temperature
1 ripe medium Florida
  avocado, pitted, peeled,
  and quartered
1 jalapeño chili, seeded and
  minced

3 tablespoons minced
  cilantro leaves (fresh
  coriander)
1½ tablespoons fresh lime
  juice
Salt to taste
1 lime, cut into wedges

1. In a small bowl mix together the Lillet, soy, brown sugar, and sesame oil. Pour the marinade over the tuna steaks in a noncorrosive shallow pan and let marinate in the refrigerator at least 3 hours.

2. Prepare the fireplace or grill for cooking. Lightly oil the grill rack.

3. Grill the fish 3 to 4 inches above the hot coals, basting with the marinade and turning once, until just cooked through, 9 to 10 minutes.

4. While the fish is grilling, prepare the avocado butter: (The butter is made at the last minute because the avocado will turn brown if it sits too long.) Place the butter and avocado in a food processor and process until smooth. Add the jalapeño, cilantro, and lime juice; process to incorporate. Season with salt.

5. Spoon a generous mound of the avocado butter onto each tuna steak as it comes off the grill. Serve at once with lime wedges.

Makes 6 servings

Shark Steaks with Fruit Salsa

— ❖ —

Consuming shark may seem better suited to double entendre in Tom Wolfe's *Bonfire of the Vanities* than to inclusion in my winter grilling chapter. Yet this splendid preparation is likely to make nervous swimmers appreciate this fearsome predator in its subdued state. If the thought of biting back at Jaws still induces trepidation, the recipe is equally delicious with salmon, swordfish, or tuna.

FRUIT SALSA

2 cups fresh or drained canned unsweetened pineapple, cut into ½-inch dice

1 ripe small avocado, pitted, peeled, and cut into ½-inch dice

3 tablespoons fresh lime juice

½ red bell pepper, stemmed, seeded, and diced

3 scallions, trimmed and minced

½ teaspoon dried red pepper flakes

⅓ cup minced cilantro leaves (fresh coriander)

2 tablespoons fruity olive oil

Salt to taste

SHARK

6 shark steaks, about 8 ounces each and 1 inch thick

2 tablespoons olive oil

Salt and freshly ground black pepper to taste

1. Prepare the fruit salsa: Toss the pineapple and avocado with the lime juice in a mixing bowl. Stir in the bell pepper, scallions, red pepper flakes, and cilantro. Mix in the olive oil and season with salt. Let sit at room temperature for 30 minutes to mellow the flavors.

2. Meanwhile prepare the grill or fireplace for cooking.

3. Brush the shark steaks lightly on both sides with the olive oil and season with salt and pepper. Grill the fish 4 to 5 inches above the hot coals, turning once, until just cooked through, 8 to 10 minutes. Serve the grilled steaks at once, topped with a liberal serving of the fruit salsa.

Makes 6 servings

Seared Squid with Tamari Beurre Blanc

— ⬧ —

I love the exotic look of grilled whole squid on a dinner plate. The Asian flavors of the marinade and sauce impart a silky counterpoint to the texturally intense squid.

MARINADE
½ cup sake (Japanese wine)
¼ cup soy sauce
¼ cup mirin (sweet rice cooking wine)

2 pounds medium to large squid, cleaned

TAMARI BEURRE BLANC
1 shallot, minced
1 tablespoon finely minced fresh ginger
¼ cup dry sherry
1 tablespoon rice wine vinegar

2 tablespoons tamari soy sauce
1¼ cups (2½ sticks) unsalted butter, cut into tablespoons

1. At least 1 hour before serving, marinate the squid: Whisk together the sake, soy, and mirin. Separate the tentacles from the squid body sacs by cutting them off just above the eyes of the squid. Toss both the tentacles and squid bodies with the marinade; let stand 45 minutes.

2. Prepare the fireplace or grill for cooking.

3. Prepare the tamari beurre blanc: Place the shallot, ginger,

sherry, vinegar, and tamari in a medium-size skillet. Boil over medium-high heat until the liquid is reduced to 2 tablespoons, 5 to 7 minutes. Reduce the heat to very low. Whisk in the butter, tablespoon at a time, incorporating the first tablespoon before adding the next. Keep the sauce warm over very low heat while grilling the squid.

4. Grill the squid bodies on a fine-mesh grill about 3 inches above the hot coals, basting with the marinade 1½ to 2 minutes per side. Remove to a platter and keep warm. Grill the tentacles, turning frequently with tongs, until tender, about 2 minutes total. Arrange the grilled squid and tentacles on serving plates and drizzle generously with the beurre blanc. Seve at once.

Makes 4 to 6 servings

SEA SMOKE

— ❖ —

Curried Lentil Soup with Chutney Butter

— ❖ —

Seared Squid with Tamari Beurre Blanc
Mixed Winter Squash Provencal
Wild Rice and Cider Pilaf

— ❖ —

Fresh Pineapple
Pine Nut Macaroons

PISCEAN
PLATTERS

"More and more we lose our ability to think as poets think, across frontiers and consecrated limits. More and more we think—or are brainwashed into thinking—in terms of verifiable facts, like money, time, personal pleasure, established knowledge. One reason I love islands so much is that of their nature they question such lack of imagination; that properly experienced, they make us stop and think a little: why am I here, what am I about, what is it all about, what has gone wrong?" —John Fowles Islands

Though I have never been one to live and breathe by my daily horoscope, I do enjoy an armchair fascination with the coincidences of astrology. Stargazers are right on the mark when they talk about seaside places attracting schools of water signs. Census takers would be amazed by how many of us—Pisces, Cancer, and Scorpio—nestle together on Nantucket. However, not only am I a Pisces lured by island living, I am also a fish with an appetite for my own fishy kin. Culinary astrologers reveal that my sign breeds the most theatrical, flamboyant, and adventurous cooks in the zodiac. Taste my renditions of Spicy Lemon Shrimp, Cider-Steamed Mussels, and Sesame-Coated Catfish, and see if you don't find that planetary alignment can affect the recipe file.

Descending from the speculative galaxy back to sea level, I find fish has increased in popularity over the last decade as the interest in eating low-fat fresh foods has soared. And, fish in the winter is both welcome and wonderful. Portuguese Pork and Clams Alentejana, Seafood Pot Pie, and Stuffed Calamari Puttanesca shine as hearty feasts, while simple preparations such as Baked Haddock with Mustard Crumbs and Shrimp Fried Wild Rice offer light relief from a cold-weather diet of sturdy soups and stews.

Solar charts and rising signs aside, these recipes will keep seafood cooks in the mainstream with fish-loving friends.

❖

Seafood Pot Pie

— ❖ —

This is the sort of winter seafood fare that is hearty and homey yet also elegant. The crust is the same delicious cornmeal and cream cheese one that envelops my Pork and Apricot Empanadas; the tarragon-laced filling strikes a nice balance between root vegetables and rich scallops, shrimp, and cod fillets. A tossed salad and a bottle of Chardonnay will complete the feast quite handsomely.

CRUST

1 cup unbleached all-
   purpose flour
½ cup yellow cornmeal
Pinch of salt
½ cup (1 stick) unsalted
   butter, chilled, cut into
   small pieces

4 ounces cream cheese,
   chilled, cut into small
   pieces

FILLING

2 medium turnips
5 tablespoons unsalted
   butter
2 fat leeks (white and light
   green parts), trimmed,
   rinsed well, and cut into
   2-inch-long julienne
   strips
2 carrots, peeled and cut
   into 2-inch-long julienne
   strips
2 teaspoons dried tarragon
2 cups dry white wine
1 bottle (8 ounces) clam
   juice

1½ cups heavy or whipping
   cream
1 tablespoon unbleached
   all-purpose flour
1 tablespoon fresh lemon
   juice
Salt and freshly ground
   black pepper to taste
1 pound medium shrimp,
   shelled and deveined
8 ounces sea scallops, cut in
   half
1 pound fresh cod, cut into
   ½-inch chunks
½ cup shredded Swiss cheese

EGG WASH

1 large egg

1 tablespoon water

1. Prepare the crust: Place the flour, cornmeal, salt, butter, and cream cheese in a food processor and process just until the mixture begins to gather into a ball. Shape the dough into a disk, wrap in plastic wrap and refrigerate at least 1 hour.

2. Prepare the filling: Place the turnips in a small saucepan,

cover with water, and boil until tender, 15 to 20 minutes. Drain, peel, and cut into ⅜-inch dice. Set aside.

3. Melt 4 tablespoons of the butter in a large skillet over medium-high heat. Add the leeks and carrots; sauté 5 minutes. Stir in the tarragon and 1 cup of the wine. Reduce the heat to medium, cover the pan, and cook 10 minutes. Uncover, increase the heat, and cook until almost all the liquid has evaporated. Remove from the heat and set aside.

4. Place the clam juice, remaining 1 cup of wine, and the heavy cream in a saucepan. Bring to a boil over high heat, then reduce the heat to medium. Cook, stirring frequently, until the mixture coats a spoon heavily, about 20 minutes. Blend the flour into the remaining 1 tablespoon butter. Whisk this mixture into the sauce and cook until smooth and quite thick. Remove from the heat and add the lemon juice, salt, and pepper.

5. Combine the sauce with the diced turnips, sautéed leeks and carrots, and the raw shrimp, scallops, and cod.

6. Preheat the oven to 400°F. Butter a round, 2-quart baking dish.

7. Transfer the filling to the prepared baking dish. Sprinkle the Swiss cheese over the top.

8. On a lightly floured surface, roll the dough out about ¼ inch thick and in a circle about 1 inch larger than the top of the baking dish. Place the dough over the top of the dish and crimp the edges. Mix the egg and water and brush over the top of the dough, then slash several steam vents in the top.

9. Bake until the crust is golden brown, 40 to 45 minutes. Let sit 5 minutes, then cut into wedges and serve.

Makes 6 servings

HAPPY AS A CLAM

— ✧ —

My Brother's Brandade de Morue

— ✧ —

Portuguese Pork with Clams Alentejana
Mixed green salad
Tangerine-Rye Rolls

— ✧ —

Lemon Squares

Iced Almonds

Portuguese Pork with Clams Alentejana

— ❖ —

This zesty combination of meat and shellfish is my idea of a great winter "Piscean" platter. In Portugal the pork is marinated in a dense red pepper paste called *massa de pimentao*. When I made the dish for the first time, I went through the lengthy process of making authentic *massa* by air drying a small fortune of imported red bell peppers over a period of three days and then puréeing the pathetic amount of pulp that remained into the precious paste. While the resulting dish was truly superb, I have since discovered that a combination of good paprika and finely minced sun-dried tomatoes mixed with a little olive oil yields a reasonable facsimile, almost equal to the original rendition.

PORK AND MARINADE

1½ tablespoons olive oil
1 tablespoon best-quality sweet Hungarian paprika
2 tablespoons finely minced sun-dried tomatoes packed in oil
1 clove garlic, minced
1 teaspoon kosher (coarse) salt

¼ teaspoon dried red pepper flakes
2 tablespoons fresh lemon juice
2 pounds boneless pork loin, cut into ½-inch cubes
1 cup dry white wine
2 bay leaves

MAIN PREPARATION

3 tablespoons olive oil
1 large onion, chopped
2 cloves garlic, minced
2 medium tomatoes, seeded and coarsely chopped
1 tablespoon tomato paste
Salt and freshly ground black pepper to taste

2 dozen littleneck clams, scrubbed well and, if necessary, soaked to remove sand and grit
¼ cup minced cilantro (fresh coriander)
Lemon wedges for garnish

1. Early in the day of or the night before serving, marinate the pork: In a small bowl whisk together the olive oil, paprika, sun-dried tomatoes, and garlic to form a paste. Season with the salt, red pepper flakes, and lemon juice. Toss the pork cubes with the paste in a non-corrosive mixing bowl; then add the wine and bay leaves. Cover and marinate in the refrigerator at least 6 hours or overnight.

2. Remove the pork from the marinade, drain it very well, and reserve the marinade. Heat the olive oil in a large skillet over medium-high heat. Add the pork in batches and brown until nicely seared on all sides, about 10 minutes per batch. Set aside the cooked batches on a warmed platter. Add the onion and garlic to the skillet and sauté until softened and beginning to brown, 5 to 7 minutes. Stir in the tomatoes and tomato paste; cook a few minutes more.

3. Add the seared pork and reserved marinade to the skillet. Season with salt and pepper to taste. Cover the skillet and simmer the mixture over medium-low heat, stirring occasionally, until the pork is tender, about 30 minutes.

4. Arrange the clams on top of the pork mixture in the skillet. Cover the pan, increase the heat to medium, and cook just until the clams open, 12 to 15 minutes. Stir in the cilantro.

5. Ladle the pork and clams into wide, shallow soup bowls. Garnish with lemon wedges and serve at once. A tossed green salad and crusty loaf of warm bread make perfect accompaniments.

Makes 4 to 6 servings

Rhode Island Clam Casserole

— ✥ —

This is my addition to the popular repertoire of New England scalloped seafood dishes. Using the Sambuca Corn Bread for crumbs makes this version extraordinary. However, if you're too harried to make the bread from scratch, Pepperidge Farm corn-bread stuffing crumbs drizzled with 3 tablespoons Sambuca can be substituted in a pinch. In any event, this casserole is guaranteed to make its eaters happier than clams!

2½ cups Sambuca Corn
  Bread crumbs (see page
  233)
½ cup (1 stick) unsalted
  butter, melted
½ cup minced fresh parsley
4 cups diced clams

1¼ cups heavy or whipping
  cream
1 teaspoon salt
1 teaspoon freshly ground
  black pepper
½ teaspoon grated nutmeg
Pinch of cayenne pepper

1. Preheat the oven to 350°F. Butter a round and deep 1½-quart baking dish and set aside.

2. Mix the bread crumbs with the melted butter and parsley. Drain the clams, reserving the juice. Combine the juice with the

cream and season with salt, pepper, nutmeg, and cayenne.

3. Sprinkle one-third of the crumbs over the bottom of the pre-pared dish. Top with half the clams. Cover with another one-third of the crumbs, then top with the remaining clams. Sprinkle the remaining crumbs over the top and pour the cream mixture over all.

4. Bake the casserole until bubbling and golden brown, about 45 minutes. Serve hot.

Makes 6 servings

Clams Casino

— ❖ —

Clams Casino are pretty much a dime a dozen on restaurant menus in my neck of the woods, but finding a really superb rendition is a whole other story. I worked hard to make this version the very best that I had ever tasted, which, in turn, tempts me to make a meal of it rather than a mere appetizer. Add a rich Caesar salad and good loaf of hot bread, then sit back and enjoy a glimpse of "Piscean" heaven.

2 tablespoons bacon fat
3 tablespoons unsalted
  butter
1 bunch scallions, trimmed
  and minced
2 cloves garlic, minced
½ red bell pepper,
  stemmed, seeded, and
  minced
½ green bell pepper,
  stemmed, seeded, and
  minced
1 cup pulverized cheese
  Ritz Crackers
1 cup fresh white bread
  crumbs

3 tablespoons minced fresh
  parsley
1½ tablespoons fresh lemon
  juice
1 tablespoon brandy
¼ teaspoon cayenne pepper
Salt and freshly ground
  black pepper to taste
8 ounces sliced bacon
36 medium cherrystone
  clams on the half shell,
  freshly opened and
  loosened slightly

1. Heat the bacon fat and butter together in a skillet over medium-high heat. Add the scallions, garlic, and bell peppers; sauté until softened, about 3 minutes. Remove from the heat.

2. Blend together the cracker and bread crumbs in a mixing bowl. Stir in the sautéed vegetables, the parsley, lemon juice, and brandy. Season the mixture with cayenne, salt, and pepper.

3. When ready to cook the clams, preheat the broiler.

4. Blanch the bacon slices in a pot of boiling water 1 minute and drain. Arrange the clams on a rack or baking sheet. Top each clam with about 2 teaspoons of the crumb mixture. Cut the blanched bacon into 2-inch pieces and top each clam with a piece of bacon. Broil the clams about 4 inches from the heat until the crumbs are browned and the bacon is crisp, 3 to 4 minutes. Transfer to serving plates and devour immediately.

Makes 3 main-dish servings, 6 first-course servings, or 12 appetizer servings

Crabmeat Casserole

— ❖ —

In my catering business, I frequently receive requests for seafood casseroles so I came up with this simple, direct, and elegantly updated rendition.

4 tablespoons (½ stick) unsalted butter

1 bunch scallions, trimmed and minced

6 sun-dried tomatoes packed in oil, drained and minced

2 teaspoons dried tarragon

3 teaspoons Dijon mustard

1½ cups milk

½ cup heavy or whipping cream

1 large egg, lightly beaten

1 pound cooked crabmeat, picked over for shell and cartilage

2 tablespoons cream sherry

Salt and freshly ground white pepper to taste

1¼ cups fresh bread crumbs

1. Preheat the oven to 375°F. Butter a 1½-quart soufflé dish or casserole.

2. Melt 2 tablespoons of the butter in a medium-size saucepan over medium-high heat. Add the scallions and sauté until softened, about 3 minutes. Add the sun-dried tomatoes and tarragon; sauté another 2 minutes. Whisk in 2 teaspoons of the mustard, the milk, and cream. Bring to a boil, then simmer uncovered 5 minutes.

3. Beat a little of the hot milk mixture into the beaten egg, then beat this mixture back into the remaining milk mixture. Stir in the crabmeat and sherry; season with salt and white pepper. Cook over low heat until all is heated through, 2 to 3 minutes more.

4. Transfer the crabmeat mixture to the prepared dish. Melt the remaining 2 tablespoons butter and swirl in the remaining 1 teaspoon mustard. Toss with the fresh bread crumbs to coat, then sprinkle the crumbs over the top of the casserole.

5. Bake the crabmeat casserole until lightly browned and bubbling, 25 to 30 minutes. Serve at once.

Makes 4 servings

Stuffed Calamari Puttanesca

— ✤ —

Marcella Hazan once wrote that squid was created "to be an incomparable container of good things to eat." I couldn't agree more and this recipe is one of my very favorites. Stuffing the squid sacs can be a bit fussy and painstaking, but I guarantee the end result will deliver to lucky diners a spectrum of exquisite flavors and textures.

PUTTANESCA SAUCE

3 tablespoons olive oil
1 large onion, coarsely chopped
4 cloves garlic, minced
1 can (35 ounces) tomatoes
½ cup dry red wine
2 tablespoons dried oregano
Pinch of dried red pepper flakes
½ cup pitted black olives
⅓ cup capers, drained

1 can (2 ounces) anchovy fillets, drained and minced
6 sun-dried tomatoes packed in oil, drained and minced
Salt and freshly ground black pepper to taste
½ cup shredded fresh basil leaves

CALAMARI AND STUFFING

16 whole large squid (including tentacles), cleaned
3 tablespoons olive oil
1 medium onion, minced
4 cloves garlic, minced
¾ cup minced fennel bulb
3 ripe tomatoes, seeded and diced
1 tablespoon finely chopped lemon zest

1½ cups fresh bread crumbs
5 tablespoons freshly grated Parmesan cheese
¼ cup minced fresh parsley
3 tablespoons shredded fresh basil leaves
Salt and freshly ground black pepper to taste
1 large egg yolk

1. Prepare the puttanesca sauce: Heat the oil in a large saucepan over medium-high heat. Add the onion and garlic and sauté until softened, about 5 minutes. Stir in the tomatoes with their liquid, the wine, and all the remaining ingredients except the basil. Crush the tomatoes a bit with the back of a wooden spoon. Simmer, stirring occasionally, 40 minutes. Stir in the basil, taste and adjust the seasonings, and cook 5 minutes more. Remove from the heat and set aside.

2. Prepare the calamari and stuffing: Rinse the squid under cold running water and drain. Separate the tentacles from the body sacs. Finely chop the tentacles and reserve the sacs.

3. Heat the olive oil in a large skillet over medium-high heat. Add the onion, garlic, and fennel; sauté 5 minutes. Stir in the chopped squid tentacles and cook 10 minutes, stirring occasionally. Stir in the tomatoes and cook another 10 minutes. Add the remaining ingredients except the egg yolk and cook, stirring frequently, 3 minutes more. Remove from the heat and stir in the egg yolk.

4. Using a small spoon, stuff each squid sac three-quarters full with the stuffing. Secure each top closed with a wooden toothpick.

5. Preheat the oven to 325°F.

6. Arrange the squid in a single layer in a baking dish. Spoon the puttanesca sauce over top. Bake until the squid are tender, about 1 hour. Serve at once accompanied with plain risotto or pasta.

Makes 6 to 8 servings

Cider-Steamed Mussels with Crispy Bacon

—— ❖ ——

A superb way to make a meal of mussels in the middle of winter. Add a basket of warm rustic bread, a tossed salad, and a cozy fire.

1 large red onion, thinly sliced
1½ cups apple cider
3 pounds fresh mussels, scrubbed and bearded (see note)
¼ cup Calvados or brandy

1½ cups heavy or whipping cream
Freshly ground black pepper to taste
8 ounces sliced bacon, cooked crisp, drained, and crumbled
½ cup minced fresh parsley

1. Place the onion, cider, and mussels in a large pot with a tight-fitting lid. Cover, bring to a boil, and cook until the mussels open, 5 to 7 minutes. Transfer the mussels with a slotted spoon to a warmed serving dish, discarding any unopened ones. Cover the dish with a warm moistened kitchen towel to help retain the heat.

2. Add the Calvados and cream to the liquid remaining in the pot. Bring to a boil and continue boiling until the liquid is reduced by half, about 10 minutes. Season with pepper. Pour the cider cream over the mussels and mix in the bacon and parsley. Scoop the mussels into individual serving bowls and serve at once.

Makes 4 servings

Note: Do not beard the mussels in advance or they will spoil.

Bay Scallops Gremolata

— ✥ —

Red-skinned potatoes are chopped into a minute dice and sautéed in olive oil to serve as a crispy bed for plump bay scallops. The mix-ture is then enhanced by the zesty Italian garnish gremolata — a blend of lemon, parsley, and garlic — to create a lusciously elegant scallop hash.

> 2 large red-skinned
>   potatoes, scrubbed but
>   not peeled
> 7 tablespoons olive oil
> 1½ pounds fresh bay
>   scallops
> 1 tablespoon finely chopped
>   lemon zest
>
> 2 cloves garlic, minced
> ½ cup minced fresh parsley
> 3 tablespoons fresh lemon
>   juice
> Salt and freshly ground
>   black pepper to taste
> Lemon wedges for garnish
> Parsley sprigs for garnish

1. Cut the scrubbed potatoes into very tiny cubes (a little less than ¼ inch). Place in a colander, rinse, and drain very well.

2. Heat 5 tablespoons of the oil in a large skillet over medium-high heat. Add the potatoes and sauté, stirring frequently, until the potatoes are light golden brown and cooked through, 10 to 15 min-utes. Remove the potatoes from the skillet and set aside.

3. Add the remaining 2 tablespoons olive oil to the skillet and heat over medium-high heat. Add the scallops and cook, shaking the pan on top of the burner, until the scallops are lightly seared and

browned all over, about 3 minutes. Add the lemon zest and garlic to the pan and cook 1 minute more. Return the potatoes to the skillet along with the chopped parsley and stir to blend. Add the lemon juice and season with salt and pepper. Cook 1 minute more to warm through. Serve at once garnished with lemon wedges and parsley sprigs.

Makes 6 servings

Scallops with Apples, Walnuts, and Sauternes

— ❖ —

The natural sweetness of Nantucket bay scallops is beautifully highlighted by amber-colored Sauternes wine. Strips of Granny Smith apple and chunky toasted walnut halves round out the harmony in this elegant entrée.

1½ tablespoons extra virgin olive oil
1¼ pounds fresh bay scallops
3 tablespoons minced shallots
⅔ cup good-quality Sauternes or Barsac wine
5 tablespoons unsalted butter, chilled, cut into small pieces

½ Granny Smith apple, unpeeled, cut into thin matchstick strips
Salt and freshly ground black pepper to taste
½ cup walnut halves, lightly toasted

1. Preheat the oven to 275°F.
2. Heat the olive oil in a large skillet over high heat until very hot. Stir in the scallops and sauté, shaking the pan vigorously over the burner to sear the scallops on all sides, just until barely cooked through, 2 to 3 minutes. Remove to a platter with a slotted spoon and keep warm in the oven while preparing the sauce.
3. Add the shallots to the skillet and cook until softened, 1 min-

ute. Pour in the Sauternes and boil until reduced to 3 tablespoons, 7 to 10 minutes. Reduce the heat to the lowest possible setting. Whisk in the butter a little at a time; it should emulsify with the mixture rather than melt. When all the butter has been incorporated, add the apple strips and season the sauce with salt and pepper.

4. Return the scallops to the skillet and stir to coat with the sauce. Finally stir in the walnuts and serve at once.

Makes 4 servings

Pan-Fried Scallops with Mustard Glaze

— ❖ —

When I spent my first winter on Nantucket almost a decade ago, this was the way I prepared the local harvest of bay scallops. It proved to be the route to a favored fisherman's heart and remains a cherished recipe today.

2 tablespoons unsalted
  butter
1½ pounds fresh bay
  scallops
½ cup Champagne vinegar
  or white wine vinegar

½ cup heavy or whipping
  cream
2 tablespoons Dijon
  mustard
Salt and freshly ground
  black pepper to taste

1. Melt the butter in a large skillet over medium-high heat. Add the scallops and sauté until just opaque, 3 to 4 minutes. Remove the scallops to a warmed plate with a slotted spoon.

2. Add the vinegar to the skillet and cook over high heat until reduced to 2 tablespoons. Add the cream and any scallop juices that may have accumulated to the skillet. Cook over medium heat until the sauce is reduced and thick enough to coat the back of a spoon, 5 to 7 minutes. Swirl in the mustard and season the sauce to taste with salt and pepper.

3. Return the scallops to the skillet and stir to coat with the sauce. Spoon the scallops onto warmed serving plates and serve at once.

Makes 6 servings

Sprightly Sautéed Scallops

— ✤ —

Scallops combine equally well with both delicate and pronounced flavors. Sun-dried tomatoes may be trendy, but when combined with scallops they truly belong. The intense flavor of the tomatoes is further complemented and strengthened by fresh rosemary, shiitake mushrooms, and toasted pine nuts. The scallops, surprisingly, are the perfect vehicle for such a sanguine mélange.

¼ cup extra virgin olive oil
4 scallions, trimmed and
  minced
1 clove garlic, minced
1 cup sliced shiitake
  mushrooms
8 whole sun-dried tomatoes
  packed in oil, drained
  and minced

1½ tablespoons coarsely
  chopped fresh rosemary
½ cup dry white wine
Salt and freshly ground
  black pepper to taste
1½ pounds fresh bay
  scallops
3 tablespoons pine nuts,
  lightly toasted

1. Heat the olive oil in a large skillet over medium-high heat. Stir in the scallions and garlic and sauté until softened, about 2 minutes. Add the mushrooms, sun-dried tomatoes, rosemary, and wine. Cook the mixture, stirring occasionally, until the mushrooms are cooked through and the wine has evaporated, about 10 minutes. Season to taste with salt and pepper. Remove from the skillet and keep warm.

2. Return the skillet to the burner and increase the heat to high. Add the scallops and sauté, shaking the pan vigorously to sear the scallops on all sides, until just cooked through, 2 to 3 minutes. Reduce the heat to medium and return the sun-dried tomato mixture to the skillet. Stir in the toasted pine nuts and cook just a minute more to heat everything through. Serve at once.

Makes 4 servings

PISCEAN PLEASURES

— ❖ —

Baby Buckwheat Popovers with Pressed Caviar

— ❖ —

Spicy Lemon Shrimp, New Orleans Style
Scalloped Tomatoes
Risotto Primavera
French Bread

— ❖ —

Pear and Biscotti Strudel

Spicy Lemon Shrimp, New Orleans Style

— ❖ —

My friend Toby secured this fantastic recipe for shrimp from Manale's Restaurant in New Orleans. In general, I would never combine butter and margarine in a dish of this nature nor use Worcestershire and Tabasco sauces, but I decided to give in and follow some advice I came across in a Cajun-Creole cookbook. It said, "Cajun-Creole foods are steadfastly untrendy.... It doesn't even matter if you use canned artichoke bottoms or garlic powder or premixed Cajun-Creole seasonings. *The taste of the completed dish is the final judge.* If it tastes wonderful, isn't that what it's all about?" I can only add that they sure are wise down there in the Bayou!

¾ cup (1½ sticks) unsalted butter

¾ cup (1½ sticks) unsalted margarine

4 cloves garlic, minced

2 tablespoons fresh rosemary, or 1 tablespoon dried, coarsely chopped

3 tablespoons Worcestershire sauce

1 to 2 teaspoons Tabasco sauce

3½ tablespoons coarsely cracked black pepper

2 teaspoons salt

3 pounds large shrimp (15 to 16 per pound) in shells

2 whole lemons, thinly sliced and seeds removed

2 loaves French bread, sliced

1. Preheat the oven to 400°F.

2. Melt the butter and margarine together in a saucepan over medium heat. Remove from the heat and stir in the garlic, rosemary, Worcestershire, and enough Tabasco to impart the desired spiciness. Add the pepper and salt.

3. Place the shrimp in a large, shallow baking dish and pour the butter mixture over them. Tuck the lemon slices in and around the shrimp.

4. Bake the shrimp, turning them once, halfway through, until tender and just cooked through, 20 to 25 minutes.

5. Place the shrimp on a trivet in the center of the dining table. Let the guests serve themselves on plates and offer plenty of bread for dunking into the delicious sauce. Be sure to have an empty dish on hand for the discarded shells.

Makes 6 main-dish or 12 to 15 appetizer servings

Shrimp Fried Wild Rice

Chinese-style fried rice makes a quick, easy, and somewhat offbeat supper. I've gone cross-cultural here by blending the classic Asian ingredients with native American wild rice. While in a global mind set, I've also found that an accompanying sip of heated Japanese sake imparts additional winter warmth to the meal.

4 tablespoons vegetable oil

2 teaspoons Oriental sesame oil

1 bunch scallions, trimmed and minced

1 red bell pepper, stemmed, seeded, and diced

2 jalapeño or serrano chiles, seeded and minced

2 cloves garlic, minced

1 tablespoon minced fresh ginger

1 pound medium shrimp, shelled and deveined

4 cups chilled cooked wild rice, about 1½ cups uncooked (see box, facing page)

1½ cups fresh bean sprouts

3 large eggs, lightly beaten

3 to 4 tablespoons soy sauce

Hot chile oil to taste (optional)

3 tablespoons minced cilantro (fresh coriander)

1. Heat 2 tablespoons of the vegetable oil and 1 teaspoon of the sesame oil in a large skillet over medium-high heat. Add the scallions, bell pepper, jalapeño chiles, garlic, and ginger; stir-fry 3 minutes. Add the shrimp and continue cooking until the shrimp are just cooked through, about 3 minutes more. Remove the mixture from the skillet and set aside.

2. Heat the remaining 2 tablespoons vegetable oil and 1 teaspoon sesame oil in the same skillet over medium-high heat. Add the wild rice and cook, stirring constantly, until heated through, 2 to 3 minutes. Add the bean sprouts and cook 1 minute more. Stir in the beaten eggs and cook, stirring constantly, until the eggs have set, about 1 minute. Stir in the reserved shrimp mixture. Season with soy sauce and chile oil, if desired. Sprinkle with the cilantro and serve at once.

Makes 4 to 6 servings

COOKING WILD RICE

— ✦ —

When cooking wild rice as an accompaniment to the meal, I have found the parboiling and baking method detailed in my Wild Rice and Cider Pilaf recipe the most successful. However, a simpler method suffices in recipes such as the Salmon and Wild Rice Fish Cakes and the Shrimp Fried Wild Rice where the cooked rice is one of many components in the recipe. This is what I suggest: Place the desired amount of wild rice in a fine sieve and rinse under cold running water 2 minutes. Drain thoroughly, place in a saucepan, and add enough fresh water to cover by 3 inches. Bring to a boil, then cook uncovered over medium heat until the rice is done, 35 to 40 minutes. Drain and use as called for in the recipes. Wild rice nearly triples in volume when cooked.

Salmon and Wild Rice Fish Cakes

— ✤ —

Fish cakes have enjoyed a resurgence in popularity. Since many of the updated recipes are jazzed with Creole flavorings, I decided to experiment with a different approach. I started thinking of Scandinavian ways with fish and ended up mixing fresh flaked salmon with rye bread crumbs, dill, capers, and horseradish. Then I borrowed the dill-mustard sauce that is served with cured gravlax. I'm now convinced that Absolut vodka isn't the only fabulous thing to come from the land of the midnight sun. These salmon cakes are spectacular!

5 cups poached or baked salmon, about 2 pounds, boned and flaked
1 cup cooked wild rice, about ⅓ cup uncooked (see box, page 325)
1½ cups fresh rye bread crumbs
1 small red onion, minced
¼ cup minced fresh dill
2 tablespoons capers, drained
1½ tablespoons prepared horseradish

2 tablespoons fresh lemon juice
2 large eggs, lightly beaten
½ cup Hellmann's mayonnaise
Salt and freshly ground black pepper to taste
½ cup unbleached all-purpose flour
1 teaspoon salt
1 teaspoon freshly ground black pepper
1 teaspoon paprika

DILL-MUSTARD SAUCE

2½ tablespoons grainy mustard
2½ tablespoons smooth honey mustard
1 tablespoon white wine vinegar

1 tablespoon honey
½ cup vegetable oil
½ cup finely chopped fresh dill
3 tablespoons unsalted butter, plus additional if needed

1. In a large mixing bowl combine the salmon, wild rice, bread crumbs, onion, dill, capers, horseradish, and lemon juice; mix well. Bind the mixture together with the beaten eggs and mayonnaise. Season to taste with salt and pepper.

2. Place the flour in a small shallow dish and season with 1 teaspoon each salt, pepper, and paprika. Using your hands, form the salmon mixture into plump patties 3 inches in diameter. Coat each patty lightly in the seasoned flour and place on a flat tray in a single layer. Repeat the process to make about 18 fish cakes.

3. Prepare the sauce: Whisk both mustards together in a small mixing bowl; then blend in the vinegar and honey. Gradually whisk in the vegetable oil in a thin, steady stream. Stir in the dill and refrigerate the sauce until serving time.

4. When ready to cook the fish cakes, melt 3 tablespoons butter in a large skillet over medium heat. Add as many salmon cakes as will comfortably fit in the pan and sauté, turning once, until golden brown on both sides, 4 to 5 minutes per side. Keep the salmon cakes warm in a low oven while cooking the rest. Add more butter to the pan if needed. Serve 2 to 3 salmon cakes per person accompanied with the dill-mustard sauce.

Makes 18 fish cakes

Sesame-Coated Catfish Fillets

— ❖ —

The freshwater catfish raised on farms in the South is quite tasty and readily available throughout the country. This crunchy preparation is both unusual and memorable.

2 cups fresh bread crumbs
¼ cup sesame seeds
¼ cup minced cilantro
(fresh coriander)
2½ tablespoons vegetable
oil
2 tablespoons Oriental
sesame oil

¾ cup unbleached all-
purpose flour
Salt and freshly ground
black pepper to taste
2 large eggs, well beaten
2 pounds fresh catfish fillets
Lemon or lime wedges for
serving

1. Preheat the oven to 350°F. Lightly oil a baking pan large enough to hold the fish fillets in a single layer.

2. Combine the bread crumbs, sesame seeds, cilantro, vegetable oil, and 1 tablespoon of the sesame oil in a wide shallow bowl; blend well. Season the flour with salt and pepper and place in another wide shallow bowl. Place the beaten eggs in a similar third bowl. Dip each catfish fillet first in flour, then egg, then roll it in bread crumbs to coat completely. Arrange in the prepared baking pan.

3. Drizzle the remaining 1 tablespoon sesame oil over the top of the fillets and bake until the fish is just opaque and the crumbs are toasty brown, about 20 minutes. Serve immediately accompanied with lemon or lime wedges.

Makes 4 servings

Cod à la Veracruzana

— ❖ —

The virtues of snow-white and fleshy codfish are often overlooked or lost in the sea of fancier and more expensive fish. Yet the best cod is available during winter months when the chilly North Atlantic waters endow the fish with firmness and hearty flavor. This recipe, with its Mexican-inspired sauce of peppers, tomatoes, capers, and olives, makes a sensational and quite thrifty winter entrée.

FISH AND MARINADE
3 large cloves garlic, finely minced
1 teaspoon kosher (coarse) salt
¼ cup fresh lime juice
2½ to 3 pounds fresh cod fillets

VERACRUZANA SAUCE
3 tablespoons olive oil
1 medium onion, minced
½ yellow bell pepper, stemmed, seeded, and diced
½ green bell pepper, stemmed, seeded, and diced
1 jalapeño chile, seeded and minced
3 medium tomatoes, seeded and coarsely diced
1 tablespoon dried oregano
2 tablespoons tomato paste
2 tablespoons capers, drained
½ cup Spanish olives, pitted and halved
½ cup dry white wine
Salt and freshly ground black pepper to taste
Dried red pepper flakes to taste
Lime wedges for serving

1. In a small bowl mash together the garlic and salt to form a paste. Stir in the lime juice. Make several ½-inch-deep slashes on the surface of the cod fillets. Place the fish in a single layer in a noncorrosive baking dish. Pour the lime mixture over the fish, making sure some of the garlic and juice gets into the slashes. Marinate in the refrigerator at least 1 hour.

2. In the meantime, prepare the sauce: Heat the olive oil in a large skillet over medium-high heat. Stir in the onion and all the peppers and the chile; sauté 10 minutes. Add the tomatoes, oregano, and tomato paste; cook 2 minutes more. Stir in the capers, olives, and wine. Season with salt, pepper, and red pepper flakes if a hotter sauce is desired. Simmer uncovered 10 to 15 minutes, then remove from the heat.

3. Preheat the oven to 350°F.

4. Spoon the sauce over and around the cod fillets. Bake until the fish is opaque throughout, 20 to 25 minutes. Serve at once accompanied by lime wedges.

Makes 6 servings

Baked Haddock with Mustard Crumbs

— ❖ —

Simply baked fish fillets with buttered bread crumbs are the essence of good New England coastal cooking and a relic from the days of Friday night fish suppers. Feel free to substitute cod or scrod in this enticing yet easy recipe.

5 tablespoons unsalted
  butter, melted
2 shallots, minced
½ cup dry white wine
1½ to 2 pounds haddock
  fillets, cut into serving
  pieces

1 tablespoon fresh lemon juice
Salt and freshly ground
  black pepper to taste
1 cup fresh bread crumbs
2 teaspoons Dijon mustard
3 tablespoons minced fresh parsley
Lemon wedges for serving

1. Preheat the oven to 400°F.

2. Pour 3 tablespoons of the melted butter into a baking dish large enough to hold the fish fillets in a single layer. Sprinkle the shallots over the butter and pour in ¼ cup of the wine. Arrange the fish fillets on top. Sprinkle each with a little lemon juice and season with salt and pepper.

3. In a small bowl toss the bread crumbs with the remaining 2 tablespoons melted butter. Mix in the mustard and parsley. Pat the bread crumb mixture evenly over the top of the fish fillets. Drizzle the remaining ¼ cup wine over the fish.

4. Bake until the fish flakes easily when tested with a fork, 15 to 20 minutes. Serve at once with lemon wedges.

Makes 4 servings

Bluefish Baked in Grape Leaves

— ❖ —

One can't live on Nantucket and write cookbooks without including at least one recipe for bluefish. On the island, the fish is almost as common as cobblestones and gray shingles. The inhabitants seem to have a love-hate relationship with it, i.e., they love the fishing but the thought of cooking and eating the catch seems to bring on the blues. This recipe seems to infuse diners with new enthusiasm for the ubiquitous yet delicious bluefish.

8 tablespoons olive oil
3 pounds bluefish fillets
2 tablespoons fresh lemon
   juice
4 cloves garlic, minced
4 whole sun-dried tomatoes
   packed in oil, drained
   and minced
2 tablespoons imported olive
   paste

½ cup freshly grated
   Parmesan cheese
¼ cup fresh basil leaves,
   shredded, or 1 tablespoon
   dried
1½ cups fresh bread
   crumbs
8 whole grape leaves packed
   in brine, rinsed and
   patted dry

1. Preheat the oven to 375°F.

2. Drizzle 2 tablespoons of the olive oil over the bottom of a large roasting pan. Arrange the bluefish fillets, skin side down, in the

pan and sprinkle with lemon juice.

3. In a small mixing bowl combine the garlic, sun-dried tomatoes, olive paste, Parmesan, basil, and bread crumbs. Add 4 tablespoons of the olive oil and mix well. Pat the bread crumb mixture evenly over the bluefish fillets.

4. Lay the grape leaves, rib side down, over the bread crumb mixture to cover it completely. Tuck any overhanging edges underneath the fillets. Brush the remaining 2 tablespoons olive oil over the grape leaves.

5. Bake the fish until the fillets are just cooked through, about 20 minutes. Cut into serving pieces with a sharp knife and serve at once.

Makes 6 servings

STORMY BLUES

— ✣ —

Bluepoint oysters grilled over a fire

— ✣ —

Bluefish Baked in Grape Leaves
Mashed Potatoes with Garlic and Olive Oil
Broccoli with Toasted Hazelnuts and Pancetta

— ✣ —

Cranberry Curd Tartlets

Red Snapper with Tomato-Kumquat Confit

— ✣ —

This unusual sauce, with its lusty hints of the sunny Mediterranean, provides an inspired use for my favorite winter citrus fruit, the kumquat. While I have provided directions for broiling whole red snapper, the fish could also be grilled or another small whole fish could be substituted for the snapper. Even meaty tuna steaks would work well sauced with this confit.

2 whole red snappers, about
    2 pounds each, scaled
    and cleaned
¼ cup olive oil
½ cup dry white wine

3 tablespoons Pernod
Salt and freshly ground
    black pepper to taste

TOMATO-KUMQUAT CONFIT

1 tablespoon extra virgin
    olive oil
1 small onion, minced
2 medium tomatoes, peeled,
    seeded, and cut into ¼-
    inch dice
8 whole kumquats, sliced
    into ¼-inch rounds and
    seeded
4 whole sun-dried tomatoes
    packed in oil, drained
    and minced
½ teaspoon sugar
1 teaspoon dried
    tarragon
½ teaspoon fennel
    seeds

2 tablespoons fresh orange
    juice
2 tablespoons fresh lime
    juice
3 tablespoons unsalted
    butter, at room
    temperature
¼ cup chopped pitted
    Niçoise olives
Salt and freshly ground
    black pepper to taste

1. Place the snappers in a broiler pan. Mix the olive oil, wine, and Pernod and pour over the fish. Season the fish inside and out with salt and pepper. Let marinate at room temperature while preparing the confit.

2. Heat the extra virgin olive oil in a small skillet over medium heat. Add the onion and tomatoes and cook 5 minutes, stirring occasionally. Stir in the kumquats and cook another 3 minutes.

3. Add the sun-dried tomatoes, sugar, tarragon, fennel, orange juice, and lime juice to the sauce; simmer uncovered 5 minutes. Remove from the heat and whisk in the butter, tablespoon by tablespoon, so it emulsifies with the sauce rather than melts. Return the sauce to low heat, stir in the olives, and season to taste with salt and pepper. Keep warm while broiling the fish.

4. Preheat the broiler.

5. Broil the snappers in the marinade 4 to 5 inches from the heat until nicely browned on the outside and just barely cooked through the center, about 7 minutes per side. Baste frequently with the marinade and accumulated pan juices to keep the fish moist.

6. Serve ½ fish per person, filleting the fish as you split it, and accompany with a generous serving of the confit alongside.

Makes 4 servings

Fish Fillets with Lemon, Capers, and Croutons

— ✛ —

This is my winter variation on the classic French lemon and butter sauce for fish known as *meunière*. The sauce is a universal favorite because it is both simple and elegant. The capers and croutons make this cold weather version a bit more hearty. If fresh dill is available, use it in place of parsley.

3 tablespoons olive oil
1 clove garlic, peeled and halved
5 tablespoons unsalted butter
½ cup cubed (¼ inch) French bread
4 sole or flounder fillets, about 8 ounces each
Salt and freshly ground black pepper to taste

1 medium lemon, thinly sliced, seeded, and each slice quartered
1½ tablespoons capers, drained
2 tablespoons chopped fresh parsley or dill

1. Heat 2 tablespoons of the olive oil in a small skillet over medium heat. Add the garlic and cook until lightly browned, 4 to 5 minutes. Discard the garlic and add the bread cubes to the skillet, tossing to coat evenly with the oil. Reduce the heat to low; cook and stir until browned and crisp on all sides, 5 to 7 minutes. Set aside.

2. Heat the remaining 1 tablespoon oil with 2 tablespoons of the butter in a large skillet over medium-high heat. Season the fish fillets with salt and pepper and add to the skillet in a single layer. Sauté just until opaque, 3 to 4 minutes per side. Remove the cooked fish to a warmed platter and cover to keep warm.

3. Add the remaining 3 tablespoons butter to the skillet and re-duce the heat to medium-low. When the butter has melted, stir in the lemon and capers. Cook, scraping up any bits clinging to the bottom of the pan, and stirring constantly, 1 minute. Add the parsley and cook 30 seconds more. Spoon the sauce over the fillets, sprinkle with the croutons, and serve at once.

Makes 4 servings

Broiled Swordfish Steaks with Clam Butter

— ❖ —

Serving fish steaks with a clam sauce has recently become fashion-able in a few upscale New England restaurants. I got the idea for this sauce when my editor raved about making my white clam sauce for pasta (in *Nantucket Open-House Cookbook*) with cilantro rather than basil. Since I share in and maybe even surpass her great affec-tion for cilantro, I was delighted with the results.

6 tablespoons fruity olive
　oil
1 bunch scallions, trimmed
　and sliced
3 cloves garlic, minced
1 small onion, minced
¾ cup fresh or bottled clam
　juice
1½ cups dry white wine
¼ teaspoon dried red
　pepper flakes
1 teaspoon dried oregano
24 freshly steamed littleneck
　clams, removed from the
　shell, or 1 cup chopped
　fresh clam meat

1 tablespoon fresh lime
　juice
½ cup chopped cilantro
　(fresh coriander)
Salt and freshly ground
　black pepper to taste
4 tablespoons (½ stick)
　unsalted butter, at room
　temperature
6 swordfish steaks, about 8
　ounces each and 1 inch
　thick
Lime slices for garnish

1. Heat 4 tablespoons of the olive oil in a medium-size skillet over medium-high heat. Stir in the scallions, garlic, and onion; sauté, stirring frequently, 5 minutes.

2. Pour in the clam juice and ½ cup of the wine. Season with the red pepper flakes and oregano. Bring to a boil, then simmer until the liquid is reduced by half, 10 to 15 minutes.

3. Add the clams to the sauce along with the lime juice and cilantro. Season with salt and pepper. Off the heat, whisk in the butter, tablespoon by tablespoon, so it emulsifies with the sauce rather than melts. Keep the clams warm over very low heat (if the heat is too high, the sauce will separate) while broiling the fish.

4. Preheat the broiler.

5. Pour the remaining 1 cup wine into a 13 × 9-inch baking pan. Rub the swordfish steaks lightly with the remaining 2 table-

spoons olive oil and place in the pan. Broil the fish 4 to 5 inches from the heat until lightly browned and cooked through, 6 to 7 minutes.

6. Transfer the swordfish with a spatula to warmed serving plates and spoon the clam sauce generously over each serving. Garnish with lime slices and serve at once.

Makes 6 servings

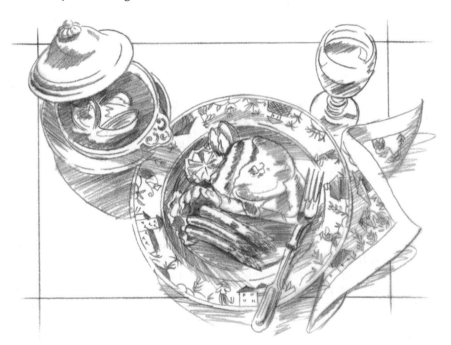

Swordfish with Toasted Pecan Béarnaise

— ❖ —

A few years ago I went into a year-long partnership running The Boarding House restaurant in the center of the town of Nantucket. The previous owners had built much of the restaurant's reputation on this fish entrée. Although my partner and I wanted to change the image of The Boarding House by going off in new food directions, we soon found that popular demand required that we keep the Swordfish with Toasted Pecan Béarnaise on the menu. And rightfully so, I might add! The following is my version of The Boarding House standby.

TOASTED PECAN BEARNAISE

2 shallots, minced
1 tablespoon dried
  tarragon
3 tablespoons tarragon
  vinegar
¼ cup dry white wine
3 large egg yolks
¾ cup (1½ sticks) unsalted
  butter, at room
  temperature

Salt and freshly ground
  black pepper to taste
½ cup pecans, lightly
  toasted and coarsely
  chopped

SWORDFISH

6 swordfish steaks about 8
  ounces each and 1 inch
  thick
Salt and freshly ground
  black pepper to taste
¾ cup milk

¾ cup unbleached all-
  purpose flour
2 tablespoons olive oil
2 tablespoons unsalted
  butter

1. Prepare the béarnaise: Place the shallots, tarragon, vinegar, and wine in a small skillet. Cook over medium-high heat until all but a teaspoon or so of the liquid has evaporated, 5 to 7 minutes. Remove from the heat. Place the egg yolks in the top of a double boiler over barely simmering water and beat until foamy. Whisk in the butter, tablespoon by tablespoon, until all is incorporated and the sauce is thick. Stir in the shallot-tarragon reduction. Season with salt and pepper, then stir in the pecans. Let stand at room temperature while preparing the swordfish.

2. Season the swordfish steaks with salt and pepper. Place the milk and flour in separate shallow bowls. Dip each steak in milk and then flour, shaking off the excess.

3. Heat the oil and butter together in a large skillet over medium-high heat. Add the swordfish and sauté, turning once, until lightly browned on both sides and just cooked through in the center, 5 to 6 minutes per side. (You may have to cook the swordfish in two batches. If so, use half the butter and oil for each batch.) Transfer the swordfish to individual serving plates and keep warm in the oven while cooking the rest. To serve, top each portion with a generous dollop of the béarnaise.

Makes 6 servings

Salt Cod
Gratinée

— ❖ —

Dried salt cod (baccala) baked with onions, potatoes, and white sauce is a typical and deliciously satisfying Portuguese specialty. Nantucket's Azorean heritage makes salt cod a readily available item in island grocery stores, but I first tried to make this casserole while wintering in Manhattan's Upper East Side. While I knew that across town Ninth Avenue was "baccala heaven," I was determined to find the formidable dried fillet of fish in my own neighborhood. Somehow I never did happen upon that Old World vendor tucked in between the Carlyle and Ralph Lauren and I'm not about to confess to how many hours I spent looking for baccala in all the wrong places. But as a result of my experience I'll just say: By all means make this wonderful dish, but first be certain the fish is available to you before planning the menu!

My version is a bit more colorful and seasoned than traditional recipes. Pale green leeks and red-skinned potatoes offset the whiteness of the dish, while fresh cilantro and a scattering of black olives impart extra oomph.

1 pound dried salt cod	1½ cups half-and-half,
3 large red-skinned	scalded
potatoes	Salt and freshly ground
½ cup olive oil	white pepper to taste
5 leeks (white and light	½ cup pitted imported
green parts), trimmed,	black olives
rinsed well, and sliced	3 tablespoons minced
into thin rings	cilantro (fresh coriander)
3 tablespoons unsalted	1 cup grated Swiss cheese
butter	
3 tablespoons unbleached	
all-purpose flour	

1. One day before cooking, place the cod in a large bowl and cover with water. Soak the cod in the refrigerator at least 24 hours, changing the water several times. Drain the cod, rinse, and drain well again. Remove any bones or skin and cut the fish into 1-inch squares. Place in a mixing bowl.

2. Boil the potatoes until just slightly undercooked. Cool and cut

into ¼-inch-thick slices. Mix with the salt cod.

3. Heat the olive oil in a skillet over medium heat. Add the leeks and sauté until soft and tender, about 15 minutes. Set aside.

4. Preheat the oven to 350°F.

5. To make the white sauce, melt the butter in a small saucepan over medium heat. Whisk in the flour and cook, stirring constantly, 2 minutes. Slowly whisk in the scalded half-and-half and cook until smooth and thick, about 5 minutes more. Season to taste with salt and white pepper. Set aside.

6. Spread the leeks over the bottom of a 10-inch gratin dish. Top with the cod and potato mixture and sprinkle with the olives and cilantro. Top with all the white sauce and then the grated Swiss cheese. Bake until bubbling and browned on top, 35 to 40 minutes. Serve at once.

Makes 4 to 6 servings

THE
TEASE
OF
SPRING

"Early spring can be cold as a witch's heart, with frost on the ground and ice crackling in the beach grass."
— *Patricia Coffin*
Nantucket

In cool coastal pockets of New England, spring is often more a state of mind than an actual happening. Sometimes sunny days in February can be warmer than rainy and raw days in April. Oh, this spring does indeed tease. That local markets begin tendering bunches of graceful green asparagus and bushels of sweet Vidalia onions does not automatically equal leaves on trees and light linen clothing on inhabitants. Surely I am not alone in witnessing Wordsworth's "hosts of golden daffodils" blanketed in primaveral snow.

On Nantucket in particular, spring and summer tend to emerge together in one fell swoop toward the end of May, though spring longings come on strong and determined just around the Ides of March. Even when outdoor temperatures fail to be appropriately mild, spring fever rules, bearing heat enough to send stew pots scurrying and fire cravings for the season's freshest and most delicate fare. Winter's monotone roasts give way to the creamy white of plump, roasted chickens and the pastel pink of shad roe. Willowy asparagus spears and sweet shelled peas become hard to resist on a daily basis, while fleeting earthy fiddleheads offer epicurean delight. Vidalia onions offer sugary surprise, and cherry-red rhubarb lets a newly awakened palate pucker with exciting repletion. The days grow longer; energy levels increase; crocuses, forsythia, hyacinths, and tulips blossom against all odds; and we souls of Northern latitudes celebrate all spring's fair flavors, even when we can't have our warming sunshine, too.

❖

Spring Rolls

— ❖ —

Asian spring rolls are the most poetic herald of spring I know. My version has a light and delicate array of crunchy vegetables wrapped in blanched cabbage leaves rather than the typical egg-roll wrappers. Freshness is further highlighted with the rolls served chilled, rather than fried, accompanied by a piquant ginger dipping sauce.

1 large head green cabbage, about 3 pounds
1 ounce dried black mushrooms
1 cup boiling water
2½ cups fresh mung bean sprouts
2 carrots, peeled and cut into thin 2-inch-long julienne strips
4 scallions, trimmed and cut into thin julienne strips
1 piece (1½ inches) fresh ginger, peeled and minced
1 boneless, skinless whole chicken breast, about 8 ounces, poached and cut into julienne strips

8 ounces deveined peeled shrimp, cooked and finely chopped
¾ cup dry-roasted peanuts, coarsely chopped
⅓ cup cilantro leaves (fresh coriander), coarsely chopped
¼ cup fresh mint leaves, minced
1 tablespoon dry sherry
1 tablespoon soy sauce
2 teaspoons Oriental sesame oil
Several drops of hot chile oil
1½ teaspoons sugar

GINGER DIPPING SAUCE

¼ cup dry-roasted peanuts
1 piece (2 inches) fresh ginger, peeled and minced
2 cloves garlic, minced
¼ cup sugar
¼ cup soy sauce
1 tablespoon Oriental sesame oil

2 tablespoons rice wine vinegar
2 tablespoons tomato paste
1½ teaspoons dry mustard
Several drops of hot chile oil
2 tablespoons sesame seeds, lightly toasted

1. Bring a large pot of salted water to a boil. Remove the core of the cabbage with a sharp knife and discard it along with any wilted outer leaves. Immerse the cabbage in the pot of boiling water. Using a fork or tongs, gently remove the outer leaves from the cabbage as they become cooked and tender. When 12 large leaves have been removed, cook the remaining head of cabbage until tender, about 5 minutes longer. Drain all well.

2. While the cabbage is cooking, soak the dried mushrooms in the boiling water 20 minutes. Drain, trim away the tough stems, and slice the caps into thin julienne strips.

3. In a large mixing bowl combine the mushroom strips with the bean sprouts, carrots, scallions, and ginger. Finely shred the small head of cooked cabbage and add it to the bowl. Mix in the chicken, shrimp, peanuts, cilantro, and mint. Sprinkle the sherry, soy, sesame oil, chile oil, and sugar over the mixture; toss well to coat and combine.

4. To assemble the spring rolls, place a cabbage leaf flat on a work surface. Spoon ½ cup of the filling mixture in a compact log shape across the lower middle of the cabbage leaf. Fold the bottom of the leaf over the filling and the sides of the cabbage leaf in, then roll it into a compact log. Place seam side down on a large plate or platter. Repeat with the remaining leaves and filling to make 12 spring rolls. Cover with plastic wrap and refrigerate at least 2 hours or up to 12 hours.

5. Meanwhile prepare the dipping sauce: Place the peanuts, ginger, garlic, and sugar in a food processor and process to a paste. Transfer the paste to a small mixing bowl and blend in the soy, sesame oil, and vinegar. Stir in the tomato paste and dry mustard until smooth. Sprinkle with chile oil to taste and mix in the sesame seeds. Transfer to a small serving bowl.

6. To serve, cut each roll into 4 thick slices and serve with the dipping sauce alongside.

Makes 12 spring rolls

DAFFODIL DAYS

— ✧ —

Spring Rolls

— ✧ —

Spinach Fettuccine with Smoked Salmon and Asparagus

Corn Bread with Carrots and Pecans

— ✧ —

Lemon Curd Tartlets

Dissolve the
Cook until the
uce over the
ole and braise
minutes. Just
at once with

Chicken

Chinese dish so named because the
soy sauce, a glass of water, and a
favorite dishes to order in New
d to create a home version for my

DE

1 teaspoon salt
1 teaspoon coarsely cracked
  black pepper
1 tablespoon cornstarch

ing, for the
forgotten.
rmeate the
Rhubarb
ter, make

UCE

2 tablespoons oyster sauce
1 tablespoon light brown
  sugar
½ cup chicken broth,
  preferably homemade
ced   2 tablespoons mirin (sweet
ed   rice cooking wine)
            2 teaspoons cornstarch
ice   1 tablespoon water
hly
ste   ¼ cup fresh cilantro leaves
rsely   (fresh coriander), minced

. Mash
he mix-
d. Rub
n, then

ast 45
roast-
erature

inutes

highs into bite-size pieces and combine them
gredients in a mixing bowl. Let marinate at
utes.
ushrooms in a small bowl and cover with the
0 minutes, then drain, reserving ½ cup of the
he excess water from the mushrooms; trim and
. Set aside.
a wok or large skillet over medium-high heat.
ken pieces and stir-fry until the chicken is lightly
7 minutes. Remove the chicken with a slotted
heatproof earthenware casserole.
er, scallions, and garlic to the wok and stir-fry 1
oyster sauce, brown sugar, chicken broth, reserved

mushroom liquid, and mirin, stirring until smooth.
cornstarch in 1 tablespoon water and stir into the sauce.
sauce is slightly thickened, 1 to 2 minutes. Pour the s
chicken and stir in the black mushrooms. Cover the casser
over medium heat until the chicken is tender, 15 to 20
before serving sprinkle the dish with the cilantro. Serve
rice or Chinese noodles.

Makes 6 servings

Roast Spring Chicken

— ❖ —

I am very fond of bringing out the flavor of bay as a season
leaves are too often tucked into a pot of stew and then
Crushed bay leaves combine with lemon zest and garlic to pe
meat of this plump and juicy roast spring chicken. Scallope
and Asparagus Vinaigrette (my favorite), both in this chap
lovely seasonal accompaniments.

1 roasting chicken, 5 to 6
pounds, rinsed and patted
dry
2 bay leaves, finely crumbled
2 cloves garlic, crushed
1 tablespoon grated lemon
zest

2 tablespoons unsalted
butter, at room
temperature
2 tablespoons olive oil
1 tablespoon fresh lemon ju
Kosher (coarse) salt and fres
ground black pepper to t

1. Preheat the oven to 325°F.
2. Loosen the breast skin from the meat on the chicker
together the bay leaves, garlic, lemon zest, and butter. Spread t
ture under the skin on each side of the breastbone. Truss the bi
the olive oil and lemon juice all over the skin of the chicke
sprinkle with salt and pepper.
3. Place the chicken breast side up in a roasting pan. R
minutes, basting occasionally. Increase the heat to 375°F; continu
ing until the skin is crisp and golden brown and the internal temp
of the thigh reaches 170°F, 45 to 60 minutes more.
4. Transfer the chicken to a platter. Let rest 10 to 15 m
before carving.

Makes 4 servings

Roast Chicken with Sweet Wine, New Potatoes, and Onions

— ❖ —

A plump roasting chicken cooks atop a bed of sliced Vidalia onions and spears of red-skinned potatoes. Sauternes wine is used as the cooking liquid to impart a subtle sweetness to this nearly one-pan meal. Add a side of asparagus or fiddleheads to make this spring chicken supper complete.

1 roasting chicken, 5 to 6
   pounds
3 cloves garlic, unpeeled
1 lemon
2 tablespoons olive oil
Salt and freshly ground
   black pepper to taste
2 large Vidalia or other
   sweet onions, peeled and
   thinly sliced

4 large red-skinned
   potatoes, scrubbed and
   each cut into 8 to 10
   lengthwise spears
1½ cups Sauternes or other
   sweet late-harvest wine

1. Preheat the oven to 350°F.

2. Rinse the chicken inside and out, then pat dry. Place the garlic in the cavity of the bird. Place the chicken breast side up in the center of a large roasting pan. Cut the lemon in half and squeeze the juice over the chicken. Place the lemon shells in the cavity. Rub the chicken skin all over with the olive oil and season with salt and pepper. Roast the chicken 45 minutes.

3. Scatter the onions and potatoes around the chicken in the roasting pan. Pour the Sauternes over all. Increase the heat to 375°F; continue roasting the chicken, basting occasionally, until the chicken is cooked through and golden brown and the vegetables are tender, about 1 hour more.

4. Let the chicken rest 10 to 15 minutes before carving. Serve with plenty of the pan-roasted onions and potatoes.

Makes 4 servings

French Bistro Chicken

— ✤ —

To my palate, this recipe embodies the essence of good, simple, and comforting French bistro fare. The whole shallots and artichoke hearts impart a mildness that reminds me of a gentle spring day.

¼ cup olive oil
2 tablespoons unsalted
  butter
2 chickens, 3 to 3½ pounds
  each, cut into serving
  pieces
1 pound shallots, peeled
⅔ cup dry white vermouth
1 tablespoon fresh lemon
  juice

2 teaspoons dried tarragon
Salt and freshly ground
  black pepper to taste
2 cans (14 ounces each)
  artichoke hearts, drained
  and quartered
1 cup chicken broth,
  preferably homemade

1. Preheat the oven to 350°F.

2. Heat the olive oil and butter together in a large skillet over medium-high heat. Sauté the chicken pieces in batches, starting skin side down and turning, until nicely browned all over. Transfer the chicken to a large baking pan and arrange the pieces in a single layer.

3. Pour off all but 3 tablespoons fat from the skillet. Add the shallots and sauté until lightly browned, 7 to 8 minutes. Add the vermouth and lemon juice; cook, stir to deglaze, scraping up any brown bits clinging to the bottom of the skillet. Stir in the tarragon and season with salt and pepper. Add the artichoke hearts and toss to combine. Pour this mixture around the browned chicken pieces.

4. Cover the pan with aluminum foil and bake until very tender, about 45 minutes. Pour the accumulated juices from the chicken into a small saucepan. Add the chicken broth and boil until reduced by half, 5 to 7 minutes. Pour the sauce over the chicken and serve at once.

Makes 6 to 8 servings

CROCUSES COMING

— ❖ —

Potage Crécy

— ❖ —

French Bistro Chicken
Asparagus with Mustard Bread Crumbs

— ❖ —

Warm Dandelion Salad

— ❖ —

Rhubarb Custard Pie

Spring Blanquette de Veau

— ❖ —

When I was traveling in France one fall, I was served a delicious veal scaloppine in a saffron cream sauce. The dish gave me the idea to enliven the normally bland and pale stew know as *blanquette de veau* with saffron. The experiment produced one of the best and prettiest stews I've ever tasted. This recipe is perfect for a March day that is more lion than lamb, when both a blanket on the lap and a *blanquette* on the stove are needed for warmth.

9 tablespoons unsalted butter

3 pounds lean veal stew meat, cut into 1½-inch cubes

3 cups chicken broth, preferably homemade

½ cup dry white wine

2 teaspoons dried tarragon

1 teaspoon saffron threads

16 small white boiling onions

12 ounces baby carrots, trimmed and peeled

8 ounces domestic white mushrooms, trimmed

4 ounces shiitake mushrooms, stems removed, caps thinly sliced

3 tablespoons unbleached all-purpose flour

½ cup heavy or whipping cream

Salt and freshly ground black pepper to taste

½ cup minced fresh parsley

1. Melt 4 tablespoons of the butter in a large stew pot or Dutch oven over medium-high heat. Sear the veal cubes in batches until lightly browned all over, 5 to 7 minutes per batch. Return all the veal to the pot and cover with the chicken broth and wine. Stir in the tarragon and saffron. Bring the mixture to a boil, reduce the heat, and simmer covered about 1 hour.

2. Meanwhile boil the onions in a medium-size pot of water for 5 minutes. Drain and peel. When the stew has cooked 1 hour, add the carrots and onions. Simmer covered until the vegetables are tender, 30 to 40 minutes more.

3. Meanwhile melt 2 more tablespoons of the butter in a medium-size skillet over medium heat. Add the whole domestic mushrooms and sliced shiitakes; sauté until softened, about 5 minutes. Set aside and add to the stew when the other vegetables are tender.

4. Pour the stew through a strainer placed over a bowl to extract the liquid. Reserve the liquid and solids separately.

5. Melt the remaining 3 tablespoons butter in a clean stew pot over medium-high heat. Stir in the flour and cook, stirring constantly, 1 minute. Gradually pour in the reserved cooking liquid; cook, stirring constantly, until smooth and thick. Stir in the cream and season with salt and pepper.

6. Return the meat and vegetables to the pot and stir to coat with the sauce. Simmer over low heat 10 minutes to heat through and blend the flavors. Serve the stew with a sprinkling of parsley over each serving.

Makes 6 to 8 servings

Baked Shad Roe in Sorrel Cream

— ✤ —

Although I'm passionate about all the caviars that come from the faraway Caspian Sea, I've never been a great enthusiast of native shad roe. However, recently when I was visiting my adorable new niece in the Rhinebeck area of New York State, we stumbled across a local shad roe festival during a Sunday stroll along the river. The sight of the fish being filleted on the spot and the smell of it grilling over a spring fire made me finally appreciate this seasonal delicacy. I find baking the roe a better method of cooking than the more common pan frying since it ensures that the fragile eggs remain intact.

4 tablespoons (½ stick)
  unsalted butter
3 tablespoons minced onion
1 large egg yolk
½ cup heavy or whipping
  cream
Salt and freshly ground
  black pepper to taste

8 ounces fresh sorrel,
  trimmed, rinsed, and cut
  into fine julienne
1 large pair shad roe, about
  12 ounces
1 tablespoon fresh lemon
  juice

1. Preheat the oven to 350°F. Place 2 tablespoons of the butter in a medium-size gratin dish. Place it in the oven to melt the butter, then remove it and set aside.

2. Heat the remaining 2 tablespoons butter in a small skillet over medium-high heat. Add the onion and sauté until softened, about 5 minutes.

3. In a small bowl whisk together the egg yolk and cream until smooth. Add the sautéed onion and season to taste with salt and pepper. Stir in the sorrel.

4. Place the whole shad roe in the gratin dish with the melted butter. Sprinkle the roe with the fresh lemon juice. Pour the sorrel cream sauce evenly over and around the roe. Bake uncovered until the roe is firm to the touch and the sauce is bubbling, 25 to 30 minutes. Divide the roe in half and serve at once napped with plenty of the sorrel cream sauce.

Makes 2 rich servings

Stracciatella with Fresh Spinach and Peas

— ❖ —

People often ask me where I get my recipe ideas. This one came to me in a dream. Although I had neither made nor tasted this Italian broth and egg soup before, one night I dreamed that I was eating it at an outdoor table along a Venetian canal. The soup tasted so exquisite in my dream that I had to get up and make it the next morning. I was not disappointed. Using a good homemade chicken broth is essential to the success of this recipe.

2 large eggs
¼ cup freshly grated
  Parmesan cheese, plus
  additional for serving
1 tablespoon fresh lemon
  juice
Pinch of grated nutmeg
4 cups homemade chicken
  broth

Salt and freshly ground
  black pepper to taste
4 ounces fresh spinach,
  rinsed well, trimmed,
  finely shredded, and
  patted dry
¾ cup shelled fresh peas

1. In a small bowl beat together the eggs, cheese, lemon juice, and nutmeg. Bring the chicken broth to a boil in a soup pot over medium-high heat. Whisk in the egg mixture, stirring gently. Cook, stirring constantly, until tiny flakes of the cooked egg appear in the stock, 1 to 2 minutes more. Season the soup to taste with salt and pepper. Remove from the heat.

2. Place the spinach and peas in the bottom of a soup tureen or serving bowl and ladle the hot soup over the vegetables. Serve at once, passing a bowl of grated Parmesan cheese.

Makes 4 servings

Sweet Minted Peas

— ✦ —

A marvelous and easy way to jazz up peas to accompany succulent roast spring lamb.

4 tablespoons (½ stick)
  unsalted butter
⅓ cup best-quality mint
  jelly

3 cups shelled fresh peas
Freshly ground black pepper
  to taste

Melt the butter and mint jelly together in a saucepan over medium heat. Add the peas and stir to coat with the sauce. Simmer covered until the peas are just barely tender, 5 to 6 minutes. Season with pepper to taste and serve at once.

Makes 6 servings

Crunchy Pea Salad

— ⬦ —

The triple crunch of fresh peas, honey-roasted cashews, and water chestnuts blends with an Oriental-inspired dressing in this fresh and light salad. Serve as a luncheon side dish on a sunny day celebrating the first blossoms of spring.

4 cups shelled fresh peas
6 scallions, trimmed and
  minced
1 can (8 ounces) sliced
  water chestnuts, drained
1¼ cups honey-roasted
  cashews
1 cup sour cream
1 tablespoon minced fresh
  ginger

2 tablespoons soy sauce
2 teaspoons Oriental sesame
  oil
2 teaspoons light brown
  sugar
2 tablespoons chopped
  cilantro (fresh coriander)
  or fresh mint leaves

1. Blanch or steam the peas just until crisp-tender, 3 to 4 minutes. Drain, cool under cold running water, and drain again.

2. In a large mixing bowl combine the peas, scallions, water chestnuts, and cashews.

3. In a small bowl whisk together the sour cream, ginger, soy, sesame oil, and brown sugar until smooth. Pour over the pea salad and stir well to bind and blend. Mix in the cilantro. Transfer the salad to a serving bowl and refrigerate until serving time, but no longer than 24 hours.

Makes 8 servings

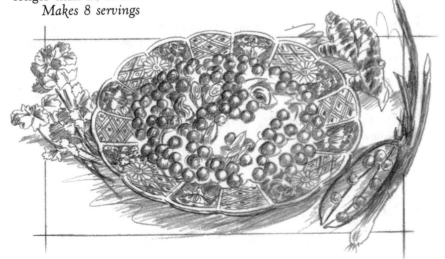

PEELING ASPARAGUS

— ✦ —

I used to think I preferred my asparagus peeled because one of my literary idols, Marcel Proust, wrote about it in the Remembrance of Things Past. *Now I know otherwise. I like my asparagus peeled simply because it adds extra glamour and grace to the spears on the plate. Fortunately, peeling asparagus is far less complex than even the shortest Proustian sentence. First snap off the tough ends of the asparagus spears where they naturally break. Next remove some of the spear's outer skin using a swivel-bladed peeler, moving the blade toward you and peeling up to 2 to 3 inches from the tip. Cook the asparagus as directed in the recipes, then enjoy the many shades of green in each cooked spear.*

My Very Favorite Asparagus Vinaigrette

— ✦ —

I can think of no more superlative recommendation for this recipe than its title. I'm happy eating it every day of asparagus season, at almost any time of the day or night.

1 tablespoon balsamic
  vinegar
1½ tablespoons fresh lemon
  juice
1 teaspoon Dijon mustard
1 small clove garlic, finely
  minced
½ cup fruity olive oil
1 plum tomato, seeded and
  diced

Salt and freshly ground
  black pepper to taste
2 pounds medium
  asparagus, trimmed and
  bottom portion of stalks
  peeled
⅓ cup freshly grated
  Parmesan cheese

1. For the vinaigrette, whisk the vinegar, lemon juice, and mustard together in a small bowl. Add the garlic. Gradually whisk in the olive oil, then stir in the diced tomato. Season to taste with salt and pepper. Let mellow at room temperature at least 30 minutes.

2. Blanch, steam, or microwave the asparagus just until crisp-tender, 3 to 5 minutes. Drain. Arrange the hot asparagus on a serving platter and pour the vinaigrette over all. Sprinkle with the Parmesan cheese. Let sit at least 10 minutes before serving. The asparagus may be served warm or at room temperature. I often make it about 30 minutes ahead of serving and let it sit while I attend to the rest of my meal.

Makes 6 to 8 servings

Oven-Roasted Asparagus with Minced Mushrooms

— ✤ —

Every once in a while a fellow cook raves to me about roasting asparagus in the oven at a high temperature. The method transforms asparagus from a delicate vegetable to a much more robust one. Roasting works best with fat stalks and is a good method to know if you are like me and eat asparagus every day when it is in season. This intense mushroom topping further accents the earthy roasted flavor of the asparagus.

1 cup finely minced domestic white, shiitake, or portobello mushrooms
4 tablespoons fruity olive oil
1 clove garlic, minced
3 tablespoons minced fresh parsley

2 pounds fat asparagus, trimmed and bottom portion of stalks peeled
Kosher (coarse) salt and freshly ground black pepper to taste

1. Preheat the oven to 500°F.

2. Place the minced mushrooms in the center of a clean kitchen towel, twist the cloth into a tight bundle, and squeeze to extract as

much liquid as possible from the mushrooms.

3. Heat 3 tablespoons of the olive oil in a small skillet over medium-high heat. Add the mushrooms and garlic; sauté until softened, 3 minutes. Stir in the parsley and cook 30 seconds more. Remove from the heat and set aside.

4. In a large shallow baking dish toss the asparagus with the remaining 1 tablespoon olive oil, coating the stalks evenly. Season with salt and pepper. Roast the asparagus, shaking the dish every 2 minutes, until crisp-tender, 8 to 10 minutes. Toss the roasted spears with the mushroom mixture and serve immediately.

Makes 4 to 6 servings

Spinach Fettuccine with Smoked Salmon and Asparagus

— ❖ —

After a winter's satiation of sturdy brown stews and roasts, both our palates and our eyes cry for clean pastel relief at the first hint of spring. The pale pink and green colors and subtle smoky and sweet flavors of this pasta dish gently ease the spirit into the taste delights of a fresh season.

4 tablespoons (½ stick)
 unsalted butter
2 shallots, minced
2 tablespoons minced fresh
 ginger
1 tablespoon grated lemon
 zest
1 cup Japanese sake or dry
 white wine
¼ cup fresh lemon juice
2 cups heavy or whipping
 cream

½ cup light cream
Salt and freshly ground
 black pepper to taste
9 ounces spinach fettuccine
1 pound thin asparagus
12 ounces thinly sliced best-
 quality smoked salmon
1 cup freshly grated
 Parmesan cheese

1. Melt the butter in a saucepan over medium-high heat. Add the shallots, ginger, and lemon zest; sauté until softened, about 3 minutes.

Pour in the sake and lemon juice. Cook until reduced by two-thirds, 7 to 10 minutes. Add the heavy and light creams and reduce again by half. Season with salt and pepper.

2. Strain the sauce to remove the solids and keep warm over low heat.

3. Bring a large pot of salted water to a boil. Add the fettuccine and cook just until al dente.

4. While the pasta is cooking, heat a medium-size pot of salted water to a boil. Trim the asparagus and cut diagonally into 2-inch lengths. Blanch the asparagus pieces in the boiling water just until crisp-tender, 3 to 4 minutes. Drain. Cut the smoked salmon into julienne strips ¼ inch wide.

5. Drain the pasta and place in a warmed serving bowl. Add the cream sauce, asparagus, salmon, and ½ cup of the Parmesan. Toss all together and serve at once. Sprinkle the top of each serving with the remaining Parmesan.

Makes 4 servings

Asparagus alla Carbonara

T his terrific recipe applies my very favorite Italian egg, bacon, and cheese sauce for pasta to pencil-thin spring asparagus. Try it paired with delicate shad roe or just as a meal in itself.

8 slices bacon, cut into ¼-inch dice
2 shallots, minced
1 clove garlic, minced
4 ounces domestic white mushrooms, thinly sliced
1 large egg, at room temperature
¼ cup heavy or whipping cream

½ cup freshly grated Parmesan cheese
Salt and freshly ground black pepper to taste
2 pounds pencil-thin asparagus, trimmed to 4½- to 5-inch lengths
1½ tablespoons pine nuts, lightly toasted

1. Fry the bacon in a medium-size skillet over medium-high heat until crisp. Remove it from the pan with a slotted spoon and drain on paper towels. Pour off all but 2 tablespoons fat from the skillet. Add the shallots and garlic; sauté just until softened, about 1 minute. Stir

in the mushrooms and sauté until lightly browned, about 5 minutes. Remove from the heat and set aside.

2. Whisk the egg and cream together in a large mixing bowl. Stir in the Parmesan and season with salt and pepper. Set aside.

3. Blanch, steam, or microwave the asparagus spears until crisp-tender. Drain thoroughly. Quickly toss the hot asparagus with the egg mixture, then stir in the mushrooms and bacon. Transfer to a serving platter, sprinkle with pine nuts, and serve at once.

Makes 6 servings

Asparagus with Mustard Bread Crumbs

— ⬧ —

An enticing variation on vegetables à la Polonaise — the mustard adds a sunny golden hue to the bread crumbs and a graceful tang to the silky taste of the asparagus

6 tablespoons (¾ stick)
  unsalted butter
1 heaping tablespoon Dijon
  mustard
1 cup coarse fresh French
  bread crumbs
2 pounds fresh asparagus,
  trimmed and bottom
  portion of stalks peeled

1 tablespoon fresh lemon
  juice
Salt and freshly ground
  black pepper to taste

1. Melt 4 tablespoons of the butter in a small skillet over low heat. Whisk in the mustard, then add the bread crumbs and toss to coat with the mustard butter. Sauté the mixture, stirring frequently, until the bread crumbs are a light and toasty golden color, about 10 minutes.

2. Blanch, steam, or microwave the asparagus just until crisp-tender, 3 to 5 minutes. Drain and toss with the remaining 2 tablespoons butter and the lemon juice. Toss with the mustard crumbs and season to taste with salt and pepper. Serve at once.

Makes 6 servings

Fiddlehead Fritters

—❖—

Although I'm never shy about ordering a mound of shoestring potato fries or a platter of crispy, frizzled onion rings at a bistro-style restaurant, I rarely, if ever, undertake deep-frying in my own kitchen. This to-die-for recipe, however, is an exception.

In this recipe the tender buds of the unfurled fern are coated in a delicate beer batter highlighted with the pink of sweet paprika and the tang of minced onion. Once fried, the fiddleheads are dusted with Parmesan cheese, cracked black pepper, and a spritz of fresh lemon juice. Serve as a special spring appetizer, an accompaniment to roast meats, or follow my lead and make a dinner of this seasonal treat.

1¼ cups unbleached all-
 purpose flour
1 teaspoon salt
1 teaspoon sweet Hungarian
 paprika
1 bottle (12 ounces)
 domestic or imported beer
3 tablespoons minced onion

Vegetable oil for deep-frying
2 pounds fiddleheads,
 trimmed and cleaned
Freshly cracked black
 pepper to taste
½ cup freshly grated
 Parmesan cheese
1 lemon, cut into wedges

1. Place 1 cup of the flour, the salt, and paprika in a food processor and process to combine. With the machine running, pour the beer through the feed tube in a thin, steady stream to make a smooth batter. Add the onion and process just to combine. Transfer the batter to a shallow bowl.

2. Pour 2 inches oil into a deep skillet and heat to 360°F.

3. Preheat the oven to 275°F.

4. Meanwhile dust the fiddleheads with the remaining ¼ cup flour. Dip them one at a time into the beer batter, shaking off any excess, and carefully drop in the hot oil. Fry the fiddleheads in batches, being careful not to crowd them. When the underside is golden, turn with a slotted spoon and cook until golden brown, about 2 minutes per batch. Remove with the slotted spoon and drain on a baking sheet lined with paper towels. Keep warm in the oven until all the fiddleheads are fried.

5. Arrange the fiddleheads on a serving platter. Season with the pepper and sprinkle with the cheese. Surround the platter with the lemon wedges, letting the guests squeeze the lemon juice over their servings. Serve hot.

Makes 6 to 8 servings

Fiddleheads Fresca

— ❖ —

An inventive and pretty salad that capitalizes on one of spring's best delicacies. While Fiddleheads Fresca is always a welcome side dish, I'm more fond of making a whole luncheon feast of fiddlehead indulgence when the vegetable is in its short season.

2½ pounds fresh
  fiddleheads, trimmed and
  cleaned
2 tablespoons balsamic
  vinegar
1 tablespoon fresh lemon
  juice
½ cup extra virgin olive oil
1 clove garlic, minced
3 tablespoons finely
  shredded fresh basil
  leaves

2 ripe tomatoes, seeded and
  diced
4 ounces thinly sliced
  prosciutto, minced
Salt and freshly ground
  black pepper to taste
¼ cup pine nuts, lightly
  toasted
4 ounces Parmesan cheese,
  shaved into thin shards
  with a vegetable peeler

1. Cook the fiddleheads in boiling water or steam over simmering water until crisp-tender, 4 to 5 minutes. Drain.

2. Whisk the vinegar and lemon juice together in a small bowl. Gradually whisk in the olive oil, then stir in the garlic, basil, tomatoes, and prosciutto. Season to taste with salt and pepper.

3. Toss the warm fiddleheads with the dressing, then mix in the pine nuts. Transfer to a serving dish and sprinkle the Parmesan generously over the top. Serve slightly warm or at room temperature.

Makes 8 to 10 servings

Fiddlehead Soufflé Sandwiches

— ❖ —

Guests won't say "Fiddlesticks!" when served these unique and scrumptious open-face sandwiches. Feature them as the main part of a spring luncheon or Sunday brunch.

1 pound fiddleheads, trimmed and cleaned
3 tablespoons unsalted butter
1 medium Vidalia or other sweet onion, minced
1 clove garlic, minced
8 ounces domestic white mushrooms, trimmed and sliced
2 tablespoons cream sherry
½ cup heavy or whipping cream
¼ teaspoon grated nutmeg

Salt and freshly ground black pepper to taste
4 English muffins, split in half
8 slices Canadian bacon (5 to 6 ounces)
3 large egg whites, at room temperature
2 cups shredded sharp Cheddar cheese

1. Cook the fiddleheads in a steamer over simmering water just until crisp-tender, 4 to 5 minutes. Set aside.

2. Melt the butter in a medium-size skillet over medium-high heat. Add the onion, garlic, and mushrooms; sauté until quite soft, 7 to 10 minutes. Stir in the sherry and cream. Bring to a low boil and continue cooking uncovered until the liquid is reduced by half and thickened, 7 to 8 minutes. Season the mixture with nutmeg, salt, and pepper. Stir in the cooked fiddleheads and keep the mixture warm over very low heat.

3. Preheat the broiler.

4. Lightly toast the muffin halves. Top each one with a slice of Canadian bacon. Spoon the fiddlehead mixture on top of the bacon. Beat the egg whites until stiff but not dry, then gently fold in the Cheddar. Spoon the cheese mixture over the tops of the sandwiches.

5. Place the sandwiches on a baking sheet. Broil 4 to 5 inches from the heat until the tops are puffed and lightly browned, about 4 minutes. Serve 2 halves per person and eat with knife and fork.

Makes 4 servings

Fiddleheads with Browned Butter

— ❖ —

This is the way I first remember my mother preparing fiddleheads and its simplicity keeps this recipe a favorite.

4 tablespoons (½ stick)
  unsalted butter
1½ pounds fiddleheads,
  trimmed and cleaned

1 tablespoon fresh lemon
  juice
Salt and freshly ground
  black pepper to taste

1. Melt the butter in a medium-size skillet over medium heat. Watching carefully, continue to cook the butter until browned but not burned. Remove from the heat.

2. Bring a large pot of water to a boil. Add the fiddleheads and boil until crisp-tender, about 4 to 5 minutes. Drain.

3. Add the fiddleheads to the browned butter in the skillet and toss to coat. Sprinkle with the lemon juice and season with salt and pepper. Serve at once.

Makes 6 servings

Warm Dandelion Salad

— ❖ —

Whether dandelion greens are plucked from a bin next to the radicchio in a fancy food store or weeded fresh from the backyard, they make a great springtime treat when bathed in a bacon-based, sweet-and-sour dressing.

8 ounces slab bacon, rind
  discarded, cut into ½-
  inch dice
¼ cup balsamic vinegar
1½ tablespoons Dijon
  mustard
2 tablespoons honey
3 tablespoons olive oil

1 tomato, seeded and diced
Salt and freshly ground
  black pepper to taste
6 to 8 cups tender young
  dandelion leaves, rinsed
  and dried
3 ounces chèvre, such as
  Montrachet, crumbled

1. Fry the bacon in a medium-size skillet until crisp. Remove it with a slotted spoon and drain on paper towels. Pour all but ⅓ cup bacon fat from the skillet. Whisk the vinegar, mustard, and honey into the skillet, then add the olive oil. Stir in the tomato and season the dressing with salt and pepper. Keep warm.

2. Toss the dandelion greens with the chèvre and bacon in a salad bowl. Pour the warm dressing over the salad and toss to coat. Serve immediately.

Makes 4 to 6 servings

Risotto Primavera

— ❖ —

I cooked this dish one night in New York when my editor came to dinner, and she commented that I had infused the tired combination of peas and carrots with new life.

3 tablespoons olive oil	1 cup dry white wine
2 tablespoons unsalted butter	1 pound asparagus, trimmed, cut into 2-inch lengths, and steamed just until crisp-tender
2 large shallots, minced	1 cup shelled fresh peas
1 cup minced fennel bulb	¾ cup freshly grated Parmesan cheese
3 carrots, peeled and minced	
2 cups Arborio rice	Salt and freshly ground black pepper to taste
5 cups chicken broth, preferably homemade	

1. Heat the olive oil and butter together in a large deep skillet over medium-high heat. Add the shallots, fennel, and carrots; sauté until the vegetables are softened, 7 to 10 minutes.

2. Stir in the rice and cook, stirring frequently, until the rice is translucent, about 3 minutes.

3. Begin adding the chicken broth 1 cup at a time, stirring constantly and allowing the broth to be fully absorbed before adding the next cup. When all the chicken broth has been absorbed, add the wine and cook in the same manner. The rice should be al dente and moist, lightly bound with a little of the cooking liquid. Total cooking time should be about 25 minutes.

4. Stir in the asparagus and peas; cook just to heat through, about 3 minutes more. Remove the risotto from the heat. Fold in the Parmesan and season to taste with salt and pepper. Serve at once.

Makes 6 to 8 servings

Vidalia Onion Casserole

— ❖ —

This recipe is inspired by a French preparation known as *soubise* — a slowly cooked blend of onions and rice served with roasted meats. It is particularly extraordinary when made with the spring crop of sweet Georgia onions and is worthy of starring in its own right as the centerpiece of a luncheon or casual Sunday supper.

6 tablespoons (¾ stick)
    unsalted butter
8 cups chopped Vidalia or
    other sweet onions (about
    6 whole onions)
⅔ cup raw long-grain
    white rice

1½ cups grated Swiss
    cheese
1 cup half-and-half
3 tablespoons dry white
    vermouth
Salt and freshly ground
    black pepper to taste

1. Preheat the oven to 325°F. Butter a 3-quart casserole and set aside.

2. Melt the butter in a large skillet over medium heat. Add the onions and cook slowly, stirring frequently, until very soft and translucent, about 20 minutes.

3. In the meantime, cook the rice for 5 minutes in a pot of boiling water. Drain well and stir into the sautéed onions. Add the cheese, half-and-half, and vermouth. Season with salt and pepper.

4. Transfer the mixture to the prepared casserole. Bake, uncovered until the rice is tender and the top is crusty brown, 1 to 1¼ hours. Let cool a few minutes.

Makes 8 servings

Oven-Roasted Vidalia Onions

— ❖ —

I adore the rustic look and flavor of these onions roasted right in their skins. Serve alongside grilled meats or on a platter with assorted cheeses and hard sausages.

6 medium Vidalia or other
    sweet onions, unpeeled
¼ cup fruity olive oil
Kosher (coarse) salt and
    freshly ground black
    pepper to taste

⅓ cup balsamic vinegar
⅓ cup fresh orange juice
2 teaspoons grated orange
    zest

1. Preheat the oven to 375°F.
2. Rub the skins of the onions generously with the olive oil. Place them in a heatproof roasting pan and sprinkle with salt and pepper. Roast the onions until soft and tender, 45 to 60 minutes.
3. Cut the onions in half through the root ends and arrange cut sides up on a serving platter. Add the vinegar and orange juice and zest to the drippings in the roasting pan. Place the pan over medium-high heat and cook the liquid until reduced to a glaze. Drizzle the glaze over the roasted onions. Serve the onions at room temperature.

Makes 4 to 6 servings

Georgia Onion Pie

— ❖ —

This pie is the savory equivalent to a deep-dish fruit pie. It is a gooey mess to serve and eat, and absolutely irresistible. Make it as soon as Georgia's crop of Vidalia onions hits the local produce shelves!

8 tablespoons (1 stick)
    unsalted butter
5 cups thinly sliced Vidalia
    or other sweet onions
    (about 3 large)
1½ cups crushed Ritz
    crackers
1½ tablespoons unbleached
    all-purpose flour
½ cup chicken broth,
    preferably homemade

2 large egg yolks
1 cup sour cream
¼ teaspoon grated nutmeg
Salt and freshly ground
    white pepper to taste
1½ cups shredded sharp
    Cheddar cheese
1 teaspoon sweet Hungarian
    paprika

1. Preheat the oven to 350°F.
2. Melt 4 tablespoons of the butter in a large skillet over medium heat. Add the onions and sauté, stirring occasionally, until quite soft and tender, about 20 minutes.

3. Meanwhile melt the remaining 4 tablespoons butter and toss with the cracker crumbs to moisten thoroughly. Press the buttered crumbs over the bottom and up the side of a 9-inch pie plate. Set aside.

4. Stir the flour into the sautéed onions and cook 1 minute. Stir in the chicken broth and cook until the liquid is slightly thickened and creamy, about 2 minutes. Remove from the heat.

5. Whisk the egg yolks and sour cream in a small mixing bowl until well blended. Season with the nutmeg, salt, and white pepper. Add the egg mixture to the onions and stir to blend thoroughly.

6. Pour the onion mixture into the pie plate. Top with the Cheddar cheese, then sprinkle with the paprika.

7. Bake the pie until lightly browned and bubbling, 35 to 40 minutes. Let cool 5 minutes. Slice the pie into wedges, as best you can, and serve at once.

Makes 6 to 8 servings

Rhubarb Muffins

— ❖ —

It takes a few tries to get rhubarb muffins just right. I finally discovered that the way to strike the perfect balance of sweet and tart is to let the rhubarb absorb the sugar before adding it to the batter. Maple syrup time up North often coincides with the first signs of rhubarb in southern New England, and, not surprisingly, the two appear to be born companions in this spring muffin.

1½ cups diced (½ inch)
*   rhubarb*
½ cup (packed) light
*   brown sugar*
2¼ cups unbleached all-
*   purpose flour*
1 tablespoon baking powder
½ teaspoon salt
2 teaspoons ground
*   cinnamon*
½ teaspoon grated nutmeg

½ cup (1 stick) unsalted
*   butter or margarine, at*
*   room temperature*
1 large egg
½ cup maple syrup
⅔ cup milk
1 tablespoon grated lemon
*   zest*
½ cup coarsely chopped
*   pecans*

1. Mix the rhubarb and brown sugar together in a small bowl. Let sit 45 minutes.

2. Preheat the oven to 350°F. Line 12 muffin cups with paper liners.

3. Mix together the flour, baking powder, salt, cinnamon, and nutmeg. Set aside.

4. Using an electric mixer, beat together the butter and egg until smooth. Beat in the maple syrup. Add the flour mixture alternately with the milk to make a smooth batter. Quickly fold in the rhubarb, lemon zest, and pecans.

5. Spoon the batter into the prepared muffin cups, filling each one almost full. Bake until lightly browned and a toothpick inserted in the center of a muffin comes out clean, 25 to 30 minutes. Serve warm or at room temperature.

Makes 12 muffins

Scalloped Rhubarb

The concept of Thanksgiving stuffing and cranberry relish makes a spring leap in this serendipitous scramble of corn bread, rhubarb, and walnuts. An absolute must with roast spring chicken!

5 cups fresh rhubarb, cut into ¾-inch chunks	1 medium onion, chopped
¾ cup sugar	3 cups Pepperidge Farm corn-bread stuffing crumbs
8 tablespoons (1 stick) unsalted butter	½ cup walnut pieces, diced
	¼ cup cassis liqueur

1. Preheat the oven to 325°F. Butter a 10- or 12-inch gratin dish or shallow casserole.

2. In a large mixing bowl toss together the rhubarb and the sugar.

3. Melt 2 tablespoons of the butter in a medium skillet over medium-high heat. Add the onion and sauté until quite soft, 10 to 15 minutes. Remove the onion from skillet and combine with the rhubarb. Melt the remaining 6 tablespoons butter in the skillet and add it to the rhubarb mixture along with the corn-bread crumbs and walnuts. Stir to combine well.

4. Spread the mixture in the prepared dish. Drizzle the cassis evenly over the top. Bake until the rhubarb juices are bubbling and the crumbs are lightly browned, 40 to 45 minutes. Serve at once.

Makes 6 to 8 servings

Rhubarb Cheese Torte

— ❖ —

This recipe is not only one of the most delicious for rhubarb that I know but also one of the very best in my dessert repertoire. Even people who normally don't eat sweets will ask for seconds of this fluffy, fruit-laced cheesecake.

4 cups diced fresh
  rhubarb
1⅔ cups sugar
⅓ cup Triple Sec liqueur
  or other orange liqueur
1 cup unbleached all-
  purpose flour
½ cup walnut pieces
2 teaspoons ground
  cinnamon
1 tablespoon orange zest

½ cup (1 stick) unsalted
  butter, at room
  temperature, cut into
  small pieces
15 ounces ricotta cheese
8 ounces cream cheese, at
  room temperature
2 teaspoons vanilla extract
3 large eggs

1. Place the rhubarb, ⅔ cup of the sugar, and the liqueur in a saucepan. Bring to a boil over medium heat, stirring occasionally, then reduce the heat and simmer until the rhubarb is cooked and thick, about 15 minutes. Set aside to cool.

2. Preheat the oven to 350°F. Butter a 9-inch springform pan.

3. For the crust, process the flour, ½ cup of the remaining sugar, the walnuts, cinnamon, and orange zest together in a food processor until the walnuts are finely chopped. Add the butter and process just until the mixture resembles coarse crumbs. Press half the crumb mixture over the bottom of the prepared pan. Reserve the remaining crumbs for the top.

4. In a mixing bowl beat together the ricotta, cream cheese, and remaining ½ cup sugar until very smooth. Beat in the vanilla and then the eggs, one at a time, beating well after each addition. Pour the rhubarb over the crumb layer in the pan. Top with the cheese layer, using a spatula to smooth and distribute it evenly.

5. Bake the cheesecake 40 minutes. Sprinkle the top with the remaining crumb mixture and bake until the top is golden brown, about 20 minutes more.

6. Let the cheesecake cool completely on a rack, then refrigerate for a couple hours before serving. Remove the side of the pan and cut into generous wedges.

Makes 8 to 10 servings

Rhubarb Custard Pie

— ✣ —

I never seem to get enough of the tart flavor and wonderful pink color of spring rhubarb. This pie is a truly luscious creation.

CRUST

1½ cups unbleached all-
  purpose flour
2 tablespoons light brown
  sugar
1 teaspoon ground
  cinnamon
1 tablespoon grated orange
  zest
Pinch of salt

6 tablespoons (¾ stick)
  unsalted butter, chilled,
  cut into small pieces
3 tablespoons unsalted
  margarine, chilled, cut
  into small pieces
2 to 3 tablespoons ice water

FILLING

5 cups diced fresh
  rhubarb
1½ cups granulated sugar
2 large eggs
1 cup sour cream

3 tablespoons tapioca
Pinch of salt
½ teaspoon almond extract

TOPPING

½ cup (packed) light
  brown sugar
1 teaspoon ground
  cinnamon
Pinch of salt
⅓ cup unbleached all-
  purpose flour

½ cup old-fashioned rolled
  oats
4 tablespoons (½ stick)
  unsalted butter, at room
  temperature

1. Prepare the crust: Place the flour, brown sugar, cinnamon, orange zest, and salt in a food processor and pulse just to combine. Add the butter and margarine; process until the mixture resembles coarse crumbs. With the machine running, add enough ice water through the feed tube to make the dough come together. Shape the dough into a thick disk, wrap it in plastic wrap, and refrigerate at least 1 hour.

2. Preheat the oven to 425°F.

3. Roll the dough out into a 12-inch circle on a floured surface. Line a 10-inch pie plate with the dough; trim and crimp the edge decoratively.

4. Prepare the rhubarb filling: Toss the rhubarb and sugar together. Beat together the eggs, sour cream, tapioca, salt, and almond extract until smooth. Add to the rhubarb and mix well. Pour the filling into the pie crust.

5. Bake the pie 15 minutes.

6. Meanwhile prepare the topping: Mix together the brown sugar, cinnamon, salt, flour, and oats in a small bowl. Blend in the butter with a fork until the mixture resembles coarse crumbs. Sprinkle the topping over the pie. Reduce the heat to 350°F and bake until the top of the pie is browned and the fruit is bubbling, about 45 minutes more.

7. Let the pie cool at least 30 minutes. Serve warm or at room temperature, cut into wedges.

Makes 8 servings

EASTER
FEASTS

Nothing gets my ethnic juices flowing like the celebration of Easter. In fact, if forced to confine my vast and varied festive energies to just one holiday, I would undoubtedly choose Easter Sunday.

Each year I begin my holiday food planning by rifling through my own family's recipe files in search of the uniquely Polish traditions of feasting which end the penitential season of Lent. My focus in the few weeks preceding Easter is on planning a travel itinerary that will put me in close proximity to a good Polish meat market to allow for securing a hefty supply of the garlicky *fresh* kielbasa special to Easter time. That accomplished, I then zero in on the time-honored customs of the nationalities of my friends, mostly Greeks and Italians, to merge my traditions with a taste of theirs.

The thrust of my entertaining efforts go toward a grand midday buffet on Easter Sunday. An assortment of boiled and sliced kielbasas takes center stage, and the usual accompaniments include dyed eggs, sweet and savory breads, and a rich dome of Russian pashka. Less traditional dishes range from pineapple gratins to fresh artichoke tarts and sauerkraut strudels. If appetite and vim permit, I like an uncomplicated evening dinner featuring roast lamb or baked ham with a colorful and light array of spring vegetables. Desserts such as lemony cheesecakes and tartlets or pineapple upside-down cake cap the festivities and ensure the sweetest of spring dreams.

❖

Polish Easter Soup

— ✣ —

This is a very complicated-sounding recipe for a rather simple and straightforward Polish borscht served traditionally at Easter. There are several steps that involve sitting and soaking over rather long stretches of time, but none are terribly difficult. The basic recipe comes from the Rumanowski family in Westfield, Massachusetts, although I have added a few elaborations of my own.

In Poland the soup is always a part of the main buffet on Easter Sunday, but I find it better suited for a homey supper following Easter since it utilizes leftovers such as sliced kielbasa and hard-boiled eggs.

2 cups old-fashioned rolled
  oats
Heel of rye bread loaf
4 cups warm water
2 ounces dried mushrooms
2 cups boiling water
2 quarts water reserved
  from cooking the Easter
  kielbasa or plain water
3 tablespoons unsalted
  butter
2 medium onions, minced
2 cloves garlic, minced

3 large eggs
2 cups sour cream
1 tablespoon prepared
  horseradish
Salt and freshly ground
  black pepper to taste
Diced cooked kielbasa for
  garnish
Chopped hard-cooked eggs
  for garnish
Boiled or skillet-browned
  potatoes for garnish

1. At least a full day before you plan to serve the soup, combine the oats and bread heel with the warm water in a small bowl. Let soak and ferment at least 24 hours. Strain and reserve the liquid; discard the solids.

2. Combine the dried mushrooms with the boiling water and let soak 2 hours. Drain and chop the mushrooms, reserving the soaking liquid and mushrooms separately.

3. In a large soup pot combine the reserved oatmeal liquid, mushroom liquid, and the kielbasa cooking water or plain water. Bring just to a boil over medium heat.

4. Meanwhile melt the butter in a medium-size skillet over medium heat. Add the onions and garlic and sauté until just beginning to turn golden, 15 to 20 minutes.

5. Beat the eggs until frothy in a small bowl. Beat in some of the hot soup liquid, then whisk all back into the soup pot, stirring constantly. At this point, it is important to keep the soup just below boiling to prevent curdling. Stir in the sautéed onion and garlic and the reserved mushrooms.

6. Put the sour cream in a small mixing bowl and gradually beat some of the hot soup into it. Return it to the soup pot and stir until smooth. Season the soup with the horseradish, salt, and pepper. Ladle the hot soup into shallow soup bowls and pass the garnishes.

Makes 10 to 12 servings

Sauerkraut and Mushroom Strudel

— ✢ —

I love the balance of sweet and savory foods that make up the all-day feast of a traditional Polish Easter. This savory strudel-like bread is the perfect accompaniment to platters of sliced kielbasa and baked ham. The appealing astringency of fresh sauerkraut (do not use canned) is also the perfect antidote to excessive jelly bean and chocolate egg consumption.

STRUDEL DOUGH
2 packages active dry yeast
1 tablespoon sugar
¼ cup warm water (110 to
  115°F)
¾ cup milk
1 tablespoon unsalted
  butter

½ teaspoon salt
½ teaspoon grated nutmeg
2 large eggs, lightly beaten
4 to 4½ cups unbleached
  all-purpose flour

FILLING
¾ cup imported dried
  mushrooms
2 cups water
2 pounds sauerkraut,
  drained
2 tablespoons unsalted
  butter
2 large onions, chopped

1 tablespoon caraway seeds
¼ cup heavy or whipping
  cream
1 cup shredded Gruyère cheese
Salt and freshly ground
  black pepper to taste
1 large egg white, lightly
  beaten

1. In a small bowl stir the yeast and sugar into the warm water. Let stand until foamy, about 10 minutes.

2. Meanwhile put the milk and butter in a small saucepan and

heat over very low heat just until the butter is melted. Pour the milk mixture into a large mixing bowl. Stir the yeast into the milk, then beat in the salt, nutmeg, eggs, and 2 cups of the flour. Stir in enough of the remaining flour to make a soft dough.

3. Transfer the dough to a lightly floured surface and knead until smooth and satiny, about 10 minutes. Place the dough in a lightly buttered bowl and cover with a damp cloth. Let rise in a warm place until doubled in bulk, 1 to 1½ hours.

4. Meanwhile prepare the filling: Place the mushrooms in a small saucepan and cover with the water. Bring to a boil, then simmer until quite soft, about 10 minutes. Strain the liquid to remove any sand and reserve. Finely chop the mushrooms and set aside.

5. Place the sauerkraut and reserved mushroom liquid in a sauce-pan. Cook uncovered over medium heat until all the liquid has evaporated, about 20 minutes. Stir frequently to prevent sticking or scorching.

6. Melt the butter in a large skillet over medium-high heat. Add the onions and sauté, stirring frequently until soft and translucent, 10 to 15 minutes. Add the sauerkraut and mushrooms and cook a few minutes more. Stir in the caraway and cream, then remove from the heat. Stir in the cheese and season with salt and pepper. Set aside to cool.

7. Preheat the oven to 350°F.

8. Punch the dough down and divide it evenly in half. On a lightly floured surface, roll each half into a 14 × 12-inch rectangle. Spread half the filling over each rectangle, leaving 1-inch borders. Roll up each rectangle jelly-roll style, starting from one long edge. Crimp the ends to seal. Carefully transfer the strudels to the lined baking sheet. Pierce the rolls in several places with the tines of a fork in order to allow steam to escape. Brush all over with the egg white.

9. Bake the strudels until light golden brown, 40 to 45 minutes. Let cool a few minutes before cutting into 1-inch slices. The strudels may also be served at room temperature.

Makes 2 strudels

Italian Artichoke Tart

— ❖ —

Making this sublime Italian-inspired quiche provides the cook with a crash course in the anatomy of an artichoke. Resist the temptation to substitute canned artichoke hearts in this recipe because the fresh hearts are what make this tart taste so extraordinary. Serve it as a part of a brunch or as the first course of a formal Easter dinner.

CRUST

1½ cups unbleached all-
    purpose flour
¼ teaspoon salt
6 tablespoons (¾ stick)
    unsalted butter, chilled,
    cut into small pieces

3 tablespoons unsalted
    margarine, chilled, cut
    into small pieces
3 to 4 tablespoons ice water

FILLING

3 large artichokes
2 tablespoons fresh lemon
    juice
4 ounces pancetta, finely
    diced
1 small onion, minced
1 bunch scallions, trimmed
    and minced
2 cloves garlic, minced
1 red bell pepper, stemmed,
    seeded, and cut into thin
    strips
¼ cup minced fresh parsley

3 tablespoons shredded fresh
    basil leaves
1 cup shredded Swiss cheese
½ cup freshly grated
    Parmesan cheese
3 large eggs
1 tablespoon Dijon mustard
¼ cup heavy or whipping
    cream
½ cup light cream
¼ teaspoon grated nutmeg
Salt and freshly ground
    black pepper to taste

1. Prepare the crust: Place the flour, salt, butter, and margarine in a food processor and process until the mixture resembles coarse crumbs. With the machine running, add enough ice water through the feed tube to bring the dough together. Shape the dough into a thick disk, wrap it in plastic wrap, and refrigerate at least 1 hour.

2. Prepare the filling: Cut the stems from each artichoke and snap off the leaves around the bottom at their natural breaking point. Cut off the top cone of leaves and scoop out the hairy chokes with a spoon. Trim any green remaining on the hearts. Cut the hearts into ¼-inch-thick slices and place in a bowl of cold water mixed with 2 tablespoons lemon juice to prevent discoloration.

3. Sauté the pancetta in a large skillet over medium-high heat until browned, 5 to 7 minutes. Reduce the heat to medium and add the onion, scallions, garlic, and bell pepper. Cook uncovered to soften the vegetables, stirring occasionally, 10 minutes. Drain the artichoke slices and add them to the skillet; cook another 3 minutes. Remove from the heat and stir in the parsley and basil. Set aside.

4. Preheat the oven to 375°F.

5. Roll out the pastry ¼ inch thick on a lightly floured surface. Line a 10-inch tart pan with the pastry; trim and crimp the edge decoratively. Sprinkle the Swiss and Parmesan cheeses evenly over the pastry; then top with the artichoke mixture.

6. Whisk together the eggs, mustard, and heavy and light

creams. Season with the nutmeg, salt, and pepper. Pour evenly over the artichoke mixture in the pastry shell.

7. Bake the tart until puffed and set, about 45 minutes. Serve hot, warm, or at room temperature.

Makes 6 to 8 servings

Pierogies
with Ricotta and Figs

— ✤ —

Italy has its ravioli, Asia its wontons, India its samosas, Austria its dumplings, and Poland its pierogies. Large parts of the world clearly enjoy the intensity of flavors that come wrapped in compact, edible packages. Most Polish cooks are very protective of family pierogi recipes and claim it is impossible to teach others to make good pierogies. Having served a couple of years of culinary penance mixing, kneading, rolling, and shaping numerous varieties of pasta dough to keep pace with the fresh pasta craze, I was not intimidated by the prospect of making pierogies without the wise and watchful eye of a long lost *cioccia* or *bacchie* (Polish aunt or grandmother).

Due to the uncertain nature of food supplies in the homeland, the resourceful Poles have devised an endless variety of serendipitous fillings for pierogies. There are savory ones filled with cabbage, pork, or mushrooms; cheese versions with ricotta and raisins, or farmer's cheese and eggs; and fruit pierogies filled with stewed cherries or blueberries. When I undertook my premier batch, I couldn't decide which type to make and ended up creating a most successful blending of all three.

FILLING

¾ cup diced (¼ inch)
   dried figs
½ cup dry white wine
2 pounds ricotta cheese

2 large egg yolks
¼ cup sugar
2 teaspoons vanilla extract
1 tablespoon caraway seeds

DOUGH

4 cups unbleached all-
   purpose flour
2 large eggs
5 tablespoons sour cream

3 tablespoons unsalted
   butter, melted
½ teaspoon salt
¾ cup water

FINAL COOKING

1⅛ cups (2¼ sticks)
   unsalted butter

4½ cups coarsely chopped onions
Sour cream for serving

1. Prepare the filling: Place the figs and wine in a small sauce-pan. Bring to a boil, then simmer about 5 minutes to soften the fruit. Let cool to room temperature. In a mixing bowl blend together the ricotta, egg yolks, and sugar. Stir in the vanilla, figs with wine, and caraway seeds.

2. Prepare the dough: Put the flour in a large mixing bowl and make a well in the center. Place the eggs, sour cream, butter, and salt in the well, then blend all the ingredients together with your hands, gradually adding the water and working the mixture into a smooth pliable dough. Divide the dough into quarters and keep the unused portions covered with a damp towel while working.

3. On a lightly floured surface, roll out one piece of the dough ¹⁄₁₆ inch thick. Cut into rounds with a 3½- to 4-inch round cookie cutter. Place a tablespoon of filling in the center of each round, fold the rounds in half, then crimp the edges together decoratively with your fingertips or seal by pressing the edges together with the tines of a fork. Place the finished pierogies in a single layer on lightly floured baking sheet. Repeat the process with the remaining dough and filling.

4. When ready to serve the pierogies (do not wait longer than 3 hours after filling the dough), bring a large pot of salted water to a boil. Cook the pierogies in batches of 8 to 10 so as not to crowd them. Drop them into the boiling water and stir gently to prevent them from sticking to the bottom of the pot. Cook over medium-high heat until the pierogies float to the surface of the water; 4 to 5 minutes. Remove with a slotted spoon and drain. Repeat the process with the remaining pierogies. (If you wish to freeze any pierogies at this point, pat them dry with a paper towel, place by the dozen in plastic bags, seal tightly, and freeze up to 1 month.)

5. Depending on how many people you are serving, sauté in 2 tablespoons butter ½ cup coarsely chopped onion per serving (6 to 8 pierogies) in a skillet over medium heat until very soft and lightly golden, about 20 minutes. Add the boiled pierogies to the pan and sauté, basting with the onions, until the pierogies are lightly browned all over, 10 to 15 minutes more. Spoon onto warmed serving plates and garnish with a generous dollop of sour cream.

Makes about 72 pierogies, serves 9 to 12

EASTER BRUNCH BUFFET

— ❖ —

Citrus Terrine
Deviled Eggs
Cold Sliced Polish Kielbasa and/
or Humpty Dumpty Ham
Ruby Horseradish Sauce
Pierogies with Ricotta and Figs
Italian Artichoke Tart

— ❖ —

Pineapple Gratin
Polish Babka
Russian Pashka
Southern Pecan Cake with Lulu's Rum Sauce

— ❖ —

Pink grapefruit mimosas
Hot Coffee

— ❖ —

Deviled Eggs

— ❖ —

I have always loved deviled eggs, and since the current hype on nutrition would have us all believing that the once simple egg could now kill us or at least clog our arteries dreadfully, I like to make my egg stuffings all the more spectacular so that they are truly worth all the guilty indulgence. The Chutney-Stuffed Eggs hint of exotic India, while the Horseradish-Stuffed Eggs reflect spring with a pretty pink color and tangy, fresh taste.

Horseradish-Stuffed Eggs

— ✤ —

6 hard-cooked eggs, peeled
2 tablespoons unsalted
  butter, at room
  temperature
2 tablespoons Hellmann's
  mayonnaise
2½ tablespoons prepared
  horseradish with beets

1 teaspoon Dijon mustard
2 tablespoons minced fresh
  chives
Salt and freshly ground
  black pepper to taste
Capers for garnish
Small fresh dill sprigs for
  garnish

1. Halve the eggs lengthwise and remove the yolks, reserving the whites. Force the yolks through a sieve into a small mixing bowl. Blend in the butter and mayonnaise until smooth. Mix in the horseradish, mustard, and chives. Season with salt and pepper.

2. Mound the yolk mixture into the cavities of the reserved whites. Press a few capers and a sprig of dill onto the top of each egg. Serve at once or refrigerate until ready to serve.

Makes 12 stuffed egg halves

Chutney-Stuffed Eggs

— ✤ —

6 hard-cooked eggs, peeled
3 tablespoons mango
  chutney, large fruit pieces
  minced
3 tablespoons Hellmann's
  mayonnaise

1 teaspoon best-quality
  curry powder
2 tablespoons minced fresh chives
2 tablespoons finely
  chopped toasted almonds,
  for garnish

1. Halve the eggs lengthwise and remove the yolks, reserving the

whites. Force the yolks through a sieve into a small mixing bowl. Blend in the chutney and mayonnaise. Season with the curry powder and chives.

2. Mound the yolk mixture into the cavities of the reserved whites. Sprinkle the top of each egg with some of the toasted almonds. Serve at once or refrigerate until ready to serve.

Makes 12 stuffed egg halves

Humpty-Dumpty Ham

— ❖ —

Since making stuffing always puts me in a good mood, this recipe lets me indulge my passion beyond Thanksgiving. The Southern savor of the stuffing is saliently accented as it absorbs the smoky juices from the ham. While it is a little tricky to bone the ham, fill the resulting cavity with the dressing, and then tie it all back together again, the flavorful masterpiece is worth the fuss for those special celebrations when going the whole hog is in order. In a pinch a prepackaged boned ham (the one that looks as if it could double as a football) could be substituted by furrowing a major tunnel through the center to house the dressing. Most ham hosts and hostesses, however, feel that the bone-in meat is more succulent.

1 bone-in ham, about 14 pounds
1 cup dried apricots, coarsely chopped
½ cup Madeira
¾ cup (1½ sticks) unsalted butter
2 large onions, chopped
4 ribs celery, chopped
12 ounces Pepperidge Farm corn bread stuffing mix
2½ cups chopped pecans, lightly toasted

1 can (20 ounces) unsweetened pineapple chunks, undrained
3 tablespoons Dijon mustard
1 large egg
1 teaspoon ground cloves
2 teaspoons ground coriander
Finely grated zest of 1 orange
1 cup fresh orange juice
1 cup cream sherry
1 cup pineapple juice
¾ cup honey

1. If you are adept with a boning knife, bone the ham or else have the butcher do it when you purchase the ham. (Save the bone

for soup.) You will end up with 2 pieces of ham that look rather like Humpty Dumpty *after* the great fall.

2. Place the apricots and Madeira in a small saucepan. Bring to a boil over medium-high heat, then simmer 10 minutes. Remove from the heat and set aside.

3. Melt the butter in a large skillet over medium-high heat. Add the onions and celery and sauté until the vegetables are soft and translucent, 10 to 15 minutes. Transfer to a large mixing bowl and combine with the corn bread stuffing, pecans, and pineapple with its juice. Stir in the apricots with any liquid. Bind the stuffing together with the mustard and egg. Season with the cloves, coriander, and orange zest.

4. Preheat the oven to 400°F.

5. Fill the hollow of the ham left from the removed bone with the stuffing mixture, then tie the ham together with kitchen string. (If there is extra stuffing, bake it separately in a buttered casserole for the last 45 minutes of cooking time.) The ham will now look like Humpty Dumpty put back together again.

6. Place the ham in a large roasting pan. Combine the orange juice, sherry, and pineapple juice and pour it around the ham. Cover the ham with aluminum foil and bake 1¼ hours. Reduce the heat to 325°F and uncover the ham. In a small bowl blend 1 cup of the pan juices with the honey. Spoon some of this mixture over the ham to glaze it and bake another hour, basting occasionally with the glaze.

7. Let the ham sit 10 to 15 minutes before carving, then slice and serve with the stuffing.

Makes 16 to 20 servings

Roast Leg of Lamb with Moroccan Spices

— ✣ —

A s much as I love the traditional roast leg of lamb with rosemary and garlic, I wanted something a little more exotic one windy spring day. My curiosity led me to explore the seasonings Moroccans use to flavor their meat tagines, or stews, and this proved to be a most exciting inspiration. The accompanying mint sauce is made as the British do with sugar and vinegar; my substitution of raspberry vinegar ties it back to the Moroccan tradition of cooking meat and fruit together in fragrant combinations. Try this recipe next time you want to infuse sophisticated pizzazz into the much loved supper of lamb.

½ cup (1 stick) unsalted
   butter, at room
   temperature
6 cloves garlic, minced
3 tablespoons minced fresh
   ginger
1 tablespoon paprika

1 tablespoon ground cumin
2 teaspoons ground
   coriander
1 leg of lamb, about 6½
   pounds
Kosher (coarse) salt
1½ cups dry red wine

RASPBERRY-MINT SAUCE

1 cup fresh mint leaves,
   torn into coarse pieces
¾ cup raspberry vinegar
½ cup rice wine vinegar

⅓ cup sugar
Freshly ground black pepper
   to taste

1. Preheat the oven to 350°F.

2. In a small bowl mash together the butter, garlic, and ginger.
Mix in the spices and blend to make a smooth spice paste.

3. If there is a lot of fat on the lamb, trim all but a very thin
layer. Make about 20 small 1-inch-deep incisions in the lamb with the
tip of a sharp paring knife. Rub the spice paste all over the lamb and
push it into the incisions. Place the lamb in a roasting pan and
sprinkle with the kosher salt. Pour the wine into the bottom of the
pan.

4. Roast the lamb 1½ hours for medium-rare meat, basting occasionally with the pan juices. Let sit 10 to 15 minutes before carving.

5. Meanwhile prepare the raspberry-mint sauce: Place the mint
in a small mixing bowl and pour in both vinegars. Whisk in the sugar
and season with pepper. Let sit at room temperature to mellow the
flavors while the lamb cooks.

6. Slice the lamb thin and arrange on a platter. Drizzle any remaining pan juices over the slices. Pass the raspberry-mint sauce in a
sauceboat.

Makes 8 to 10 servings

Lemony Leg of Lamb, Greek Style

— ❖ —

If anyone is an expert at cooking fabulous tasting lamb, the Greeks
are. Lots of lemon, garlic, rosemary, and oregano infuse this spring
roast.

1 tablespoon grated lemon
    zest
1 tablespoon dried oregano
1 tablespoon dried
    rosemary, coarsely
    crumbled
3 cloves garlic, minced
⅓ cup unbleached all-
    purpose flour
6 tablespoons fresh lemon
    juice

Salt and freshly ground
    black pepper to taste
1 leg of lamb, 5½ to 6
    pounds, excess fat
    trimmed
¾ cup water

1. Preheat the oven to 425°F.

2. In a small mixing bowl combine the lemon zest, oregano, rosemary, garlic, and flour. Stir in the lemon juice to make a paste, then season with salt and pepper. Make ½-inch-deep slits all over the leg of lamb. Rub the lemon paste all over the leg, making sure it gets into the slits.

3. Put the lamb on a rack in a roasting pan and pour the water into the bottom of the pan. Roast the lamb 30 minutes. Reduce the heat to 325°F and continue roasting until a meat thermometer registers 145°F for medium-rare meat, 1 to 1¼ hours longer.

4. Transfer the lamb to a cutting board and let sit 10 minutes before carving. Skim the fat from the pan juices and spoon over the sliced lamb.

Makes 8 servings

Couscous with Mushrooms and Mint

To my mind, this soothing couscous is the perfect match for roast spring lamb since it mirrors the color of the season's first forsythia and daffodil blossoms.

¼ cup olive oil
1 bunch scallions, trimmed
  and minced
1 yellow bell pepper,
  stemmed, seeded, and
  diced
½ teaspoon saffron threads
1 teaspoon ground
  cinnamon
8 ounces shiitake or
  domestic white
  mushrooms, sliced (only
  the shiitake caps)

3 tablespoons pine nuts,
  lightly toasted
2½ cups chicken broth,
  preferably homemade
4 tablespoons (½ stick)
  unsalted butter
12 ounces couscous
½ cup fresh mint leaves,
  coarsely chopped
Salt and freshly ground
  black pepper to taste

1. Heat the olive oil in a large skillet over medium-high heat. Add the scallions and bell pepper and sauté until softened, about 5 minutes. Stir in the saffron and cinnamon; cook 30 seconds more. Add the mushrooms and continue sautéing until all the mushroom juices have evaporated, 10 to 15 minutes. Remove from the heat, stir in the pine nuts, and set aside.

2. In a medium-size saucepan bring the chicken broth to a boil. Add the butter and stir until melted. Quickly stir in all the couscous. Cover the pot and remove from the heat. Let stand undisturbed for 5 minutes. Uncover and stir in the sautéed vegetables and fresh mint. Season with salt and pepper. Serve at once.

Makes 8 servings

IMAGINING EASTER AND MATISSE IN MOROCCO

— ❖ —

Bowl of mixed marinated olives
Pita toasts

— ❖ —

Leg of Lamb with Moroccan Spices
Couscous with Mushrooms and Mint
Sweet Minted Peas

— ❖ —

Pineapple Upside-Down Cake

Braised White Beans

—✧—

W̲hite beans braised with a healthy array of minced spring vegetables are one of my favorite accompaniments to lamb. If you can find
the fresh sage, it will add a typically Italian flavor to the recipe.

8 ounces small white beans,
  picked over for pebbles
  and soaked in water to
  cover overnight
3 tablespoons fruity olive
  oil
1 fat leek (light green and
  white parts), rinsed well,
  trimmed, and minced
1 carrot, peeled and minced
1 rib celery, minced

4 cloves garlic, minced
2 ounces thinly sliced
  prosciutto, minced
3 tablespoons tomato paste
¼ cup minced fresh parsley
3 tablespoons coarsely
  chopped fresh sage leaves
  (optional)
Salt and freshly ground
  black pepper to taste

1. Drain and rinse the soaked beans. Place them in a pot and
cover with fresh water. Bring to a boil, then simmer uncovered until
just barely tender, 35 to 40 minutes. Drain, reserving ½ cup of the
cooking liquid.

2. Meanwhile heat 2 tablespoons of the olive oil in a medium-
size skillet over medium-high heat. Add the leek, carrot, celery, and
garlic; sauté until the vegetables are quite soft, about 10 minutes. Stir
in the minced prosciutto and cook 1 minute more.

3. Preheat the oven to 325°F.

4. Combine the vegetable mixture, beans, and ½ cup cooking
liquid in a 2-quart casserole. Stir in the tomato paste, parsley, sage,
and remaining 1 tablespoon olive oil. Season with salt and pepper.

5. Bake the beans until piping hot and quite tender, about 30
minutes. Serve hot.

Makes 6 servings

WE HAD A LITTLE LAMB

— ❖ —

Fiddleheads Fresca

— ❖ —

Lemony Lamb, Greek Style
Cinnamon Onion Marmalade
Baked Cherry Tomatoes Provençal
Comfort Carrots

— ❖ —

Galatoboureko

Baked Cherry Tomatoes Provençal

— ❖ —

By early spring my taste for a garden tomato is almost unbearable. I've found that cherry tomatoes yield much better flavor at this time of year than the sickly hothouse varieties still proliferating on supermarket shelves. This Provençal preparation not only ensures the greatest concentration of rich tomato flavor but also is a born companion to roast lamb.

1½ pints ripe cherry
   tomatoes
Salt and freshly ground
   black pepper to taste
1 teaspoon dried oregano
2 large cloves garlic, peeled

2 large slices white bread,
   preferably homemade
½ cup coarsely chopped
   fresh parsley
¼ cup fruity olive oil

1. Preheat the oven to 400°F.
2. Slice the top off each tomato and arrange them compactly in a single layer in an ovenproof dish. Sprinkle the tomatoes with salt, pepper, and oregano.

3. Place the garlic, bread, and parsley in a food processor and process until finely minced. With the machine running, pour the olive oil through the feed tube and process until well blended. Sprinkle the bread crumb mixture evenly over the tomatoes.

4. Bake until the crumbs are crusty brown and the juices from the tomatoes are bubbling, about 45 minutes. Let cool a few minutes. Serve hot, warm, or at room temperature.

Makes 6 servings

Comfort Carrots

— ❖ —

This unusual method of parboiling carrots with a vanilla bean induces a magical and delicate flavor transformation in this most common of vegetables. The fluffy orange purée with wisps of bright green chive goes superbly with roast spring lamb or chicken.

*2 pounds carrots, peeled
  and cut into 1-inch
  chunks
1 vanilla bean
2 tablespoons unsalted
  butter, at room
  temperature
⅔ cup light cream*

*1 tablespoon grainy
  mustard
2 tablespoons minced fresh
  chives, plus additional for
  garnish
½ teaspoon grated nutmeg
Salt and freshly ground
  black pepper to taste*

1. Place the carrots and vanilla bean in a saucepan and cover generously with water. Bring to a boil, then simmer uncovered until the carrots are very tender, 15 to 20 minutes. Drain well and discard the vanilla bean.

2. Place the carrots in a food processor, add the butter, and process to a smooth purée. With the machine running, slowly pour the cream through the feed tube and process until completely blended. Blend in the mustard. Add the chives, nutmeg, salt, and pepper; process just to combine.

3. Serve the purée immediately or gently reheat it in a double boiler over simmering water at serving time. Garnish with an extra sprinkling of snipped chives just before serving.

Makes 6 to 8 servings

Polish Creamed Beets

— ✛ —

You can't be Polish and not serve beets on Easter Sunday. This rich preparation makes a lovely vegetable accompaniment for a sit-down dinner.

2 bunches (4 beets each)
medium beets, rinsed and
greens removed
3 tablespoons unsalted
butter

1 tablespoon light brown sugar
1 tablespoon red wine vinegar
Salt and freshly ground
black pepper to taste
1 cup sour cream

1. Place the beets in a large saucepan and add cold water to cover. Bring to a boil, then simmer until the beets are fork-tender, about 30 minutes. Drain and peel the beets in the sink under running water. Cut into ¼-inch-thick slices.

2. Melt the butter and brown sugar together in a large skillet over medium heat. Add the beets and toss to coat with the butter mixture. Sprinkle with the vinegar and season with salt and pepper.

3. Just before serving, fold in the sour cream. Cook over low heat just until warmed through. Serve at once.

Makes 8 servings

Ruby Horseradish Sauce

— ✛ —

A demitasse spoonful of nose-tingling horseradish has always been a traditional part of the Polish Easter breakfast feast in my family. The powerful little mouthful acts as a vernal equinox for the body as it spritzes the system out of winter hibernation into a jolt of spring awakening. Ever the chef, I couldn't resist transforming the ritual spoonful into something a bit more refined. This vibrant-colored and -tasting sauce is the palatable result of my experimentation. The kick of the horseradish is retained but also balanced by a sweetness and slight bitterness that remind me of a Campari aperitif. Serve warm or at room temperature with sliced kielbasa, baked ham, or corned beef.

1 cup dry red wine
⅔ cup port
½ teaspoon ground
    cinnamon
½ teaspoon grated nutmeg
½ teaspoon ground allspice
1 tablespoon finely grated
    lemon zest

1¼ cups finely grated or
    chopped fresh horseradish
    (see note)
1 jar (10 ounces) red
    currant jelly

Place the wine, port, cinnamon, nutmeg, allspice, and lemon zest in a small saucepan. Bring to a boil, then reduce the heat and simmer until the mixture is reduced by half, 12 to 15 minutes. Stir in the horseradish and the currant jelly; cook over low heat 10 minutes to blend and mellow the flavors. Transfer to a sauceboat and serve hot or at room temperature.

Makes about 2 cups

Note: During preparation, fresh horseradish can give off very strong fumes. Keep your face away from the horseradish while you grate it.

Cinnamon-Onion Marmalade

This is a simple yet rather unusual homemade condiment to serve as an embellishment to lamb.

4 tablespoons (½ stick)
    unsalted butter
2 large onions, thinly sliced
½ cup water
3 tablespoons dried currants

1½ teaspoons ground
    cinnamon
2 tablespoons pine nuts,
    lightly toasted

1. Melt the butter in a large skillet over medium-high heat. Add the onions and sauté, stirring constantly, 5 minutes. Add the water and currants and reduce the heat to low. Cover the pan and cook, stirring occasionally, until the onions soften almost to a purée, 45 to 60 minutes.

2. Stir in the cinnamon and pine nuts. Cook 5 minutes more to marry the flavors. Serve hot in a sauceboat.

Makes about 2½ cups

Pineapple Gratin

— ❖ —

This unusual combination of ingredients—pineapple, Cheddar cheese, and brown sugar—makes a delightful accompaniment to sliced Easter meats at an Easter brunch. The sunny yellow color of the dish adds to the celebration of spring.

2 tablespoons unsalted
   butter, melted
½ cup unbleached all-
   purpose flour
¾ cup (packed) light
   brown sugar
1 pound sharp orange-
   colored Cheddar cheese,
   shredded

1 can (1 pound)
   unsweetened crushed
   pineapple, drained, juice
   reserved
2 cans (1 pound each)
   unsweetened sliced
   pineapple, drained, juice
   reserved

1. Preheat the oven to 325°F. Pour the melted butter over the bottom of a shallow, 2-quart casserole. Set aside.

2. Place the flour, sugar, and Cheddar in a mixing bowl and toss to combine. Make a layer of half the crushed pineapple in the baking dish. Top with a third of the cheese mixture. Spread the remaining crushed pineapple over the top and sprinkle with another third of the cheese mixture. Arrange the pineapple slices attractively on top and sprinkle with the remaining cheese mixture. Drizzle the reserved juice over all.

3. Bake 1¼ hours. Serve hot.

Makes 10 to 12 servings

Sweet Potato Biscuits

— ❖ —

One Easter when much of my family was off enjoying the splendors of spring in Portugal and I was in Manhattan trying to concentrate on several different projects, my catering comrade, Pat Powers, invited me up to Weston, Connecticut, to share in a cooking and eating extravaganza with her food-loving family. With the exception of one essential clothing foray to the local Loehmann's, we spent all of our time in the kitchen scheming up wonderful menus and meals.

Even Pat's daughter Julie, a newly minted MBA, was able to escape the grueling hours of the corporate finance department at Citibank to add these delightfully moist biscuits to our feasting frenzy. "Awesome," as Pat's other daughter, Little Sarah, would say!

2 large sweet potatoes or
yams, peeled
½ cup (1 stick) unsalted
butter, at room
temperature
½ teaspoon salt

1¼ to 1½ cups unbleached
all-purpose flour
¼ cup sugar
1½ teaspoons baking
powder

1. Put the sweet potatoes in a saucepan with water to cover. Boil until very tender, 30 to 40 minutes. Drain the sweet potatoes and place them in a mixing bowl. Add the butter and beat, using a hand-held electric mixer, until smooth. Add the salt and set aside to cool to room temperature.

2. Preheat the oven to 450°F.

3. Using a wooden spoon, beat 1¼ cups flour into the sweet potatoes. Stir in the sugar and baking powder. If the dough seems too sticky, add the remaining flour.

4. On a lightly floured surface, roll the dough out 1 inch thick. Using a 2½-inch round cookie cutter, cut the dough into biscuits and arrange on an ungreased baking sheet. Gather up the scraps, reroll, and cut out as many more biscuits as possible.

5. Bake the biscuits until lightly golden on top, 15 to 20 minutes. Serve warm with whipped sweet butter.

Makes 12 to 16 biscuits

Angel Biscuits with Dill

— ❖ —

My guess is that these Southern biscuits get their name from the heavenly lightness that the three leavening agents—baking powder, baking soda, and yeast—impart. I like the herby taste of the feathery dill, but it may be omitted if a plain biscuit is preferred.

1½ teaspoons active dry yeast
¼ cup warm water (110 to 115°F)
1 cup buttermilk
¼ cup finely minced fresh dill
2½ to 3 cups unbleached all-purpose flour
2 tablespoons sugar
¼ teaspoon salt

1½ teaspoons baking powder
½ teaspoon baking soda
6 tablespoons (¾ stick) unsalted margarine, chilled, cut into small pieces

1. In a medium-size mixing bowl, stir the yeast into the warm water and let stand until dissolved, 5 to 10 minutes. Stir in the buttermilk and dill until completely blended.

2. Place the flour, sugar, salt, baking powder, soda, and margarine in a food processor and process until the mixture resembles coarse crumbs. Using a fork, blend this mixture with the yeast mixture to form a dough.

3. Transfer the dough to a floured surface and knead, adding more flour if the dough is sticky, until soft and smooth, about 5 minutes. Place the dough in a plastic bag, fasten it loosely, and refrigerate at least 1 hour or up to 24 hours.

4. Preheat the oven to 400°F. Line baking sheets with parchment paper.

5. Roll out the dough ½ inch thick on a lightly floured surface. Cut into 1-inch rounds with a cookie cutter. Arrange the rounds ½ inch apart in rows on the lined baking sheets. Gather up the scraps, reroll, and cut out as many more biscuits as possible. Cover with a kitchen towel and let rise in a warm place 30 minutes.

6. Bake until puffed and golden, 10 to 12 minutes. Serve warm or at room temperature.

Makes about thirty 1-inch biscuits

Italian Pecorino and Prosciutto Bread

— ❖ —

This is a traditional Italian Easter specialty known as *torta di pasqua*. It makes a tasty and savory addition to a brunch bread basket, and any left over make inspired post-holiday sandwiches.

2 packages active dry yeast
½ cup warm milk (110 to 115°F)
4 large eggs
¼ cup fruity olive oil
¼ cup (½ stick) unsalted butter, melted and cooled
3½ to 4 cups unbleached all-purpose flour
½ teaspoon salt

1 teaspoon freshly ground black pepper
1 cup freshly grated Pecorino Romano cheese
½ cup shredded Swiss or Fontina cheese
4 ounces thinly sliced prosciutto, cut into thin shreds

1. Stir the yeast into the milk in a large mixing bowl and let stand until dissolved, 5 to 10 minutes. Beat in the eggs, olive oil, and butter until well blended. Combine 3½ cups flour with the salt and pepper, add it to the yeast mixture, and stir to form a dough. Work in the cheeses and the prosciutto.

2. Transfer the dough to a floured work surface and knead, adding more flour if the dough is too sticky, until smooth and satiny, 7 to 10 minutes. Shape the dough into 1 round and bulbous loaf. Place on a baking sheet lined with parchment paper. Cover with a clean kitchen towel and let rise in a warm, draft-free place until doubled in bulk, 1½ to 2 hours.

3. Preheat the oven to 400°F.

4. Bake the bread until the loaf sounds hollow when tapped on the bottom, 30 to 40 minutes. Let cool on a wire rack.

Makes 1 loaf

Polish Babka

—❖—

Babka is a luscious bubble bread that translates from the Polish as Grandmother's sweet bread. It is as integral to a Polish celebration of Easter as our jelly-bean-bearing bunny. The Poles, a hearty, robust people, never write a babka recipe that yields less than two loaves. If you're not sharing Easter breakfast with the town or every relative you have, the second babka will freeze nicely if wrapped securely.

3 packages active dry yeast
1 cup plus 1 tablespoon sugar
¾ cup warm water (110 to 115°F)
8 to 9 cups unbleached all-purpose flour
1½ cups milk
1 cup (2 sticks) unsalted butter
¾ cup golden raisins
¼ cup golden rum

6 large eggs
2 large egg yolks
2 teaspoons vanilla extract
1 teaspoon salt
1 teaspoon ground cardamom
1 tablespoon grated orange zest
2 teaspoons grated lemon zest
2 large egg whites
1 tablespoon water

TOPPING
4 tablespoons (½ stick) unsalted butter, at room temperature
⅓ cup (packed) light brown sugar

1 teaspoon ground cinnamon
½ cup slivered almonds
½ cup unbleached all-purpose flour

GLAZE
2 large egg whites
1½ cups sifted confectioners' sugar

½ teaspoon fresh lemon juice

1. Lightly butter two 10-inch tube pans. Set aside.

2. Stir the yeast and 1 tablespoon sugar into the warm water in a small mixing bowl. Let stand until foamy, about 10 minutes. Whisk in ½ cup of the flour, cover with plastic wrap, and let stand in a warm place until the mixture has doubled in volume and is bubbly, about 10 minutes.

3. Place the milk and butter in a small saucepan and heat over medium heat just until the butter has melted. Let the mixture cool until just slightly warm to the touch.

4. Put the raisins and rum in another small saucepan. Bring to a boil over medium-high heat, then simmer 2 minutes and remove from the heat.

5. In a large mixing bowl beat together the eggs, egg yolks, and remaining 1 cup sugar until thick and lemon colored. Beat in the cooled milk mixture, the raisins, the yeast mixture, vanilla, salt, cardamom, and orange and lemon zests. Gradually beat in 5 cups of the flour, then stir in enough of the remaining flour to make a soft dough.

6. Transfer the dough to a well-floured surface. Gently knead the dough making sure the raisins are distributed evenly. Continue kneading the dough until it is smooth and satiny, about 5 minutes more.

7. Divide the dough evenly in half. Arrange a ring of dough in each prepared pan. Cover each pan with a damp cloth and let the bread rise in a warm, draft-free place until doubled in bulk, about 1½ hours.

8. Meanwhile prepare the topping: Cream together the butter and brown sugar in a mixing bowl. Add the cinnamon, almonds, and flour and stir until the mixture is crumbly. Set aside.

9. Preheat the oven to 350°F.

10. When the dough has risen, beat the egg whites and 1 tablespoon water together and brush over the top of the dough. Sprinkle the topping evenly over each babka.

11. Bake the babkas until golden brown and hollow sounding when tapped lightly with the fingers, 50 to 60 minutes.

12. Let the breads cool 5 minutes in the pan, then turn out onto wire racks to cool completely.

13. Meanwhile, prepare the glaze: Place the egg whites in a medium-size mixing bowl and beat until frothy. Gradually beat in the confectioners' sugar and continue to beat until very glossy, about 10 minutes more. Beat in the lemon juice. Drizzle the glaze fancifully over the tops of the cooled babkas.

Makes two 10-inch babkas

Russian Paskha

— ❖ —

My sister, Holly, made this Russian Easter specialty—a celestial spread of creamy dairy products, candied fruits, and toasted almonds—several years ago, and it instantly became an Easter breakfast tradition in our household. It is the perfect gilding for a plump slice of Polish babka or other festive Easter bread. While paskha represents the renewal of spiritual life in Russia, the list of ingredients may make it seem more like instant hardening of the arteries to health-conscious Americans. Yet with all the hard-boiled eggs and other delectables that go into the ritual feasting of this springtime holiday, counting cholesterol on Easter Sunday is almost as perverse as trying to live by a watch when traveling in Mexico!

1 pound farmer's or pot cheese, crumbled into small pieces	1½ cups sugar
	2 teaspoons vanilla extract
	2 teaspoons grated lemon zest
1 pound cream cheese	2 teaspoons grated orange zest
1 cup (2 sticks) unsalted butter	4 ounces candied citron, chopped
	½ cup golden raisins
1 cup heavy or whipping cream	¼ cup Grand Marnier or other orange liqueur
2 large egg yolks	½ cup lightly toasted slivered almonds
1 large egg	

1. Have all ingredients at room temperature. Using an electric mixer, beat the farmer's cheese, the cream cheese, and butter together in a large bowl until well blended. With the mixer running, pour in the cream in a thin, steady stream. Beat this mixture at least 10 minutes more, for a very smooth texture is essential to the success of pashka.

2. Meanwhile in another bowl beat together the egg yolks, egg, and sugar until very thick and light, 3 to 4 minutes. Gradually beat the egg mixture into the cheese mixture until well blended and smooth. Beat in the vanilla and lemon and orange zests.

3. Place the citron and raisins in a small saucepan. Add the Grand Marnier and bring to a boil over medium-high heat. Reduce the heat and simmer a few minutes, then remove from the heat to cool. Blend the cooled fruit into the cheese mixture. Add the almonds and mix to distribute evenly.

4. Thoroughly wash and dry a new 7-inch, 6-cup clay flowerpot. Line the pot with a couple layers of dampened cheesecloth, letting 4 to 5 inches of extra cloth hang over the edge of the pot all around. Pour the paskha mixture into the pot and press it down to make a compact mass. Fold the cheesecloth over the top of the paskha.

5. Place a plate that is slightly smaller than the top of the flowerpot on top of the paskha. Place a weight such as a large can or brick on top of the plate. Set the pot in a shallow dish to drain and refrigerate 24 hours.

6. When ready to serve, remove the weight and plate. Pour off the liquid in the dish. Invert the flowerpot onto a serving plate, unmold, and carefully peel away the cheesecloth.

7. The paskha may be decorated with pieces of candied fruit and

almonds set into the mold in a decorative pattern or the base simply may be surrounded with a ring of fresh strawberries or raspberries and mint sprigs. Let each person mound a generous spoonful on a serving plate to spread on slices of eggy Easter bread.

Makes 12 to 15 servings

Lemon Curd Tartlets

— ✣ —

These dainty and exquisite tartlets were always a favorite in my Que Sera Sarah shop. They make a particularly welcome and cleansing dessert after a lamb feast. In this version the almond tart shells add a crunchy contrast to the ultrasmooth lemon curd. When spring violets are in season, use them as a lovely garnish on top of each tartlet.

Almond Crust (see
  page 121)
12 large egg yolks, at room
  temperature
2 cups sugar
1 cup fresh lemon juice
1 cup (2 sticks) unsalted
  butter, at room
  temperature, cut into
  tablespoons

2 teaspoons finely grated
  lemon zest
1 teaspoon finely grated
  lime zest
1 teaspoon finely grated
  orange zest

1. Roll out the pastry ⅛ inch thick on a lightly floured surface. Cut twelve 3½-inch rounds from the dough and line twelve 3-inch tartlet pans with the rounds, trimming and crimping the edges decoratively. Prick the bottoms of the shells with a fork and place in the freezer at least 30 minutes.

2. Preheat the oven to 400°F. Line each tart shell with a small square of aluminum foil and fill with dried beans or pie weights.

3. Bake the tart shells 12 minutes. Remove from the oven and take out the foil and weights. Return to the oven and bake until nicely browned, about 5 minutes more. Let cool completely, then carefully remove the shells from the pans.

4. Whisk together the egg yolks, sugar, and lemon juice in a medium-size, noncorrosive saucepan. Cook over medium to medium-low heat, whisking constantly, until very thick, 10 to 15 minutes. Do not allow the mixture to boil at any point and be sure to keep stirring to prevent it from sticking and burning on the bottom of the saucepan. (This recipe requires concentration!) When the mixture is thick, remove it from the heat.

5. Stir the butter into the hot mixture, 1 tablespoon at a time, until all is incorporated. Stir in the citrus zests. Transfer the curd to a bowl, cover, and chill at least 2½ hours.

6. Fill a pastry bag fitted with a decorative tip with the chilled lemon curd. Pipe the curd into the baked tart shells. Serve at once or store the tartlets in the refrigerator until ready to serve, but no longer than 12 hours.

Makes twelve 3-inch tartlets

Polish Easter Cheesecake

The traditional Polish Easter cheesecake is always baked in an oblong pan. It is not too sweet, very lemony, and, I think, absolutely delicious. This is my preferred version.

CRUST
¾ cup unbleached all-
  purpose flour
¼ teaspoon baking
  powder
Pinch of salt
¼ cup granulated sugar

¼ cup (packed) light
  brown sugar
4 tablespoons (½ stick)
  unsalted butter, chilled,
  cut into small pieces
½ cup finely chopped walnuts

FILLING
1 pound cream cheese, at
  room temperature
1 pound farmer's or skim
  ricotta cheese
1¼ cups granulated sugar
5 large eggs

2 lemons
¼ cup unbleached all-
  purpose flour
1½ tablespoons vanilla extract
½ cup light cream

1. Preheat the oven to 325°F. Lightly butter a 13 × 9-inch glass baking dish.

2. Prepare the crust: Place the flour, baking powder, salt, both sugars, and the butter in a food processor and process just until the mixture begins to hold together. Add the walnuts and pulse to combine. Press the dough evenly over the bottom of the prepared dish. Bake until lightly browned, 12 to 15 minutes. Let cool.

3. Prepare the filling: In a large mixing bowl beat together the cream cheese and farmer's cheese until light and fluffy. Beat in the sugar, then add the eggs, one at a time, beating well after each addition.

4. Finely grate or chop the zest of the lemons. Squeeze the juice from the lemons and strain. Add the zest and juice to the cheese mixture. Add the flour, vanilla, and light cream and beat until smooth. Pour the filling over the baked crust.

5. Bake the cheesecake until a wooden toothpick inserted in the center comes out clean, 1 hour to 1 hour and 10 minutes. Cool, then cover and refrigerate at least 12 hours. Cut into squares to serve.

Makes 12 to 15 servings.

Pineapple Upside-Down Cake

— ❖ —

Years of experimentation with the recipe for this classic American cake have convinced me that the very best version in the world comes from those coveted files of my Polish grandmother. This cake's secret of success is the lengthy beating of the batter and the moistening of the cake with pineapple juice. The saffron and pine nuts are my esoteric additions and may be omitted by traditionalists.

1 cup (packed) light brown
    sugar
½ cup (1 stick) unsalted
    butter
2 tablespoons Grand
    Marnier or other orange
    liqueur
1 can (20 ounces)
    unsweetened pineapple
    slices, drained, ½ cup
    plus 2 tablespoons juice
    reserved

2 tablespoons pine nuts,
    lightly toasted (optional)
3 large eggs, separated
1½ cups granulated sugar
1 teaspoon vanilla extract
1½ cups unbleached all-
    purpose flour
½ teaspoon salt
2 teaspoons baking powder
1 teaspoon saffron threads
    (optional)

GARNISHES

1 cup heavy or
    whipping cream,
    whipped

3 tablespoons finely
    chopped crystallized
    ginger (optional)

1. Preheat the oven to 350°F.

2. Put the brown sugar, butter, and Grand Marnier in a heat-proof 10-inch cake pan or ovenproof skillet. Cook over medium heat, stirring constantly, until the butter has melted and the mixture is smooth. Remove from the heat and arrange the drained pineapple slices in a decorative pattern over the butter-sugar mixture. Sprinkle the pine nuts in the gaps between the fruit slices. Set the pan aside while preparing the cake batter.

3. Place the egg yolks, granulated sugar, 2 tablespoons reserved pineapple juice, and the vanilla in a mixing bowl. Using an electric mixer, beat at high speed until the sugar is nearly dissolved and the mixture is very light and fluffy, at least 10 minutes.

4. Sift together the flour, salt, baking powder, and saffron. Gently fold the flour mixture into the batter in 2 or 3 additions, alternating with the remaining ½ cup pineapple juice. Beat the egg whites until stiff but not dry and gently fold into the batter. Pour the batter evenly over the pineapple slices in the prepared pan.

5. Bake the cake until a toothpick inserted in the center comes out clean, 50 to 60 minutes. Let the cake cool 10 minutes, then carefully invert it onto a serving platter. Serve the cake warm or at room temperature, garnished with whipped cream and ginger.

Makes 8 to 10 servings

Greek Galatoboureko

— ❖ —

On a recent visit to Boston, my great Greek friend, Olga, introduced me to the pleasures of galatoboureko, a custard cousin to the better known baklava. While it has taken me at least a month to perfect my pronunciation of the dessert, it took me less than an instant to know that I adored the taste. This is Olga's recipe.

SUGAR SYRUP
2 cups sugar
1 cup water
3 tablespoons fresh lemon
  juice

1 slice orange

CUSTARD
2 quarts milk
1 cup sugar
1 cup farina or Cream of
  Wheat cereal

½ cup (1 stick) unsalted butter
Pinch of salt
12 large eggs
2 teaspoons vanilla extract

PHYLLO PASTRY
½ cup (1 stick) unsalted
  butter, melted

1 pound phyllo dough,
  thawed

1. Prepare the syrup: Place all the ingredients in a heavy saucepan and boil 10 minutes, skimming off any froth that rises to the surface. Remove and discard the orange slice. Set aside to cool.

2. Prepare the custard: Scald the milk with the sugar in a deep saucepan over medium-low heat, stirring with a wooden spoon. Gradually stir in the farina. Add the butter and salt. Continue cooking and stirring until the butter has melted and the mixture is thick and smooth. Remove from the heat and let the mixture cool to room temperature.

3. Beat the eggs and vanilla together in a large bowl until light, about 2 minutes. Stir in the cooled farina mixture and blend thoroughly.

4. Preheat the oven to 350°F.

5. To assemble, brush a 17 × 11-inch baking pan with a thin coating of the melted butter. Unwrap the phyllo dough, lay it out flat on a clean surface, and cover it with a slightly damp kitchen towel to keep it from drying out. Lay 1 sheet of phyllo dough on the bottom of the pan and brush it with a thin coating of melted butter. Continue layering and buttering the dough in the same manner for 8 sheets.

6. Pour in all the custard and spread it evenly. Cover the custard with 8 more layers of buttered phyllo dough. Puncture the top sheets with a sharp knife in several places to allow the custard to breathe during baking.

7. Bake until the custard is set and the pastry shakes loose from the pan, 45 minutes to 1 hour.

8. Let cool 30 minutes, then pour the sugar syrup over the pastry. Let cool completely. Serve slightly chilled or at room temperature, cut into small diamonds with a sharp knife.

Makes about 48 diamonds

Southern Pecan Cake with Lulu's Rum Sauce

This dense, nut-and-fruit-laden bundt cake makes a great finish for a smoky Southern ham dinner. The fabulous rum sauce comes from another one of the Powers' sisters, my Nantucket cooking clone and the inimitable blond bombshell—Lulu!

CAKE

1 cup (2 sticks) unsalted
  butter, at room
  temperature
1 cup (packed) dark brown
  sugar
1 cup granulated sugar
6 large eggs, separated, at
  room temperature
3½ cups cake flour
4 teaspoons baking powder

1½ teaspoons grated
  nutmeg
½ teaspoon salt
1 cup bourbon
4 cups pecan halves
1 cup dried apricots, diced
2 cups golden raisins
½ cup unbleached all-
  purpose flour

LULU'S RUM SAUCE

1 cup (packed) dark brown
  sugar
½ cup dark corn syrup
½ cup heavy or whipping
  cream

4 tablespoons (½ stick)
  unsalted butter
¼ cup golden rum
1 teaspoon vanilla extract

1. Preheat the oven to 325°F. Grease and lightly flour a 3½-quart bundt pan. Set aside.

2. Cream the butter and both sugars together in a large mixing bowl until light and fluffy. Add the egg yolks, one at a time, beating well after each addition.

3. Sift the cake flour, baking powder, nutmeg, and salt together. Add the flour mixture to the batter in 4 additions, alternating with the bourbon and beating just until blended after each addition.

4. Toss the pecans, apricots, and raisins with the all-purpose flour, then stir them into the batter. Beat the egg whites in a large clean bowl until stiff but not dry and gently fold into the batter. Transfer the batter to the prepared pan.

5. Bake the cake until a toothpick inserted in the center comes out clean, 1¼ to 1½ hours. Let cool in the pan 10 minutes, then invert onto a wire rack to cool completely.

6. Meanwhile prepare the rum sauce: Combine the brown sugar, syrup, cream, and butter in a medium-size heavy saucepan. Cook at a low boil 10 minutes. Remove from the heat and stir in the rum and vanilla. Let cool to room temperature.

7. To serve, cut the cake into 1-inch-thick slices and pass the rum sauce separately.

Makes 12 servings

INDEX